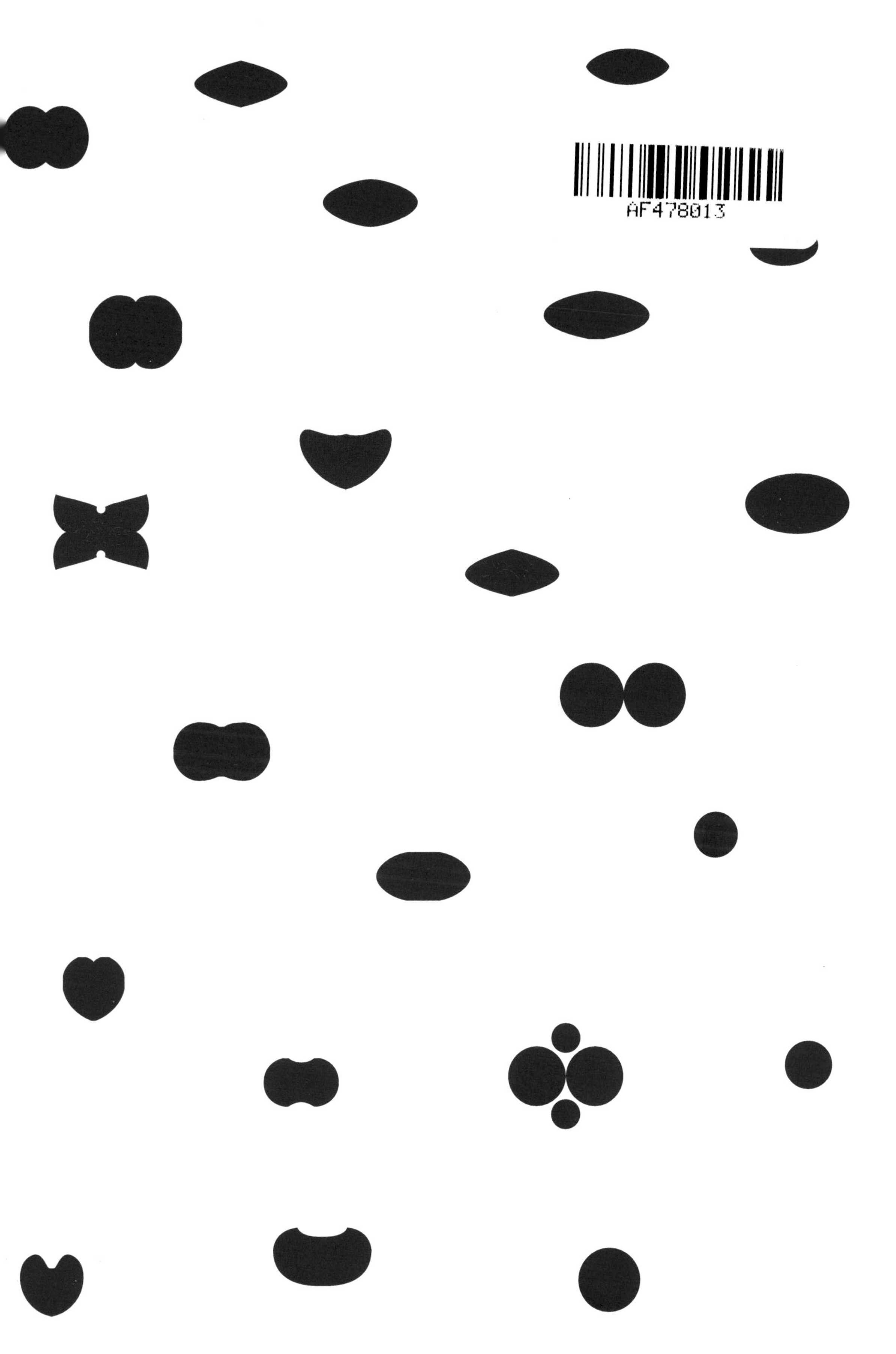
AF478013

World Art Studies: Exploring Concepts and Approaches

Edited by:
Kitty Zijlmans
Wilfried van Damme

Valiz, Amsterdam

CONTENTS

It must have been an extraordinary sight, seeing the earth rise on the horizon of the moon, and seeing for the first time with human eyes planet Earth as a little blue ball floating in the vast surrounding universe. The crew of Apollo 11 was the first to experience this spectacular view, but glued to their TV screens millions of people were able to share the moment. It was immediately clear how tiny our globe is, and indeed how fragile, but this panorama from space also emphasized our planet's singularity and unity.

In the same fashion, we believe, art should be contemplated as a global human enterprise, and it is this conviction that motivated us to produce this book. Our particular approach was also driven by a sense of urgency fueled by various recent developments, including the ongoing processes of globalization, the vast range of contemporary art production worldwide that draws in part on an equally vast range of local art traditions, and the re-evaluation of the discipline of art history in today's postcolonial era. Also, recent archaeological findings in Africa underscore the intimate interconnection between art and human beings; the visual arts may well be as old as *Homo sapiens* and have richly developed in multifarious directions once humans began to spread across the globe.

The new field of investigation known as world art studies first and foremost acknowledges art as a panhuman phenomenon. As such it aims to study art from all times and all regions of the world in an integrative manner and from a variety of disciplinary perspectives. Within this framework new concepts and approaches need to be developed and applied. This book represents the first effort devoted to this pursuit. Over the last few years, the editors organized a number of workshops at Leiden University to discuss and evaluate the structure and contents of this volume. The basic assumptions of these preparatory meetings were both sweeping and straightforward: art is global and can be approached from many disciplinary angles. This is why we invited colleagues from different fields of expertise (art history, anthropology, archaeology, and philosophy) to participate. We would like to thank all discussants for their suggestions and support.

To the contributors of this volume we express our sincerest gratitude for their willingness to engage in this exploratory undertaking. The volume has been longer in the making than we anticipated, and this is why we would also like to thank them for their patience.

The overall structure of the book elucidates the global and multidisciplinary approach we advance. The first section is devoted to the historiography of the study of art on a worldwide basis, the second to the meeting of disciplines and their multiple perspectives on the study of art. These sections are succeeded by three sections that focus on three guiding themes: the origins of art, intercultural comparison, and interculturalization in art. While paving the way for an art history conceived as world art studies, this volume also aims to open up the debate about art as a basic feature of our shared humanity, and thus to enhance our self-understanding as human beings. We hope that the journey through this volume may evoke some of the awe and wonder experienced by the first space-travelers.

Leiden, April 2008
Kitty Zijlmans and Wilfried van Damme

We dedicate this book to all art scholars who aspire to look beyond their horizons

BEN-AMI SCHARFSTEIN

Prelude: Keeping the World Together

What's a world? Just now, the most direct example is ourselves, me and you, you in the singular and the plural, all together in this book. We're a world because as writer and readers we're related to one another by a common immediate interest and are either present in or reading the pages of the same book. Outside of this one book-world on the subject of world art, there are other book-worlds on roughly the same subject, adjacent book-worlds, dealing with the art of one or another culture, or, more broadly, world culture, and on to I don't know how many kinds of books. Each book is of course contained within a home, library, or bookstore, each of which is located in some defined geographical area we for the moment call a world and is set on the surface of the world of all these worlds, that is, the earth, which is in turn inside the "world" of the solar system, which is on an outer arm of the Milky Way galaxy, which is in a certain defined region of the universe, and so on I don't know how many containing places or how far.

To make this notion of a world—a bounded complex whole the elements of which are related to one another—even more starkly obvious, let me offer ourselves as examples. Each of us constitutes a world in himself or herself, and, though a unity, contains very many other, different worlds, among them a brain, which, seen with one of the new imaging devices, would now be visibly active in its left, linguistically attentive area, and in its right, melodically attentive area—melody is integral to language—not to speak of its necessary visual areas. I will not press the point by going down to our individual cells, genetic filaments, and so on successively I don't know how many or how small. But I will add as an example of a small verbal world, a poem, any poem, and the even smaller world of a monorheme, a single sentence-word such as the "mommy" spoken with a particular intonation by a small child, which has a content equivalent to that of a full sentence.

To come closer to my main subject, visual art, each picture or sculpture is a world, and so is each artist, each approximately coherent group of artists, each coherent fraction of an art tradition, the art tradition or the culture as a whole, and, to speak of the world that concerns me most, the visual art of all the human cultures regarded as a single human-art world. But the unity of each of these worlds, small or large, is deceptive and may threaten to break up into discordant parts. Take as an example a single versatile artist. Picasso continued to create in several quite different styles, from the simple or romantic realism that might signal the entry of a new woman into his life, to the expressionistic that signaled her exit, to a modernized kind of Neo-Classical, and a Cubist, and a Surrealist style. Given no more evidence than the pictures minus his signature, it would be easy to divide his work into that of several different artists. Picasso was an exception, but if I look no further than the incomparably lesser art that I myself practice —I use this example only because I am so familiar with it—I am surprised that the pictures I made were all my work. Can this violently red sunset reflected in the water, painted in 1972, be by the same artist who made the sad, washed-out face in a watercolor self-portrait of 1996? Could either of these be by the person who, in 2002, painted this sketchy blind white rooster against a flat black background, his sharp beak open and his sharp claws extended to attack the flower in front of them, to symbolize blind aggression?

I suppose that it is plain information that is often necessary to keep the work of an artist attributed to him or her with certainty, and the absence of information that creates sometimes-painful doubts. But supposing that a variety of works is all by the same artist allows one to sharpen one's perceptions by noticing the possible changes in nature of the curves used, the quality and angles of the lines, the centers of gravity, and so on, and correlate all these particulars with one another, and by doing so enable the visual, historical, and conceptual understanding of the artist as a more complicated, more interesting whole.

Yet to grasp the visual unity of a particular artist is, if I may hazard the adverb, infinitely easier than to grasp the unity of a whole art tradition or culture. The art cultures of the West, of India (and adjacent countries), and of China (along with Japan, Korea, and other adjacent countries) each encompass varying, unclearly delimited areas, show in different places the effects of different external influences, including the influences they have exerted on one another. They have also had different conceptions of high and low in art, different basic aesthetic conceptions, and considerable internal conflict. What does an ancient Greek potter or pottery painter have to do with a Byzantine painter of icons, a Baroque sculptor or painter, a French Impressionist, a German Expressionist, or, to name names, a Jackson Pollock, or a Duchamp; or, for that matter, what have any of these to do with any of the others?

In India, what does the guild craftsman, with his prescribed procedures and low social status, have to do with the Sanskrit poets and dramatists who both reflected and created the aesthetic doctrines of upper-class appreciation of art, or what have any of these to do with the Mughal miniaturists, who worked at the pleasure of their Muslim employers? In China, the literati, who wrote poetry and practiced calligraphy and painting learned to look down not only on the potter, however expert, but also on the professional painter, who committed the spiritual sin of painting for the sake of money and the lesser but still considerable sin of excessive decorativeness and ostentatious virtuosity. I have excluded the sometimes-sharp differences among the literati, but must ask again, what has all of this to do until recently with the art and artists of Europe and India?

Each of the worlds I have mentioned, one sees, is as easy to conceive as many as it is as one, and it is easy to contend that it can only confuse matters if we try to make a really single world of each art tradition, and all the more confusion if we try to make a single world of all the art traditions. Yet to show that they are also one, or to keep them together as a world, is exactly my ambition. This ambition leads to a clash not only with the relativists, who in the present generation are called "postmodernists," but with those experts who are so aware of local details and so convinced of the need for further local research that they are skeptical of any summary of great bodies of what they take to be unreliable observations and of the assumption that enough is known to make a plausible attempt to see all human art as a world. I concede that their specialization is essential to perceiving the art world reasonably as one. I do not want to deny the specialists their superior grasp of detail but to unite the fragments into which they break each artworld, and refuse the view that each artist, each fragment of each tradition, and each tradition is incommensurable with any other. Instead, the specialists' knowledge should be used to show how and why the world can be rebuilt, and how much we can gain by rebuilding it. Doubts always remain, but to allow them to keep the world fragmented is like being afraid to go far from home or to climb to a point where much of the scenery is visible at once because an accident might happen on the way. However, I agree that the world may be de-natured by forcing unity on it too ruthlessly.

There are contemporaries, though still not many, who share the ambition I have expressed, and there have been similar ambitions in neighboring fields of study, such as history, anthropology, and philosophy. Scholars who would like to fulfill such an ambition usually share it among themselves by composing anthologies of their essays, each dealing with a subject narrowed to fit their individual research. Only few of them are willing to attempt a serious view of the whole that is the collective object of the anthology. Each of them who tries to clarify some limited example of, say, the relations between the art of one culture and another acts as a thinking mirror; but each mirror has its personal aberrations, and no one reader can join all the individual views because the scholars' varying individualities—their singular aberrations—do not sum up into any clear full view. But joining, an act quite different from summing up, becomes natural as one practices it and, after while, an inescapable source of interest.

I use this conclusion to justify my resolve not to lessen the pleasure in the flow of my thought or yours by distracting it with notes and bibliographical details. I will mention, but only mention, a few of the relatively recent thinkers whose creative boldness influenced me personally, even though I disagreed strongly with most of them. In history, I would recall only Arnold Toynbee, who wrote of the rise and fall of whole civilizations in accord with their responses to the challenge of their environments, and of the religions that provided the soil for civilizations and transcended them. In philosophy, the great integrator was the learned Hegel, whose writings on philosophy and art suffer from sad prejudices (though he had the integrity to retract his very negative opinion of Indian philosophy) and a megalomaniacal-appearing hierarchy of philosophies that culminate in his own. In anthropology, I will not single out any individual anthropologist but the collective fostering of the ability to see strange cultures in the light of their own perceptions no less than (or perhaps more than) our perceptions of them. In aesthetics and the history of art, I remember Élie Faure's *History of Art*, which related art to civilizations, especially in its last, poetically sensitive volume; René Grousset, who helped to open Indian, Chinese, and Japanese art for me; and André Malraux, whose latest biographers have shown him up as a tireless poseur but whose dramatically illustrated art books and grand or grandiose generalizations on world art impressed me. I'm tempted to name present-day thinkers, some of them my friends, but refrain out of the fear of doing an injustice to those I leave out.

These preliminaries bring me to the central issue I want to discuss, which is the need to react to the various traditions of art in a spirit of empathic decency that helps to keep the world together. Although I stress the degree to which human traits and abilities are universal, I see no contradiction between this universality and the endless variety of ways in which it is expressed. The endless variety, which overlies and often conceals the unity, is essential to the sensuous experience of art; but for understanding in the abstract sense, it is more helpful to become aware of how the endless variety makes up endlessly rich sets of variations on common human themes. It is therefore much more rewarding to accept the assumption that the visual art of all human cultures is to some extent accessible to members of all others, not only because all seeing humans have more or less similar eyes and visual systems, but also because they have such a receptive power of empathy, an instrument for grasping art no less important than vision because it by nature makes so much of human experience as contagious as laughing and crying. Just as a color-blind person is not capable of a full appreciation of color in art, an emotion-blind person (blind by reason of narrow-mindedness, narcissism, or autism) has a deficient appreciation of the art of his or her own tradition and certainly of other, strange traditions. If the reach of empathy is amplified by the study of context, we even become able to respect art to which we may not feel emotionally close or intuitively admire. A richer web of associations is created, which makes it possible to see works of art from many points of view, ask and answer many questions about them, discover in them characteristics that are otherwise hidden, remember them more easily, and, altogether, grasp them more fully and subtly.

Having pointed out the advantages and limitations of keeping the world of art together, I want to emphasize the advantages by means of a series of modest subtractive fantasies. They are modest because they concern only the last few centuries and confine themselves to what fits the proportions of this essay.

Now, first, I use my fantasy power to make Japanese and African art disappear from the early history of modern art, that is, become invisible to Europeans, and when I feel like it, I'll make the European art invisible too. What disappears immediately is the enthusiasm with which nineteenth-century Frenchmen fell in love with everything Japanese, including kimonos, erotic prints, and food. This love spread from France in every direction. Everything about the prints attracted the French painters who found their own tradition no longer satisfying. What attracted them? The affectionately simplified episodes of daily life, the rocks jutting out of the ocean, the rounded bridges and straight waterfalls, the delicately bold flowers, the heroically enlarged sexual organs, the bright, hardly modulated colors, the decorative patterns on kimonos, the freely undulating curves, and the waves made of imaginatively varied linear undulations. The French artists also appreciated and copied the long, narrow Japanese formats, the compositions made up of diptychs and triptychs, the silhouetted foreground masses, the dramatic diagonals from one corner to another corner, and the dramatic truncations, especially of foreground figures. Both the diagonals and the truncations were similar to those observed in photographs, Japan and Europe converging in this instance as if by providence.

Among the French Impressionists, the deepest influence of the prints was on Degas and Monet. Both of them loved and bought the prints, which were cheap, both had access to large collections, and both looked to the prints for new subjects, compositions, and points of view. Degas's women bathing, drying themselves, and combing themselves and being combed are borrowed from Kiyonaga, whose diptych of women bathing hung in his bedroom, from Hokusai, and perhaps from Utamaro. The near-parodic nudes Degas drew in monotype also recall the Japanese. From the Japanese (and from photography) he learned to break the time-honored centrality of human figures and cut them off at the frame, show them from behind, from above, from below, at close range, and reduced to shadows; and from both sources he learned to create depth by means of sharply opposed diagonals. Monet, like Degas, adopted the Japanese downward- or upward-viewing, and he cut boats off at the frame and extended boats over more than one leaf of a print. It was maybe from Hokusai's series *Thirty-six Views of Mount Fuji* that he learned to paint things—poplars, haystacks, water lilies, cathedrals—in series. His masses of water lilies growing in a pond are composed in Japanese asymmetry. However, the most profound of the influences or parallels was the dissolution of humans and nature into one another experienced as the intermingling of cosmic forces.

Gauguin, who borrowed from everywhere, borrowed figures quite literally from Kuniyoshi and Hokusai. Van Gogh, who at one time planned to go into business with his brother selling Japanese prints, copied three paintings and many themes from them. Attentive to the Japanese space-filling techniques, such as Hokusai's dot-and-stroke method, he used them when he drew with reed pens on absorbent paper. He envied the Japanese the clearness which everything had in their work. Their work, he said, is as simple as breathing. Van Gogh preferred to live in the south of France because he saw in it a second Japan in its sunlight, color, and simple inhabitants; and he dreamed of a community of artists who would refresh their spirits and humanity by returning periodically from the city to live in Japanese fellowship. Like Van Gogh, Toulouse-Lautrec found in the Japanese a dream-ideal. His portraits of actors and his erotic scenes, not to speak of his style and mode of composition, are reminiscent of the Japanese. Hokusai's *Manga* stimulated him to portray momentary and yet typical gestures, precarious equilibriums, and people stretching, lying, and lolling, in every pose.

Now, for the sake of our shared fantasy, subtract all these Japanese influences and without quibbling, which ruins fantasies, ask yourself what has changed. Degas, the later Monet, and Toulouse-Lautrec are hardly the artists we used to know. Van Gogh has lost his most telling technique of drawing and his ideal of Japanese fellowship; and Toulouse-Lautrec the artist has disappeared, I am afraid.

And now we will, by the fiat of our fantasy, subtract Africa from European art. Ensor can't discover African sculpture anywhere, and De Vlaminck can't find or even see and, a fortiori, can't sell an African mask to Derain, who has no mask or other African object to show to Matisse and to Picasso. Now the shape of a Gabonese (Fang) mask will no longer show up in the paintings of all three artists. Picasso will no longer say of an African sculpture that it is more beautiful than the Venus de Milo or borrow African shapes for his paintings. Nor will Picasso go to the Trocadéro and discover that African sculptures were magic weapons, like his own, directed against unknown threats, nor would the idea of *Les*

Demoiselles d'Avignon, his first exorcism painting, he said, have come to him that day.

It therefore makes good dramatic sense to date the beginning of the end of the European tradition to about that time, 1910. Reacting to Monet's huge paintings of water lilies set in multicolored, shapeless spaces and to Bonnard's "potpourri of indecision" that made things melt together, Picasso wanted to make strong, "ballsy" paintings, to take possession of things by fragmenting, faceting, flattening, massing, and illuminating them from everywhere, and by rebuilding and exhibiting them like an architect who had bent or cut them into their angled shapes. Picasso, as he once said, saw that one had to break with the past and start at zero. African sculpture, with its simplified, symbolically proportioned shapes and often-sharp adze-cut planes was a factor in the invention of Cubism. Cubism, it hardly need be said, departed from the modern European tradition of art in a way far more profound and disruptive than any artistic change that had preceded it. In Cubist paintings all things seemed to have been broken up —could you hear the things being cracked apart to make more angles?—and reassembled with a new, dull-colored angularity. Cubism treated appearances with what looked like inexplicable, outrageous violence. Some contemporary Africans have gone so far as to claim that Cubism and, with it, the whole radical break in the European tradition was caused by the influence of African art on Picasso and his circle. However that is, in our subtractive fantasy we conclude, with a fantasy's arrogance, that in the absence of African art there would have been no Cubism and no violent disruption of the European tradition.

Now I will use my imagination to subtract not a culture but an institution, the British Museum, and, by doing so, subtract Henry Moore from the history of European art. He recalls that his first year in art school, when he was twenty-one, passed in a dream of excitement—not because of the school, the Royal College of Art, but because every room in the British Museum revealed a new world of art. At first, Moore was most impressed by the monumentality of Egyptian sculpture, which was closest to familiar Greek and Renaissance ideals; but the hieratic stylization, academic obviousness, and "rather stupid love of the colossal" ended by alienating him from much of the Egyptian. Other rooms that remained attractive were the archaic Greek, with life-size female figures, "grand and full like Handel's music"; the Sumerian, with its bull-monsters and its contained sculptural energy; the prehistoric period and Stone Age, with the free but very human richness of its female figures (and its tender, thumbnail-sized carving of a girl's head); the African, its figures statically patient, resigned to unknown powers, vertical and rooted in the earth like the trees they were made from, one of the figures, from Azande, as deliberate and, to the sculptor who made it, Moore says, as pleasurable an achievement as the writing of a poem; the Mexican, its figures tremendously powerful and yet sensitive, astonishingly fertile in form-invention, and notably three-dimensional; and the Oceanic, more two-dimensional and pattern-conscious than the African, and in its New Ireland examples with a unique, bird-in-a-cage form. Moore says that the deepest impression was made on him by early Mexican art, although Romanesque or early Norman also spoke deeply to him. He could not, however, assimilate these influences in peace. Instead, he underwent a crisis, the result of a six-month trip during which he was exposed to the masterpieces of European art. He could not shake off the new impressions without denying everything he had believed in before, and he found himself helpless and unable to work. Only gradually did he begin to feel his way out of his quandary, the way out leading back toward ancient Mexican art. When he adventured in a museum, he might happen on a non-European sculpture he would like to but could not, he felt, equal. Not unfairly, our subtractive fantasy leads to the omission of any recognizable Henry Moore from the history of European art,

Come to think of it, we might turn, though very briefly, to see what the subtraction of European art might do to the art of Japan or China. In still traditional Japan, I'd want to subtract Hokusai (1760–1849) because he exemplifies the undeniably creative borrower from Europe. Full of curiosity, he took whatever he wanted from wherever he found it. His desire was to grasp the living quality of everything he drew, which for him included the bone structure of birds, fish, animals, and insects. When young he experimented with European projection and perspective, and he educated himself to understand both European and Sino-Japanese shading, which are, he wrote, "as different as front and back and equally important." To judge by Hokusai's own standard of the creation of "life and death in everything one paints," his fusion was quite successful. So if there is no Europe in Japan, there is not much of Hokusai there either.

For that matter, if there had been no European prints or Jesuit artists in seventeenth century China, then there would have been no Tseng Ching (Zeng Jing) (1568–1650), who was an extraordinarily realistic portraitist by Chinese standards. A contemporary source praises his portraits as like images reflected in a mirror and explains that the faces "would glare and gaze, knit their brows or smile, in a manner alarmingly like real people.... When one stood looking at such a face one forgot both the man and oneself in a moment of spiritual comprehension." Tseng's technique of adding "tens" of washes on washes was also the attempt to gain a European intensity of color. But it is interesting that the praise of realism I have quoted is justified, in Chinese fashion, by its ability to induce self-forgetfulness and spiritual comprehension.

Tseng is said to have had many followers. So no Europe in China, no Tseng. Also, I add, no Chia Ping-ch'en (Jia ping-chen), who was versed in topography and astronomical measurement, knowledge that must have helped him to achieve his reported

ability to paint striking effects of depth—mountain ranges showing
enormous distances—daylight, and mist. The description of his
painting continues with praise for "the Western method" employed
by Chia. It excels, the description says, in painting shades. He is said
to dissect a picture into minute parts so as to distinguish yin and
yang, front and back, slanting and upstanding, long and short, and
to apply colors either light or heavy, bright or dark, according to the
distribution of shades. Therefore, viewed from a distance, figures,
animals, plants and houses, all seem to stand out and look rounded.

The mutual criticism of the Chinese and the Europeans naturally reflected their traditional values. The painter Wu Li, though
converted to Christianity, was not impressed by the Europeans'
ability to represent distances by special rules of light and shade, or
by their brushwork or their painstaking attempts at realism. The
European criticism of Chinese painting was usually that it lacked
perspective, shadows, and knowledge of human anatomy. Yet it
was a Jesuit who wrote that the paintings in the Imperial palace had
"a great deal to teach our painting as to the way to treat a landscape, to paint flowers, to render a dream palpable, to express pas-
sions, etc." The very Emperor considered Giuseppe Castiglione, a
Jesuit missionary and a painter, as the equal of the great Chinese
painters, in particular, without a rival as a painter of horses.

When Christianity fell into disfavor, so did European painting. The mixed European-Chinese style of the missionary painters
was thought foreign and vulgar by Chinese connoisseurs and was
ridiculed by Europeans as well. Yet it appears that there was a
pronounced European influence on certain able Chinese painters
who remained distinctively Chinese. These painters, of the early
seventeenth century, lived in or near Nanking. One of them, Wu
Pin (Wu Bin) (active 1576–1616) became a court artist and is likely to have seen the European paintings and illustrated books presented to the Emperor in 1601. A near contemporary writes that
"he never followed old models, but always depicted real scenery."
His landscapes struck viewers with amazement. Extraordinarily
for China, the claim was made that he had painted them directly
from nature. The angles from which he viewed the landscapes,
the way he cut off structures and trees, his use of reflections in water, and his rainy or cloudy skies, sunsets, and chiaroscuro, all
suggest European influence. Analogously, the very forceful landscapes of Kung Hsien (Gong Xian) have been taken to argue an
acquaintance with European engravings. A similar acquaintance is
likely to have helped Chang Hung (Zhang Hung) (1577–c. 1652)
to make landscapes that were thought mysteriously natural. They
do have a new, unusually empirical quality, which is an attempt to
paint as if from a European kind of perspective, dominated by a
single viewpoint, and new ways of dotting to represent forms. His
departures from Chinese tradition, which influenced Chinese critics to rank him low, do not deter a European historian of Chinese
art from ranking him high.

I skip many intervening years and end my report on Chinese painters with a contemporary, Zao Wou-ki. He was born in Beijing in 1921 (Wou-ki in its Chinese position is Zao-Wou-ki's first name, while Zao, the second name, is the French version of Tsao). He learned both traditional Chinese painting and calligraphy and the Western academic method of drawing first from plaster casts. But he felt neither happy nor successful. Influenced by reproductions of Cézanne, Picasso, and especially Matisse, he painted in the contemporary French manner, and when critics ridiculed his work, he reacted defiantly. He and his first wife Lan-Lan moved to Paris in 1948. He spent the afternoon of the day he arrived in Paris at the Louvre, whose art flooded him with joy but did not answer his creative needs. He tried a mixed Chinese-French style, aroused little interest, and then tried turning completely French but discovered, guiltily, that he kept on using traditional Chinese colors. He grew to feel that his paintings had become flowerless, unindentifiable. In the end, it took some four years for Zao to overcome this renewed spell of anxiety. Since then, his paintings have become more nearly realistic. They are often large landscape-like vistas, generally seen from above, in colors that suggest both Monet and Turner. His finally very successful career demonstrates how painful it may be to meet the challenge of unifying such different worlds of art. But what concerns our fantasy most is that Zao could not survive the subtraction of either Chinese or Western painting.

My comments on the subtraction of Japanese and Chinese painters from European art require me to add that, along with them, there go much of Mark Tobey, Morris Graves, and Isamu Noguchi. See their biographies for a nuanced verdict.

I've run out of space for detailed fantasizing. My subtractive magic has affected the following European artists: Degas, Monet, Gauguin, Van Gogh, Toulouse-Lautrec, Picasso, Moore, Tobey, Graves, and Noguchi. Among Chinese artists, those affected are Wu Li, Castiglione (a more or less Sinified European), Wu Pin, and Chang Hung. You would be right to suppose that I could have included very many more names, but I have to distinguish between a fantasy and an encyclopedia. The subtraction pales all of these artists and must make some of them unrecognizable or make them even vanish from view (I see too dimly into my fantasy to be sure). The general implication is clearly that the active contact of one world of art with another enriches it, fecundates it, and renews its body and spirit.

That said, I close my eyes and try to imagine what it would be like if all the art of all the non-European traditions vanished. I recommend that you too try imagining the loss to yourselves. As for me, I'm appalled. Even my precious library is more than half emptied, and my life is partly emptied as well. I counter the prospect of loss by trying to remember, in the usual random way that memory works, what I would most miss. Maybe because of the book I was looking at a short while ago, I miss the dramatic,

sometimes glitteringly gorgeous simplicity of Japanese screens
(the names that come to my mind by themselves are Sotatsu and
Korin). The screens recall the different/similar, more plebian
woodblock prints of gorgeous courtesans, theatrically posing war-
rior-actors, colorful travel scenery, and a lot of Mount Fujis. Japan
of course brings China to mind, and China, ink paintings of grandly
upright pines, wintry old trees (portraits of their painters), and
wispy scenes of mountain paths. The supple sobriety or mad spon-
taneity of Chinese calligraphy reminds me then of the decorative
beauty of Muslim calligraphy, which reminds of Bizhad and Persian
miniatures, with their extraordinarily skillful, delicately detailed
drawing, chords of color like musical chords, and arabesque compositions, based on flowering vines. The Persian miniatures remind of
the Mughal ones and of the Emperor Akbar, who out of his desire
to know the world insisted on the miniatures' documentary value.
As I remember now, Akbar said that a painter has especial means
of recognizing God because in devising limbs for his miniatures
the painter must come to feel that he cannot bestow full individuality on his work—Leonardo, who was more ambitious than
Akbar's imagined painter, favored painting because it led the painter to recreate the universe by learning it in detail.

What else does my mind dredge out of its memories? Statues of Dancing Shivas with flaming haloes around their heads; the
benignly graceful Bodhisattvas, with their graceful entourages, of
the Ajanta Caves; and the loving sculptured pairs of Khajuraho. I
shut off my memory before it takes me to the temple-mountain
of Angkor Wat or the mile-long reliefs of the life of Buddha and
his disciples at the great temple of Borobudur.

It is one of the banes of my life that my memory does not
serve me nearly as well as I would like, but even so, the loss I can
remember overwhelms me now. It's easy to point out that, as individuals, we're worlds in ourselves; and it should be easy to recognize that the act of keeping the world together makes art far more
interesting for each of us. We want to learn the eyes, colors, compositions, interests, minds, imaginations, and memories of humans
from everywhere. One can excuse this ambition by saying that it is
close to the moral aim of universal understanding or, less flattering-
ly, an indulgence in the temptation of aesthetic omniscience. I find
neither these excuses false but stand on my right, felt almost as an
obligation, to share what has filled my own life with interest and
pleasure.

Can I press this point home by speaking of our common
hunger for art? Once, when I tried to answer why we all experience
this hunger, I gave this answer: art strengthens the desire to live
by enhancing the quality of life of those who experience it, whether
by creating art or by enjoying it and in a sense recreating it. It
strengthens the desire to live by countering boredom, lassitude,
and depression. It does so by enriching experience or, in the simplest words, by making experience more interesting. In particular,

art enriches experience by using perception, emotion, memory, and association to make the embodied equivalent of whatever it is that we want to experience, whether or not it has a literal existence. Seen in this light, the function of art is to enhance the quality of life by satisfying the hunger for experience in all of its actual and imaginable variations.

It follows that our hunger for experience, for the sake of which we use art to create or recreate all the actual and imaginable variations of life, is best satisfied when the art is as rich, varied, and encompassing as possible.

I can't say more than I have, and I can't say it better.

WILFRIED VAN DAMME

Introducing World Art Studies

Let us first have some music. From the tunes a mother sings to her child to the sounds produced and songs performed in countless cultures at an individual's death, music is a prominent part of human existence. In celebration and in sorrow, people sing songs and play instruments; both courtship and battle may be accompanied by music. Music occurs in myriad forms and in countless settings, and may induce a whole range of moods or mental states. Pacifying, exciting, or triggering imagination and reflection, its impact and allure are used for a variety of purpose. Music communicates between humans, but it may also address perceived nonhuman entities, honoring gods or attracting spirits. These entities in turn are sometimes believed to communicate to humans through music.

The various deployments and effects of music have led thinkers and educators in numerous times and places to regard music as both morally uplifting and morally degrading, to want some forms banned, while encouraging other forms as edifying. Indeed, some music is condemned as seductively manipulative or corrupting, other music is praised as the highest achievement of human creativity and the most lofty expression of the human soul, considered fit to educate the mind and inspire exemplary behavior in its listeners.

Found in fields and factories, concert halls and courts, places of worship and of commerce, musical forms range from simple to complex in their overall organization and in any or all of their constituent parts, such as rhythm, melody, and harmony. Musical compositions may be conceived as rigid, their structure, instrumentation, and performance tightly prescribed, or they may allow for considerable variation and improvisation. Music can be transmitted aurally and orally, by means of notation, or both, and its composers and performers may vary from occasional amateurs to fulltime professionals. Many people find pleasure in making music, collectively or individually, and frequently the distinction between performers and audience is blurred. Musical forms are classified in various ways in various traditions, and often traditions do not consider "music" a separate phenomenon or analytical category, conceptualizing some of its manifestations as inextricably linked to the performance of dance or poetry (to introduce two more general categories used in present-day Western classifications of human expression).

Some people not only experience music, by making or perceiving it, they examine it. Even the brief characterization provided above suffices to suggest that music constitutes a vast and varied field of study. Requiring a firm basis of conceptual, epistemological, and methodological considerations, its examination encompasses attention to the origins and evolution of various musical forms; the human voice and other instruments used to produce music, including their range, timbre, and other acoustic properties; the various characteristics of the resulting aural products, compositional and otherwise, and their possible relationships with words sung and bodies moving; the creation, performance, perception, and reception of musical products; the various occasions, contexts, and purposes of their occurrence; and the nature, qualities, and effects ascribed to musical forms by those who make, experience, use, and indeed study them.

The range of questions to be asked is formidable (from the supposedly trivial to the mind-bogglingly elusive) and the prospect of comprehensively studying music in human life seems, as result, daunting. This has not, however, discouraged scholars from suggesting unified and encompassing approaches to the examination of music as a multifaceted phenomenon in human existence. Thus, in 1885, when the division of labor in Western academia was still in full swing, the young musicologist Guido Adler outlined a systematic perspective on the study of music. He presented his comprehensive view in a paper that opened the first issue of the *Vierteljahrschrift für Musikwissenschaft* (Musicology Quarterly).

Adler systematized the study of music by dividing it into two sections: historical musicology and systematic musicology, each with four subdivisions and various auxiliary sciences. Whereas Adler's first section deals mainly with methodically organizing existing practices in studying the history of music, systematic musicology in his proposal consists of various forms of theory that ultimately aim at inductively establishing "laws" in the field of music. One of the subdivisions of systematic musicology concerns the intercultural comparative study of music—called a new branch, it is discussed only briefly, yet characterized as "very rewarding." Among the auxiliary sciences of systematic musicology we find acoustics, physiology, psychology, and aesthetics. Adler suggests, in short, that musicology draw on all contemporary types of research relevant to our understanding of music as a phenomenon in human life. In today's terms, Adler's essay could be typified as promoting musicology as the worldwide and multidisciplinary study of music.

Adler's programmatic essay is generally regarded as crucial to the establishment of musicology as an academic discipline.[1] Moreover, as musicologist Bruno Nettl notes, the idea that musicology cover, from diverse disciplinary perspectives, all the varying aspects of music, whatever its forms and from whatever tradition in time or space, has remained a cornerstone of the discipline. In Nettl's assessment, it is largely thanks to Adler that "in over a century, musicology, despite some internecine strife and a lot of attitudes, has remained a single field in which most individuals recognize that the rest, however far-flung their musical interests, are colleagues" (2002, 20).

Wondering About the Visual Arts

A prospective student of the arts may well expect to find a parallel academic discipline addressing corresponding topics and questions in the visual realm. One might imagine her as being intrigued by the human tendency to make images, particularly those of a more arresting type, whether figurative or abstract. To continue the phantasy, our student wonders about the imagination and skill that go into producing such images, especially after having herself tried her hand at both painting and photography. She notes that many other people are equally fascinated by images, and that they may have a strong effect on human beings. Examples are not hard to find, living as she does in a metropolitan multicultural environment and spending most summers in her father's home town on another continent. Her horizon has been further expanded by books and documentaries acquainting her with the visual art forms of various other cultural worlds in the present and the past. She notices that images have played and continue to play prominent roles in such contexts as religious and political propaganda, and, increasingly, the commercial propaganda called advertising—all of these contexts implying the profound impact of visual imagery on its viewers.

TV footage and personal experience have also made her aware that frequently people not only create and behold images but relate to them in various other ways, including actual handling or manipulation. She has seen, for example, statues being carried around on litters among crowds of devotees—dangerously tilting, adorned with flowers, and accompanied by the sounds of instruments and human voices. When not part of such dynamic and dramatic performances, these same statues may be the focus of attention in architectural settings where fragrant substances are burnt and where the images are prayed to, touched, and kissed.

This is considerably different from the decontextualized and static presentation of visual images from various times and places encountered in most art books and museums, although such presentation allows for a better inspection of the works themselves.

1
Adler's article was not without its predecessors, however. In discussing the study of music at the time of Adler's influential publication, a publication which has led to a "holistic musicology" with various subdivisions that may now seem "old hat," Bruno Nettl mentions "parallel stirrings elsewhere ... in Russia, in France, even of a sort in the USA" (2002, 20–21). He singles out as Adler's most obvious predecessor Friedrich Chrysander, "who for a few years beginning in 1863 published his *Jahrbücher für musikalische Wissenschaft*, in whose preface he asserts that this "*Wissenschaft*" has several branches: history, aesthetics, theory, folk music scholarship (including intercultural comparison) ... Chrysander tells the reader that however many concerns are represented among scholars involved with music, they have much in common and ought at least to share a period-ical" (2002, 21). In 1884, Chrysander, "the distinguished biographer and editor of Handel's work," and Philipp Spitta, "the great biographer of Bach," teamed up "with the youthful Adler ... in founding the new *Vierteljahrschrift für Musikwissenschaft*. There was no fly on the wall, but I like to imagine the older, established scholars permitting Adler, with his youthful energy and enthusiasm, to be the principal architect of this venture, while also leaving him most of the work" (ibid.). Nettl concludes that "In some ways, [Adler's paper] reads like the work of a seasoned scholar, stating its points with authority and even majesty. But on the other hand, to lay out a field with courage and conviction, from scratch, may have been the characteristic approach of a young man" (ibid.). The contents of the first issue of the *Viertelschrift für Musikwissenschaft* suggest that the interest both in various disciplinary approaches and in cultures outside the West was indeed in the air (Nettl 2002, 29–30).

Close visual examination might lead one to marvel about the talent and dedication that went into the making of some images, clearly lifting them, or so it would seem, above others created in a similar style and for a similar purpose. One might then wonder whether such transcultural assessments coincide with those of the people who originally made and evaluated these works. Are there perhaps aesthetic universals, and how could they be explained? How might one account for the cultural diversity in views on artistic quality that seems all the same unquestionable?

And why indeed do visual images, for all their particularities, so often appear to be made in a specific style, a visual idiom that we somehow seem to recognize and that may allow us to situate a statue, painting, textile, or any other artistic object, in a particular time and place? Where do styles come from, and what is in fact their relation to a given locality and time period? Why do styles sometimes last for many generations, and why do they sometimes change more than once within in a lifetime? How and why do some art styles travel not only in time but also in space? And what about the relationship between style and subject matter? How do visual images manage to convey "meaning," and why is it that some pictures are worth "more than a thousand words"?

Also, being well-acquainted with various cultural spheres, it has occurred quite naturally to our prospective student that humans often make themselves into living images—by the pigments they apply to their faces and bodies, and the clothes and ornaments they wear; by the way they dress their hair, and perhaps scar their skin; and even by the way they gesture and move about. Aesthetics or cosmetics and the communication of individual and collective identities by means of local visual codes are both likely to be involved, but these notions would seem to provide only the beginnings of an analysis of what is going on, and why.

So what is it with humans and the visual images they create that are intended to have an impact on others—principally conspecifics, but at times also nonvisible personified entities? When, how, and why did all this start? What roles has visual imagery taken on in human life, and how do images manage to have their effect on perceivers?

These questions may make one curious as to what various forms of contemporary scholarship have to say about the human engagement with imaginatively designed visual images. Thoughts may wander from psychological studies of perception of form and color to anthropological analyses of the sociocultural uses of imagery to humanistic interpretations of formally complex and semantically dense visual creations designated as "high art." And what about the advances in neuroscience and evolutionary studies that one so frequently hears about these days? Do these disciplines shed any light on the origins and underpinnings of human creativity and the making, use, and perception of art? At the other end of the spectrum, yet by no means unrelated, how does scholarship deal with today's processes of globalization in the arts as well as the various new media that have become available to artists? In looking for an academic field that may accommodate and indeed deepen such interests and questions, what would a future art scholar find?

Towards a Comprehensive Study of Art Worldwide

One of Adler's motives in presenting his encompassing musicological approach was his impression that the study of music was lagging behind the study of the visual arts (Mugglestone 1981, 2). Yet no scholar before or any time soon after Adler would seem to have suggested an analogous systematic program for studying the visual arts. Recent historiographic analyses, to be sure, make it increasingly clear that at the turn of the previous century, and especially in the German-speaking world, within the framework of *Kunstwissenschaft*, the study of the graphic and plastic arts was much more globally oriented and was more multidisciplinary in character than has previously been generally thought (see Marlite Halbertsma and, especially for the role of various disciplines, Ulrich Pfisterer, this volume).

Kunstwissenschaft shared in the same positivistic, and optimistic, intellectual climate that produced *Musikwissenschaft*. But whereas scholars of music, despite changing opinions, would con-tinue to regard their multifaceted field as an intellectual unity under the flag of musicology (at least in Nettl's perhaps slightly over-optimistic interpretation), no "artology" developed that could have safeguarded scholars of the visual arts from seeing their shared subject matter fragmented into epochal, regional, and disciplinary specialties whose practitioners hardly communicate with each other. World art studies, a concept and approach first proposed and promoted by the art scholar John Onians (1996), may be considered an attempt to remedy this situation. As it is interpreted here, largely in line with Onians, world art studies suggests doing for the visual arts what musicology does for music—or what, for example, linguistics does for language or religious studies for religion: to approach its subject matter from a global perspective across time and place and to study it from all relevant disciplinary viewpoints imaginable, ranging from evolutionary biology to analytic philosophy.

This volume sets out to advance the idea of world art studies as the global and multidisciplinary examination of the visual arts. In addition to broaching the intellectual history of this type of examination, it will introduce readers to a number of disciplinary approaches that might be fruitfully applied in studying art as a worldwide phenomenon. The consideration of various relevant perspectives at the same time provides one opportunity to explore concepts necessary for rethinking the study of the visual arts along the lines of world art studies. In order to operationalize some of these approaches and concepts, and especially to give focus to

the budding study of art as a worldwide phenomenon, the editors
have decided to highlight, in this initial phase, three fundamental
topics that warrant our attention once we start looking at the visual
arts across time and place.

The first of these concerns the origins of art, meaning its
appearance in human evolution. When, at the turn of the previous
century, the study of art was becoming professionalized in the
West, the basic questions of when and how the visual arts had come
into being, and had developed through time, received quite some
attention from students of art history, archaeology, and anthropology. They thereby continued, in effect, a longstanding Western
scholarly interest in the origin and evolution of the visual arts. For
most of the twentieth century, however, the issue of origins was
relegated to the margins of academic concern, in part because of
the highly speculative character of the various theories that were
proposed in view of what might have happened in the dim and distant past. Today, with many recent archaeological discoveries and
various new theories to account for these and earlier findings,
questions concerning the origins of art have become topical again,
although speculation remains. In the study of music, language,
literature, and religion, too, the arrival of new conceptual tools, interpretative frameworks, research methods, and data, together
with an increasingly global orientation in present-day scholarship,
has led to parallel revivals in pursuing questions of origins.

Once having come into being, the visual arts would develop
an enormous variety of forms, embody a host of themes, and be
used in a wide range of contexts, for various purposes and with
various effects. The extensive examination of the numerous dimensions of visual artistic behavior in the world's many disparate
cultures is of course a primary task of world art studies. Fortunately,
it is a task to which art historians, anthropologists, archaeologists,
and other scholars have already made substantial contributions,
although this may well have gone unnoticed outside specialist fields
due to the lack of an overarching global framework in the study of
art. The absence of such an integrative framework might explain in
part why very few scholars so far have subjected the available cross-
cultural data to systematic secondary analyses.

This brings us to our second topic: intercultural comparison.
As we will see, the idea of comparing art in various human
contexts or settings worldwide is a theoretically complicated and
contested issue. Intercultural comparison is also a large issue, in
that it may assume numerous forms. Its objectives may vary from
highlighting cultural differences to discerning regional patterns
to establishing and accounting for universal commonalities in art
and artistic behavior. Subjects of comparison may range from the
creation of art to its violent destruction. Indeed, humans beings in
varying times and places are known to have attacked works of
art—iconoclasm has occurred in places and contexts as different as
the Low Countries, Rapa Nui (Easter Island), and, more recently,

Afghanistan. Under what conditions do humans violently destroy
visual images, either figurative ones or those, such as flags, that are
nonfigurative? What does this type of behavior tell us about the
interaction between human beings and images? Intercultural comparison, however problematic and controversial, may open up a
whole range of fundamental questions concerning the place and
role of the visual arts in human existence.

Looking at art around the globe, both diatopically and diachronically, not only leads to discerning a variety of spatiotemporal
traditions (if such may be initially distinguished for the sake of
analysis without neglecting internal diversity and change), each with
its own particularities, though often sharing similarities with others; it also leads to the observation that the world's various artistic
traditions have only rarely developed in complete isolation.
The third theme of this volume therefore concerns the artistic influences that are exerted by one culture or tradition on another,
or the mutual artistic crossfertilization that occurs between two or
more such analytical entities. Artistic exchanges between cultures,
or between more or less discrete sociocultural contexts or settings,
have obviously become vary salient in recent years, yet such exchanges have been occurring in one form or another for most of
human history—Egyptian influences on ancient Greek art, Chinese influences on Japanese art from the sixth century CE onward,
and the two-way interactions between African and European art in
the twentieth century are but a few and relatively recent examples.

Coeditor Kitty Zijlmans has suggested to conceptualize
such exchanges between varying settings as interculturalization in
the arts. Pending further elucidation, interculturalization may in
our case be provisionally characterized as referring to the processes of visual artistic exchange between two or more cultures or
contexts, including their preconditions, nature, and consequences.

HUMAN ARTISTIC BEHAVIOR

The mental processes and manual activities involved in what in
today's English is often referred to as "visual representation," are
late arrivals in human evolution. Drawing, painting, sculpting, or
otherwise creating visual stimuli that evoke perceptual and/or
semantic referents in a human beholder (a bird, a deity, the concept
of ten, and so on), is a behavior that is associated almost exclusively with the most recent human species, *Homo sapiens*. Within the
genus *Homo*, the same would seem to apply, by and large, to related
activities that seem to require less neurocognitive sophistication of
both creator and perceiver, activities such as modifying human
bodies and objects so as to give them heightened visual interest by
means of shape, color, or line. Clearly, the boundaries between
these two analytical sets of activities are often hard, if not impossible, to establish, as when modification of the human body's appearance implies both aesthetic effects and signaling social status.

In fact, it is for a particular field of overlap between these two sets of activities that many people today reserve the word "art," with numerous contemporary definitions of the term in one way or another mentioning both "aesthetics" (denoting, say, high quality or captivating visual appearance) and "meaning" (referring to some high quality or captivating referential content) as diagnostic features—although here, too, any clear-cut distinction between the two appears unwarranted, if only since there is no signified without a signifier (cf. Van Damme 1996). Visual artistic behavior would then refer to the creation of any material or, now, virtual object displaying these two features, as well as the use of such objects in a given context (which may involve senses other than the visual, a tangible environment, intangible ideas, and so on). In order to cast our net as widely as possible in exploring human visual artistic behavior, including its ingredients or building blocks, one may propose to direct attention to any object made or modified by humans and capable of engaging perceivers' attention because of its appearance and/or any references or associations it might evoke.

A category of carefully produced handaxes that were made by the ancestors of modern humans from around 1.6 million years ago onwards, may well prove to be an exception to the idea that activities aimed at increasing visual appeal and attention are exclusive to *Homo sapiens* in the history of human evolution. By 500,000 to 400,000 years ago, these pear-shaped stone tools displayed a striking symmetry, both *en face* and in profile. Some of these exquisitely crafted objects have other intriguing features: they show no traces of use-wear, even under a microscope, and some are too big, or too small, to perform the practical tasks they appear to be designed for.

Archaeologists Marek Kohn and Steven Mithen (1999) have suggested an interesting but controversial interpretation of these objects by drawing on evolutionary theory and specifically the concept of sexual selection, which concerns mate choice and its effects. Kohn and Mithen propose that the carved stones served to signal to members of the opposite sex that their maker, probably male, has "good genes": he is able to secure resources, capable of planning ahead, skillful, has endurance, and enough leisure to engage in the production of nonutilitarian objects. (This signaling need not involve a deliberate intention on the part of the maker, or a conscious or even an unconscious consideration on the part of the beholder—let alone that it requires knowledge of genetics. Evolutionary thinking suggests that members of the opposite sex who happened to be drawn to "sexy handaxe" producers as mates, made advantageous choices when it came to the survival of their genes in the physical and sociocultural environments of the time-frame concerned. The competitive offspring of the admirers and creators of the objects—creators who might have simply been enjoying what they did well—would then inherit the same interest in the production of handaxes. The objects could in sum be considered "indexes" of certain motor and mental capacities, as determined by an analyst, in a way not unlike conceptualizing a peacock's tail as an index of the animal's genetic qualities and an attractor to peahens, although in human evolution associations and deliberations are likely to play an increasingly important role.)

As to the conspicuous symmetry of the objects, Kohn and Mithen argue that, although making the artefact sit comfortably in the hand, the imposed symmetry goes beyond utilitarian requirements (stone tools taking less time and skill to produce are said to do as well). Its presence in the context of females sexually selecting males (or perhaps vice versa) is elucidated with reference to a "perceptual bias" for symmetry. By this it is meant that early humans had already evolved a sensitivity to symmetry as a property of stimuli other than made objects, such as the human body (where symmetry counts as an index of stable development and good health). "The makers of handaxes, we argue, were simply tapping into this perceptual bias, making artefacts that caught the attention of, and were most probably attractive to, members of the opposite sex" (Kohn and Mithen 1999, 523).[2]

Discussion of these issues aside, it needs to be observed that *homo aestheticus*, who in his or her most basic form discriminates between visual or other sensorial stimuli in terms of perceived agreeableness (human bodies, berries, sounds, landscapes, and so on), is indeed likely to be much older than *homo faber* or *homo artifex*, the maker of things, let alone *homo pictor*, the creator of images or visual representations.[3] The symmetrical handaxes may then present the first material evidence we have for what might be called *homo faber aestheticus*. Applying the very broad conception of visual art hinted at above, one could even suggest that these conspicuous handaxes signal the arrival in the archaeological record of *homo artisticus visualis*, a point of view perhaps first defended by the historian Joseph Alsop (1982, 33ff).

The art historian David Summers (2003) has the history of art in fact begin even earlier, around 2.5 million years ago, when *Homo habilis*, handy human, began producing simple stone tools in East Africa: the first evidence we have of what Summers calls "facture," referring to things made, or artifacts.[4] Rudimentary as the stone tools of *Homo habilis* may be (their manufacture involves but a few blows with one stone producing sharp edges in another, as well as usable flakes), they do present the first material witnesses of the human capacity to transform a medium, although it would take hundreds of thousands and indeed some two million years or more before the evolution of this capacity would result in the creation of anything that we might broadly recognize as artistic.

The stone tools produced by *Homo habilis* (whose brain was less than half the size and no doubt differently organized from today's human brain) present an intriguing moment in the development of hominid manual and cognitive capacities. Today we know that various species of living primates, as well as many other

2
According to Kohn and Mithen, symmetrical handaxes became less prominent when, due to the increase in brain size between 300,000 and 200,000 years ago, children were born earlier and matured more slowly, making mothers more dependent on males for protection and providing food. Female mate-choice criteria changed, placing more emphasis on the relationships with mates and their ability to provision resources (rather than their genes alone). This made it no longer worthwhile for males to invest in the manufacture of conspicious handaxes, and they started concentrating instead on the production of more functionally effective varied toolkits.

3
The concept of *homo pictor* was introduced by Hans Jonas in 1961. There is as yet no consensus on what the English words "picture" and "image," or the cognate German *Bild*, exactly mean. The same goes for "representation," a term that in the context of the visual arts might be replaced by "presentation," in the sense that a visual stimulus (*representing* something or not) is presented or offered to a beholder—in whose brain this stimulus is then "represented," as neuroscientists say (to complicate matters further). Recent and variously conceived discussions on the definition and nature of images can be found in, for example, Mitchell 2005; Boehm 2006 [1994], 2007; Hyman 2006; Stafford 2007.

4
Since making tools had long been considered a feature typical of any being broadly defined as human, *Homo habilis* was designated the first species of the genus *Homo*. Some paleontologists now reclassify this small-brained species as belonging to the older genus *Australopethicus*. Dated between c. 4.5 and 1.5 million years ago, this family of "southern apes" from Africa is comprised of various species, the best known of which is *Australopithecus afarensis*, most famously represented by the skeleton of "Lucy," who lived some 3.2 million years ago. Once considered the ancestor of present-day humans, *Homo habilis* is now generally regarded as an evolutionary dead-end. It is presently thought that more recent species have descended from *Homo ergaster*, a somewhat younger but partly contemporaneous hominid that also made stone tools. From this early human evolved a species known as *Homo erectus*, who as early as 1.8 million years ago, it is now estimated, left Africa to colonize Asia. Its 1000 cc brain almost double the size of that of *Homo habilis*, and having mastered fire, *Homo erectus* would thrive there for hundreds of thousands of years. Some of its descendants may well have lived up to 12,000 years ago, if the

animals, use tools, too, such as the stones that some groups of chimpanzees utilize to crack nuts. Unlike *Homo habilis*, however, none of these tool-using animals seem to use one tool to create another. At some point in hominid evolution, then, we see the emergence of a brain whose neural circuitry not only allows for particular capacities and experiences but for combining these into the behavior of beating one stone against another and then putting the resulting products to work to solve problems, facilitate the execution of certain tasks, or indeed modify yet other objects. Allowing for some sense of drama, the arrival of stone tools thus also signals the rudimentary beginnings of the human capacity to shape the world and in the process be shaped by it (cf. Spivey 2005).

Brains, then, are not only restricted or selective when it comes to collecting information from the outside world; they are also very selective in *connecting* this information (hard stones and closed nuts; the sharp edges produced by beating stones and the cutting of carcasses; and so on). This should make us aware not only of how much we may be missing out on today, by failing to absorb and creatively combine information, but also may help us to appreciate the incremental steps in neurocognitive development that would be taken later, leading up to the imaginative creation and meaningful perception of increasingly complex visual images—an evolution, also, that would at some point lead to the development of writing systems and that has spawned the virtual worlds of our digital age. It is easy to take for granted a brain capable of performing all the operations involved—operations native to us, members of *Homo sapiens*, but apparently absent in human evolution until quite recently. Precisely what these operations are, and how modern brains facilitate them, however, are matters that will occupy scholars for some time to come.

AFRICAN ORIGINS

Modern dating techniques and genetic research would seem to converge in suggesting that "anatomically modern humans" arose in Africa some 200,000 years ago. Discussions remain of what is in any case a gradual process; but more challenging to present-day scholars is the question of when humans became "cognitively" and "behaviorally" modern: at what moment in time did they not only "look like us," but did they start thinking and behaving in ways we would consider characteristic of the humans populating the earth today? Unsurprisingly, there is no consensus on what exactly differentiates the thought and behavior of "modern" humans (*Homo sapiens*) from those of "premodern" humans. In order to identify in the archaeological record the arrival of cognitive and behavioral modernity, scholars have drawn up lists that include such characteristics as the presence of microlithic technology, tools made from bone rather than stone alone, indications of long distance trade, and elaborate burials—all seen as material evidence of significant mental and behavioral changes in human evolution.[5]

Enumerations of cognitive and behavioral modernity's traits commonly include some reference to "art and decoration." In these cases, art usually denotes any human-made figurative image, while decoration particularly refers to what is interpreted as personal ornamentation. Figurative imagery and personal decoration are awarded special significance because they are considered, along with ritualized burials, as the first material evidence of "symbolic behavior," which is typically seen as the most defining trait of human modernity (and to which language also prominently belongs). It should be noted, however, that the qualifier "symbolic" is often poorly defined and loosely applied in prehistoric contexts (cf. Currie 2004, 120ff; but see Hovers et al. 2003).

In addition to the question of what makes humans cognitively and behaviorally modern, visual artistic behavior and their attendant mental processes notably included, scholars also examine the questions of when and how (or why). Did cognitive and behavioral modernity coincide with the appearance of an altered anatomy, which in modern humans comprises a brain case whose shape suggests an enlargement of the prefrontal cortex, site of the "higher" cognitive functions? Or did various forms of modern thought and behavior have to await genetic mutations and reorganizations of the brain that are still more difficult to establish than "hard" anatomical changes? Some scholars are less concerned with neurocognitive preconditions, stressing instead the effects of environmental pressures acting on preexisting cognitive capabilities (the presence of which must then be accounted for as well). Still others emphasize the inventions of individuals whose innovations were then transmitted by means of what we tend to call culture or tradition. This view, while pointing to what is undeniably a major force in human existence, nonetheless needs to acknowledge that the inventions were enabled by a certain type of brain. It must also allow for other humans around who were neurocognitively able " to get the idea," as well as to imitate and transmit the inventions that would otherwise have been lost, unless reinvented.

Geometric Engravings

Scholars concerned with these matters have only started to digest the latest archaeological discoveries in Africa and ponder their implications. Central to present-day discussions, especially where visual artistic behavior is concerned, are the recent finds from Blombos Cave, situated some 30 meters above sea-level at the southernmost strip of the African continent. Excavations led by Christopher Henshilwood have yielded, among other things, a piece of flattened ochre showing a series of engraved X-shaped or crosshatched marks. The engravings appear to be framed on the two longest sides by incised lines, while another line seems to run across the middle of the design (Henshilwood et al. 2002; images

6

A piece of engraved flint from the site of Qafzeh, Israel, showing a series of what could be roughly described as semicircular, nested markings, is older, dated to 100,000 to 90,000 years ago (d'Errico et al. 2003, 20), but it is also more contentious. Even more controversial are the markings on an elephant bone found in Bilzingsleben, Germany, estimated to be 400,000 to 350,000 years old, and said to have a series of 7 and a series of 14 regularly spaced engraved lines (Mania and Mania 1988). Many scholars do not regard these marks as deliberate but as the accidental result of activities such as cutting meat; but see, for example, Hodgson (2006a, 63), who also draws attention to "the first documented 'intentional' marks (a meandering line and cupele), from Auditorium cave, Bhimbekta, India (c. 500,000 to 200,000 bp) ...."

7

It should of course be noted that in both the Blombos case and the case of the earlier symmetrical handaxes, the contemporaneous visual appeal of the properties concerned—the symmetry but also the patterned surface texture and sometimes glistening black stone in case of the handaxes, and the cross-hatched pattern on the Blombos piece—is inferred by present-day viewers on the basis of their own responses, precariously but not altogether unreasonably in light of cross-cultural empirical data on human visual preferences and their suggested evolutionary origins (see Van Damme 1996, chap. 3; Voland and Grammer 2003; Eibl-Eibesfeldt and Sütterlin 2007).

can be found on the internet). There appears no doubt that we are dealing here with markings of a deliberately patterned type. Dated to c. 75,000 years ago, the engraved Blombos piece is generally considered the earliest unquestionable example of a human-made geometric pattern known so far.[6]

The announcement of its discovery in late 2001 led to considerable attention in the popular press. Paper headings hailed the Blombos ochre as "the world's oldest art object," and a *Nature* science update claimed that because of this find "art history doubles" (Whitfield 2002)—an assertion referencing the figurative cave paintings of Chauvet in southern France, discovered in 1994 and said to be some 32,000 years old. Claims such as these make one wonder about the tacit definitions of art involved. One possibility concerns an "aesthetic" definition that conceives of visual art as the purposeful modification of a medium such that the resulting properties please the human eye. A characterization like this would indeed be in keeping with a still widespread Western conception of art as referring to human-made beauty. If one were effectively to apply such a definition, the symmetrical handaxes discussed earlier might qualify instead as the oldest art forms presently known.

If the art-status of the Blombos piece depends on its assumed aesthetic properties,[7] one needs to ask not only why the object's patterned lines would be considered attractive, but also what enabled and what prompted the creator of the engravings to "beautify" a piece of ochre. Existing theories and views on human evolution, perception, and art-making may shed some light on these questions—questions that are crucial to any attempt to account for the arrival of human mark-making or geometric pattern creation in aesthetic terms.

Thus one might take a clue from the idea of "perceptual bias," suggesting in this case that the human brain is attuned, for good evolutionary reasons, to finding regularities in nature and experiencing these as pleasing, however mildly perhaps. This is what Derek Hodgson (2006a) has recently done, although he does not use the term perceptual bias, starting instead from the concept of "neurovisual resonance." Following earlier researchers, Hodgson suggests that in order to make sense of their visual environment, humans and other primates long ago evolved a sensitivity to such features as straight lines and repetitive patterns (as well as such other visual properties as color contrast). Purified and concentrated versions of these and other geometric features would then hyperstimulate the brain and increase the pleasure that "rewards" the detection of visual regularity. This may explain in part Paleolithic humans' interest in the crystals they are known to have collected, but the brain's innate response to visual patterning might also shed light on the question of why humans started creating geometric designs.

With regard to their appearance on durable materials,

Hodgson proposes that the arbitrary scratch-marks left on hard surfaces by the use of stone tools (for example, when defleshing bones) will have accidentally assumed the form of a regular pattern at times. Provided the neurocognitive development of sufficient measures of visual memory, awareness, visuo-motor-control, and concentration, as well as the necessary neural connections between the brain parts enabling such capacities, these accidental patterns may have inspired humans to intentionally create durable visual patterns for the intrinsic pleasure they provide to the evolved human brain. Hodgson further suggests, in line with Ellen Dissanayake's work (e.g., this volume), that the making of stable geometric designs may have led to feelings of control and reassurance in a world characterized by flux and uncertainty.

Once having come into existence, geometric designs may have acquired additional significance or complementary effects. If we continue our emphasis on visual impact, and draw on existing approaches, one might then ask, for example, whether the creation of geometric designs also came to serve, in analytical retrospect, as a way of "showing off," "sexy handaxe hypothesis"-like (see Miller 2000 for an extended discussion of sexual selection and art). Or, one might interpret geometric patterns, like those on the Blombos piece, as instances of "making special" (Dissanayake, this volume), an activity aimed at emphasizing the extraordinary character of (in this case) an object, or the context in which it is used.

The presence of arresting geometric patterns, moreover, might also have led to assigning some form of "meaning" to them, turning a geometric design into a visual signifier that stands for some agreed-upon signified. The creation of geometric patterns would then additionally (some would say predominantly) present an act of intentional visual referentiality, a major step in human cognitive evolution, especially if the relationship between signifier and signified is established on a conventional or arbitrary basis (that is, when it is "purely symbolic").

This brings us back to our original question. Calling the engraved Blombos ochre art might also imply a tacit "semantic" definition of art as first and foremost displaying "visual symbolism" —in keeping with the oft-heard characterization of art as "symbolic representation" (a characterization that would include visual stimuli not generally considered "art," stimuli such as particular hand-signs or numerals having an agreed-upon meaning). Whether or not they consider the Blombos design an instance of art, the majority of archaeologists—including excavator Henshilwood and his team—appear to interpret the patterned lines as "unequivocally symbolic" (Mithen 2005, 252). Although it remains unclear what the design might refer to, this symbolism would demonstrate that the Blombos people were capable of "abstract thought" and "association by convention," and that that they were able to store as well as retrieve information outside the brain. The mental capacities involved are in themselves often held to presuppose the existence of syntactical language, not so much because it is similarly symbolic but rather because language would be required to establish by intersubjective agreement the link between the engraving and its stipulated meaning.

Proponents of a symbolic interpretation of the geometric pattern from Blombos like to point out that in this cave a second piece of ochre was found with roughly the same design, showing similar X-shaped engravings but no framing or dividing lines. The repetition of the pattern would suggest the existence of a shared "symbolic code." This seems not very convincing evidence, but a further seven pieces of engraved ochre from Blombos are said to be under study (d'Errico et al. 2005, 6).

Beads

Adherents of a symbolic reading of the Blombos ochre also draw attention to another find in the cave: some 40 deliberately perforated estuarine shells (*Nassarius kraussianus*) that show signs of having been strung and worn as beads (d'Errico et al. 2005). Beads are almost universally regarded as symbolic by archaeologists, who, inspired by studies in ethnography, emphasize the social role of beads in signifying individual and collective identities. Specifically, beads may signal the wearer's age, kin group, marital status, and so on, thus visually marking and accentuating social differentiations.

When the finding of the Blombos shells was first announced in 2004, this was considered a discovery as spectacular as that of the ochre, in that the perforated shells, likewise dated to 75,000 years ago, were generally held to have almost doubled the age for human bead-production — not counting a few disputed cases previously known only to a handful of specialists, such as the 90,000 year-old perforated and ochered marine shells from the site of Qafzeh, Israel.[8] This led to claims that the Blombos shell beads were too anomalous to allow any significant conclusions about human behavior to be drawn during the time period concerned. Meanwhile, 13 deliberately perforated shells, some of which are ochered, have been discovered in a cave in Taforalt, in northeastern Morocco, and they have been firmly dated to some 82,000 years ago (Bouzouggar et al. 2007). A few other perforated shells from northern Africa and adjacent parts may even be older.[9] Interestingly, all these beads are made from *Nassarius* shell, as are the Blombos beads from southern Africa, and they were found up to 200 km from the sea, implying transport and probably exchange or trade; similarly, the Blombos shells are said to haven been collected originally some 30 km from the cave in which they were found.

Although archaeologists consider beads to be symbolic, in describing their probable use in necklaces, or bracelets, they do use terms like "ornament" or "decoration," implying that the wearing of beads also had an aesthetic effect. Indeed, the shells used as beads in Paleolithic contexts seem to have been selected for such

8

The site of Qafzeh represents a temporary intrusion of modern humans into what archaeologists tend to call the Levant. The shells were found in association with burials that are dated to between 100,000 and 90,000 years ago (d'Errico et al. 2003, 20). The evidence of these *Glycymeris* shells having been worn as beads, however, is considered to be unresolved, since they may also have served as ochre containers (d'Errico et al. 2005, 3–4).

9

Following the Blombos finds and the ensuing controversy, a team of scholars redated, by means of chemical analysis, a few shell beads found decades earlier at other sites. It is now suggested that two perforated shells from the Skhul rock shelter in Israel date to between 135,000 and 100,000 years ago, while a single shell bead from Oued Djebbana in Algeria may be some 90,000 years old (Vanhaeren et al. 2006).

visual qualities as bright color and luminosity (Balme and Morse 2006, 801). One may also note the repetitive pattern that emerges when similar-sized beads are strung together; alternation of color might add as well.

Aesthetic and symbolic functions do not necessarily rule each other out. For example, the making and wearing of beads might have started off as an aesthetic or a playful behavior (meaning that beads might have had their origins in intrinsically rewarding experiments in the material-visual realm), only later having social signaling added to their meaning. Such a hypothetical transformation may have come about because of increased associative capacities that enabled people to link the making of eye-catching beads to the qualities of those individuals who managed to secure particular types of shell and were dexterous enough to make them into beads by means of perforation—a feat not easily accomplished by present-day experimenters (Balme and Morse 2006, 808). These individuals might have worn these precious possessions themselves—a form of visual display demonstrating self-awareness—but they might also have presented them to others, for example in the context of courtship; beads could as well have been instrumental in creating and maintaining intergroup contacts (see also below). If worldwide practices today are anything to go by, the wearing of shells or other pendants might also have early acquired an apotropaic or protective function, or served to bring good luck.

Ochre

As do some older perforated shells, four of the 75,000-year-old Blombos beads show traces of red ochre. This may be the result of deliberate coloring or could be due to the shells having been worn on ochered bodies, among other possibilities (d'Errico et al. 2005, 16). Ochre is found in large quantities at African archaeological sites associated with anatomically modern humans, although its first use predates the arrival of modern humans by at least tens of thousands of years (McBrearthy and Brooks 2000, 528; Barham 2002). Some pieces of ochre, at times called "pencils" or "crayons," have clearly been rubbed against surfaces. It has been suggested that ochre might have been used for preparing hides, for medicinal reasons, or as an adhesive (McBrearthy and Brooks 2000; Wadley 2005). More popular, however, is a "symbolic" interpretation for the use of this material, with many archaeologists assuming that ochre was applied especially to human bodies in ritual contexts. Although this interpretation is mainly based on contested ethnographic analogies,[10] ochre might indeed have had some "significance" for early modern humans. This is suggested, for example, by the ochre-stained bones of an infant who was buried some 100,000 years ago in Border Cave, South Africa, together with a perforated shell that is thought to have been worn as a pendant.[11]

10
As Wadley (2005, 58) points out, "The common assumption about the use of large quantities of ochre in the MSA [Middle Stone Age in Africa, c. 250,000–40,000 years ago] is that red coloring was used for symbolic body decoration. This conjecture is based on analogy with modern hunter-gatherers living tens of thousands of years later. For example, red body-paint was used for puberty and marriage rituals by !Kung girls in northwestern Botswana in historic times .... There is, however, no way of testing whether ancient people practiced body painting, and the application of hunter-gatherer ethnography to the deep past can be problematic ... ethnographic analogy cannot be used as both a building block of a model and a test of the same model."

11
McBrearthy and Brooks 2000, 526, 528; cf. Mithen 2005, 252; Hoven et al. (2003) similarly argue for a symbolic use of ochre found in association with 100,000 to 90,000-years-old burials in Qafzeh.

12
It has been argued that the stone's grooves and abrasions, which microscopic analysis suggests to be human-made, have been added to enhance the object's natural "female" features (see d'Errico et al. 2003, 20). Mithen (2005, 229), however, objects that the incisions may have resulted from entirely utilitarian practices, such as blunting a razor-sharp blade.

The application of ochre to surfaces would at some point also result in geometric and figurative images. Figurative imagery brings us to a subject that some call "iconic representation"—the two- or three-dimensional rendering of humans and other animals, or to be more precise, the representation of things resembling those in the external world, or indeed imaginary worlds, fauna and flora especially, but also topographical features, built environments, and other human-made objects.

Specialists seem agreed that it is cognitively less exacting to produce and perceive three-dimensional figurative images than it is to create and make sense of two-dimensional iconic depictions (see Hodgson 2006a, 64). We may therefore begin by considering what we presently know about the first human creation of figurative or iconic images in the round. There is as yet no unambiguous evidence that early modern humans in Africa produced three-dimensional figurative imagery, although the few indications we do have give some credence to the speculation that they might have done so using such perishable, nonrecovered, but more easily modified media as mud or vegetal materials, including wood. Similarly, for this period we lack information on any ephemeral forms of modifying the body's appearance, involving, say, flowers, feathers, and plaited fibers, but also hairdressing, or about such possible practices as drawing in, and perhaps with, sand.

With respect to early iconic representation, one could mention two controversial modified stone objects that both date, in fact, to before the arrival of anatomically modern humans as presently conceived. One of these is an object recently discovered near the Moroccan town of Tan Tan (Bednarik 2003). It was found in layers that are provisionally dated to between 500,000 and 300,000 years ago. The so-called Tan Tan figurine is a small stone whose natural shape resembles that of a human being (at least to present-day eyes). Some of the object's natural grooves, which are in part responsible for its anthropomorphic appearance (e.g., a groove separating the "legs"), seem to have been accentuated artificially in what is interpreted as an attempt to enhance the human semblance. Interestingly, red pigment appears to have been applied to the object's surface. The "Berekhat Ram figurine," found in present-day Israel in an archaeological context dated to 233,000 years ago, presents a similar but even more controversial case of semi- or protosculptural activity.[12]

Exceptional and controversial as these objects may be, there are indications that hominids have long been capable of discerning human features in natural (meaning nonanthropogenic) objects. The oldest indication to date is a naturally weathered pebble resembling a hominid face that was found at a three-million-year-old occupation site in Makapansgat in South Africa, probably having been brought there from a riverbed a few kilometers away (Dart 1974). Given humans' evolved sensitivity to the visual appearance of the human body, particularly for mate choice, it is not all that surprising, in retrospect, that the increased capabilities of modifying materials, by means of stone tools or otherwise, would at some point lead to the further elaboration of objects that happen to bear a natural resemblance to human features. The late arrival in hominid evolution of this type of behavior, however, should warn us not to think too lightly of the combined capacities involved.

A similar thing appears to have happened with natural objects, such as cave walls, suggesting the shapes and outlines of especially animals (see also Onians, this volume). As for the latter, the archaeologist Sheila Coulson has recently reported on a large piece of rock—six meters long and two meters high—found in a cave in the Tsodilo Hills in Botswana and resembling the body and head of a python (press reports, late 2006). The surface of the rock shows hundreds of artificial indentations that might have been applied to suggest a snake's scales. The indentations appear to have been made by stone tools excavated in the cave, and which are provisionally dated to more than 70,000 years ago.

AFRICA AND BEYOND

Somewhere between perhaps 80,000 and 60,000 years ago, modern humans left Africa to colonize the rest of the world (where present, earlier humans, such as descendants of *Homo erectus* in Asia, would gradually be replaced by these newcomers having an evolutionary edge). Following a coastal trajectory, groups of humans are likely to have migrated along the present-day Arabian peninsula via India to southeast Asia and on to Australia, a continent that in all likelihood had not yet been populated by hominids. Other migrants, at some point turning north, would colonize Eurasia, probably following river courses at first.

Perhaps the exodus was engendered in part because of the consequences of climate changes that took place from c. 80,000 years ago onward, when temperatures dropped and the environment became more arid (Mellars 2006). This trend would have been enforced by the eruption of Mount Toba on Sumatra some 73,000 years ago. According to paleoanthropologist Stanley Ambrose (1998, 2003), this supereruption (the biggest in the last two million years and estimated to have been 3000 times as powerful as the 1980 Mount St. Helens eruption) caused a "volcanic winter" that may have lasted six years. This was followed by "an instant Ice Age" bringing drought, and famine, for at least a thousand years. Ambrose suggests that the drastic climate changes caused by the Toba eruption may have been responsible for the "bottleneck" that geneticists argue humans must have gone through at some fairly recent point when the population of modern humans is thought to have decreased to a mere ten thousand individuals or even less.

According to Ambrose, the remaining pockets of humans

13
As Mithen (2005, 250) notes, summariz-
ing the data provided by McBrearthy
and Brooks (2000), "Their age is
contentious. Radiocarbon dating of the
archaeological layer in which they
were found gives a date no older than
28,000 year ago. But fragments of os-
trich eggshell from the layer above the
slabs have been dated to 59,000 ago,
which agrees better with the types of
chipped-stone artefacts found with the
slabs. So the radiocarbon dates may
have been contaminated with more
recent material." As McBrearthy and
Brooks (2000, 525) point out more
generally with regard to the preservation of ancient paintings in Africa,
"subsaharan Africa contains few deep
limestone caves which can provide
the alkaline conditions conducive to
preservation. Prehistorically occupied
rockshelters are often no more than
overhangs with walls exposed to the
elements. [T]he earliest mural rock
paintings in Africa have probably long
since been lost through exfoliation
and the natural collapse of shallow cave
systems, and only rare discoveries of
buried pieces of painted rock provide
an indication of the true antiquity of
the tradition ...."

(thought to be situated in East Africa primarily) were under a
strong selection pressure for both intra- and intergroup cooperation and the sharing of information in order to survive. The exchange of beads may have been instrumental in fostering social
relationships among human groups. It is suggested that it was
the demand for ingenuity created by adverse circumstances, together with cooperation and the exchange of information, that led to
the development of more sophisticated technologies. These new
technologies then permitted the survivors' descendants to explore
more risky environments in Africa, and eventually enabled
modern humans to colonize the rest of the world.

There is presently some consensus that the exodus from
Africa took place around 65,000 years ago. This exodus is estimated
to have involved no more than a few hundred colonists, known to
geneticists as the "L 3 group" and said to present one wave of emi-
gration only (Mellars 2006). It has been argued, however, that both
genetic evidence (Oppenheimer 2004) and stone tools recently
found in India in a pre-Toba layer (Petraglia et al. 2007) suggest
that modern humans left Africa before the massive volcano eruption; the tools are currently a topic of debate among specialists.

Various forms of behavior that we would broadly recognize
as artistic seem to have accompanied *Homo sapiens* in its exodus
from Africa. Thus, in Australia, where modern humans arrived at
least 45,000 ago (O'Connell and Allen 2004), shell beads in all likelihood continued to be worn, with the oldest finds so far including
perforated shells that are dated to more than 30,000 years ago
(Balme and Morse 2006, 802). From around this time we also have
burials containing human bones covered with ochre. Red ochre
was used as well for what is claimed to be the oldest evidence for
rock painting in the world today: an ochered piece of rock, found
at Carpenter's Gap, Kimberley, in northwestern Australia, and
dated to around 40,000 years ago (Morwood 2002, 19).

Is this indeed the first evidence we have of humans applying
paint to rock? If so, could this mean that this type of behavior
developed only after modern humans had left Africa? Africa's oldest rock paintings yet discovered were found in the Apollo 11
Cave in Namibia (its name referring to the first moon landing that
took place during initial excavations in 1969). Several images of
animals appear on slabs of rock, with the most famous one showing
a quadruped whose hind legs are interpreted by some as human
(it is unclear whether the painted slabs have fallen off the roof or
wall of the cave, or whether they were originally made as "portable
art"). The paintings are traditionally dated to c. 28,000 years ago,
which at the time of their finding and first dating in the early 1970s
meant that they were almost twice as old as the oldest paintings
then known, from Altamira and Lascaux in Europe. It is now suggested that the paintings from the Apollo 11 Cave may in effect be
some 60,000 years old.[13] If so, this increases the possibility that
Africa is the birthplace of two-dimensional figurative imagery.

(Botswana's Tsodilo Cave, showing signs of sculptural activities around 70,000 years ago or more, also boasts paintings of an elephant and a gir-affe, but no announcements have yet been made as to their possible age.) This would suggest in turn that the ability to produce such imagery may well have been part of the neurocognitive (although not necessarily behavioral) repertoire of modern humans moving out of Africa.

As noted, there is as yet no unquestionable evidence that preexodus modern humans created three-dimensional imagery. For the oldest indisputable examples of figurative sculptures discovered so far we must turn to western Eurasia. Here modern humans were to gradually replace the Neanderthals, descendants of the hominid relatives their predecessors had branched off from in Africa some 300,000 years earlier. Recent excavations of the oldest levels of the Upper Paleolithical site of Kostenki, on the river Don in present-day Russia, suggest that modern humans first arrived in western Eurasia at least 45,000 years ago. The excavations have yielded shell beads and a worked piece of mammoth ivory that may represent a human head; if it does, it is the oldest figurative sculpture known so far (Anikovich et al. 2007).

Less ambiguous are recent finds from Vogelherd in south-western Germany, including a small ivory figure of a woolly mammoth and an animal interpreted as a lion, showing crossed incisions along its spine (similar X-shaped marks occur as well on other animal sculptures from Upper Paleolithic Europe). The figures were found in sediments that are dated to between 38,000 and 32,000 years ago (Conard et al. 2007). From roughly the same period are the figures that were discovered a few years ago in Hohlen Fells cave, also in southwestern Germany. Here archaeologists dug up three small ivory carvings: the oldest known representation of a bird, the head of an animal resembling a horse, and a sculpture interpreted as therianthropic, combining felid and human traits—the object is compared to the roughly contemporaneous, but much larger figure known as the *Löwenmensch* or "Lion Human" from Hohlenstein Stadel, found in 1939 (Conard 2003).

Other relatively well-known European finds from this period include a small ivory horse sculpture that was discovered in Vogelherd already in 1931 and that may have been worn as a pendant (it has a perforation between the forelegs), and, somewhat later, the delicately carved ivory head of a woman showing a long neck and a patterned hairdo or cap, found in Brassempouy in France.[14] The misleadingly labeled "Venus figurines" from Upper Paleolithic Europe, typically representing corpulent or obese women, appear to be somewhat more recent, too, with the most famous example, found in Willendorf in 1908, being dated to c. 25,000 years ago. This limestone figure, fitting in the palm of a hand, is covered with red ochre.

Like their relatives who migrated to Australia, the newly arrived modern humans in Europe not only made shell beads (as

14
For monographic surveys of Upper Paleolithic art in Europe, see Lorblanchet 1999; Bahn and Verlut 2001; White 2003; and Guthrie 2005.

well as other beads and pendants) but their activities included engraving and painting images on rock, as is testified, among others, by the depictions of animals and geometric designs found in Chauvet Cave, the earliest of which are estimated to be some 32,000 years old (Clottes 2003). Until very recently, Europe was in fact considered the cradle of human artistic behavior, with scholars employing such expressions as "creative explosion" (part of a more general "cognitive revolution") for what was regarded as the sudden advent of bead-making, painting, and sculpture in this human outpost some 30,000 years ago.

Farther afield, in Mal'ta, to the west of Lake Baikal in Siberia, were found ivory sculptures depicting the human form and birds, which are assumed to be some 23,000 years old. Of the 30 anthropomorphic figures unearthed, 20 are complete, and the majority of them seem to represent women. Most of the 15 avian sculptures depict birds in flight (they are interpreted as swans, geese, and ducks). Like some of the human figures, they are perforated. By analogy with nineteenth- and twentieth-century Siberian hunter-gatherer practices, the perforated sculptures have been interpreted as "spirit helpers" that were attached to a "shaman's costume" (Schlesier 2001).

Interpreting Paleolithic Art

The recent Hohle Fels findings, too, are interpreted in the context of shamanism, this time with reference to David Lewis-Williams's (2002) intriguing theory on the beginnings of human image-making. Lewis-Williams suggests that the images characteristic of Upper Paleolithic art, namely animals and geometric designs, find their origin in hallucinations and other "altered states of consciousness," especially as experienced by "shamans" in a state of trance (induced by ritual, sensory deprivation, or psychotropic drugs).

In proposing his theory, Lewis-Williams draws on shamanistic practices found today in hunter-gatherer societies all over the world. He thereby argues that present-day humans have basically the same brains as their Paleolithic ancestors tens of thousands of years ago. Now when we perceive the world it is ultimately the brain that generates the images we experience. The brain may in fact produce images even in the absence of external visual stimuli, as in mental visualization and perhaps more vividly in dreams or other altered states of consciousness (but also, for example, when one slightly pushes the eyeball, resulting in the visual experience of various geometric or abstract shapes in different colors, something experienced more intensely by people suffering from migraine).

It is suggested, furthermore, that the images generated and experienced by the brain in trance-like conditions (such as images of animals) would have been interpreted as pertaining to phenomena existing on another plane, as glimpses or visions of beings populating "alternative realities." Indeed, Lewis-Williams argues that the modern human brain is not only able to self-generate images; it is also able to remember these and to share and discuss them with others through both verbal language and visual images—images that on this view were created by shamans as records of what was powerfully experienced when sojourning in "other realms."

These neurocognitive developments and their implications would at the same time present the beginnings of "religion" (and of "religious specialists," potentially also wielding sociopolitical power). The new and extended view of "reality" that resulted, originating in socially shared experiences of altered states of consciousness, may have included the belief in an afterlife spent in a "spirit world," which could explain the arrival of ritualized burials in anatomically modern humans.

Shamanistic rituals are said to involve not only experiencing spirits in the form of animals, but also the shaman's transformation into such a spirit being, which might shed light on the occurrence of therianthropic images in Paleolithic art. It has been objected, however, that not all artefacts interpreted as therianthropic represent actual mixtures of humans and other animals —the so-called Lion Human of Hohlenstein Stadel, for example, might as well be a depiction of a bear standing upright (Guthrie 2005, 446)—and that some of these images may in fact depict a human in disguise, pretending to be an animal in the context of the hunt (see Hodgson 2006b, who provides a more general critical appraisal of Lewis-Williams's neuropsychological theory, arguing, for example, that the literature on hallucinations is less supportive of its claims than suggested).

An alternative account of Upper Paleolithic art has been presented by R. Dale Guthrie (2005), who does not, however, address the preconditions or origins of human image-making. Guthrie, focusing on Ice Age Europe, proposes that the images of animals on cave walls and other objects result from their creators' fascination with the local wildlife. Countering the prevailing "magico-religious paradigm" in prehistoric art research (as does Onians, this volume), Guthrie suggests that many images might in fact have been made by male adolescents who were inspired by what he calls "testosterone moments," such as the excitement of the hunt or the confrontation with large predators (Guthrie additionally argues that most of the handprints found in caves are those of male teenagers). This profane perspective on Paleolithic art-making is also deployed to elucidate the sexual imagery frequently found in cave paintings and rock engravings but also on portable objects made of ivory and other materials. Featuring mainly women and female sexual organs, this prehistoric "graffiti" could present young men's sexual fantasies or experiences.

Paleolithic art has always been and continues to be a fascinating field of competing interpretative theories. One currently debated topic concerns the question of whether or not early art forms had an adaptive function, meaning whether or not artistic behavior contributed to the survival and reproduction of those who practiced it. Could it be that, once having come into existence, the tendency to create visual art was selected, and therefore able to spread, because it turned out to confer some evolutionary advantage on individuals or groups so inclined?

Among the proponents of an adaptionist perspective on art, a distinction may be made between those who favor an explanation of art's role in the competition among individuals (specifically for mates) and those who argue for the social benefits of art's presence, such as its effects on group solidarity, cooperation, and the intergenerational transmission of knowledge (for example, by making messages more memorable). Scholars who deny that the visual arts may be ascribed an adaptive value usually suggest that these arts have evolved as by-products of capacities and activities that in themselves are probably adaptive (or at least have been so in the past). This is not to deny that the visual arts, once there, had particular effects on human communities, but it is to deny that these effects facilitated survival and reproduction, at least in some direct sense. These issues are further elaborated upon in Dissanayake's contribution to this volume.

CULTURAL AND ARTISTIC DIVERSIFICATION

As in the western part of Eurasia, modern humans first arrived in present-day Siberia when climatic conditions allowed them to, which was likely to have been several millennia earlier than the Mal'ta finds mentioned above. From the northeast of Eurasia humans would go on to colonize the Americas, although it is still unclear exactly when this first happened (estimates vary from 35,000 to 12,000 years ago, with most scholars appearing to prefer the later dates).

To the south of Eurasia, colonization of new territories by modern humans went on until recently. Setting out from present-day Taiwan, which they seem to have occupied from China, the seafaring people known as Austronesians spread out over insular southeast Asia and island Melanesia from around 6000 years ago. Most parts of this area were already inhabited by modern humans following the exodus from Africa tens of millennia earlier, but migrating Austronesians or their descendants were the first humans ever to populate the western Pacific (Fiji, Tonga, Samoa), with estimates of their arrival varying between 1500 and 800 BCE. From there, at the end of the first millennium CE, they would colonize more isolated islands, including Hawai'i to the north. Rapa Nui or Easter Island in the southeast Pacific, like Aotearoa New Zealand in the southwest, may have been first populated by humans as recently as 1200 CE (Hunt and Lipo 2006). Incidentally, Rapa Nui boasts rock engravings and cave paintings, in addition to its famous stone statues.

While adapting to their new environments—from

Australian deserts to Eurasian steppe to tropical islands, not to mention the diverse ecologies of the Americas—modern humans would in time develop an increasing variety of ways of life and worldviews. So did those modern humans who had remained in Africa, migrating and occupying various ecological niches, or who would at some point reenter the continent.

Agriculture, having been invented independently at various places in the world after the last Ice Age some 10,000 years ago, would have a profound impact on the life styles and value systems of those populations who adopted it, creating sociocultural differences between them and those who remained hunter-gatherers. After the introduction of agriculture, social and political organization would take on new and more complex forms. Social differentiation intensified as a result of extended group size and increased specialization. In many places in the world, sedentary humans became organized into ever-larger political structures—in the terms of evolutionist scholars: from villages to chiefdoms to early and, then, modern states.

What are the implications of these developments for the production of the visual arts and their use? In what is still one of the very few attempts to study art as a global phenomenon across time and place, art historian Esther Pasztory (2005) has recently tried to link varying types of sociocultural organization to the forms assumed and the roles performed by the visual arts in these diverse settings. As to their roles or functions, Pasztory argues that among hunter-gatherers, in village-based societies, and in states relying on oral tradition, the visual arts hold a prominent place as central forms of communication (in each of these cases the arts serve specific communicative functions and assume different forms). With the large-scale introduction of writing, texts become privileged, and the visual arts lose some of their significance, develop complex relations with texts, and tend to become aestheticized. When the mass media, made possible by today's modern technology, take center stage in sociocultural communication, argues Pasztory, there is a twofold development: whereas the visual arts of previous times are collected and worshipped in museums, contemporary forms are marginalized because addressing and received by no more than a very small audience.

Pasztory's pioneering analysis on a worldwide scale is presented in such a way that it might serve as an invitation to scholars to join the debate on systematic, contextualized cross-cultural comparisons in the visual arts. The perspective adopted by Pasztory tallies well, incidentally, with the approach that the anthropologist Donald Brown (this volume) has developed for the study of portrait styles—naturalistic or stylized—in relation to the sociopolitical contexts in which they occur.

The changed nature of socioeconomic and sociopolitical organization among sedentary humans also meant that in many societies certain individuals could spend a considerable amount of their time creating visual imagery, for a variety of purpose. Thus, Mesoamerican Aztec society from the fourteenth to the early sixteenth century included a class of people referred to as *toltécatl*, those who specialized in sculpture, painting, pottery, and metalwork. These were individuals well versed in the practices and ideals of *toltecáyotl*, or "artistry," a term that for the Aztecs evoked the much-admired artistic skills of the Toltec culture that flourished in Mesoamerica before 1300 CE.[15] Similarly, the Yoruba of West Africa have for centuries had their *onisona*, individuals who have mastered *ona*, the ability to skillfully and imaginatively design two- or three-dimensional figurative and abstract images in any visual medium.[16] Akin to the Yoruba concept of *ona* is the English word *art*, especially as used in the previous few centuries, with its practitioners being referred to as *artists*.[17] Many other cultural ways of conceptualizing image-makers exist. Some traditions, for example, conceive of painters/calligraphers as thoroughly different from those who create figurative or geometric images in wood, stone, or metal.

The conditions required for individuals to become specialists in the visual arts and the ways in which image-makers are conceptualized then present interesting topics for both cultural-particularistic and intercultural comparative research. So do a host of other issues relating to visual artists and artistry, including the use of materials (which mostly exhibit a mixture of visual qualities and economic and symbolic values, with the latter including those associated with their gendered use); the training of producers of imagery, including attention to the tools and techniques applied and the instruction into stylistic and iconographical matters as well as artistic and aesthetic standards; the extent of individuality manifest in the works created; the role of artistic innovation; "artist-patron" relationships; the social status of the creators of images; the personalities of artists or image-makers; and so on.

The presence of "art" and "artists" has in many societies worldwide led to reflections on the nature of artistry and its products. Given particular conditions, these reflective practices may give rise to culturally recognized specialists pondering such matters as the nature, creation, and qualities of the visual arts. Thus, to return to our three disparate examples, the Aztecs had their *tlamatinime*, thinkers whose speculations on ultimate reality included deliberations on the nature of the various arts; the Yoruba have their *amewa*, "knowers of *ewa*, beauty or artistic quality"; and Western cultures their *philosophers of art* (sometimes also known as *aestheticians*) and *art critics*.[18]

Besides reflecting on the nature of images, visual qualities, artistic talent, and so on, there are of course numerous other ways of examining the visual arts. Examination may ascribe artistic objects to a particular time and place, analyze their materials, study their composition, clarify their symbolic references, elucidate their function, and so on. Obvious as they may perhaps seem to readers

15
Kubler 1991, 2, drawing on Léon-Portilla 1980. Many Aztec visual artists were in fact subjugated Toltec (Anderson 2004 [1990], 153).

16
See, for example, Adepegba 1992, and Abiodun, Drewal, and Pemberton 1991, 13.

17
For a history of the Western concepts of art and artist, see Shiner 2001.

18
For the Aztec, see Anderson 2004 [1990], 148ff, drawing on the codices published by, among others, Léon-Portilla 1966. The Yoruba *amewa* are briefly discussed by Abiodun (1990, 65ff), who notes that these individuals acquire their knowledge by "walking with the elders." The *amewa* would seem to function primarily as "art critics," who are traditionally known among the Yoruba also by various other labels, including *gbenugbenu*, "'one who carves with one's mouth (voice)'—a sculptor of words" (Yai 1999, 32). For more on the rich Yoruba vocabulary pertaining to matters of visual art, artistry, and aesthetic, see, for example, Abiodun 1990 and Lawal 2001.

of a volume like this, performing any of these or related examinations in any systematic sense appears to be peculiar to certain times and places, and would indeed seem far less common than reflecting on the arts. In his book *The Rare Art Traditions* — one of the isolated efforts from the second half of the twentieth century in what we would today call world art studies, or world art history — Alsop (1982) suggests that at least the historical study of the visual arts, which he argues goes hand in hand with art-collecting, is found only during certain time periods of a few discrete traditions: Chinese culture, with an offshoot in Japan; the Western tradition, especially Greco-Roman antiquity and the period from the Renaissance onwards; and the Islamic world. Mapping, analyzing, and comparing scholarly engagements with the visual arts in various traditions in time and space may then be considered one of the many future tasks of world art studies (see also Elkins 2007 and Cao Yiqiang, this volume).

Artistic Diversity and Its Intercultural Study

The relatively rare practices of studying art would seem to have limited their attention by and large to examining the art forms of the tradition that gave rise to these practices. Indeed, studying the visual arts from traditions other than one's own is even rarer. Yet this is, of course, what we are witnessing today. This type of intercultural study of the arts raises fundamental epistemological questions. Is it indeed possible for a member of one culture to arrive at some minimal understanding at least of the art forms of another tradition, as is assumed in any attempt at intercultural examination? Or have human cultures over time become so diverse and idiosyncratic that this no longer presents a realistic prospect, as radical relativists would have it? In defending the latter position, scholars usually highlight what they consider the untranslatability of a tradition's core concepts, thereby suggesting that cultures present conceptually and semantically closed universes that are forever inaccessible to cultural outsiders. In more moderate views, studying a tradition's central concepts is suggested to provide bridges between cultures and thus increase transcultural understanding.

Now it will be clear that all concepts from a given tradition, including those that are relevant to this tradition's art, have their own histories and their own semantic fields, being couched within their own conceptual frames of reference. (Moreover, each of these concepts is likely to be interpreted more or less differently by different native speakers at any given moment in time.) The above examples from the vocabularies of Nahuatl (the Aztec language), Yoruba and English suggest, however, that there may well be a significant semantic overlap between various cultures' concepts used in relation to the visual arts, although other examples could be given that show only a minimal correspondence or perhaps none at all. Provided proper elucidation and contextualization, in analyses of visual art written in a language other than

the one spoken by the producers and users of that art, key concepts
and other crucial terms could then be retained in their original
forms, in order for their meanings or semantic resonance to remain
intact as much as practically possible.

For example, discussions in English centering on early
twentieth-century art and culture in west Central Africa may retain
the Kikongo concept of *nkisi* (as specialized scholars tend to do,
after an appropriate introduction to the idea of "power object"),
while analyses in Chinese of seventeenth-century Dutch painting
might want to preserve the term *stilleven* in reference to images
that, in what is but one interpretation, aim to arrest life by means
of compositions of natural and human-made objects. Hindu practices of visually interacting with statues regarded as divine are
characterized better by a properly presented notion of *darsan* than
by the first part of this sentence, just as "supernatural power" is a
poor translation of the *mana* held to be inherent in certain Polynesian sculpted objects, and so on.

More generally, studying traditions' artistic and aesthetic
vocabularies and the conceptual frames in which they are embedded may provide a fascinating entry into other cultural worlds,
throwing a unique light on the creation, use, and experience of the
visual arts in varying semantic and affective universes (see also
Ben-Ami Scharfstein's essay on comparative aesthetics, this volume). Such examinations are then also likely to put into relief
the terminologies used to discuss and study the visual arts in the
tradition and language that the analyst is most familiar with,
thus raising one's awareness of the historical contingency and cultural embeddedness of all concepts used in relation to art.

The proposition to thoroughly consider, whenever possible,
a culture's conceptualizations when studying its art, is likely to be
regarded as quite uncontroversial, although problems of transcultural understanding remain (and extreme particularists will
continue to stress the futility of any attempt at intercultural comprehension). Causing more debate today, now that the study of art
is becoming evermore intercultural, is the question of whether
and to what extent the specialized terminology of various traditions
can contribute to the conceptual apparatus or analytical framework for the study of art generally (see the animated discussions in
Elkins 2007).

Discussants would thereby seem to acknowledge that the
prevailing metalanguage in the study of art today is based on various Western intellectual traditions, with its vocabulary, inextricably linked to the largely tacit worldviews and theoretical biases of
these traditions, deriving particularly from ancient Greek, Latin,
French, German, and English. Specifically, it would seem to be taken
for granted that, for the time being, the international language for
communication in art scholarship is English. Having absorbed ideas
from various European traditions of thought, its specialized analytical framework is constantly being adapted or enriched by

conceptual contributions that include neologisms coined specific-ally for visual art studies or borrowed especially from other schol-arly domains in the Western humanities.

Can the analytical apparatus of art scholarship be similarly enriched by concepts deriving from intellectual traditions outside the West (see also Cao, this volume)? There would seem to be no reason why this could not be the case. Given the underdetermined nature of many of the basic terms with which we presently ap-proach the study of the visual arts, and try to communicate trans-culturally—fundamental terms such as "image," "representation," or "creativity," "aesthetic experience," and so on—there is indeed plenty of room for semantically more precise terms, as well as for terms filling semantic gaps (that we may not even be aware of until a suitably refined concept is proposed). It should, however, be ob-served that any proposal for the cross-cultural applicability of a term developed in a particular system of thought does not sit well with the insistence on the cultural contingency of concepts. Ideally, such proposals should be made by representatives of the tradition or culture concerned, in order to minimize the everpresent risk of accusations of appropriation.

Still, it would seem advisable to consider various traditions' concepts for their analytical usefulness in studying art worldwide, even if this means giving up some of the nuancing of these con-cepts' original meanings, although they remain intact in their origin-al contexts. One is reminded here, in a related analytical frame-work, of the Austronesian concept of *tapu* that has, as "taboo," use-fully entered religious and social analyses in anthropology (and is now also used in everyday parlance in the West and beyond), albeit its conceptual uprooting for cross-cultural analytical purposes has inevitably led to some semantic loss. Indeed, and more generally, the worldwide study of art now faces some of the same problems that the discipline of anthropology has wrestled with for a much longer time in its attempts to study cultures around the globe.[19]

Continuities

The unmistaken diversification in art, its uses, and conceptualiza-tions that has taken place over the last ten thousands of years does not mean that there are no continuities. Thus, the practice of visu-ally marking or decorating the body has remained a constant in vir-tually all human societies. Unsurprisingly, it has taken a variety of forms and, to some extent, acquired different meanings, depending on such contextual factors as the availability of raw materials and such features of societal organization as economic specialization and the structure and content of various forms of sociopolitical hierarchy. Similarly, however much the use of materials and modes of production may have changed, humans still add eye-catching features to a variety of objects, ranging from everyday items to ob-jects of special significance, whether religious or political. They also still design tools in ways that transcend their practical efficacy in

19

In the second half of the twentieth century, anthropologists increasingly realized that they operate within a legacy of a Western intellectual tradi-tion, with its attendant conceptual frameworks and theoretical biases. While most anthropologists soldiered on, trying to be aware as much as possible of the problems of translation and tacit analytical frames, others opted for a more radical approach and concluded that there is simply no way of getting to know "the other." In the most recent contribution to the de-bate, Veronica Strang (2006) sets out to redress the balance after a decade of two of hyperrelativism in some circles of cultural anthropology. She argues that anthropology has always been dialogical and that this intercul-tural exchange has at all times led to a synthesis of theories and bodies of knowledge (although the results were usually expressed eventually in a Western language). According to Strang, contemporary anthropology should continue along these lines and "incorporate the conceptual frames, the analytical tools, the forms of knowledge, the pedagogy of a multi-plicity of different worldviews" (2006, 985). Colloboration between scholars of various backgrounds (a more realis-tic perspective today than it ever was, now that power relations between the "West and the Rest" have in many cases become less unequal and the technical means of communication and dialogue have definitely im-proved) may then lead to "a cultural Esperanto," "a shared conceptual vocabulary that can be employed by anyone willing to learn the discipli-nary *lingua franca*. Collectively com-posed and designed to permit cross-cultural translation of ideas, it is sub-ject to continual evolution through the incorporation of new information and understandings of its users" (2006, 990).

order to be pleasing to human sight and touch.

The human form (representing humans or anthropomorphized entities) and animal shapes (depicting real or imaginary animals and at times representing zoomorphized beings) have continued to dominate the imagery of countless artistic traditions across time and place, and to this day humans are found to create images combining features of humans and other animals. Again, contexts may have changed considerably, affecting material, style, meaning, use, and function, thereby offering countless topics of study for a globally oriented art scholarship. Also, some traditions would come to discourage or ban the production of images of living beings, while others would enlarge the range of artistic themes by adding, for example, flora and topographical features (including so-called land- and seascapes) to the repertoire. Still other traditions, although quite exceptionally, would give a whole new meaning to abstract images, conceiving of noniconic arrangements of color and form as expressive of their creator's emotions.

Similarly, however varied their functions and contexts of use, most of the visual arts today still serve a communicative purpose, as they have done for millennia. They relay messages of, for example, a social, political, or ideational nature among humans (signaling statuses and roles, impressing subjects, conveying visualized thought). Or they allow people to contact and be contacted by what they perceive to be realms beyond earthly human existence.

THE WESTERN STUDY OF ART FROM OTHER CULTURES

The systematic study of the visual arts has until recently been associated particularly with what has come to be known as the Western tradition. So let us now turn to the "western cape of Eurasia," and very briefly review some of the scholarly concerns with the arts that developed there. What interests us here most is Western scholars' engagements with visual art forms deriving from traditions they consider to be other than their own.

Perhaps the first writer in the West to pay attention to sculptures, architectural forms, and personal decoration in other cultural spheres, is the Greek historian and ethnographer Herodotus of Halicarnassus (484–c. 425 BCE), although he usually mentions these art forms merely as an aside to phenomena considered more significant to his accounts of Egypt, Western Asia, and beyond. The same can be said of subsequent writers from the Greco-Roman tradition who took an interest in "barbarian" worlds, meaning the ways of life of people not speaking Greek or Latin.

After the Arabic conquest of Spain in the eighth century, and from the time of the Christian crusades from the end of the eleventh century onward, Islamic architecture and decorative arts came to the attention of the West, and they influenced its art forms. Descriptions entered travel accounts and other writings from medieval Europe, while a few reports on elements of visual culture from Central Asia, China, and India became available as well. However, these were not generally times encouraging scholarly analysis of art forms whatsoever.

The European view of the world considerably widened when in the fifteenth century Portuguese and Spanish rulers started sponsoring overseas explorations, which were made possible in part by such inventions as the compass. Portuguese navigators first sailed south along the African coasts, at times bringing back figurative and decorative items, some of which would end up in the so-called cabinets of curiosity of European rulers and rich merchants (Bassani 2001). European explorers (Portuguese, Dutch, English) would go on and reach India and China by sea, intensifying trade with cultural worlds whose products, artistic among them, had already filtered into Europe by means of overland trade in Central and Western Asia (Lach 1970). The contacts between Europe and Africa and Asia implied in turn that European objects entered realms beyond the West. In human history, such intercultural encounters and exchanges have of course occurred countless times, on varying scales and to varying degrees of intensity (see also the introductions in the present volume to the sections on comparison and interculturalization).

The most astounding revelation to European minds during "the age of discovery," however, occurred in the early 1500s, when it was becoming clear that Christopher Columbus and subsequent navigators had hit upon a whole continent the existence of which had not been anticipated by anyone in the West at that time. A decade after Columbus had reached the "West Indies" in 1492, Europeans would set foot on the Mesoamerican mainland. Tens of thousands of years after their ancestors had split up, with some groups eventually turning to the west of Eurasia and others moving to the east of the continent, descendants of these migrating modern humans were now facing each other in Mesoamerica.[20]

The dramatic consequences of this and subsequent meetings in the Americas are well known. Here we may note that, whatever the amount of differences, there are a number of striking similarities between the societies and cultures these two groups of people had developed at the time. These include economies based on agriculture, elaborate hierarchical systems of political and social organization, with a dominant role performed by religious specialists, and large-scale architecture. Also, for example, members of both populations played ball games, made music, and told tales; they turned their bodies into socially differentiated visual displays, and they worked such raw materials as stone and metal into human and animal forms.

Western references to the visual arts of the Americas occur from the logbooks of Columbus onwards. Sailing westwards, Guanahani, in what is now called the Bahamas, was the first island Columbus reached, on October 12, 1492. Some two weeks later he

20
On a far more limited scale this had already happened some five centuries earlier when small groups of Norse migrants had settled on the northeast coast of North-America. Memories of these events would not seem to have made it into Renaissance Europe's public consciousness. A report of an even earlier transatlantic crossing was available, though, in the form of the "legend of St. Brendan," the sixth-century CE Irish monk who set out to find the "Land of Delight."

21
The first Western account of visual art forms in the Americas—not mentioned in Kubler's historical survey—had already been written in the mid-1490s by the friar Ramón Pané, after a two-year stay in a northern chiefdom on the island "Hispaniola," present-day Haiti and Dominican Republic (Pané 1999). As for the Western scholarly engagement with art forms from outside the West in this period, Claire Farago (1995) has made an attempt to investigate how cultural contacts with the Americas, especially, influenced not only sixteenth-century Italian artistic practices but also Renaissance theoretical discussions of the arts, an influence that in the latter case, however, does not seem attestable in any direct sense (cf. Farago 1995, 11). See also the introduction to the section on comparison, this volume.

landed on Cuba and reported that the inhabitants possess both wooden statues with a female shape and well-carved heads or masks. In his entry for October 29, Columbus makes the following intriguing note: "I do not know whether they regard these as beautiful or for worship" (Kubler 1991, 42).

Since the original logbooks of Columbus have been lost, we are forced to rely on the partial transcripts made by Bartolomé de las Casas (c. 1474–1566). Dominican bishop of Chiapas in southern Mexico, De las Casas is known above all for his defense of the full humanity of the inhabitants of the Americas—most famously during the Valladolid Debate of 1550 and 1551, where his adversary, the Jesuit Juan Sinés de Sepúlved claimed that "Indians" had no "souls" and could therefore be treated a slaves. In order to prove the rationality of the "Indians," De las Casas also wrote his *Apologética historia de las Indias* ("In Defense of the Indians") between 1552 and 1559. As art historian George Kubler (1991, 49) reports, chapters 61–65 of this history are devoted to a description of visual arts and crafts in Mesoamerica, making parallel comparisons between "New World" achievements and the accomplishments of the "Old World," both past and present. These descriptive and comparative efforts led Kubler to conclude that De las Casas "wrote a rudimentary history of world art" (1991, 5).

Although the claim is obviously exaggerated (most of the world is still missing in De las Casas's account, which was, of course, never meant to be comprehensive in global terms), Kubler's observations do make us aware that writing the history of cross-cultural art studies has only just begun.[21] Seen from a Western perspective, such exercises in intellectual history should include the way in which European philosophers and others in later centuries dealt with the art forms of traditions considered foreign, digesting (or not) the data coming in from the Islamic world, various Asian traditions, the Americas, the Pacific, and other regions of the world—for example Jean-Baptiste Dubos (1719) drawing on cross-cultural examples in his examination of the influence of climate on artistic production, but also Reynolds reflecting on Cherokee personal decoration, Kant on Maori tattoos, Hegel on Chinese painting and Indian architecture, and so on.

Philosophers Hegel and Herder are among the scholars (including also the globally oriented geographer Alexander von Humboldt) who are said to have influenced the German art historian Franz Kugler in his attempt to provide what is generally considered the first survey of world art ever, in his *Handbuch der Kunstgeschichte* ("Handbook of Art History") published in 1842. Kugler does indeed summarize much of what was then known about the visual arts and their history around the globe, emphasizing European and Asian traditions, but also including the Americas, and even spending a few pages on Polynesia. Most noticeably absent, however, is Sub-Saharan Africa, which may be due in part to a relative lack of information at that time, but which may also reflect the influence of Hegel, who notoriously proclaimed Africa to be outside history (Kugler is not, however, generally considered a Hegelian).[22]

Following in Kugler's wake, several surveys of art history were published in German that went beyond the West to varying extents (see Schwarzer 1995 for a discussion of especially Carl Schnaase's and Anton Springer's works), with the most comprehensive coverage provided by Karl Woermann's multivolume *Geschichte der Kunst aller Zeiten und Völker* ("History of Art of all Times and Peoples"), first published between 1900 and 1911. (For more on global art history surveys published in German prior to World War II, see Halbertsma and Pfisterer, this volume.)

As for the first English-language surveys of world art, one might mention the all-but-forgotten book *Comparative Art* (and later versions), published by the prolific writer, Antarctic explorer and art lover Edwin Balch in 1906. Of this work, Balch would later write: "This, as far as I know, was the first attempt ever made to examine into and classify the fine arts of all races" (Balch and Balch 1920, xiii).[23] The first edition of Helen Gardner's *Art Through the Ages*, published in 1926, contained chapters on Indian, Chinese, and Japanese art, as well as a chapter on "Aboriginal American Art," later to be extended with the arts of Africa and Oceania (cf. Elkins 2002, 73). Now in its twelfth edition (Kleiner and Mamiya 2006; the thirteenth edition is announced as *Gardner's Art Through the Ages: A Global History*), this voluminous survey of world art has more recently been joined by equally massive one-volume multiregional overviews, most notably Hugh Honour and John Fleming's *A World History of Art*, published in North-America under the title *The Visual Arts: An Introduction* (first published in 1982, seventh edition 2005) and Marilyn Stokstad's *Art History* (first published in 1995, third edition 2007).

The earlier German multivolume projects attempting to cover all the world's visual arts have been succeeded by various endeavors, including the imposing *Enciclopedia Universale dell'Arte* (Salmi et al. 1958), published in English as *Encyclopedia of World Art*, and the even more impressive *Dictionary of Art*, which similarly aims at a "comprehensive coverage of the history of all the visual arts worldwide, from prehistory to the present" (Turner 1996, vii).[24]

The existence of these various globally oriented European-language surveys from the twentieth century should not obscure the fact that in this period art history as a Western academic discipline remained concerned primarily with Western art (one need but check the contents of the various leading journals in the field). Art forms other than those from Greek antiquity onward did draw the attention of Western scholars, and increasingly that of scholars outside the West, but these arts were usually studied in academic fields at the periphery or indeed beyond the purview of the discipline of art history. The study of "prehistoric art" — a term mainly

22
Although Kugler's scholarship has received quite some attention of late (e.g., Locher 2001, 244 ff.; Karlholm 2004, passim), his global aspirations have not yet been addressed in any comprehensive sense; but see Kubler 1991, 130ff; Schwarzer 1995, 25ff; and Farago 1995, 82, who chastises Kugler for being "very patronizing" in his "esthetic recognition" (George Kubler's term) of pre-Columbian art, for deploying, like other European writers, "assimilative mechanisms," and for being evolutionistic, setting up cultural hierachies in art production.

23
Together with his spouse Eugenia, Balch wrote a follow-up studein 1918 titled *Art and Man*, which was also published in German in 1921. They later produced *Arts of the World* (1920), an extended version of *Art and Man*. Consisting of over 300 pages, the book is divided into four parts: Europe (a mere 78 pages, half of which are devoted to prehistoric art), Africa (including Egypt), Asia (including Mesopotamian cultures; the Asian section takes up some 100 pages), Australasia (insular South-East Asia and the Pacific), and the Americas. Remarkably, the book does not have illustrations (it does have 5 maps).

24
Other twentieth-century multivolume surveys of world art in European languages include the German series *Propyläen Kunstgeschichte*, the French series *Histoire d'Art* (Elie Fauré's project) and *L'univers des formes* (under the direction of André Malraux), and the Spanish series *Summa Artis: Historia General del Arte*. English-language introductory series to art history that comprise volumes dedicated to art forms outside the West include World of Art (Thames and Hudson), Pelican History of Art (Yale), Art and Ideas (Phaidon) and the Oxford History of Art series. The Japanese language "Sinchô Encyclopedia of World Art," a single-volume publication to which 500 specialists contributed, published in 1985, appears limited to Oriental and Western art (Inaga 2007, 264).

used at the time to refer to "Ice Age art" from Europe—was large-ly left to prehistorians, usually people trained in archaeology or paleoanthropology and publishing in journals and books not gener-ally found on the shelves of art history libraries (at a time when this counted more than in today's digital age). Archaeologists, sometimes joined by art historians, also dealt with the artistic re-mains uncovered from a variety of pre-, proto- and historic trad-itions outside Europe, applying the methods and interpretations paradigmatic of their own regionally and temporally specialized disciplines.

The calligraphy, figurative paintings, sculptures, and other visual arts from various so-called Oriental traditions were the sub-ject matter of scholars (trained art historians among them) whose analyses were often firmly embedded in the tradition of culture-historical and textual examinations characteristic of the scholarly fields focusing on Indian, Chinese, Japanese, and Islamic culture. The study of the visual arts from cultures with an oral rather than a textual tradition in Africa, Southeast Asia, Oceania, and the Amer-icas was at first left mainly to cultural anthropologists. During the second half of the twentieth century these art forms were increas-ingly examined by art historians as well, who also carried out local research. Art historians "doing fieldwork" adopted to a large ex-tent the methods and approaches of anthropologists, favoring so-ciocultural contextualization in the study of art. They tended not to publish in mainstream art historical journals.

ENTER WORLD ART STUDIES

It is against this background that in the early 1990s John Onians proposed the idea of world art studies. He first wrote about this new concept and approach in a brief article entitled "World Art Studies and the Need for a New Natural History of Art," pub-lished in the prominent art historical journal *The Art Bulletin* in 1996. Onians starts by recognizing that the visual arts are a world-wide phenomenon across time and place, seeing them as integral to the behavior of *Homo sapiens* (although he argues that other ani-mals may display art-like activities as well). Onians acknowledges that his recognition of the global occurrence of art was inspired in large part through a 1975 gift to the University of East Anglia in Norwich, where he taught, of a collection of visual art objects from around the world. The confrontation with the Sainsbury collection in the then School of Art History raised the question of how to come to scholarly terms with the totality of human visual artistic production. Although Onians considers art history the foremost academic discipline concerned with the visual arts, he has to con-clude that this discipline has been very parochial in confining itself to the arts of the Western tradition (and especially the so-called high arts, whose agenda of study, moreover, is often set by nationalistic motives). So, as a first step, Onians suggests that conventional art history be transformed into a discipline with a global coverage across time and space.

This spatiotemporal extension implies inviting scholars from outside the West to become involved in the study of art worldwide. These scholars may bring not only valuable expertise on the art forms of their respective traditions, but also fresh perspectives on the examination of art from whatever time or place. In doing so, they may alert Western colleagues to the inevitable biases in their work while at the same enriching art scholars' repertoire of approaches. Although the editors of the present volume were not as successful as they had hoped in engaging scholars who identify with traditions outside the West, the dialogue between art historians from various cultural backgrounds is now underway (see, for example, Elkins 2007).

The proposed transformation of art history into a discipline with global coverage also entails giving attention to the work of archaeologists and anthropologists who study the visual arts of places and times not usually addressed by mainstream art history. Importantly, the introduction to the work of archaeologists and anthropologists also provides opportunities to learn from the various approaches applied in these scholars' disciplines. Onians stresses that the acquaintance with both other cultures' arts and the way they are studied, allows Western students to look at their traditional subject matter and scholarly practices in a new light, putting into relief the many contingent peculiarities of the West's visual arts and the way they are analyzed. Indeed, as the psychologist and philosopher William James suggested a century ago, one profitable strategy of scholarship consists in "making the natural seem strange."

In addition to becoming more global and multidisciplinary, Onians suggests that the study of art also cast its net more widely when it comes to the types of objects it examines. He proposes that art scholars take into account folk and popular art as well—in fact, he suggests that they focus their attention on all forms of "visually interesting material culture" (1996, 206). If we wish to examine the visual arts as a phenomenon in human existence, we should indeed adopt a wide-ranging point of view that goes well beyond considering relatively rarefied objects only.

What is emerging here is a new framework or vantage point in the study of the visual arts from which to raise many new questions and address older ones afresh. In order to further develop the idea of world art studies, in 2000, Onians organized two major scholarly events. The first of these was a conference entitled "Compression vs. Expression: Containing and Explaining the World's Art," held at the Clark Art Institute in Williamstown, Massachusetts, USA (see Onians 2006 for the published proceedings). This conference dealt in large part with questions concerning the spatiotemporal extension in the study of art: to what extent do the various sectors of art history as an institutional field deal

25
A second conference on world art studies, entitled "World Art: Ways Forward," was held at the University of East Anglia in September 2007. Meanwhile, Eric Venbrux and Pamela Rosi had edited a special issue of the *International Journal of Anthropology* on the theme of "Conceptualizing World Art Studies" (Venbrux and Rosi 2003). Already in 1986, the 26th conference of the International Committee for the History of Art (CIHA) was dedicated to "World Art: Themes of Unity in Diversity" (for the proceedings, see Lavin 1989). An early deliberation on the need and prospects of global perspectives in art history was provided by Oleg Grabar (1982). The idea of world art studies is also addressed in some of the contributions in Golden 2001.

26
See, for example, also Volkenandt 2004, focusing specifically on art history's engagement with present-day "international art," or *Weltgegenwartskunst*.

with the visual arts as a worldwide phenomenon? How do we arrive at a more balanced representation of art from different times and places in museums, university courses, publications, libraries, bibliographies, and theory-building?[25]

The Clark conference thus addressed basic topics in what some today also call "world art history," or "global art history," and what in German has already been known for some time as *Weltkunstgeschichte*. Unlike the term world art studies, these latter labels (emphasizing history, in the singular) might unwittingly suggest the idea that historical developments in the world's various art traditions ultimately present one homogeneous story, with its attendant unilinear and teleological connotations (Hegelian or otherwise) that might lead to the portrayal of these various traditions as steps on an evolutionary ladder, with some traditions lagging behind others.

David Summers distances himself from such an interpretation when he writes: "The World Art History of the subtitle [of Summers's book *Real Spaces*] is not a global history (which I think is both undesirable and impossible), but the discipline of art history itself, now faced with the task of providing the means to address as many histories as possible nearly enough in their own terms to permit new intercultural discussion" (Summers 2003, 12). It is in this sense also that James Elkins appears to be using the term when, in his extensive review of Summers's book, he observes that "Far and away the most pressing problem facing the discipline of art history today is the prospect of world art history" (2004, 373). In the present volume, John Clark, Elkins, and Zijlmans continue the discussion of issues that arise when the Western discipline of art history confronts the prospect of becoming more globally oriented.[26]

In 2000, Onians also organized the Getty-sponsored "Summer Institute in World Art Studies," which took place at what since 1992 has been called The School of World Art Studies and Museology of the University of East Anglia in Norwich, UK. This Summer Institute was a four-week meeting of minds, attended by some 30 participants from around the world and featuring a host of speakers, most of them internationally renowned. As did the participants, speakers came from the disciplines of art history (e.g., Hans Belting, Hubert Damisch, Griselda Pollock), archaeology (e.g., Stephen Bahn, Ian Hodder, Steven Mithen, Colin Renfrew), and anthropology (e.g., Jack Goody, Michael Rowlands, Marilyn Strathern, Nicholas Thomas). Whereas the Clark conference basically set out to examine where we stand and what could be improved in terms of *world* art studies, the Norwich Summer Institute might be characterized as taking the first steps in exploring the multidisciplinary character of world art *studies*.

In order to advance the intellectual exchange on the idea of studying art in a multi- or interdisciplinary way, all scholars involved were asked to consider a set of questions that included the following: "What are the strengths and limitations of art history, anthropology, archaeology and related disciplines as frameworks for understanding art?"[27] They were also asked to ponder the following two opposed queries: "How effective across the disciplines are cultural/social/ideological explanations of artistic activity?" and "How effective across the disciplines are natural/biological/ecological explanations?" The latter question, rather disturbing to many participants at the time,[28] already takes us some way from mainstream art history, cultural anthropology, and, to a lesser extent, archaeology. A similar observation can be made of the final and most challenging leading question for the Summer Institute: "How can current explanations be integrated and developed to create a larger theoretical framework?"

These fundamental questions are still with us, and they will be for some time to come. It is one of the aims of this volume to try and add to the discussion of the merits of various disciplinary approaches in the study of art, and to examine their possible integration. As suggested as well by Onians's reference to a "natural history of art" and by some of the questions he formulated for the Norwich Summer Institute, in considering the contributions that diverse disciplinary perspectives might make to an understanding of the visual arts, our attention need not be confined to art history, anthropology, and archaeology. Especially in the West during the last one and a half centuries or so, the visual arts have indeed been studied from a wider range of disciplines. Some of these disciplines will be briefly presented in the introduction to the second section of this volume, where specialists will explore particular disciplinary perspectives in more depth.

Contributors to the first section of this book address the history of global approaches in the study of art and discuss some of the promises and problems of present-day attempts to develop worldwide perspectives on the visual arts. The third section examines the foundations of human art-making and perception by considering these activities from bioevolutionary and neuropsychological perspectives. In doing so, the contributors to this section continue the exploration of disciplinary approaches in the study of art, while at the same extending in a theoretical manner the more descriptive introduction provided above to the origins of visual artistic behavior. The fourth and fifth sections, finally, deal with the two other issues introduced above as key topics in world art studies, namely, intercultural comparison and interculturalization in the visual arts. Each of these two sections is prefaced by an introduction that provides a larger framework for exploring the issues addressed by their individual contributors.

ACKNOWLEDGMENTS

I would like to thank Kitty Zijlmans for having taken the initiative for this volume and inviting me to join her as coeditor. For these

27
The five leading questions for the Summer Institute in World Art Studies were mentioned on the poster announcing this event. The question just referred to in the text is the second one. The first one read: "How complete is our knowledge of art (including visual and material culture) worldwide from prehistory to the present?" The three remaining questions will be discussed shortly.

28
Although none of the Williamstown conference speakers, which included the present writer, were intended to double for the Summer Instititute, I happened to be present at the latter as well as a last minute stand-in. During this meeting's third week, dealing with anthropological perspectives on the study of art and aesthetics, I gave a seminar that tried to integrate "culturalist" and "naturalist" approaches to aesthetics (cf. Van Damme 2000; see Ridley 2003 for a lucid exposition on the interaction between biological inheritance and sociocultural environment more generally, an exposition that should put to rest discussions that posit "nature" and "nurture" as autonomous or mutually exclusive categories; compare also Richerson and Boyd 2005). This seminar was skeptically received. I was told that the bioevolutionary and neuropsychological approaches applied in Steven Mithen's and John Onians's seminars were equally objected to by many participants.

introductory notes I have drawn on lectures I prepared for a
course on world art studies that I have been fortunate to teach at
Leiden University from 2004. The first three generations of students who took this course I thank for their sense of adventure and
for encouraging me to clarify certain issues and not forget others.
I am also grateful to colleagues who at some point served as guest
lecturers for the course and deepened my knowledge of their
areas of expertise: Jan Baptist Bedaux (ethology), Raymond Corbey
(evolutionary anthropology), Erik Dormaels (neurosciences),
Pieter ter Keurs (cultural anthropology), and Alexander Verpoorte
(archaeology). A special word of thanks is due to Jean Borgatti,
who not only read and commented on the penultimate version of
this introduction but volunteered to smoothen my English. I am
also grateful to Ben-Ami Scharfstein for last minute discussions on
a few disparate topics.

REFERENCES

ABIODUN, ROWLAND. 1990. The future of African art studies: An African perspective. In *African art studies: The state of the discipline*, Rowland Abiodun et al., 63–89. Washington, DC: The National Museum of African Art.
—, Henry J. Drewal, and John Pemberton. 1991. *Yoruba: Art and aesthetics in Nigeria*. Zurich: Museum Rietberg.

ADEPEGBA, CORNELIUS O. 1992. *Ona*: The concept of art among the Yoruba. In *Yoruba culture*, Cornelius O. Adepegba et al., 1–6. Ibadan: The Nigerian Field Society.

ADLER, GUIDO. 1885. Umfang, Methode und Ziel der Musikwissenschaft. *Vierteljahrschrift für Musikwissenschaft* 1: 5–20. (See Mugglestone 1981 for an English translation)

ALSOP, JOSEPH. 1982. *The rare art traditions: The history of art collecting and its linked phenomena wherever they have appeared*. New York: Harper and Row.

AMBROSE, STANLEY H. 1998. Late Pleistocene human population bottlenecks, volcanic winter, and the differentiation of modern humans. *Journal of Human Evolution* 34 (6): 623–51.
—. 2003. Did the super-eruption of Toba cause a human population bottleneck? Reply to Gathorne-Hardy and Harcourt-Smith. *Journal of Human Evolution* 45 (3): 231–37.

ANDERSON, RICHARD L. 2004. *Calliope's sisters: A comparative study of philosophies of art*. 2nd, rev. ed., 1st ed. published 1990. Upper Saddle River, NJ: Prentice Hall.

ANIKOVICH, MICHAEL V. et al. 2007. Early Upper Paleolithic in Eastern Europe and implications for the dispersal of modern humans. *Science* 315 (5819): 223–26.

BAHN, PAUL G., AND JEAN VERLUT. 2001. *Journey through the Ice Age*. Los Angeles: University of California Press.

BALCH, EDWIN S., AND EUGENIA BALCH. 1920. *Arts of the world: Comparative art studies*. Philadelphia: Lane and Scott.

BALME, JANE, AND KATE MORSE. 2006. Shell beads and social behaviour in Pleistocene Australia. *Antiquity* 80 (310): 799–811.

BARHAM, LAWRENCE S. 2002. Systematic pigment use in the Middle Pleistocene of South-Central Africa. *Current Anthropology* 43 (1): 181–90.

BASSANI, EZIO. 2001. *African art and artifacts in European collections: 1400–1800*. London: British Museum Press.

BEDNARIK, ROBERT G. 2003. A figurine from the African Acheulian. *Current Anthropology* 44 (3): 405–13.

BOEHM, GOTTFRIED, ed. 2006. *Was ist ein Bild?* Bild und Text 1. 1st ed. 1994. Munich: Wilhelm Fink.
—. 2007. *Wie Bilder Sinn erzeugen*. Berlin: Berlin University Press.

BOUZOUGGAR, ABDELJALIL et al. 2007. 82,000-year-old beads from North Africa and the implications for the origins of modern human behavior. *Proceedings of the National Academy of Sciences of the United States of America* 104: 9964–69.

CLOTTES, JEAN. 2003. *Return to Chauvet cave: Excavating the birthplace of art*. London: Thames and Hudson.

CONARD, NICHOLAS J. 2003. Palaeolithic ivory sculptures from South-Western Germany and the origins of figurative art. *Nature* 426 (6965): 830–32.
—, et al. 2007. Einmalige Funde durch die Nachgrabung am Vogelherd bei Niederstotzingen-Stetten ob Lontal, Kreis Heidelheim. *Archäologische Ausgrabungen in Baden-Württemberg* 2006, ed. Jörg Biel, 20–24. Stuttgart: Theiss.

CURRIE, GREGORY. 2004. The representational revolution. *Journal of Aesthetics and Art Criticism* 62 (2): 119–28.

DART, RAYMOND A. 1974. The waterworn pebble of many faces from Makapansgat. *South African Journal of Science* 70 (6): 167–69.

D'ERRICO, FRANCESCO et al. 2003. Archaeological evidence for the emergence of language, symbolism, and music: An alternative multidisciplinary perspective. *Journal of World Prehistory* 17 (1): 1–70.
— et al. 2005. *Nassarius kraussianus* shell beads from Blombos cave: Evidence for symbolic behavior in the Middle Stone Age. *Journal of Human Evolution* 48 (1): 3–24.

DUBOS, JEAN-BAPTISTE. 1719. *Réflexions critiques sur la poésie et sur la peinture*. Paris: Pissot.

EIBL-EIBESFELDT, IRENÄUS, AND CHRISTA SÜTTERLIN. 2007. *Weltsprache Kunst: zur Natur- und Kunstgeschichte bildlicher Kommunikation*. Vienna: Brandstätter Verlag.

ELKINS, JAMES. 2002. *Stories of art*. New York: Routledge.
—. 2004. Review of *Real spaces: World art history and the rise of Western modernism* by David Summers. *The Art Bulletin* 86 (2): 373–80.
—, ed. 2007. *Is art history global?* The Art Seminar 3. New York and London: Routledge.

FARAGO, CLAIRE, ed. 1995. *Reframing the Renaissance: Visual culture in Europe and Latin America 1450–1650*. New Haven, CT and London: Yale University Press.

GOLDEN, LAUREN. ed. 2001. *Raising the eyebrow: John Onians and World Art Studies. An album amicorum in his honour*. Oxford: Archaeopress.

GRABAR, OLEG. 1982. On the universality of the history of art. *Art Journal* 42 (4): 281–83.

GUTHRIE, R. DALE. 2005. *The nature of Paleolithic Art*. Chicago and London: The University of Chicago Press.

HENSHILWOOD, CHRISTOPHER S., et al. 2002. Emergence of modern human behaviour: Middle Stone age engravings from South Africa. *Science* 295 (5561): 1278–80.
—, and Curtis W. Marean. 2003. The origin of modern human behaviour: A review and critique of models and test implications. *Current Anthropology* 44 (5): 627–51.

HODGSON, DEREK. 2006a. Understanding the origins of Paleoart: The neurovisual resonance theory and brain functioning. *PaleoAnthropology* 2006: 54–67.
—. 2006b. Altered states of consciousness and Palaeoart: An alternative neurovisual explanation. *Cambridge Archaeological Journal* 16 (1): 27–37.

HONOUR, HUGH, AND JOHN FLEMING. 2005. *A world history of art*. 7th ed., 1st ed. published 1985. London: Laurence King.

HOVERS, ERELLA, et al. 2003. An early case of color symbolism: Ochre use by modern humans in Qafzeh cave. *Current Anthropology* 44 (4): 491–522.

HUNT, TERRY L., AND CARL L. LIPO. 2006. Late colonization of Easter Island. *Science* 311 (5761): 1603–6.

HYMAN, JOHN. 2006. *The objective eye: Color, form, and reality in the theory of art*. Chicago and London: The University of Chicago Press.

INAGA, SHIGEMI. 2007. Is art history globalizable? A critical commentary from a Far Eastern point of view. In *Is Art history global?* The Art Seminar 3, ed. James Elkins, 249–79. New York and London: Routledge.

KARLHOLM, DAN. 2004. *Art of illusion: The representation of art history in nineteenth-century Germany*. Bern: Peter Lang.

KLEINER, FRED S., AND CHRISTIN J. MAMIYA. 2006. *Gardner's art through the ages*. 12th ed., 1st ed. published 1926. Belmont, CA: Wadsworth.

KOHN, MAREK, AND STEVEN MITHEN. 1999. Handaxes: Products of sexual selection? *Antiquity* 73 (279): 518–26.

KUBLER, GEORGE. 1991. *Esthetic recognition of ancient Amerindian art*. New Haven CT, and London: Yale University Press.

KUGLER, FRANZ THEODOR. 1842. *Handbuch der Kunstgeschichte*. Stuttgart: Ebner & Seubert.

LACH, DONALD F. 1970. *Asia in the making of Europe*. Vol. II: *A century of wonder, Book 1: The visual arts*. Chicago and London: The University of Chicago Press.

LAVIN, IRVING, ed. 1988. *World art: Themes of unity and diversity (Acts of the 26th International Congress of the History of Art)*. University Park: Pennsylvania State University Press.

LAWAL, BABATUNDE. 2001. *Àwòrán*: Representing the self and its metaphysical other in Yoruba art. *The Art Bulletin* 93 (3): 498–526.

LÉON-PORTILLA, MIGUEL. 1966. Pre-Hispanic thought. In *Major trends in Mexican philosophy*, Mario De La Cueva et al., 2–56. Notre Dame, in: University of Notre Dame Press.
—. 1980. *Toltecáyotl, aspectos de la cultura náhuatl*. Mexico City: Fondo de Cultura Económica.

LEWIS-WILLIAMS, DAVID. 2002. *The mind in the cave: Consciousness and the origins of art*. London: Thames and Hudson.

LOCHER, HUBERT. 2001. *Kunstgeschichte als historische Theorie der Kunst 1750–1950*. München: Wilhelm Fink.

LORBLANCHET, MICHEL. 1999. *La naissance de l'art: genèse de l'art préhistorique dans le monde*. Paris: Editions Errance.

MANIA, DIETRICH, AND URSULA MANIA. 1988. Deliberate engravings on bone artefacts of Homo Erectus. *Rock Art Research* 5: 91–97.

MCBREARTHY, SALLY, AND ALLISON S. BROOKS. 2000. The revolution that wasn't: A new interpretation of the origin of modern human behavior. *Journal of Human Evolution* 39 (5): 453–563.

MELLARS, PAUL. 2006. Why did modern human populations disperse from Africa *ca.* 60,000 years ago? A new model. *Proceedings of the National Academy of Sciences of the United States of America* 103: 9831–36.

MILLER, GEOFFREY. 2000. *The mating mind: How sexual selection shaped the evolution of human nature*. London: Heinemann.

MITCHELL, W. J. THOMAS. 2005. *What do pictures want? The loves and lives of images*. Chicago and London: The University of Chicago Press.

MITHEN, STEVEN. 2005. *The singing Neanderthals: The origins of music, language, mind and body*. London: Weidenfeld and Nicolson.

MORPHY, HOWARD. 2008. *Becoming art: Exploring cross-cultural categories*. Sydney: University of South Wales Press.

MORWOOD, MICHAEL J. 2002. *Visions of the past: The archaeology of Australian aboriginal art*. London: Allen and Unwin.

MUGGLESTONE, ERICA. 1981. Guido Adler's "The Scope, Method, and Aim of Musicology" (1885): An English translation with an historico-analytical commentary. *Yearbook for Traditional Music*, vol. 13, 1–21. [New York]: International Council for Traditional Music.

NETTL, BRUNO. 2002. *Encounters in ethnomusicology: A memoir*. Warren, MI: Harmonie Park Press.

O'CONNELL, JAMES, AND JAMES ALLEN. 2004. Dating the colonization of Sahul: A review of recent research. *Journal of Archaeological Science* 31: 835–53.

ONIANS, JOHN. 1996. World art studies and the need for a new natural history of art. *The Art Bulletin* 78 (2): 206–9.
—, ed. 2006. *Compression vs. expression: Containing and explaining the world's art*. Williamstown, MA: The Clark Art Institute.

OPPENHEIMER, STEPHEN. 2004. *The real eve: Man's journey out of Africa*. New York: Carroll and Graf.

PETRAGLIA, MICHAEL, et al. 2007. Middle Paleolithic assemblages from the Indian subcontinent before and after the Toba supereruption. *Science* 317 (5844): 114–16.

PANÉ, RAMÓN. 1999. *An account of the antiquities of the Indians*, rev. ed., with an introductory study, notes, and appendices by José Juan Arrom, trans. Susan C. Griswold. Durham and London: Duke University Press.

PASZTORY, ESTHER. 2005. *Thinking with things: Toward a new vision of art*. Austin: University of Texas Press.

RICHERSON, PETER J., AND ROBERT BOYD. 2005. *Not by genes alone: How culture transformed human evolution*. Chicago and London: The University of Chicago Press.

RIDLEY, MATT. 2003. *Nature via nurture: Genes, experience, and what makes us human*. New York: HarperCollins.

SALMI, MARIO, et al., eds. 1958. *Enciclopedia universale dell'Arte*. Venice and Rome: Istituto per la Collaborazione Culturale (Published in English as: *Encyclopedia of world art*. New York: McGraw Hill, 1959–1968).

SCHLESIER, KARL H. 2001. More on the "Venus" figurines. *Current Anthropology* 42 (3): 410–12.

SCHWARZER, MITCHELL. 1995. Origins of the art history survey text. *Art Journal* 54 (3): 24–29.

SHINER, LARRY. 2001. *The invention of art: A cultural history*. Chicago and London: The University of Chicago Press.

SPIVEY, NIGEL. 2005. *How art made the world*. London: BBC Books.

STAFFORD, BARBARA MARIA. 2007. *Echo objects: The cognitive work of images*. Chicago and London: The University of Chicago Press.

STRANG, VERONICA. 2006. A happy coincidence? Symbiosis and synthesis in anthropological and indigenous knowlegde (with peer comments). *Current Anthropology* 47 (6): 981–1008.

STOKSTAD, MARILYN. 2007. *Art history.* 3rd ed., 1st ed. published 1995. Upper Saddle River, NJ: Prentice Hall.

SUMMERS, DAVID. 2003. *Real spaces: World art history and the rise of Western modernism,* London and New York: Phaidon.

TURNER, JANE. ed. 1996. *The dictionary of art,* 34 vols. London: Macmillan.

VAN DAMME, WILFRIED. 1996. *Beauty in context: Towards an anthropological approach to aesthetics.* Philosophy of History and Culture 17. Leiden, New York, and Cologne: Brill.
—. 2000. Universality and cultural particularity in visual aesthetics. In *Being humans: Anthropological universality and particularity in transdisciplinary perspectives,* ed. Neil Roughley, 258–83. Berlin and New York: Walter De Gruyter.

VANHAEREN, MARIAN, et al. 2006. Middle Paleolithic shell beads in Israel and Algeria. *Science* 312 (5781): 1785–88.

VENBRUX, ERIC, AND PAMELA S. ROSI, eds. 2003. *Conceptualizing world art studies.* Special issue, *International Journal of Anthropology* 18 (4).

VOLAND, ECKART, AND KARL GRAMMER, eds. 2003. *Evolutionary aesthetics.* Berlin: Springer.

VOLKENANDT, CLAUS, ed. 2004. *Kunstgeschichte und Weltgegenwartskunst: Konzepte – Methoden – Perspektiven.* Berlin: Reimer.

WADLEY, LYN. 2005. Putting ochre to the test: Replication studies of adhesives that may have been used for shafting tools in the Middle Stone Age. *Journal of Human Evolution* 49 (5): 587–601.

WHITE, RANDALL. 2003. *Prehistoric art: The symbolic journey of humankind.* New York: Harry N. Abrams.

WHITFIELD, JOHN. 2002. Art history doubles. *Nature Science Update,* 11 January.

WOERMANN, KARL. 1900–1911. *Geschichte der Kunst aller Zeiten und Völker.* 6 vols. Leipzig: Bibliographisches Institut.

YAI, OLABIYI BABALOLA. 1999. Tradition and the Yoruba artist. *African Arts* 32 (1): 32–35, 93.

I

Historiography: Envisioning Global Approaches in the Study of Art

ULRICH PFISTERER

Origins and Principles of World Art History— 1900 (and 2000)

At first glance, David Summers's 2003 *Real Spaces: World Art History and the Rise of Western Modernism* and John Onians's 2004 *Atlas of World Art*—although both attempts to encompass world art history; although both similarly monumental books—could not appear to be more different in concept, methodology, and presentation. Of the many more comparable features which do emerge on closer reading, here I primarily wish to emphasize only one: both works present themselves as absolutely innovative.[1] Onians claims to be taking "a whole new approach to the subject" of art; whereas, Summers declares that prior "formalist, contextual and post-structural approaches to art cannot provide the basis for a truly global and intercultural art history," therefore he "mean[s] to make it possible for traditions of art (and art history) to address one another in new ways."[2] For both authors, premises of methodological novelty and of originality make it superfluous even to pose the question of earlier historical attempts to deal specifically with world art—though Summers in particular commences with a lengthy review of art historical thinking and frequently brings the luminaries of European intellectual tradition, from Plato and Aristotle to Kant and Hegel, to bear in his arguments.

1

These claims seem to be over-stated: "absolute innovation" is a characteristic quality of the self-proclaimed avant-garde artist/intellectual, as shown by Krauss 1985; equally available are the "absolute" paradigm shifts in the sciences, see Kuhn 1962.

2

Summers 2003: dust jacket and p. 13; but see also p. 15ff his claim to have broken with "all that has gone before"; Onians 2004, 10. To name just some of the more important reviews: Elkins 2004; Silver 2004; Kemp 2005.

3
Obviously, this is not meant to deny that there are — in other contexts — excellent discussions of the "history of the study of non-European art," as for example the chapter of the same name in Gerbrands 1957, 25–65.

4
The bibliography on these questions is overwhelming; two comprehensive books are Torgovnick 1990 and Connelly 1995.

5
The state of research (with further bibliography) may be found in Halbertsma 2003 and Müller 2003; for Asian art history, see also Von Erdberg 1985.

6
This is to claim for art history what Bunzl and Penny 2003, 1ff has outlined for the anthropological (and historical) disciplines in an excellent contribution, albeit with a slightly different chronology of the decisive changes and a tendency to undervalue the factor of "psychology."

This tendency to overlook older art historical research on the theme of world art is a characteristic displayed not only by Summers and Onians.[3] Naturally, at least since the period in which Early Modern *Kunst- and Wunderkammern* were pieced together, examples of "exotic handicraft" have been the topic of discussions across Europe. It was a topic which accrued even more intense interest in the nineteenth century when new means of transport became available, international expositions were held, the systematic acquisition of colonies by almost all *Kultur-Nationen* was in full swing and the first attempts to establish ethnological museums were made. Ever since the Enlightenment, there has been a self-consciously high regard and nostalgia for the "noble savage" and the "original" — qualities which from a European perspective both contemporary indigenous and prehistoric peoples alike seemed to offer. The heirs to this nostalgia in a certain sense were movements of the intelligentsia and the modern artists of the late nineteenth and twentieth centuries which were enthusiastic about appropriating indigenous arts and cultures.[4] All this seems to have been the focus of research for quite a long time. Today, nevertheless, most of these products of art history and other disciplines, at least as practiced up to the 1970s, appear to bear the stamp of colonial appropriation and Eurocentrism, to such an extent indeed that most research today can proceed only under the banner of "postcolonial studies" — and only by radically distancing itself from its forerunners (Schmidt-Linsenhoff 2003; Errington 1997; Thomas 1999; Volkenandt 2004; Brückner 2004).

As a consequence of this, the first efforts to arrive at a world art history by German-language writers have until now largely been seen in direct relation to the acquisition, beginning in the 1880s, of German colonies.[5] The purpose of my contribution is to argue against this assumption by revealing three additional aspects and sketching in the details to make a more complex picture[6]: my first point is that the beginnings of German research on world art, dating back to the 1880s and 1890s, derived from the interdisciplinary context of texts and discussions which so far have been virtually or entirely ignored by art history, namely, cultural anthropology and psychology. My second contention is the fact that nineteenth-century art historians initially focused on these apparently uncommon questions can hardly have been the outcome solely of "colonialist thinking," but may also be attributed to the methodological and institutional crises which agitated German art history during these years. The third point about which I wish to speak is to make at least a passing reference to why these beginnings of world art history in the German-speaking realm received little international notice, and, after c. 1930, fell into such complete oblivion that today it is necessary to discover these discussions anew. Furthermore, a certain kind of question asked is comprehensible only if very distinct, nationally particular historical trajectories such as that in Germany and Austria at the turn of the twentieth century are taken into account. When this step is taken, such studies on the historiography of art history are transformed into an analytical tool (not an antiquarian quest) in the search to understand our own cultural-intellectual situations, conditions, and concepts of thinking.

Needless to say, some of the following ideas suggested can hardly claim to do anything more than just hint at topics of interest. In the complex intermingling texture of nineteenth-century theories, my argument has to concentrate on the main context, the psychological, anthropological, and institutional foundations of a world art history. I will introduce the reader to certain marginalized authors and texts, which most explicitly demanded a world art perspective and consequently a methodical revision of traditional art history in the first place.

KUNSTWISSENSCHAFT, ANTHROPOLOGY, AND THE PSYCHOLOGY OF ART

The fundamental crisis in German art history in the decades around 1900 can be characterized summarily as a battle between *Kunstgeschichte* ("art history") and *Kunstwissenschaft* ("the science of art"). Whereas the adherents of *Kunstgeschichte*—Karl Friedrich von Rumohr among others—concentrated on studying and accumulating individual historical data, the defenders of *Kunstwissenschaft* sought in these newly accumulated facts binding principles of art (*Grundbegriffe*) and overarching rules governing its development– on a strictly "scientific" methodological basis and without falling back on idealistic constructions of the late eighteenth and early nineteenth centuries or other traditions of deductive aesthetic and philosophical speculation.[7]

The latter group's claims were given extra impetus by the institutional situation in the field which required dual legitimation. As a recently created university discipline, the study of art history had to demonstrate its "scientific" dimension in comparison with other human sciences—and it had to fulfil the requirements of a "science," primarily expressed as holistic explanatory models and laws (Dilly 1979; König and Lämmert 1999; Locher 2001, esp. 378–397). Simultaneously, art history had to secure an independent profile in order to contrast itself to the discipline of history, which had provided the most important methodological model for the positivist *Kunstgeschichte* in the tradition of Rumohr. This predominance of history as a discipline loomed even more threateningly in the 1880s and thereafter, when a growing tendency towards the writing of an all-embracing "cultural history" emerged. This included the study of art as a subfield and thereby attempting to incorporate art history into itself as a kind of secondary discipline (Haas 1994).

Probably the most decisive attempt to solve this dilemma on the part of *Kunstwissenschaft* involved an orientation towards the natural sciences, initially based on their classification systems,

7
See Heinz 1970; Nachtsheim 1984; Henckmann 1985; Mallgrave and Ikonomou 1994; Locher 1999 and Locher 2001, 203–97); for the overriding tradition of formal, nonspeculative aesthetics, with special emphasis on R. Zimmermann and Herbartianism, see Wiesing 1997.

8
Kuper 1988, 2 (esp. for Germany 129ff); for the importance and popularization of Darwin's ideas on the whole range of "the human sciences" see Young 1995 (esp. for psychology 56–78) and Daum 1998. See for a very selective discussion of the influence of Darwin on nineteenth-century art historical writings, Golden 2001. In the decades around 1900, the terms "anthropology," "ethnology," "ethnography" and the like were not yet precisely defined, see for example Haddon 1910, preface.
9
See Hauser 1985 and Mallgrave 1985; the modifications of Semper's original theories by, for example, E.E. Viollet-le-Duc and A. Choisy, are outlined in Kruft 1985, 321–328.

most famously developed for paleontology by Georges Cuvier. Then Charles Darwin's theory of evolution began to exert an influence (nevertheless the traditionally very prominent German philological traditions continued to play an important role, not least because the research on anthropology and prehistory pertaining to newly found relics of prehistoric life prior to the advent of Darwin and the mid-nineteenth century, was carried out mainly by "comparative linguistics"). In a nutshell: Darwin's (and others') ideas about physical anthropology had to be extended and complemented by a new anthropology of culture. A "scientific programme," to which history, religious studies and linguistics, as well as the new disciplines of the "human sciences" (such as art history, ethnology, prehistoric archaeology, psychology, and others) were eager to contribute. The fact that Darwin's triumph stimulated a very "un-Darwinian anthropology" (often more indebted to Jean-Baptiste de Lamarck and Herbert Spencer, to name just two) need not concern us here in detail.[8]

Out of these exemplary scientific models and their concomitant inductive method, art history initially gained a "functional materialism" in the trend of Gottfried Semper, who, commencing with the primitive beginnings of art (their "Urformen"), tried to explain the increasingly complex development of art forms and ornaments by their function in relation to materials, techniques and other social and cultural factors.[9] When this influential theory quickly came under fire, a second attempt was prompted—one decisive to my question, which has so far received too little attention. It was constructed on the then widely popular "empirical psychology," which borrowed a mechanical and mathematical model. Its foundations were laid by the philosopher Johann Friedrich Herbarth (rejecting the older theory of *a priori* mental "faculties"). This new psychology received decisive impulses through a growing interest in the natural sciences, historical anthropology, and cultures worldwide (Leary 1977; Arens 1989). Matters of investigation were the origins of the imaginative, creative, moral and cultural potentials of the human soul/intellect on the one hand, and their evolutionary developments and different stages on the other, that is, human "psycho-history," which manifests itself in the totality of cultural output of humankind.

Two aspects made this question scientifically so attractive: first of all, psychology presented itself as the "missing link" between human physiology and culture; or to phrase it slightly differently: the new psychology seemed to make it no longer possible to separate mind and culture (the "subjective") from the domain of scientific law (the "objective"). In research in art history and aesthetics, especially after the 1850s, this led to the development of a new methodological approach, which we might perhaps call "psychological aesthetics," of which the Herbartian Robert Zimmermann, Robert and Theodor Vischer, Gustav Theodor Fechner and others were protagonists. Surprisingly, these figures personally showed little interest in the problem of "primitive art," even though their theories would assume a central importance in the initial discussions on world art history (Drüe 1983; Allesch 1987; Mallgrave and Ikonomou 1994; Wiesing 1997). Secondly, and at least for a certain group of scientists, the quest for the human psyche promised to deliver a common "anthropological basis"— that is, a point of departure which would be the same for all humans; one which could provide objective scientific grounds of comparison, thereby allowing the cultural and individual developments and deviations from this to be determined (for example, these might result from local geographic or socioeconomic conditions or from "racial differences"). Since it was easier to study the basics and principles of these psychic mechanisms on such "primitive" human beings as prehistoric or indigenous peoples or children than on complex European high cultures, the results of their research in those areas gained the highest respect.[10]

Incidentally, Johann Gottfried Herder had already attempted something very similar with his collection of fairy tales: he sought to discover characteristics and connections between peoples which could be grasped in more uncorrupted form in folk art and literature than in "high art." Moreover, Herder—in contrast to the then dominant Enlightenment doctrine of a *raison universelle* manifesting itself in all humans alike—already favored the idea of a plurality of cultures and individual histories of peoples. Wilhelm von Humboldt would develop Herder's concept in his *Plan einer vergleichenden Anthropologie* ("Plan of a Comparative Anthropology," 1795/97; remained unpublished the first time) (Broce 1986; Bunzl 1996; Zimmerman 1998, 102–5).

By mid-century, most of these thoughts seem to have been common currency in German scientific discussions: they were, for example, succinctly presented and discussed between 1859 and 1871 by Theodor Waitz in the six volumes of *Anthropologie der Naturvölker*, which the first was translated into English as early as 1863 as *Introduction to Anthropology* (Waitz 1863, esp. 380ff). Right in the very first pages, the relevance of psychology is introduced as the only possibility to facilitate a truly scientific research into the cultural phenomena of humankind. Furthermore, Waitz claims a "general uniform intellectual capacity in all human populations" from the Greeks to the Hottentots—a uniform capacity which had only a short while before been questioned, most prominently by Gobineau in his thesis about the "inequality of races," a thought which had been and was to be shared by several other influential "polygenist thinkers," who argued for multiple origins of human races (and thereby tried to establish a "scientifically proven" fundamental difference between the Europeans and other peoples).[11] Among the representatives of the idea of uniform intellectual capacity themselves, many parties still held rather contradictory views on more or less any other question which happened to arise. The majority of the followers of Anglo-American

10
A short summary of this idea is given by Bastian 1874. See also Bastian 1868 and Waitz 1863. Finally, when research into the human psyche became psychoanalytical, even the drawings of neurotics were, in imitation of Freud, included in this argumentation, see Von Sydow 1927, esp. 39.

11
Gobineau (1853–1855); the first German translation appeared only in 1898–1901 under the titel *Versuch über die Ungleichheit der Menschenracen*.

For the complex history of polygenist theories from the eighteenth century to the Nazis and the initially slow reception of Gobineau in Germany, which until c. 1900 remained, at least for the majority of the physical anthropologists, the country of monogenism, see Stocking 1982, 42–68; Massin 1996; Weikart 2004.

12

See Stocking 1987 and Sanderson 1990, esp. 1–35; for the importance of Franz Boas and (to a lesser extent) W. H. R. Rivers in rejecting evolutionism and introducing (German) diffusionist ideas into Anglo-American anthropology, see Kuper 1988, 125–51, 162–65 and 171ff.

13

The literal translation of *Völkerpsychologie* would be "psychology of peoples," Franz Boas proposed "folk psychology." Lazarus and Steinthal 1860; outlined already in Lazarus 1851; both texts now edited in Lazarus 2003. See the excellent analyses of Belke 1982; Whitman 1984; Kalmar 1987, Bunzl 2003, and Diriwächter 2004.

14

Bastian himself stated the formative importance of Lazarus's and Steinthal's theory and those of Waitz's writings, on his thoughts, see Bastian 1881, 32ff. However, he subordinated linguistics and philology as they were tinged with instability and therefore not very reliable sources for his ethnology of material culture. For Bastian's theories in general see Köpping 2005; also Zimmerman 1999, 206 on Bastian and art.

anthropology (led by Edward B. Tylor) stated a severely unilinear, materialist evolutionism for all stages of the human race. Consequently, in their eyes an innate "artistic consciousness" of primeval humankind, unchanged in principle over the centuries, was out of question. Considering the early and "savage" manifestations of human handiwork (including ornament, painting and the like), preponderantly the necessities of survival and society (and prompted scarcely at all by any genuine aesthetic impulse) were accepted as possible motivations. Nevertheless, the long and short of it was that the European was believed to epitomize the teleological aim and indisputable role model of all developments.[12]

In contrast to this, especially in the context of German-speaking discussions, the postulation of a uniform mental capacity in all human populations led to the genesis of a further idea: if all peoples shared the same intellectual conditions in the first place, why should these varying cultures all follow the European model? And were they not so profoundly different from each other and in their characteristics that they should be studied without applying preconceived Eurocentric categories and evaluations? This final step was eventually taken up by the German-Jewish founders of *Völkerpsychologie*, the philosopher and psychologist Moritz Lazarus and the linguist and philologist Heymann Steinthal.[13] Their programme of a "psychic ethnology," developed during the 1850s, was based on systematic research into language, religion/mythology, art, and other similar systems of all peoples—since, they argued, only these manifestations of collective genius finally seen in synthesis offered the clue to the driving forces and governing principles of various historical trajectories. Lazarus and Steinthal traced a theoretical demand (based especially on their interests and professional training in the field of language, which appeared to them to be the main unifying psychological essence of a people) which was modified only slightly later (since 1860) and actually applied to the whole range of research on "primitive peoples" (now primarily their material cultures) by the founder of German ethnology, Adolf Bastian.[14]

Bastian's universal relativism was founded on the idea of the "psychic unity of humankind," which implied equal intellectual capacities and assumed that all cultures could ultimately be reduced to the same mental principles or elementary thought patterns (*Elementargedanken*). These basic common psychic foundations and innate human universals never actually occurred as such, but were subject to modification through an equally innate "propensity to change" as well as through geographically, chronologically and socially divergent overlays on different *Völkergedanken* (patterns of thought of a people). For this reason no culture could be transformed into another. Every people existed in their own right, in their own context and with their own categories—though within different stages of development. So, with Lazarus, Steinthal, and Bastian the superiority of Europeans, at least theoretically, was eclipsed. Only decades later, in 1910, Lucien Lévy-Bruhl formulated an idea even more radical than that of psychic unity and equal cultures: he postulated there is a fundamental alterity of "primitive," prelogical thinking, or in other words: in Lévy-Bruhl's eyes even cognition is relative.[15]

Here is not the place to pursue other, later receptions and modifications of these theories of *Völkerpsychologie* (by, for example, Wilhelm Wundt, who eventually gave it a nationalist turn) or its (partial) rejection by a younger generation of German "diffusionist ethnologists" after 1904, who tried to explain similarities of cultures to only a very limited extent by common psychic foundations, but attributed these mainly to direct transmissions. Consequently they argued for limited, more in-depth research into *Kulturkreise* and of human differences for their own sake Whitman 1984; Bunzl 2003; Penny 2003, esp. 110–24). Nor can we pay adequate tribute to folk psychology's importance to the field of sociology (Georg Simmel) or research on history, where it contributed to efforts to construct a "cultural" or "universal history" (Karl Lamprecht) (Lamprecht 1896; Lamprecht 1905; Breysig 1896; Ratzel 1904; Chickering 1991; Köhnke 1990; Haas 1994).

The only fact of relevance here is that there were some radical implications in all this for art history: Germany especially had quite a number of scientists and intellectuals who acknowledged the "artistic impulse" as a kind of innate human universal and thereby conceded the people known as primitives "real art" (Hirn 1900; Rothfuchs-Schulz 1980). This led to the problem that, if all cultures around the world produced "real art" which adequately expressed the respective attitudes and claims in its own right, this obviated the existence of any obligatory canon of aesthetic norms. The ancient European ideals of beauty, which had sought their legitimacy by referring to God, Nature, or Classical antiquity, were robbed of their validity. Aesthetic principles should be ascertained empirically by the application of perceptual psychology, using categories of a shared human psychic constitution, but modified through time, place and cultural traditions.

Two further aspects of "primitive art" should have made this very attractive to art historians: the enormous expansion of the range and objectives of the discipline and the presumed "history-lessness" among prehistoric and indigenous peoples. "Primitive" peoples seemed to live without a historical consciousness, without written history. As no written testimonials existed, it seemed that only art and the products of handicrafts could offer information on the stages of their cultures.[16] This unique anthropological approach allowed the protagonists of *Kunstwissenschaft* to believe that it could finally be emancipated from the confines of historical and philological research and concentrate on methodological independence and security of "form," namely, on what was genuinely "visual" and "artistic." In this the champions of *Kunstwissenschaft* saw the chance for it to become one of the leading "human

15
Lévy-Bruhl's theories were most probably not generated by German writings on anthropology, but should be seen primarily as a reaction to E. B. Tylor's unilinear evolutionism, see Scott Littleton 1985. For an explicit reaction to Lévy-Bruhl in the context of German art history see Vatter 1926, 23–34.

16
Consistently, after the "Introduction" Lubbock 1870 begins with a chapter on "Art and Ornament." Also Schweinfurth 1875, X: "A people, as long as they are on the lowest rung of their development, are far better characterized by their industrial products ["Kunstfleisses"] than they are either by their habits, which may be purely local, or by their own representations, which (rendered in their rude and unformed language) are often incorrectly interpreted by us. If we possessed more of these tokens, we should be in a position to comprehend better than we do the primitive condition of many a nation which has now reached a high degree of culture." In contrast, only a few years earlier, Prichard (1848) did not even mention art and art history.

An indication of the success of art history in its quest for disciplinary acceptance is given by the historian Lamprecht 1905, 118ff and esp. 123.

sciences" of the future.

In sum: if it were natural for the human "psyche" to produce art, as the new anthropological research tried to demonstrate, only a consideration of all the products of art worldwide—the "art of all times and peoples"—could deliver definitive conclusions about the origins and fundamental principles of art in its entirety. This paved the way to a central motivation for world art history around 1900. It also once again makes it apparent that it was a specific constellation of anthropology, psychology and discussions about cultural evolution in Germany which influenced the positions in the new *Kunstwissenschaft*. Another strand of arguments led to the same result: German art history in the late nineteenth and early twentieth century could seemingly only succeed as a "science" in the canon of university fields—that is, as a discipline explaining the rules and fundamental principles of all connections and developments in art—by adopting the new empirical and inductive methods of the natural sciences. This late, law-oriented objectification of artistic production, reception, and development could only be achieved in connection with the concept of a universal human psyche. Now, in order to determine these "basics" from the millennia of cultural histories, the art of "primitives"—namely, children, prehistoric and indigenous peoples—suddenly acquired a central interest. Hence world art history received a second decisive impulse from the methodological and institutional crisis of the discipline in the late nineteenth century. This is not to say, of course, that the "colonial interests" should be dismissed from their claim to be another important factor—especially since expeditions and colonies provided the material for studying the art of world peoples.

"PRIMITIVE ART" AND THE SURMOUNTING OF "OLD EUROPEAN PREJUDICES"

Following this brief sketch of the principal lines of thought, how did the art historical discussion go into detail? Three preliminary remarks are necessary to set the stage.

First of all, the separation between "principle thinking" and the "art historical discussion in detail" is only necessary because none of the texts I discuss below really develops the interconnections I have laid out above giving due weight to their full implications. None the less, all these texts, even if it is not obvious they do relate directly to this discussion, at least allude unmistakeably to these "psychological" theories, which seem to have been delivered through various, widely dispersed channels. Therefore, the contemporary "horizon of discourse" in this case must be reconstructed; this lack of any obvious, direct connection may also be one of the reasons these texts have received so little attention over the years.

The idea of undertaking research into the art of all cultures without any comparative evaluation was formulated by authors who will be designated "relativists" in this discussion. Their considerations always relate to other contemporary art historical reflections on non-European art. Consequently, the two additional alternatives—namely the theories of "evolutionists" and "nationalists"—also deserve a brief introduction, even more so as a clearcut separation of these three camps is impossible to achieve without some ambiguity creeping in.

Finally, the names of quite a number of art historians and authors of the late nineteenth and early twentieth century, which usually occur in art historical discussions on the beginnings of a literary and scientific estimation of non-European art, will be mentioned only in passing. This is not to deny the relevance of Edmond de Goncourt, Aby Warburg, Roger Fry, Guillaume Apollinaire, Carl Einstein and Wilhelm Worringer, among others, for offering important aspects for a new view on world art. In the context of a psychic conception of artistic production worldwide, however, they do not occupy a central position. Therefore, it seems justifiable that this article concentrate primarily on the lesser known writers who have pleaded most explicitly for a worldwide art history and the end of Eurocentric aesthetic categories, and who have anticipated some of the central claims made in present-day discussions with their demands for a methodological renewal of the subject of art history. All that can be done is to acknowledge that, because these texts both cover many different subjects and were published over a long time period (c. 1860–1930), the selection here could quite definitely be expanded.

The art historical "evolutionists" presented themselves as the successors to the age-old theories on the historical progress of humanity, which were formulated most cogently by Hegel and which had already led to the situation that, in Franz Kugler's *Handbuch der Kunstgeschichte* in 1842, for the first time non-European art had received an astonishingly "objective" appreciation in the context of an "entire art history."[17] Just in this period, the new scientific classificatory systems, especially Darwin-inspired theories, offered a role-model which was also eminently suitable for arranging works of art according to morphological principles and in sequences of development. This was underlined by the fact that the majority of "primitive art" known in the nineteenth century consisted of ornaments, which could be arranged and illustrated particularly well in series set closely together. Ralph Nicholson Wornum's *Analysis of Ornament* of 1856 and Owen Jones's *Grammar of Ornament* from the same year were both born of attempts to detect eternally stable foundational and developmental principles from a complete comparison of world ornament (as the basic "language" of all different styles).[18] In 1861 Semper presented his most authoritative formulation of the origins and early functionalist developments of art forms and ornaments, which he argued begin with abstract-geometric forms and end with the most naturalist ornament. As early as 1879, in a short paper entitled the *Anfänge der Kunst: anthropologische Beiträge zur Geschichte des*

17
For the context of Kugler see Locher 2001, 208–66; on art historical ideas of progress Hazan 1998; Errington 1997. Of special interest in this context is also the history of "world architecture"; published under different titles and in different forms since 1855 this was initially done by James Fergusson, who included an introductory chapter "Ethnography as Applied to Architectural Art" (Fergusson 1865–1867, 42–74).

18
In France, slightly later Charles Blanc commenced publishing his project of compiling a *Grammaire des arts*; for a concise summary of these developments see Locher 2001, 328–78.

Ornaments ("Beginnings of Art: Anthrolopological Contributions to the History of Ornament"), in Munich the anthropologist Johannes Ranke would attempt to link these materialist explanations to anthropological-ethnological considerations, based on the newly published materials gathered from all over the world.[19] However, it was especially in Great Britain and the Scandinavian countries that unilinear evolutionism found its most faithful supporters: Augustus H. Lane-Fox Pitt-Rivers, Henry Balfour, H. Colley March, Alfred C. Haddon and K. Hjalmar Stolpe.[20] In opposition to Semper and his followers, they formulated an early history of ornamentation which led from naturalistic to abstract forms ("degeneration theory"). At this point, at least two Scandinavian scholars should be mentioned briefly: the Swedish historian Hans O. Hildebrand, a specialist in early history who published drawings and carvings of the Inuit peoples in 1883, and foremost among them, the Danish archaeologist Julius Lange who was one of the first to compare not merely ornaments but the monumental sculpture of several "primitive cultures," including Greek archaic sculpture, and who concluded most importantly that the "law of frontality" had been a universal principle of form at this point in plastic representation.[21] Nevertheless, the decisive aspect in this case is that invariably in all these evolutionist theories, the analyses of ornaments and other art forms supplied interesting information concerning early human history, but such artefacts were always thought to be hopelessly inferior to later products. Ornamental decorations especially were regarded simply as craft objects and even seen partly as a "pictographic writing system," but basically not regarded as "real art."

As an objection to this, it seems to have been a trait of German-speaking ethnological research to emphasize the artistic character of ornaments even in the most "primitive level" of cultures. In 1890–1891, Alois R. Hein explicitly pointed out the aesthetic qualities of "savage" ornament and distinguished between the material culture of a civilization and the quality of its art (partially this idea had already been widespread earlier, for instance, in Owen Jones and Ralph Nicholson Wornum).[22] Only two years later, in 1893, Alois Riegl presented his groundbreaking criticism of Semperian materialism and offered a new account of the historical development of (ancient) ornament. As is well known, slightly later, in *Spätrömische Kunst-Industrie* (*Late Roman Art Industry*, 1901), he also introduced the concept of "Kunstwollen," a psychological force behind all artistic developments (and obviously influenced by the theories of *Völkerpsychologie*).[23] Since these considerations demanded the abandoning of normative aesthetic categories and evolutionist imaginings of art's development, Riegl at this point had already become a "relativist."

Now a brief word needs to be said about the "nationalists." Obviously it was an easy step from the conception of an ever more perfect series of stages in art forms and cultures to "nationalist"

19

Ranke 1879; for an explicit, if somewhat critical discussion of Semper see pp. 16–24.

However, Ranke later disputed the "dignity of science" of non-European anthropology, see Zimmerman 1998, 35ff and 87.

20

A. Lane-Fox Pitt-Rivers 1874–1875 contributions are reprinted in Pitt-Rivers 1906; Balfour 1890 and Balfour 1893; taking the art of New-Guinea as his starting point, Haddon 1895, 306ff: "There are two ways in which art may be studied—the aesthetic and the scientific. The former deals with all manifestations of art from a purely subjective point of view, and classifies objects according to certain so-called 'canons of art.' These may be the generally recognised rules of the country or race to which the critic belongs, and may even have the sanction of antiquity, or they may be due to the idiosyncrasy of the would-be mentor. In criticizing the art of another country it must be remembered that racial tendencies may give such a bias as to render it very difficult to treat foreign art sympathetically. Western Europe and Japan are cases in point. Dogmatism in aesthetics is absurd, for, after all, the aesthetic sense is largely based upon personal likes and dislikes.... We will now turn to a more promising field of inquiry, and see what can be gained from a scientific treatment of art. This naturally falls into two categories, the physical [including: "psychology"] and the biological."

For a discussion of Haddon's ideas and their transference to all artistic products see Colley March 1896; his ideas on ornament in Colley March 1889. Stolpe's articles of the 1890s are collected in Stolpe 1927.

21

Hildebrand 1885; Lange 1899, V–XXXI; the expression "Gesetz der Frontalität" is not Lange's own, but was coined by the editor Furtwängler, who regarded its discovery as a "kunstgeschichtliches Resultat ersten Ranges, der Entdeckung eines Naturgesetzes vergleichbar."

22

Hein 1891 was reviewed by Alois Riegl: Riegl 1892.

23

The best succinct summary of Riegl's thinking is given by Kemp 1990.

(and racist) schemes. In the German-speaking world, since the efflorescence of Pan-Germanism and *völkisch* movements in the 1890s, some scholars had postulated the superiority of (German-) Aryan art to "primitive" art. The rub was that a second argument also had to be brought to bear in order to discredit the artistic traditions of ancient Italy and Greece, previously celebrated as the foundation and perfection/apotheosis of Western art. As there was little to criticize in the products, instead of vilifying them, writers contested their priority. Therefore, they directed attention to the Near East, the "cradle of the Aryans," and attempted to locate the origin of central art forms there—consequently, in a seemingly paradoxical fashion, a new point of view on non-European art tailored to nationalist purposes emerged. An early example of this can be found in the writings of Friedrich Seesselberg in 1897.[24] The best-known example is certainly Josef Strzygowski, beginning with his 1901 publication of *Orient und Rom*. His interest in non-European art would later be employed for nationalist ends (Jäggi 2002; Kite 2003).

The third and most important group was that of the "relativists." In 1875, Georg Schweinfurth was already implying that the "civilization" of the world by the West could be understood as a double-edged narrative—of progress, but also as a history of loss: "Speed is of the essence as the destructive tendency which is generated when our industrial productions obtrude themselves upon all the nations of the earth, threatens, sooner or later, to sweep away the last vestiges of indigenous arts, even in Africa."[25] Yet shortly afterwards, the technically advanced works of art from Benin—looted during a British penal expedition in 1897— not only dramatically justified Schweinfurth's lament, they also conclusively upset ideas about "primitive" African art.

The real discussion was actually opened by an exceptional intellectual achievement in 1894: the 300-page treatise by Ernst Grosse on *Die Anfänge der Kunst* (*The Beginnings of Art*). In contrast to its title, in reality it presents itself as an attempt to found anew the discipline of *Kunstwissenschaft* on a strictly objective and scientific basis as a kind of "comparative ethnological method applied to art history"; this revised *Kunstwissenschaft* aspired to analyse in order to make "individual manifestations" its primary goals (p. 9), but to define the overarching cultural-historical, and socioanthropological hypotheses pertaining to the art forms of body decoration, ornament, sculpture, dance, poetry, and music, all objects which Grosse regarded—at least in their early stages— as having been heavily determined by their socioeconomic functions.[26] Behind all this of course lies Darwin's evolutionist theory: "The development of art, too, is accomplished under the great law of natural selection" (p. 14). Grosse argued that "humanity ... by no means moves along a single line in a single direction; rather, as different as the living conditions of peoples are, so different too are their paths and destinations." And therefore "the present

24
Seesselberg 1897 is most explicit in the "Conclusion," p. 141; for the origins of "northern" and "southern" European art in Near Eastern "world art" see pp. 4–15.
25
Schweinfurth 1875, X; the book has a dedication "Seinem vielverehrten Freunde Prof. Dr. A. Bastian, dem Gründer der Deutschen Gesellschaft zur Erforschung Aequatorial-Afrikas." For the (German) tradition of criticizing Eurocentric historiography and Western "materialism" see Marchand 1997.
26
Grosse 1894; the English translation of 1897 went through five more editions in 1898, 1899, 1900, 1914 and 1928; a French translation appeared in 1902 under the title *Les débuts de l'art*. A short discussion of the merits and (evolutionist) limitations of Grosse's theory is in Gerbrands 1957, 47ff.

27
Schmarsow 1907, 310–12. Also relevant
in this context are Schmarsow 1910
and Schmarsow 1919. For the tradition
of German anthropology to collect
materials and facts, without theoretical
a priori" see Zimmerman 1998, 54–64.
28
Verworn 1907, 5–7. For Hegel see
Locher 2001, 206.
29
Worringer 1919 [1907], 70ff. On the
same pages, he praises Japanese art. See
also his later rejection of the idea of
"art" as a human universal in Worringer
1956; whereas in Worringer 1911, 6–9,
he argued against the dominance of a
(European) canon of classical beauty.

history of art [has] made the field of its research too narrow to the detriment of foreign arts" (p. 2). "The science of art should extend its researches to all peoples; but it should apply itself especially to those groups which it has formerly most neglected. All forms of art are equally endowed with a claim to their own intrinsic interest" (p. 23). Once again the summary states the central idea of artistic potential as a human universal: "Our investigation has proved what aesthetics has hitherto only asserted: that there are, for the human race, at least, generally effective conditions governing aesthetic pleasure, and consequently generally valid laws of artistic creation. In contrast to this fundamental agreement, the differences between primitive and higher art forms appear to be more of a quantitative than a qualitative sort. The emotions represented in primitive art are narrow and rude, its materials are scanty, its forms are poor and coarse, but in its essential motives, means, and aims the art of earliest times is one with the art of all times" (p. 307).

The new investigations into world art reached a first climax in 1907: in this year August Schmarsow tried to devise a first systematic summation of the meaning of *Völkerpsychologie* and anthropology for a new *Kunstwissenschaft*.[27] The point of departure adopted by Schmarsow was Grosse's book, which he linked with the theories of Yrjö Hirn (*The Origins of Art*, 1900) and Wilhelm Wundt (*Völkerpsychologie*, 1900). To avoid the problem of how to differentiate between art and other artefacts made by these peoples, Schmarsow pleaded for an unprejudiced and general inclusion of all handicrafts from a culture. In the same year, Max Verworn developed the programme of an art psychology of the "primitives," in which he also modified (unconsciously?) a *dictum* by Hegel that art could sometimes give the deepest insight into the nature of a people (or could even allow exclusive insight if the people are illiterate).[28] Furthermore, the reader should be reminded of the fact that in 1907 Wilhelm Worringer's enormously influential PhD thesis on *Abstraktion und Einfühlung* (*Abstraction and Empathy*) was published; his work was also based entirely on the tradition of psychological-formal aesthetics and changed the general acceptance of abstract forms of art radically. Despite his pioneering effort, Worringer could still continue to dismiss all prehistoric and indigenous arts as "not yet really art."[29] If Carl Einstein's publications on *Negerplastik* (1915/1920) and *Afrikanische Plastik* (1921) are pointed out at this stage, this is done for reasons beyond the newly researched and remarkable formal analysis of these works of art. Indeed, as one of the first, Einstein seems to have recognized the dangers of the psychological *Kunstwissenschaft*, because its central term "empathy"—against all previous intentions and with Worringer as the latest to modify it—began to be endowed with an increasingly subjective-speculative component (Einstein 1981, 65ff).

After 1918—after the eclipse of Imperial Germany and the loss of the colonies—the demands for a world art history were able to become even more radical. The year 1923 seems to have marked a second climax in the attempt to develop a world art history: in this year Herbert Kühn published a substantial book on *Die Kunst der Primitiven* ("Art of the Primitives"), which embraced the entire spectrum of prehistoric and indigenous art forms: the products of Aztecs, Bushmen, Eskimos, Africans and so forth. In contrast to other books about the "art of all times and peoples," Kühn did not espouse the idea of a superior development of the art derived from the so called *Kultur-Nationen*. His introductory conviction was instead that "the art of the primitives is not in truth primitive — men of the time lived primitively … — but their art is the purest expression of their world …. We must thus look at them from an entirely different point of view. Winckelmann and Goethe's concepts are no longer adequate for interpreting the art of aboriginal and indigenous peoples. A time when Greek antiquity and the Renaissance alone appeared to be the epitome of art and when every stylization seemed a corruption would have no understanding for an art of primitive peoples" (Kühn 1923, 7; this and subsequent translations are mine). Kühn added an acute analysis of the historiography of the topic stretching from Semper to Riegl to the ethnologists — in order to pursue a Marxist-related theory of all-determinative forms of economic organization.

In 1923, Josef Strzygowski also presented a systematic summary and elaboration of his thoughts, which he had been developing since the publication of his controversial book *Orient und Rom* in 1901.[30] If his work had not included unabashedly anti-Semitic attacks against the "Jewish world conspiracy" and if we had not known about Strzygowski's later nationalistic instrumentalization of his theories, his *Krisis der Geisteswissenschaften* ("Crisis of the Humanities") may have been regarded as one of the fundamental methodological texts of a world art history (taking its place alongside Grosse's and Schmarsow's publications). In explicit opposition to a Eurocentric "humanistic tradition" and a view of the whole world obtained by means of a "strictly scientific" three steps of "tidings, nature, development," Strzygowski attempted to assert that a "comparing/comparative art research" would be a leading discipline of the future human sciences: "It seems to me that we have been taught to think in a certain 'humanistic' way, dominant since the Renaissance, a kind of superstition…. This is how I see the situation of the humanities when all and sundry is viewed from the perspective of philosophy, Classical philology and the historiography of Europe…. If we were to let the objects speak for themselves, to see ourselves simply in the service of those projects who have their own character…, then we might perhaps begin to reach out for each other around the globe in friendship…. If there were a science which would embrace the entire circle of the globe, mankind in the entire course of its existence, and in addition in all of its societal stratifications, and which would finally strive to understand its inner values as common to its universal character, it will show the way to the other disciplines in the humanities. This science,

30
The book is based on eight lectures given by the Vienese art historian in the USA; see Strzygowski 1923, the following quotations on pp. 2 and 31. See also Marchand 1994 and Wood 2004.

31
Beyer 1923, the book went through
three printings in this one year.
32
For Grosse's *Kunstwissenschaftlichen
Studien*, published in 1900, see Heinz
1970, 210–13; his publications on East
Asian sculpture, East Asian ink painting, and the art collections in Tokyo, etc.
contributed significantly to making this
art widely known in Germany, see Von
Erdberg 1985.
33
On Kühn see his partly "autobiograph-
ical" Kühn 1976.

it seems to me, could indeed be the investigation of the arts."

Finally, in the same year, in his small book *Welt-Kunst: von der Umwertung der Kunstgeschichte* ("World Art: The Reevaluation of Art History"), Oskar Beyer attempted to dethrone classical Greco-Roman and Renaissance art completely: Beyer, too, strove to establish a "world perspective" and an "surmounting of old European prejudices" with help from the "previous work and findings of the [ethnological, anthropological and archeological] sciences." But he only went as far as to designate the art of classical Greece, on the basis of its manifest "individualistic principle of art" — that is, its production of singular artist-geniuses in competition with one another and therefore no longer representatives of the community as a whole — as the beginning of artistic (and with it, of ethical and societal) decline.[31]

As a digression it should be mentioned that in the following year, at the second *Kongreß für Ästhetik und allgemeine Kunstwissenschaft* (Berlin 1924), the sociologist Alfred Vierkandt presented arguably the best summary on the competing theories so far developed and the problems confronting the new anthropological-psychological art research. However, he addressed his methodological conclusions and demands only to ethnology, and did not draw attention to the implications of a new world art history (Vierkandt 1925). This may also have been connected with the fact that those years were marked by a contest which was apparently taking place between art history and anthropology, disputing which discipline had discovered "primitive art" and whose task it was to investigate and document it. *Kunstwissenschaft* seemed to be winning out at first with its "aims for a universal History of Art of all times and peoples … which will make possible the discovery of universal laws of artistic creation, the origin and change of style, as well as the conditions for the individual psychology, the sociology and culture of artistic creation" (Vatter 1926, 7ff).

In trying to make sense of the fact that all these works obviously play no part at all in today's art historical discussions, at first sight it is tempting to conclude that most of the authors could be considered marginal figures of art history: Grosse (1862–1927) studied philosophy and literature and in 1894 became a professor of philosophy in Freiburg; beginning in 1896–1897 he specialized in researching and collecting East Asian art.[32] Kühn (1895–1980), who had written his PhD on *Die Grundlagen des Stilwandels in der modernen Kunst* in 1918, became a professor in 1929 — of prehistory and early history, an area of study to which mainstream art historians paid little attention.[33] Beyer (1890–1960) spent his entire life working as an independent scholar and writer. Only Schmarsow (1853–1936) and Strzygowski (1862–1941) may be considered important academic art historians in Germany and Austria of their time, but they were both also very idiosyncratic and controversial figures: the contemporary critique bemoaned the lack of careful factual research in Schmarsow's extensive published *oeuvre*, touching upon a wide range of topics as well as methodical questions. Strzygowski unfortunately stated his subversive ideas of Eastern influence on European art very uncompromisingly and pugnaciously; he also brought discredit upon himself through his already mentioned anti-Semitic and nationalistic remarks.

Nevertheless, this impression of marginalization is complicated by the fact that some of their publications were obviously very popular and had a wide readership; some — for example Grosse's — were even translated into English and French.[34] The prehistoric and indigenous art in the German multivolume manuals on the art of all times and peoples (Woermann, Springer, *Propyläen*, very selective: *Handbuch der Kunstwissenschaft*) were at least intended in part for the *Bildungsbürgertum*; and also the steadily increasing production of "coffeetable books" on these topics seemed to be a parallel phenomenon to the various editions of popular "world histories" in the Germany of the Emperor Wilhelm II (Bergenthum 2002). Other factors were also unquestionably important: the very common *Völkerschauen*; the founding of ethnological museums; the growing antiquarian market; and even the first exhibitions of non-European art are pertinent indications that World Art experienced a kind of heyday in the early 1900s.[35] In 1924–1925, finally, the first German-speaking specialist journals — *Jahrbuch der asiatischen Kunst*, *Artibus Asiae* and *Jahrbuch für prähistorische & ethnographisch Kunst (Ipek)* —, which operated exclusively outside of the established art historical canon, were founded.

That these impulses did not really penetrate the Anglo-American realm is attributable to a variety of theoretical and methodological developments: the domination of unilinear evolutionism in the late nineteenth century, whose strongest supporters were Tylor and Frazer; the historical particularism of the German-Jewish émigré Franz Boas (in our context especially his 1927 published *Primitive Art*); and, finally, the increasing hegemony after the 1940s of structural-functionalism propagated by Bronislaw Malinowski and A.R. Radcliffe-Brown. Paradoxically, Boas's (at least temporary) overwhelming influence on American anthropological research made his name a virtual substitute for the German research tradition and all earlier forms of cultural relativism were gradually subsumed under it.[36]

Nevertheless, probably the most decisive break with and "neglect" of the early German impulses in world art history should be set (and not surprisingly) in Germany itself: attributable to the changing ideals undergone by ethnology in the years after 1900 (abandoning among other pursuits the search for fundamental elements of the human psyche); the growing nationalism of the Weimar Republic and the general crisis of *Geisteswissenschaften* during these years; and especially in the 1930s, when the Nazis begin to force a radical racism of research and insist on a severance

34
See also the positive contemporary evaluations of Grosse's book, for example by Frobenius 1897, 12.
35
See Penny 1999. This search for a world art history might even be set in relation to the idea of "modern art" around 1900 becoming a "world language [of art] … beyond natural differences in place and time," as Julius Meyer-Graefe put it; see Gillen 2002.
36
This does not imply that Boas himself ever formulated this claim; see Bunzl 1996; Massin 1996; Bunzl and Penny 2003, 5–7 and 22.

37
For the "ethnological" dimensions of
this change see Penny 2003 and Bunzl
and Penny 2003.
    38
Instead, within the discipline of
anthropology/ethnology a subfield
"anthropology of art" was established,
see Haselberger 1969; Kreide-Damani
1992; Morphy 1994; Hatcher 1985.
    39
Onians 2004, 11ff. For a concise summary of the actual discussions on
human universals see Brown 2004.

with all earlier liberal approaches.[37] This did not happen in a vacuum: analogues in neighbouring disciplines, for example, the cultural historian Karl Lambrecht and his Institut für Kultur- und Universalgeschichte (Institute of Cultural and Universal History) in Leipzig, founded in 1909 and closed by the Nazis in 1933 may also be pointed out (Haas 1994, 229–42).

After 1945, German art historians avoided dealing with the recent past. Hence, the controversial topic of world art was simply expunged from the art history curriculum.[38] Cogently, the conceptual reworking of the second edition of *Propyläen Kunstgeschichte* (1966) turned back to Winckelmann, insofar as it allowed the history of art in Volume One to begin once again with the Greeks—and no longer as in the first edition (1923) with the early cultures and indigenous peoples, which were divided over the supplementary volumes (Paul 2003).

TOWARDS 2000

In many respects, the re-awakening of interest in world art in the 1970s and 1980s astonishingly resembles the situation in the decades around 1900: since the 1970s and during the 1980s, cultural historical and anthropological questions and methods have also celebrated a comeback. As in the years at the beginning of the twentieth century, today we pose questions about the possible connections between and common principles in the objects of world art—not to do so would make world art history appear to be nothing more than an accumulation and linear regimentation of art forms, without making clear, for example, what a comparison between an Inca temple and Michelangelo's dome for St Peter's should contribute to our understanding. Even today, the solution to the problem consists in taking recourse to the "psychic unity of mankind" and to human universals: in Hans Belting's 2001 *Bild-Anthropologie*, thoughts of death, memory, and substitution form the foundation for all representations. In the work of Summers, "real space" (an idea also heavily reliant on anthropology and basic human-psychology concepts) and "post-formalist art history" assume this role. In the case of Onians, finally, it is "nature," and when he specifies that "[t]he nature referred to here is one familiar to people of all cultures. It is nature as a set of resources and constraints, principally those embodied in the nature of the earth, of time and of man"[39]—his work almost reads as an unmediated sequel to Bastian's theory of the divergent overlays of the *Völkergedanken*. In other words: we are still wrestling with what has been the greatest problem ever since the initial European ideas about World Art, namely the "ennobling" category of "art" itself and the tensions between its deeply Eurocentric connotations contrasted with its potential to be understood as a human universal.

Finally, interestingly the institutional conditions framing world art history in Germany in 1900 and 2000 also display parallels: if the original issue was the establishment of *Kunst-geschichte/Kunstwissenschaft* in the university landscape, today it is the survival of art history in the context of newer, purportedly more interdisciplinary fields like *Bildwissenschaft*, visual studies or media studies, all competing for the distribution of scarce resources and funds. Taking account of the historiographical beginnings of the subject, namely the origins and principles of world art history around 1900, can alert our consciousness to points relevant to the current discussions, with regard both to methodological and to institutional conditions, possible solutions and self-imposed apori.

ACKNOWLEDGEMENTS

Rainer Donandt, Patricia Gilson, Wolfgang Kemp, Charlotte Schoell-Glass, Wilfried van Damme, and Kitty Zijlmans have each made important suggestions for modification or correction—my thanks to all of them. A complementary aspect to this essay —the discovery of prehistoric art in the latter part of the nineteenth century—is outlined in: Ulrich Pfisterer, "Altamira—oder: die Anfänge von Kunst und Kunstwissenschaft". *Vorträge aus dem Warburg-Haus* 10. Berlin: Akademie Verlag, 2007, 13–80.

REFERENCES

ALLESCH, CHRISTIAN G. 1987. *Geschichte der psychologischen Ästhetik: Untersuchungen zur historischen Entwicklung eines psychologischen Verständnisses ästhetischer Phänomene.* Göttingen, etc.: Verlag für Psychologie Hogrefe.

ANDRÉE, RICHARD. 1878. *Ethnographische Parallelen und Vergleiche.* Stuttgart: Maier.
—. 1887. Das Zeichnen bei den Naturvölkern. *Mittheilungen der Anthropologischen Gesellschaft in Wien* 12: 98–106.

ARENS, KATHERINE. 1989. *Structures of knowing: Psychologies of the nineteenth century.* Dordrecht: Kluwer Academic Publishers.

BALFOUR, HENRY. 1890. The origin of decorative art as illustrated by the art of modern savages. *Midland Naturalist* 13: 189–201.
—. 1893. *The evolution of decorative art: An essay upon its origin and development as illustrated by the art of modern races of mankind.* London: Rivington, Perceival & Co.

BASTIAN, ADOLF. 1868. *Das Beständige in den Menschenrassen und die Spielweite ihrer Veränderlichkeit: Prolegomena zu einer Ethnologie der Culturvölker.* Berlin: Reimer.
—. 1874. Review of *Völkerkunde* by Oscar Peschel. *Zeitschrift für Ethnologie* 6: 148ff.
—. 1881. *Die Vorgeschichte der Ethnologie: Deutschlands Denkfreunden gewidmet…* Berlin: Dümmler.

BELKE, INGRID. 1982. Die Begründung der Völkerpsychologie in Deutschland. *Rivista di Filosofia* LXXII (22–23): 192–233.

BELTING, HANS. 2001. *Bild-Anthropologie: Entwürfe für eine Bildwissenschaft.* Bild und Text. Munich: Fink.

BERGENTHUM, HARTMUT. 2002. Weltgeschichten im wilhelminischen Deutschland: Innovative Ansätze in der populären Geschichtsschreibung. In *Weltgeschichtsschreibung im 20. Jahrhundert.* Comparativ. Leipziger Beiträge zur Universalgeschichte und vergleichenden Gesellschaftsforschung 12 (3), ed. Matthias Middell, 16–56. Leipzig: Leipziger Universitätsverlag.

BEYER, OSKAR. 1923. *Welt-Kunst: von der Umwertung der Kunstgeschichte.* Dresden: Sybillen-Verlag.

BITTEL, KURT, ed. 1966–1983. *Propyläen-Kunstgeschichte: in achtzehn Bänden.* Berlin: Propyläen-Verlag.

BOAS, FRANZ. 1927. *Primitive art.* New York: Dover 1955 (1st ed. Oslo: Aschehoug).

BREYSIG, KURT. 1896. Über Entwicklungsgeschichte. *Deutsche Zeitschrift für Geschichtswissenschaft* 1: 161–74, 193–211.

BROCE, GERALD. 1986. Herder and ethnography. *Journal of the History of Behavioral Sciences* 22: 150–170.

BROWN, DONALD E. 2004. Human universals, human nature & human culture. *Daedalus: Journal of the American Academy of Arts & Sciences 133* (Fall), 47–54.

BRÜCKNER, WOLFGANG. 2004. Museale Kontinuitätskonstruktion von "les arts premiers". In *Gründungsmythen, Genealogien, Memorialzeichen: Beiträge zur intitutionellen Konstruktion von Kontinuität,* ed. Gert Melville and Karl-Siegbert Rehberg, 241–60. Cologne, Weimar and Vienna: Böhlau.

BUNZL, MATTI. 1996. Franz Boas and the Humboldtian tradition: From *Volksgeist and Nationalcharakter* to an anthropolocial concept of culture. In *Volksgeist as method and ethic: Essays on Boasian ethnography and the German anthropological tradition.* Vol. 8 of *History of Anthropology,* ed. George W. Stocking, Jr., 17–78. Madison: University of Wisconsin Press.
—. 2003. *Völkerpsychologie* and German-Jewish emancipation. In *Wordly provincialism: German anthropology in the age of empire,* ed. Matti Bunzl and H. Glenn Penny, 47–85. Ann Arbor: University of Michigan Press.
—, and H. Glenn Penny. 2003. Introduction: Rethinking German anthropology, colonialism, and race. In *Wordly provincialism: German anthropology in the age of empire,* ed. Matti Bunzl and H. Glenn Penny, 1–30. Ann Arbor: University of Michigan Press.

BUSSE, KARL H. 1914a. Die Ausstellung zur vergleichenden Entwicklungsgeschichte der primitiven Kunst bei den Naturvölkern, den Kindern und in der Urzeit. In *Bericht: Kongress für Ästhetik und Allgemeine Kunstwissenschaft.* Stuttgart: Enke, 79–82.
—. 1914b. Vergleichende Entwicklungspsychologie der primitiven Kunst bei den Naturvölkern, den Kindern und in der Urzeit. In *Bericht: Kongress für Ästhetik und Allgemeine Kunstwissenschaft* Stuttgart: Enke, 232–45.

CHICKERING, ROGER. 1991. Karl Lamprechts Konzeption einer Weltgeschichte. *Archiv für Kulturgeschichte* 73: 437–52.

COLLEY MARCH, HENRY. 1889. The meaning of ornament, or its archeology and its psychology. *Transactions of the Lancashire and Cheshire Antiquarian Society* 7: 160–92.
—. 1896. Evolution and psychology in art. *Mind: A Quarterly Review of Psychology and Philosophy* 5 (20): 441–63.

CONNELLY, FRANCES S. 1995. *The sleep of reason: Primitivism in modern European art and aesthetics, 1725–1907.* University Park: Pennsylvania State University Press.

DAUM, ANDREAS W. 1998. *Wissenschaftspopularisierung im 19. Jahrhundert: bürgerliche Kultur, naturwissenschaftliche Bildung und die deutsche Öffentlichkeit, 1848–1914.* Munich: Oldenbourg.

DE GOBINEAU, J. ARTHUR 1853–1855. *Essai sur l'inégalité des races humaines.* 4 vols. Paris.

DILLY, HEINRICH. 1979. *Kunstgeschichte als Institution: Studien zur Geschichte einer Disziplin.* Frankfurt a.M.: Suhrkamp.

DIRIWÄCHTER, RAINER. 2004. Völkerpsychologie: The synthesis that never was. *Culture & Psychology* 10 (1): 85–109.

DRÜE, HERMANN. 1983. Die psychologische Ästhetik im Deutschen Kaiserreich. In *Ideengeschichte und Kunstwissenschaft: Philosophie und bildende Kunst im Kaiserreich.* Kunst, Kultur und Politik im Deutschen Kaiserreich 3, ed. Ekkehard Mai, Stephan Waetzoldt and Gerd Wolandt, 71–98. Berlin: Mann.

EINSTEIN, CARL. 1981. Afrikanische Plastik. In *Werke 2,* ed. Marion Schmid, 62–144. Berlin: Medusa-Verlag.

ELKINS, JAMES. 2004. Review of *Real spaces: World art history and the rise of Western modernism* by David Summers. *The Art Bulletin* 86 (2): 373–81.

ERRINGTON, SHELLEY. 1997. *The death of authentic primitive art and other tales of progress.* Berkeley and London: University of California Press.

FERGUSSON, JAMES. 1865–1867. *History of architecture in all countries: From the earliest times to the present day.* 2 vols. London: John Murray.

FINEBERG, JONATHAN, ed. 1998. *Discovering child art: Essays on childhood, primitivism and modernism.* Princeton, NJ: Princeton University Press.

FROBENIUS, LEO. 1897. Die bildende Kunst der Afrikaner. *Mittheilungen der Anthropologischen Gesellschaft in Wien* 27: 1–17.

GERBRANDS, ADRIANUS A. 1957. *Art as an element of culture, especially in Negro-Africa.* Trans. Gertrude E. van Baaren-Pape. Leiden: E.J. Brill 1957.

GILLEN, ECKHART. 2002. German art—national expression or world language?: Two visual essays. In: *The two art histories: The museum and the university,* ed. Charles W. Haxthausen, 87–101. New Haven, CT, and London: Yale University Press.

GOLDEN, LAUREN. 2001. Science, Darwin and art history. In *Raising the eyebrow: John Onians and world art studies: An album amicorum in his honour,* ed. Lauren Golden, 79–90. Oxford: Archaeopress.

GROSSE, ERNST. 1894. *Die Anfänge der Kunst.* Freiburg i.Br. and Leipzig: J. C. B. Mohr. English trans. *The beginnings of art.* New York: Appleton, 1897.

HAAS, STEFAN. 1994. *Historische Kulturforschung in Deutschland 1880–1930: Geschichtswissenschaft zwischen Synthese und Pluralität.* Münstersche historische Forschungen 5. Cologne, etc.: Böhlau.

HADDON, ALFRED C. 1895. *Evolution in art: As illustrated by the life-histories of designs.* London: Walter Scott.
—. 1910. *History of anthropology.* London: Watts.

HALBERTSMA, MARLITE. 2003. Fremde Welten und vertraute Methoden: die deutsche Weltkunstforschung des frühen 20. Jahrhunderts. *Kritische Berichte* 31 (2): 28–36.

HASELBERGER, HERTA. 1969. *Kunstethnologie: Grundbegriffe, Methoden, Darstellung.* Vienna and Munich: Schroll.

HATCHER, EVELYN PAYNE. 1985. *Art as culture: An introduction to the antropology of art.* 2nd ed. 1999. Westport, CO, and London: Bergin & Harvey.

HAUSER, ANDREAS. 1985. Der "Cuvier der Kunstwissenschaft": Klassifizierungsprobleme in Gottfried Sempers *Vergleichender Baulehre.* In *Grenzbereiche der Architektur. Festschrift Adolf Reinle,* ed. Thomas Bold, 97–114. Basel, etc.: Birkhäuser.

HAZAN, OLGA. 1999. *Le mythe du progrès artistique: étude critique d'un concept fondateur du discours sur l'art depuis la Renaissance.* Montréal: Presses de l'Université de Montréal.

HEIN, ALOIS RAIMUND. 1890. *Die bildende Kunst bei den Dayaks auf Borneo.* Vienna 1890
—. 1891. *Mäander, Hakenkreuze und urmotivische Wirbelornamente in Amerika: ein Beitrag zur allgemeinen Ornamentgeschichte.* Vienna: Hölder.

HEINZ, RUDOLF. 1970. Zum Begriff der philosophischen Kunstwissenschaft im 19. Jahrhundert. In *Der Wissenschaftsbegriff: Historische und systematische Untersuchungen,* ed. Alwin Diemer, 202–37. Meisenheim am Glan: Hain.

HENCKMANN, WOLFHART. 1985. Probleme der allgemeinen Kunstwissenschaft. In *Kategorien und Methoden der deutschen Kunstgeschichte 1900–1930. Aus den Arbeitskreisen "Methoden der Geisteswissenschaften" der Fritz-Thyssen-Stiftung,* ed. Lorenz Dittmann, 273–334. Stuttgart: Steiner-Verlag Wiesbaden GmbH.

HILDEBRAND, HANS. 1885. Beiträge zur Kenntnis der Kunst der niederen Naturvölker. In *Studien und Forschungen, veranlasst durch meine Reisen im hohen Norden: ein populär-wissenschaftliches Supplement zu: Die Umsegelung Asiens und Europas auf der Vega,* ed. Adolf E. von Nordenskiöld, 289–386. Leipzig: F. A. Brockhaus. Originally published as *Studier och forskningar föranledda af mina resor i höga norden: ett populärt vetenskapligt behang till "Vegas färd kring Asien och Europa"* (Stockholm, 1883).

HIRN, YRJÖ. 1900. *The origins of art: A psychological & sociological inquiry.* London: Macmillan & Co.

JÄGGI, CAROLA. 2002. Ex Oriente Lux: Josef Strzygowski und die "Orient oder Rom": Debatte um 1900. *Okzient und Okzident. Special issue, Sanat Tahiri Defterleri [Kunsthistorische Hefte]* (6): 91–111.

JONES, OWEN. 1856. *Grammar of ornament.* London: Day and son.

KALMAR, IVAN. 1987. The *Völkerpsychologie* of Lazarus and Steinthal and the modern concept of culture. *Journal of the History of Ideas* 48 (4): 671–90.

KEMP, WOLFGANG. 1990. Alois Riegl (1858–1905). In *Altmeister moderner Kunstgeschichte.* Kunstgeschichte zur Einführung. 2nd. ed. 1999, ed. Heinrich Dilly, 36–60. Berlin: Reimer.
—. 2005. Aesthetikkolumne: Die Idee der Weltkunst in East Anglia. *Merkur* 59 (669): 49–55.

KITE, STEPHEN. 2003. "South opposed to East and North": Adrian Stokes and Josef Strzygowski: A study in the aesthetics and historiography of Orientalism. *Art History* 26 (4): 505–32.

KÖHNKE, CHRISTIAN. 1990. Soziologie als Kulturwissenschaft: Georg Simmel und die Völkerpsychologie. *Archiv für Kulturgeschichte* 72 (1): 223–32.

KÖNIG, CHRISTOPH, AND EBERHARD LÄMMERT, eds. 1999. *Konkurrenten in der Fakultät: Kultur, Wissen und Universität um 1900.* Fischer 14262: Forum Wissenschaft. Frankfurt a.M.: Fischer.

KÖPPING, KLAUS-PETER. 1983. *Adolf Bastian and the psychic unity of mankind: The foundations of anthropology in nineteenth-century Germany.* St. Lucia, London and New York: University of Queensland Press.

KRAUSS, ROSALIND. 1985. *The originality of the avantgarde and other modernist myths.* Cambridge, MA: MIT Press.

KREIDE-DAMANI, INGRID. 1992. *KunstEthnologie: zum Verständnis fremder Kunst.* DuMont-Taschenbücher 291. Cologne: DuMont.

KRUFT, HANNO-WALTER. 1985. *Geschichte der Architekturtheorie: von der Antike bis zur Gegenwart.* München: Beck.

KUGLER, FRANZ. 1842. *Handbuch der Kunstgeschichte.* Stuttgart: Ebner & Seubert.

KÜHN, HERBERT. 1923. *Die Kunst der Primitiven.* Munich: Delphin-Verlag.
—. 1976. *Geschichte der Vorgeschichtsforschung.* Berlin and New York: De Gruyter.

KUHN, THOMAS S. 1962. *The structure of scientific revolutions.* Chicago and London: The University of Chicago Press.

KUPER, ADAM. 1988. *The invention of primitive society: Transformations of an illusion.* London and New York: Routledge.

LAMPRECHT, KARL. 1896. Was ist Kulturgeschichte?: Beitrag zu einer empirischen Historik. *Deutsche Zeitschrift für Geschichtswissenschaft* 1: 75–150.

—. 1905. Universalgeschichtliche Probleme vom sozialpsychologischen Standpunkte. In *Moderne Geschichtswissenschaft: Fünf Vorträge*, 103–30. Freiburg im Breisgau: Heyfelder.

—. 1914. Einführung in die Ausstellung von parallelen Entwicklungen in der bildenden Kunst. In *Bericht: Kongress für Ästhetik und Allgemeine Kunstwissenschaft*. Stuttgart: Enke, 75–78.

LANGE, JULIUS. 1899. *Darstellung des Menschen in der älteren griechischen Kunst,* ed. Adolf Furtwängler. Trans. from the Danish by Mathilde Mann. Strassburg: Heitz (1st Danish ed. 1892/1898).

LAZARUS, MORITZ. 1851. Über den Begriff und die Möglichkeit einer Völkerpsychologie. *Deutsches Museum: Zeitschrift für Literatur, Kunst und öffentliches Leben* 1 (July), 112–26.

—. 2003. *Grundzüge der Völkerpsychologie und Kulturwissenschaft.* Philosophische Bibliothek 551, ed. with an introd. by Klaus Christian Köhnke. Hamburg: Meiner.

—, and Heymann Steinthal. 1860. Einleitende Gedanken über Völkerpsychologie, als Einladung zu einer Zeitschrift für Völkerpsychologie und Sprachwissenschaft. *Zeitschrift für Völkerpsychologie und Sprachwissenschaft* 1: 1–73.

LEARY, DAVID. 1977. *The reconstruction of psychology in Germany, 1780–1850.* PhD diss., University of Chicago.

LOCHER, HUBERT. 1999. Wissenschaftsgeschichte als Problemgeschichte: die "Kunstgeschichtlichen Grundbegriffe" und die Bemühungen um eine "strenge Kunstwissenschaft". In *Disziplinen im Kontext: Perspektiven der Disziplingeschichtsschreibung.* Erlanger Beiträge zur Wissenschaftsforschung, ed. Volker Peckhaus and Christian Thiel, 129–62. Munich: Fink.

—. 2001. *Kunstgeschichte als historische Theorie der Kunst 1750–1950.* Munich: Fink.

LUBBOCK, JOHN. 1870. *The origins of civilisation and the primitive condition of man.* London: Longmans, Green & Co.

MALLGRAVE, HARRY FRANCIS. 1985. Gustav Klemm and Gottfried Semper: The meeting of ethnological and architectural theory. *Res: Journal of Anthropology and Aesthetics* 9 (Spring): 68–79.

—, and Eleftherios Ikonomou, 1994. Introduction. In *Empathy, form, and space: Problems in German aesthetics, 1873–1893,* ed. Harry Francis Mallgrave and Eleftherios Ikonomou, 1–85. Santa Monica, CA: Getty Center for the History of Art and the Humanities.

MARCHAND, SUZANNE L. 1994. The rhetoric of artefacts and the decline of classical humanism: The case of Josef Strzygowski. In *Proof and persuasion in history. Special issue History and Theory* 33 (4): 106–30.

—. 1997. Leo Frobenius and the revolt against the West. *Journal of Contemporary History* 32 (2): 153–70.

MASSIN, BENOIT. 1996. From Virchow to Fischer. Physical anthropology and "modern race theories" in Wilhelmine Germany. In *Volksgeist as method and ethic: Essays on Boasian ethnography and the German anthropological Tradition.* Vol. 8 of *History of Anthropology,* ed. George W. Stocking, Jr., 79–154. Madison: University of Wisconsin Press.

MORPHY, HOWARD. 1994. The anthropology of art. In *Companion encyclopedia of anthropology: Humanity, culture and social life,* ed. Tim Ingold, 648–85. London and New York: Routledge.

MÜLLER, CLAUDIUS. 2003. La reconnaissance des arts premiers en Allemagne: un trajet bien particulier? *Arquivos do Centro Cultural Calouste Gulbenkian* 45: 75–83.

NACHTSHEIM, STEPHAN. 1984. *Kunstphilosophie und empirische Kunstforschung 1870–1920.* Kunst, Kultur und Politik im deutschen Kaiserreich 7. Berlin: Mann.

ONIANS, JOHN, ed. 2004. *Atlas of world art.* London: Laurence King Publishing.

PAUL, BARBERA. 2003. Schöne heile Welt(ordnung): zum Umgang der Kunstgeschichte in der frühen Bundesrepublik Deutschland mit aussereuropäischer Gegenwartskunst. *Kritische Berichte* 31 (2): 5–27.

PENNY, H. GLENN. 1999. *Cosmopolitan visions and municipal displays: Museums, markets, and the ethnographic project in Germany, 1868–1914.* PhD diss., University of Illinois.

—. 2003. Bastian's museum: On the limits of empiricism and the transformation of German ethnology. In *Wordly provincialism: German anthropology in the age of empire,* ed. Matti Bunzl and H. Glenn Penny, 86–126. Ann Arbor: University of Michigan.

PITT-RIVERS, AUGUSTUS HENRY LANE-FOX. 1906. *The evolution of culture and other essays,* ed. John Linton Myres, introd. by Henry Balfour. Oxford: Clarendon Press.

PRICHARD, JAMES COWLES. 1848. On the relations of ethnology to other branches of knowledge. *Journal of the Ethnological Society of London* 1: 301–29.

RAMPLEY, MATTHEW. 2005. The ethnographic sublime. *Res: Anthropology and Aesthetics* 47: 251–63.

RANKE, JOHANNES. 1879. *Anfänge der Kunst: Anthropologische Beiträge zur Geschichte des Ornaments.* Berlin: Habel.

RATZEL, FRIEDRICH. 1904. Geschichte, Völkerkunde und historische Perspektive. *Historische Zeitschrift* 93: 1–46.

RIEGL, ALOIS. 1892. Review of *Mäander, Hakenkreuze und urmotivische Wirbelornamente in Amerika* by Alois Raimund Hein. *Mittheilungen der Anthropologischen Gesellschaft in Wien* 22: 120ff.

—. 1893. *Stilfragen: Grundlegungen zu einer Geschichte der Ornamentik.* Berlin: Siemens.

—. 1901. *Spätrömische Kunst-Industrie nach den Funden in Österreich-Ungarn in Zusammenhang mit der Gesammteintwicklung der Bildenden Künste bei den Mittelmeervölkern.* Wien: Verlag der Kaiserlich-Königliche Hof- und Staatsdruckerei.

ROTHFUCHS-SCHULZ, CORNELIA. 1980. *Aspekte der Kunstethnologie: Beiträge zum Problem der Universalität von Kunst.* Berlin: Reimer.

SANDERSON, STEPHEN K. 1990. *Social evolutionism: A critical history.* Cambridge, MA: Blackwell.

SCHMARSOW, AUGUST. 1907. Kunstwissenschaft und Völkerpsychologie: ein Versuch zur Verständigung. *Zeitschrift für Ästhetik und Kunstwissenschaft* 2: 305–39, 467–500.

—. 1910. Anfangsgründe jeder Ornamentik. *Zeitschrift für Ästhetik und Kunstwissenschaft* 5: 191–215, 321–55.

—. 1919. Kunstwissenschaft und Kulturphilosophie mit gemeinsamen Grundbegriffen. *Zeitschrift für Ästhetik und Kunstwissenschaft* 13: 165–258.

SCHMIDT-LINSENHOFF, VIKTORIA. 2003. Postkolonialismus. *Metzler-Lexikon Kunstwissenschaft: Ideen, Methoden, Begriffe,* ed. Ulrich Pfisterer, 278–82. Stuttgart and Weimar: Metzler.

SCHWEINFURTH, GEORG. 1875. *Artes Africanae: Abbildungen und Beschreibungen von Erzeugnissen des Kunstfleisses Centralafrikanischer Völker: Illustrations and Descriptions of Productions of the Industrial Arts of Central African Tribes.* Leipzig: F. A. Brockhaus; London: S. Low, Marston, Low, and Searle.

SCOTT LITTLETON, C. 1985. Lucien Lévy-Bruhl and the concept of cognitive relativism. In Lucien Lévy-Bruhl, *How Natives think* [1910], trans. Lilian A. Clare, introd. by Lucien Lévy-Bruhl. Princeton, NJ: Princeton University Press.

SEESSELBERG, FRIEDRICH. 1897. *Die früh-mittelalterliche Kunst der germanischen Voelker unter besonderer Beruecksichtigung der skandinavischen Baukunst in ethnographisch-anthropologischer Begruendung.* Berlin: Wasmuth; the second volume was published under the title *Die skandinavische Baukunst der ersten nordisch-christlichen Jahrhunderte in ausgewählten Beispielen bildlich vorgeführt von Friedrich Seesselberg.* Berlin: Wasmuth.

SILVER, LARRY. 2004. Atlas of world art. Review of *The atlas of world art* by John Onians and *Toward a geography of art* by Thomas DaCosta Kaufmann. *The Art Bulletin* 86 (4): 783–87.

SPRINGER, ANTON. 1895–. *Handbuch der Kunstgeschichte.* 6 vols. Leipzig: Seemann.

STERNE, CARUS [ERNST KRAUS]. 1891. *Natur und Kunst: Studien zur Entwicklungsgeschichte der Kunst.* Berlin: Allgemeiner Verein für Deutsche Literatur.

STOCKING, GEORGE W., JR. 1982. *Race, culture, and evolution: Essays in the history of anthropology.* 1st ed. published 1968. Chicago and London: University of Chicago Press.
—. 1987. *The Victorian anthropology.* New York: Free Press.

STOLPE, HJALMAR. 1927. *Collected essays in ornamental art.* 2 vols. Foreword by Henry Balfour. Stockholm: Aftonbladets Tryckeri.

STRZYGOWSKI, JOSEF. 1901. *Orient und Rom: Beiträge zur Geschichte der spätantiken und frühchristlichen Kunst.* Leipzig: Hinrichs.
—. 1923. *Die Krisis der Geisteswissenschaften.* Vienna: A. Schroll & Co.

SUMMERS, DAVID. 2003. *Real spaces: World art history and the rise of Western modernism.* London and New York: Phaidon Press.

THOMAS, NICHOLAS. 1999. *Possessions: Indigenous art, colonial culture.* London and New York: Thames and Hudson.

TORGOVNICK, MARIANNA. 1990. *Gone primitive: Savage intellects, modern lives.* Chicago and London: The University of Chicago Press.

VATTER, ERNST. 1926. *Religiöse Plastik der Naturvölker.* Frankfurt a.M.: Frankfurter Verlagsanstalt.

VERWORN, MAX. 1907. *Zur Psychologie der primitiven Kunst: Ein Vortrag.* Jena: Fischer.

VIERKANDT, ALFRED. 1925. Prinzipienfragen der ethnologischen Kunstforschung. *Zweiter Kongreß für Ästhetik und Kunstwissenschaft: Bericht.* Stuttgart, 338–55.

VOLKENANDT, CLAUS, ed. 2004. *Kunstgeschichte und Weltgegenwartskunst: Konzepte – Methoden – Perspektiven.* Berlin: Reimer.

VON ERDBERG, ELEANOR. 1985. Die Anfänge der ostasiatischen Kunstgeschichte in Deutschland. In *Kategorien und Methoden der deutschen Kunstgeschichte 1900–1930. Aus den Arbeitskreisen*

"Methoden der Geisteswissenschaften" der Fritz-Thyssen-Stiftung, ed. Lorenz Dittmann, 185–207. Stuttgart: Steiner-Verlag Wiesbaden GmbH.

VON SYDOW, ECKART. 1927. *Primitive Kunst und Psychoanalyse: Eine Studie über die sexuelle Grundlage der bildenden Künste der Naturvölker.* Leipzig etc.: Psychoanalytischer Verlag.

WAITZ, THEODOR. 1863. *Introduction to anthropology,* ed. J. Frederick Collingwood. London: Longman, Green, Longman, and Roberts. Originally published as *Anthropologie der Naturvölker* (Leipzig: Fleischer, 1859–1871).

WEIKART, RICHARD. 2004. *From Darwin to Hitler: Evolutionary ethics, eugenics, and racism in Germany.* New York: Palgrave Macmillan.

WHITMAN, JAMES. 1984. From philology to anthropology in mid-nineteenth-century Germany. In *Functionalism historicized: Essays on British social anthropology,* ed. George W. Stocking, Jr., 214–29. Madison: University of Wisconsin Press.

WIESING, LAMBERT. 1997. *Die Sichtbarkeit des Bildes: Geschichte und Perspektiven der formalen Ästhetik.* Reinbek bei Hamburg: Rowohlt.

WOERMANN, KARL. 1900–. *Geschichte der Kunst aller Zeiten und Völker.* 6 vols. Leipzig: Bibliographisches Institut.

WOOD, CHRISTOPHER. 2004. Strzygowski und Riegl in den Vereinigten Staaten. *Wiener Jahrbuch für Kunstgeschichte,* 53, ed. Hans Aurenhammer and Michael V. Schwarz, 217–33. Wien: Böhlau.

WORNUM, RALPH NICHOLSON. 1856. *Analysis of ornament.* London: Chapman & Hall.

WORRINGER, WILHELM. 1919. *Abstraktion und Einfühlung.* 8th ed., 1st ed. published 1907. Munich: Piper.
—. 1911. *Formprobleme der Gotik.* Munich: Piper.
—. 1956. ARS UNA? In *Fragen und Gegenfragen: Schriften zum Kunstproblem: (Zum 75. Geburtstag v. Wilhelm Worringer).* Munich: Piper, 155–63.

WUNDT, WILHELM. 1900. *Völkerpsychologie: eine Untersuchung d. Entwicklungsgesetze von Sprache, Mythus und Sitte.* Leipzig: W. Engelmann.

YOUNG, ROBERT M. 1995. *Darwin's metaphor: Nature's place in Victorian culture.* Cambridge: Cambridge University Press.

ZIMMERMAN, ANDREW. 1998. *Anthropology and the place of knowledge in imperial Berlin.* PhD diss., University of California.
—. 1999. Geschichtslose und schriftlose Völker in Spreeathen: Anthropologie als Kritik der Geschichtswissenschaft im Kaiserreich. *Zeitschrift für Geschichtswissenschaft* 47 (3): 197–210.

MARLITE HALBERTSMA

The Many Beginnings and the One End of World Art History in Germany, 1900–1933

In the early twentieth century, non-European art was a much-debated issue in Germany.[1] Although described and illustrated in reference books on art history, non-Western art was mostly left to outsiders in the art historical community, in some cases not art historians at all. In 1929, the various strands were drawn together in the impressive volume *Die aussereuropäische Kunst* ("Non-European Art"), part of the prestigious series *Handbuch für Kunstgeschichte* (Glaser 1929a). In this book, non-Western art forms are regarded as the equivalents of the art of the West, each with its own history and context. However, a critical reading of its text will reveal that even the most advanced art historical methods of that time could not prevent a certain bias and contradictions.

Around 1900 Central Europe was the homeland of art history. Nearly all new ideas on and methods of art history were formulated

[1]
This article is based on a lecture held in 2002 at the University of Leipzig at the conference "Global Players? Kunstgeschichte und die Gegenwartskunst der Welt." See Halbertsma 2003 for an abridged version of this lecture.

2
Non-European art was already included in the first handbook of art history, Franz Kugler's *Handbuch der Kunstgeschichte*, Stuttgart 1842, and its many reprints and revisions, but in the context of this article I do not go into the details of nineteenth-century art historical writing, see in this volume the article by Ulrich Pfisterer.

by Austrian, German, and Swiss scholars in various monographs, surveys, and journals published in German. To obtain a clear and representative picture of early twentieth-century ideas about the art and its history of non-European peoples in Germany, means having to examine the various reference books which appeared at that time. A good summary of German art history around 1900 is Karl Woermann's *Geschichte der Kunst aller Zeiten und Völker* ("History of Art of all Times and Peoples"), published between 1900–1911, second edition 1915–1922.[2] The second volume of the 1915 edition is dedicated to the "art of the primitive peoples and other non-Christian primitive peoples, including the art of the Islam."

Woermann operates within a clear-cut scheme which puts art and culture on the same level. "Civilized peoples" are acquainted with a multiform and naturalistic art in various disciplines and techniques; primitive peoples, and only "semi-civilized peoples" (*Halbkulturvölker*), do not. In Woermann's opinion, "primitive peoples" represented a less developed phase in general human culture. He believed culture unfolded itself in the same direction worldwide, but not at the same rate: "Mankind shows the same basic artistic skills and the same basic artistic decorations under identical circumstances at the same phase of its development" (Woermann 1915–1922, II, 2; all translations from the German are mine).

Woermann counted decoration as the oldest art, which connects various phases of artistic development, including the art of Western Antiquity. To Woermann ornament meant two things: a form of art of itself and a link between different phases in and places of art history. The connecting function of ornament is not confined to older European art, but is, as Woermann emphasized, also important in later European and non-European art, including Chinese silks of the fourteenth century, landscape architecture in the eighteenth century, and Moresque architecture in the nineteenth century. He mentioned the influence of non-European ornament, for example Japanese, on European art and crafts of the late nineteenth century. Woermann made a point by stating that Cubism and abstract art originated from the interest in the ornaments and the art of primitive peoples, "…and at this time we have seen an exhibition of 'Cubist' painting vindicated by putting an exhibition of real or assumed Negro art alongside it" (Woermann 1915–1922, II, 3–4).

Woermann's opinion on the important role of ornament in the history of art was strongly influenced by the contemporary interest in the history and development of ornament, which considered "primitive" more or less identical with "ornamental" (Gombrich 1979; Simon Thomas 1996). Ornament was the focus of various scientific disciplines, and the history of art and culture of "primitive" peoples was principally written as the history of ornament. Many great and innovative art historical publications of the

nineteenth and early twentieth centuries, such as the publications
of Semper, Riegl, Worringer, and Strzygowski, are books on ornament. The same applies to Warburg, who defined "Pathosformel"
as an expression frozen in ornament.

In the nineteenth century, ornament could be construed as
the "good" side of non-European art. Three-dimensional objects,
interpreted as idols, personified its bad side. Their form and content
were conceived as less developed, no more than a kind of caricature, not as serious art (cf. Connelly 1995; Perry 1993; Barkan and
Bush 1995; Rhodes 1994). In contrast to this view, avant-garde artists of the late nineteenth century used both the "good" ornament
and the "bad" idol as alternatives to academic art. Ornament signified unspoilt, pure, and fresh art forms and as such promised a new
beginning for modern art, drawn from the sources of "primitive"
peoples. Artists using non-European art forms based on idols criticized the empty, self-indulgent and superficial salon art (Connelly
1995, 113–14).

The modern art of the early twentieth century was no longer
interested in ornament, as the expression of non-European art as
a *whole* became more important to it. The interest in non-European
art shifted from mainly two-dimensional art to three-dimensional
art as well, a change in course which contributed to a less prominent interest in decoration.

The art critic Carl Einstein, who wrote the booklet *Negerplastik* ("Negro Sculpture") in 1915, was not interested in ornament (Einstein 1920 [1915]). Nor was he interested in the relationship between art and the stages of cultural development of humankind. Einstein saw African sculptures as works of art, independent
of the conditions in which they originated, not depicting aspects
of concrete reality. "The concrete objects and the associations with
the real they generate, have to be eliminated and the forms have
to be to analyzed as forms of art. Try to see how the formal aspects
of the sculptures produce a general form on which the artistic
aspects are based," Einstein wrote (1920 [1915], vii). In his eyes,
analogies between modern art and African sculpture were a coincidence. Ever since the Cubists discovered the fundamental aspects
of spatial representation, people recognized the same qualities in
African sculpture (Einstein 1920 [1915], xi). Consequently, Einstein
notes no concrete details of the African sculpture illustrated,
such as its size, material, pedigree, age, representation, and location
(Einstein 1928).[3]

In Einstein's *magnum opus*, *Die Kunst des 20. Jahrhunderts*
("The Art of the Twentieth Century"), published in 1926, the relationship between modern and African art is again described as coincidental, not causal (Fleckner and Gaehtgens 1996). Picasso was
not influenced by African art when he painted the *Demoiselles
d'Avignon*, Einstein writes. And Kirchner's fascination with non-
European art is treated very unspecifically by Einstein. Einstein
does not give exact dates and places, but writes only that Kirchner

3

In a second work on the same subject
in 1928 Einstein gives more, including anthropological details (Einstein
1928). This book was very well received by the scientific community.

4
Kirchner's studio in Dresden was already lavishly decorated with a mixture of African and Javanese forms in 1910; in 1911 "real" Africans, members of the Zirkus Schumann, which was visiting Dresden, were invited to pose for Kirchner (cf. Rhodes 1994, 99–101 and Perry 1993, 77–78). In their mixture of different "primitive" styles Kirchner's interior as well as his painting *Negro Couple* (1911) are akin to fashionable interiors of that period.

saw primitive art in a museum in Dresden in 1904 and showed illustrations of Indian wall paintings to his friends (Fleckner and Gaehtgens 1996, 127, 212).

For Einstein, modern art was a completely new art without any ties to the past. Modern and non-European art might have some formal resemblances, as those who produced it came to identical solutions along different paths. The possibility of the direct influence of African or other non-European arts on modern artists was unthinkable to him. His sketchy description of Kirchner's contacts with non-European art was a conscious strategy to keep his distance from contemporary fashions in costumes and home decorations in exotic forms (Heinrichs 1998, 63).[4] Later Kirchner openly admitted that he had been influenced by Micronesian art. Kirchner saw these paintings in the Anthropological-Ethnographical Museum in Dresden (then in the Zwinger Building, an annex to the Dresden Art Gallery) in 1903, not 1904. By dating this influence to 1904, when Kirchner's Expressionism was well under way, Einstein diminishes any possible influences on Kirchner's development as the foremost German Expressionist painter. The works Kirchner saw in the Dresden Museum were Micronesian wall paintings from Palau, at that time a colony of the German Empire. They are illustrated in the second volume of Woermann's *Geschichte der Kunst aller Zeiten und Völker*. As Woermann's book was important to Kirchner, so did Einstein's book on Negro art influence another German Expressionist, Schmidt-Rottluff (Gordon 1984, 373, 393). These are both good examples of the interlaced strands between art historical texts and modern art.

Avant-garde art paved the way for an appreciation of non-European art in the wider circles of the educated public, as abstract forms made up the stock of various adaptations in design and fashion, mingling freely with the exotic. The outcome of this process was that non-European art was valued as art *per se*. This led to a new interest in it in anthropological circles, which began to see non-European art as a separate cultural category, not invariably identical with religion and not linked to specific phases of development.

Art historians tried to deal with non-European art as a serious branch of art, which had to be studied using methods identical to those used to the study of European art. However, this interest was restricted to a small circle of German art historians—some of whom will be discussed below—as the majority of art historians in Germany and Austria saw non-European art as a minor interest. This could be left to art historians who worked in the periphery of the discipline, including art historians outside universities and art museums, or to the colorful assembly of missionaries, art critics, and anthropologists. It is telling that the first serious book on modern art as well as the first serious book on African art in Germany were written by the art critic Carl Einstein, then seen as the foremost German expert in both fields.

In the 1920s, many attempts were made to establish a kind of world art history at various German universities, but these came to nothing, in contrast to the activity which at the beginning of the century had let to the founding of new museum departments for non-European art in Berlin and a new museum for the art of East Asia in Cologne (Wiesner 1977; Ledderose 1989; Marchand 1994). The defeat of Germany in 1918, the economic difficulties in the Weimar Republic, and the political and cultural breakdown after 1933 hindered the development of art history in general and of world art history in particular. The Nazi government favored the figurative European art of former centuries and its contemporary academic versions and banned all abstract art and other "entartete Kunst" (degenerate art), including "primitive" non-European art as art of inferior races. For the art historical community this meant that the focus of art history was increasingly narrowed to the art of Germany and its European neighbors, although in the circles around Heinrich Himmler, commander of the SS, the fascination with prehistoric Indo-German cultures and their abstract decorations continued (Kater 1997). Academic art history after 1933 adopted the methodological notion of "Kunstgeographie," a then internationally fashionable, mildly racist, art historical methodology which tried to link European art forms to European geography (Kaufmann 2004). These developments forced art historians with other interests or with Jewish origins to lay low or to emigrate.[5]

Only in Austria did Josef Strzygowski, one of the most authoritative scholars of Early Christian Art in the Near East of his generation, try earnestly to establish a fusion between European and non-European art history. He founded an East Asian Department at his Institute of Art History of the Vienna University in 1912.

Strzygowski split world art in two antagonistic groups. The classic art of the Greeks and Romans conflicted with the Aryan-German art of the East and the North. Eastern art, the art of the Indo-Germanic "Altai Iran," oriental, ornamental, and abstract, is the oldest, but was subjugated by the naturalistic, urban, "Semitic" art of Greek and Roman Mediterranean culture.[6] In his view, world art history was the history of a perpetual racist conflict, with Rome-based art and culture as the oppressors of "Aryan" values. Strzygowski argued for a revision in the canonical identification of Greece and Rome as the locus of European inspiration. "Germany and the North, he claimed, was the ultimate site of the production of great art," states Annabel Wharton in a summary of Strzygowski's ideas (Wharton 1995, 10).

However curious these theses may look today, Strzygowski must be accorded due credit as being one of the first art historians to consider non- or peripheral European art forms as part of *one*, dynamic and competing system of world art. Strzygowski was very tolerant towards research on non-European art and many

5
See for the developments of German art history after 1933 Dilly 1988; Wendland 1999; Held and Papenbrock 2003; Doll, Fuhrmeister and Sprenger [2005]. For the developments in world art history in postwar Germany see Paul 2003.

6
For a summary of his views see Strzygowski 1923. See recently on Strzygowski: Marchand 1994; Wharton 1995; Elsner 2002.

7
Like Alfred Salmony (1890–1958),
curator and deputy-director of the
Cologne Museum of East Asian Art
and from 1933 professor of Asian Studies at New York University, or Stella
Kramrisch (1898–1993), who, after her
studies with Strzygowski, went to Oxford for a few years and became lecturer on Indian art at the University of
Calcutta in 1922. Leaving India in 1950,
she worked as a curator and a professor
in Philadelphia, only resigning in 1982
(Trubner 1977; Stoler Miller 1983).
8
In this article, I discuss mostly literature on African art, because of the
overwhelming amount of texts.

students in his institute were trained as experts in East Asian art.[7] Taking a negative tack, it could be stated that most German art historians were not interested in non-European art. Looked at it from a positive angle, however, it could be pointed out that non-European art at that time was the scientific subject of a broad community of scholars, not necessarily art historians. Studies of non-European art can be found at places one does not expect them to be present: in anthropological publications or in the memoirs of missionaries. Anthropological texts are especially very rich sources, because in many cases their writers were interested in the art they discovered *in situ* in modern Africa and the German colonies in the Pacific, not only that in museum collections.[8]

Seen from this perspective, Oskar Nuoffer's booklet *Afrikanische Plastik in der Gestaltung von Mutter und Kind* ("African Sculpture of Mother and Child"), published in 1926, is to be preferred to Einstein's publications, as Nuoffer placed these sculptures in the everyday context of contemporary Africa. In contrast to Einstein, Nuoffer saw African sculpture as contemporary art and as African art, not as an art conceived in the nonhistorical, nongeographical realm of three-dimensional forms.

A sculpture, which would never have found its way into the pages of Einstein, is Nuoffer's illustration no. 45, a sculpture from Senegambia; a Madonna. It is, following Nuoffer, an African interpretation of Roman Catholic sculptures imported into Africa by the Portuguese from the seventeenth century. Nuoffer describes how this exuberant Baroque Christian art was brought to Africa, and embarked on a period of transition at the moment the power of the Portuguese and Roman Catholic Church dwindled in the eighteenth century. This Christian inspired art reevolved as an African art, into what Nuoffer calls "fetish art," for example the sculptures studded with nails, a view no longer held today. As the missionaries returned in the nineteenth century, sculptures of saints came to Africa again. Nuoffer writes that the figure of the Madonna was Africanized, as can be observed in the way mother and child do not look at each other. Their relationship is revealed in the food, which is offered (a fruit), and the way the child is suckled by its mother. Representing the Madonna in the nude, as is the case here, would be unthinkable in European art.

The memoirs of the German missionary Johannes Emonts, *Ins Steppen- und Bergenland Innerkameruns: Aus dem Leben und Werken deutscher Afrikamissionare,* ("In the Steppes and Mountains of the Interior Cameroon. From the Life and Work of German Missionaries") 1922, are fascinating. Emonts was not a scholar: his book has the fresh flavor of the adventurous. Emonts possessed keen powers of observation and described the Africans and their culture as contemporaries, living in a region inhabited by Africans, Europeans, and Arabs. The chapter on "The Blacks and their Art" is enthralling. Emonts describes in detail how a "chief-artist" (*Künstlerhauptmann*) in Babanki, Cameroon, worked in ivory and wood and how he organized his workshop. This—unfortunately nameless—artist was a very famous creator of beautiful thrones and stools which Emonts illustrates with photographs in his text. Emonts drew a portrait of the chief artist as a modern artist, who happened to live in Africa. He bowed to the wishes of his clients, but argued, dressed and behaved like an European artist (Emonts 1922, 170). Emonts was surprised by the quality of his art and he bought various thrones and stools for the Missionary Museum, but these acquisitions perished when the German colonies were occupied by the English in the Great War. Emonts ended his story as follows: "These and other moments made me wonder and forced me to consider how to evaluate the possibility of educating the blacks of this region, who, if Christian culture is brought to them, could create great things" (Emonts 1922, 174). Emonts's view of the Africans as *modern* people, not as descendants of a perhaps great, but as yet vanished culture, was probably influenced by his Christian belief that all people are equal in the eyes of the Lord. At that time, racists believed that people had a fixed identity, embedded in the immutable characteristics of their race. This view does not admit the possibility to change people or convert them, and so we can assume that Emonts's optimism about educating the Africans was related to his missionary zeal.

It may come as a surprise that I choose to discuss here the famous work of the American anthropologist Franz Boas, *Primitive Art* (1927). Boas's publication is a good example of the "art historical turn" in the humanities in the 1920s, and the title of his book could be read as a statement that the creative products of the Native American cultures are to be regarded first and foremost as art.

    At the beginning of the twentieth century—a situation never to be repeated—various disciplines drew inspiration from the new methods in art history, such as working with simple sets of formal typologies not bound to historical periods, but to the different positions humans could take toward the real. Even sociology adapted this "ideal typical" method (Halbertsma 1992, 46ff, 195). The history of art was written as a parallel to the intellectual history of humankind (*Kunstgeschichte als Geistesgeschichte*). Within the context of this interpretation, art did not develop in one direction, but was the outcome of conflicting ideas about the status of the real and the ideal world.

    Franz Boas (1858–1942) was born in Minden, Germany, and must have been an avid reader of the publications of the German art historians, art theoreticians, and psychologists of his day.[9] In Boas's view, all humans are equal, and mental processes all over the world are fundamentally identical. Culture is the outcome of specific historical processes, and therefore cultural products, like art, are different in time and place. This triggers a recognition of Wölfflin's "twin source of styles" ("doppelter Wurzel des Stils"). Wölfflin saw works of art as the outcome of a continuous process

9

Boas 1927: Riegl on p. 11 and 16, Fechner and Wundt on p. 13, Semper on p. 15. See on Boas: Hyatt 1990; Rodekamp 1994; Jonaitis 1995; Stocking 1996.

of alternating opposite art forms on the one hand, and the specific historical, racist, and local context in which the artists work, on the other.

Boas could not accept the idea that art developed from "primitive" to more cultivated stages, as the formal "sets" the artist chooses to work in, do not vary in time. It is other, cultural and material factors, which make works of art different, compounded by the many ways artists influence each other, adopting foreign motifs and techniques for their own purposes. Changes in form and technique are the outcome of interaction, not of evolution. Another parallel to art historians of his time (Riegl) are his ideas on ornament as an artistic choice, not necessarily preceding or following naturalism.

Boas distinguished three families of forms, "formats," as we would call them today: formal art; representative art; and symbolism. These three formats are subsequently evaluated from the perspective of style and technique, influenced by geographical, material, and individual conditions. In his analysis Boas used art historical methods to look at the interaction between individual and communal forms, grouped into several styles belonging to different peoples. No local style can be understood without a knowledge of related forms in the region, but primitive art does not have a relationship with prehistorical and historical European and Asian art. It is not possible for a style to develop by itself in isolation: "There is probably not a single region in existence in which the art style may be understood entirely as an inner growth and an expression of cultural life of a single tribe" (Boas 1927, 176).[10]

The self-made anthropologist, explorer, and prolific writer Leo Frobenius is more or less an antithesis to the subtle and concisely formulating Boas. Frobenius's publications exerted a very strong influence on the debate on African art, and not only in Germany.

Frobenius was a friend and follower of the philosopher Spengler, author of *Der Untergang des Abendlandes* ("The Decline of the West"). Frobenius saw the contemporary culture of Africa as a dying culture, unable to develop any further. In various publications Frobenius presented a kind of organic cultural philosophy, "Kulturmorphologie." His theory states that the human spirit undergoes a development from youth to old age, and that each people contributes to the stage in which this spirit unfolds itself at a particular moment. To Frobenius Africa meant the youth of humankind, expressing its irrational and unformed mind in myths and stories (Frobenius 1898, x–xi; see also Frobenius 1933; Heinrichs 1998, 21; Haberland 1973; Sylvain 1996; Marchand 1997). In some aspects, the African spirit was akin to the German spirit, as the Germans, a young and unspoilt race, were on the brink of taking the lead in new developments in world culture and world politics.

The various forms of African art are explained by Frobenius in terms of this historical development. Frobenius saw culture as a dynamic process, each culture a part of a cultural circle ("Kultur-kreis") related to other cultures, but never losing its essential character ("paideuma"), in this case the "African psyche." Because of the long history of African culture, more taking than giving, African culture is interrelated in various ways with other cultures, mostly the culture of the Mediterranean, which spread itself over the African continent in waves.

In Frobenius's opinion, the culture of Africa was not able to create greatness in the field of technology. Architecture and bronze-casting had had to have come from outside (Frobenius assumed a link between the vanished culture of Atlantis and the art of the Yoruba). Although the moment of Africa was over, it was the task of the explorer to collect and sift the "documents" of the history of humankind before they perished (Frobenius 1989, ix). Frobenius collected these documents on a grand scale being especially interested in myths, folk tales, rock paintings, and sculptures.

Frobenius's position in the scholarly world of his day was based on his intimate knowledge of the immense amount of material he collected during his many trips to the African continent. No other German knew so much of Africa; no other German explorer had been there so many times; and no anthropologist had such good ties with the German Foreign Office and the German Emperor (Heine 1980).[11]

In the 1930s, Frobenius's emphasis on the irrational and intuitive sides of African culture was very appealing to intellectuals from the French African colonies who studied in Paris. Frobenius was invited to Paris in 1933, where he gave lectures and showed photos of African rock paintings. These photographs made a huge impression on French surrealists. In 1936 Frobenius's voluminous and muddled *Kulturgeschichte Afrikas* ("The Cultural History of Africa"), was translated into the French, the resultant work being an abridged and well-written text, palatable to French intellectuals. Out of these contacts grew the "Négritude Movement" of "Young Africa" which openly borrowed from Frobenius (Heinrichs 1998, 106, 108, 113ff, 117ff).

In his memoirs, Léopold Senghor writes that a group of black students from the French African and Caribbean colonies launched the "Négritude Movement" in Paris in the early 1930s. They had a wealth of arguments to summon Africans and Blacks to take part in an actual renaissance of black culture. They had jazz, Senghor continues, blues, dances, and of course the art—art, as he remembered—which influenced Picasso and the Surrealists. But they had failed to find convincing arguments and a theory, until they stumbled across the writings of Frobenius, flattered to see African culture compared positively with German culture (cited in Heinrichs 1998, 119–20). In the words of Senghor: "'Emotion,' 'intuitive reason,' 'art' and 'poetry,' 'image' and 'myth,' these are words or concepts or synonyms which we confront when we are considering Negroes, and their study is pertinent. We shall con-

11
Frobenius acted as a spy for the German government from November 1914 to April 1915, trying to expand Germany's influence in the Sudan to hinder the English, but his expedition stranded in Eritrea, at that time an Italian colony. After the war, Frobenius and the German Kaiser continued to see each other in Doorn in the Netherlands, where the Kaiser lived in exile.

12
See his first publication on African art (Von Sydow 1921), followed by an attempt to use psychoanalysis to analyze non-European art (Von Sydow 1927).

nect the first two words with German words, such as *Einfühlung*, *Gefühl*, *Wesenheit* and *Weltanschauung*, for which corresponding expressions can be found in the Negro African languages and which interpret some of the fundamental values of the German soul: of *Germanité*…. Nevertheless we had to wait for Leo Frobenius before the affinities between the 'Ethiopian,' that is the Negro African, and the German soul could be made manifest…. Frobenius tells us that, like individuals, ethnic groups are diverse, even opposed, like the Hamites and the Ethiopians, in their feelings and their ideas, their myths and their ideologies, their customs and their institutions; that each ethnic group, having its own *paideuma*—once again, its *soul*—reacts in its own peculiar way to the environment and develops autonomously; that, though they may be at different stages of development, Germans and 'Ethiopians' belong tot the same spiritual family…. It is easy to guess the consequences of this discovery and the increased self-confidence which it gave us" (Senghor 1973, x–xi; also Harney 2004). In this way young Africans discovered their own culture outside Africa, presented to them by the French avant-garde and the German anthropologist Frobenius.

Frobenius had a positive, more or less romantic anti-imperialist opinion of Africa as an old, primitive culture, and he was concerned about the influences of Islam and the modern effects of French and Belgian colonialism. His critique on the modernization of Africa is part of the German observation of the fragility of European rule outside Europe and the fragility of European culture and "the West" (Marchand 1997, 156). Frobenius's romantic anti-imperialism is typical of the German view of non-European cultures in general. The colonial politics of Germany in Africa and its contacts with the Near East were different to those of other empires, like the French or the English, which can be described as a policy of distance, not as a cautious, inquisitive approach. German colonialism in Africa as well as Germany's contacts with the Ottoman Empire in the Near East, displayed the characteristics of a latecomer on the imperial stage and should be regarded on its own merits (Marchand 1996, 302–3).

In the 1920s, two voluminous reference books on non-European art came on the German market. The first, *Die Kunst der Naturvölker und der Vorzeit* ("Primitive and Pre-Historic Art") was written by Eckart von Sydow in 1923 and had four reprints (the last in 1938) before the Second World War (Von Sydow 1938 [1923]). Von Sydow was an art historian, and his books show the transition from a purely aesthetic to a more anthropological and psychological perspective.[12]

Von Sydow's book appeared as part of the prestigious Propyläen series on art history. In its layout (399 full page illustrations, some in color, preceded by an introduction of some hundred pages), it was addressed to a bourgeois lay public, although the descriptions (separate from the photographs) meet academic standards.[13]

In its title the same evolutionist approach of non-European art can be recognized, as the use of the notion "Naturvölker" implies that they are the counterpart of "Kulturvölker," literate cultures. The treatment of "primitive art" of non-European peoples in the same breath as European prehistoric art (in this case the art of illiterate Europeans, including Germanic and Nordic cultures, until the eleventh century CE) suggests the equivalization of the "primitive" non-European cultures with European "primitive" stages of development. Von Sydow was convinced of the idea that the non-European art of his own day was only a shadow of a great past, "Instead of the rosy dawn and its seemingly endless promises, we saw the fantastic evening clouds, lit only weakly by the setting sun" (1938 [1923], 102).

In his book, Von Sydow explains non-European art from a psychological perspective, as an art which is rooted in emotions, not in intentions, as it is in modern humans. "The emphasis in primitive culture is on emotion, in modern mass culture on intention. … primitive spiritual life is more or less static, that of the modern mass more dynamic" (1938 [1923], 12). Von Sydow saw the art of the primitives for the most part as an art related to religion, although he recognized the fact that some art was created for secular purposes, but it is telling that he referred only to secular art as ornament made just for the fun of it (1938 [1923], 19).

The assumption that non-European art is a part, not the prehistory, of world art history and—as art—has to be analyzed using the same methods as European art, is the point of departure of the reference book *Die aussereuropäische Kunst* ("Non-European Art"), edited in 1929 by Curt Glaser, I referred to in the beginning.[14] The book is designed as an academic arthistorical study, with illustrations in the text, not separate. The title is neutral: non-European, not "primitive."

In his introduction Glaser states: "In the last few decades non-European art has become the focus of general interest.… In former times, only the unfamiliar and hostile was discerned in the idols and tools of far away continents, but later its aesthetic values were recognized. Artists led the way, amateurs, and collectors followed, and in the end scholarship had to find a new appreciation of the collections in ethnographical museums. Until then, these collections served mostly for anthropological studies, but from a certain moment, the interest of scholars was attracted to the meaning, origin, and development of the formal aspects of non-European art. So began the much-debated new orientation of anthropological museums, which to a great extent changed from collections for the study of customs and religions to museums of non-European art. In this way, large new fields are now opening up to art history, and its foundations and its horizon are being broad-

13
Von Sydow had a subordinate position at the University of Berlin (until his death in 1942), as "beauftragter Dozent," and gave lectures on "primitive art." Starting in the summer of 1935 however, these lectures were announced as general introductions to the "art of primitive peoples and their racial foundations" ("Allgemeine Einleitung in die Kunst der Naturvölker und ihre rassischen Grundlagen." http/www.rz.uni-karlsruhe. de/~kunstgeschichte/projekte/kgns/ lektographie/berlin.htm (accessed May 7, 2005).

14
Curt Glaser (1879–1943) was trained as an art historian and was the head of the Staatliche Kunstbibliothek in Berlin. He was expelled from his post by the Nazis in 1933 and went to the United States in the same year.

Frobenius and Germann knew each other well, Germann went with Frobenius on a research trip to Africa in 1914. Paul Germann was a curator at the Museum für Völkerkunde in Leipzig.

ened to an inconceivable degree. Thinking in terms of world history is typical of contemporary historical disciplines, and it is obligatory for art history too. Freedom has to be sought from the traditional clinging to the undisputed canonical forms of Mediterranean Classical and Renaissance art, as well from the aesthetic rules they set. The recognition of difference is equally important to the study of the interrelated artistic influence and fertilization between peoples" (Glaser [1929a], vii).

Reading this citation from 1929 it might have been concluded that the aim of an all inclusive world art history appeared to have been achieved. Thanks to modern art and modern art history, anthropology and the ethnographical museums had abandoned their limitations. Yet, the articles which followed Glaser's introduction show otherwise. Characteristic of the 1920s debate on non-European arts was the emphasis on influences; whether this be Frobenius's "Kulturkreise" or Boas's view that all art is connected to the art of other cultures. Glaser's authors were determined to connect all art forms to other art forms on a global scale. Changes or innovations must inexorably have been caused by extraneous influences. "We know for sure that there is no connection between the fanciful stylized monsters of the three early dynasties and the immediately recognizable freely moving representations of animals of the Han period. It is also plausible that a fresh and strong impulse turned Chinese art in a new direction at that time," Glaser was writing about Chinese art of the first century CE. This new impulse is presumed to have come from Scythian art, just as the ornamental art of that period was influenced by the art of Western Antiquity. "It is striking, how free Chinese art has generally been from imitating models which were foreign to its nature and how Chinese art, especially in the Han period, shaped its own vocabulary of forms by assimilating adopted goods and changed these in its own characteristic ways" (Glaser [1929b], 8, 19).

In his contribution to the book, Paul Germann writes the art history of Africa as a parallel to its history, but in the end it is this historical approach which locks Africa in the past, an endorsement that corresponds to Frobenius's views (Seige 1996).[15] The amazing wall paintings of the Bushmen in the southernmost part of Africa must have been made many centuries ago, Germann argues, since the present African population was incapable of such efforts (Germann [1929], 561–62). Echoing Frobenius, Germann says that the bronzes of Benin must have been influenced by Mediterranean art. "What nowadays is cast in the old technique at the courts of the chiefs in the grasslands of Cameroon and in the city of Ilorin in Yoruba, just as the modern products of Benin itself, show characteristic traits of decline in style and skill" (Germann [1929], 575). This emphasis on influences is coupled with the constantly returning question of the origins of art. How can art commence without impulses from outside? Many chapters in this book address this question as one of the most important issues in the art they discuss, for example in the chapter on the art South America it is said: "Actually, the greatest difficulty is the origin of the high cultures of Ancient America" (Ubbelohde-Doering 1929, 650).

Just as the question of the origin of art could not be answered convincingly, nor can the question of the end of art. In all chapters, the view persists that non-European art nourishes itself more or less on the energy and influence of the art of other peoples, until it dies of European art. No chapter has anything to say about art after 1850, or only in terms like the "waning of the creative energy of the nation" (Glaser [1929b], 121). Ernst Kühnel remarks on Ottoman art: "Here too, the very close relationship with the West proved fatal, as it paved the way to foreign elements and engendered a powerless rigidity in architecture, surrendering totally to modern European styles in architecture. The arts and crafts deteriorated to soulless mass production of bazaar goods for the Western market" (Kühnel 1929, 525).

In some ways, the authors in Glaser's *Die aussereuropäische Kunst* elaborate on the anti-Western notions we saw earlier in the work of Frobenius (cf. Errington 1998). However, the authors are not consistent. They looked for the origin of art, but their method presupposed that art could only develop itself by assimilating art forms from elsewhere. They believed that art could only grow by borrowing foreign forms and adapting them, but they could not accept European influences on non-European art after 1850. Why was non-European art unable to develop in new directions after the contact with nineteenth-century Western art, as Chinese and Indian art blossomed after their contact with the art of Western Antiquity? Why could European art reinvent itself around 1900 by turning to non-European art, while non-European art died from the contagion of European art?

The answer to this antithesis is the double standard with which Glaser's authors operate. Their notion of art as a permanent cultural practice which develops with time, nurtured by many sources, is in its essence based on the history of European art, as an art with no definite formal characteristics, without a clear and once-only, easy recognizable "beginning," but with many endings. The authors could not free themselves fully from the notion that non-European art is its opposite. They saw non-European art as an art with well-defined and permanent characteristics, with a clear beginning and hence with a definite end.

Conflating these two views brought the study of world art history in Germany to a halt; it is impossible to have an art history believing the history of art is the history of flux and borrowings and an art history, which presupposes the permanent identity of people and their culture at the same time. What was needed then, as it is now, was a fully new theory of art and art history rethinking the production of artefacts by recognizing the possibility that "art" is not a given category of culture, but a process of labeling on the one hand and appropriation—in a literal meaning too—on the other.

REFERENCES

BARKAN, ELAZAR, AND RONALD BUSH, eds. 1995. *Prehistories of the future: The primitive project and the culture of modernism*. Stanford, CA: Stanford University Press.

BOAS, FRANZ. 1927. *Primitive art*. Oslo: Aschehoug.

CONNELLY, FRANCES S. 1995. *The sleep of reason: Primitivism in modern European art and aesthetics, 1725–1907*. University Park: The Pennsylvania State University Press.

DILLY, HEINRICH. 1988. *Deutsche Kunsthistoriker 1933–1945. Kunstgeschichte und Gegenwart*. Munich and Berlin: Deutscher Kunstverlag.

DOLL, NIKOLA, CHRISTIAN FUHRMEISTER, AND MICHAEL H. SPRENGER, eds. [2005]. *Kunstgeschichte im Nationalsozialismus: Beiträge zur einer Wissenschaft zwischen 1930 und 1950*. Weimar: VDG.

EINSTEIN, CARL. 1920. *Negerplastik*. 1st ed. published 1915. München: K. Wolff.
—. 1928. *Afrikanische Plastik*. Leipzig: Wasmuth.

ELSNER, JÁS. 2002. The birth of Late Antiquity: Riegl and Strzygowski in 1901. *Art History* 25 (3): 358–79.

EMONTS, JOHANNES. 1922. *Ins Steppen- und Bergland Innerkameruns: aus dem Leben und Werken deutscher Afrikamissionare*. Aachen: Xaveriusverlag.

ERRINGTON, SHELLY ELIZABETH. 1998. *The death of authentic primitive art and other tales of progress*. Berkeley and London: University of California Press.

FLECKNER, UWE, AND THOMAS W. GAEHTGENS, eds. 1996. *Die Kunst des 20. Jahrhunderts*. Vol. 5 of *Carl Einstein: Werke*, ed. Hermann Haarmann. Berlin: Fannei & Walz.

FROBENIUS, LEO. 1898. *Der Ursprung der afrikanischen Kulturen*. Berlin: Gebrüder Borntraeger.
—. 1933. *Kulturgeschiche Afrikas: Prolegomena zu einer historischen Gestaltlehre*. Zurich: Phaidon.

GERMANN, PAUL. [1929]. Die afrikanische Kunst. In *Die aussereuropäische Kunst*. Vol. VI of *Handbuch für Kunstgeschichte von Anton Springer*, ed. Curt Glaser, 549–91. Leipzig: Kröner.

GLASER, CURT, ed. [1929a]. *Die aussereuropäische Kunst*. Vol. VI of *Handbuch für Kunstgeschichte von Anton Springer*. Leipzig: Kröner.
—. [1929b]. Die ostasiatische Kunst. In *Die aussereuropäische Kunst*. Vol. VI of *Handbuch für Kunstgeschichte von Anton Springer*, ed. Curt Glaser, 2–230. Leipzig: Kröner.

GOMBRICH, ERNST H. 1979. *The sense of order: A study in the psychology of decorative art*, 2nd ed. 1994. Oxford: Phaidon.

GORDON, DONALD E. 1984. German Expressionism. In *"Primitivism" in 20th Century Art: Affinity of the Tribal and the Modern*, vol. II, ed. William S. Rubin, 368–403. New York: Museum of Modern Art.

HABERLAND, EIKE, ed. 1973. *Leo Frobenius 1873–1973: An Anthology*. Wiesbaden: F. Steiner.

HALBERTSMA, MARLITE. 1992. *Wilhelm Pinder und die Deutsche Kunstgeschichte*. Worms: Wernersche Verlagsgesellschaft.
—. 2003. Fremde Welten und vertraute Methoden: die deutsche Weltkunstforschung des frühen 20. Jahrhunderts. *Kritische Berichte* 31 (2): 28–36.

HARNEY, ELIZABETH. 2004. *In Senghor's shadow: Art, politics, and the avant-garde in Senegal, 1960–1995*. Durham, NC: Duke University Press.

HEINE, PETER. 1980. Leo Frobenius als politischer Agent: Ein Beitrag zu seiner Biographie. *Paideuma* 26: 1–5.

HEINRICHS, HANS-JÜRGEN. 1998. *Die fremde Welt, das bin ich: Leo Frobenius: Etnologe, Forschungsreisender, Abenteurer*. Wuppertal: P. Hammer.

HELD, JUTTA, AND MARTIN PAPENBROCK, eds. 2003. *Kunstgeschichte an den Universitäten im Nationalsozialismus*. Göttingen: Vandenhoeck und Ruprecht Verlag.

HYATT, MARSHALL. 1990. *Franz Boas: social activist: The dynamics of ethnicity*. New York: Greenwood Press.

JONAITIS, ALDONA, ed. 1995. *A wealth of thought: Franz Boas on native American art*. Seattle: University of Washington Press.

KATER, MICHAEL H. 1997. *Das "Ahnenerbe" der SS, 1935–1945: ein Beitrag zur Kulturpolitik des Dritten Reiches*. Munich: Oldenbourg.

KAUFMANN, THOMAS DACOSTA. 2004. *Toward a geography of art*. Chicago and London: The University of Chicago Press.

KÜHNEL, ERNST. [1929]. Die islamische Kunst. In *Die ausser europäische Kunst. Vol. VI of Handbuch für Kunstgeschichte von Anton Springer*, ed. Curt Glaser, 373–548. Leipzig: Kröner.

LEDDEROSE, LOTHAR. 1989. Kunstgeschichte und Weltkunst geschichte. *Saeculum* 40 (2): 136–41.

MARCHAND, SUZANNE L. 1994. The rhetoric of artefacts and the decline of classical humanism: The case of Josef Strzygowski. In *Proof and Persuasion in History*. Special issue, *History and Theory* 33 (4): 106–30.
—. 1996. Orientalism as Kulturpolitik. German Archeology and Cultural Imperialism in Asia Minor. In *Volksgeist as method and ethic: Essays on Boasian ethnography and the German anthropological tradition*, ed. George W. Stocking, Jr., 298–336. Madison: University of Wisconsin Press.
—. 1997. Leo Frobenius and the revolt against the West. *Journal of Contemporary History* 32 (2): 153–70.

NUOFFER, OSKAR. 1926. *Afrikanische Plastik in der Gestaltung von Mutter und Kind*. Dresden: Carl Reissner.

PAUL, BARBARA. 2003. Schöne heile Welt(ordnung): zum Umgang der Kunstgeschichte in der frühen Bundesrepublik Deutschland mit aussereuropäischer Gegenwartskunst. *Kritische Berichte* 31 (2): 5–27.

PERRY, GILL. 1993. Primitivism and the "Modern." In *Primitivism, Cubism, Abstraction: The Early Twentieth Century*, ed. Charles Harrison, Francis Frascina, and Gill Perry, 3–86. New Haven, CT and London: Yale University Press in association with The Open University.

RODEKAMP, VOLKER, ed. 1994. *Franz Boas (1858–1942): ein amerikanischer Anthropologe aus Minden*. Bielefeld: Verlag für Regionalgeschichte.

RHODES, COLIN. 1994. *Primitivism and modern art*. World of Art. London: Thames and Hudson.

SEIGE, CHRISTINE. 1996. Paul Germann (1884–1966): In memor-

iam. In *Jahrbuch des Museums für Völkerkunde zu Leipzig,* vol.
XLII, 47–79. Leipzig: Harrassowitz.

SENGHOR, LÉOPOLD S. 1973. The Lessons of Leo Frobenius. In
Leo Frobenius 1873–1973: An anthology, ed. Elke Haberland, vii–
xiii. Wiesbaden: F. Steiner.

SIMON THOMAS, MIENKE. 1996. *De leer van het ornament:
Versieren volgens voorschrift 1850–1930.* Amsterdam: De
Bataafsche Leeuw.

STOCKING, GEORGE W., JR., ed. 1996. *Volksgeist as method and
ethic: Essays on Boasian ethnography and the German anthropological tradition.* Madison: University of Wisconsin Press.

STOLER MILLER, BARBARA. 1983. Stella Kramrisch: A biograph-
ical essay. In *Exploring India's sacred art: Selected writings of
Stella Kramrisch,* ed. Barbara Stoler Miller, 3–34. Philadelphia:
University of Pennsylvania Press.

STRZYGOWSKI, JOSEF. 1923. *Die Krisis der Geisteswissenschaften.*
Vienna: A. Schroll & Co.

SYLVAIN, RENEE. 1996. Leo Frobenius: From *Kulturkreis* to *Kulturmorphologie. Anthropos* 91 (4): 483–94.

TRUBNER, HENRY. 1977. Alfred Salmony (10 November 1890–29
April 1958). In *Zur Kunstgeschichte Asiens: 50 Jahre Lehre und
Forschung an der Universität Köln,* ed. Roger Goepper, 17–20.
Wiesbaden: Steiner.

UBBELOHDE-DOERING, HEINRICH. [1929]. Die indianische
Kunst Amerikas. In *Die aussereuropäische Kunst.* Vol. VI of
Handbuch für Kunstgeschichte von Anton Springer, ed. Curt
Glaser, 592–658. Leipzig: Kröner.

VON SYDOW, ECKART. 1921. *Exotische Kunst. Afrika und
Ozeanien.* Leipzig: Klinkhardt & Biermann.
—. 1927. *Primitive Kunst und Psychoanalyse: eine Studie über die
sexuelle Grundlage der bildenden Künste der Naturvölker.* Leipzig:
Internationaler Psychoanalytischer Verlag.
—. 1938. *Die Kunst der Naturvölker und der Vorzeit.* 4th ed., 1st ed.
published 1923. Berlin: Propyläen-Verlag.

WHARTON, ANNABEL J. 1995. *Refiguring the Post Classical city:
Dura Europos, Jerash, Jerusalem, and Ravenna.* Cambridge, MA:
Cambridge University Press.

WENDLAND, ULRIKE. 1999. *Biographisches Handbuch
deutschsprachiger Kunsthistoriker im Exil: Leben und Werk
der unter dem Nationalsozialismus verfolgten und vertriebenen
Wissenschaftler.* Munich: Saur.

WIESNER, ULRICH. 1977. Die Geschichte der Abteilung Asien.
In *Zur Kunstgeschichte Asiens: 50 Jahre Lehre und Forschung an
der Universität Köln,* ed. Roger Goepper, 3–16. Wiesbaden: Steiner.

WOERMANN, KARL. 1915–1922. *Die Kunst der Naturvölker und
übrigen nichtchristlichen Völker einschliesslich der Kunst des
Islams.* Vol. II of *Geschichte der Kunst aller Zeiten und Völker.* 6
vols., 2nd. rev. ed., 1st ed. published 1900–1911. Leipzig and Vienna:
Bibliographisches Institut.

JAMES ELKINS

Can We Invent a World Art Studies?

The study of the worldwide conditions and prospects of art history —what I call "globalism" in art history—is growing so fast that it can scarcely be captured in monographs. During the two or three years it takes to conceive, gather, edit, and publish a collection of essays, the subject can change radically, even fundamentally. When I accepted the invitation to write this essay, I had been at work on several projects having to do with twentieth-century painting around the world. Those—especially a book project, *Success and Failure in Twentieth-Century Painting*—are still ongoing.[1] I had been giving papers with titles such as "On the Limits of Writing the Art History of Non-Western Cultures," intended to make the general point that belatedness and differing values has made much of the world's art invisible to the discipline of art history.[2] I had also given a paper called "Is Art History a Global Discipline?" at the opening of the Irish Art Research Centre at Trinity College, Dublin, May 2004; when I got the editors' invitation, I thought that could be the basis of this essay.[3] Now, in early summer 2006, I find that it is necessary to completely rewrite that talk. There have been four relevant developments:

1. The Clark Art conference for 2000 is, at last, being published; it concluded with a session on art historians who had tried "to put the world in a book."[4] My paper for that conference has also had to be revised several times in light of the many changes since 2000.[5] It is now a survey of the ways that modernist art made in countries like Paraguay, Uzbekistan, Estonia, and Slovenia can be made to seem important, and even crucial, to art historians who normally work only with Western European and North American modernism. Despite tremendous amounts of interest in international postmodernism and biennale art, and with a few

1
In addition to the texts mentioned in the next footnote, there are: Elkins 2004a, which concerns ways of judging art conventionally excluded from serious consideration because it seems historically insignificant; and an unpublished essay on strategies in dealing with belatedness, "How Much of the World is Behind the Times in Painting?" CIHA conference, London, 2000, session chaired by Cao Yiqiang and Craig Clunas; repeated at the Vancouver Art Gallery, October 2000; and in Bratislava, January 2003.

2
"On the Limits of Writing the Art History of Non-Western Cultures," invited lecture, Getty Center, March 2000; repeated at the Second Clark Conference, chaired by John Onians, April 2000; University of Washington at Seattle, October 2000; Duke University December 2000; and for Richard Vinograd's seminar on Chinese painting, Stanford University, February 2001. The material in those talks informed problems I tried to open in a review of Steven Mansbach's *Modern Art in Eastern Europe*, in Elkins 2000; and see Elkins 2002b.

3
It was rewritten for the "Beijing Forum," August 2004 (the paper was not given), and again in c. 2005 for the publication of the commemorative volume of the launch of the Irish Arts Research Centre (forthcoming).

4
This is John Onians's phrase; the conference was called "Compression vs. Expression: Containing and Explaining the World's Art," and was held April 6–8, 2000. It is now available

as John Onians, ed., *Compression vs. Expression: Containing and Explaining the World's Art* (Williamstown, MA: Clark Art Institute, 2006).

5
It is now called "Writing About Modernist Painting Outside Western Europe and North America," in Onians 2006. For related material see: Elkins 2003a, with English summary provided by the editors; Elkins 2002a; and a version in English and Slovenian: Elkins 2002d. Some of this material was also given as "Writing About World Art: Philosophic and Political Problems," three invited lectures, given at Mohile Parikh Centre for the Performaing Arts in Mumbai, and at the Sanskriti Foundation in Delhi, November 2003.

6
University of Maryland at College Park, November 2005.

7
The correspondence followed the publication, in Chinese, of my book on the ways Chinese landscape painting has been studied. See Elkins 1999 (unpublished in English). The paper at the conference, which will be published by Jason Kuo, is "Problems with the Project *Chinese Landscape Painting as Western Art History*."

exceptions—John Clark, Steven Mansbach—there is still virtually no scholarship written in Western Europe or North America on modernisms in the rest of the world. Such art appears belated, unnecessary, provincial, or otherwise not crucial for accounts of modernism, and that fact continues to concern me.

2. In 2005 I had a public discussion with Jim Cahill, about the ways that Chinese and Western scholars write about Chinese art.[6] That followed an Afterword I had written to a book of interviews with Chinese art historians, edited by Jason Kuo (Elkins 2006a). As I write this, Cahill and I are corresponding about the issue, with the intention of publishing the results. The central issue is whether Western scholars have a distinguishably Western way of interpreting Chinese painting—or to put it differently, whether there is an indigenously Chinese way of writing about Chinese painting that can be of interest *as* art history to a Western scholar, and yet be distinct from Western methodologies. The question has an easy answer (Chinese scholars have been traditionally interested in colophons and textual sources at the expense of what Western scholars like Cahill think of as detailed formal analysis) and a hard answer (Chinese scholars practice a kind of "connoisseurship," mingled with "aesthetics," which may or may not be an identifiably different discourse).[7]

3. I have edited a book, *Is Art History Global?* which will be, I think, the most comprehensive on its subject; it has nearly forty contributors from around the world. A version of the Irish Art Research Centre paper is one of its opening essays—hence it wouldn't be appropriate to republish that here. The book, *Is Art History Global?* centers on a roundtable conversation held in Ireland in 2005. The roundtable is in the book, along with five previously unpublished essays by the participants. I then sent the roundtable to over sixty scholars in over thirty-five countries. Their Assessments—including one written by an editor of this book, Kitty Zijlmans—appear in the book following the roundtable. There are also two conclusions (one written by an anthropologist, the other by an art historian) and an introduction.

4. In 2004 the University College Cork assembled the largest database of art history departments worldwide—almost 800 institutions. Some of that information is published in a volume edited by Anna Brzyski, on the subject of the canons of art history (Elkins 2007b). The database also underlies the emphases of *Is Art History Global?* because it enabled me to invite scholars from places such as Macau, South Africa, Benin, Paraguay, Venezuela, Georgia, and Uzbekistan, whose art historians had not previously participated in Western European or North American congresses, or published in Western languages.

At this point in the discussion of "world art studies" or "global art history," I think it is reasonable to say that there are certain texts and certain academic programs that should probably now be considered required reading. They form the background of the current discussion, so that this book, or *Is Art History Global?*, should not be taken as introductory texts but as contributions to an ongoing discussion. Such "required readings" might include David Summers's *Real Spaces*, perhaps along with my review (Summers 2003; Elkins 2004b). There are also studies of the world art market by Julian Stallabrass, Charlotte Bydler, and others.[8] "Required readings" should probably also include neurological, neuropsychological, and Darwinian studies by John Onians, Ellen Dissanayake, Barbara Stafford, and others.[9] And as background, the discussion in art history certainly assumes familiarity with the larger debates about globalism, such as Michael Hardt and Antonio Negri's *Empire* (2000) and Gayatri Spivak's *Critique of Postcolonial Reason* (1999). I would like to think that the present book, in particular, along with *Is Art History Global?* will set the stage for a fair amount of the discussion to come.

Some universities are emerging as centers of the study of globalism in art and art history, and they can also be conceived as "required reading" in the sense that it is important to be familiar with their programs in order to assess the state of the field. In addition to the program in Leiden, there is John Onians's program of World Art Studies at the University of East Anglia. Many other major universities try, in effect, to cover the world: I might name Sussex, the University of California at Los Angeles, the University of Chicago, Copenhagen University... but such a list would be unhelpfully open-ended. What matters is how the initiatives form themselves philosophically; and unfortunately, at present it seems most do not have coherent philosophic agendas other than hiring lecturers to cover increasing swathes of the world. (The University of East Anglia program is unified by its members' desire to be more than an aggregate of specialists, but aside from John Onians —whom I will discuss a little below—they have yet to issue a position paper or present collaborative work.)

In light of all this, it is hard to know exactly what contribution will be most timely and useful for the present volume. In this brief essay, I would like to review some questions that I think remain outstanding.

I. PLACES WHERE ART CRITICISM IS THE ONLY HISTORICAL PRACTICE

The book *Is Art History Global?* is volume 3 of a series called *The Art Seminar*. The idea of the series is to capture *incoherent* conversations on ill-defined topics. (The other volumes are on such contentious topics as *Photography Theory, The Renaissance*, and *Art History versus Aesthetics*.) The thirty or forty Assessments in each volume of the *Art Seminar* are deliberately as diverse as possible, and as editor, I make no particular attempt to choose people whom I know or whom I can trust. The result is a kind of chaos, but one that hopefully mirrors the worldwide state of conversation on the given topic. In *Is Art History Global?* some people who wrote Assessments were concerned to defend the internationalism of their own institution; others wanted to show that their country or region had effectively produced its own kind of writing, thus vitiating the problem.

Among the various perspectives on the roundtable conversation, several stand out as especially poorly resolved. One such is the difference between art history and art criticism. This was raised explicitly in the roundtable conversation itself, and some respondents picked up on it. The question, in the roundtable, concerned countries and regions that have no art historians, and where newspaper art criticism becomes, de facto, the principal form of historical writing. We discussed that question as an initial way of getting at what might count as "art history." The theme reemerged in the Assessments, sometimes as a point to be argued, but also as something *invisible to the writers*. This is a bit tricky to explain: what I mean is that some people writing Assessments simply took what we were calling "art criticism"—more or less ephemeral, journalistic writing—to *be* art history. Those writers did not engage the question of what might divide art history from criticism, not because they believed that all art history has a critical dimension, or even because they had a principled position about the relation between the two, but because they had such minimal contact with what the roundtable panelists were considering as art history that they did not recognize it as potentially different from what the roundtable panelists thought of as art criticism. Of course I do not want to name those writers, or even their countries: but I think it is very important to acknowledge that some people who identify themselves as art historians are so far outside of American and European protocols of scholarship that they cannot yet engage the discussion we had set up. It is, I think, a cardinal danger in conversations about "world art history" that "we" (however that pronoun might be configured in any given instance) assume that people who are interested in art and its history *can* engage in the kinds of discussions that interest us. Some people —as we discuss in the roundtable—work in places where they have no slides, no books, and virtually no students, and where there is no local literature on art's history. They do not know Wölfflin, Baxandall, Clark, and the many others who form the variable background of our conversations; and often, of course, they do not know Derrida, Foucault, Benjamin, and the others who enable us to speak so confidently about the possible differences between art history and criticism.

I want to make sure I am not misunderstood here: I do not at all think that there is a single decisive difference between art history and art criticism, or even a set of plausible alternative theories.[10] I just mean that if the net is thrown widely enough, to include writers from smaller third-world countries—and some from larger and more prosperous countries—then conversations about art history or "world art studies" will come to include senses of "art history" so far outside of the usual spectrum of warring methodologies that they may just appear to be misguided. I notice that the contributors to this volume, including myself, are all people who already have a sense that they might have a stake in the conversation. Some of our respondents from smaller third-world countries and from disadvantaged areas were not at all able to engage with questions that concerned choices between social art history and semiotics, or postcolonial theory and archival research: they were outside, or *before*, the sum total of those questions. I think it is both fair and neutral to say those authors *missed the point* made in the roundtable, and mistook the art critical practices in their countries for art history. This poses an interesting challenge for conversations about the globalization of art history: to what degree is this really a conversation among the empowered, in the West and in areas with sufficient Western contact?

II. THE POSSIBILITY THAT SCIENCE MIGHT PROVIDE THE COHERENCE OF A WORLD-WIDE PRACTICE OF ART HISTORY

Several people who wrote Assessments for the book proposed that art historians should look to the sciences for ideas that might work cross-culturally. Ladislav Kesner, who was on the roundtable itself, has an interest in cognitive psychology and neurobiology, and he is currently exploring what those sciences might contribute to art history. Barbara Stafford (who wrote an Assessment) and several other historians have also pointed to an alarming lack of interest in science among people in the humanities, even if she (and others) do not think of science as something that might unify culturally disparate discourses. I mentioned Dissanayake and Onians at the beginning; they have different, but perhaps equally scientific, ideas about how artistic practices might be studied across cultural boundaries. Dissanayake is a Darwinian interested in explaining art as an evolutionary phenomenon. Onians is an empirical materialist, interested in neuropsychology—the study of changes made in the brain on the timescale of individual generations. Onians says that for him, the program at the University of East Anglia is different from those in larger US universities, even though they have comparable numbers of specialists (two or three China and Japan specialists; several southeast Asian specialists; several Africanists, and so forth). For Onians, the expression "world art studies" —which he coined—implies an obligation to understand how art has arisen as a worldwide phenomenon. Art started in a number of places, independently, around 30,000 BP, and that calls for an

11
This information comes from a visit to UEA in May 2006. I thank John Onians for inviting me, and letting me sit in on one of his postgraduate seminars.
12
See Hyman's website in Oxford; the paper is at http://www.queens.ox.ac.uk/academics/hyman/files/art_and_neuroscience.pdf.
13
This argument—that a scientific explanation may not count *as* an explanation because it changes the terms of the debate—is developed and defended in Elkins, forthcoming.
14
I elaborate and defend this in two forthcoming papers: in Elkins, forthcoming; and in the introduction to an edited volume, *Visual Practices Across the University* (work in progress).

explanation. Onians's project is called "neuroarthistory," and he is the only one in the UEA group who pursues it as a central interest. (The first chair of World Art Studies in UEA, John Mack, has other interests.[11])

Further afield one might mention E.O. Wilson or Vilayanur Ramachandran, although the latter's theories have been well critiqued by John Hyman.[12]

In the context of *Is Art History Global?* those interested in science—as I am, in other contexts—are a small but distinct minority. I wonder if scientific explanations aren't by definition marginal to the debates about the globalization of art history, just because they involve *changing the subject*—replacing talk about value, context, and interest with talk about optimal response, conditioned behavior, and evolutionary advantage.[13] I wonder, in other words, if some scientific explanations might be at one and the same time largely or wholly correct, and largely or wholly beside the point. I wonder: but the discussion on that subject has not yet begun, perhaps because many scholars in the humanities prefer simply to avoid engaging science and its empirical arguments.[14]

III. THE WESTERNNESS OF THE QUESTION

Some of those writing Assessments in *Is Art History Global?* felt that the question itself presupposed Western ways of thinking that rendered any possible answer unreliable. Any kind of world art studies or global art history that might fairly be seen as a response to the kinds of questions that books like this one pose were taken, by those respondents, as inherently ideologically loaded. In his Assessment Craig Clunas describes his own program, SOAS in London, in such a way that it appears that what counts as "art history" might or might not appear along with many other interests and in many different contexts. Suman Gupta wrote an Assessment, but he effectively declined to join the debate; he says instead that art history as it is constituted renders the kinds of questions we meant to ask at the roundtable inherently unanswerable or circular. My own position, which I do not articulate in *Is Art History Global?* is close to theirs. Art history, as it currently is practiced, is itself certainly an impediment to thinking about worldwide ways of telling art's history. The roundtable conversation in *Is Art History Global?* kept to questions recognizable as art history, but as Clunas, Gupta, and others implied, or argued, some things can't be solved without thinking more widely. Art history can't diagnose its Westernness without taking on other perspectives, and without being willing to see itself dissolve.

It helps to dissect this problem into three parts: methodologies, institutions, and leading terms. This is artificial, but it has the virtue of clarity. I'll return to the argument in section VII.

IV. THE WESTERNNESS OF METHODOLOGIES

We can certainly see beyond our interpretive agendas—our semiotics, deconstruction, literary theory, anthropology, linguistic theory, psychoanalysis—but it is not clear that we can recognize what we find beyond those limits as viable alternates to the interpretive methods we currently employ. In *Visual Studies: A Skeptical Introduction*, I argue that it would be an important step for visual studies to adopt as many new interpretive strategies as possible (Elkins 2003b). Visual studies should experiment with avoiding Benjamin, Lacan, Foucault, Derrida, and the rest, and try taking indigenous texts as interpretive languages—Indian or Chinese texts, for example, or even "unusual" Western texts such as Leibniz, Vico, Bruno, Pico, Bayle, or any number of others. The idea would be to see what might happen to our concept of adequate or appropriate interpretation when the discourses are no longer the familiar ones.

It is interesting how few scholars do this. Consider, for example, the fact that Gayatri Spivak, with her deep interests in Bengali language and culture, continues to employ a strictly faithful version of Derrida's philosophy in order to interpret Bengali culture. Or that Slavoj Žižek continues to alternate between Marxist and Lacanian models, no matter what subject matter he encounters. I have argued this elsewhere in a little more detail: what I want to register here is the fact that even the most reflective, multinational, multicultural writers do not move beyond Western interpretive methods (Elkins 2003b). This is all the more true of art history. The art of all nations continues to be interpreted using the toolbox of twentieth-century Western European and North American art history: structuralism, formalism, style analysis, iconography, patronage studies, biography. I agree with Vinay Lal that an enormous challenge awaits a more adventurous historical practice, one that would try to explain artworks using indigenous, non-Western texts.[15] Such an art history would risk seeming ineffectual, idiosyncratic, or misguided, and it is likely that it would not be perceived as an art history at all. Yet the risk is worth taking, if historical accounts of art are to finally pull free of the mire of Westernness.

This isn't to say I am sanguine about the possibility of changing interpretive methods. I have myself experimented by using a sixteenth-century Persian text to interpret images, and I have also used precontact Chinese texts, and several earlier Indian texts.[16]

The results, I think, are interesting, and they certainly sound unusual. But as far as I know, they have hardly been noticed, and in general art history and visual studies keep to the usual twentieth-century Western theorists.

V. THE WESTERNNESS OF INSTITUTIONS

Part of Gupta's argument entails the observation that institutional structures of art history—its departments, seminar structures,

15
My review of David Summers's *Real Spaces*, Elkins 2004a, quotes Lal and develops this idea.

16
In the chapter "Different Horizons for the Concept of the Image," in Elkins 1998b. An earlier version is Elkins 1998a, and the ideas are reviewed in Elkins 2002c.

refereed journals, examinations, essays and vivas, international conferences, visiting professorships, and archival protocols—are more pervasive than some of us in the roundtable imagined them to be. I agree with that, too, and I would say that the institutions of art history can make it nearly impossible to *recognize* a non-Western interpretive practice as an instance of art history. I have only a little to say about this because virtually *all* contributions to the problem of globalism are written by scholars who work in Western-style universities. We all (for once the "we" is not contentious) attend conferences, publish in refereed journals, attend international conferences, and write according to international protocols. We are all of us inside that bubble. I know only two exceptions, both people who wrote Assessments for our book. One is from Ghana, and the other Benin, and they work largely (but not completely) outside such structures. Disappointingly, then, they do not engage these problems: instead they write in ways that open the question of the difference between art history and criticism (as in my first point).

So if rethinking art history for world art involves a critique of institutions, I am afraid we are all stuck.

VI. THE WESTERNNES OF TERMS

This was an object of protracted debate throughout *Is Art History Global?* The central issue was this: Should art historians continue to use Western terms such as space and form, or should it be the business of historians to learn the relevant languages and adopt their critical terms? Very approximately speaking, David Summers's *Real Spaces* suggests that an optimal way to address the full range of art-making practices across different cultures is to attend to the fundamental terms that structure embodied human experience, terms like *space*, *axis*, and *center*. His book is a monumental rethinking of those terms, most of them classical and many originally Greek or Latin, so that they can be made flexible and open enough to address works made outside of Western traditions. In my review of his book, I noted that most postcolonial theory goes in a different direction: it opts for local concepts, taken from indigenous—and often non-Western—languages. In our roundtable conversation, Summers became increasingly unhappy about this possibility.

I am still undecided on the question—both sides have compelling arguments in their favor—but I am more interested in looking at unusual, non-Western terms than I am in revisiting the oldest Western concepts. That bias came out in the roundtable, although we ended on a conciliatory and indecisive note in order to make way for the people who would write the Assessments. They, in turn, mostly doubted the project of finding "new," non-Western terms to describe non-Western artworks; but—to sum up an enormous variety of responses, hints, and even evasions— they also kept their distance from Summers's approach. There are some brilliant Assessments on this question, most especially one by the Japanese scholar Shigemi Inaga, who proposes a complex "elliptical" model of translations that involves three languages rather than the usual two. For many scholars, the question is solved, effectively, by deferring it: my sense of the Assessments as a whole is that most scholars do not see non-Western terms and Western terms *as a choice:* rather they take a mixed, local, and opportunistic attitude, hoping to find the best terms in any given context. I am not convinced that is a coherent position, especially given that any practice that mixes discourses has to assume that concepts can be safely excerpted from traditions that might well be inherently, deeply, immiscible. (How can *space*, to name just one example, be disentangled from Western metaphysics?) The issue looms over any future art history that continues to grant a place to discourses identified as Western, and those seen as somehow outside that tradition.

Kitty Zijlmans's Assessment in *Is Art History Global?* advocates an intercultural perspective formed in part by the development of several key themes, including a rethinking of center and periphery, frames and contexts, and the concept of multiple cultures. Her project is to found a multidisciplinary study of art, as a panhuman phenomenon. Her terms are the culture's broadest and deepest terms, including "culture" itself, and her purpose is to find common ground, and to develop a broad, open-ended sense of the ideas that bind artmaking around the world. Her approach is, from that perspective, allied to Summers's. My skepticism, then, comes from the Westernness of the terms, but also from the sense that those terms are not sufficiently capacious or malleable to embrace world art production. My sense of the words "space," "form," and "culture" is that they are moored in the deep waters of the recent Western past, and that our confidence in their capacity to shift and metamorphose and rediscover themselves in new settings is itself a symptomatic overconfidence that has been built into Western metaphysics since Plato.

VII. WESTERNNESS, CONCLUDED

Those last three sections were brief looks at three dimensions of the Westernness problem. My own notion is that non-Western methodologies (point IV) and non-Western terms (point VI) are interesting ways forward, even if we remain trapped within academic institutional structures (point V). I think that about half the people participating in the book *Is Art History Global?* would agree with some versions of those positions.

But I think I am probably in a small minority in another respect. The overwhelming majority of contributors feel that it is time to let go of the discipline of art history, and begin experimenting with new writing. I agree. But they also assume that by doing new work, we will release ourselves from the clinging remnants of older disciplines and find new ways of writing and thinking. I doubt that.

A very wide spectrum of writers, who otherwise might share relatively few claims—Zijlmans, Onians, Clark, Matthew Rampley, many others—might agree to the proposition that things change, and that soon writing about art might take very different shapes. The world is changing, and so are disciplines, and in fifty years art history may look wholly different. If I am skeptical about those hopes, it is because I think the methods, concepts, and institutions of art history exert a tidal pull. We hardly know how to think about art's history without them, and just when we think we are furthest away—when we are experimenting with some new anthropological approach, or studying things no one has thought of studying before—just then the tidal pull is strongest. I do not think that anyone has invented effectively new ways of thinking about art in relation to history that can be recognized *as* ways of thinking about art's history. We are not as inventive as we like to think, and we are not as free.

That is why I think we need to continue to study the forms of the "old" art history, even if that means that our writing appears to be nostalgic, conservative, or old-fashioned. I do not believe that it is possible to find new ways of interpreting art just by looking at art with increasing sensitivity. I do not believe that a study of, say, modern art in Indonesia can proceed without considering its indebtedness to the very idea of an art history—an idea which is entirely Western in origin, and which continues to be developed according to Western models.

An adventurous Assessment cowritten by Atreyee Gupta and Sugata Ray takes me to task for underestimating the flexibility of non-Western *responses* to art history, especially Indian ones. Gupta and Ray note that, "the fact that Spivak draws her methodologies from Derridean poststructuralism and Kapur from Lyotard is sufficient to mark them (for Elkins) as fundamentally dependent on 'Western interpretive models.' Kapur and Spivak's potent critiques of Euro-American imperialism are lost in Elkins's quest for a 'multicultural' world art history" (Elkins 2006b).

I need to register a stubborn inability here. I have read, I think, everything of Kapur's that is available in the West. She will be contributing to another book series I am editing, *Theories of Modernism and Postmodernism in the Visual Arts*. I find her answers to the narratives of Western modernism and postmodernism to be among the best and most cogent developed anywhere. And yet I have not seen evidence that her sense of Indian modernist painting has been taken seriously anywhere outside of two very particular communities: those already engaged in modern Indian painting, and those—such as Fred Jameson, Homi Bhabha, Spivak, Sarat Maharaj, and others—who comprise a worldwide community of postcolonial theorists *outside art history*. I do not say this in any way as a critique of Kapur's ideas, and I hope that my interest in them is sufficiently clear from the fact that I invited her to participate in the book series. What I want to signal is that *even this optimal account*—optimal in its eloquence, intelligence, resourcefulness, and historical purchase—has not had any effect that I can see on worldwide models of art in the twentieth century. As far as I am aware, her responses have not been taken up in the principal English, French, German, Italian, Chinese, South African, or Spanish textbooks or curricula, and they have not been noticed in colloquia or university curricula on modernism. In short, I don't see her critiques as "potent." I see them as *necessary*, and as optimal, and probably even as unimprovable, but not as efficacious. The West continues to win.

It may well happen that the discipline of art history melts away, and that we start to see it as an ideological fossil, the way modernist artists saw the old academies. It may well be that new interests, new ways of thinking about artworks, take us far from the places we once were. It may not be too many years before we look back with amusement on scholars of our generations who worried about optimal forms of Lacanian interpretations, or anthropological interventions, or the perpetually unfinished, perpetually new field of visual studies. We may study things very differently in just a few years. Books like Craig Clunas's excellent *Art in China*, or Georges Didi-Huberman's fabulously inventive *l'Image survivante*, may come to be seen as exemplars of a new independence, a new freedom from the past.

But if all that happens, and I hope and expect that it will, we will still be chained to the old art history. We will be shackled to identifiably art historical assumptions about the significance of art and its history, to received ideas about how certain objects are expressive and why they matter, and to immovable convictions about the significance and capaciousness of concepts like "space" and "form." We will still be addicted to scholarship, academies, culture, value, art, and the writing of art's history. We need to go backwards, into our own past, in order to see why we are so optimistic about the idea that we can escape our own histories by looking into the future.

REFERENCES

BYDLER, CHARLOTTE. 2004. *The global art world inc.: On the globalization of contemporary art.* Figura Nova Series 32. Uppsala: Acta Universitatis Upsaliensis. PhD diss., Uppsala University.

CLUNAS, CRAIG. 1997. *Art in China.* Oxford History of Art. Oxford: Oxford University Press.

DIDI-HUBERMAN, GEORGES. 2002. *L'Image survivante: Histoire de l'art et temps des fantômes selon Aby Warburg.* Paradoxe. Paris: Minuit.

DISSANAYAKE, ELLEN. 1992. *Homo aestheticus: Where art comes from and why.* New York: Free Press, etc.

ELKINS, JAMES. 1998a. Different horizons for the concept of the image. *Zeitschrift für Ästhetik und allgemeine Kunstwissenschaft* 43 (1): 29–46.
—. 1998b. *On pictures and the words that fail them.* Cambridge: Cambridge University Press.
—. 1999. *Xi fang mei shu shi xue zhong de Zhongguo shan shui hua* [*Chinese landscape painting as western art history*]. Trans. from the English by Pan Yaochang and Gu Ling. Hangzhou: Zhongguo mei shu xue yuan chu ban she [National Academy of Art].
—. 2000. Review of *Modern art in Eastern Europe: From the Baltic to the Balkans, ca. 1890–1939* by Steven A. Mansbach. *The Art Bulletin* 82 (4): 781–85.
—. 2002a. [Why it is not possible to write the art history of non-Western cultures]. Trans. into Chinese by Ding Ning. *Mei yuan/Journal of the Lu Xun Academy of Fine Arts* [Beijing] 3: 56–61.
—. 2002b. Response [to Anthony Alofsin's letter regarding the review of Mansbach's *Modern art in Eastern Europe*]. *The Art Bulletin* 84 (3): 539.
—. 2002c. *Stories of art.* New York: Routledge.
—. 2002d. Why it is not possible to write the art history of non-Western cultures. In *Minulost'v Prítomnosti: Súcasné umenie a umeleckohistorcké myty/The past in the present: contemporary art and art history's myths,* ed. Ján Bakoš, 229–55. Bratislava: Nadácia-Centrum Súcasného Umenia [sic: 2003].
—. 2003a. Ako je mozné písat' o svetovom umení? [How is it possible to write about the world's art?]. *Ars* [Bratislava] 2: 75–91.
—. 2003b. *Visual studies: A skeptical introduction.* London and New York: Routledge.
—. 2004a. Two forms of judgement: forgiving and demanding (the case of marine painting). *Journal of Visual Art Practice* 3 (1): 37–46.
—. 2004b. Review of *Real spaces: World art history and the rise of Western modernism* by David Summers. *The Art Bulletin* 86 (2): 373–80.
—, ed. 2005. *Art history versus aesthetics.* The Art Seminar 1. New York and London: Routledge.
—. 2006a. Afterword. In *Discovering Chinese painting: Dialogues with art historians.* 2nd ed., ed. Jason C. Kuo, 249–56. Dubuque, IO: Kendall/Hunt Publishing.
—. 2006b. Writing about modernist painting outside Western Europe and North America. In *Compression vs. expression: Containing and explaining the world's art,* ed. John Onians, 188–214. Williamstown, MA: Clark Art Institute.
—, ed. 2007a. *Is art history global?* The Art Seminar 3. New York and London: Routledge.
—. 2007b. Canon and globalization in art history. In *Partisan canons,* ed. Anna Bryzki, 55–77. Durham, NC: Duke University Press.
—, ed. 2007c. *Photography theory.* The Art Seminar 2. New York and London: Routledge.
—, and Robert Williams, eds. 2008. *Renaissance theory.* The Art Seminar 4. New York and London: Routledge.
—. Forthcoming. Aesthetics and the two cultures: Why art and science should be allowed to go their separate ways. In *Rediscovering aesthetics,* ed. Julia Jansen, Francis Halsall, and Tony O'Connor. New York: Columbia University Press.

HARDT, MICHAEL, AND ANTONIO NEGRI. 2000. *Empire.* Cambridge, MA: Harvard University Press.

ONIANS, JOHN, ed. 2006. *Compression vs. expression: Containing and explaining the world's art.* Williamstown, MA: Clark Art Institute.

ONIANS, JOHN. 2007. *Art between culture and nature.* London: Pindar Press.

SPIVAK, GAYATRI. 1999. *Critique of postcolonial reason: Toward a history of the vanishing present.* Cambridge, MA: Harvard University Press.

STAFFORD, BARBARA MARIA. 2007. *Echo objects: The cognitive work of images.* Chicago and London: The University of Chicago Press.

SUMMERS, DAVID. 2003. *Real spaces: World art history and the rise of Western modernism.* London and New York: Phaidon.

CAO YIQIANG

World Art Studies and the Historiography of Chinese Art

The idea of world art has its origin in the concept of universal history, an intellectual product of nineteenth-century Europe. The introduction of the concept of universal history into China at the dawn of the twentieth century inspired many Chinese radicals to attack the traditional historiography developed from the time of Confucius through Si Maqian, Ban Gu, and down to their own time. Liang Qichao and He Bingsong, who were the champions of this "new historiographical revolution," even went so far as to claim that all the historical books surviving from the past did not deserve the very name of history because they merely involved masses of isolated and undigested facts that failed to account for a comprehensive and linear progression of Chinese civilization.[1]

Art scholars who were at the forefront of this new battle not only agreed with Liang Qichao's evolutionist view, but also came to realize that a true history of Chinese art could only be meaningful if situated in the context of world art. In 1917, Jiang Danshu published a brief history of both Chinese art and Western art. In the former, he pointed out that the old Chinese art history only paid attention to literati painting and neglected other genres such as sculpture, architecture, and applied art; and, even worse in his view, this history was unsystematic in its recording of paintings while also failing to trace "the origin, transformation and evolution"[2] of Chinese art as a whole. In 1929, Zheng Wu Chang echoed Jiang's view by publishing *The Comprehensive History*

[1]
See He Bingsong, *New Meaning in Universal History,* originally published in 1928, republished by Guangxi Normal University Press, 2005. He studied history and politics in the United States and returned to China in 1916. He first taught at Beijing University and next at Shanghai Guanghua University and Jinan University in Guangzhou. He was the first Chinese scholar to introduce systematically Western historiography into China. Also see Liang Qichao, *Methodologies of Chinese Historical Studies,* based on his lectures in 1921, 1st ed. published 1922. All publications mentioned in the notes are published in Chinese; the titles have been translated into English by the author.

[2]
Preface to *A History of Art,* now in *Jiang Danshu's Miscellaneous Writings on Art Education* (Zhejiang: Zhejiang Education Publishing House, 1991) 1.

3
The Comprehensive History of Chinese Painting and its Theories. 2nd ed. (Shanghai: Shanghai Calligraphy and Painting Press, 1983) 2.

4
Ibid.

5
See Xie Hai Yan's Foreword to the second edition of Zheng's book, p. 1, and also Zong Bai Hau's review, *The Book Reviews*, Peiping [Beijing], 1,(1934) 2.

of Chinese Painting and its Theories, the title of which was already meant to be a manifesto. In his Preface, Zheng argued the need for a systematic history of Chinese painting that should comprise every stage Chinese art has passed through, as opposed to such precedents as Zhang Yanyuan's *Record of Famous Paintings* (ninth century CE). Having mentioned a great number of previous books on art history, Zheng also claimed:

> If we look at all these books and examine their structures, we find that what is said and recorded in them is confined either to one place, one period, one artist and one event or to one system and one method; they merely give a tabulation of artists' names, their place of origin or the place where they lived without anywhere considering the sequence of time; they just jumble together different works and different opinions of various ages without anywhere explaining the origins of different schools. Hence, although there are so many famous books, they have only very limited functions and values, for none of them was written according to a scientific method, that is, observing the sequence of time and the course of artistic developments, collecting, analyzing and combining theories and opinions of all kinds; framing and defining the origins of different schools and their relationship with politics, ethics and religion.

Zheng suggested in other words that "we Chinese have not yet possessed a scholarly history that is systematically and coherently written."[3]

What he attempted was to write just such a coherent history. He divided the whole development of Chinese art history into four stages. It began with what he called the "utilitarian period," which was followed by the "ritual period" that covers the arts produced before the Han Dynasty (206 BCE–220 CE). After this stage, Chinese art entered "the age of religion," and since the Tang Dynasty (618–907) Chinese painting has developed into "the era of literature." This particular historical conceptualization also allowed the author to divide each one of these periods into four subsections: a general account of the rise and decline of the various schools, a description of the famous paintings made in each period, a biographical narrative of the great painters within each period, and a discussion of theories on the art of painting by other painters and connoisseurs within each period. In addition, the appendix includes a bibliography of the books on Chinese paintings of various periods, together with some biographical notes on contemporary painters and what the author called "proportional lists of the number of painters active in different areas and of the vicissitudes of different schools."[4]

Zheng's work, which is usually held to constitute a milestone in Chinese art historical studies,[5] provides the first framework for a general survey of Chinese art from its beginnings up to the present time, as opposed to offering merely a conventional periodical narrative. His study, however, was soon embraced as a standard account and blindly copied by a great number of succeeding writers; above all, it gave rise to a desire for completeness which has culminated in our own day and age.

In retrospect, we cannot avoid the conclusion that the desire of these art historians for a "complete" history of Chinese art was inspired not so much by an earnest acceptance of a so-called "scientific historical method" as by nationalist feelings, which were particularly strong during the time when Zheng was writing his book because of the impact of China's domestic cultural decline and external assaults from the West. Zheng himself claimed to be extremely disappointed when hearing that Chinese scholars could not fully answer questions about the history of Chinese painting put to them by such famous Westerners as Bertrand Russell on their visits to China, and that he was equally embarrassed knowing that the Japanese had preceded us in supplying the world with a complete history of Chinese art. He felt it to be humiliating for the Chinese, partly in view of the fact that

> in this world there only exist two systems of painting; one is the Eastern, the other the Western.... The Eastern system originated in the mainland China ... then ... spread to Japan. While the motherland of Western painting is Italy, the fatherland of Eastern painting is China. This is the place that our Chinese painting occupies in the world history of art![6]

These words, too, have found their way into the works of succeeding generations of writers on Chinese art history. It is safe to argue that all studies on the subject written in China between 1929 and today start from this claim. If the door to world art had always been closed, however, it was this nationalistic noise that forced a breakthrough, which has in turn led us to reconsider the legacy of Chinese historiography and its possible contribution to world art studies to which this volume is devoted.

CHINESE HISTORIOGRAPHY OF ART

From a global perspective, Chinese literature on painting is unmatched in terms of its preeminence, consistency and quantity (as is true of Chinese historical documents in general). By the time Vasari launched European art history in the mid-sixteenth century with his *Lives*, China had already produced a long series of writings on art.

Traditionally, Chinese writings on art were roughly divided into four categories: 1. "Classification," which groups painters in grades before describing their lives and works, in many ways analogous to the art criticism practiced in eighteenth-century France,

7
Zhu Jingxuan, 'Preface,' in *Chinese Theories of Painting,* ed. Wu Mengxia (Anhui: Anhui Fine Art Publishing House) 50.

albeit in a completely different form. 2. "Discussions," which can now be called theory of art; 3. "Histories of painting," which will be the focus of my paper; and 4. "Cataloguing," which is mainly concerned with connoisseurship and collecting. Although in actual practice these four methods have been applied more or less in combination with each other since the Tang Dynasty, the first two have usually been more closely connected by their tendency towards critical discrimination, while the last two have been more historically inclined.

Chinese historiography of art well reflects the evolution of art. Early Chinese painting served a didactic and ritual function, while its main concern was with figure painting, and thus with representation. For these purposes, a system was developed of classifying painters according to their merits and faults. As early as in the sixth century, Xie He composed his *Classification of Painters*, and set forth the Six Laws or canons of painting for assessing the quality of the work of individual artists. The first law stresses the vividness and lifelikeness of painting, the second requires the method of vigorous brushwork, the third is concerned with likeness of the subjects painted, the fourth is about the use of color according to the kinds of the objects, the fifth applies to composition, and the sixth is about copying. Xie He thus divided the painters he managed to trace into six classes, each corresponding to one of the six laws. With the passing of time, the system of classification on the basis of merit became a more and more sophisticated critical tool. Li Sizhen of the late seventh century developed a nine-fold division of quality in a sequel to the text by Xie He and Yao Zui. But in his *Later Classification of Calligraphers* he introduced a new category, which is called "*I*," meaning free from all restraints, intended for those talents which did not seem to fit into any one of the other categories. This was to be incorporated into the most influential order system established by the official scholar Zhu Jingxuan in his *Record of Famous Painters of the Tang Dynasty*: the Four Classes which consist of the divine, the wonderful, the skillful, and the spontaneous. And in each of these he distinguished three levels: upper, middle, and lower. What was new in his work is not so much his order system, which was derived from his predecessors, but his brief introductory descriptions of specific painters' subjects and styles which were strictly based on his own experience. "Since I am fond of painting," he wrote in his preface, "I have been trying to track down the existing paintings. But I do not make a record of any paintings which I do not see, but only those which I have seen with my own eyes."[7] This approach, strictly based on the writer's own experience of works of art, makes his record reliable and allows us to reconstruct those pictures and pieces of calligraphy that are now lost, and it was to become a permanent art historical method.

The development of classifications is of vital importance to historical studies because it reflects, like a mirror, the rise of new genres of painting as well as the shifts in taste. It also affected the art market; the price of a painting was settled according to the class its maker was credited with, which in turn stimulated a zeal for collecting because to own works from superior painters carried with it a sign of moral virtue.

Chinese painting reached its peak in every genre during the Song Dynasty (960–1279). This development was accompanied by a highly sophisticated critical discrimination based on incorporating short biographies of earlier artists. Furthermore, the methods of classifying grew more diverse. For example, Liu Daochun divided painting into six subject categories—figures, landscapes, animals, birds and flowers, demons, and houses and trees—and put artists into one of the three traditional classes on the basis of their performance within each particular genre. This system permitted a subtler degree of discrimination in judging quality. However, this method only represents a transitional stage between the evaluative classification based on personal merits and the separation into categories in terms of the subject depicted, because it was rarely to become the main principle of organization. The more influential and, indeed, one of the most original contributions to the classification system was made by Huang Xiufu who placed the spontaneous class at the head of the listing, rather than at the end as in Zhu Jingxuan's system. This modification was soon to change the whole course of Chinese art history. Amateur scholar painters with a more spontaneous approach to painting replaced their professional counterparts, while landscape and bird-flower painting done in a more free style replaced figure painting that had been classified as the most difficult genre, and formal likeness was rejected in favor of spontaneous brush strokes.

We now move into the Ming Dynasty (1368–1644) in order to emphasize the importance of the so-called spontaneous spirit. Dong Qichang, who was a high official, painter, theorist and historian, divided the landscape painters from the Tang Dynasty to his own age into a Southern school and a Northern school, regardless of historical truth and actual stylistic differences shown in the existing paintings. Painters were put into one school or the other in such a way that all those who, according to him, represented superior artistic qualities belonged to the Southern school, while the painters placed into the Northern school were denied all genius.

This theory had a decisive influence on Chinese historiography because for the first time an attempt was made to describe the development of different artistic schools from a historical viewpoint by introducing, or, rather, inventing the contrast between them, which in some ways is analogous to mobilizing the "ism"-versus-"ism" model in the practice of modern European art history.

HISTORIES OF PAINTING

This brings us to the third category of our traditional writing on art: History of Painting. Linguistically, it seems the nearest thing

8
His own Preface to *Annotated Bibliography of Books on Calligraphy and Painting,* (Zhejiang: Zhejiang People's Publishing House, 1982).
9
Comprehensive Bibliography of Books on the History of Painting (Shanghai People's Fine Art Publishing House, 1962).

comparable to the history of art as we understand it today. In the Chinese historical context, however, it actually involved another version of the cataloguing approach. The first book entitled *History of Painting* appeared in China in the late eleventh century. It was written by Mi Fu, who created the so-called "Mi style" which applied the splashing technique to its logical extreme. Mi Fu was above all an antiquarian and collector. His *History of Painting* was to be as influential in later Chinese literature on art as his Mi style was in painting. The book's lasting impact, however, is explained by the great precision with which Mi recorded and described the paintings he saw. He was able to distinguish, with a rare flair, what was genuine and what was fake. At the same time, he discussed the methods of collecting and mounting pictures, while also giving his opinion on how to ascertain authenticity. No wonder, his study has become the bible of Chinese connoisseurs and collectors. Subsequent books of this kind all shared the same features, but they presented far fewer insights with much less authority. In fact, most of them only consist of anecdotes and brief artist biographies.

Of course, as we saw at the beginning of this essay, the question of "what is art history" never occurred to most previous generations of Chinese art historians, but with the arrival of Western influence the issue gained urgency. In 1931, when editing his *Annotated Bibliography of Books on Calligraphy and Painting,* the eminent Chinese scholar Yu Shaosong found himself confronted with this problem simply because he had become familiar with the Western definition of art history through the historical work recently produced by such art historians as Tan Gu who was trained in Germany. There was no problem when putting recent writings under the heading of what he labeled "Comprehensive history of art." But regarding the classification of studies produced prior to the twentieth century, he soon ran into great difficulties because, as he wrote, "our country has never possessed any true history of painting and calligraphy" which "narrates the whole development of different schools through the ages and describes their success and failure, rather than only recording the practice and behaviour of the painters and calligraphers."[8] But since he had become familiar with the Western definition of art history, and for the sake of being scientific—a catchword prevalent at the time— he had to begin his bibliography with a historical section. In so doing, he started from three headings: periodical history, specialized history, and brief biography. Three decades later, in 1962, Yu Anlan edited a *Comprehensive Bibliography of Books on the History of Painting,*[9] in which he added a fourth category: periodical history, regional history, genre history and anecdotal notes. Arbitrary as it is, this framework can be of some help for us to bring out some distinguishing characteristics of Chinese art history.

From an array of books included by modern scholars in the "Histories of Painting" genre, I would like to single out a few examples and look at them more closely. First, Zhang Yanyuan's *Re-*

cord of Famous Painters of Successive Dynasties, which appeared in the ninth century, seven centuries before Vasari's *Lives*. Our knowledge of early Chinese paintings is exclusively derived from this most informative and sophisticated art historical text ever written. More importantly, to this day this work served as an indisputable model in China for writing about art—one to which all subsequent books in the field can be regarded as sequels or footnotes. Because of its extreme importance, I will discuss it in more detail below, but let me turn first to another influential book written by a minor official at the Song capital at the beginning of the eleventh century: Guo Ruoxu's *Account of the Paintings Seen by Myself*. From the outset this author clearly stated that he conceived his study as a kind of sequel to Zhang's *Record of Famous Paintings* and that he attempted to present a more comprehensive survey of Chinese painting. For this reason he only provided condensed entries on the artists from the end of the Tang era to the year 1074. The scope of the text also allowed him to dispense with classification on the basis of quality for practical reasons. In addressing the contemporary masters of the Northern Song, he felt it appropriate to divide them into four specialized subject groups. The striking novelty of this grouping lies in its pioneering application to art history of the practice of ranking biographies in the dynastic histories by social status. In his groupings, an emperor, thirteen nobles, and scholar-officials are placed at the very beginning. This method would be extensively applied by Guo's followers, and such distinctions anticipate an elitist view of that elevated Xie He's "lifelikeness" to "spiritual consonance" as a kind of innate talent that reflects a man's character and social condition. Guo wrote that one may master other painting skills by study, but "the spiritual consonance can certainly not be acquired by skill or dexterity, nor can one arrive at it through months and years of study. It is secretly blended with the soul; one does not know how, yet it is there."[10] It follows that if your character is noble, your painting must be superior. Thus, in the wake of his predecessor Zhang Yanyuan, Guo opened his histories with a chapter on the moral significance of painting in relation to the nature of "spiritual consonance," and then proceeded to discuss the standards to be achieved in each genre and the proper approach to brushwork. Because of the acute historical perceptions embodied in the text, this work is rather a true history of painting than a simple compilation of biographies.

The unique practice of making a sequence of painting histories followed the pattern of Chinese official histories. Shortly before the fall of the Northern Song Dynasty (960–1127), a typical official history of art was compiled collectively by scholar officials at the court of Huizong. As usual, this work contained biographies of artists, placed in various sections according to the subjects of their paintings and then given in chronological order. Special emphasis was put on the meaning of pictorial subjects as indicated in

10
Account of the Paintings Seen by Myself. In *Chinese Theories of Painting*, ed. Wu Mengxia, 1995, 308–9.

11
Unpublished paper, which was sent to the present writer in 1997.

the *Books of Changes* and the *Book of Songs*, early classics in the Confucian canon. In terms of its genre, however, this work is more like a catalogue than a history of painting, as is also suggested by its title, *Catalogue of Painting in the Xuanhe Imperial Collection*. A consciously conceived and comprehensive history of painting was to appear in the late Yuan period (1271–1368). This work, entitled *Precious Mirror for Examining Painting*, has extensively absorbed the sources of previous writings, including all the books I have discussed so far.

After this period, the scope of art historical writing in China became more limited and specialized. This shift gave rise, for example, to so-called "regional histories," such as *Paintings Seen in the Yue* [Modern Hangzhou] *Area*. Moreover, scholars began to focus on writing histories of special subjects. These studies included *A Record of Court Paintings of Qing Dynasty*, *A History of Women Painters*, and many other histories of specific topics, such as a religious figure, bamboo, and the ink plum flower.

Considered as a whole, the so-called "histories of painting" do not offer a comprehensive image of Chinese literature on art; these histories in fact represent the least powerful form of Chinese writing on art, notably when compared to art criticism, art theory, connoisseurship, and art collecting. It is for this reason that one of the most learned and elderly scholars in China today cannot agree with those who have put Zhang Yanyuan's *Record of Famous Paintings* into this category, as was done by Yu Shaosong in his 1931 volume mentioned above. In an article written right before he died, Professor Yuan Po argued strongly against Yu Shaosong's view. The article's title is characteristic: "The Nature and Quality of *Record of Famous Paintings*: Blending Histories of Painting with Art Criticism, Art Theory and Cataloguing."[11] This prolonged debate in twentieth-century Chinese art historical circles about the definition of art history, or the justification of its name, may appear utterly tiresome and meaningless to an European reader, but it has deep roots in Chinese historiography. It is ironic, though, that this dispute has largely resulted from overlooking precisely this historical fact, which gave birth to the unique traits of Chinese art history not seen in Western historiography.

What makes Chinese historiography unique is its emphasis on the constitutional utility of history. According to this view, history makes sense only if it can serve as a means by which the former dynasty's constitutional system can be inherited and the present system can be handed down to posterity; it makes sense only if it can furnish practical directives for action or supply correct information upon which action can be wisely based. Therefore, the specialized role of the historian became recognized as part of the civil service. As early as the eleventh century BCE, the Chinese court employed so-called Left and Right History Officials: the Left Officials were responsible for recording the utterances of the Emperor while the Right Officials were in charge of recording the business he conducted on a day-to-day basis. Confucius, with his emphasis on the moral content of lessons, formed part of this universal belief in the practical value of history. One of the duties he promoted was the scrupulous transmission of authentic records. When, some centuries after his death, the unified Imperial state began to recruit its bureaucracy from among Confucian scholars, the recording of all the necessary information and careful preservation of records constituted one of the main functions of the Chinese government, both at the central and local levels. During the Tang Dynasty, a History Office was set up that became an indispensable tool of the government. The great mass of Chinese history was written by bureaucrats for bureaucrats. After antiquity, this appears to have become prominent again only in nineteenth-century Europe, when many active politicians and statesmen — such as Guizot, Macaulay, Mommsen, and Thiers — began to write history. But whereas Western politician-historians made use of history in order to explain what was currently going on, the main function of traditional Chinese historiography was to justify the dynastic genealogy or the continuation of the Celestial Empires mandated by Heaven — that is, in modern terms, to use the past to justify the present, the kind of history which Butterfield would call "the Whig interpretation."[12] The consequence of this utilitarian function is that Chinese history, as standardized by Si Maqian's *Histories* and Pan Ku's *History of the Former Han Dynasty*, includes not only records of imperial events, chronological tables, monographs, annals of vassal princes, and biographies of all sorts of famous and worthy people, but also observations of astronomical phenomena, hydrography, studies of geography, political economy and music, etc. The practice of history moved beyond its own realm into what today we call the natural sciences, and it basically came to serve as an Encyclopedia — in its true sense — to be consulted by the government. As such it was never intended to provide an organic narrative, as pursued by European historians, which is why it lacks, by modern Western standards, historical synthesis.

The characteristics of official dynastic histories significantly determined the traditional approach to art in China. In fact, Zhang Yanyuan, with his *Record of Famous Paintings* has often been compared with Si Maqian, who has been called the inventor of official history, as the initiator of Chinese art history. Evidently, the format and the wide scope of Zhang's book is largely modeled on that of official dynastic histories. It begins with three preliminary books of essays on historical developments and more specific subjects: it contains chapters on the vicissitudes of the art of painting in connection with the dispersal of both private and imperial collections and the destruction of the mural paintings in the Buddhist and Taoist temples brought about by wars and religious disputes; on the six elements of painting and the origin and development of different schools with reference to individual artists' training, their stylistic derivation, and their individual brushwork; and there are

12
Butterfield 1931; see especially the second chapter, 'The Underlying Assumption'.

13
Record of Famous Painters of Successive Dynasties. In *The Chinese Theories of Painting*. Vol. I, 99.

technical sections on the materials and methods used by artists; on how to paint mountains and waters, trees and rocks. There are chapters on connoisseurship, collecting, preservation, and appreciation; on colophons and private and public seals and the signatures to be seen on ancient and modern paintings. There is a section on the price of paintings.

Furthermore, there are seven successive books containing the biographies of painters arranged by their respective dynasties. Within each dynasty the ranking of artists roughly appears to approximate their official status, with members of the imperial court placed first.

Like Si Maqian, Zhang included an autobiography in his book, from which we know that he had been collecting works of art from his earliest days. Like Vasari, his Italian counterpart of seven centuries later, Zhang Yanyuan received a double education: both in writing and in painting. And like Vasari, Zhang was more accomplished as a writer than as a painter, which he attributed to the inaccessibility of ancient masterpieces. "Since I have but few genuine works of calligraphy, I have not been able to learn good brush methods … In Painting too my work does not come up to my idea of what it should be."[13] No single trace of his painting and calligraphy has come down to us, but his *Record of Famous Paintings* has become a lasting source both for art writers and artists in all ages. Despite all he said about the impossibility of seeing paintings and works of calligraphy, we have no more reliable sources of the history of art from the ancient mythical era to the Tang Dynasty; no sounder judgments about the individual artists are to be found in subsequent ages. It is no exaggeration to say that without this encyclopedic book, our knowledge of pre-Tang and Tang art, as well as the writings on it (Zhang's book provides source references, which is uncommon in Chinese writing), would be a complete blank and that all later writers have imitated and repeated the commentaries by Zhang.

What to modern eyes further distinguishes Zhang Yanyuan from all others, before and after him, is his historical sense. Remember that he lived in the mid-ninth century, brought up in a tradition that, paradoxically enough, felt strongly self-conscious about its past, but never really tried to explain it historically. This renders it all the more extraordinary that he was capable, as we will see in the following, to incorporate a historical or, to be specific, evolutionistic point of view into both his arrangement of the biographies of the painters included and his technical discussion of artistic matters! Given that art history as a whole in China seems to have been lagging far behind the West, for reasons which I will try to bring out at the end of this essay, it would certainly do injustice to Zhang Yanyuan in many respects if I were to compare his work only with early Western writings such as Lorenzo Ghiberti's *Commentaries* and even Vasari's *Lives*. After all, the scope of Zhang's book and the subtlety of his critical terms and arguments are incomparable. However, superficial though it may be, a limited comparison may be of some help in understanding the creativity and novelty of his work and appreciating how some ideas transcend time and space and present themselves universally.

Zhang Yanyuan's account of the evolution of Chinese art up to his own time is strikingly similar to that of Vasari. He surveyed this development from the point of view of a gradual improvement in painting skill as well as in representing natural life. Moreover, he associated each forward step and the establishment of particular genres with the names of individual masters, while also attributing artistic progress and decline to the exhaustion of artistic possibilities as well as to social and territorial changes. His very compilation of this work may have been part of his reaction to the loss of the works of art and the destruction of many mural masterpieces in temples (only known to us through his descriptions) during the Buddhist persecution of 845.

Take the example of his survey of Chinese landscape painting. He observed that all the famous paintings surviving from the Wei and Jin periods (317–420) which he himself had seen were rather clumsy. Pointing to the painting by Gu Kaizhi, he claims: "The peaks were painted like the teeth of a pearl-inlaid comb of rhinoceros horn; the waters were not flowing; the human figures were larger than the mountains; the trees and rocks were stiff, like stretched-out fingers and arms."[14] He then tells us that it was not until the beginning of the Tang Dynasty (his own era) that great painters such as the Yan Liben and Yan Lide brothers and Zhang Zi Qian demonstrated improved skills in painting buildings and trees and rocks. Regardless, "their rocks still looked as if they were sharply cut like cracks in the ice made by an axe, and their trees as if roughly engraved. It appeared that the more labor they applied to them, the more clumsy they became!" With the arrival of the master Wu Daozhi, "who was endowed by the Divine with an inspiring brush" and had a talent for keen observation of nature, came the next improvement in landscape painting. Since Wu Daozhi drew his landscape painting directly from nature, in his works "the rocks looked as though one could actually touch them and the rushing torrents as though one could actually dip into them." Thus, "Wu initiated this transformation and then the father and son Li Sixun and Li Zhaodao accomplished the genre. And with Wei Ou, the rendering of trees and rocks became exquisite and Zhang Tong finally exhausted its possibilities."[15]

But, unlike Vasari, who in order to glorify Florence as his adopted city (and, perhaps, his patrons, the Medici family) interpreted art history as a three-stage process (the rise of art in antiquity, its decline in the Middle Ages, and its revival in Tuscany, with the art of Michelangelo as heroic culmination), Zhang Yanyuan did not offer such an all-embracing theory, nor did he seek to praise the art of his own age. On the contrary he looked at his own era with a critical mind, hoping that the art that had been brought

14
Idem, 89.
15
Idem, 89.

to a decline by the barbarous acts he witnessed would be revived in the future. This is the main purpose of his writing, i.e. using the highest achievements from the past to serve as models for the present and the future. He did not only want to preserve, in words, the memory of the works of art (both those that had survived and those that had perished), but also to pass on to posterity the techniques invented by the old masters on every possible matter concerning art, as listed at the beginning of my discussion of his work.

This true historical sense only finds its distant echoes in much later developments. If for the sake of brevity we say that the Song period after the Tang was an age of art criticism and the Yuan period that succeeded it was an era of compilation, one might consider the Ming period as a time when the history of art was flourishing, notably because so many volumes of so-called histories of painting and calligraphy were written. However, a mere glance at their content, rather than their titles, will reveal that they are primarily concerned with connoisseurship and collecting, instead of with historical description. A genuine historical approach is only to be found in a personal collection of reflections on art by Wang Shizhen, whom Osvald Sirén in his *The Chinese on the Art of Painting* called "one of the best informed art historians of the Ming period" (Sirén 1936). Wang owned an important collection of paintings and had thorough knowledge of historical sources. His narrative is brief, but systematic, closely corresponding to the actual development of every genre in painting; his judgment of individual artists is perceptive and fair, without Dong Qichang's literate bias. Wang died in 1593 and Dong in 1636. After them, Chinese literature on art continued to flourish, but it moved more and more into the direction of monographs on specific subjects and genres and methods for painting and calligraphy—or, for that matter, pattern-books. Connoisseurship and the compilation of catalogues especially flourished in the Qing period. Among them the most valuable book is An Qi's descriptive catalogue of his own wonderful collection. What our forefathers named "Histories of Painting" degenerated further into a mere (sometimes hasty) compilation of artists' short biographies taken from the preceding writers, such as *A History of Mute Poetry*.

In this essay I have suggested that one of the main reasons why art history, as understood in the West and in China today, is poorly developed in traditional Chinese writings on art—while, conversely, connoisseurship, art criticism, and cataloguing are quite strong—is tied to its deep roots in Chinese historiography in general. This longstanding historical tradition aims to encompass all knowledge and has largely been geared toward moral and utilitarian purposes, as a governmental system that can be carried on through history, as a didactic instrument that can be put to practice, or as an encyclopedia that can be consulted, somewhat reminiscent of the eighteenth-century French encyclopedia. This particular tradition, however, was never meant to serve some rational plan or

pursue theoretical synthesis as a goal in its own right. At this point,
I agree with Butterfield who commented that Chinese historians
have focused on man's achievements and have refrained from seeking broader causal explanations. This was the main point inherent
in Chinese historiography on which "the early twentieth-century
new history movement," led by such radical reformers as the
ones mentioned at the start of this essay and influenced by modern
Western ideas, launched a devastating attack. As far as historical
narrative is concerned, if, as a Frenchman in 1599 observed, history
has passed through four stages (poetry, myth, annals and "a perfect history"), Chinese historiography never went beyond the stage
of annals; no coherent and organic narrative in the manner of
Herodotus or Thucydides was ever produced in China prior to the
twentieth century. It is obvious that the Chinese approach to the
development of art largely inherited its characteristics from its tradition of historiography in general.

Another reason for the weakness of the so-called "History
of Painting" is that in Chinese history few significant men were
involved in the subject, whereas many great literary and artistic
figures and historians—such as Du Fu, Ou Yangxiu, Song Lian,
Guo Xi, Dong Qichang, to name but a few—passionately engaged
in art criticism, art theory, connoisseurship, collecting, and artistic
practice. Apparently, this has to do with the moral function of art
that Confucian philosophy set forth, implying that a gentleman
should elevate his spirit and character through artistic enjoyment
and practice. But, as I would like to point out once again, the lagging behind of Chinese art history should largely be understood as
a product of the overall tradition of Chinese historiography. In
1993 my teacher Professor Haskell published a great book, *History
and its Images*. It revealed to me how eminent Western historical
writers—from Hippolyte Taine and Michelet to Burckhardt and
Huizinga—had consciously made use of art as historical evidence
in their interpretation of the past, which in turn paved the way
for, or even gave the impetus to, the rise of Western art history as a
humanistic discipline. This reliance on art has been marginal in
our Chinese tradition of history writing. There have been some disputes over the moral implications of the portraits of the great
men of the past, which go back to the Han period, and history as a
discipline has certainly expanded its scope by including *Tu Pu*
(illustrative pictures and atlases) since the Song period, while *Ji
Shi* (inscriptions on ancient bronzes and stone tablets) or even
decorative patterns on ancient mirrors and inkstones were increasingly used by Qing historians in their attempt to correct the cor-
rupt texts of historical books. But unlike their European counterparts, Chinese historians did not capitalize on the arts as historical
sources or documents to account for historical development or
progress in the representation of reality.[16] Consequently, the scholarly approach to art in China has taken radically different routes.
However, because of the emphasis on art theory, art criticism, and

16
See my own articles, The Validity and
Fallacy of the Use of Visual Images
as Historical Evidence. In *Perspectives
on Art History, Theories, Methodolo-
gies and Meaning of Visual Studies*, ed.
Cao Yiqiang (Hangzhou: The National
Academy of Art Press, 2007) 3–14.

17
Personal conversations with the present writer, October, 1997.

connoisseurship in China, together with the many treatises written by Chinese artists themselves, we are still left with an extremely rich legacy—one that, I believe, not only provided us with rich materials for our historical studies, but also with effective linguistic terms which, as Michael Baxandall[17] has claimed, enable us to address the visual aspects of art more adequately.

If we take world art studies to be a new form of the old idea of universal history, my argument in this essay underscores that its gains and losses for Chinese historiography in art are obvious. The perpetual dilemma of world art studies is how to render a universal or global significance to national art and its history without diminishing the importance of its uniqueness. It is here that the great historian Johan Huizinga, who from 1915 to 1942 was a professor of history at Leiden University, academic home to the editors of this volume, can greatly inspire us. Throughout his life Huizinga sought to stress the importance of what he called "aesthetic elements in historical thought." He regarded history as an intellectual form imposed by historians upon the past, which, in turn, produced and determined the different forms of history writing. Every civilization created and altered these forms according to its own peculiar style. So if our grandfathers discussed in this essay had known Huizinga's definition of the concept of history, they certainly would not have been so radical, but more rational towards our traditional historiography. Based on both their knowledge of history and their experience of historical research, they would readily agree with their great Dutch contemporary's view of history as "the intellectual form in which a civilization renders account to itself of its past" (Klibansky and Paton 1936, 9). This definition, I feel, has a lasting significance for our approach to world art.

REFERENCES

BUTTERFIELD, HERBERT. 1931. *The whig interpretation of history*. London: G. Bell and Sons.

HASKELL, FRANCIS. 1993. *History and its images: Art and the interpretation of the past*. New Haven, CT and London. Yale University Press.

KLIBANSKY, RAYMOND, AND HERBERT J. PATON, eds. 1936. *Philosophy and history: Essays presented to Ernst Cassirer*. Oxford: The Clarendon Press.

SIRÉN, OSVALD. 1936. *The Chinese on the art of painting*. Peiping [Beijing]: H. Vetch.

KITTY ZIJLMANS

The Discourse on Contemporary Art and the Globalization of the Art System

Having been considered a long time as a predominantly European affair, the discipline of art history changed considerably in the last decades of the twentieth century. Not only did North America definitively emerge as an important place for art historical research, especially because of the wide acceptance of French postmodern thinking; the focus also shifted from an emphasis on the work of art as a unique object towards a more dynamic field of art historical practices with a variety of aims, contextualizations, and interdisciplinary orientations. Critical awareness was raised by what since the early 1980s has been called New Art History. It comes as no surprise that after twenty-five years the "new" has become somewhat tarnished. However, New Art History has been crucial to the discipline for at least two reasons. The first is the shift it introduced in the focus of research to social context and power structures, to ideology, and subsequently to politics, feminism, psychoanalysis, cultural identity—topics and approaches often subsumed under the heading of "theory." The second reason is the alleged objectivity it brought in the research by taking the basic assumption that knowledge is constructed—that art history is produced, conveyed and maintained by art historians. Moreover, this

1

This question was central to the
Visual Studies Questionnaire of *October's* 1996 summer edition and has
been strenuously discussed ever since.
(Cherry 2004; Rampley 2005)

2

The concept of art of Niklas Luhmann,
or rather his concept of the art system,
includes all art forms, ranging from the
visual arts, design, architecture, literature and film to music and theatre.

change meant that the exclusion of the "non-West" from art history and the Euro-American attitude towards other cultures in general (Orientalism, cultural imperialism) has been subjected to criticism.

Its profound impact on the transformation of art history into a more critical discipline notwithstanding, New Art History has been challenged by such new scholarly disciplines as cultural studies. Despite its critical attitude, New Art History was still focusing on the time-honored canon of art works; and the so-called bourgeois gaze and the notion of art as value were still intact. Rather than prioritizing this limited subject matter of art history, cultural studies focuses on the analysis of cultural products in order to study underlying structures of social groups and the construction of cultural and social identities (race, class, gender, ethnicity). Nevertheless, however successful cultural studies was in gaining a foothold in the discourse at art schools and art institutions, in the last decade it has had to face up to the challenge posed by the new outgrowth of visual (culture) studies. Here, the focus shifts from the role of race, class, and gender in cultural practice to *visuality*, visual production, and the critical study of the history and theory of the media involved, which include photography, digital imaging, film, video, multimedia and the like (cf. Mirzoeff 1999; Sturken and Cartwright 2001; Elkins 2003).

Where does this leave the discipline of art history? Is it part of visual studies, or conversely, is visual studies part of art history, and/or are visual culture studies art history's good conscience and critical antipode?[1] In my opinion, these positions are less polarized than is sometimes suggested; the fundamental changes which have taken place within art history have provided enough firm art historical methods, which have been complemented by a wide range of theoretical positions and interdisciplinary approaches from outside the discipline of art history. This also applies to one of today's most pressing questions in art history, its global scope. In this contribution I would like to present German sociologist Niklas Luhmann's theory of dynamic social systems and related concept of art[2] as an evolving system in an attempt to grasp contemporary art as a global issue. First, however, I would like to sketch the hard road to acknowledgment taken by (contemporary) non-Euro-American art.

INCLUSION/EXCLUSION

It may seem a contradiction to what I stated earlier, but in Germany and Austria in the late nineteenth and early twentieth century, non-European art and the concept of world art were widely debated by art historians (see Halbertsma and Pfisterer, this volume). However, under the influence of rigid modernist thinking, everything non-European dropped out of the discourse, or in other words, was excluded from the canon of art history and the art his-

torical survey texts. Western art dominated the canon and filled up
the art museums, while the "Restern," predominantly what were
generally known as traditional and tribal art, was consigned to
ethnol- gical museums, at least this was, and still is the case in Western Europe. This Euro-American bias became particularly manifest in the post-World War Two era of political turbulence, decolonization, and the emancipation of the former colonies, when a
major contemporary, that is *modern* art production from non-
Euro-American nations emerged which demanded attention and
evaluation. Because of the inability to respond to this art production effectively, this partiality has become even more glaringly apparent with the increasing movement of immigrants to (in this
case) Western Europe. These new "immigrant-artists" and indeed
the second generation immigrant artists are facing a vacuum in the
art world. Often they are viewed upon as a synecdoche of the
country of origin and their art is confined to their alleged "own culture." Consequently, stigmatized by their "otherness," these artists
are left out of the dominant discourse. Conversely, when reviewed
within that context, they are often castigated as Western epigones.

In the climate of globalization, visual culture studies seem to
be the key by which to effect an escape from this deadlock because
it offers equal treatment of all visual productions irrespective of
their origin — but why should art history not do the same? Art history covers more than just High Modernist Art, under whose narrow-
minded, medium-related definition far more art of the twentieth
century was excluded than was ever included. Weighed on the
scale of a global art production, Modernism contributes only a
tiny fragment; but because of the Euro-American institutionalization of the art world and its subsequent appropriation of Modernism, it has become the dominant discourse. In addition, it seems
ironic that precisely at the time that when the world is facing the
emergence of a global modern art production, the notion of art
is losing its validity and is being replaced by "visual culture."

The replacement of the term "art" by that of "visual culture"
seems to offer too easy a way out. In the first instance, the modernist concept of art will not be challenged and will continue to be
constrained within the confines of its narrow definition. Outdated
and limited as it may be, in many cases it still is and will remain the
point of reference. Secondly, modern art may have been born in
the West, but that does not make it especially or exclusively Western. Adopting the reductionist view, modern art is denied the
enrichment of the fact that it was also nurtured by impulses from
other civilizations and that we are confronted with at least a plurality of modernisms or modernities (cf. Clark, this volume). As
Toni Maraini points out in her discussion of contemporary Moroccan art: "From its birth the modern movement saw itself as international. However, with the exception of certain isolated individuals, modern Western art has not been keen to admit into its artistic system (galleries, venues, museums, collections) contemporary

groups and movements from other cultures" (Maraini 1989). This is also the central issue in *Third Text* editor Rasheed Araeen's objection to the writing of the history of our modern culture. It is the possessive pronoun "our" which is problematical, as its scope is largely determined by who is using it and what it designates. In his opinion, and he has a point there, when reference is made to "our modern culture," it usually indicates the Western mainstream — white — culture, and the modern art canon, without any reference to contemporary "Other" influences on the development and constitution of Modern Art and consequently Modernism (Araeen, Cubitt and Sardar 2002). What is lacking is the acknowledgment of the "non-Western" contemporary artists' role in the construction of Modernism. Instead of seeing a multitude of sources and interconnected developments which contribute to make up the field of modern art, one single development has been isolated by Western Art History and is viewed as if it were autonomous; as if it were the sole development. In the opinion of Gerardo Mosquera, Adjunct Curator at the New Museum of Contemporary Art in New York, this Euro-centrism refers not only to the ethnocentrism exercised by a specific culture but also to the often forgotten fact that the worldwide hegemony of a specific culture has allowed it to impose its own ethnocentrism as a universal value, and for a long time has persuaded us that this is right (Mosquera 1992–1993). Consequently, this "sole" development has become overvalued; preponderating over the other ones (cf. the feminist striving for acknowledgment) and this trend has lead to a one-dimensional, simplistic vision of the development of modern art. Trading the concept of art for that of visual culture completely ignores this issue, and endorses only the exclusion of the other participants of the field.

In the eyes of Bourdieu, it is precisely this definition of the limitations of the field which acknowledges legitimate participation in the struggles. Denying the modern non-Western artists' share in the formation of modern art and Modernism is tantamount to refusing it a legitimate existence, excluding it from the game, excommunicating it (Bourdieu 1990). Simply incorporating the Other into the existing discourse will not solve the problem of dominance; the centre would simply expand its bulk by the expedient of gobbling up the other modernities, thereby denying their Otherness (in German "Andersartigkeit"). Taking this "own-ness" — not as essentialism but as a distinction and as self-description — as a point of departure presupposes that modern art is multifarious. Modern art did not emerge everywhere simultaneously, nor did it spring from one source. Every modern art development has its own genesis, tempo, and development process, and must therefore be viewed within its own past and to be envisioned within its own future. On a global scale, we see a dissimultaneity of comparable processes which are relative to each other and are mutually connected. Yet, the singling out of one development is precisely what happened.

PERIOD CODES

Few words have been the cause of so much confusion as the concept of art, loaded as it is with valuation, ideology, and institutionalization (cf. Nelson and Shiff 2003). Used in its reduced, specific (and relatively recent) Kantian meaning of an autonomous, self-reflective aesthetic, it is worlds apart from the more pragmatic use as a designation of a specific category of practices and artefacts to be found in all cultures of the world and at all times (cf. Dissanayake, this volume). By narrowing down the temporal concept to the modern period—as I shall do here—barely diminishes its complexity; rather it increases it by adding yet another complex notion, that of "modern." Modern, from which the concepts of "modernity" and "m/Modernism" are derived, is a problematic concept not only because of its wide use and potentiality of meanings, but also because of its rapid change in valuation within the humanities. From a positive connotation referring to resisting tradition and parochialism and favoring a contemporary, technology-based, positive and openminded attitude towards life, in the post-World War Two era it shifted to a negative implication of being exclusively white Western and male bourgeois-elitist, subsequently indicating but a small fragment of the cultural production. Again this seems to coincide with the emergence of the modern State in many of the countries which were going through the process of decolonization and/or the (re)gaining of independence, including the Central and Eastern European countries. Albeit often used indiscriminately, the concepts of "modern," "modernity" and "m/Modernism" only partly overlap (cf. Harrison 2003 in his concise survey of the concept of modernism).

Whereas modernism in general is used to refer to distinguishable characteristics of Western culture (the processes of industrialization and urbanization seen as principal mechanisms of transformation in human experience) from the mid-nineteenth until at least the mid-twentieth century, with the concomitant positive inclination to "modernize" and to experience "modernity"; in its more specialized and reduced sense it refers to the distinguishing of a supposedly dominant tendency in modern culture. The latter concept of Modernism points toward "high" art's aesthetic adagio "art for art's sake" set against traditional, academic, popular and other forms of art, and it is far removed from the concept of modernity as the indication of the patterns of change in modern society. These painters and their art are referred to by the adjective modern*ist*, not modern. To complicate matters, Modernist (with a capital M) is often used to signify a critic whose judgments reflect a specific set of ideas and beliefs about art and its development, a direction of thought which Greenberg commandeered, and which firmly established itself in the discourse of modern art. With the blurring of the various concepts, controversy about the meaning of modernism has become central to the debate about the meaning and value of art and culture (Harrison 2003). In the discourse on art,

3

To attempt to translate the German term *Wissenschaft* by the English term *science* is confusing, because the German concept of *Wissenschaft* refers to both the sciences and the arts as the combined scholarly field of academic knowledge, whereas science refers only to the natural sciences and not to the arts and humanities. I shall therefore refer to the science system with the German term *Wissenschaft*.

"Modernism" as the univalent and unifying period code referring to the Euro-American fine art production of approximately 1860–1960, is far behind us. Modernism, or rather the emergence of *modern* art, is a worldwide phenomenon, and its diversity and multiculturality confronts art history with an interesting challenge: art is global, why should art history also not be so? Precisely this question was at issue in the roundtable conversation held at the University College Cork in Ireland in 2005, which resulted in the volume *Is Art History Global?* (Elkins 2007). Besides the full transcript of The Art Seminar and a few essays which had been written in advance to distribute to the participants of the seminar, a large number of scholars who did not attend the seminar were asked to write an assessment in which to offer a consideration of the conversation from a distance. Hence the production of *Is Art History Global?* staged a truly international/global discussion on the subject of global thinking within and around the discipline of art history.

ART AS A SOCIAL SYSTEM

Seen from a metatheoretical point of view, the practice of art history is not part of the art system itself. Art history produces art history, not art—it observes and describes what occurs in the art system. To explain this relationship between art and art history, or in Niklas Luhmann's terms, between the art system and the *Wissenschaft* system,[3] I need to introduce some of the concepts which are basic to the idea of looking upon modern society as being differentiated into functional systems. Whereas the initial formulation of his theory in itself already consists of a 500-page volume (Luhmann 1995 [1984]), followed by a large number of extensive books on the various functional systems (and not counting the hundreds of articles), I can only touch upon the complexity and ingenuity of his theory. In my opinion, however, his concept of art as a social system, the art system's self-description and art history as an observation of the second and third order, can definitely be productive in understanding the relationship between art and art history in the era of globalization. I am not alone in this opinion. Since the translation from German into English in 1995 of his fundamental work *Social Systems*, followed in 2000 by *Art as a Social System*, the work of Niklas Luhmann is witnessing a growing acceptance, understanding, and application in field of art history (Halsall 2007; 2008; Rampley 2005; Rampley, forthcoming).

The emergence of what Luhmann considers to be present-day modern society (in contrast to segmented and stratified societies) occurs when, in order to be able to process the amount of information produced, society's ever-increasing complexity evolves into a differentiation into such functional systems as economy, law, politics, religion, education, science, media, and art. Luhmann built his theory of evolving social functional systems grafted onto the model of evolution of the Chilean biologists Humberto Maturana

and Francisco Varela, which describes the self-creation of biological living systems and their increasing capability of processing
complex information. In the context of a theory of evolution, it is
possible to show that changes within socially stable conditions
generate possibilities for variation and selection which are left to
their own internal dynamic and lead to a rapidly accelerating, self-
generated structural change (Luhmann 2000, 237–38). As a result
of this, various autonomous functional systems have emerged, and
mutatis mutandis an autonomous art system as the double-bind
effect of society's differentiation on the one hand and an internal
evolution within art on the other.

All systems realize operative closure and self-organization:
they are self-generating or autopoietic,[4] a term Luhmann adopted
from neurobiology. Each functional system is a particular operation and manifestation of society (of society's whole), a specific
function, and each evolves out of a specific communication as its
leading principle. The art system is seen by Luhmann as a *specific*
social system because it operates on the basis of a *specific* coded
communication which cannot be taken over by any of the other
social systems — after all, they all have their own particular function. The code which governs the art system is the binary opposition
of "beautiful/ugly." Not surprisingly, this binary code has been the
cause of much misunderstanding. The code "beautiful/ugly," however, is not fixed or immutable, nor is it ontological; it is a set of positions in which the one "side" (beautiful) means that the utterance
is successful for the art system, and the other (ugly) means that it
has failed for the art system. It does not mean that the one artwork
is beautiful and the other *is* ugly, but that the one utterance elicits
more response (be it negative or positive) than the other. From
this point of view, there can never be such a mechanism at work as
a *Zeitgeist*, a period code, or any other teleological force driving
society, since it is impossible to predict which utterance will generate reactions. The system operates in a highly contingent way.

Consequently, an *art* communication is not a political one; if
it is taken as a political utterance, it is part of the system of politics.
Because of a system's specific communication, each system distinguishes itself from the other functional systems; at the same time,
they derive their identity from their distinction from the other systems. In other words, the functional systems constitute each other's
environment (*System/Umwelt*). To determine themselves, the systems distinguish between "self-reference" and "hetero-reference."
This distinction takes place between the various social systems
(system/environment), as well as within a system itself. The operation of self-description (self-reference) yields the distinction between describing and the described within the same system. So, the
art system itself "decides" what is part of it and how it operates its
self-description. Below, I shall continue this line of thinking. Within
the context of this text it is not my aim to elaborate more specifically upon the intricacies of Luhmann's functional systems theory,

4

Autopoiesis, literally "self-making, self-
generating," means that the elements
of the system are produced within the
network of the system's elements, that
is, through recursions (Luhmann 2000,
49). To put it more simply: social systems generate themselves and develop
through communication.

but to focus upon the workings of the art system and the perspective on it from the viewpoint of art history in the context of globalization processes (cf. Luhmann 2000 [1995]).

Art, as a particular function of modern society, has evolved into a self-emerging, autopoietic system at an operative and structural level. Or to put it simply: society has left art to take care of itself, of its own communication, what it is about, to self-regulate, proceed, and develop. As briefly pointed out above, this does not mean that there is no interconnectedness between art and other functional systems; the art system—as all other functional systems—remains dependent on its social environment (system/environment distinction), and such dependency, for example of an economic nature, can increase. The art market is a good example. A specialized art market couples the art system and the economic system, but in this market, artworks are traded as capital investments or as extremely expensive goods. An artwork may be considered a masterwork because of its artistic value within the art system, in the economic system this valuation is expressed in money, not in laudatory words; as a financial communication it is part of the economic system. At the same time, however, the environment cannot determine what counts as art and how artworks will be judged. The abundance of communicative possibilities which emerges from this state of affairs can be processed only within the art system. This includes the problem of how the distinction between art and non-art is made on the basis of the system's operational code, and how it is to be controlled. It is left to the expertise of the art system itself to determine its own boundaries and not to a guiding hand, be that transcendental, political, or educational (Luhmann 2000, 314). The decision to see Marcel Duchamp's readymades as art was neither an art dealer's nor an art historian's. However, once this was established within the art system, Duchamp's *Bottle Rack* (1914), *Fountain* (1917) and other once massproduced objects and their resulting discourse became part of the system's self-description and were exhibited in art museums, traded (how many original readymades may exist?), and canonized into art history.

The mode of operation by which the art system generates its internal identity, is self-description, that is, description of the system by the system. This means that the system observes and describes its own operations (becomes its own theme), for example in the form of art programs, treatises, art theory, and criticism. These self-descriptions are observations of the second order: the system observing its own workings. Self-descriptions are not the sum total of all that is happening in the system, but are selective and contingent. They are also concerned with what Luhmann describes as "the question of how to relate to the past within a system that has become autonomous; how to mediate between past and future, between memory and the freedom to change sides, in all of the systems distinctions. ... The art of the past was no longer a model, an exemplary standard, or a reservoir of *paradigmata* or examples. Instead, it offered the possibility for a hetero-reference that does not interfere with the autonomy of art." He concludes: "The art of the past has become history" (Luhmann 2000, 303).

I find it intriguing to consider the question of when the art of the past begins to be seen as *history* as happens in newly emerging art systems. It implies awareness of the self, of identity and continuity, in other words, the emancipation of an autonomous, self-evolving art system which both regulates and observes its own "making." This occurs within the transition of society to a system of primarily functional differentiation, an order in which art must eventually claim a place of its own which cannot be determined by outside forces. Cases in question are the "new" countries of the European Union, as I shall discuss further on.

GLOBALIZATION OF THE ART SYSTEM

Communication systems do not stop at national borders or at the rim of a continent. As observed above, the occurrence of an autonomous art system is the effect of an internal evolution within art, which as such is part of the emergence of society's functional differentiation. These developments are doubly bound: art evolves into an autonomous system as an effect of society's functional differentiation, and society's functional differentiation occurs when its complexity leads to selectivity in the processing of information, and consequently to the emergence of functional differentiated systems. In this respect, the emergence of a global modern art production can be viewed as exemplary for the increasing functional differentiation of societies on a global scale. Following this line of reasoning, the rise of a modern art production (in Luhmann's terms: communication, and hence of an art system) in the non-Euro-American world, is not so much the result of the spheres of influence of this art, but rather of the development of an evolving functional differentiation of societal systems worldwide.

This does not happen everywhere at the same time, or in the same way. In Western Europe, the German Democratic Republic is a case in point. From 1949 until the fall of the Berlin Wall in 1989, the GDR was part of the totalitarian system of the Soviet Union. Referring to art under totalitarian regimes, Luhmann remarks: "Art has very few direct effects on other functional systems, and this is why society rarely responds to the differentiation and autonomy of the art system. It tends to attract attention when certain functional systems fail to recognize or accept their own specificity and therefore consider developments within the art system to be an encroachment or mistake that needs to be corrected. A notorious case is the reaction of the Catholic Church in the wake of the Counter Reformation or, more accurately, in the wake of the Council of Trent. Other examples are the political reactions of twentieth-century totalitarian regimes, especially in the Soviet

5
See the 2004 Edinburgh workshop "Art History in National Contexts: Structures and Institutions of Scholarship" of the European Science Foundation Network *Discourses of the Visible: National and International Perspectives* (DVNIP). See www.esf.org.

Union and in Germany under National Socialism" (Luhmann 2000, 181–82). But even under the rigid system of the Soviet-regulated GDR there seem to have been some stirrings.

In his systems theoretical analysis of the literature of the (late-)GDR period, literary theorist Ekkehard Mann cogently argues that militating against all repression and countermovements, even within the Soviet period an autonomous art (literature) system was emerging in the GDR. He takes as his point of departure the thesis that the Soviet-regulated GDR resembled a stratified, premodern society, but that especially in the 1970s yielding inexorably to societal change, the cultural domain was becoming polarized into various ideological parties—in what also seemed to be a generation conflict—and their different literatures. This was one of the incentives, Mann states, of the emergence of an autonomous literature system as part of an autonomous art system which ultimately set in motion the events of 1989. Mann sees the social function of this "Other" (autonomous, self-referential) literature for the GDR society as a whole precisely in this communicative limitation and restriction—literature as communication on literature, individual positions, complexity—which helped to set in motion the breaking up of the GDR system (Mann 1996). The case of the GDR may help us to understand the processes occurring in the many other countries of the former Soviet Union. It also shows that even under repressive systems "blood is thicker than water."

In the post-Soviet era, similar processes can be seen everywhere in such "new" EU countries of Central and Eastern Europe as Slovenia, the Czech Republic, Croatia, Estonia, Latvia, Lithuania and the like. Simultaneously with the unification of Europe, national and regional identities are consolidated, amongst other actions by the founding of art museums and museums of national history, by drawing up a list of national heritage monuments, and by writing the *national* art history, to underline the ownness of the country's cultural identity. Of course, these projects are made possible and stimulated, even commissioned by the Government, but for the internal state of affairs with respect to the content (selfregulation) of what is in- and excluded (self-description), the expertise is entrusted to art experts, (art) historians, that is, to an emerging *Wissenschaft* system, which parallels that of the art system. At the 2004 Edinburgh workshop "Art History in National Contexts: Structures and Institutions of Scholarship" organized by the ESF Network "Discourses of the Visible. National and International Perspectives," scholars from Slovenia, Estonia, and Latvia sketched the changes (and problems) in their countries in the post-Soviet process of simultaneously building up self-awareness and self-esteem, and becoming part of the EU.[5] It is an example of the dissimultaneity of evolving art systems that these countries are simultaneously struggling to forge national cultural identities and subsequently a national history and canon of art; the concept of canons of art are heavily contested by the discourses of the dom-

inant Euro-American art system and are thrown overboard. In
Western Europe and North America, the art system has established itself in the course of time in such a way it can permit itself
these self-questioning and even self-endangering discourses
without threatening its continuation; on the contrary, such debates
even underline the system's independence. In a more recent
emerging art system with a lesser degree of complexity, the situation is different. In such a new system, the art system's self-
description is aimed at building its identity in contrast to hetero-
reference, what is considered outside or other.

Comparable situations occur on a global scale. Within Asia,
Japan witnessed an emerging art system which began in the 1880s,
while its giant neighbor China has only very recently loosened its
governmental grip on the art production and regulation (cf. Clark
1998). In the post-Mao era the authorities have intervened time
and again when art got out of hand in their eyes. Notwithstanding a
degree of relaxation in governmental control under Deng
Xiaoping (1979–1997), in 1989 the Ministry of Culture closed down
the controversial modern art exhibition "China/Avant-garde" curated by Gao Minglu and Li Xianting. Supporters of the exhibition
were banned from any further art activities, curators were forbidden to work, and the magazine *Fine Art in China* was closed down.
Followed by the Tiananmen massacre on June 4, 1989, many
Chinese artists left the country (Erickson 2005, 19–23). Not until
the mid-1990s were the bonds loosened to create a situation in
which China could see the development of an autonomous art system. Too blatant references to sex and politics are still taboo —
in the exhibition catalogue *On the Edge*, Britta Erickson illustrates
this state of affairs by pointing out that the Ministry of Culture
claimed the need to approve of Britney Spears's stage costumes
prior to her tour of Beijing and Shanghai in 2005 (Erickson 2005,
31). These State-interferences do not have to prohibit the art
system to allow it to develop further into an autonomous, self-
generating system; art will find ways to skirt the forbidding finger
of authority, come what may. In China, the emancipation of the
art system has only been endorsed by recent developments in art
in which artists use shocking media (corpses) and express a fierce
resistance to "the West," ultimately to decide from within what
is art and what not. Contemporary modern art has begun to be included in the art system's self-description, and it will be an internal decision how the present state of affairs is connected to the art
of the past and to "hetero"-art and visual culture, and how eventually art histories will be written. However, there is another side
to the story.

During the 1990s, to the frustration of Chinese artists, the
outside world had a blind spot where modern Chinese art was concerned, a situation which contrasted blatantly the helter-skelter
rush to embrace contemporary Chinese art by the international art
world in the past few years. Whereas in the mid-1990s not a single

Chinese artist was listed as invitee for the prestigious Documenta X international exhibition in Kassel (Germany) in 1997, only two years later, contemporary Chinese art was suddenly catapulted into the orbit of the international art scene in the 48th Venice Biennale in 1999 at the instigation of Harald Szeemann (Fibicher 2005). A greater contrast would be hard to imagine. Only a few years before, the absence of Chinese artists on the Documenta X-list had prompted the artists Hong Hao and Yan Lei to fake an invitation for an additional, entirely Chinese exhibition allegedly adjoining the Documenta. Many Chinese artists responded eagerly, even incurred expense to be able to participate, and they were not at all pleased when they found out that it was all a hoax (Erickson 2005, 94–97). The "Invitation" (1997) is now presented at such exhibitions as *On the Edge* (Stanford 2005), and is seen as a conceptual artwork referring to the capriciousness of the dominant art institutions. Within the art system, the art institutions seem to have won an increasing authority; they are—contested though it may be—entrusted with the power to decide what is to be included and hence excluded of the dominant discourse. By incorporating "Invitation" as an artwork immediately signifies the "artification" of the protest, now creating and elaborating information about the art system *within* the art system, and the inclusion of contemporary Chinese art as part of the system's self-description. It also shows the contingency of the art system's differentiation and evolution. Unlike any other functional system, it has the capacity to integrate the most heterogeneous modes of operation into an "autopoietic functional nexus." In a way the art system is surprisingly isolated from other functional systems, and this might explain why modern art is capable of developing a symbolization of fundamental social problems of modern society. Art is a "playful" doubling of reality; this is both the result and the condition of its evolution, and offers a plurality of possible self-descriptions (Luhmann 2000, 178, 242).

ART HISTORY'S LOOKING AT ART

The need felt by the countries of the former Baltic states and the Eastern Bloc, and the same situation applies to former European colonies, to designate their own names (Slovakia, Estonia, Myanmar) in their efforts to build a self-identity as a nation-state, a related national art history, and their own canon of art is not surprising considering the age-old history of various occupations, subdivisions and rearrangements. It is also an example of the self-formation, self-description, and identity-formation of a society. The differentiation of the art system can be inferred from what it demarcates and specifies as relevant in the environment (in the cases in question, native vs. foreign). Some relationships become important, others are neglected and that means that distinctions are being made. By the mode of self-description, the art system generates its internal identity. Because of the art system's complexity and abundance, this is only possible when the system observes its own operations and distinguishes internal *leitmotivs*. These second-order observations do not describe all that is going on — that would mean a duplication of the grand total of the art system — but are selective (i.e. in- and exclusive) and contingent. Also, these processes are not directed from the outside; they are the reflection upon art within the art system which shapes its critical judgment. Because of the systems' own evolution, they differ at various places and times, and so does the distinction between self-reference and hetero-reference. Artworks constitute their own programs, modern art even in a superlative way by continuously challenging the boundaries of the tolerable as well as current systems of valuation criteria. There is an abundance of past art and art programs; in other words, the art system has history.

The availability and recollection of the past is connected to the emergence of art history as a scholarly discipline alongside the evolution of the art system, and both "demarcate an era by virtue of their operations and their observations" (Luhmann 2000, 230). Art history is a field of observation *of* the art system (from the point of view of the *Wissenschaft* system) and not from *within* the art system — not a self-description but a hetero-description. Apart from observing and describing the complexities and functions of the art system, art history also observes and describes its own operations, namely its methods and operations. This is an ongoing discourse. The "old" art historical methods such as style analysis, iconography, social art history, semiotics, and deconstructivist approaches and more recent approaches such as cultural studies and visual studies are all modes of observation within the *Wissenschaft* system: they all observe the operations of the art system but employ different distinctions. The point of departure of art history lies at what the art system communicates as art. In a globalizing art system, the concept of art differs and expands all the time. Art history needs to keep up by developing new approaches to grasp the changing self-descriptions within the art system. Leaving behind the long-ruling ways of the "old art history" marks the rejection of an identification of art with one particular style of self-description, that is reflection on unity rather than on difference. Difference invariably implies distinction, and how does the art system handle that? What is involved (artistically, politically, socially, and ideologically) when distinctions are applied, and what happens when they are changed? And, in addition, what does it mean for the scholarly field of art history?

A case in question is what Holland Cotter in his article in the *New York Times* of 30 March 2005 refers to as "Outside In," the "Non-Western art is being taken out of its niche and being treated as art first, non-Western second". What is discussed here is the complex problematic of changing distinctions and identity formation in the contemporary US art world and the role of the museums. Two distinctions are basic here, the "Western/non-Western" and the "high art/visual culture" distinction. Although thematized and discussed on a large scale, neither in fact has been dislodged; moreover, now they are being interwoven. Even when such a major museum as the Museum of Fine Arts in Boston recently opened permanent galleries devoted to the arts of Africa and Oceania and increasingly African, Latin-American and Asian art exhibitions are included as part of museums' programs, the dissimilarity between us/them (Western/non-Western) persists. Paradoxically both solutions proposed to remove this distinction can have a negative effect: either the two realms of the "Western" and the "non-Western" become one whole with the concomitant loss of alleged identities—and this is often seen as the triumph of the West because it is the dominant system which opens its arms to enfold the other, and so far there are no museums explicitly named Museum for Western (or Euro-American and so forth) Art; or ethnic/cultural-specific distinctions are emphasized, which at it best resolves in equal treatment of the various (non-Western) parties.

The latter has resulted in the rise of such museums as the Museum for African Art in New York, the Asian Art Museum in San Francisco, and the National Museum for the American Indian in Washington, to mention just a few. The last recently changed from an art museum into a cultural history center, designed for American Indians by American Indians. This change from art to cultural history makes sense in a way, as Cotter observes, because "many objects in question do not conform to Euro-American definitions of art as a passive medium of contemplation and exchange." There are pros and cons to this argument, but the fact remains that in doing so culture-differences are underscored and Euro-American definitions still prevail. Matters become even more complicated when contemporary art is concerned; where would a contemporary American Indian artist go: to the Museum of Modern Art or the National Museum for the American Indian in New York? Does s/he wish to be in the NMAI and/or would he be allowed into the MoMA? After all, the new Modern still celebrates the "art-object-speaks-for itself formalism," and according to Holland Cotter "a huge revisionist task [is] to be undertaken if the Modern is to fully justify its name." That would imply an "institutional acknowledgement of a global modernism, of which Western European and North American modernism were a tremendous important part, but only a part." To begin equalizing the collection of modern art, Cotter suggests stopping collecting vertically and to start collecting horizontally, which means "filling out the yawning international gaps in its 20th-century Modernist collection." However, the Western bias would still prevail because "the Other" would only fill in the holes.

Taken in conjunction with the evident globalization of the art system and the emerging awareness of art's cultural diverse practices within the realm of the museums, consequently art history will evolve into a globally oriented discipline, looking at and

reflecting upon the multifarious developments of art worldwide.
The discipline of art history has to assume equal tasks in reflecting
upon its methods and descriptions of in- and exclusion, to disen-
tangle the discourse which brought the discipline to where it is now,
and to deploy distinctions other than the ones employed previously.

REFERENCES

ARAEEN, RASHEED, SEAN CUBITT, AND ZIAUDDIN SARDAR, eds. 2002. *The third text reader: On art, culture and theory*. London and New York: Continuum.

BOURDIEU, PIERRE. 1990. The intellectual field: A world apart. In *Theory in contemporary art since 1985*, ed. Zoya Kocur and Simon Leung. London: Blackwell.

CAMNITZER, LUIS, JANE FARVER, AND RACHEL WEISS, eds. 1999. *Global conceptualism: Points of origin, 1950s–1980s*. New York: Queens Museum of Art.

CHERRY, DEBORAH. 2004. Art: History: Visual: Culture. *Art History* 27 (4): 479–93.

CLARK, JOHN. 1998. *Modern Asian art*. Sydney: Craftsman House; Honolulu: University of Hawaii Press.

COTTER, HOLLAND. 2005. Outside In. *New York Times*, March 30, Special Section on Museums.

ELKINS, JAMES. 2003. *Visual studies: A skeptical introduction*. London and New York: Routledge.
—, ed. 2007. *Is art history global?* The Art Seminar 3. New York and London: Routledge.

ENWEZOR, OKWUI, ed. 2001. *The short century: Independence and liberation movements in Africa 1945–1994*. Munich, London and New York: Prestel.

ERICKSON, BRITTA. 2005. A fleeting introduction to contemporary Chinese art. In *the edge: Contemporary Chinese artists encounter the West*. Stanford, CA: Iris & B. Gerald Cantor Center for Visual Arts at Stanford University.

FIBICHER, BERNHARD. 2005. Kulturelle Partnerschaften, vielleicht auch mehr: zur Rezeption chinesischer Gegenwartskunst im Westen. In *Mahjong: Chinesische Gegenwartskunst aus der Sammlung Sigg*, ed. Bernhard Fibicher and Matthias Frehner, 41–49. Ostfildern: Hatje Cantz.

HALSALL, FRANCIS. 2007. Niklas Luhmann (1927–1998). In *Art: Key contemporary thinkers*, ed. Diarmuid Costello and Jonathan Vickery, 187–90. Oxford and New York: Berg.
—. 2008. *Systems of art*. Oxford: Peter Lang.

HARRISON, CHARLES. 2003. Modernism. In *Critical terms for art history*. 2nd. ed., ed. Robert S. Nelson and Richard Shiff, 188–201. Chicago and London: The University of Chicago Press.

KAPUR, GEETA. 2000. *When was modernism: Essays on contemporary cultural practice in India*. New Delhi: Tulika Books.

KRAUSS, ROSALIND, et al., ed. 1996. Visual studies questionnaire. *October* 77 (Summer): 27–28.

LUHMANN, NIKLAS. 1995. *Social systems*. Trans. John Bednarz, Jr., with Dirk Baecker. Stanford, CA: Stanford University Press. Originally published as *Soziale Systeme: Grundriss einer allgemeinen Theorie* (Frankfurt am Main: Suhrkamp, 1984).
—. 1997. *Die Gesellschaft der Gesellschaft*. 2 Vols. Frankfurt am Main: Suhrkamp.
—. 2000. *Art as a social system*. Trans. Eva M. Knodt. Stanford, CA: Stanford University Press. Originally published as *Die Kunst der Gesellschaft* (Frankfurt am Main: Suhrkamp, 1995).

MANN, EKKEHARD. 1996. *Untergrund: Autonome Literatur und das Ende der DDR: eine systemtheoretische Analyse*. Frankfurt: Peter Lang.

MARAINI, TONI. 1989. Morocco. In *Contemporary art from the Islamic world*, ed. Wijdan Ali, 211–18. London: Scorpion Publishers (on behalf of the Royal Society of Fine Arts in Amman).

MIRZOEFF, NICOLAS. 1999. *An introduction to visual culture*. London and New York: Routledge.

MOSQUERA, GERARDO. 1992–1993. The Marco Polo syndrome: Some problems around art and eurocentrism. In *Theory in contemporary art since 1985*, ed. Zoya Kocur and Simon Leung, 218–25. London: Blackwell: 2005.

NELSON, ROBERT S., AND RICHARD SHIFF, eds. 2003. *Critical terms for art history*. 2nd ed. Chicago and London: The University of Chicago Press.

RAMPLEY, MATTHEW, ed. 2005. *Exploring visual culture: Definitions, concepts, context*. Edinburgh: Edinburgh University Press.

RAMPLEY, MATTHEW. 2005. Systems aesthetics: Burnham and others. *Vector [e-zine]* b # 12, http://virose.pt/vector/b_12/rampley.html.
—. 2008. Art as a social system: The sociological aesthetics of Niklas Luhmann. *Telos* [2008].

STURKEN, MARITA, AND LISA CARTWRIGHT, eds. 2001. *Practices of looking: An introduction to visual culture*. Oxford: Oxford University Press.

SUMMERS, DAVID. 2003. *Real spaces: World art history and the rise of Western modernism*. London and New York: Phaidon.

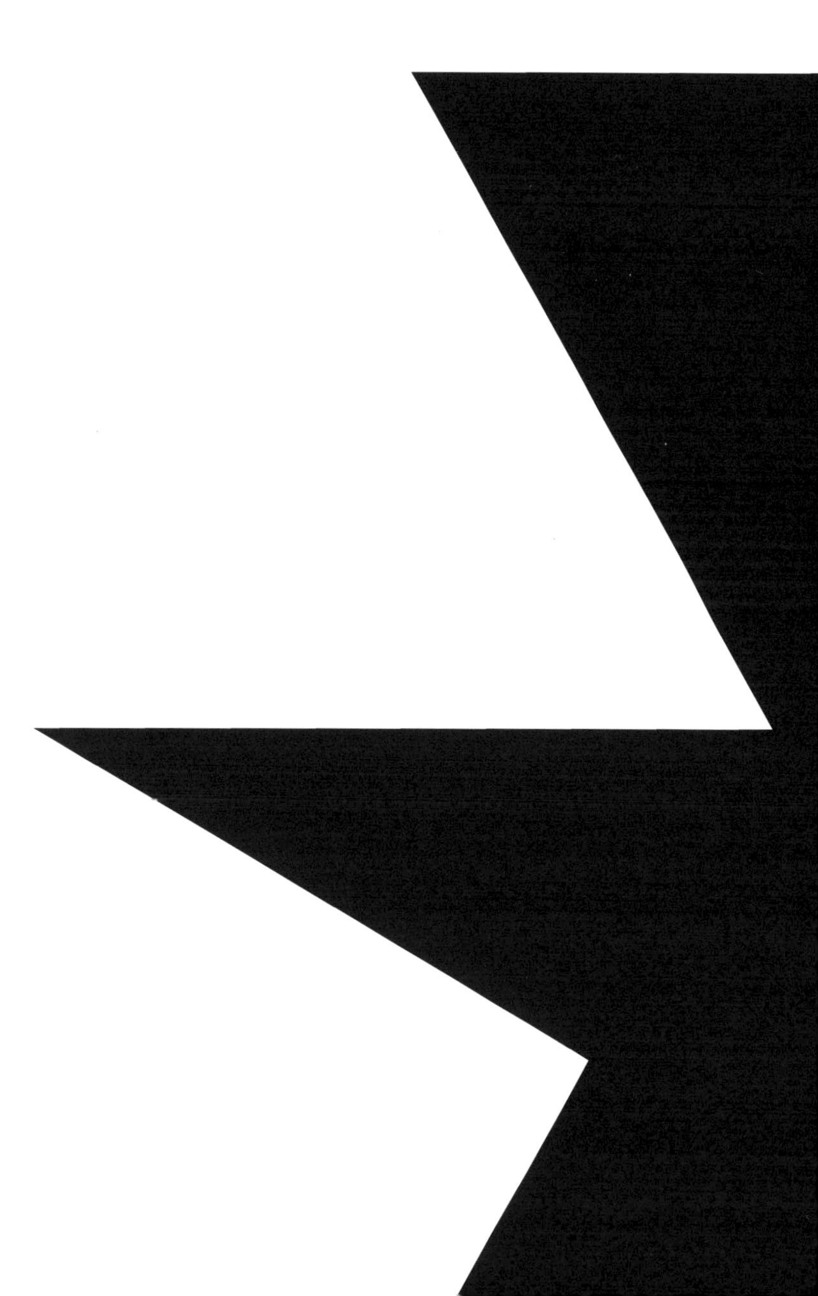

II

Disciplines Meeting: Multiple Perspectives on the Study of Art

Art and the Academic Disciplines

The study of the visual arts has traditionally been associated particularly with the discipline of art history. However, especially during the last one and a half century or so, art has also been an object of study in various other scholarly fields that each construe their subject matter somewhat differently, ask different questions, and apply different methods. World art studies proposes that we try to integrate the endeavors and results of these varying disciplines in order to thus enhance our understanding of the visual arts in human existence. By way of introduction to this admittedly bold objective, we may briefly look at some of the academic fields that have been concerned with the visual arts, with a few suggestions as to how their approaches and insights might contribute to the development of world art studies as a multi- and interdisciplinary, and ultimately perhaps, indeed, an integrative, transdisciplinary field of study (compare also Van Damme 2006 for a more systematic attempt to develop a transdisciplinary framework for the study of visual aesthetics worldwide).

Art history—taking this disciplinary label, in the grand scheme of things, in a literal but limited sense—may be said to conceive of art first and foremost as a historical phenomenon, both in the sense that attention is directed towards art forms of the past (usually in literate Western contexts) and in the sense that art forms are examined in a diachronic perspective. In response to the latter, art historians have developed various methodologies and sensibilities in dealing with questions that concern the development of style, and to a somewhat lesser extent, iconography and subject matter in art. In part by drawing on the research methods and insights of historical scholarship more generally, art historians have also acquired an aptness in addressing questions that relate to the interpretation of the various aspects of the visual arts in their historical contexts. Art historical research has been concerned with such topics as patronage, use, function, and contemporary reception, but in more culture-historical studies, too, issues of style and subject matter would seem to have predominated in conventional art history, until at least the 1960s and 1970s. This type of examination, while sometimes aimed at authentification and attribution, has resulted in rich interpretations that remain close to the visual object, analyzing and contextualizing its multidimensionality in a manner that often subtly combines form and meaning.

From the point of view of world art studies, one might examine how, and to what extent, art historians' expertise in making painstaking and compelling visual-semantic analyses of works of Western art could be applied in other cultures and related disciplinary contexts. Art historical methods have in fact already been adopted elsewhere for quite some time, especially in archaeology, a discipline sharing many of its historical roots with art history (for a recent discussion of archaeological dealings with art, see Corbey, Layton, and Tanner 2004). Art historical expertise in analyzing images is also called upon in various forms of visual and media studies, as well as in the related field of *Bildwissenschaft* in the German-speaking world. The relationship between art history and visual cultural studies is briefly addressed by Kitty Zijlmans in her contribution to this volume; for discussions of the development of visual studies and *Bildwissenschaft* as comprehensive multidisciplinary fields investigating visual images of all sorts, the reader might consult Sachs-Hombach 2005 and Elkins 2008, among many other recent publications dealing with the place and role of "visuality" in human existence from a wide range of perspectives.

Vernon Hyde Minor (1994), Eric Fernie (1995) and Donald Preziosi (1998) are among those who have surveyed the topics and interpretative strategies of Western art historical inquiry over the last few centuries. More recent accounts, stressing theoretical trends that have been in vogue during the previous two decades, are provided by Anne d'Alleva (2005) and by Michael Hatt and Charlotte Klonk (2006). They focus on the application in art historical analyses of a range of approaches that are collectively known as "critical theory" — Marxism, feminism, gender theory, queer theory, psychoanalysis, deconstructionism, and postcolonial theory among them. Art history may then be said to have to some extent evolved into a multidisciplinary endeavor, in the sense that it has increasingly incorporated in the last few decades perspectives that originally developed outside its own perimeters, an incorporation that notably includes semiotics as well. Reflecting the present-day opening up of Western art history to other traditions, d'Alleva, herself a historian of Pacific art, also explores in some cases the value of applying more recent approaches to the study of art forms outside the West.

Marxism had already influenced art historians concerned with the "social history of art," for example Arnold Hauser in *The*

Social History of Art (1951). The visual arts, their producers, patrons, consumers, institutions, and so on, have, from the mid-nineteenth century onward, also been topics of analysis for sociologists proper, Marxist or otherwise. Conceptualizing art as a primarily social phenomenon, sociologists of art direct their questions to the place and role of artistic practices in various societal configurations in both historical and especially present-day Western settings (with an emphasis on what are known as "art worlds").

In his overview of the sociology of art, Jeremy Tanner (2003) emphasizes that art history and the sociology of art share the same nineteenth-century intellectual roots, but notes that the two fields developed in separate directions during the twentieth century. As Barbara Aulinger has suggested in another survey, the sociology of art "is primarily concerned with the study of art as a means of understanding society, [while] the main aim of the social history of art is a deeper artistic understanding, and sociologists of art and social historians of art often stress the differences between their approaches" (1996, 915). The topics highlighted and the perspectives applied by social historians and sociologists of art in their study of the West could then prove inspirational to scholars examining art forms outside the West, especially anthropologists. These scholars may in turn enrich the examination of Western art by bringing into play the questions and approaches developed in their respective disciplines and areas of study.

Throughout the twentieth century, intellectual exchange between sociologically inspired students of Western art and anthropologists dealing with art in settings outside the West has been limited. This may be due in part to the lack of interest in art displayed by *social* anthropologists (one late but notable exception is Gell 1998), leaving the study of art to *cultural* anthropologists. Be that as it may, there is of course considerable overlap between the concerns of social historians, sociologists, and anthropologists of art, with all these scholars sharing a general interest in the socio-cultural contextualization of art forms, their producers, audiences, and institutions.

Two essays in this section familiarize readers with anthropological approaches to the visual arts. Richard Anderson provides a concise intellectual-historical survey of cultural anthropological studies of art and aesthetics, and points to potential future developments, thereby suggesting how the anthropology of art might connect to the developing field of world art studies. In her contribution, Paula Girshick elaborates on some of the themes that the anthropology of art has focused on particularly during the last two decades: cultural identity, cultural representation, and globalization — topics that are indeed very much still on the minds of anthropologists concerned with art (see Venbrux, Rosi, and Welsch 2006).

Readers interested in recent considerations of what it might mean to study the visual arts from an anthropological perspective,

1
It seems significant also that the highly philosophical *Journal of Aesthetics and Art Criticism* has recently devoted a special issue to naturalistic approaches to art and aesthetics (see Levinson and Robertson 2004).

may also refer to the various suggestions discussed by Wilfried van Damme (2003) and Maruška Svašek (2007) and in Westermann 2005, Morphy and Perkins 2006, and, specifically for the anthropological study of contemporary art, Schneider and Wright 2006. The volume edited by Mariët Westermann signals the growing interest of historians of Western art to engage in dialogues with anthropologists. This interest seems inspired in part by art historians' increased attention to the art forms of cultures with which anthropologists are traditionally associated, but it would also seem to reflect an increased emphasis on sociocultural contextualization in the study of Western art.

A discipline perhaps not readily connected to the study of art in most present-day readers' minds is geography, including human (or social and cultural) geography. Yet geographical considerations have accompanied Western writing on art from its very beginnings in Greco-Roman antiquity (from giving attention to the availability of raw materials to considering the influence of climate on art production). Having been unpopular during the last half-century or so, geographical and ecological approaches are regaining interest now that scholars have started looking at art from the perspective of planet Earth. These approaches hold the promise of providing refreshing insights not only into the materials used but also the style and subject matter of art forms produced in varying physical environments (see also John Onians, this volume). The conceptual tools of social and cultural geography, for their part, might be instrumental, for example, in analyzing the movements of groups of people and the resulting convergence of influences that characterize many forms of "diaspora art," both past and present.

Starting from the observation that the visual arts, in addition to being situated in time, are made in a given place, Thomas Da-Costa Kaufmann in his contribution to this section introduces readers to the "geography of art," its intellectual history, its topics of research, and its prospects. Elisabeth de Bièvre presents several case studies that serve to illustrate the value of a related, more specifically ecological approach that she introduces in this section as "green art studies." Onians's *Atlas of World Art* (2004) has recently highlighted as well the influences of geographical and ecological circumstances on the production and circulation of art objects.

The attention to available material resources and ecological contexts may be considered part of what might be called a naturalistic trend in present-day studies of art and aesthetics. This trend is perhaps seen most clearly in the increasing number of studies that in examining art-making and aesthetic response draw on the insights and approaches of one or more bioevolutionary disciplines such as neuroscience, ethology, and evolutionary psychology (recent examples include Eibl-Eibesfeldt and Sütterlin 2007; Onians 2007; Stafford 2007; Dutton 2008; and Scharfstein 2008).[1] Varied as these disciplines may be, what they have in common is that they conceive of humans as organic beings that are the products of bio-

logical evolution via the processes of random genetic change and
non random environmental selection. When applied to the study of
art and aesthetics, these various bioevolutionary approaches thus
proceed from the realization that both the creation and perception
of art are inextricably tied to the evolved human body-cum-ner-
vous system. This conceptualization leads to asking fundamental
questions that are clearly relevant to world art studies as the comprehensive examination of the visual arts in human existence.

For example, what biomechanical and cognitive-perceptual
properties of human beings make the production and perception of
art possible in the first place? When and why did these properties
evolve (hand-eye coordination, conjuring up mental images and
holding them in the mind's eye, planning ahead, image-recognition,
referential and associative thinking, and so on)? Do other species
also display art-like activities? How does artistic behavior develop
in human children? What is the nature and evolutionary origin
of imagination and creativity? To what extent have human brains
been programmed by evolution to respond stereotypically to
certain visual stimuli (not only stimuli that tend to induce pleasurable feelings, but also those that inspire repulsion, fear, or awe)?
How do artists the world over employ humans' in-built responses
to these stimuli? To what extent and in what manner do physical
and sociocultural environments influence the neural mechanisms
involved in the creation and perception of art? What are the
effects of making, using, and beholding art on the human brain?

The various naturalistic approaches to art and aesthetics,
while offering promising avenues to a better understanding of
fundamental dimensions of human art-making and aesthetic
response, are still in their infancy, and their development is being
critically monitored (see, e.g., Hyman 2006 on "neuroaesthetics").
Varying aspects of these approaches are further introduced by
Onians's and Ellen Dissanayake's contributions to the next section of this volume.

To a certain extent, these new developments draw on earlier
work in the psychology of art, another field of study that originated
in the nineteenth century, and one that has tended to focus on
experimental research in visual perception (e.g., Arnheim 2004),
with some attention being paid to creativity as well (e.g., Lindauer
1998). The art historian Ernst Gombrich applied insights from this
field in several books, including his cross-cultural investigation of
ornament, *The Sense of Order: A Study in The Psychology of Decorative Art* (1979). This analysis, being both interdisciplinary and
globally oriented in time and space, may be considered a pioneering study in world art studies.

Until very recently, the psychology of art only seldom took
into account evolutionary and neuroscientific findings on creativity and visual perception, but it is now catching up (see Solso 2003,
Locher, Martindale, and Dorfman 2006, and Martindale, Locher,
and Petrov 2007). Naturalistic approaches, taking as their starting

point the shared cognitive, affective, and motivational heritage of humans as evolved beings, are now also being applied in the study of architecture (e.g., Hildebrand 1999; Smith 2003), music (e.g., Peretz and Zatore 2004; Mithen 2005; Levitin 2006; Sacks 2007) and literature or fictional narrative (e.g., Carroll 2004; Eibl 2004; Gottschall and Wilson 2005; Flesch 2008).

At the other end of the spectrum — or so tradition has it — we may also ask how various forms of philosophy can be instrumental in coming to grips with the visual arts as a phenomenon in human life. Although Western philosophers of art have often claimed universal value for their propositions, at least implicitly, they have in fact based their reflections and analyses almost exclusively on Western art. As suggested in the introduction to this volume, an exception can be made for a few eighteenth- and nineteenth-century philosophers, at least to some extent. Their deliberations on art from outside the West may have been limited, but then so was the information available to them. Although Western knowledge of these art forms steadily increased during the twentieth century, Western philosophy paid little attention — developments in Western philosophy of art parallel those in Western art history in this respect.

Yet, as in art history, things have begun to change. The first present-day philosopher to systematically draw on data from a variety of cultures worldwide in his reflections on art is Ben-Ami Scharfstein, in *Of Birds, Beasts, and Other Artists: An Essay on the Universality of Art* (1988). Other philosophers who are breaking out of the Western mold and consider cross-cultural examples in their theorizing about art include Denis Dutton (e.g., 2006), who has a long-standing interest in the visual arts from "small-scale societies," Cynthia Freeland (2001), and David Carrier (2008). In addition to providing creative intellectual contributions to our understanding of art in human existence, one important role that philosophers may fill in the emerging field of word art studies is that of "theoretical watch dogs" who scrutinize the use of concepts, examine explicit and implicit epistemological assumptions, and monitor the methodologies being developed.

A quite different, although not wholly unrelated, contribution to world art studies from the field of philosophy comes from those scholars who study non-Western systems of thought concerning the arts and their qualities. Especially in the second half of the twentieth century, a small number of Western and Eastern philosophers started paying attention to the way in which artistic and aesthetic phenomena are reflected upon in Indian and later also in Chinese, Japanese, and Islamic traditions of thought. Known as "comparative aesthetics," this subfield in the philosophy of art continues to exist (e.g., Elberfeld and Wohlfahrt 2000; Hussain and Wilkinson 2006). Especially during the last decade, and frequently under the banner of "transcultural aesthetics," some philosophers and humanistic scholars have endeavored to extend this field to include the reflections on art and aesthetics of all human cultures in time and space (e.g., Benitez 1997; Marchianò and Milani 2001; Benitez 2005; compare also Feagin 2007); for an introductory discussion of this field, which was pioneered by the philosopher Scharfstein (1988) and the anthropologist Anderson (2004 [1990]), see Van Damme 2006, 171ff.

From the perspective of world art studies, it is then particularly interesting to examine the extent and manner in which systematic thought on the visual arts (including deliberations on art's origins, ontology, qualities, functions, and effects) influences the creation and use of visual art forms in a given context. Conversely, one might wish to examine, for example, specifically which artistic practices in a particular tradition are at the basis of that tradition's reflections on art. In this volume, Scharfstein exemplifies the new globally oriented approach in philosophical aesthetics by comparing the artistic principles of not only various Western and Eastern cultures, but an African tradition as well.

—WvD

REFERENCES

ANDERSON, RICHARD L. 2004. *Calliope's sisters: A comparative study of philosophies of art.* 2nd, rev. ed., 1st ed. published 1990. Upper Saddle River, NJ: Prentice Hall.

ARNHEIM, RUDOLF. 2004. *Art and visual perception: A psychology of the creative eye,* rev. and enlarged ed. Los Angeles: University of California Press.

AULINGER, BARBARA. 1996. Social history of art. In *The dictionary of art,* Vol. 29, ed. Jane Turner, 915–17. London: Macmillan.

BENITEZ, EUGENIO, ed. 1997. *The Pacific rim conference in transcultural aesthetics.* Sydney: University of Sydney. (free version available online)
—, ed. 2005. *Before Pangaea: New essays in transcultural aesthetics.* Special issue, *Literature and Aesthetics* 15 (1). (free version available online)

CARROLL, JOSEPH. 2004. *Literary Darwinism: Evolution, human nature, and literature.* New York and London: Routledge.

CARRIER, DAVID. 2008. *A world art history and it's objects.* Philadelphia: Pennsylvania State University Press.

CORBEY, RAYMOND, ROBERT LAYTON, AND JEREMY TANNER. 2004. The archaeology of art. In *A companion to archaeology,* ed. John L. Bintliff, 357–79. London: Blackwell.

D'ALLEVA, ANNE. 2005. *Methods and theories of art history.* London: Lawrence King.

DUTTON, DENIS. 2006. A naturalist definition of art. *Journal of Aesthetics and Art Criticism* 64 (3): 367–77.
—. 2008. *The art instinct: Beauty, pleasure, and human evolution.* London: Bloomsbury.

EIBL, KARL. 2004. *Bausteine einer biologischen Kultur- und Literaturtheorie.* Paderborn: Mentis Verlag.

EIBL-EIBESFELDT, IRENÄUS, AND CHRISTA SÜTTERLIN. 2007. *Weltsprache Kunst: zur Natur- und Kunstgeschichte bildlicher Kommunikation.* Vienna: Brandstätter Verlag.

ELBERFELD, ROLF, AND GÜNTER WOHLFART, eds. 2000. *Komparative Ästhetik: Künste und ästhetische Erfahrungen zwischen Asien und Europa.* Cologne: Edition Chora.

ELKINS, JAMES. 2008. *Six stories from the end of representation: Images in painting, photography, astronomy, microscopy, particle physics, and quantum mechanics, 1980–2000.* Stanford: Stanford University Press.

FEAGIN, SUSAN L., ed. 2007. *Global theories of art and aesthetics.* Special issue, *Journal of Aesthetics and Art Criticism* 61 (1).

FERNIE, ERIC, ed. 1995. *Art history and its methods: A critical anthology.* London: Phaidon.

FLESCH, WILLIAM. 2008. *Comeuppance: Costly signaling, altruistic punishment, and other biological components of fiction.* Cambridge, MA: Harvard University Press.

FREELAND, CYNTHIA. 2001. *But is it art?* Oxford: Oxford University Press.

GELL, ALFRED. 1998. *Art and agency: An anthropological theory.* Oxford: Oxford University Press.

GOMBRICH, ERNST H. 1979. *The sense of order: A study in the psychology of decorative art,* 2nd ed. 1994. London: Phaidon.

GOTTSCHALL, JONATHAN, AND DAVID SLOAN WILSON, eds. 2005. *The literary animal: Evolution and the nature of narrative.* Evanston, IL: Northwestern University Press.

HATT, MICHAEL, AND CHARLOTTE KLONK. 2006. *Art history: A critical introduction to its methods.* Manchester: Manchester University Press.

HAUSER, ARNOLD. 1951. *The social history of art.* London: Routledge and Kegan Paul.

HILDEBRAND, GRANT. 1999. *Origins of architectural pleasure.* Berkeley: University of California Press.

HUSSAIN, MAZHAR, AND ROBERT WILKINSON, eds. 2006. *The pursuit of comparative aesthetics: An interface between the East and the West.* Aldershot and Burlington, VT: Ashgate.

HYMAN, JOHN. 2006. *Art and neuroscience.* www.interdisciplines. org/artcognition/papers/15.

LEVINSON, JERROLD, AND JENEFER ROBINSON, eds. 2004. *Art, mind, and cognitive science.* Special issue, *Journal of Aesthetics and Art Criticism* 62 (2).

LEVITIN, DANIEL J. 2006. *Your brain on music: The science of a human obsession.* New York: Dutton.

LINDAUER, MARTIN S., ed. 1998. *Interdisciplinarity, the psychology of art, and creativity.* Special issue, *Creativity Research Journal* 11 (1).

LOCHER, PAUL, COLIN MARTINDALE, AND LEONID DORFMAN, eds. 2006. *New directions in aesthetics, creativity, and the arts.* Amityville, NY: Baywood.

MARCHIANÒ, GRAZIA, AND RAFAEL MILANI, eds. 2001. *Frontiers of transculturality in contemporary aesthetics.* Milan: Trauben. (free version available online)

MARTINDALE, COLIN, PAUL LOCHER, AND VLADIMIR PETROV, eds. 2007. *Evolutionary and neurocognitive approaches to aesthetics, creativity, and the arts.* Amityville, NY: Baywood.

MINOR, VERNON HYDE. 1994. *Art history's history.* Englewood Cliffs, NJ: Prentice Hall.

MITHEN, STEVEN. 2005. *The singing Neanderthals: The origins of music, language, mind and body.* London: Weidenfeld and Nicolson.

MORPHY, HOWARD, AND MORGAN PERKINS, eds. 2006. *The anthropology of art: A reader.* Oxford: Blackwell.

ONIANS, JOHN, ed. 2004. *Atlas of world art.* London: Laurence King Publishing.
—. 2007. *Neuroarthistory: From Aristotle and Pliny to Baxandall and Zeki.* New Haven, CT and London: Yale University Press.

PERETZ, ISABELLE, AND ROBERT J. ZATORE, eds. 2004. *The cognitive neuroscience of music.* New York: Oxford University Press.

PREZIOSI, DONALD, ed. 1998. *The art of art history: A critical anthology.* Oxford and New York: Oxford University Press.

SACKS, OLIVER. 2007. *Musicophilia: Tales of music and the brain.* New York: Knopf.

SACHS-HOMBACH, KLAUS, ed. 2005. *Bildwissenschaft: Disziplinen, Themen und Methoden*. Frankfurt am Main: Suhrkamp.

SCHARFSTEIN, BEN-AMI. 1988. *Of birds, beasts, and other artists: An essay on the universality of art*. New York: New York University Press.
—. 2008. *Art without borders: A philosophical exploration of art and humanity*. Chicago and London: The University of Chicago Press.

SCHNEIDER, ARND, AND CHRISTOPHER WRIGHT, eds. 2006. *Contemporary art and anthropology*. Oxford: Berg.

SMITH, PETER F. 2003. *The dynamics of delight: Architecture and aesthetics*. London and New York: Routledge.

SOLSO, ROBERT L. 2003. *The psychology of art and the evolution of the conscious brain*. Boston: MIT Press.

STAFFORD, BARBARA MARIA. 2007. *Echo objects: The cognitive work of images*. Chicago and London: The University of Chicago Press.

SVAŠEK, MARUŠKA. 2007. *Anthropology, art and cultural production*. London and Ann Arbor, MI: Pluto Press.

TANNER, JEREMY, ed. 2003. *The sociology of art: A reader*. London: Routledge.

VAN DAMME, WILFRIED. 2003. Anthropologies of art. *International Journal of Anthropology* 18 (4): 231–44 (adapted version published as Anthropologies of art: Three approaches. In *Exploring world art*, ed. Eric Venbrux, Pamela S. Rosi, and Robert L. Welsch, 69–81. Long Grove, IL: Waveland Press, 2006).
—. 2006. World aesthetics: Biology, culture, and reflection. In *Compression vs. expression: Containing and explaining the world's art*, ed. John Onians, 153–87. Williamstown, MA: Clark Art Institute.

VENBRUX, ERIC, PAMELA ROSI, AND ROBERT L. WELSCH, eds. 2006. *Exploring world art*. Long Grove, IL: Waveland Press.

WESTERMANN, MARIËT, ed. 2005. *Anthropologies of art*. Williamstown, MA: Clark Art Institute.

THOMAS DACOSTA KAUFMANN

The Geography of Art: Historiography, Issues, and Perspectives

Historical methods deal with events or objects (including art and architecture) chronologically, considering their antecedents, causes, and effects. But explanations of human actions or the man-made may also concentrate on their spatial instead of their temporal aspects. Approaches that consider spaces, locations, or other environmental features including climate may be called geographical.

A dictionary definition holds that geography is the "science of the earth and its life, especially the description of land, sea, air, and the distribution of plant and animal life including man and his industries." From this initial definition, it is evident that geography in theory may encompass all the world. Hence its immediate pertinence to world art studies.

Since the beginning of the twentieth century a more specialized area of human geography has also developed. Human geography (*Anthropogeographie, géographie humaine*) considers the impact of the physical environment on, and in general its relation to, human beings. This approach specifically deals with the man-made, hence the relation to culture, which stands as a complement to nature. A field of cultural geography thus also came into being:

it deals with the definition and spread of human cultures, however the term be understood, over the globe.

The conception of spread or diffusion implies a notion of a development that occurs in time as well as through space. Although critical reflection may distinguish between what Immanuel Kant deemed the basic categories of understanding (space and time), they are of course inseparable in existence; and an important school of cultural geography has indicated that considerations of geography can not be extricated from those of history. One of its founders already recognized that cultural geography was in effect cultural historical (Sauer 1963). It can also be argued that cultural history (including art history) is inextricable from cultural geography.

Geography has in fact intersected with many other discourses, and scholarship in several disciplines of the human (or cultural) sciences has proposed that a geographical accompany a historical method. For instance, a geography of literature originated when the idea of landscape, a concept that conjoins nature (land, earth, ground, and other environmental features) with human culture, was applied to literary works. Even though *Landschaft* was at first conceived in a way that questionable terms such as *Volk* or *Stamm* designated the determinants of German literature (Nadler 1912), the interconnections between history and geography have been discussed in relation to other literatures, notably Italian (Dionisotti 1967), and the notion of cultural landscapes (linguistic, literary, or artistic) has persisted. A geography of Europe's intellectual life has also been posed, an expanded view of geography in which thinkers are related to the social and political circumstances of the countries in which they lived (Mandrou 1978, 213–28). It has been recognized that even the seemingly universal enterprise of science occurs in specific places: recently an argument has been made that scientific knowledge has its own geographies, comprising the venues, sites, regions, and forms of circulation of scientific knowledge (Livingstone 2003).

All these and other products of human endeavor are manifest in forms of material culture. For example, literature and intellectual history are presented in books. Interest in the history of the book is growing, and this discourse might thus well be regarded as involving geographical concerns when it deals with such issues as the location of printing presses or the circulation of books (Darnton 1976, 1979). The geography of science entails attention to laboratories, gardens, and instruments, among other entities. All these have also gained increasing scholarly attention. But the study of material culture that most immediately deals with the relation of the natural to the cultural and hence most directly takes into account geographical considerations is that of (visual) art and architecture.

In general, considerations of space may be regarded as fundamental to architecture and art. Buildings shape the space in which they exist; they relate directly to their environment, which they in turn form (Scully 1991). The pictorial and plastic arts often strive to create the illusion of space, and consequently these questions have engendered a large literature on perspective and on the psychology of visual representation, among other things. In the twentieth century a widely read aesthetics or poetics of space was also excogitated that related human sensory experience of space to the response to objects and environments (Bachelard 1994 [1964]). Furthermore, a discourse on space in relation to art and architecture has recently been elaborated that stresses the distinctive character of the "sacred space" created near and around holy objects and sites; a new field of "hierotopy" has thus arisen (Lidov 2004). A newly published theory of space has been even more fully elaborated which argues that a world history of art may be founded on the thesis that the visual arts are all essentially related to real spaces (Summers 2003).

However, these theories do not bear directly on issues of the geography of art as described here, because artistic geography entails considerations of place. Although both space and place are notoriously difficult to define, the concept of place represents something more specific. According to one recently formulated distinction, places considered in art history may be distinguished from spaces as "definite areas distinguished from their surroundings by hominid construction" (Summers 2003, 117). In any event, the geography of art treats places as distinctive locations in relation to art.

Along with conceptualizations of history, geographical notions are inherent in some of the most basic ideas that frame approaches to the history of art and architecture. Objects are usually categorized with terms such as "baroque architecture" which relate them to historical epochs, whereby stylistic labels are utilized to designate particular periods. Yet they are also related either to specific (the School of Pont Aven) or to general locations (African art), indicating that geographical categories are also employed. Most often, of course, the two categories are conjoined (as in French Gothic). The idea that art is related to geography is implicit in such labels, whether or not they are explicitly analyzed. Throughout the historiography of art and architecture geographical ideas that have entered into these and many other assumptions about the place of art have indeed often been articulated, analyzed, and debated.

The geography of art may thus be related to cultural and human geography, and further defined. To restate some descriptions, the geography of art investigates how art results from or expresses a response to geographical circumstances, either directly, or in the way that such conditions have shaped human differences that have led to the production of distinctive kinds of objects (Kaufmann 2005a, 1–2). It raises such questions as how art and architecture are related to, determined by, or determine, or are affected by or affect the place in which they are made; how art (and architecture) are identified with a people, culture, region, nation, or state; and how art or architecture in various places are to be inter-related, through spread, or contact. It involves concerns about how areas of study are to be delimited, spatially as well as chrono-logically, in relation to a particular place (Kaufmann 2004, 7–8).

In the early twentieth century in the German-speaking lands the geography of art was conceptualized as *Kunstgeographie*, and was advanced as a field distinct from that of the history of art, *Kunstgeschichte*. While *Kunstgeographie* never succeeded in becom-ing an independent field, discussion of the geography of art never-theless seems to be regaining some of its vigor in the discourse on art and its history. Moreover, the geographical dimension of what came ultimately to be called art and architecture was discussed long before the history of art was conceptualized as such, and certainly long before it became institutionalized as a discipline. This essay presents a brief account of the historiography of the geography of art in the western tradition (although it is pertinent to Chinese historiography, as well: see Purtle 2005), followed by a survey of some of the basic problems with which it continues to be con-cerned; it concludes with an overview of some current perspectives.

HISTORIOGRAPHY

In the western (European and American) tradition, views of the relation of artifacts to their location have long been expressed in both proscriptive and descriptive terms. In the only treatise on the visual arts from antiquity that has survived intact, Vitruvius (Book I) called for careful consideration of the siting of a city or a building in relation to heat, moisture, water, and wind. He also correlated human physical and cultural differences with their geographical, that is physical, location and climate (Book VI, 1, 7ff). This thesis probably derives from the tradition of Hippocrates, who had argued (*Airs, Waters, Places*) that human temperaments were affected by climate. Hippocratic conceptions, whether mediated through Vitruvius or otherwise, later had an immense impact on architectural theorists since L. B. Alberti, who for instance stated that the site of construction should be selected ac-cording to climate, atmosphere, elevation, and water. They have also been echoed by a long line of thinkers (e.g. Bodin, Montes-quieu, and Taine) who have postulated that climate, location, topography, and hence materials available have affected human beings and what they have made (Glacken 1967).

The descriptive tradition of topography also originated in antiquity. Topography is defined as the configuration of a surface including its relief and the position of its natural and man-made features, and as the accurate or detailed delineation or description of a particular place or places. Topography is thus clearly related to geography, and already in antiquity it touched upon discussions of works of art and architecture. The origins of these discussions are seen in writings such as the description (*periegesis*) of Greece by Pausanias, which describes works of art and architecture according to the places where they are found. Their heritage survives to the present in the form of guidebooks or surveys of monuments.

This approach may be related to other modes of discussion in ancient Greek and Latin literature, where buildings or types of objects are associated with particular peoples or places. Authors such as Herodotus, Lucian (as in Περι του οίκου 5), and Athenaeus (*Deipnosophistae*) related art works to the peoples who had produced them, or according to the places where they had been made. The Roman writer Pliny (*Natural History* 35) also organized works according to where they were found or crafted.

However, geography is to be distinguished from topography, in that it ascribes importance to the place of origin or location in its procedure of characterization, and assigns place a role in the determination of the existence or appearance of a work of art. In this light, elements in Pliny and even Vitruvius may be found that more closely approximate the geography of art as it was to develop. Pliny classified painting according to "schools" (called *genera*), and he also elsewhere assigned historical significance to the locations where works of art originated. Vitruvius also offered some historical information related to geography, albeit briefly and in quasi-mythical form, when he discussed how the architectural orders had originated and were named according to the places where they had been invented.

Along with the topographic tradition (in the form of pilgrims' handbooks, for instance) geographical ideas connected with art—that climate influences the visual arts, and that buildings or types of objects are to be associated with particular peoples or places—were passed on through the middle ages. When some of the first statements which are usually identified with the origins of the modern historiography of art were formulated in sixteenth-century Italy, they also contained geographical notions. For a potential world art history it is noteworthy that even though the historiography of art has often subsequently taken on local dimensions, such views of art and its history, like other examples of early modern historiography, were also potentially global in their scope, in that they proposed a model of universal history which theoretically comprised all times and places. In his seminal *Vite*, as seen especially in the preface to this work, Giorgio Vasari thus outlined a universal history of the arts of *disegno*. Notoriously, however, Vasari distinguished the art of Tuscany and especially Florence from and above that of other centers; he treated the history of *disegno* largely as a narrative of the fate of the arts in Florence, often disparaging what was made in other places, most conspicuously that of the Germans (see further Brough 1985, 103–31).

Vasari's geographical prejudice evoked reactions from subsequent writers, who, even if they at times adopted his model of universal history, shaped their treatments according to the place where they were writing (hence the origins of histories of the arts in Bologna, Genoa, Venice, etc.). In the seventeenth century writers on art also began to adopt Pliny's ideas of genera for the notion of local or regional schools (Mahon 1947, 245ff), and these ideas later became standard in art historical discourse. Geographical explanations were accordingly often called upon to account for local or regional differences. Moreover, cases continued to be made for the causal effect of climate and geography on human society and culture, and hence on art.

Thus were laid some of the foundations for Winckelmann's history of ancient art, a work which, though not the first of its kind as it claimed to be, helped mightily to establish the discourse and discipline of *Kunstgeschichte*, art history. Winckelmann argued that Greek art had been determined in good measure by the Greek environment, because of the effects of Greek climate on the Greeks' ability to see and imitate the (nude male) human form (Winckelmann 1764, 19, 111). This sort of geographical presentation was also expressed elsewhere in later eighteenth-century discussions of art. The late eighteenth-century Swedish architect and author Carl August Ehrensvärd averred for instance that the nearer to Italy, and especially to Naples, the better art was, because Naples was closest to the qualities of Greek art, but the farther north one traveled, the uglier art and people became. Hence beautiful art was impossible in Sweden (Ehrensvärd 1925).

While not all thinkers shared such opinions, when more structures were constructed for the discipline of art history in the nineteenth century, prejudices in favor of the classical norm were of course widespread, and, more than that, geographical ideas often formed the basis for further arguments. For instance, the idea that art expressed the spirit of a nation or people found in a particular place, or that there was a spirit of a place manifest in art, became commonplace. The study of national characteristics in art thus became a major concern for art history. This also happened because the era in which art history was institutionalized in the form of university chairs and museums was one in which many modern nation states were founded, and accordingly nationalism grew. Works of art and architecture were thus often invoked in efforts to define the identity of newly invented states.

In the nineteenth century nation was also by no means simply a neutral geographical concept. Besides being related to discussions of climate, and especially of the earth and its political or physical delimitations, ideas of nation were mingled with those of race. Hence along with geographical location race came to be counted among the determinants of human existence and culture: the two are combined for instance in the philosophy of Hippolyte Taine (as "race, moment, milieu") (Taine 1964).

Thus it was that when a self-conscious *Kunstgeographie* was articulated at the beginning of the twentieth century, many writers wove not only physical and cultural elements, but national, ethnic, and racial determinants into the discourse of the geography of art.

Kunstgeographie drew from *Anthropogeographie*, as defined by Friedrich Ratzel (its counterparts are *géographie humaine* and human geography). Ratzel associated Darwinian notions of anthropology, such as the survival of the fittest and the struggle for existence, with geographical considerations of space. Ratzel also coined the idea of *Lebensraum* (Ratzel 1912).

Kunstgeographie of the earlier twentieth century often related the origins and spread of works of art to their physical circumstances as well as to the ethnic origins of people who made them. For writers on the geography of art continued to believe that along with the physical features of the earth, ethnic origins determined the limits and spread of artistic traditions. Both sets of factors were thought to delimit or determine cultural phenomena. Another basic method of *Kunstgeographie* was also formulated at this time. The geographer who coined the term *Kunstgeographie*, Hugo Hassinger (Hassinger 1912), stated that one of the methods of the geography of art would be the cartographic representation of the spread of the forms and styles of houses. The distribution of forms as indicated on a map was supposed to reveal essential features about the place of art. Adapting a standard geographic procedure, Hassinger was quite specific about the central role of mapping in the project of the geography of art, and cartography consequently became one its main methods. Scholars in many countries who espoused artistic geography thus argued they were applying this method when they traced the spread of artistic phenomena through maps (Kaufmann 2005b).

Many prominent scholars of the first half of the twentieth century, including Josef Strzygowski, Paul Frankl, Henri Focillon, and Dagobert Frey presented a variety of ideas or methods that may be associated with the geography of art. For many of them, as for other contemporaneous scholars, a basic concern of artistic geography was to determine the constants that existed in space over a long period of time, independent of history. These constants were associated with a city, region, state, or nation, and described as characteristic of a people (*Volk*), tribe (*Stamm*), landscape (*Landschaft*), or race. While not identifying themselves as geog-raphers of art, many other thinkers, including several associated with the second Vienna school of art history, such as Karl Maria Swoboda, Otto Pächt, and Hans Sedlmayr, shared such views of national constants, and some of their students and followers continued to advance them (Kaufmann 2004, 68–104).

In the 1930's some other important ideas were also promoted that have continued to resonate in discussions of the geography of art. In an effort to clarify the spatial concepts he saw being utilized in art history, Paul Pieper both reviewed the historiography of artistic geography, and proposed some outlines for its future study. He asserted that the geography of art sought for the cultural geographical laws that determined the spread of styles over a region from a cultural center (Pieper 1936).

Although before the Second World War several scholars sharply criticized treatments of art in relation to race or nationality (even Pieper, while ultimately utilizing the concept of *Stamm*, also rejected racial explanations), they could do little to stem other tendencies of the time, which were overtly concerned with national expression (as is for instance indicated by the theme of the international congress International Congress of the History of Art held in Stockholm in 1933). Nationalist movements and arguments and even more significantly beliefs such as the Nazi adaptation of the ideology of *Blut und Boden*, the Spenglerian thesis of blood and soil, tinged *Kunstgeographie* with an ideologically charged and often racist coloration. Disastrous consequences resulted, for much more than scholarship.

Despite the calamities of the Second World War, even afterwards many prominent scholars still continued to apply essentialist and racist notions of ethnicity in discussions of geographical questions. Among these, the nature of a continuing or constant national art continued to be paramount. Treatments of the Englishness of English art by émigré scholars like Nikolaus Pevsner or Erwin Panofsky in this regard bear remarkable resemblance to the continued and racist utterances of Dagobert Frey, who had been a Nazi propagandist and who was also reportedly involved in the destruction and despoiling of Polish monuments (Pevsner 1956; Panofsky 1963; Frey 1942, 1946, 1955; Kaufmann 2004, 86, 91ff).

Not until the later 1960's did a number of scholars including Rainer Hausherr, Horst Bredekamp, and Herbert Beck deliver a strong critique of *Kunstgeographie*. Pointing to the unhistorical and often racist assumptions that underlay them, they undermined the premises for previous premisses concerning stylistic or structural constants, unvarying climate, cultural landscape, and perpetual national or regional differences. They called instead for an understanding of geographical questions that would not project backward current national or political differences, but seek to explain the historic dimension and changing character of regions, and to find rational explanations for them. And in so doing they also called for a consideration of artistic centers and their involvement in the transmission of art, which occurred through workshops, the migration of artists, and the import and export of works of art (Hausherr 1970; Beck and Bredekamp 1975).

In the meantime, up through the mid-1960's George Kubler had been expressing a wide variety of ideas that also could have been potentially fruitful for the geography of art. Among the topics Kubler illuminated were questions of center versus periphery, of metropolis versus province, of city and region, of the difference between artistic and political regions, of artistic mixtures, and of the transfer of artistic ideas and personalities. Yet in his later work Kubler changed his focus. Until quite recently, moreover, Kubler's ideas have gone largely unheeded, except by a few scholars like Jan Białostocki (see Kaufmann 2004, 272–99).

In more general terms, a reorientation in thinking about geographical issues may be observed since the late 1960's from discussions of questions of the national in art to that of regional issues. This shift is noticeable in the choice of regions and regional styles as the theme of the 1969 International Congress of the History of Art in Budapest. Notable contributions to the discussion of artistic geography were also made during the 1970's and 1980's by Dario Gamboni, Enrico Castelnuovo, and Carlo Ginzburg, who helped redefine several issues (Gamboni 1987; Castelnuovo and Gamboni 1984; Castelnuovo and Ginzburg 1979). Jan Białostocki also published important essays on vernacular qualities (versus provincial ones), on the positive aspects of the artistic periphery, and on the Baltic area as an artistic region: in his treatment of the Baltic physical position, materials (or lack thereof, namely stone), and social background are deemed to be determining factors (Białostocki 1965, 1976, 1989).

ISSUES

These and other writings have left a legacy for the geography of art. Out of the plethora of potential issues, several questions in effect dominate recurrent discussions. Among these are notions of identity, regions, centers, metropolises, diffusion, circulation, and forms of exchange, or mixture.

One of the most debated is identity. A work of art or architecture may be said to obtain an identity when it is linked with a particular place, or time, or a particular artist. Identity is conceived geographically, when it is associated with a place, as in Venetian art. But this simple process also may become more elaborate, since it is also inherent in efforts to find geographical constants in art, cultural invariants that are to be associated with a location, a nation, or people. Much as the relatively unvarying features are said to characterize a landscape, so the characteristics that link a work with a place are often regarded as ahistorical or transhistorical.

Art historical literature continues to be haunted by such ghosts, among them the spirit of the place (Norberg-Schulz 1979). These may be found in the attempts to employ works of art as signs of a "visual culture," which may be defined in national or ethnic terms (Alpers 1983). Even if such conceptions occasionally assume historically specific characteristics, they still seem to depend from assumptions about a culture or ethnic group remaining identifiable independent of historical circumstances. Apart from inherent conceptual flaws, the history of the twentieth century should have sufficiently revealed the problems with such assumptions.

In any case, personality psychology and postmodern critiques have revealed problems with the notion of coherent identity. The term "identity" should be used in the plural, and historical investigations also suggest as much. For example, even notions of popular identity may involve a sense of membership in a nation, a region, a town or village, a craft, and finally a class (Burke 1992, 305). When identities are far from fixed or unchanging, to search for something as complicated and contradictory as national or even regional identity in art thus seems more than questionable. Many forms of artistic identity may exist in the same place and at the same time, making it difficult to define any single such identity.

Nevertheless, efforts may be made to try to find features of localities, their built environments, that are shaped by place as well as in time. One recent essay has suggested that there is a *longue durée* in the formal preferences found across styles in the history of French architecture (Guillaume 2005). Other attempts have argued for a distinctive character of Dutch cities and their art, which result from geology, geography, and climate and the history and commerce that these environmental factors support (e.g. De Bièvre 2005; also in this volume).

Cities may also be considered as centers, or metropolises. In regional geography, which is closely related to cultural geography, such cities in turn define regions. A region may be defined as an area dominated *by* a metropolis or center. Regions may thus also be considered to be provinces, in the sense that they constitute a province in relation to a center, a core, or capital; centers also imply the existence of peripheries found towards the limits of their influence.

This argument has offered geographers a fruitful alternative to theories that explained cultural forms as determined by race, ethnicity, or nation, and it has accordingly also been productive for considerations of art. Notions of center and periphery or province are of course present in much art historical literature, where the importance of sites such as ancient Rome, Renaissance Florence, nineteenth-century Paris, or contemporary New York are deemed important, and other sites consequently ignored, disregarded as dependent on them or provincial, or dismissed as geographically peripheral.

Art historians utilize such ideas in discussions of centers and peripheries. Informed by geography, other social sciences, and historiography, Ginzburg and Castelnuovo provided a cogent definition of artistic metropolises as places of innovation, where paradigms were first created that would come to determine the course of art. Artists, workshops, academies, patrons, and information determined the fate of these cities as centers of innovation and production, which stood in contrast with their peripheries (Castelnuovo and Ginzburg 1979, 305–6).

A problem here is one of perspective. For what happens to areas outside of Europe, or even areas in eastern Europe, which do not belong to traditional art historical discourse? They may be condemned to neglect, or second-rate status, even remain hard to define as regions, and historical developments in them remain hard to study (Bakoš 1991). In any case, just as political borders around states and regions change, so do political, cultural, and artistic centers. Metropolises change with time, and many centers do not last long. Like any locality, metropolises must be considered in relation to historical circumstances, and historical change. Their function may often change, and the production of art in them, or its importance, accordingly.

The conception of centers also assumes ideas about artistic diffusion. Diffusion is defined as the "spread of ideas or knowledge" from their origins to areas where they are adopted (De Blij and Murphy 1997, 12). Applied to objects, diffusion has long been a tool of the geography of art, and indeed has served art history as another way to express influence; as such it helps explain why in effect art does not remain constant, but changes in history. Art is said to be diffused from a center to its peripheries, as in the instance of Italian Renaissance art (and artists) abroad.

As art historians have increasingly recognized, however, concepts of diffusion may overlook several important factors. Diffusion does not account for local differences. That is because like the concept of influence the notion of diffusion concentrates on one side of the transaction, ignoring or underestimating the other. But reception is also involved in the process, and recipients are not simply passive. Cultural goods are assimilated in a variety of processes (Kaufmann 2004, 187–216).

One process affecting diffusion is circulation. According to geographers such as Paul Vidal de la Blache, circulation is a dynamic process by which regions change, as new ideas, techniques, materials, and persons are introduced into different milieus (Vidal de la Blache 1926, 349ff). In artistic geography notions of circulation involve considerations not only of dissemination but of the assimilation of artistic and architectural forms, subjects, techniques, and materials. These are circulated by artists, travelers, objects themselves, reproductions, and collections. In this way itinerant masons in the Renaissance, medieval pilgrims, gifts of Netherlandish paintings, prints sent to Asia, and conversely collections such as the *Kunstkammer* all helped circulate a variety of forms and content of art and architecture in early modern Europe.

Just as they are not static, and just as the milieu in which something is assimilated is important, these processes are not one-sided, either. Art history and art geography have thus become increasingly concerned with issues of cultural transfer, or better, cultural exchange. And in the process in which goods and ideas are exchanged, travel does not occur just in one direction. Hence conceptions such as transculturation have come to replace ideas like acculturation that were earlier linked with diffusion: accordingly artistic ideas are not simply regarded as being transferred to the Americas in forms of churches or paintings, but transported back to Europe, in feather paintings and conch compositions, or seen in the Americas to take on distinctive forms in the often discussed, seemingly hybrid artistic creations called *tequitqui* or *mestizo* that are found in viceregal Mexico and Peru. The terms with which these phenomena are discussed and the processes involved in them have touched off a lively debate (Kaufmann 2004, 272ff).

PERSPECTIVES

By the mid-1990s a broader revival of interest in questions of place and space had begun. The growth of interest has recently been evinced by a week-long symposium on artistic geography held in 2005 in Cortona. Previously, a symposium has explicitly revisited *Kunstgeographie* (Murawska-Muthesius 2000). A critical overview of the historiography and approaches to the field has appeared (Kaufmann 2004). The cartographic method has also gained renewed attention, marked by the appearance of several atlases, most notably in 2004 (Onians 2004). The preliminary choice of the question of national styles as the theme for the 1996 International Congress to be held in Amsterdam, although it was not ultimately accepted, indicates that even this issue could be revived. Perhaps a better indication of growing interest in all kinds of geographical issues is given by the submission of over ninety proposals to a section devoted to the geohistory of art at the International Congress of the History of Art held in London in 2000, of which a few out of the final selection have been published (see Kaufmann and Pilliod 2005). The theme of the 2004 congress in Montreal was "sites and territories" of the history of art, and that in Melbourne in 2008 focussed on issues of cultural exchange, hybridity, and world art history, and many issues pertaining to the geography of art were discussed.

Grand theories about geography and the environment have also returned to discussions of art, as more generally to histories of culture or civilization (Diamond 1999; Fernández-Armesto 2001). Strongly restating the argument for the existence of artistic constants, John Onians has traced them to Paleolithic origins (Onians 2000). In his introduction to a new atlas of art, Onians also argues that the production of art springs from man's biological nature, and further relates visual responses to inherent neural networks. Consequently artistic traditions are seen to result from direct responses to the physical environment, which provides a set of resources and constraints. These are interrupted and caused to change only by outside forces, military, commercial, ideological and religious (Onians 2004, 11–130).

David Summers has laid out an opposing case. While considering Paleolithic material, and much else, Summers argues strongly against the conflation of notions of national, regional, and ethnic character with style. He presents a powerful critique of the identification of peoples with characters in art, and against the derivation of ideas about culture from some particular essence (Summers 2005). Instead, he adumbrates his own grand theory of how style works by defining group practices and expectations as they are accommodated to spaces. In brief, Summers theorizes how artefacts interact with places—shaping and determining them (Summers 2003). The implications of these arguments for further geographical considerations of art have yet to be drawn.

However, most others writers on the geography of art, including authors involved in projects to which Onians and Summers have also contributed, demur from proposing overarching principles or general laws. Explicitly eschewing a grand theory of the geography of art, the present author has for instance called for attention to specific cases, for descriptive analysis instead of statements of laws, for a concern with places in which the historical and the transhistorical, that is change in relation to places of origin and circulation, would be studied. By reintroducing human agency into the equation, he has argued instead for a new conceptualization of the geographical in history, renamed the geohistory of art (Kaufmann 2004, 351; see also Kaufmann and Pilliod 2005).

Emphases have also been radically redirected in the geography of art. Rather than being regarded as marginal, areas that from one point of view might appear to be borderlands or frontier regions have been studied for their own particular qualities, and how they might cause the geography of art to be redefined (Murawska-Muthhesius 2000; Castelnuovo 2000, 15–66). The existence of distinctive and original forms of art on what is supposed to be a frontier has thus led to questioning the validity of the older model of center-periphery (Bargellini 2005). Beyond questions of centers and peripheries, a view of a "post-nationalistic geography" has also challenged the notion that there are clearly definable lines and networks of communication for art (Piotrowski 2000 and esp. 2005).

Perspectives onto a potential geography of art may also be derived from the maps in the new atlas of art (Onians 2004). Their cartographic representations suggest a host of topics for investigation. Among them are the location of types of monuments; the circulation of goods; objects and artists; materials used; their sources, and transport; the relation of trade and culture; trade and innovation; and correspondingly the distribution of centers and of wealth. While many of these subjects have been discussed in the past, the arrangement of the atlas suggests something different. It has been remarked that the structure of the atlas offers something new, and more truly global, by emphasizing contact between regions and cultural change rather than constancy as the objects of study (Silver 2004, 784).

These approaches point to a growing interest in the transregional or intercontinental aspects of global exchange. A large vocabulary has been created for them: negotiation, hybridization, accommodation, creolization, convergence (Burke 2003). And the products of cultural exchange, for which the evidence provided by Jesuit art and architecture throughout the world provides a particularly good example, have also been variously defined: as hybrids, mestizo forms, and much more (Bailey 1999). Cultural transfer engenders a variety of reactions: they may be negative, in the form of resistance (as revealed in Japanese *fumi-e* [Kaufmann 2004, 303–40]) or positive, in the form of adaptation seen in the creation of Chinese export porcelain. The end effects of such processes of transfer on a global scale have also been variously described: as resulting in counterglobalization, cultural bilingualism, cultural homogenization, and the creolization of world culture (Burke 2003). While the significance of all these ideas for cultural and hence artistic geography remains to be elaborated, in the end they suggest the existence of many new perspectives not only for the geography of art, but also for the foundation of a new world art history.

REFERENCES

ALPERS, SVETLANA. 1983. *The art of describing: Dutch art in the seventeenth century*. Chicago and London: The University of Chicago Press.

BACHELARD, GASTON. 1994. *The poetics of space*. Trans. Maria Jolas, foreword John R. Stilgoe. 1st ed. published 1964. Boston: Beacon Press.

BAILEY, GAUVIN ALEXANDER. 1999. *Art on the Jesuit missions in Asia and Latin America 1542–1773*. Toronto, Buffalo and London: University of Toronto Press.

BAKOŠ, JÁN. 1991. Peripherie und kunsthistorische Entwicklung. *Ars* 1:1–12.

BARGELLINI, CLARA. 2005. At the center on the frontier: The Jesuit Tarahumara missions of New Spain. In *Time and place: Essays in the geohistory of art*, ed. Thomas DaCosta Kaufmann and Elizabeth Pilliod, 113–34. Aldershot and Burlington, VT: Ashgate.

BECK, HERBERT, AND HORST BREDEKAMP. 1975. Die mittel-rheinische Kunst um 1400. In Kunst um 1400 am Mittelrhein: ein Teil der Wirklichkeit, ed. Herbert Beck, Wolfgang Beeh, and Horst Bredekamp, 30–109. Frankfurt a. M.: Liebieghaus Museum alter Plastik.

BIAŁOSTOCKI, JAN. 1965. Mannerism and the vernacular in Polish art. In *Walter Friedländer zum 90. Geburtstag: eine Festgabe seiner europäischer Schüler, Freunde und Verehrer*, ed. Georg Kauffmann, 47–57. Berlin: De Gruyter.
—. 1976. The Baltic area as an artistic region in the sixteenth century. In *Hafnia: Copenhagen papers in the theory of art*, 11–23. Copenhagen: University of Copenhagen, Institute of Art History.
—. 1989. Some values of artistic periphery. In *World art: Themes of unity and diversity: Acts of the XXVIth international congress of the history of art*, vol. 1, ed. Irving Lavin, 49–58. University Park, PA: Pennsylvania State University Press.

BROUGH, SONIA. 1985. *The Goths and the concept of Gothic in Germany from 1500 to 1750: Culture, language and architecture*. Frankfurt and New York: Peter Lang.

BURKE, PETER. 1992. We, the people: popular culture and popular identity in modern Europe. In: *Modernity and identity*, ed. Scott Lash and Jonathan Friedman, 293–308. Oxford and Cambridge, MA: Blackwell
—. 2003. *Hibridismo cultural*. Trans. Leila Souza Mendes. São Leonardo: Editora Unisinos.

CASTELNUOVO, ENRICO. 2000. *La cattedrale tascabile: Scritti di storia dell'arte*. Livorno: Sillabe.
—, and Dario Gamboni. 1984. Die Schweiz als Kunstlandschaft: Kunstgeographie als fachspezifisches Problem. *Zeitschrift für Schweizerische Archäologie und Kunstgeschichte* 41: 65–136.
—, and Carlo Ginzburg. 1979. Centro e periferia. In *Materiali e problemi*. Vol. 1 of *Storia dell'arte italiana: Questioni e metodi:*, ed. Giovanni Previtali, 285–352. Turin: Einaudi.

DARNTON, ROBERT, ed. 1976. *The widening circle: Essays on the circulation of literature in eighteenth-century Europe*. Philadelphia: University of Pennsylvania Press.
—. 1979. *The business of the Enlightenment: A publishing history of the Encyclopédie 1775–1800*. Cambridge, MA, and London: The Belknap Press of Harvard University Press.

DE BIÈVRE, ELISABETH. 2005. Alchemy of wind and water: Amsterdam, 1200–1700. In *Time and place: Essays in the geohistory of art*, ed. Thomas DaCosta Kaufmann and Elizabeth Pilliod, 87–112. Aldershot and Burlington, VT: Ashgate.

DE BLIJ, HARM J., AND ALEXANDER B. MURPHY. 1977. *Human geography: Culture, society, and space*. New York: Wiley.

DIAMOND, JARED. 1997. *Guns, germs and steel: The fate of human societies*. New York: Norton.

DIONISOTTI, CARLO. 1967. *Geografia e storia della letteratura italiana*. Turin: Einaudi.

EHRENSVÄRD, CARL AUGUST. 1925. *Skriften*. Svenska författare utgivna av Svenska Vitterhetssamfundet, 10, ed. Gunhild Bergh and Andrea Delen. Stockholm.

FERNÁNDEZ-ARMESTO, FELIPE. 2001. *Civilizations: Culture, ambition, and the transformation of nature*. New York: Free Press.

FREY, DAGOBERT. 1942. *Das englisches Wesen in der bildenden Kunst*. Stuttgart: Kohlhammer.
—. 1946. *Kunstwissenschaftliche Grundfragen: Prologomena zu einer Kunstphilosophie*. Vienna: Rohrer.
—. 1955. Geschichte und Probleme der Kultur- und Kunstgeographie. *Archeologia Geographica* 4: 90–105.

GAMBONI, DARIO. 1987. *Kunstgeographie*. Ars Helvetica: Die visuelle Kunst der Schweiz 1. Disentis: Desertina.

GLACKEN, CLARENCE J. 1967. *Traces on the Rhodian shore: Nature and culture in Western thought from ancient times to the end of the eighteenth century*. Berkeley and Los Angeles: University of California Press.

GUILLAUME, JEAN. 2005. Styles and manners: Reflections on the longue durée in the history of architecture. In *Time and place: Essays in the geohistory of art*, ed. Thomas DaCosta Kaufmann and Elizabeth Pilliod, 37–58. Aldershot and Burlington, VT: Ashgate.

HASSINGER, HUGO. 1910. Über Aufgaben der Städtekunde. *Dr. A. Petermanns Mitteilungen aus Justus Perthes' geographischer Anstalt* 56: 289–94.

HAUSHERR, RAINER. 1970. Kunstgeographie: Aufgaben, Grenzen, Möglichkeiten. *Rheinische Vierteljahrsblätter* 34: 158–71.

KAUFMANN, THOMAS DACOSTA. 2004. *Toward a geography of art*. Chicago and London: The University of Chicago Press.
—. 2005a. Introduction. In *Time and place: Essays in the geohistory of art*, ed. Thomas DaCosta Kaufmann and Elizabeth Pilliod, 1–19. Aldershot and Burlington, VT: Ashgate.
—. 2005b. Adam Miłobędzki: Mapping and the geography of art. In *Rocznik Historii Sztuki* [Yearbook of Art History] XXX , 23–30. Warsaw: Polish Academy of Sciences.
—, and Elizabeth Pilliod, eds. 2005. *Time and place: Essays in the geohistory of art*. Aldershot and Burlington, VT: Ashgate.

LIDOV, ALEXEI, ed. 2004. *Hierotopy: Studies in the making of sacred spaces: Material from the international symposium*. Moscow: Radunitsa.

LIVINGSTONE, DAVID N. 2003. *Putting science in its place: geographies of scientific knowledge*. Chicago and London: The University of Chicago Press.

MAHON, DENIS. 1947. *Studies in seicento art and theory*. London: Warburg Institute, University of London.

MANDROU, PIERRE. 1978. *From humanism to science 1480–1700*. Trans. Brian Pearce. Harmondsworth: Penguin.

MURAWSKA-MUTHESIUS, KATARZYNA, ed. 2000. *Borders in

art: Revisiting "Kunstgeographie": University of East Anglia, Norwich, 1998: The proceedings of the Fourth Joint Conference of Polish and English art historians. Warsaw: Institute of Art.

NADLER, JOSEF. 1912. Literaturgeschichte der deutschen Stämme und Landschaften. 3 vols. Regensburg: Habbel.

NORBERG-SCHULZ, CHRISTIAN. 1979. Genius loci: Towards a phenomenology of architecture. New York: Rizzoli.

ONIANS, JOHN. 2000. The biological and geographical bases of cultural borders: the case of the earliest European prehistoric art. In Borders in art: Revisiting "Kunstgeographie": University of East Anglia, Norwich, 1998: The proceedings of the Fourth Joint Conference of Polish and English art historians, ed. Katarzyna Murawska-Muthesius, 27–33. Warsaw: Institute of Art.
—, ed. 2004. The atlas of world art. London: Laurence King.

PANOFSKY, ERWIN. 1963. The ideological antecedents of the Rolls Royce radiator. Proceedings of the American Philosophical Society 107: 273–88.

PEVSNER, NIKOLAUS. 1956. The Englishness of English art. London. Architectural Press.

PIEPER, PAUL. 1936. Kunstgeographie: Versuch einer Grundlegung. Neue deutsche Forschungen 61. Berlin: Junker & Dünnhaut.

PIOTROWSKI, PIOTR. 2000. The geography of Central/East European art. In Borders in art: Revisiting "Kunstgeographie": University of East Anglia, Norwich, 1998: The proceedings of the Fourth Joint Conference of Polish and English art historians, ed. Katarzyna Murawska-Muthesius, 43–50. Warsaw: Institute of Art.
—. 2005. Between place and time: A critical geography of "new" Central Europe. In Time and place: Essays in the geohistory of art, ed. Thomas DaCosta Kaufmann and Elizabeth Pilliod, 153–71. Aldershot and Burlington, VT: Ashgate.

PURTLE, JENNIFER. 2005. Placing Chinese painting history: The cultural production of the geohistory of painting practice in China. In Time and place: Essays in the geohistory of art, ed. Thomas DaCosta Kaufmann and Elizabeth Pilliod, 135–51. Aldershot and Burlington, VT: Ashgate.

RATZEL, FRIEDRICH. 1912. Die Geographische Verbreitung des Menschen. Vol. 2 of Anthropogeographie. 2nd ed. Stuttgart: Engelhorns.

SAUER, CARL ORTWIN. 1963. Land and life: A selection form the writings of Carl Orwin Sauer, ed. John Leighly. Berkeley, Los Angeles: University of California Press.

SCULLY, VINCENT. 1991. Architecture: The natural and the man-made. New York: St. Martin's Press.

SILVER, LARRY. 2004. Review of The atlas of world art by John Onians and Toward a geography of art by Thomas DaCosta Kaufmann. The Art Bulletin 86 (4): 783–87.

SUMMERS, DAVID. 2003. Real spaces: World art history and the rise of Western modernism, London and New York: Phaidon.
—. 2005. Arbitrariness and authority: how art makes cultures. In Time and place: Essays in the geohistory of art, ed. Thomas DaCosta Kaufmann and Elizabeth Pilliod, 203–16. Aldershot and Burlington, VT: Ashgate.

TAINE, HIPPOLYTE. 1964. Philosophie de l'art: Voyage en Italie: Essais de critique et d'histoire. Ed. Jean-François Revel. Paris: Hermann.

VIDAL DE LA BLACHE, PAUL. 1926. Principles of human geography. Ed. Emanuel de Martonne, trans. Millicent Todd Bingham. New York: Holt.

WINCKELMANN, JOHANN JOACHIM. 1764. Geschichte der Kunst des Alterthums. 2 vols. Dresden: In der Waltherischen Hof-Buchhandlung.

ELISABETH DE BIÈVRE

Green Art Studies and the Local Subconscious

Why does art look different all over the world? Most of us are aware that the place where an artwork originates has something to do with the distinctiveness of its appearance. But we rarely give the place itself prominence in our explanations of this phenomenon. Instead, most academic disciplines which deal with art—whether archaeology, anthropology or art history—tend to see the object as embedded less in a place, more in a society. They thus explain the distinctive properties of objects in terms of specificities that are social and historical rather than geographical. They draw attention to political, religious, and economic factors, rather than to such conditions as geology, hydrology, and climate. They certainly never fully acknowledge the role of these conditions in shaping political, religious, and economic life in the first place; even less the possible influence on aesthetic preferences and technical choices. The social environment is treated as if independent of the natural environment, which of course it isn't. What we need is an approach that requires us to consider the influence of the local geographical environment on the economic, social, and historical context. That is why we need "Green Art Studies."

Green Art Studies does not deny the role of history, economics, religion, or society, but it does not see them as primary influences. Instead they are seen as shaped by the natural environment to start with. The distinctiveness of the natural setting of a place has to be defined before the distinctiveness of its history, its culture—and thus its art—can be appreciated and understood. Since during most of human history and even today the majority of people stay close to home, it is useful to think of "place" in terms of an area with a radius of up to about fifty miles. Clearly this is not an exclusive classification and where appropriate areas both much larger, such as an ocean or river system, and much smaller, such as a village or even a street, should be considered.

It is important to recognize at the outset that even geography has a history, which is why I talk of it being "long" or "short," by analogy with the "long" and "short" history of the Annales school (De Bièvre 2005, 88). The "long geography" of a place is defined by its geology below and its climate above, as well as the flora and fauna they support. These elements change over time either by natural interferences such as earthquakes, floods or draught, or by human intervention, such as building of dams or bridges, digging of canals or irrigation systems, deforestation or agriculture, war or internal legislation. That is what I call "short geography." I find it also useful to differentiate the "situation" of a place from its "position." The manner in which a community interacts with its environment is thus shaped by both the initial circumstances of its geographical "situation"—on either a river or coast, in the desert or in a jungle—and its geographical "position," in relation to other parts of the world, either facilitating or preventing interaction. It is these geographical circumstances that are in fact the prime movers behind the shaping of all social conditions, of history, of culture and so, too, of art.

Well aware that "art," like "history," is a far from universal category and should in each particular instance be clarified anew—like "place" itself—I want to define it here as "anything material, still or in movement, made or chosen intentionally or unintentionally any where in the world at any time by an individual or a group, to be of interest for its autonomous visual properties and the beliefs and values these may carry, whether aesthetic, religious or spiritual, secular or sociopolitical, private, public or otherwise."

GREEN ART STUDIES
AND ITS CONSEQUENCES

These definitions throw into relief further consequences of approaching art through the framework of Green Art Studies. One consequence is that it involves attaching a greater emphasis to the shared experiences of makers and users. We are used to seeing these activities as the separate prerogatives of the maker (or artist) and the user (or public/patron) in their respective, relatively active and passive roles. Green Art Studies, instead, requires us to stress what the maker and user share by living in the same physical and mental environment. Besides, each is conscious of the other. The maker not only usually has the potential user in mind, but also is him/herself one of the users in the habit of continuously making choices in a particular context. The user, on the other hand, by his/

her expectations and experiences comes to identify with the artist.

Another and more important consequence of adopting this framework is that it draws attention away from individual intention and instead gives prominence to experiences shared on the subconscious level (De Bièvre 1995). Our academic disciplines familiarize us with the conscious, as they teach us to use texts, the spoken word, and material remains to recover the beliefs and social systems of communities, which in turn are often broken down into groups categorized according to class, religion, gender, profession, family, lineage or kinship. The subconscious, by contrast, is an area with which we are ill at ease, which is why we frequently underestimate the extent to which a community is shaped by the sum of physical circumstances, both natural and man-made and historical events that it has collectively experienced. The fact that these circumstances often continue through time and that historical events are remembered across generations ensures that their impact is enduring and gives rise to a set of distinctly "local" assumptions. What Green Art Studies remind us of is the degree to which all these subconscious assumptions are profoundly affected by the natural situation in which they are formed. Every aspect of a community's life, from its economy to its social organization, from its food supply to its building materials, from its defensibility in war to its vulnerability to fire, flood, or drought, depends ultimately on natural resources. It is by these that the values and expectations, the hopes and fears of the inhabitants of any particular place are shaped, a collective psychology formed.

VISUAL EXPERIENCE AND THE SUBCONSCIOUS

It is easy to sum up the process in this way, but how are we to describe it in detail and in terms of its relevance to the study of art in its broadest sense? Clearly stories and other verbal commentaries have an important role, but when we talk of the subconscious we have to pay more attention to other forms of exposure, especially the sensual and above all the visual. In doing so we have to dispose of substantial obstacles, which have long hindered enquiry in the European tradition. From Plato onwards the senses have been repeatedly marginalized by a prejudice that placed them outside of and indeed in opposition to the intellect or mind, the superiority of the latter being made apparent by its exploitation of the medium of language. Plato's grading of the senses as inferior to the mind has until recently remained largely unchallenged in spite of Immanuel Kant's influential scheme reconfiguring the relationship between the senses, the intellect, reason and ideas. In Kant's system the senses are like perfect machines transferring perceptions to the mind, which then transforms them into verbal thoughts and ideas. In effect he brought them so close to other aspects of the mind as to lose their separate identity and strengths.

Not that the Platonic tradition went uncontested. Aristotle already recognized the vital importance of the senses and especially the sense of sight, which he called the "first gate of the intellect," and today his opinion receives the backing of the latest cognitive neuroscience. The link between the eye and the mind is now defined by a new understanding of the process of visual perception. For example, it is crucial that nerve cells in the retina of the eye do not go to the area of language production (Wernicke's area in the left posterior temporal lobe) but send their impulses to the primary visual area (the occipital lobe), from where networks lead to other areas of the brain. There the information they carry about objects and scenes is not just catalogued but acquires emotional associations either from the immediate context or from memory. Mirror neurons too, identified as such by a group of scientists in Parma, underline how we are inclined to almost automatically imitate things and beings we observe (Rizzolatti, Fadiga, Gallese and Fogassi 1996, 131–41). Whether or not the purely visual experiences are brought to consciousness and verbal articulation, they remain, all the same, as autonomous influences on each individual.

Many of these visual experiences are likely to find an expression in art, architecture and the other material culture of a community, where they in turn feed back into visual experience. Once captured in art in this way, they then serve to perpetuate and intensify the values and emotions out of which they arose. The forms this art can take and the responses it can evoke are as many as there are environments, art objects and observers all over the world. They may affect an individual or a group in a number of different ways: they may prompt hate or love, greed or revulsion; they may arouse or eliminate fear, sorrow or melancholy. They may inspire awe, amazement or devotion, even obsession or entrapment. They may terrify, console or pacify. And by any of these they may contribute to creating a state of either order or chaos. They also may give pleasure either by producing a sense of laughter or by stirring erotic longings or encouraging dreams. They may satisfy or intrigue by their sheer being and the consideration of beauty or the sublime. In this way they may anchor a sense of security and belonging or impose feelings of alienation and puzzlement.

These reactions are usually place- and culture-bound. Nudity means one thing to a Greek or an African, another to an Andean Inca or Arctic Inuit. Often the same object can evoke opposing feelings in neighboring populations because of differences in their ecology. The Great Wall meant one thing to the settled Chinese, another to the galloping Mongolian nomads. In Central Australia a rock sticking out in the desert may evoke the buttocks of an ancestor from the Dreamtime and so respect, while in central, agricultural Italy a rock in the field will stand as a hindrance to the plough and will be removed in disgust. Any sign of water in the Arabian dessert will be treated with the utmost reverence, while a Dutch person will see water as an ambivalent resource to dominate and to exploit. For the same reasons, dreams and even erotic reveries differ from place to place. A person in the Congo will probably conjure up large bodies, while a Southern Californian may be haunted by images of slender creatures. All these reactions are — of course — not a straightforward product of a cause and effect relationship, but are a result of the interplay between nature, time, and culture.

THE GEOGRAPHY OF ART: HISTORIC PROBLEMS

The need for Green Art Studies as proposed here emerges most forcefully out of a review of art geography such as Thomas DaCosta Kaufmann has presented most recently. In the excellent overview of the literature in his *Toward a Geography of Art* (2004) he highlights the length and the strength of the European tradition of so-called art geography.[1] During classical Antiquity the predominant emphasis was on categorization in terms of race/tribe, language, region, state, or city. Hence Vitruvius' identification of architecture as Doric, Ionic, or Corinthian, Cicero's differentiation of rhetoric as Attic or Asiatic and Pliny's distinction between Helladic, Asiatic, and Sicyonian painting. If there is a common theme it is one of cultural difference. Problems arise with the associations evoked by the terms used for describing these differences. These often depend on the value systems of the author, as with Cicero relating Attic with elegance and Asiatic with opulence. In a similar spirit, in sixteenth century Italy Vasari and others differentiate Florentine and Venetian painting, identifying one with line and the other with color. Implicit values intertwined with these epithets remain un-outspoken. However, what for Cicero is positive, may for his Asiatic counterpart be negative, and vice-versa. Neither is the question posed why a particular place at a particular time becomes interested in a particular style, be it elegant or opulent, linear or colorful. While each author categorizes a group of works of art under a stylistic common denominator and gives the style a geographical name — Attic, Asiatic, Florentine, Venetian — none of them enters into a more elaborate discussion of the various factors which make each place unique and which influence the outlook and expectations of the local population and thus their cultures.

Only by the eighteenth century were natural factors taken into serious consideration in cultural analysis. Although Charles-Louis de Montesquieu in his *De l'esprit des lois* (1748) saw climate and soil as major influences on societies, he did not discuss art. Similarly, Johann Winckelmann (1764) does not elaborate on many different facets of the environment when proposing that the excellence of marble statues in Greece was due to its climate, the warm sun allowing Greek people to walk around without clothes. Although the French thinker Hippolyte Taine (1866; 1869) and others in the nineteenth century widened the subject, they were still generalizing. Some writers didn't go far enough, others went

1
Only in his work of 2005 jointly edited with E. Pilliod (2005) Kaufmann has adopted the term geohistory of art and thus accepts the possibility of discussing culture in simultaneous chronological and geographical term.

2
Ehrensvärd quoted in Kaufmann 2004.
Ehrensvärd's evaluative ideas were first
attacked by Castelnuovo and Ginzberg
1979. See also Hadjinicolaou 1983,
36–56.

too far. The latter applies to the so-called "Blut und Boden" approach as it was advocated in the twentieth century by Strzygowski (1918), Spengler (1923) and others, with its disastrous connotations in relation to Nazi racial politics. This approach gives a primary role to the geographical conditions of the earth as unchanging determinants both for peoples or races and their art production. Clearly shunning such reductivist explanations, Green Art Studies rather seeks to analyze the lively relationship between constantly changing geographical conditions, altering historical inputs, and the local art production.

Some of the descriptive categories of which Green Art Studies is equally skeptical are the stylistic names used by early modern and modern art historians. Terms such as Classical, Romanesque, Gothic, Renaissance, Impressionist, Modernist, refer principally to formal traits. They may carry political or cultural associations, but are seldom connected with causes in the natural environment. They are also problematic in terms of Green Art Studies for being normative and hierarchic. Any reference to a Gothic or Modernist work is likely to imply that there is a prototypical work of that style to which all others can be related, usually as derivatives or lesser examples. They also assume regional norms. A Gothic or Impressionist work in Paris may thus be seen as the standard by which all others are judged. In this they share a weakness with the general concepts of "centre" and "periphery."[2] The "centre," where a style originates and is represented at its most pure, is usually the economic, political, and militarily most powerful place. The "periphery," on the other hand, often carries derogatory connotations: it may be territory conquered or colonized by a "centre" or may just be remote geographically and isolated economically. The "periphery" typically uses the stylistic features of the "centre" in a way that is considered either impure or imperfect, in either case inferior to the original, central canon. Since art can represent peoples, so-called "peripheral" or "impure" works of art can too easily be identified with "peripheral" or "impure" peoples. Other concepts related to the "centre" and "periphery" classification, which are employed by twentieth century art historians such as diffusion and the idea of the "metropolis," have to be treated with similar caution. In analyzing any work, which seems to be influenced by imported (or "diffused") forms and ideas, the observer can either concentrate exclusively on these or more judiciously pay equal attention to that which is discernibly local. Many of these problems are now acknowledged. For example, the importance of local components in so-called colonial art and architecture has recently been recognized and these are now valued as highly as the imported ones or even recognized as dominant. After all, in most relationships both the roles and the labels of "master" and "slave" are interchangeable.

This, though, still understates the power of place, the focus of Green Art Studies. The main reason for avoiding both the concept of hierarchy in "centre" and "periphery" and the inversion of that hierarchy in recent critiques, is that we need to pay more attention to the impact that each environment has on its production regardless of its social prestige. Besides, even when hierarchies are addressed they should be seen as principally local in their formation and neither regional nor universal. Equally distracting are the often connected assumptions in relation to quality. These Green Art Studies sets aside until it has analyzed all "green" circumstances surrounding the genesis of the object. Since all values emerge out of particular environments, it is with these local values that Green Art Studies is primarily concerned. This is why it seeks to promote the analysis and study of those categories of criticism which each community — consciously or subconsciously — uses for making and understanding its own objects, instead of just applying categories of evaluation conceived in the European tradition.

GREEN ART STUDIES: THE TEST CASE OF THE SEVENTEENTH CENTURY NORTHERN NETHERLANDS

It is possible, indeed desirable, to apply the Green Art Studies approach to the art of all areas of the world, but it may be helpful in the first instance to try it out in one, as an example. The art of the seventeenth century Northern Netherlands is a particularly appropriate and challenging test case. There are two reasons for this. One is that the art of this area is usually seen as a single phenomenon, so-called Dutch Art. The other is that this "Dutch Art" is explained in principally social terms. Both these tendencies come out in the two most admired recent works on the topic by Svetlana Alpers and Simon Schama (Alpers 1983; Schama 1987). What Green Art Studies reveals is that there is no single phenomenon, Dutch Art, but rather a set of different arts of different cities, such as Leiden, Delft, Amsterdam, etc.[3] What it also brings to the fore is that although there is social differentiation between the cities, this differentiation is not a result of different social systems as such but has its roots in their geographies, both "long" and "short," and in their "situation" and "position," which were in each case different.

These cities in and around the delta of the rivers Rhine and Maas are sometimes not further apart then twenty miles, but each grew out of different geologies and geographical situations and each developed different cultural patterns, most strikingly during the seventeenth century. Admittedly they all generated large painting productions (Van der Woude 1991) but detailed scrutiny of these reveals that in each town production is in a different idiom. Characteristic attributes of these paintings, such as the format, technique, the use of material, use of color, use of perspective, and choice of subject matter, were particular to the city where they were manufactured and for more than 60% bought (Montias 1991, 347). These characteristic features, which were informed by the

3
Exhibitions and exhibition catalogues on the seventeenth century painting production of separate cities have been organized over the last twenty years. However, in none of these enterprises connections are made between the long and short geographical data and the geographical situation and position of the cities and different aspects of their art production.

4
For specialized maps see: Stichting
Wetenschappelijke Atlas van Neder-
land, *Atlas van Nederland*, The Hague:
Staatsuitgeverij 1963–1977.

taste of the buyer, the practice of the studios and the native tradition—all of which need to be studied in their own right—can be
connected to local circumstances, both natural and man-made. The
circumstances themselves turned out to be formed over a long
period of time, often going back to the very beginnings of the community and the reasons for the community first settling in that
particular place.

Habitation developed relatively late in this coastal region and
remained sparse even under the Roman occupation during the
first centuries of our era. It was only by the tenth century that the
terrain became ready for a growing population after large parts
of its geography had, during the intervening centuries, been affected by natural disasters which first changed land to water and then
back to land again. The administration and responsibility for the
infrastructure of the territory fell successively under the empires
of the Franks, the Germans, and the Spanish, in each case the
centres of power being at a considerable distance from the feudal
territory itself. Possibly even because of this situation—and also
for many other reasons—the local population at the end of the
sixteenth century established by force a political and economic independence from its feudal sovereign, King Philip II, residing in
Madrid. A federation was formed known at the time as the Republic of the Seven United Provinces. Besides being one of the first
postmedieval European republics within a large area dominated
by kings and aristocrats, it became one of the wealthiest communities of early modern times, with an unusual high amount of cities
with fast growing populations of between 20.000 and 200.000 inhabitants. With both domestic and institutional architecture flourishing—but sculpture in a back seat—the cities acquired renown
for their uniquely large production of images painted in oil on
panel or canvas. Such works, earlier reserved for the altars of Catholic churches and a few noble halls, now started to cover the walls
of the (predominantly) protestant merchants' houses, their format,
technique, subject matter and style being adapted to the specific
demands of the local clientele. It is the influence of the different
geographies of the individual towns on these demands that is the
concern of Green Art Studies.

MAPPING THE GEOLOGY
OF THE NETHERLANDS

Earlier these geographies could only be sensed and experienced.
Nowadays we can study them in specialized maps.[4] On a geolog-
ical map of the Northern Netherlands we can read detailed soil
differences: we can discriminate old and young dunes; areas of peat
and those made up out of marine or lagoon sediments as well
as combinations of the two; also marine deposits in erosion gullies
coinciding with river courses, and many other mixtures of soil
structure. A map showing the groundwater shows strong variations

in the presence of water and the level of water, the depths of
which in some extreme cases can reach to 16 to 20 ft. Another map
shows the principal waterways. The sea itself is kept at bay by a
wall of sand-dunes, but these are in some places several miles thick,
in others barely existent.

Climatological differentiations can also be mapped. Variations in rainfall and in the amount of sunshine or thunderstorms
can occur over short distances. The impact of these variables on
the potential of the local soil can then be registered in differences
in the flora and fauna. And it is of course on these plants and animals that man depends, as well as on the water and waterways. It is
these variations in ecology that produce the variations in material
and behavioral cultures registered, for example, in the maps of
farm types and dialects. Each combination of climate and geology
encourages a different lifestyle. But, more important for the argument here, it is these factors that influence the origins and histories
of the cities, whose cultures and art productions—we will see—
show a direct response to these different "Green" factors.

THE FIVE CITIES

Of these cities five, all in the province of Holland, became most
famous. Dordrecht, where the painter Aelbert Cuyp (1620–1691)
worked; Haarlem, known for its landscape painters such as Salomon
van Ruisdael (c.1600–1670) and merry portraits by Frans Hals
(1582–1666); Delft above all known through the work of Johannes
Vermeer (1632–1675); Leiden, best represented by works of Gerrit
Dou (1613–1675), and Amsterdam, most associated with the work
of Rembrandt (1606–1669). In the following I will present a swift
outline of factors in each specific environment, which seem to have
influenced the particular character of each local art production.[5]

An excellent example of the way in which social values are
rooted in natural factors is offered by Dordrecht, whose seniority as the oldest city in Holland was based only upon its privileged
natural situation (Fig. 1). An island surrounded by the waters
of the rivers Maas and Rhine (called Merwede near Dordrecht) its
situation was exceptionally strategic. Secure from attack it could
control water-born trade with the rest of the county of Holland,
the German lands and territories to the South, as well as with the
British Isles and Scandinavia. These natural advantages motivated the Count of Holland to grant its citizens a lucrative monopoly,
the privilege of levying tolls on all goods coming down the rivers.
This vital toll-right was enforced from a huge tower. Rising high
over the rest of the town as symbol of their civic pride, its image
was used for their city seal.

5
The present author is finishing a book,
which demonstrates in fuller detail the
premises here summarized.

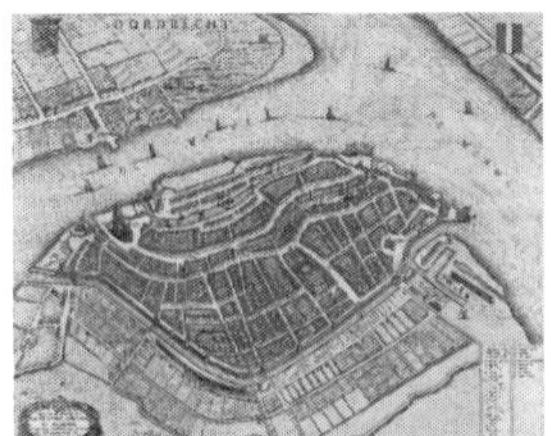

Figure 1
Frans Hogenberg, Map of Dordrecht, before 1574.

With such natural endowments and so well protected by law, it is not surprising if the town's richer citizens came to view their wealth almost as a natural condition. While communities elsewhere had to show initiative or work hard, the inhabitants of Dordrecht felt superior and at ease. This sense was reinforced by the river's generosity in supplying record numbers of fish and water birds. The rights to these ample food supplies were carefully kept in the hands of the ruling classes, as were the rights to lease the stalls on the fishmarket shown in one of the first large and splendid secular paintings produced in Dordrecht by the local artist Jacob Cuyp in 1627.[6] The fisherman behind his stall also testifies to another local tradition sustained by the town's unique situation. While in other places fishermen had to spend most time at sea in dangerous conditions leaving the fish stalls in the hands of their women, in Dordrecht the easy access to a constantly renewable river harvest meant that men could be involved in its sale as well. Not that the access to the river fisheries was free. That, too, was leased from local landowners, creating relationships such as that shown in a portrait by Jacob's son Aelbert Cuyp. There the mounted *Pieter de Roovere, Lord of the Manor of Hardinxveld* is shown inspecting a salmon brought to him in tribute by one of his fishermen. Such a feudal relationship arranged around a local resource is rarely so elaborately portrayed outside Dordrecht.

Equally rare were portraits on horseback. In Dordrecht they were almost the norm as horses were a local resource as well. The seventeenth century historian Gerard Vossius points out that the land around Dordrecht has always been renowned for horse breeding and that this even gave the name to the surrounding area. This was called the Merwede, meaning in Dutch "Mer," "merrie," mare or horse, and "weide" for field or meadow.[7] Today we know that the soil being so appropriate for horse breeding was due to a so-called "tidal accumulation" by which deposits of seashells, rich in lime, had become mixed with layers of heavy clay left by the frequently flooding rivers. The same meadows were equally ideal grazing for cows producing calcium-rich milk. Both types of animal were often painted by Aelbert Cuyp set against buttery skies, reminding the citizens of one of the sources of their well-being. These buttery skies were as unique to Dordrecht as its soil and water. The town's situation close to the sea in an environment where separate areas of land alternated with large stretches of water created highly unstable weather patterns. Golden sunlight alternated

with black thunderclouds and both were not only reflected in and
reinforced by the wide water surfaces surrounding Dordrecht,
but often captured in Cuyp's paintings (Fig. 2). His sunlit reflections
of Dordrecht's west-facing harbor and its wide ship-filled river, or
his stormy landscapes filled with well-fed cattle, each dominated by
the profile of the city, represent the realities of the local ecology.
They were also well calculated to satisfy the subconscious desires
of his exclusively local clients to see their unique environment
eternalized in a visual memory system.[8]

8
Aelbert Cuyp's paintings were not
sold outside Dordrecht until the eigh-
teenth century.
9
Gerard David, *Forest Landscape*,
outer wings of a triptych, The Hague,
Mauritshuis; Geertgen tot St. Jans,
St John the Baptist in the Wilderness,
Berlin, Staatliche Museen.

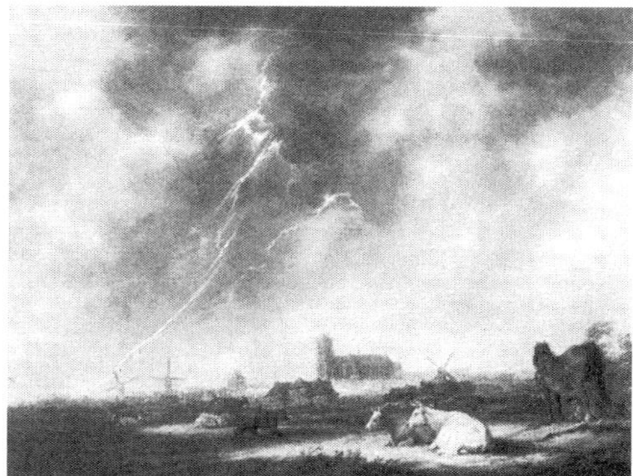

Figure 2
Albert Cuyp, *A Horse and Cattle
outside Dordrecht in a Thunder-
storm*, c. 1644.

The natural realities that attracted the first settlers to Haarlem, the
town second in seniority and only thirty miles to the north of
Dordrecht, were completely different: a wealth of land rather than
water. A wide band of dunes offered protection against the North
Sea and both these dunes and the sandbanks behind were richly
forested. Dunes and forest together supplied the settlers with
game to eat and wood for fires and for the building of houses and
ships. Large trees were a unique feature in Holland's soggy marsh-
land and trees played a major role in the formation of Haarlem's
reputation. Its unique ecology attracted the count to set up a
principal residence and later brought many other special visitors.
Already in the fifteenth century, the Haarlemmers exploited this
image for their identity on their city seals, using a tree in full leaf
(Fig. 3). They also celebrated their landscape in an unparalleled
series of urban eulogies, the earliest dated around 1400. Each text
glorified the local countryside and especially the neighboring
forest. And so did the earliest known painters from fifteenth century Haarlem. Albert van Ouwater, Gerard David, and Geertgen
tot St. Jans were specially praised around 1600 by authors such as
Guicciardini and Van Mander for their interest in landscape
and topography, examples of which can still be admired in several collections.[9]

In the early seventeenth century laudatory verses about
Haarlem's natural surroundings increased, coinciding with the impressive expansion of the local tradition of landscape imagery.
A true rage for Haarlem landscapes developed and many painters
and engravers from elsewhere in the Netherlands flocked to the

town in the 1610's to learn the canon. This was elaborated later
by local painters such as Solomon van Ruisdael and Pieter de
Molijn. Solomon's young nephew, Jacob van Ruisdael, by moving
to the more lively art market in Amsterdam could formulate the
archetypical Haarlem landscape, which became known in short as
Haarlempje, "little Haarlem," as the environs of Haarlem became
established as an "ideal" landscape.

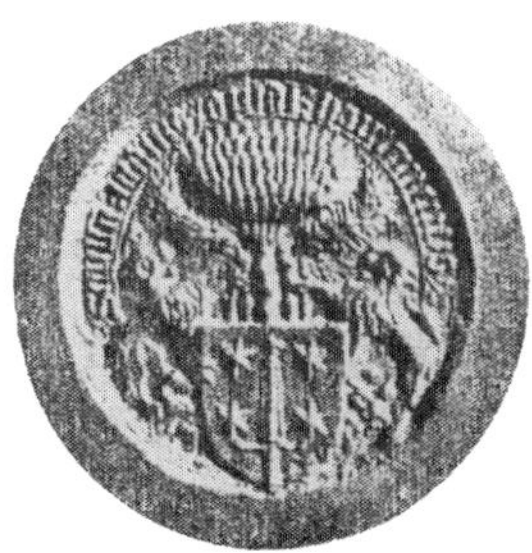

Recreation in the leisurely curves of the Haarlem dunes
brought enjoyment, which was celebrated and reinforced by the
many so-called *Merry Companies* (Vrolijke Gezelschapjes)
by painters such as Dirck Hals. The same sentiment can be seen in
close-up in Dirck's brother, Frans Hals' portrayal of Haarlem
citizens. The easy-going smile of *The Laughing Cavalier* expresses
an easy-going disposition, which we find in most of Hals' Haarlem
sitters—both identifiable and anonymous (Fig. 4). They are shown
more often than not with big, extrovert grins, a mode of expression seldom portrayed in the other cities. *The Smiling Couple in the
Outdoors* is a perfect example of a sunny Haarlem dune landscape reflected in the beaming faces of the young sitters. Even the
thick impasto of Hals' lively brush strokes contributes to the
atmosphere of joyful vitality.

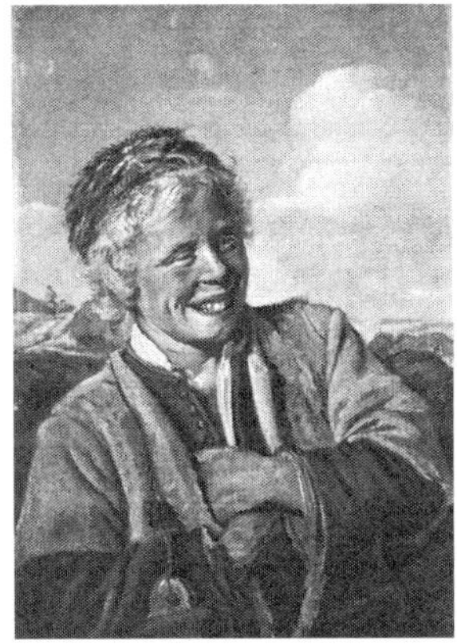

The ecology of Delft, the third city in seniority, was different
again. Not on a river and away from the dunes, it developed on
a manmade canal, dug to facilitate the drainage of the surrounding marshes, from which it took its name. "Delft," from the

Dutch verb "delven," "to dig," was the designation of the city's principal straight waterway, which was shown first as streaming water, but later as an increasingly abstract straight stripe on the city's earliest seals (Fig. 5). The city's ground plan well illustrates how this artificial beginning on the canal became the inspiration for an almost geometrical grid of canals with at its centre a wide rectangular piazza, unparalleled elsewhere. The citizens of Delft were used to long straight vistas and one of those citizens, the painter Vermeer, captured the city's distinctive geometrical aesthetic in his crisp and clean city views and elegant interiors, constructed according to strict linear perspective.

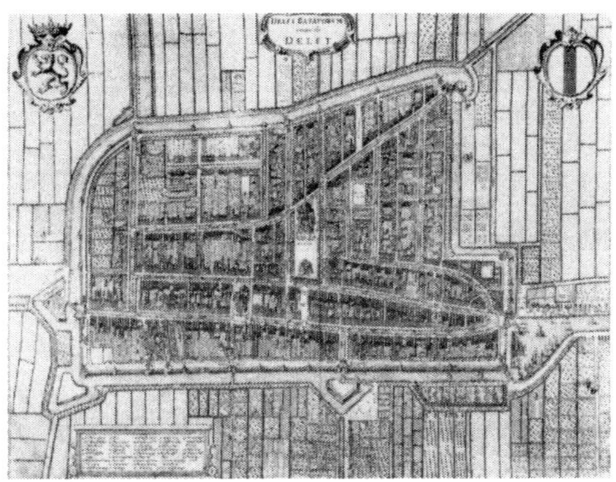

Figure 5
Joan Blaeu, Map of Delft
(from *Stedenatlas*), 1649.

Equally characteristic and influential on the formation of this taste, was the surrounding saliferous soil. It produced a quality of grain ideally suited for fermentation, and this, when combined with the local marsh-water, supported a capital-intensive, brewing industry. To ensure a supply of clean water, special legislation was passed requiring streets to be kept clean, an activity again documented by Vermeer in his *Little Street*. In the mean time Delft became more and more well-to-do, clean and conservative and its pride in the man-made came out in its architectural paintings, a genre above all developed and produced in Delft by painters such as E. de Witte and G. Houckgeest, greatly outnumbering those of landscape (Fig. 6). A remarkable characteristic of the Delft paintings, both those of the domestic and the church interiors, was the use of primary hues. This feature can be related to two other capital-intensive industries, tapestry weaving and the faience production, which Delft developed in the seventeenth century. At the time the tapestries were specially praised for their closeness to the art of painting and even considered superior to painting in their liveliness of color (Brom 1907, 461). Due to its soil and situation, Delft could sustain nonlabor intensive industries, which by discouraging immigration in turn preserved the architecture in uncluttered urban spaces, a luxury Leiden, only fifteen miles away, could not afford.

Leiden was situated on a river like Dordrecht and, like Haarlem, was close to the dunes, but neither resource was substantial. The

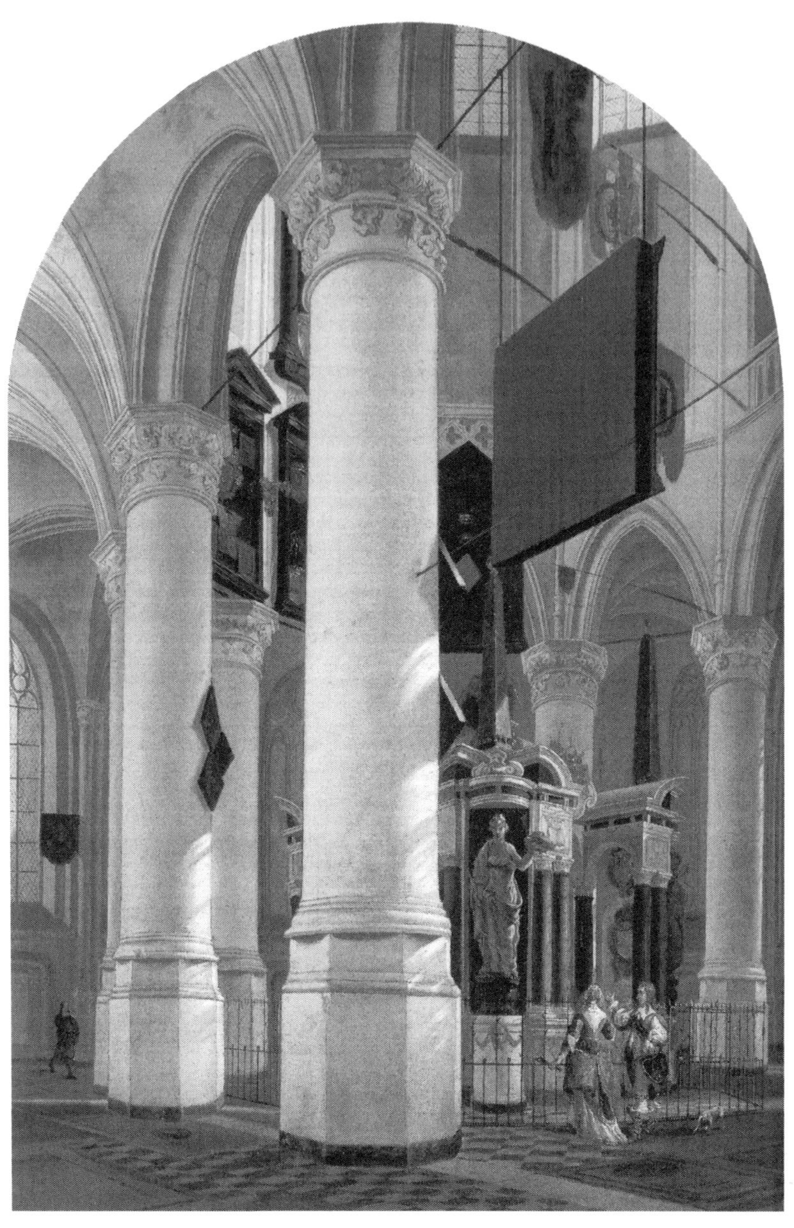

river was small and brought no great trading privileges. The band of dunes was narrow and relatively treeless. The river, however, not only initially connected Leiden via the North Sea to England and to its supplies of raw wool, it also supplied the running water that was the life-blood of the city's water-polluting wool manufacturing industry. Leiden became the biggest cloth-producing centre of the Northern Netherlands, making it after Lyon the second largest industrial town in Europe. As the wool industry is not only polluting,

but also highly labor-intensive, Leiden soon became one of the
most overcrowded urban communities in Holland (Fig. 7). While
the congested population caused problems of law and order, the
many stages of cloth production required strict and complex regulation and both regulatory aspects may be alluded to by the city's
early seal (c. 1300), where, underneath St Peter, the city's patron
saint, we meet images of the community's eight magistrates.

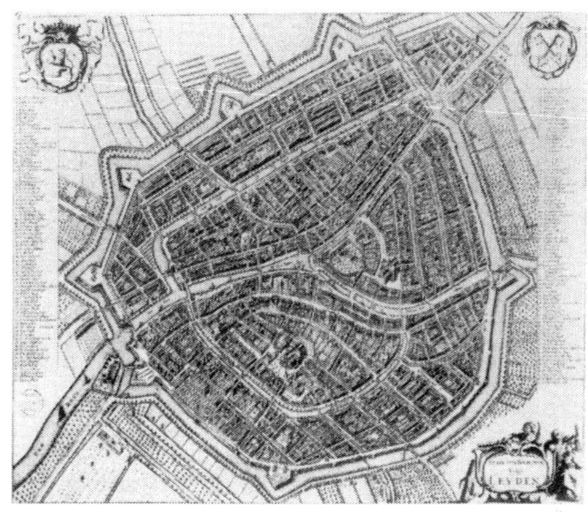

Figure 7
Johannes Jansonius,
Map of Leiden, c. 1650.

Another consequence of the overcrowding and pollution was
disease and with that death. The population suffered more than
elsewhere from contagious epidemics and was regularly decimated
by the plague, a situation made far worse by the Spanish siege in
1572, in which three quarters of the population died. The trauma
of this event is captured in the decoration of the town hall in the
1590's, where a skull was prominently carved on the balustrade of
the entrance stair. The cumulative longterm impact of these pressures is palpable in the work of Leiden's most famous seventeenth
century painter, Gerrit Dou. In many of his small, compact compositions—such as his *Self Portrait with Skull*—the skull strikes a
morbid note and the space is as dark and restricted as the city
had become by its industrial overcrowding. Indeed, in general, in
Leiden not only were many more still-life paintings with skulls
produced than in any other city but also many more small-format
dark compressed compositions. Another characteristic of these
works was their almost invisible brushstrokes, a stylistic feature
that can, perhaps surprisingly, be connected to the special values of the cloth industry. After all, the success of this enterprise,
which fed the whole population, was dependent on the flawless
weave of the finished cloth, which could not be sold until checked
by the wool masters. These officials regularly visited the weavers'
houses and held the cloth against the light for inspection of its
spotless surface. The surface of the city's paintings had to be as unblemished as that of its cloth.

The labor-intensive aspect of the wool industry encouraged
many women into the labor market, and the diversity of the locations of the manufacturing process brought these female workers

onto the streets to transport materials between stages. Most, though, were confined in sunless workshops, which probably explains why Guicciardini in the sixteenth century comments on the city's "very beautiful and white women" (1612, 206). A few years later paintings of women at work became one of the specialties of Leiden's painters, such as the early example from 1607 of *Women Spinning and Weaving* by I. van Swanenburgh, commissioned for public display in the Cloth Hall, and the numerous *Kitchen Maid*'s by Dou and his contemporaries, their subjects characteristically always peeping out of a shallow dark room, clearly based upon the reality of urban overcrowding. (Fig. 8). The latter compositions, in true Leiden manner, allowed the whiteness of the women to stand out against dark backgrounds, a simple formula that inspired hundreds of local variants. Even the monotonous, dark hues prevalent in many of the obscure interiors and developed in the monochrome landscapes by Jan van Goyen during the 1620's can, perhaps, be connected to both the overcrowded gloomy housing and the grey and brown dyes of the woolen cloths.

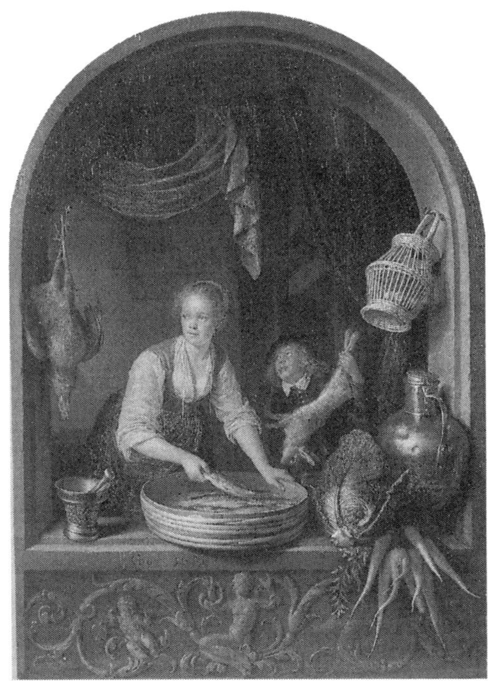

It is not just for rhetorical effect that we turn to Amsterdam last. Amsterdam developed after the other communities, which had occupied all the higher, drier, safer and more fertile sites first. The later generations who looked for new land had to content themselves with an, at first sight, less advantageous location with fewer obvious resources. They had little soil and what there was was water-logged. As a result the immigrants, who came to live on a narrow area of bog-land at the mouth of the river Amstel on the shore of the Zuyder Zee, needed a more positive and imaginative attitude to make both their homes and their living.

Being squeezed between two feudal territories, the Amsterdam settlers also needed to fight for their freedom from competing overlords. And such freedom was vital for their exploitation of the two capricious elements in which they were rich, the wind that swept in from the West and the water of the adjoining sea. Since the environment supplied so little in terms of food or other raw materials, these had to be acquired from far away, and this encouraged the early community of fishermen to use the power of the wind to conquer not just the Zuyder Zee but the remote Baltic by developing an efficient marine transport-industry, backed by the use of armed force. All these risky activities required an unprecedented individual strength, entrepreneurship and leadership. This combination of attributes is represented on the city's early seals with their association of sailing ships and heavily armed men (Fig. 9).

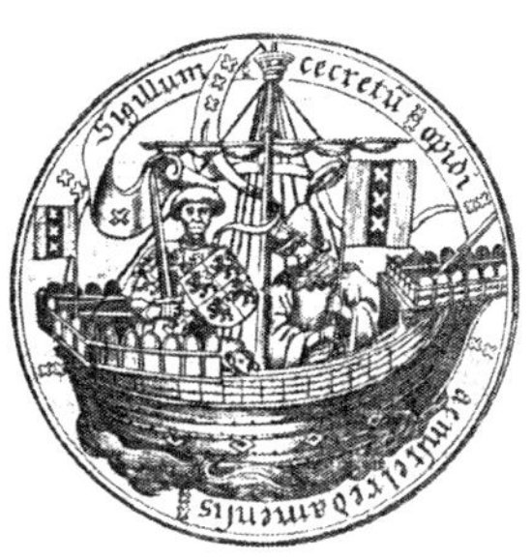

Figure 9
Amsterdam city seal, c. 1450.

If Amsterdam had a much later start than its older siblings, it also had a much more rapid growth. By the sixteenth century their equal, it soon overtook them. In the first quarter of the seventeenth century the city almost doubled its population from about 60 to 110 000, raising its property market to unknown heights both in quantity and quality. This unprecedented success story and the human skills on which it depended called for both celebration and justification, and this resulted in the appearance of a new type of small panel painting with subjects from history, above all from the Old Testament relating the histories of the tribes of Israel. With such subjects the Amsterdammers demonstrated that they too felt privileged by God. Such was the importance of history painting that the genre became by far the most popular in Amsterdam, making up at least 44% of the total output between 1620 and 1629 (Montias 1991, 352). The Amsterdam-born Pieter Lastman established the genre, and the opportunity to excel in this most admired field of painting inspired other enterprising young artists to move to the city. Of these Rembrandt from Leiden became the most influential, and by reducing the elaboration of the compositions of his teacher Lastman, and concentrating on one, two or three protagonists from the obligatory Old Testament narratives using the sober coloring from his Leiden home background, he could reveal and elevate the qualities of individual- and group-enterprise in which Amsterdammers excelled.

The field in which such individual and group resources are best captured is portraiture. A powerful figure such as burgomaster Andries Bicker appears as canny as a fox and as strong as a boar in the portrait by Bartholomeus van der Helst (Fig. 10). But even more typical are the group portraits, which advertized at once the talents of leadership and collaboration. Most striking were the militia groups, which developed earliest and in largest numbers in independent, militaristic Amsterdam and became far more popular there than anywhere else. Rembrandt's *Nightwatch*, only the most famous such militia portrait, is in composition light years away from the early city seal with the ship and the two heavily armed military men, but, in fact, they both reflect the similar impact of a particular natural environment on a particular community. Only a landless city needed to place such emphasis on the importance of armed forces on sea and on land.

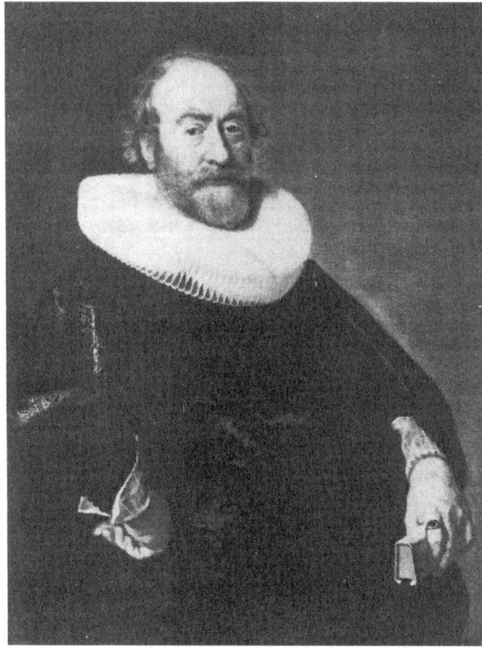

The Amsterdammers did not get rich by military strength alone. They also needed to understand the variety of cultures with which they came into contact, an understanding which they documented on maps, matching the costumes, habits and lifestyles shown in the margins to the different regions and capitals of Europe. This really meant appreciating a culture's relation to its geographical origin. In the case of the burghers of Amsterdam, this awareness of the relation between culture and context was vital to their economic success. Increasingly their voyages took them to the ends of the earth and as they traveled they noted not only the soils and climates, temperatures and humidities but also the flora and fauna and the goods that the peoples, who lived in them,

produced. This knowledge embracing the whole world they recorded in guide- and travel-books and maps. In this they almost anticipated Green Art Studies as a dimension of world art studies.

How then might Green Art Studies itself approach the whole
world? We can begin by extending our view of the Netherlands
to take in two cities one to the South and one to the North of those
we have looked at so far. Flower-pieces were developed by
Ambrosius Boschaert and Balthasar van der Ast in Middelburg in
Zeeland, which, near the extreme westerly point of the island of
Walcheren, combines a special miniclimate of more sunshine hours
a year than anywhere else in the Republic, with a soil famed for
flower cultivation. No such flower paintings were produced in the
city of Kampen, on the cold north eastern shore of the Zuyder Zee,
close to where the famous Elfstedentocht, the ice races linking
eleven cities, are run to this day. Instead, Hendrick Avercamp and
later his nephew Barent specialized in ice scenes. These two paint-
erly subjects, which were for a time particularly associated with
these two cities, were nourished by specific climates and geologies.
Similar relationships can be discovered in other places and regions
around the globe, as art works everywhere tend to reflect in their
style or subject matter the influence of both natural realities and the
cultural priorities these engender.

REFERENCES

ALPERS, SVETLANA. 1983. *The art of describing: Dutch art in the seventeenth century*. Chicago and London: The University of Chicago Press.

BROM, GERARD, AND LAMBREGT ABRAHAM VAN LANGERAAD, eds. 1907. *Diarium van Arend van Buchell*. Amsterdam: Müller.

CASTELNUOVO, ENRICO, AND CARLO GINZBURG. 1979. Centro e periferia. In *Materiali e problemi. Vol. I of Storia dell' arte italiana: Questioni e metodi,* ed. Giovanni Previtali, 283–352. Turin: Einaudi.

DE BIÈVRE, ELISABETH. 1995. The urban subconscious: The arts of Delft and Leiden. *Art History* 18 (2): 222–52.
—. 2005. Alchemy of wind and water: Amsterdam 1200–1700. In *Time and place: Essays in the geohistory of art,* ed. Thomas DaCosta Kaufmann and Elizabeth Pilliod, 87–113. Aldershot and Burlington, VT: Ashgate.

GUICCIARDINI, LUDOVICO. 1612. *Beschryvinghe van alle de Neder-landen, anderssins ghenoemt Neder-duytslandt.* Trans. by Cornelius Kilianus. Amsterdam: Willem Jansz. Originally published as *Descrittione di tutti I Paesi Bassi, altrimenti detti Germania Inferiore* (Antwerp, 1567).

EHRENSVÄRD, CARL AUGUST. 1925. Skriften. In *Carl August Ehrensvärd (1745–1800): An original Swedish aesthetician and an early functionalist.* Holger Frykenstedt. Uppsala, 1965.

HADJINICOLAOU, NICOS. 1983. Kunstzentren und periphere Kunst. *Kritische Berichte* 11: 36–56.

KAUFMANN, THOMAS DACOSTA. 2004. *Toward a geography of art.* Chicago and London: The University of Chicago Press.
—, and Elizabeth Pilliod, eds. 2005. *Time and place: Essays in the geohistory of art.* Aldershot and Burlington, VT: Ashgate.

MONTIAS, JOHN, MICHAEL. 1991. Works of art in seventeenth century Amsterdam. In *Art in history, history in art: Studies in seventeenth-century Dutch culture,* ed. David Freedberg and Jan de Vries, 331–77. Santa Monica, CA: The Getty Center.

RIZZOLATTI, GIACOMO, LUCIANO FADIGA, VITTORIO GALLESE, AND LEONARDO FOGASSI. 1996. Premotor cortex and the recognition of motor actions. *Cognitive Brain Research* 3 (2): 131–41.

SCHAMA, SIMON. 1987. *The embarrassment of riches: An interpretation of Dutch culture in the Golden Age.* New York: Knopf.

SPENGLER, OSWALD. 1923. *Der Untergang des Abendlandes: Umriss einer Morphologie der Weltgeschichte.* 2 vols. Munich: Beck.

STRZYGOWSKI, JOSEF. 1918. Vergleichende Kunstforschung auf geographischer Grundlage. *Mitteilungen der geographischen Gesellschaft in Wien* 61: 20–48, 153–58.

VAN BEVERWYK, JOHAN. 1644, *Epistolicae quaestiones cum doctorem responsis: Accedit ejusdem, nec non Erasmi, Cardani, Melanchthonis, Medicinae encomium.* Rotterdam: A. Leers.

VAN DER WOUDE, AD. 1991. The volume and value of paintings in Holland at the time of the Dutch Republic. In *Art in history, history in art: Studies in seventeenth-century Dutch culture,* ed. David Freedberg and Jan de Vries, 285–329. Santa Monica, CA: The Getty Center.

VAN MANDER, KAREL. 1603–1604. *Het schilder-boeck … Daer nae in dry deelen t'leven der vermaerde doorluchtighe schilders des ouden en nieuwen tyds.* Haarlem.

RICHARD L. ANDERSON

Art, Aesthetics, and Cultural Anthropology: Retrospect and Prospect

Inasmuch as "anthropology" refers to the systematic study ("-ology") of humans ("anthro-"), it is hardly surprising that since the late nineteenth-century inception of the field, scholars have often included art, as well as indigenous ideas about art, within the scope of their research and writing on the many and varied societies of the world. Looking back over the history of the cultural anthropological study of art and aesthetics, two recurrent themes are apparent: The effort to discover and pursue questions that simultaneously are interesting and feasible, and the extent to which such activities are colored by broader intellectual movements.

The first generation of anthropologists tried to answer the question, how did human cultural institutions evolve down through the millennia into their present forms? With regard to the visual arts, the Americans W. H. Holmes, Frank Cushing, and Otis Mason speculated that the earliest decorations on artifacts were the coincidental result of technique. Some very early ceramic pots, for example, had surfaces covered with cross-hatch patterns because they were made by forming clay inside of baskets. As time passed (this theory went), meanings were attached to such patterns, and eventually these meaningful designs and figures came to be recreated for their own sakes. Thus, it was said, abstract art gradually evolved into representational art. Other scholars, however, such as the Swedish anthropologist Hjalmar Stolpe, made the opposite claim: The first art was representational, Stolpe surmised; but as time passed, figures were simplified, original meanings were lost, and the eventual results were abstract designs that were devoid of any reference to the visible world around us.

ART ANTHROPOLOGY IN THE MODERN ERA

Undoubtedly, such unilineal theories of cultural evolution were developed in the shadow of the evolutionary ideas that were revolutionizing the biological sciences. It gradually became apparent, however, that explanations that worked well for plants and animals were inadequate for human institutions. Franz Boas led the movement away from evolutionary theories in anthropology in the United States by pointing out two of their shortcomings: first, such theories, whether about art, marriage, religion, or anything else, often were based on mistaken or superficial information, a problem latter addressed by the development of the methodology of intensive anthropological fieldwork.

Second, Boas faulted the evolutionary theorists for their tendency to assume ethnocentrically that the institutions of Europe and America are on the top rung of a hypothetical evolutionary ladder and that the more unlike something is from its Western counterpart, the less evolved it is and the lower the rung of the ladder it should occupy. From 1903 onward, Boas, who had started the first American program in academic anthropology at Columbia University, argued his case with regard to art to a generation of American anthropologists, and he eventually published his ideas in the highly influential book, *Primitive Art* (1927). The outcome of all this was a great deal of research and writing that sought to describe, if not necessarily understand, many non-Euro-American (albeit often Native American) art traditions. Today, however, it could be argued that whereas the project of the earlier evolutionists was interesting but not feasible, the ethnographic descriptions of Boas and his students, while feasible, are now of limited interest, at least for the light they shed on the role of art in human culture and thought.

Just as the Darwinian revolution in biology was echoed in nineteenth-century theories of unilineal cultural evolution in anthropology, the modernist movement that emerged in the Euro-American fine arts community in the early twentieth century may have had consequences for the subsequent study of art in anthropology. During the period when Boas and his students were documenting the details of cultures that were thought to be on the verge of extinction, the paradigm of sociocultural functionalism was being formulated in Europe by Bronislaw Malinowski, A. R. Radcliffe-Brown, and others. The functionalists' concern was to understand the ways in which traditional institutions and beliefs fit together to form an integrated social order as well as the ways in which specific practices contribute to that integration. The central premise of twentieth-century modernism in the fine arts was that the highest response to art is as art for art's own sake; viewing art as a handmaiden to religion, ideology, or even representation was definitely déclassé. Perhaps because this notion was so prominent in the Euro-American intellectual milieu for the first half of the twentieth century, the seminal functionalist writers spent relatively little time thinking about the functions of art.

Cross-cultural interest in art and aesthetics began to revive in the 1960s, however, with some scholars beginning to look at art from a functionalist perspective. Roy Sieber's "Masks as Agents of Social Control" (1962) and the essays in *African Art and Leadership* (Fraser and Cole 1972), for example, reflect a growing realization that, the tenets of modernism notwithstanding, art *can* play a significant role in human life. (Sieber, an art historian, sagely remarked that African art is made "for life's sake" rather than "for art's sake" [Sieber 1962, 8].)

But it was an increased interest in the psychological dimension of human culture that engendered much of the new research and writing by anthropologists on the subject of non-Western art. 1971 saw the publication of *Anthropology and Art: Readings in Cross-cultural Aesthetics* (Charlotte M. Otten, ed.) and *Art and Aesthetics in Primitive Societies: A Critical Anthology* (Carol F. Jopling, ed.), each with two dozen substantial essays ranging from the descriptive and archaeological (e.g., Frank Willett's discussion of early sculpture traditions in Nigeria) to the sociocultural (e.g., Erna Gunther's "Northwest Coast Indian Art"), but with special emphasis on the cognitive, symbolic, and philosophical dimensions of art (e.g., John L. Fischer's "Art Styles as Cultural Cognitive Maps" and James W. Fernandez's "Principles of Opposition and Vitality in Fang Aesthetics"). By the mid-1980s, three surveys of the field had been published by anthropologists (Anderson 1989 [1979]; Hatcher 1999 [1985]; Layton 1991 [1981]), each one attempting to summarize the most significant anthropological findings to date on non-Western art with regard to topics such as artists, stylistic traditions, symbolism, and the functions of art.

Another significant development during this period was the increased interaction between previously separate academic disciplines. For example, philosophers such as Denis Dutton and Donald Keene also began making significant contributions to the study of non-Western art and aesthetics.

THE AESTHETIC EXPERIENCE

One outcome of this heady cross-disciplinary dialogue was an increasing interest in the comparative study of *aesthetics*, that is, indigenous philosophies of art, as well as the relationship between such theories of art and those that have existed in the West. A fundamental debate has had to do with whether or not the word "art," with all of its Western cultural baggage, should be used with reference to the expressive cultures of non-Western peoples. For some, the answer has been "no," if for no other reason than that many of the world's languages do not have a word that can be directly translated into the English "art." In light of this fact, Jacques Maquet (1986) equated "art" with the "aesthetic experience," that is to say, the distinctive psychological state of mind brought about (in a properly attuned person and under the right circumstances) by apprehending the art work *as* an art work, rather than responding to it on a cognitive, practical, or personal level. By this line of reasoning, if one focuses on an item as a utilitarian means to some material end, perhaps as an accoutrement to religious or political practice, or even simply as a cipher in the world of commerce, one is not responding to it as an art work. As Maquet remarked with regard to art works, "to be beheld is their proper and only use" (1986, 17); aesthetic objects, he wrote, "stimulate a total disinterested vision" (1986, 33).

Using this definition of "art," Maquet concluded that most of the world's societies have little or no art, arguing that outside of contemporary, urban settings, artifacts for the most part are made to serve instrumental purposes, with only a few — if indeed any — noninstrumental features added. "Objects we have labeled 'primitive art,'" Maquet wrote, "were not art for those who made them. Did they make other objects with no other use than visual enjoyment? Yes, but they were few and of minor importance" (1986, 66).

Maquet's approach echoes the modernist aesthetic of formalism, in which the aesthetic — that is, the formal — dimension of art works is central; and his work was valuable in testing the limits of formalism's application to non-Western art. It could even be argued that inasmuch as contemporary Westerners have grown up in a milieu where formalist thinking prevails in the fine arts, Maquet does explicitly what all of us have some tendency to do, namely, to privilege the art-induced transcendental experience in which the apprehension of an art work sweeps one away — not because of its technical, social, or monetary value but because of its singular form.

NON-WESTERN AESTHETIC SYSTEMS

A useful approach to non-Western art and philosophies of art can be derived from a seminal article by the philosopher Morris Weitz (1967 [1956]). Weitz pointed out that although many intelligent and thoughtful people have long tried to identify a single, definitive trait of "art," none of their efforts have stood the test of time. Therefore, instead of a single-trait, "closed" definition, Weitz proposed an "open" definition, that is, one composed of *several* traits, which he called "recognition criteria," that are generally associated with most or all of the things associated with "art" in a particular place and time. In a book entitled *Calliope's Sisters: A Comparative Study of Philosophies of Art* (Anderson 2004 [1990]) I modified somewhat Weitz's list of recognition criteria to propose a definition of art as being "culturally significant meaning, skillfully encoded in an affecting, sensuous medium" (2004 [1990], 277).[1] This is an extremely broad definition in that art's "culturally significant meaning" can be in the realm of the sacred or the secular; the artist's exceptional (compared to his or her peers) "skill" can be manual, but also may be conceptual and imaginative; the possible "sensuous, affecting" responses to art range from the purely physical to the thoroughly psychological; and the "media" in which art is produced includes visual, performing, and literary activities. This definition not only reflects the way that most people in the West think about most of the things they call "art," but equally well *it fits the way that people elsewhere think about certain special things in their own cultures*, things that are recognized as being special and falling into a (named or unnamed) category that is distinguished from other things (cf. Freeland 2001, 77; Dissanayake 1992).

With regard to the bugaboo regarding cultures that do not have a word paralleling the English word "art," it should be noted that many cultures also lack words that translate directly into the English words "kinship" and "language." Needless to say, such cultures not only *have* kinship and language systems, but also their members recognize the difference between kin and nonkin and between language and nonlanguage. Similarly, even in cultures that have neither professional aestheticians nor an explicit philosophy of art, examination of their material and intellectual cultures reveals identifiable ideas regarding the fundamental nature of art, the role of art in human affairs, and, sometimes, the criteria used to distinguish good art from not-so-good art (cf. Anderson 2004 [1990]). Some examples will illustrate this important point.

THREE CASE STUDIES
IN NON-WESTERN AESTHETICS

The various Inuit groups of the North American Arctic traditionally made art in several media: Although most men carved materials such as ivory, a few were recognized for their exceptional abilities in that activity. Some ivory carvings were made as toys; others, as amulets, gave the owner special abilities. Women in some groups decorated their bodies with tattoos, often to make themselves more pleasing to look at, sometimes to insure a better future for themselves and their children. Music and dance, too, were highly valued by the Inuit, especially during the long, cold, dark months of winter. Thus, traditional Inuit peoples were well aware of art's special importance in their lives.

The Inuit valued art not only for its material benefits but they also seem to have conceived of the arts as providing a means

1

Although Maquet (along with some others) attach central importance to the psychological mode known at the "aesthetic experience," this quality is absent from the definition I have proposed. The reasons are two: first, although some people may feel that they unequivocally recognize an aesthetic experience when they have one themselves, the transcendental and fleeting nature of the experience make it impossible to define with sufficient explicitness to allow someone to find out if and when *other* people—especially those who live in different cultures—experience it. Second, some things that are commonly considered to be art, by Westerners or by others, rarely, if ever, prompt the rarified "aesthetic experience." See Anderson 1989, 14–16.

whereby the separate and distinct worlds of the supernatural, the human, and the natural were articulated with each other. In a nineteenth-century Inuit story, for example, Raven, a mythic being, encountered First Man. Seeing him, Raven "raised one of its wings, pushed up its beak, like a mask, to the top of its head, and changed at once into a man" (Nelson 1899, 451). Raven then modeled a figure out of clay, "and after the image had dried in his hand, he waved his wings over it ... and a beautiful young woman arose and stood beside Man" (Nelson 1899 454). Thus, by removing an art work, a mask, Raven turns himself into a man; and by another artistic act Raven changes inanimate earth into a living woman. This theme of artistic transformation is found elsewhere in Inuit ethnography: in the Inuit aesthetic paradigm, art permits communication between nature, humans, and the supernatural (cf. Anderson 2004 [1990], 50–52).

Horticultural societies have aesthetic systems too, and often they are more explicit and complex than those of hunting and gathering peoples such as the Inuit. For example, the twenty-five million Yoruba who live in West Africa have long made a distinction between the men (called *gbenegbena*) who carve the masks needed for various important dance rituals, versus men (called *gbegibe-gi*) who carve practical, mundane items such as mortars (Bascom 1973, 64). The Yoruba language includes a vocabulary for discussing the strengths and weaknesses of carved wooden figures, made up of words, such as *didón* (shining luminosity), that are used by Yoruba art critics, that is, individuals who, although they derive their livelihood from other endeavors, are nonetheless widely recognized for their acute abilities to talk about art (Thompson 1966, 1968, 1973, 1974). A Yoruba aesthetic complex has been revealed through the efforts of several scholars, some of whom are Yoruba themselves (cf., e.g., Abiodun 1987; Lawal 1974; Thompson 1971; see also Anderson 2004 [1990], 138–63). This system of thought addresses such things as the relationship between art and beauty, between art and ethical goodness, and between the ephemeral art of this world and the timeless art of the spiritual realm.

Finally, complex societies outside the Western tradition have had their own unique systems of aesthetic thought. The Aztec empire, which flourished in Mesoamerica during the century and a half before the arrival of the Spanish, was ruled by an elite class, a small group of whom were called *tlamatinime* (singular, *tlamatini*) — people we would call philosophers. An Aztec poem describes the *tlamatini* in these terms:

> He is the way, the true guide of others...
> teacher of the truth, he never stops reproving...
> He holds a mirror before others,
> he makes them mindful and judicious...
> He shines his light on the world....
>
> (*Codice Matritense 1907* fol. 118rx, cited in León-Portilla 1971, 448)

Like Western philosophers, some of the *tlamatinime* turned their inquiring minds to questions about art. The central axiom of Aztec popular religion was that the world would be created and destroyed five times, that four such obliterations had already occurred, and that the fifth and final destruction of the world was imminent. The ultimate cataclysm could not be prevented, but it was widely believed that ritual practices, especially those involving blood sacrifice, might at least postpone the day of reckoning. The more speculatively-minded *tlamatinime*, however, put forward an alternative idea, suggesting that in this world where everything else is destined to end, where, as one of them put it, "jade shatters [and] the quetzal feather tears apart" (*Cantares Mexicanos*, 1904, fol. 12v, cited in León-Portilla 1971, 448), the one thing that is eternal is *art*, which they poetically referred to as "flower and song."

How did art have the unique power to do this? Some *tlamatinime* simply believed that the gods who would someday destroy the world might be temporarily "bought off," as it were, by gifts of the finest art. Others more thoughtfully asserted that although the material substance of art might be ephemeral, its abstract essence, its eternal spirit, would live on. Still others observed that when one is totally absorbed by an art work, time stops; and if time halts, the future, along with the cataclysmic end of everything, can get no closer, a profound insight indeed (cf. Anderson 2004 [1990], 169–85).

These capsule summaries of the aesthetic systems of three non-Western societies do not do justice to the cultures they come from. In every case, ideas about art are more complex than can be described here, and the application of such ideas to actual artistic practice is itself a complicated subject. The information does, however, lead to several conclusions regarding aesthetics in general, conclusions that are supported by additional ethnographic cases:

– Aesthetic principles, that is, abstract beliefs that provide a conceptual basis for art production, seem to be part of every culture.

– Philosophies of art vary significantly from one society to the next. In some places, for example, more emphasis may be placed on the potential spiritual dimension of art whereas in others art is more at work in the secular realm. Such differences do not, however, follow any simple pattern: some small-scale societies and some complex societies emphasize the former while other small-scale societies and other complex societies attach greater importance to the latter.

– Although no cross-cultural pattern is apparent with regard to the *content* of aesthetics systems, their *structure* does seem to vary in a fairly regular fashion. The aesthetic systems of complex societies tend to be more explicit, intricate, and the domain of a small cadre of specialists; philosophies of art in small-scale societies, on the other hand, are for the most part relatively less so. (The word "relatively" must be emphasized, however, in that all three of the qualities just noted are present to a degree in small-scale societies as well [cf. Anderson 2004 [1990], 255–76].)

– Far from being a nonutilitarian icing on the cultural cake, art conveys significant meaning in every society, be it the Inuit idea of art providing a connection between the natural, human, and supernatural worlds, or the Aztec belief that the inevitable destruction of the world may be postponed by giving gifts of "flower and song" to the gods.

– The exceptional *skill* with which the artist works, the *sensuous* qualities of the medium in which an art work is executed, and the *style* in which art is produced and that is characteristic of its time and place of origin—all have an impact on aesthetic production and as such merit attention in the study of world art.

– Finally, aesthetic information such as this helps one understand and appreciate art works from other cultural traditions. Nothing prevents a person from responding to alien works as no more than found objects, mere Rorschach patterns upon which to project ideas and sentiments from one's own culture; and needless to say, each individual inevitably has a unique and personal reaction to every art work. But aesthetic information of the sort described above can only broaden this reaction.

RECENT DEVELOPMENTS

During the 1990s, the literature on non-Western art and aesthetic systems grew, but the currents of interest split into two uneven channels. The descriptive, empirical tradition that had long characterized anthropological studies of non-Western cultures continued in limited fashion, as in the work on the arts of Australia: the massive *Oxford Companion to Aboriginal Art and Culture* (2000) is exemplary for the breadth of its coverage. Maturation of the discipline is also evident in such art historical texts as *Native North American Art* by Janet C. Berlo and Ruth B. Phillips (1998).

However, as we have noted, the study of art inevitably reflects ambient intellectual trends; and by 1990, the postmodern movement had become the source of a second, larger direction of inquiry in which there was less examination of actual art works and talking to their flesh-and-blood makers and correspondingly more examination of the discipline itself, along with the theoretical frameworks that its students have adopted. The hoary question about whether or not words such as "art" and "aesthetics" can be applied to non-Western cultures was raised again. Moreover, the very name of the discipline was—and continues to be—debated exhaustively, with calls for "world art studies," "world aesthetics," "transcultural aesthetics," and "intercultural aesthetics," each with somewhat different boundaries and emphases. (For an extended discussion of this terminological issue, see Van Damme 2006.)

The internecine battle between empiricists and postmodernists, which was so heated during the 1990s, abated during the first years of the twenty-first century, and it would seem that we now can glean the best from both paradigms to forge a discipline (or multidisciplinary effort) that is *empirically grounded* but still highly conscious of the importance and inevitability of the *political and subjective dimensions* of the enterprise.

Postmodern analysts also effectively demolished the convenient fiction of there being pure, authentic societies, free of the taint of outside influences, and at the same time they introduced the challenge of trying to understand human lives and interaction in a postcolonial world where globalization and technology have combined to shrink time and space.

PROSPECT: NON-WESTERN ART ON THE GLOBAL STAGE

One way to meet this challenge with regard to art and aesthetics is to look at what is happening today in those societies that we once thought of as being traditional. On examination, facile claims of "culturecide" generally turn out to be far too simplistic. Consider, for example, the three groups whose aesthetic systems were briefly described above.

The Inuit people of arctic North America continue to have a distinctive culture and to produce equally distinctive art, but both are very different than in the past (cf. Anderson 2004 [1990], 56–62). In Alaska, Inuit carvers have been carving craft items and selling them to foreign visitors since the Gold Rush brought men and money to their land in the late 1800s. Some pieces were ivory copies of Western artifacts—cribbage boards were especially popular for a while in Nome. The "billikin," however, is more interesting in terms of the global flow of art and art ideas. Invented (and in fact patented) in 1908 by a Kansas City school teacher and dubbed "the god of things as they ought to be," the plump, Buddha-like figure was adopted as the symbol of the 1909 Alaska-Yukon-Pacific Exposition. Soon, Inuit carvers in Alaska were turning out hundreds, then thousands, of the small ivory figures. But whereas traditional Inuit art was conservative, with artistic styles changing only very slowly, century by century, the twentieth-century Alaskan carvers exercised considerable creativity with the billikin, producing imaginative figures in a bewildering array of variations, such as "milikins" with breasts (Ray 1977, 45). Billikin innovations occurred in other ways, too: While still today a collector's item in North America, the presumably Eastern-inspired image also has returned to the Orient so that in Japan one can buy billikin ice cream, make a wish before a foot-high billikin in an Osaka shrine, or perhaps see the 1996 comedy film entitled *Birrikin*, in which the central character has the power to grant people's wishes.

As in Alaska, the Canadian Arctic has had its share of unpredictable artistic developments. By the 1920s the Canadian Handicrafts Guild and the Hudson's Bay Company were promoting and marketing Inuit-made ivory models of tools and figures. Then in 1948 a Canadian artist named James Houston encouraged men in Port Harrison (now Inukjuak) to start carving figures in soapstone, a medium that was more readily available and softer than ivory from walrus tusks. Subsequently, Houston introduced printmaking techniques including stencil, intaglio, and lithography in the Inuit community of Cape Dorset. The consequence of these two innovations was a revolution in Inuit art production. As in Alaska, the central Canadian Inuit have exercised great creativity in their new media, and their efforts have been rewarded by markets in the south, making the sale of art works the largest single source of income in a region otherwise ravaged by the colonial experience.

Although it is popular in the modern West to decry the effects of the marketplace on non-Western arts, two factors should be borne in mind. First, similar criticisms are rarely leveled at Western artists who sell enough art to pay their bills; and, as Ingo Hessel (1998) has pointed out, the sale of art works provides an income that allows Inuit to maintain other, more traditional lifeways that otherwise probably would disappear.

To a great degree, Inuit "market art" derives from a different set of aesthetic values than did traditional art. For one thing, contemporary Inuit artists take more self-conscious pride in creativity and technical skill than in the past. Also, arctic artists recognize market art as a vehicle for expressing Inuit identity. Every art-producing community has a distinctive style that, residents are pleased to say, sets them apart from their neighbors. Also, the Inuit are proud that their art works are a positive contribution to the way non-Inuit people think of the Inuit. Thus, a Baker Lake artist, Ruby Angrnanaaq, says, "Prints and drawings are our way of sharing our thoughts of the past and present life with the southern people; they are the messages that we are sending out to the rest of the world" (Seidelman, Turner, and Swinton 2001 [1994], 143). (It should also be noted that today some Inuit carvers have become "artists" in a more restricted sense of the word: they place greater emphasis on form than on narrative message, and their sculptures and paintings are exhibited and sold in museums and fine art galleries.)

With regard to West Africa, Robert Farris Thompson has observed that at one time, "Yoruba traditional culture and religious art had seemed destined for total obliteration in the wake of the slave trade, civil wars, and modernization" (1983, 16). Fortunately, Yoruba art has not disappeared, as Thompson himself has shown. For one thing, the Yoruba who came to the Americas as slaves brought their culture and art with them, and soon these were syncretized with elements of other West and Central African cultures as well as Western European culture to produce unique, hybrid art forms. Some of these, such as the visual arts of *vodun* remain (cf. Thompson 1983, 161–91) relatively isolated, but others, such as the African influence on Western popular music, permeate not only the West but also much of the rest of the world.

Meanwhile, back in Nigeria, a number of Yoruba artists have merged Yoruba art with Western fine art traditions. Perhaps the best known is a man who works under the name of Twins Seven-Seven, who began painting after meeting members of the Mbari Mbayo Club in the town of Oshogbo. Oshogbo itself is an example of the heady intercultural art exchanges that have been taking place in many places around the globe. Although traditional arts had disappeared from Oshogbo by the mid-twentieth century, the town did have several "Brazilian" or "San Salvador" houses that had been built in an architectural style brought back to West Africa by slaves who returned to Nigeria in the nineteenth century. This, along with Oshogbo's being the site of an important annual festival, led an Austrian painter named Suzanne Wenger to move to Oshogbo in 1950 to study Yoruba poetry and philosophy. Later, German-born Ulli Beier and his British artist wife, Georgina Beier, also came to live in Oshogbo; and by the 1960s the three-some was organizing printmaking workshops, and their Mbari Mbayo Club became a hotbed of all sorts of artistic activity, producing numerous now-famous Yoruba artists, including the aforementioned Twins Seven-Seven (cf. Kennedy 1992, 58–86).

For the Aztecs, the prediction that their world would soon come to an end did come true, although not in the way foretold by the codexes. The codexes *were* right, however, in that insofar as pre-1521 Aztec culture attained any immortality, it was largely by means of the arts: The famous "Sun Stone" and the image of an eagle perched on a cactus with a snake in its beak, both of which had symbolic significance for the Aztecs, are perhaps the best known national symbols of Mexico today. Identification with Aztec art is not mere political rhetoric, either. For example, visit Mexico City's *zócalo*, or main square, today and you will see young people performing Aztec dances that are as historically accurate as the source materials allow. If you are there during the day, they will be dressed in Aztec costumes, the shell rattles on their legs adding a eerie background drone to the powerful beat of the drum, all within sight of the excavated ruins of Tenochtitlán's main pyramid and a museum displaying Aztec sculpture, feather mosaics, and other visual arts. The dancers, happy to take donations, are of great interest to tourists, of course, although it should be born in mind that most of the onlookers are *Mexican* tourists. Visit the *zócalo* after dark, however, and you will find an even larger group of young people dancing for their own pleasure and for the satisfaction of connecting with their indigenous, Aztec roots. Although most of them wear Western clothes as they perform the vigorous traditional dances, they dance with the Aztec-style shell rattles on their legs.

Aztec art lives on in other forms, as well. Diego Rivera, José Clemente Orozco, David Alfaro Siqueiros and other members of the Mexican mural movement, arguably the most important fine art movement in the history of Latin America, often incorporated pre-Hispanic themes in their powerful, politically charged works; and the same is true of the contemporary Latino artists who create large wall paintings and graffiti in many cities to this day. Also, modern-day Mexican food, not only in Mexico but also the United States and the many other countries were it is popular, echoes indigenous Mesoamerican cuisine: Tortillas and tamales, moles and other salsas, were as characteristic of traditional Aztec fare as they are of Mexican food today.

But if Aztec art lives on in some forms, the Aztec aesthetic of "flower and song" seems to be gone, even among the million or more people still living in Mexico who speak the Aztec language of Nahuatl. A study done in the 1960s in a fairly remote Aztec village found that the people there valued pottery, not as a gift to the gods that might at least temporarily save the world, but rather as examples of fine craftsmanship and, when figurative, for its portrayal of people of robust good health and endurance (Golde 1963; Golde and Kraemer 1973).

Inuit, Yoruba, and Aztec: three examples of traditional societies creatively adapting to the contemporary, postcolonial, globalizing world; examples, I believe, of one of the most exciting challenges for those who study art and aesthetics today. The amount of empirical investigation of such changing traditions is far from adequate, mostly consisting of material collected as an afterthought to other concerns. Furthermore, if data is scant, synthesis is nearly nonexistent (but see Cowen 2002, Graburn 1999, and Taylor 1997). Perhaps this is a consequence of the longstanding history of anthropologists taking more interest in the exotic Other than in cultures that combine indigenous and foreign elements; or maybe it is because whereas sources of "authentic" traditional arts are becoming more rare (and hence the art works themselves become more sought after), market arts continue to proliferate in quantity, their novelty making them unlikely candidates for museum collections and connoisseurs.

In the face of calls for "world art studies," to ignore market art is to ignore most of the art produced in the world today. The eminent student of East Asian aesthetics, Eliot Deutsch, once wrote, "Aesthetic theory has often been pretentious.... Each theory has to do with a possibility of art, but not, as they have often claimed, to do with 'Art.' This is especially evident when the arts of non-Western cultures are included in the art world, a not unreasonable request" (1975, x–xi). Now, in the twenty-first century, it is, I believe, equally reasonable to request inclusion of market art within the purview of world art studies — and for two reasons.

First, the distinction between market art and traditional art is blurry at best. On the one hand, market arts have their own traditions, their own histories, sometimes reaching back hundreds of years; and on the other hand, traditional art has often been made for a "market," whether it be a Yoruba wooden mask commissioned by members of an ancestor cult that needed new masks for use in an annual dance performance, or else an artist in any of a great number of cultures making an art work because a visiting anthropologist said he or she would pay or trade something of value for it. Certainly there are extremes — at the one end of the spectrum, the Inuit father who carves a toy harpoon for his son to play with; at the other end a Mexican potter who goes through all of the laborious work of digging and processing clay, forming vessels, and then gathering fuel to fire them, all because the only source of income is selling pots to outsiders. But between those extremes, there is a continuum of motivations for art-making, none of which should be dismissed as being unimportant or uninteresting.

Moreover, the makers of market art typically have more to say about their art than simply, "I want to sell it." For decades the destinations for the great majority of Navajo weavings has been off the Navajo Reservation. Nonetheless, as Gary Witherspoon (1977, 1981, Witherspoon and Peterson 1995) has shown in great detail, Navajo weaving is created within a philosophical context that is both complex and subtle. Similarly, in my own research (Anderson 2000), I found American popular art to be grounded in a discernible, multifaceted and enduring set of aesthetic principles.

A second reason for giving increased attention to market art on the global stage is simply that there are so many interesting and important questions to pursue. Among them are:

– The interplay between art and other cultural forces, the most important of which would seem to be government/politics, economics/technology, and cultural identity.

– When one culture is impacted by another, any one of three things can happen. Some elements of culture may be rejected, and others might be adopted without change. However, far more common — and more interesting, in my opinion — are cases that result in the emergence of *hybrid* art forms that resemble but do not duplicate their cultural heritage and in which some foreign elements are accepted but only after having undergone changes that make them compatible with the receiving culture. The results of such re-interpretation may be ephemeral, but more often they emerge with a new and enduring identity in their new home.

– Debates regarding the concept of "authenticity" cannot be avoided. As Dutton has shown (2003), it is no easy matter to ascertain the extent to which an art work is or is not "authentic," in any of the several plausible meanings of the word.

– Two issues that frequently come up in discussions of economic and political globalization (cf., e.g., Llewellen 2002) are also relevant to global interactions in the arts. First, with the contraction of space and time made possible by contemporary technology, are the arts changing in ways that are qualitatively different from the kinds of changes they underwent in the past? And second, are the arts of the world becoming more homogeneous or more heterogeneous with the passage of time? Although it is commonly assumed that the former is the case, Cowen (2002) has pointed out that even though differences *between* cultures have been lessening, the diversity of life (and artistic) options *within* any particular culture has been increasing.

CONCLUSIONS

The systematic, cross-cultural study of art and aesthetics has come a long way during the hundred plus years of its existence. We now have more information on these topics and we also have more ways of thinking about that information. But art is constantly changing, more rapidly now than ever in the past. As a result, a great and exciting challenge lies ahead, namely, describing and understanding the many arts and theories of art that are coming into existence around the world.

REFERENCES

ABIODUN, ROWLAND. 1987. Verbal and visual metaphors: Mythical allusion in yoruba ritualistic art of Orí. *Word & Image* 3 (3): 252–70.

ANDERSON, RICHARD L. 1979. *Art in primitive societies.* Englewood Cliffs, NJ: Prentice Hall.
—. 1989. *Art in small-scale societies.* 2nd, rev. ed. of *Art in primitive societies.* (originally published 1979). Englewood Cliffs, NJ: Prentice Hall.
—. 2000. *American muse: Anthropological excursions into art and aesthetics.* Upper Saddle River, NJ: Prentice Hall.
—. 2004. *Calliope's sisters: A comparative study of philosophies of art.* 2nd, rev. ed., 1st ed. published 1990. Upper Saddle River, NJ: Prentice Hall.

BASCOM, WILLIAM R. 1973. A Yoruba master carver: Duga of Meko. In *The traditional artist in African societies,* ed. Warren L. D'Azevedo, 62–78. Bloomington: Indiana University Press.

BERLO, JANET CATHERINE, AND RUTH B. PHILLIPS. 1998. *Native North American art.* New York: Oxford University Press.

BOAS, FRANZ. 1927. *Primitive art.* New York: Dover, 1955 (1st ed. Oslo: Aschehoug).

CANTARES MEXICANOS. 1904. BNMex 1928bis, ff. 1–85.

CÓDICE MATRITENSE DE REAL PALACIA. 1906. A facsimile edition of Vol. VI (Part 2) and Vol. VII by Francisco del Paso Y Troncoso. Madrid: Hauser y Menet.

COWEN, TYLER. 2002. *Creative destruction: How globalization is changing the world's cultures.* Princeton, NJ: Princeton University Press.

DEUTSCH, ELIOT. 1975. *Studies in comparative aesthetics.* Monographs of the Society for Asian and Comparative Philosophy 2. Honolulu: University Press of Hawaii.

DISSANAYAKE, ELLEN. 1992. *Homo aestheticus: Where art comes from and why.* New York: Free Press, etc.

DUTTON, DENIS. 2003. Authenticity in art. In *The Oxford handbook of aesthetics,* ed. Jerrold Levinson, 258–274. New York: Oxford University Press.

FRASER, DOUGLAS, AND HERBERT M. COLE, eds. 1972. *African art and leadership.* Madison: University of Wisconsin Press.

FREELAND, CYNTHIA. 2001. *But is it art?* Oxford: Oxford University Press.

GOLDE, PEGGY. 1963. *Aesthetic values and art styles in a Nahua pottery producing village.* PhD diss., Harvard University.
—, and Helena C. Kraemer. 1973. Analysis of an aesthetic values test: Detection of the inter-sub-group differences within a pottery producing community in Mexico. *American Anthropologist* 75 (5): 260–75.

GRABURN, NELSON. 1999. Ethnic and tourist arts revisited. In *Unpacking culture: Art and culture in the colonial and post-colonial worlds,* ed. Ruth Phillips and Christopher Steiner, 335–53. Berkeley: University of California Press.

HATCHER, EVELYN PAYNE. 1999. *Art as culture: An introduction to the anthropology of art.,* 1st ed. published 1985. Westport, CT: Bergin & Garvey.

HESSEL, INGO, DIETER HESSEL (Photographer) AND GEORGE SWINTON. 1998. *Inuit art: An introduction.* New York: Harry N. Abrams.

JOPLING, CAROL F., ed. 1971. *Art and aesthetics in primitive societies.* New York: Dutton.

KENNEDY, JEAN, et al. 1992. *New currents, ancient rivers: Contemporary African artists in a generation of change.* Washington, DC: Smithsonian Institution Press.

KLEINERT, SYLVIA, AND MARGO NEALE, eds. 2000. *Oxford companion to aboriginal art and culture.* New York: Oxford University Press.

LAWAL, BABATUNDE. 1974. Some aspects of Yoruba aesthetics. *British Journal of Aesthetics* 14 (3): 239–49.

LAYTON, ROBERT. 1991. *The anthropology of art.* 2nd ed., 1st ed. published 1981. New York: Cambridge University Press.

LEÓN-PORTILLA, MIGUEL. 1971. Philosophy in ancient Mexico. In *Archaeology of Northern Mesoamerica,* ed. Gordon F. Ekholm and Ignacio Bernal, 447–51. Vol. 10 of *Handbook of Middle American indians,* ed. Robert Wauchope. Austin: University of Texas Press.

LLEWELLEN, TED C. 2002. *The anthropology of globalization: Cultural anthropology enters the 21st century.* Westport, CT: Bergin & Garvey.

MAQUET, JACQUES. 1986. *The aesthetic experience: An anthroplogist looks at the visual arts.* New Haven, CT and London: Yale University Press.

NELSON, EDWARD. 1899. *The Eskimo about Bering Strait.* Washington, DC: 18th Annual Report-Bureau of American Ethnology.

OTTEN, CHARLOTTE M., ed. 1971. *Anthropology and art: Readings in cross-cultural aesthetics.* Garden City, NY: Natural History Press.

RAY, DOROTHY JEAN. 1977. *Eskimo art: Tradition and innovation in North Alaska.* Seattle: University of Washington Press.

SEIDELMAN, HAROLD, JAMES TURNER, AND GEORGE SWINTON. 2001. *The Inuit imagination: Arctic myth and sculpture.* Reprint, 1st ed. published 1994. Seattle: University of Washington Press.

SIEBER, ROY. 1962. Masks as agents of social control. *African Studies Bulletin* 5 (11): 8–13.

TAYLOR, TIMOTHY D. 1997. *Global pop: World music, world markets.* New York: Routledge.

THOMPSON, ROBERT FARRIS. 1966. An aesthetic of the cool: West African dance. *African Forum* 2 (2): 85–102.
—. 1968. Esthetics in traditional Africa. *Art News* 66 (9): 44–45, 63–68.
—. 1971. *Black gods and kings.* Los Angeles: UCLA Museum of Ethnic Arts.
—. 1973. Yoruba artistic criticism. In *The Traditional Artist in African Societies,* ed. Warren L. d'Azevedo, 19–61. Bloomington: Indiana University Press.
—. 1974. *African art in motion: Icon and act in the collection of Katherine Coryton White.* Berkeley: University of California Press.
—. 1983. *Flash of the spirit: African and Afro-American art and philosophy.* New York: Random House.

VAN DAMME, WILFRIED. 2006. World aesthetics: Biology, culture, and reflection. In *Compression vs. expression: Containing and explaining the world's art,* ed. John Onians, 153–87. Williamstown, MA: Clark Art Institute.

WEITZ, MORRIS. 1967. The role of theory in aesthetics. In *Aesthetic inquiry: Essays on art criticism & the philosophy of art,* ed. Monroe C. Beardsley and Herbert M. Schueller, 3–11. Belmont, CA: Dickenson. Originally published in *Journal of Aesthetics and Art Criticism* 15 (1956): 27–35.

WITHERSPOON, GARY. 1977. *Language and art in the Navajo universe.* Ann Arbor: University of Michigan Press.
—. 1980. Language in culture and culture in language. *International Journal of American Linguistics* 46 (1): 1–13.
—. 1981. Self-expression and self-esteem in Navajo weaving. *Plateau* 52 (4): 29–32.
—, and Glen Peterson. 1995. *Dynamic symmetry and holistic asymmetry in Navajo and Western art and cosmology.* New York: Peter Lang.

PAULA D. GIRSHICK

Envisioning Art Worlds: New Directions in the Anthropology of Art

Art studies in anthropology go back to the nineteenth century beginnings of the discipline. For Victorian scholars like A. H. L. F. Pitt-Rivers and Alfred Court Haddon in England and Franz Boas and his followers in the United States, art was central to their analyses of culture, for the British scholars as a prime indicator of cultural evolution and for the American as a marker of cultural contact and an expression of the deepest cultural values. But as the focus within the discipline changed to kinship and sociopolitical structure, art was relegated to the sidelines (see Morphy 1994). Only towards the end of the twentieth century have anthropologists begun to regard art as important again, and they have done so (in fact, have predominantly done so) in relation to four issues that are central to the discipline today: representation, globalization, consumption, and identity. These issues emerged as a response to scholarly trends inside and outside the discipline as well as changes in the world at large.[1]

From the 1960s — and particularly in the 1980s and 1990s — anthropologists began to question their foundational analytical concepts and to rethink their own contributions to supporting

[1]
There have been several overviews of the anthropology of art in this period: Anderson (this volume), Morphy 1994, Neich 1984, Plattner 2004.

colonial power structures. Influenced by postmodernism, postcolonialism, feminism, and political economy, new perspectives emerged in the discipline as a whole and in art studies in particular. These new perspectives are the focus of this essay.

REPRESENTATION AND THE ART-CULTURE SYSTEM

By the mid-1980s anthropologists were concerned about what was being termed "a crisis in representation" (Marcus and Fischer 1986), which drew its inspiration in part from the writings of the French historian and philosopher Michel Foucault (1980). Foucault called attention to how disciplinary discourses (he especially concentrated on medicine and psychology) should be understood as systems of knowledge which were supported by institutions and practices. This knowledge constituted a form of power – the power to shape what was widely accepted to be normal, right, and real. In responding to Foucault, anthropologists (and scholars in other humanistic disciplines) began to question the ways in which their academic disciplines represented the people they studied, most particularly, how their definitions and classifications of others aided colonial and postcolonial power structures.

These questions were immediately relevant to art studies. In his seminal essay, "On Collecting Art and Culture," James Clifford (1988) provided a framework for conceptualizing "the art-culture system"—the specifically twentieth-century institutions and classifications by means of which exotic objects have been "contextualized and given value in the West" (1988, 223–26). The power relations that enabled Western modernism to appropriate objects from other cultures as "art" are seen by scholars like Sidney Kasfir (1992) as imperialistic. Sally Price (2001 [1989], 5), in particular, goes so far as to compare the plight of objects captured and transported to the West to that of Africans captured in the slave trade.

The art-culture system establishes the relative value and institutional context for these objects and in so doing determines their authenticity. According to Clifford, "tribal" objects enter the Western system and are classified along two axes: art/culture and authentic/inauthentic.[2] Along the first axis are placed objects that are original and singular—and therefore can be considered "art"—or traditional and collective and therefore constitute "culture." Along the second axis objects are either authentic, that is, certifiably art or artifact, or inauthentic—fakes, reproductions, tourist arts, commodities, and curios. Each category has its own institutional setting (ethnographic museums, art museums, curio shops, etc.). Objects can move across categories, but only in certain ways; for example, an authentic cultural artifact can be reconceptualized as authentic fine art, as when Australian Aboriginal acrylic painting moved into the category of fine art (Myers 1995). These paintings were amenable to such a shift, Myers shows, precisely because they fit the criteria of the modern art system which, as Kirschenblatt-Gimblett (2001, 261) has so clearly defined, "privileges painting, formal concerns, art's autonomy, artistic intention, faith in the universality of art, and circulation within a national and international art system."[3] Similarly, as Clifford points out, commodities can become collectibles as is the case with green glass coke bottles (1988, 25).

Actual "moments" of classification can be found in the literature; for example, Williams (1985) shows how pre-Columbian artifacts in nineteenth-century Paris had such an ambiguous status that they were shifted between the Louvre, the Bibliothèque Nationale, and the Musée Guimet, finally being settled in the Trocadéro as "ethnographic" artifacts. In the same vein, Steiner (1995) describes the early twentieth-century struggles of a New York art dealer to get a modernist Brancusi sculpture destined for an art gallery past Customs in New York City, where it had been classified and taxed as a piece of metal.

Museums and galleries have been key transformational institutions, particularly in the format of blockbuster exhibitions which, as Morphy (1995, 212) points out, involve the collaboration of a range of national institutions—art galleries, government organizations, corporations, and academics. One example is the Exposition of Indian Tribal Arts at the Grand Central Art Galleries in Manhattan in 1931 which functioned to shift formerly ethnographic artifacts into the category of fine arts (Mullin 2001; see also Morphy 1995).

While objects can shift between categories, their very functionality insures these shifts are marked as such. These objects are not counted as "merely" ethnographic because they have great formal appeal. Yet they do not meet modernism's expectations that art objects are freed from utility. Thus they are called "art," but always accompanied by a qualifying label as "primitive," "tribal" or "non-Western."

Errington (1998) traces the history of the entry of "primitive art" into the modern Western art world. According to her, the category of "primitive art" was formed and its canon established between the two world wars. Interest was spearheaded by the avant-garde who wove it into the mainstream of modernism. Their support of museum exhibitions, particularly the 1982 opening of the Rockefeller wing of the Metropolitan, played an enormous role in defining these objects as "art." This redefinition has presented its own problems. As Shiner (1994, 226) points out, "Ironically, it has been the success of the European and American elevation of ritual artifacts to the status of Art that has created the heavy demand and rise in prices which led to the inevitable incidence of 'fakes,' particularly in the booming African sculpture market."

In Clifford's terms, the art-culture system is a "machine for making authenticity" (1988, 224). As he and other scholars (Kasfir

---

3
The issues of Primitivism and aesthetics are discussed elsewhere in this volume by Colin Rhodes and will be omitted here.

4
A number of excellent recent studies of
tourist art can be found in Phillips and
Steiner 1999.

1992; Steiner 1992, 1996) demonstrate, the concept of authenticity functions to mark boundaries and establish value — and has done so for some time. For example, McCracken (1988, 38) traces the symbolic significance of patina — a characteristic marker of authenticity in the West — to medieval and early modern England where it functioned as a "visual manner of determining where families stood in the process of gentrification and social mobility." It was the space where money was transformed into status.

Today authenticity plays an important role as a boundary marker of indigenous people at sites around the world — tourist markets, galleries, museums, and overseas exhibitions (Venbrux and Rosi 2004, 220). The criteria for authenticity in the global market are: age (preferably precolonial), evidence of ritual usage, absence of production for gain or export, and in some cases, previous residence in a prestigious collection (Clifford 1988, 222; Kasfir 1992, 2003; Price 2001 [1989], 100–7; Shiner 1994; Steiner 1996; Venbrux and Rosi 2004, 220). Certain kinds of objects do not meet these criteria and are defined as tourist arts, hybrid arts, or studio arts (Steiner 1996).

Kasfir (1992) point outs that the claims for authenticity in "tribal" art depend on a view of tribal societies as being small, closed, and slow to change. When their artistic production becomes swamped with Western iconography or produced for Western consumption, they lose their authenticity.

The notion of authenticity rests on two sets of dichotomies: purity versus corruption and singularity versus mechanical reproduction. The first — purity — means freedom from the corruption of outside, primarily Western, influences — a clearly unrealistic expectation as cultures have been in contact for centuries. As Welsch (2004), Schildkrout and Keim (1998), and Thomas (1991) all point out, some of the nineteenth and early twentieth centuries items considered most authentic were already made for export, making it impossible to ever establish a baseline.

The second underlying dichotomy is between creativity/ singularity versus "mechanical reproduction," associated primarily and negatively with tourist art. According to Kasfir (1992, 48), the Western connoisseur imagines that contemporary workshops work with a kind of "machine-like efficiency…with assembly lines" and their products, thus, are inauthentic. This view has been challenged by several scholars (Ben-Amos 1977; Jules-Rosette 1984; Kasfir 1992).[4] Most recently, Steiner (1999) has drawn on Walter Benjamin's 1936 essay "The Work of Art in the Age of Mechanical Reproduction" to argue that serial production occurs with "any art form that is embedded in a wider economy and subject to the market forces of production and consumption." In this view, tourist art is not a unique form of art produced in colonial and postcolonial encounters but fits into "a more generalized model of producer-consumer relations including other major innovations in mechanical reproduction, mass production, and the universal dissemination of popular culture." Redundancy is an important factor in contact situations as tourists find validation in recognizable forms (see also Ben-Amos 1977).

In addition to fine arts and tourist arts, there are a range of cultural productions which have been difficult to define and label. Nelson Graburn was the first to attempt a classification of these productions in his 1976 *Ethnic and Tourist Arts: Cultural Productions from the Fourth World*. In his Introduction he classifies them as commercial fine arts, souvenir (tourist or airport) arts, reintegrated arts, or popular arts. In the literature since then, terms like "transitional" and "hybrid" have been used but each of these terms has problems. Transitional implies a unilinear preordained development (Nettleton 1988) while hybrid, according to Thomas (1996, 9), "enables critics and curators to celebrate their own capacity for acknowledging cultural difference, while refraining from engaging with the stories and works that emerge from ground remote from their own" (see Graburn 1999, 343–44). An alternative offered by Szombati-Fabian and Fabian (1976) is based on the fact that "artists and consumers of [contemporary Zairian painting] neither define the forms and contents of this art *against* a tradition nor *toward* modernization. Their ordinary existence is in the middle of both, making it a daily task to transform seemingly disparate elements into coherent and consistent action" (1976, 18). Such an approach is in line with Phillips and Steiner's rejection of classificatory attempts. According to them, scholars should stop trying to define art: "no longer treatable as distinct and separate categories, the art-artifact-commodity triad must now be merged into a single domain where the categories are seen to inform one another rather than to compete in their claims for social primacy and cultural value" (1999, 16).

TOWARDS NEW PERSPECTIVES

The late twentieth-century critique of anthropology's underlying assumptions about the nature of culture and art brought about a new paradigm in which dichotomies of time and space were transcended. One of the most influential works was Johannes Fabian's *Time and the Other* (1983) which exposed how anthropological discourses, particularly nineteenth-century evolutionism and twentieth-century ethnographic presentism, had constructed non-Western people at a temporal distance, denying them coeval existence with us. As against the view of these cultures as self-contained and isolated from the main streams of world interaction, works such as Immanuel Wallerstein's *The Modern World System* (1974) and, especially, Eric Wolf's *Europe and the People Without History* (1982) demonstrated how longstanding and profound were global economic and political interconnections. A major focus of research has become how objects circulate in this system. Arjun Appadurai's "Introduction" and Igor Kopytoff's essay on "The

Cultural Biography of Things" in Appadurai's edited volume
The Social Life of Things (1986) look at the cultural definitions of
things at different points in their social life and how they are circulated in and out of commodity status. Readers are asked to consider the "candidacy" of things for specific states and the social are-
nas in which the particular state occurs. Kopytoff argues that in every society there are things that are publicly precluded from being
commoditized, at least in theory. This process, which he calls "sin-
gularization," is at the heart of art collecting. Their approach leads
directly to issues of the politics of value, demand, and consumption.

Art studies in anthropology have moved in new directions,
particularly the politics of collecting and representation in historical perspective, the global art market with special reference to the
relationship between art and commodity, and, lastly, art and ethnic
and/or national identity. At the heart of these new perspectives is
the trope of movement, one example being the title of a special
issue of *Ethnos* organized by Kenneth George (1999): "Objects on
the Loose." The notion of an art world, originally developed by the
philosopher Arthur Danto (1964) and the sociologist Howard
Becker (1982), has proven useful as a way to conceptualize a range
of these new issues involving concepts of time, space and new
forms of relationships.

THE POLITICS OF COLLECTING
AND REPRESENTATION
IN HISTORICAL PERSPECTIVE

The field of postcolonial studies, especially the work of Edward
Said (1978) and Homi Bhabha (1990), influenced anthropologists
into looking more closely at the role objects played in our representation of "the Other." The historical trajectory of collecting in
Africa is addressed by Schildkrout and Keim (1998), who trace the
development from fifteenth-century Portuguese commissions of
ivory carvings on the West African coast, through nineteenth-century curio collecting, to trophy collection, to scientific expeditions,
each with its own characteristics. They talk about a massive scramble for artifacts in the beginning of the twentieth-century in the
then Belgian Congo. Similar scrambles occurred simultaneously or
somewhat earlier in the Northwest Coast of America (Cole 1985),
the American Southwest (Dubin 2001; Mullin 2001; Rushing 1995),
Alaska (Lee 1999) and New Zealand (Allen 1998, 144–52). Collecting was stimulated by—and was complicit in—the development of museums and the foundation of the field of anthropology
(Clifford 1988; Coombes 1994; Fabian 1983; Stocking 1985).

Circulating goods and increasing trade were primary motivations for imperial expansion and, thus, objects were at the heart
of colonial endeavors and relationships, as Gosden and Knowles
(2001) point out. They argue that given the unequal power relationships and lack of common understanding, the resulting situation

was one of instability, experimentation, and novelty (see also
Barringer and Flynn 1998 and MacClancy 1997). From the beginning, local people were agentive, they were highly selective of
what they sold as they catered to tastes of Europeans (Cole 1985;
Fabian 1998; Gosden and Knowles 2001; Schildkrout and Keim
1998; Thomas 1991) while resisting when force was used to carry
away their objects, as Allen (1998) describes for the Maori. It is
clear that local people were active participants in a global market
which they manipulated as best they could. According to Schildkrout and Keim (1998, 5), "Artifacts and the texts that came with
them were an important part of the process of economic redefinition—new scales of value developed as different sorts of wealth,
both material and immaterial, entered into the economy." As
Thomas (1991) ably demonstrates, through the appropriation and
exchange of goods between Pacific Islanders and Europeans, new
forms of difference emerged with radically transformed meanings.[5]

In the metropole, the objects collected in the colonies,
whether through purchase or as war booty, played an important
role in defining images of the Other and effecting their relationships before, during, and after colonialism. Annie Coombes (1994)
shows how the reportage, especially photographs, of the looting
and subsequent display of the "bronzes" and ivories from the Benin
Kingdom fed into the complex and fundamentally ambivalent
notions about Africa at that time—promoting both an image of
a savage people needing to be civilized and an appreciation, indeed,
a sense of marvel, at the skill and beauty of their art. Objects
continue to act as representatives of an imaginary Other long after
colonialism, as Clifford (1988), Errington (1998), and Price (2001
[1989]) clearly demonstrate in their analyses of the 1984 blockbuster exhibition entitled *"Primitivism" in 20th Century Art: Affinity of the Tribal and the Modern* at the Museum of Modern Art in
New York City.

GLOBALIZATION AND THE ART WORLD

The notion of an art world, originally aimed at the networks of artists, dealers, scholars, critics and museums in the urban centers of
the Euro-American world, has been extended outside of centers to
peripheries at home and abroad. What constitutes an art world?
Sullivan (1995, 257) uses Benedict Anderson's (1991) definition to
describe the art world as an "imagined community" of "tiered commercial, communicative and social networks spread across the
globe." The participants are linked by commercial dealings and an
ideology about the nature of art and how to evaluate it (for discussions of the rise of modernism and the contemporary art world,
see Errington 1998; Marcus and Myers 1995; Sullivan 1995).

In analyzing this global art world, the focus has been on the
centers, particularly New York (Marquis 1991; Sullivan 1995;
Errington 1998), London (MacClancy 1988) and Paris (Moulin

5
The issue of appropriation has been
dealt with extensively; see Hart 1995,
Muller 1995, Schneider 1996, 2003,
among others.

1987), but more recently attention has turned to internal peripheries like the American Southwest (Dubin 2001; Gordon 1988; Mullin 2001; Wade 1985) and Midwest (Plattner 1996) and to areas outside of the United States such as the Low Countries (Corbey 2000), Southern and Eastern Africa (Fongue 2002 and Jules-Rosette 1986, respectively) and, especially, Australia (Morphy 1994, 1995, 2001 and Myers 1994, 1995, 1999, 2001, 2002). Centers are seen as determining the shape of the art world by defining its boundaries of inclusion and exclusion and by establishing value in their main art institutions. This is vividly expressed by Morphy (1995, 211) in his claim that "[i]t is in the nature of the Western category of art to expand anaconda-like by swallowing the products of its neighbors and its own and other people's pasts. Thus it changes not only its own criteria of existence but also transforms the meaning and value of the objects that it swallows up."

The fine art market is portrayed as a special kind of arena where, as Plattner (1996, 195) points out, value is "mysterious, socially constructed, and impossible to predict a priori." Ambiguity arises because there is no standard accepted formula for evaluating objects. Instead, provenance and other culturally-defined attributes are important, perhaps more so than the material and appearance.

The art market is also a special case because the modernist ideology of art's autonomy conflicts with its commodity status. Bourdieu (1984 [1979], 197) characterizes art and its collection as "a sacred island systematically and ostentatiously opposed to the profane everyday world of production; it offers a sanctuary for gratuitous, disinterested activity in a world of money." The ambiguous role of art as both treasure and commodity presents problems for the players; for example, academics and museum personnel are not "allowed" to talk about monetary value while collectors want to see themselves "as connoisseurs uncontaminated by a search for profit" (Plattner 1996,181–82).

Scholars dealing with these ambiguities and conflicts have raised questions about who are the gatekeepers, who controls the classification of an object as "art" or "artifact," and who determines authenticity and who the monetary value. Graburn (1999, 349) argues that the gatekeepers are the middlemen who transmit the physical art object and control the flow of information about its origin, age, meaning and producer. Bystryn (1978), Marquis (1991), and Plattner (1996) are in agreement with him that gallery owners are the pricemakers, tastemakers, and, in the case of "tribal" arts, culture brokers (Steiner 1994). In his study of British collectors, MacClancy (1988) notes that so-called "primitive art" is valued by collectors for its "spirit, power, magic, mystery—modern variants of the noble savage" and suggests that these qualities are so ephemeral that those who can use the terminology, who "have the eye," have great power. "In this market, a dealer with eye surrounded by buyers who are learning their way has far more power in determining taste then one in Renaissance painting." Not all dealers are successful and Plattner (1996, 195) adds that these gate-keepers themselves are arranged hierarchically and the elite galleries can spoil the sales of lesser galleries by denying legitimacy to their art.

Steiner (1994) has done groundbreaking work on the role of African middlemen in Côte d'Ivoire. These traders remove objects from their original context and circulate them among dealers and collectors where they become global commodities and aesthetic objects. The traders act as culture brokers, describing to the producers the preferences of the Western clientele and expressing to the purchasers a particular image of African art and culture (1994, 15). Complementing Steiner's African focus, Stoller (2003) has looked at West African traders in the USA and explores their kinship organization and socioeconomic practices in New York City. He explains how they have adjusted their long standing trade practices in West Africa to the realities of the American market.

Auction houses like Sotheby's and Christie's play an important role as the sole public source for art prices (Marquis 1991, 251). Indeed, Sullivan (1995, 273) asserts that since the 1970s they have begun "usurping dealers' power to 'curate' longterm and international clusters of art." Corbey (2000, 99) characterizes auctions as "rich sources of information about the movements of ethnographics, the formation of collections and changes in taste, fashion and market value." (See also Benthall 1987; Geismar 2001; Marquis 1991; Plattner 1996; Satov 1997.) Geismar (2001) builds on Appadurai's notion of a "tournament of value" (1986, 21)[6] to trace the social practices occurring from the catalogue sale through viewing to auction itself. During this process, she claims, "object identities, criteria of authenticity and transaction histories are manipulated by buyers and sellers in order to influence value" (2001, 26).

Auction houses promote a notion of a canon of aesthetic appeal, suitability for display, rarity, fashionableness, nationalistic appeal, illustrious provenance, degree of scholarship and documentation available in order to enhance value. The catalogue is a key factor in their efforts to stress authenticity (Benthall 1987, 10; Corbey 2000; Geismar 2001; Satov 1997). Gorgeous color photographs, discussions of ethnographic context, and most especially, establishment of the "pedigree" of objects (their history of ownership) are determining factors. Auctioneers, however, are too connected to the commodity side of the art/commodity conflict and so seek to acquire academic credibility by drawing on existing scholarship in their catalogues.

In this way the market is tied to institutionalized academic knowledge in museums and universities (Geismar 2001). In fact, in Britain the auction house and the academic/museum nexus draw on the same recruits, who have similar schooling but differ in how they deal with the conflicted relationship between art and commodity based, on the one hand on connoisseurship, and, on the oth-

6

Appadurai (1986, 21–22) defines tournaments of value as "complex periodic events that are removed in some culturally well-defined way from the routines of economic life. Participation in them is likely to be both a privilege of those in power and an instrument of status contests between them."

er, commodity marketability (Benthall 1987, 9). Academics and curators, on their part, often distance themselves from the financial world of the auction.[7] Curators rely on a form of mystification which Sullivan (1995) aptly describes as drawing a veil across their decision-making practices. Sullivan (1995, 269) argues that it is the curators who are the "pivotal linchpin of the system" where "new ideas become corporeal and objects are invested with historical significance."

There has been much discussion of the motivations of collectors (Belk 1995; Elsner and Cardinal 1994; Pearce 1995, 1998). MacClancy (1988), for example, argues that cultural usage, age, and patina are not as important to the British collector as the tactile sensations, the act of possessing (with its sexual overtones). "Love, touch, greed, fear, courage, passion, ownership, devotion, taste… the whole person is involved in serious collecting" (1998, 164). But, it is clear, not financial gain. As Appadurai (1986, 28) has shown, once an object takes on the value of a collectible it must not be used or exchanged—though its commodity potential always exists. The value that it now embodies is not monetary but rather related to the quest. While collectors know how much they paid and how much they insured the object for, they nevertheless choose to ignore that aspect.

Collecting of art tends to be an elite, middle and upper class pattern of consumption (Belk 1995; Bourdieu 1984 [1979]; Gans 1974; Gordon 1988; Halle 1993; Lee 1999; McCracken 1998; Plattner 1996; Vogel 1988a). The issue at stake for these collectors is what Bourdieu has called "cultural capital," the perceived worth of objects, behaviors, or ideas based on values such as aesthetic quality, symbolic significance, historical importance, uniqueness, social function, and such. In a fascinating analysis of how a cultural elite developed its status and influence in Boston, DiMaggio (1991) demonstrates how the definition of high culture (and its opposite) and the institutionalization of this classification was the work of "cultural capitalists"—the capitalists and the professionals among them, who founded the museums and orchestras that embodied and elaborated the high cultural ideal. The collecting of "tribal art" may involve other factors. In his 1993 study of the personal meaning of art in 160 homes in the NYC area, Halle asked a sample of wealthy, middle, and working class families about various genres of art found in their homes—landscapes, portraits, and for our purposes, tribal/primitive art. He found that the collector's motivations for the latter were primarily based on ethnic identity and political leanings rather than prestige issues.

Artists are in the weakest position in the global art-culture system. With the exception of Anderson's 2000 ethnography of a range of sixty four American artists, most studies have concentrated on the special problems experienced by indigenous creators (Babcock 1995; Morphy 1995, 216–17; Venbrux and Rosi 2004, 219–22; Myers 2002). Graburn (1999, 347) sees the artists who create for the world art system as living "in a minefield of rules that they overstep at their peril." With the exception of the minority of Native artists who are able to attend art schools, the majority are "rarely socialized into the symbolic and aesthetic system of the consumers who support them" (for example, see Wade 1985, 189). Not all would agree with Graburn. For example, in his sensitive and detailed study of Aboriginal painters, Myers (2002) shows how these artists have used their art to reformulate their position in contemporary Australian society. While, as Graburn has claimed, many of the discussions about indigenous artists depict them as overpowered by a system beyond their control, Myers (2002, 5) shows how Pintupi artists have used acrylic paintings as a way to "objectify their political aspirations and identity," successfully transforming their work into widely accepted fine art which conveys meaning to both Pintupi and whites.

ART AND IDENTITY

Art has become a major arena for the negotiation of identity as people seek to recreate themselves first in the colonial project and currently in the postcolonial situation (MacClancy 1988; Marcus and Myers 1995; Phillips and Steiner 1999). This is true because art is a readily recognizable, economically relevant way for groups to try to control how they are represented. As Myers (2001, 30) explains, "Art is an institution that purports to judge, place, and define a range of differences within its own hierarchy of value. As a medium of objectification, the materiality of art and its meaning have made it particularly productive in the context of modernity, as an arena for constituting and considering human difference and value."

Studies show how these identity projects operate in a variety of contexts—class, regional, national, and global. Small, marginalized groups, like the Inuit painters described by Berlo (1999, 191) or the Iatmul carvers on the Sepik River in Papua New Guinea by Silverman (1999), create idealized versions of themselves or their material culture as they existed in "the old days" in an effort to support their sense of identity. Others, like the Amazonian activists described by Conklin (1997), use traditional body painting to play off of Western stereotypes of primitivism and exoticism as political tools in their interethnic politics.

The art of indigenous people can be appropriated by local and national elites, as Svašek (1997, 75) demonstrates for Ghana, where these elites reappropriate notions of African art from Western discourse and use them for their own ends. Thomas (2001, 139) argues that similar things occur in antipodean settler colonies, where "anxieties around national identities have often been negotiated through art, and conversely, the value of art has often been adjudicated on the basis of its local authenticity and its adequacy as a vehicle for national distinctiveness. One of the most obvious routes to such national distinctiveness has been reference to, or appropriation of, elements of the indigenous art traditions of these colonial societies."

Similarly, Dubin (2001) and Mullin (2001) have shown how in the American Southwest, early twentieth-century elite white women used native American art to create a distinctive American artistic identity in contrast to the dominant European one of the East Coast elite.

CONCLUSION

The approaches discussed here have not been accepted uncritically (or universally, for that matter). Some of their proponents have been criticized for essentializing the West (Dutton 1995), for not attributing sufficient agency to local people (Schneider 1996) or for making the process of appropriation seem a specifically Western imperialistic behavior (Beidelman 1992). While these criticisms hold in some of the more extreme cases, in the main the studies discussed here have made important contributions to the anthropology of art by offering a serious challenge to the insistence on the purity and autonomy of art, by exploring new sites and new institutions, and by giving art a role in key socioeconomic processes in the contemporary scene.

REFERENCES

ALLEN, NGAPINE. 1998. Maori vision and the imperialist gaze. In *Colonialism and the object: empire, material culture and the museum,* ed. Tim Barringer and Tom Flynn, 144–52. London: Routledge.

ANDERSON, BENEDICT. 1991. *Imagined communities: Reflections on the origin and spread of nationalism.* London: Verso.

ANDERSON, RICHARD. 2000. *American muse: Anthropological excursions into art and aesthetics.* Upper Saddle River, NJ: Prentice Hall.

APPADURAI, ARJUN. 1986. Introduction: Commodities and the politics of value. In *The social life of things: Commodities in cultural perspective,* ed. Arjun Appadurai, 3–63. Cambridge: Cambridge University Press.

BABCOCK, BARBARA. 1995. Marketing Maria: The tribal artist in the age of mechanical reproduction. In *Looking high and low: Art and cultural identity,* ed. Brenda Jo Bright and Liza Bakewell, 124–50. Tucson: The University of Arizona Press.

BARRINGER, TIM, AND TOM FLYNN, eds. 1998. *Colonialism and the object: Empire, material culture and the museum.* London: Routledge.

BECKER, HOWARD 1982. *Art worlds.* Berkeley: University of California Press.

BEIDELMAN, TOM O. 1992. Authenticity and appropriation [Dialogue section]. *African Arts* 24 (3): 24–26.

BELK, RUSSELL W. 1995. *Collecting in a consumer society.* London: Routledge.

BEN-AMOS, PAULA. 1977. Pidgin languages and tourist arts. *Studies in the Anthropology of Visual Communication* 4 (2): 128-39.
—. 1989. African visual arts from a social perspective. *African Studies Review* 32 (2): 1–53.

BENJAMIN, WALTER. 1955 [1969]. The work of art in the age of mechanical reproduction. In *Illuminations,* ed. and intro. Hannah Arendt, trans. Harry Zohn, 59–67. New York: Shocken Books. Originally published as *L'Œuvre d'art à l'époque de sa reproductibilité technique* (1935).

BENTHALL, JONATHAN. 1987. Ethnographic museums and the art trade. *Anthropology Today* 3 (3): 9–13.

BERLO, JANET CATHERINE. 1999. Drawing (upon) the past: Negotiating identities in Inuit graphic arts production. In *Unpacking culture: Art and commodity in colonial and post-colonial worlds,* ed. Ruth B. Phillips and Christopher B. Steiner, 178–96. Berkeley: University of California Press.

BHABHA, HOMI. 1990. *Nation and narration.* New York: Routledge.

BLIER, SUZANNE P. 1989–1990. Art systems and semiotics question of art, craft, and colonial taxonomies in Africa. *The American Journal of Semiotics* 6 (1): 7–18.

BOURDIEU, PIERRE. 1984. *Distinction: A social critique of the judgment of taste,* trans. Richard Nice. Cambridge, MA: Cambridge University Press. Originally published as *La distinction: critique sociale du jugement* (Paris: Minuit, 1979).
—, and Alain Darbel. 1990. *The love of art: European art museums and their public.* Trans. Caroline Beattie and Nick Merriman. Cambridge: Cambridge University Press.

BRIGHT, BRENDA JO, AND LIZA BAKEWELL. 1995. Introduction: Art hierarchies, cultural boundaries and reflexive analysis. In *Looking high and low: Art and cultural identity,* ed. Brenda Jo Bright and Liza Bakewell, 1–18. Tucson: The University of Arizona Press.

BYSTRYN, MARCIA. 1978. Art galleries as gatekeepers: The case of the abstract expressionists. *Social Research* 45: 390–408.

CLIFFORD, JAMES. 1988. *The predicament of culture: Twentieth century ethnography, literature, and art.* Cambridge, MA: Harvard University Press.

COLE, DOUGLAS. 1985. *Captured heritage: The scramble for Northwest Coast artifacts.* Norman: University of Oklahoma Press.

COLEMAN, ELIZABETH BURNS. 2001. Aboriginal painting: Identity and authenticity. *Journal of Aesthetics and Art Criticism* 59 (4): 385–402.

CONKLIN, BETH A. 1997. Body paint, feathers, and VCRs: Aesthetics and authenticity in Amazonian activism. *American Ethnologist* 24 (4): 711–37.

COOMBES, ANNIE E. 1994. *Reinventing Africa: Museums, material culture and popular imagination.* New Haven, CT: Yale University Press.

CORBEY, RAYMOND. 2000. *Tribal art traffic: A chronicle of taste, trade and desire in colonial and post-colonial times.* Amsterdam: Royal Tropical Institute.

DANTO, ARTHUR C. 1964. The artworld. *Journal of Philosophy* 61 (19): 571–84.

DIMAGGIO, PAUL. 1991. Cultural entrepreneurship in 19th-century Boston. In *Rethinking popular culture,* ed. Chandra Mukerji and Michael Schudson, 374–97. Berkeley: University of California Press.

DUBIN, MARGARET. 2001. *Native America collected: The culture of an art world.* Albuquerque: University of New Mexico Press.

DUTTON, DENIS. 1995. Mythologies of tribal art. *African Arts* 26 (4): 32–43

ELSNER, JOHN, AND ROGER CARDINAL, eds. 1994. *The cultures of collecting.* Cambridge, MA: Harvard University Press.

ERRINGTON, SHELLY. 1998. *The death of authentic primitive art and other tales of progress.* Berkeley: University of California Press.

FABIAN, JOHANNES. 1983. *Time and the other: How anthropology makes its object.* New York: Columbia University Press.
—. 1998. Curios and curiosity: Notes on reading Torday and Frobenius. In *The scramble for Central Africa,* ed. Enid Schildkrout and Curtis Keim, 79–81. Cambridge: Cambridge University Press.

FONGUE, J. NDEFFO. 2002. The market for works of art: The case of African cultural goods. *South African Journal of Economics* 70 (8): 1320–43.

FOUCAULT, MICHEL. 1980. *Power/knowledge: Selected interviews and other writings 1972–1977,* ed. Colin Gordon. New York: Pantheon.

GANS, HERBERT. 1974. *Popular culture and high culture: An analysis and evaluation of taste.* New York: Basic Books.

GATHERCOLE, PETER. 1987. Anthropology and auction houses: Thatcherite anthropology? *Anthropology Today* 3 (2): 22.

GEISMAR, HAIDY. 2001. What's in a price: An ethnography of tribal art at auction. *Journal of Material Culture* 6 (1): 25–47.

GEORGE, KENNETH M. 1999. Objects on the loose: Ethnographic encounters with unruly artefacts. *Ethnos* 64 (2):149–50.

GORDON, BEVERLY, WITH MELANIE HERZOG. 1988. *American Indian art: The collecting experience.* Madison: University of Wisconsin Press.

GOSDEN, CHRIS, AND CHANTAL KNOWLES. 2001. *Collecting colonialism: Material culture and colonial change.* Oxford: Berg.

GRABURN, NELSON, ed. 1976. *Ethnic and tourist arts: Cultural expressions from the fourth world.* Berkeley: University of California Press.
—. 1999. Ethnic and tourist arts revisited. In *Unpacking culture: Art and commodity in colonial and postcolonial worlds,* ed. Ruth B. Phillips and Christopher B. Steiner, 335–53. Berkeley: University of California Press.

HALLE, DAVID. 1993. *Inside culture: Art and class in the American home.* Chicago and London: The University of Chicago Press.

HART, LYNN M. 1995. Three walls: Regional aesthetics and the international art world. In *The traffic in culture: Refiguring art and anthropology,* ed. George E. Marcus and Fred R. Myers, 127–50. Berkeley: University of California Press.

JULES-ROSETTE, BENNETTA. 1984. *The messages of tourist art: An African semiotic system in comparative perspective.* New York: Plenum Press.
—. 1986. Aesthetics and market demand: The structure of the tourist art market in three African settings. *African Studies Review* 29 (1): 41–59.

KASFIR, SIDNEY L. 1992. African art and authenticity: A text with a shadow. *African Arts* 25 (2): 40–53, 96–97.
—. 2003. Thinking about artworlds in a global flow: Some major disparities in dealing with visual culture. *International Journal of Anthropology* 18 (4): 211–18.

KIRSCHENBLATT-GIMBLETT, BARBARA. 2001. Reflections. In *The empire of things: Regimes of value and material culture,* ed. Fred R. Myers, 257–68. Santa Fe: School of American Research.

KOPYTOFF, IGOR. 1986. The cultural biography of things: Commoditization as process. In *The social life of things: Commodities in cultural perspective,* ed. Arjun Appadurai, 3–63. Cambridge: Cambridge University Press.

LEE, MOLLY. 1999. Tourism and taste cultures: Collecting native art in Alaska at the turn of the twentieth century. In *Unpacking culture: Art and commodity in colonial and postcolonial worlds,* ed. Ruth B. Phillips and Christopher B. Steiner, 267–81. Berkeley: University of California Press.

MACCLANCY, JEREMY. 1988. A natural curiosity: The British market in primitive art. *RES: Anthropology and Aesthetics* 15: 163–76.
—, ed. 1997. *Contesting art: Art, politics, and identity in the modern world.* Oxford: Berg.

MARCUS, GEORGE E. 1995. Middlebrow into highbrow at the J. Paul Getty Trust, L.A. *Looking high and low,* ed. Brenda Jo Bright and Liza Bakewell, 173–98. Tucson: The University of Arizona Press.
—, and Michael M. J. Fischer. 1986. *Anthropology as cultural critique: An experimental moment in the human sciences.* Chicago and London: The University of Chicago Press.

—, and Fred R. Myers. 1995. The traffic in art and culture: An introduction. In *The traffic in culture: Refiguring art and anthropology,* ed. George E. Marcus and Fred R. Myers, 1–51. Berkeley: University of California Press.

MARQUIS, ALICE GOLDFARB. 1991. *The art biz: The covert world of collectors, dealers, auction houses, museums, and critics.* Chicago: Contemporary Books.

MCCRACKEN, GRANT. 1998. *Culture and consumption: New approaches to the symbolic character of consumer goods and activities.* Bloomington: Indiana University Press.

MORPHY, HOWARD. 1994. The anthropology of art. In *Companion encyclopedia of anthropology: Humanity, culture and social life,* ed. Tim Ingold, 648–85. London: Routledge.
—. 1995. Aboriginal art in a global context. In *Worlds apart: Modernity through the prism of the local,* ed. Daniel Miller, 211–39. London: Routledge.
—. 2001. Seeing aboriginal art in the gallery. *Humanities Research* 8 (1), www.anu.edu.au/hrc/publications/hr/issue1_2001/article05.htm.

MOULIN, RAYMONDE. 1987. *The French art market.* Trans. A. Goldhammer. New York: Routledge.

MULLIN, MOLLY H. 1995. The patronage of difference: Making Indian art "art," not ethnology. In *The traffic in culture: Refiguring art and anthropology,* ed. George E. Marcus and Fred R. Myers, 1–51. Berkeley: University of California Press.
—. 2001. *Culture in the marketplace: Gender, art, and value in the American Southwest.* Durham, NC: Duke University Press.

MYERS, FRED R. 1994. Culture making: Performing aboriginality at the Asia Society Gallery. *American Ethnologist* 21 (4): 679–99.
—. 1995. Representing culture: The production of discourse(s) for aboriginal acrylic paintings. In *The traffic in culture: Refiguring art and anthropology,* ed. George E. Marcus and Fred R. Myers, 55–95. Berkeley: University of California Press.
—. 1999. Objects on the loose. *Ethnos* 64 (2): 263–73.
—. 2001. The wizards of Oz: Nation, state and the production of aboriginal fine art. *The empire of things,* ed. Fred Myers, 165–206. Santa Fe: School of American Research.
—. 2002. *Painting culture: The making of an aboriginal high art.* Durham, NC: Duke University Press.

NEICH, ROGER. 1984. Some recent developments in the anthropology of the visual arts. *Pacific Arts Newsletter* 19: 24–42.

NETTLETON, ANITRA. 1988. The myth of the transitional: Black art and white markets. *South African Journal for Cultural and Art History* 2 (4): 301–10.

PEARCE, SUSAN M. 1995. *On collecting: An investigation into collecting in the European Tradition.* London: Routledge.
—. 1998. *Collecting in contemporary practice.* London: Sage.
—, and Christopher B. Steiner 1999. Art, authenticity, and the baggage of cultural encounter. In *Unpacking culture: Art and commodity in colonial and postcolonial worlds,* ed. Ruth B. Phillips and Christopher B. Steiner, 3–19. Berkeley: University of California Press.

PHILLIPS, RUTH B. 1998. *Trading identities: The souvenir in Native North America, 1700–1900.* Seattle: University of Washington Press.

PLATTNER, STUART. 1996. *High art down home: An economic ethnography of a local art market.* Chicago and London: The University of Chicago Press.
—. 1998. A most ingenious paradox: The market for contemporary fine art. *American Anthropologist* 100 (2): 482–93.

—. 2004. Anthropology of art. https://ep.eur.nl/retrieve/1335/towse%20ebook.

PRICE, SALLY. 2001. *Primitive art in civilized places*. 2nd edition, 1st ed. published 1989. Chicago and London: The University of Chicago Press.

RUSHING, W. JACKSON. 1995. *Native American art and the New York avant-garde: A history of cultural primitivism*. Austin: University of Texas Press.

SAID, EDWARD. 1978. *Orientalism: Western conceptions of the Orient*. New York: Pantheon.

SATOV, MURRAY. 1997. Catalogues, collectors, curators: The tribal art market and anthropology. In *Contesting art: Art, politics, and identity in the modern world*, ed. Jeremy MacClancy, 215–41. Oxford: Berg.

SCHILDKROUT, ENID, AND CURTIS KEIM. 1998. Objects and agendas: Re-collecting the Congo. In *The scramble for art in Central Africa*, ed. Enid Schildkrout and Curtis Keim, 1–36. Cambridge: Cambridge University Press.

SHINER, LARRY. 1994. "Primitive fakes," "tourist art," and the ideology of authenticity. *Journal of Aesthetics and Art Criticism* 52 (2): 225–34.

SCHNEIDER, ARND. 1996. Uneasy relationships: Contemporary artists and anthropology. *Journal of Material Culture* 1 (2): 183–210.
—. 2003. On "appropriation": A critical reappraisal of the concept and its application to global art practices. *Social Anthropology* 11 (2): 215–29.

SILVERMAN, ERIC. 1999. Tourist art as the crafting of identity in the Sepik River (Papua New Guinea). In *Unpacking culture: Art and commodity in colonial and postcolonial worlds*, ed. Ruth B. Phillips and Christopher B. Steiner, 51–86. Berkeley: University of California Press.

SPOONER, BRIAN. 1986. Weavers and dealers: The authenticity of an oriental carpet. In *The social life of things*, ed. Arjun Appadurai, 195–235. Cambridge: Cambridge University Press.

STEINER, CHRISTOPHER B. 1992. Fake masks and faux: The modernity crisis of misrepresentation [Dialogue section]. *African Arts* 25 (3): 18–19.
—. 1994. *African art in transit*. Cambridge: Cambridge University Press.
—. 1995. The art of the trade: On the creation of value and authenticity in the African art market. In *The traffic in culture: Refiguring art and anthropology*, ed. George E. Marcus and Fred R. Myers, 141–65. Berkeley: University of California Press.
—. 1996. Can the canon burst?, *The Art Bulletin* 78 (2): 213–18.
—. 1999. Authenticity, repetition, and the aesthetics of seriality: The work of tourist art in the age of mechanical reproduction. In *Unpacking culture: Art and commodity in colonial and post-colonial worlds*, ed. Ruth B. Phillips and Christopher B. Steiner, 87–103. Berkeley: University of California Press.

STOCKING, GEORGE W., JR., ed. 1985. *Objects and others: Essays on museums and material culture*. Madison: The University of Wisconsin Press.

STOLLER, PAUL. 2003. Circuits of African art/paths of wood: Exploring an anthropological trail. *Anthropological Quarterly* 76 (2): 207–34.

SULLIVAN, NANCY. 1995. Inside trading: postmodernism in the social drama of *Sunflowers* in the 1980s art world. In *The traffic in culture: Refiguring art and anthropology*, ed. George E. Marcus and Fred R. Myers, 256–301. Berkeley: University of California Press.

SVAŠEK, MARUŠKA. 1997. Identity and style in Ghanaian artistic discourse. In *Contesting art: Art, politics, and identity in the modern world*, ed. Jeremy MacClancy, 27–61. Oxford: Berg.

SZOMBATI-FABIAN, ILONA, AND JOHANNES FABIAN. 1976. Art, history, and society: Popular painting in Shaba, Zaire. *Studies in the Anthropology of Visual Communication* 1 (1): 1–21.

THOMAS, NICHOLAS. 1991. *Entangled objects: Exchange, material culture, and colonialism in the Pacific*. Cambridge, MA: Harvard University Press.
—. 1996. Cold fusion. *American Anthropologist* 98 (1): 9–16.
—. 1997. Collectivity and nationality in the anthropology of art. In *Rethinking visual anthropology*, ed. Marcus Banks and Howard Morphy, 256–75. New Haven, CT: Yale University Press.
—. 1999. *Possessions: Indigenous art, colonial possessions*. London and New York: Thames and Hudson.
—. 2001. Appropriation/appreciation: Settler modernism in Australia and New Zealand. In *The empire of things*, ed. Fred R. Myers, 139–64. Santa Fe: School of American Research.

VENBRUX, ERIC, AND PAMELA ROSI. 2004. Confronting world art: An introduction. *Visual Anthropology* 17 (3/4): 217–28.
—, and Robert L. Welsch, eds. 2006. *Exploring world art*. Long Grove, IL: Waveland Press.

VOGEL, SUSAN M. 1988a. *The art of collecting African art*. New York: Center for African Art.
—. 1988b. Introduction. In *ART/artifact*, Arthur Danto et al., 11–17. New York: Center for African Art.

WADE, EDWARD L. 1985. The ethnic art market in the American Southwest 1880–1980. In *Objects and others: Essays on museums and material culture*, ed. George W. Stocking, Jr., 167–91. Madison: University of Wisconsin Press.

WALLERSTEIN, IMMANUEL. 1974. *The modern world system: Capitalist agriculture and the origins of the European world economy*. New York: Academic Press.

WELSCH, ROBERT L. 2004. Epilogue: The authenticity of constructed art worlds. *Visual Anthropology* 17 (3/4): 401–6.

WILLIAMS, ELIZABETH A. 1985. Art and artifact at the Trocadero: Ars Americana and the primitivist revolution. In *Objects and others: Essays on museums and material culture*, ed. George W. Stocking, Jr., 146–66. Madison: University of Wisconsin Press.

WOLF, ERIC. 1982. *Europe and the people without history*. Berkeley: University of California Press.

III

The Arts and Our Shared Humanity: The Bio-evolutionary Basis of Art-Making and Perception

ELLEN DISSANAYAKE

The Arts after Darwin: Does Art Have an Origin and an Adaptive Function?

Like medieval cosmology, which placed the earth and man at the center of the universe, the long philosophical tradition of Western art history and aesthetics considered Western man and his accomplishments to be the measure of all things. This chauvinism was due in part to necessary ignorance: our scholarly forebears could not have known about the cognitive complexity of the languages and kinship systems of the people they considered to be "savages." Nor could they have been acquainted with other of these people's intellectual and artistic achievements—the richly-carved *masawa* (or ceremonial seagoing canoes) of the Trobriand Islanders, the soaring facades of the *haus tambaran* of the Sepik River area of northern New Guinea, or the impressive *bisj* poles of the Asmat of coastal Irian Jaya, to mention only a few. The founders of Western art theory were necessarily also unaware of the astonishing galleries of Paleolithic cave paintings in France, Spain, and elsewhere.

Although many twenty-first-century scholars in the arts and humanities now wish to incorporate the works and worldviews of non-Western humans into their studies, they remain encumbered by another legacy of their 2500-year-old intellectual heritage. I refer to the Western humanities' ignorance of and resistance to the implications of Darwinism—the news that humans have evolved over millennia from simpler forms. Yet it is only by accepting this momentous fact of nature that today's scholars can truly broaden the humanities to include *humanity*—the lives, minds, and works of people in all societies and historical periods, including prehistory. Such broadening requires that one understand the human species' evolutionary history and its evolved psychology—in particular, that engagement with the arts is an integral and necessary (adaptive) part of a common human nature.

To adopt a human nature (or "adaptationist") point of view—accepting that human bodies, brains, and behavior (including making and experiencing the arts) evolved to enable individual survival and reproduction in ancestral environments—is a revolution in worldview for the humanities that can be likened to replacing a geocentric with a heliocentric perspective in cosmology. Having adopted such a perspective, one can go on to study particulars and levels far more specialized than the cosmic or taxonomic but will have gained new tools for framing questions and can avoid spending time on fruitless Ptolemaic paths. For example, knowledge of how and why the brain has evolved to work as it does brings new perspectives to bear on some classical philosophical problems (e.g., how we perceive and "know" aesthetic objects) and disposes of others (e.g., the assumption of mind-body dualism or of the duality of cognition and emotion in aesthetic response).

The adaptationist principle of the unity of species nature is able to provide an underlying framework in which to address what is now an incoherent mishmash of concerns within the humanities about identity, authenticity, relativism, the crisis of representation, and the consequences of globalization. Influential organizing principles of nineteenth- and twentieth-century intellectual discourse such as Marxian interpretation of history, Freudian psychoanalysis, Jungian archetypes, or structuralist mythographies can be reframed (or discarded—see Scalise Sugiyama 2001c, 2003) when one recognizes that principles of human action arise fundamentally from an evolved human nature; different circumstances produce different responses in different individuals, but these individuals have the same underlying psychobiological needs. Jared Diamond's compendium of world history, geography, and biology in *Guns, Germs and Steel* (1997), is a brilliant example of understanding human diversity, including artistic expression, within an underlying framework of species unity.

In this essay I shall briefly (i) suggest that art is an adaptation, (ii) counter misconceptions about evolution and one of its core concepts—"function," (iii) survey four major current adaptationist hypotheses for the evolutionary origin and function of the arts, (iv) propose a common denominator of art and introduce the notion of "making special," (v) expand upon and defend this hypothesis, and (vi) suggest implications of adopting a humanity-centered art history and aesthetics.

I. CONSIDERING ART AS AN ADAPTATION

There are two major problems with considering art to be an evolved (adaptive) component of human nature. The first problem is shared with all who hope to say anything useful about art: what is it that one is talking about? What is art? For now let us simply include in this concept the activities that are commonly and loosely thought of as "the arts"—music, dance, literary language, visual ornamentation and representation, dramatic performance—and return to the question again in Section IV.

The second problem is restricted to evolutionary psychologists ("adaptationists"), who view all physical and psychological effort as being directed toward the ultimate ends of survival and reproduction: what is art's adaptive function? The ability to make a weapon or a canoe presumably contributes to personal welfare and fitness, but careful decoration of these objects would seem to take time and effort that could be better used in more obviously beneficial activity. The arts—singing, dancing, drumming, complex performances, and the lavish ornamentation of bodies or surroundings—are costly, highly-energetic activities whose ultimate benefits are not immediately apparent. One eminent evolutionist has, in fact, forcefully declared that music (and by implication the other arts) is not an adaptation, but rather a byproduct of other adaptations (Pinker 1997, 2002).

Yet certain observations suggest that art (the arts) might well be adaptive.

A. They are observable cross-culturally in members of all known societies regardless of their degree of economic or technological development.

B. Their traces are evident in our ancestral past, as we find from at least 100,000 years ago with the use of red ochre (Watts 1999) and subsequent material artifacts.

C. Their rudiments are detectable and easily fostered in the behavior of young children, as when babies and toddlers spontaneously move to music, sing along or alone, make marks, decorate their bodies and possessions, play with words, find pleasure in rhythm and rhyme, or enjoy make believe.

D. They are generally attractants and sources of pleasure, like other adaptive behaviors such as mating, parenting, resting,

1
According to evolutionary psychologists Leda Cosmides and John Tooby (1992, 165), adaptations are characterized by economy, efficiency, complexity, precision, specialization, reliability, and affect. According to my hypothesis (see IV and V), art meets these criteria, but this essay is not the place to elaborate my case.

or being with familiars in warm and safe surroundings.

E. They occur under appropriate and adaptive conditions or circumstances—that is, they are typically "about" important life concerns, as in ceremonies that mark stages of life or that concern prosperity, safety, and subsistence.

F. They are costly: large amounts of time, physical and psychological effort, thought, and material resources are devoted to the arts as to other biologically-important activities such as sex, finding, preparing, and consuming food, socializing and gaining social acceptance, helping close kin, talking with friends, and acquiring useful information. Especially in small-scale or subsistence societies, art behavior consumes resources far beyond what one would expect for an unimportant activity.

A trait, activity, or behavior meeting these requirements is a candidate for being considered adaptive.[1]

II. MISCONCEPTIONS ABOUT EVOLUTION AND FUNCTIONALISM

Evolutionary theory is the central unifying concept in modern biology. For a century and a half its claims have been tested by countless scientists who overwhelmingly accept its validity and fruitfulness. (Controversies within the field concern not the *fact* of evolution but rather the *mechanisms* by which it operates [Gilman 2003].) The theory has been essential to developments in modern medicine, epidemiology, agriculture, and pharmaceuticals on which our daily lives depend. Yet most people are both uninformed and skeptical about the very idea, particularly when it is applied to humans. Half of American adults, for example, deny evolution as a fact of nature (Gross 2002) and for nearly a century in the United States religious zealots have sought to restrict or even ban the teaching of evolution in the public schools.

Unfortunately, serious misunderstandings about the claims of evolutionary theory are as widespread and pernicious in the academy as they are in popular culture where the word "Darwinian" is synonymous with cut-throat competition. Terms such as "survival of the fittest," "nature red in tooth and claw," "genetic determinism," or "selfish" were not used by Darwin himself and poorly convey the complexity of the theory they are thought to encapsulate. It should not be necessary to remind readers that current evolutionary thinking about humans, unlike that of some nineteenth-century proponents, is neither hierarchical (with white European males at the top) nor determinist (see Dissanayake 2003, 253–54). Individuals are not in a perpetual struggle of each against all: sympathy, generosity, and cooperation are as much a part of human nature as are self-interest, xenophobia and aggression.

Evolutionists know that both environment and experience affect genetic expression so that the concept of genetic (or any other) "determinism" should be abolished along with the phrase "nature or nurture." Culture ("nurture") is not an alternative to but is part of biology ("nature"): every human is born with an unstoppable preparedness to become cultural. Babies come into the world ready to interact socially with those around them, to learn to speak, to imitate and wish to please, to accept the beliefs of their associates, and to play. These behaviors are evolved—adaptive—predispositions—the means by which every human becomes enculturated in the ways of the group into which he or she is born.

In contemporary anthropology, the concept of function has been discarded along with the explanatory models of Durkheim, Malinowski, and Radcliffe-Brown, whose wide-ranging "functionalist" interpretations of society and culture have been replaced with less ambitious and more focused and individualized studies. As used by evolutionists today, however, functional explanations of human behavior bear little resemblance to anthropologists' assumptions about functionalism. They do not suggest, for example, that all parts of a society are interrelated or that individual behaviors within a society perform some intrinsic function specific to that society. The concept of adaptive function need not be inflexible, hierarchical, or determinist, nor will it force individual instances of a functional (adaptive) behavior, such as art, into a Procrustean bed of Western presuppositions. Quite the contrary—the adaptationist idea is that behaviors are evolved predispositions that can be expressed in a variety of cultural and individual manifestations (Dissanayake 2003).

Adaptationist thinking *requires* functional explanation, as when noting that anatomical features have functions: hands are used for handling and making and eyes for seeing. Similarly, behaviors such as smiling, laughing, playing, or speaking, and behavioral categories such as courtship, mating, parenting, aggression, or food-sharing have an adaptive function, often several functions. Over evolutionary time, apathetic and unsociable babies would not have thrived as well as their more interactive age-mates, who would leave more of their genes to future generations.

Adaptive explanations of behavior distinguish between two levels of functional explanation—"proximate" reasons for the behavior (its ostensible motivation and immediate emotional or psychological effect—usually "this feels good or right") and its "ultimate" selective value (its biologically adaptive end of contributing to individual fitness—survival or reproductive success). Obviously one rarely acts from a conscious decision or intention to survive or transmit one's genes to future generations. It is proximate emotional desires and satisfactions that motivate and reward adaptive behaviors such as courtship and mating, caring for children, defending against an aggressor, sharing food with one's kin and intimates, and participating in art. These desires and satisfactions, products of brain activity, have evolved to motivate adaptive behavior. People engage with the arts for many proximate reasons—to express their inner selves, to demonstrate their devotion to a deity, to earn a living, to assure a successful hunt, to please a client, to impress others, to while away the time, for entertainment and pleasure. One can quickly compile a long list from looking at examples of the arts in various small-scale societies as well as from examining aesthetic theories proposed by people who had no interest in a biological or adaptationist explanation.

An adaptationist view of art should seek to describe a proximate function (or functions) of art that can plausibly be shown to fulfill the ultimate function of contributing to survival or reproductive success.[2] It is not necessary that each instance of art contribute to these ends, no more than each instance of altruism or mating. However, in the way of life in which the adaptation evolved, those who possessed the adaptation would have tended to survive and reproduce better than those who did not.

III. CURRENT ADAPTIVE HYPOTHESES OF ART

Since about 1990, a growing number of scholars with an evolutionary grounding have published book-length and shorter treatments about the evolutionary function of one or another art—some of which are summarized in this paragraph for readers who are interested in exploring the subject.[3] Considerable interest has been shown in a Darwinian view of literature or narrative (e.g., Carroll 1995, 2004; Cooke 2001, 2002; Gottschall and Wilson 2005; Scalise Sugiyama 1996, 2001a-c, 2003; Storey 1996). The origin and adaptive function of music in humans has been addressed in papers by Brown (2000a, b), Cross (1999, 2003), Dissanayake (2000a, b), Hagen and Bryant (2003), Merker (2000), Morley (2002), and Miller (2000a, b)—see also essays by Dissanayake, Merker, and Morley and Cross in Malloch and Trevarthen (forthcoming). Visual art has been treated in books by Aiken (1998a) and Coe (2003), and art in general by Dissanayake (1988, 1992, 2000a) and Miller (2000a).

Rather than describe each author's claims individually, I have apportioned their evolutionary hypotheses of art into four general adaptive functions that the arts are said to serve in human evolution. Some views straddle categories and I am aware that particular proponents of a hypothesis may feel that I have oversimplified or overgeneralized their position.

A. Improving cognition: *the arts contribute to problem-solving and making better adaptive choices*

This function includes proposals from several bioevolutionary approaches to the arts. Self-labeled "Darwinian" (or "evolutionary") aesthetics (which despite its label has little if anything to do with aesthetics as philosophers have used the term) addresses preferences for features that influence choices of desirable habitats, healthy and fertile sexual partners, and other judgments that would affect fitness in ancestral environments. For the range of subject matter see the essays and bibliographies in Voland and Grammer (2003). Although they do not deal directly with art works or art activities, some of these studies have contended that present-day responses to the arts may be derived from the ancestrally-adaptive preferences (e.g., for symmetry of bodies and faces) that they investigate.

In a related vein, neurologists of vision who practice "neuroaesthetics" (Zeki 1999) show how evolved perceptual psychology underlies our appreciation of visual art (see also Ramachandran and Hirstein 1999; Solso 1994). For Zeki (1999, 9–10), the function of art is "to represent the constant, lasting, essential and enduring features of objects, surfaces, faces, situations, and so on, and thus allow us to acquire [a deeper knowledge of them]." These neurocognitivists do not treat the sorts of multimedia and participative arts that presumably characterized early humans but use examples from masterpieces of Western visual art to illustrate their claims.

A third cognitivist approach addresses the human appetite for fictional stories, which on the face of it would seem to be maladaptive in a species that relies on the transmission of accurate information. Following Darwinian aesthetics theorists (and early theorists of children's play), these hypotheses claim that fiction safely presents vicarious experience of adaptive information to cognitive systems that are involved with foresight, planning, and empathy, thereby providing risk-free practice for later life when similar circumstances might arise (e.g., Tooby and Cosmides 2001). Scalise Sugiyama (2001a) has examined folktales from around the world to demonstrate that in fictional narrative people acquire accurate information about local habitats that may contribute to their fitness.[4]

> B. Propaganda: *the arts are used to manipulate,*
> *deceive, indoctrinate, or control other people*

Insofar as art directs attention and emotion to messages, it can be used subversively to the benefit of the artmaker (Aiken 1998a, b; Eibl-Eibesfeldt 1988). Surveying a wide folklore literature, Scalise Sugiyama (1996) makes a case for storytelling as a means of political manipulation and fitness-enhancement. Power (1999) offers an unusual argument, supported by studies of rituals described in sub-Saharan African ethnographies, that visual art and dance originated when ancestral females (participating as a group) painted their bodies with red ochre in order to attract males (who assumed they were menstruating and hence fertile — receptive to courtship and eventual insemination), thereby gaining gifts of meat, a valuable resource.

[4] I regret that the general theme of this essay and its space restrictions does not allow consideration of the comprehensive, integrated, and well-argued cognitivist view of the adaptive function of literature by Carroll (see, e.g., 2004, 2007).

C. Sexual display: *the arts promote mating opportunity through display of desirable qualities (e.g., physical beauty, intelligence, creativity, prestige) which denote fitness*

At present the most popular and influential evolutionary explanation of the adaptive value of art is the *sexual selection hypothesis*, derived from Darwin's speculations about the extravagant plumage or elaborate songs of some male birds (Darwin 1871). Noting that these conspicuous excesses would seem to impede locomotion or attract predators and therefore be nonadaptive, Darwin suggested that splendidly colorful tails or lusty songs must instead be courtship devices for attracting the attention and sexual favors of females. A twentieth-century examination of such "costly signals" by Zahavi and Zahavi (1997) proposed that they "honestly" convey (to prospective mates and to potential predators) that their owners have unusual vigor. Weak or sickly males could not "fake" such clear signs of vitality which for them would be handicaps rather than advertisements. The ornamental character of plumes, crests, tails, and songs provides an obvious analogy with human arts, which are claimed also to be honest, costly signals since the strength, vitality, intelligence, skill, and creativity required for their display cannot be faked by those who are less well-endowed (see Miller 1999, 2000a, 2001; Voland 2003). The arts thus are seen to be an arena for competition—advertising fitness and therefore leading to reproductive opportunity through female choice.

D. Reinforcing sociality: *The arts enhance cooperation and contribute to social cohesion and continuity*

Despite the popularity of the sexual selection hypothesis, countless ethnographic accounts attest to the contribution of the arts to sociality and cooperation. Evolutionary psychologists have then attributed to art important social functions such as augmenting the impact of ritual, thereby strengthening religion's power to cement group cohesion (Boyd 2005), indicating group membership with dress or badges (Aiken 1998a), enabling behavioral coordination and neural entrainment through rhythmic movement and ritualized participation in temporally-organized performances (Dissanayake 1992, 2000a, b), and inculcating "descent amity" (Coe 2003). Based on extensive fieldwork in Spain, Colombia, Ecuador, and the southwestern United States, Coe's "ancestress hypothesis" describes how the visual arts transmit traditions within kin groups, especially by mothers to children, and encourage cooperation among those identified as codescendants of a common ancestor (see also Aiken and Coe 2004). Carroll (2004, xxii) puts the general argument well when he argues that "the arts are indispensable ... for the organization of shared experience that makes collective cultural life possible."

It is obvious that all four hypotheses are plausible in at least some instances—everyone can think of examples that appear to perform these functions and each function can be shown to contribute to survival or reproductive success. All make welcome contributions to a greater appreciation of the deep-rootedness and variety of artful characteristics in our species. Yet I maintain that most of the arguments for the hypotheses are inadequate for understanding art as a broader evolved and adaptive phenomenon. Some are too narrow—focusing on one art (e.g., body decoration) or one evolved capacity (e.g., visual perception). Most are conceptually vague, using the word "art" imprecisely and frequently conflating it with other concepts with which art is often but not universally associated or equated.

For example, in some of the cognitivist explanations, art is treated as being synonymous with or equivalent to "beauty"—defined (circularly) as pleasurable (and thus adaptive) sensory or cognitive preferences (e.g., Thornhill 2003), or art is located in visual stimuli that excite perceptual responses to color, line, and form. Yet in experiences of art one responds to more than adaptive preferences (say, for salubrious landscapes) and to more than single qualities such as color, shape, and line. By considering aesthetic response to be any adaptive preference and by defining beauty as what is highly preferred and enjoyed, Darwinian aesthetics does not distinguish experiences of art from any other pleasurable or adaptive experience.[5] Similarly, Scalise Sugiyama's discussions of narrative are wide-ranging, useful, and well-supported, but the adaptive advantages she notes lie in the information content of any narrative—not in what about it might be art (Scalise Sugiyama 2001a, b). Few would consider a newspaper story, a museum guide to an exhibition, a diary entry, an electronic message, or a joke art, even though all are narratives or stories that provide useful knowledge or can manipulate others' behavior.

Advocates of the sexual selection hypothesis focus on art as being a costly display of the artist's beauty, virtuosity, skill, and creativity. Yet these features too are not in themselves art, but broader entities that some but not all instances of art may have or use. Conversely, they are also to be found outside the arts as later examples will show. Granted, art is frequently beautiful, skillful, or costly—as in the ritualized presentation of beautifully garbed marriageable young women, the tireless dancing of impressively masked and costumed males, the displays of wealth such as decorated yams in New Guinea or the prestige of feather headdresses of Polynesian chieftains. But so are other things—a colorful bird or a field of wildflowers, a perfectly-executed gymnastic feat, an ingot of gold. What specifically makes artful instances of beauty, virtuosity, skill, and creativity different from nonartful examples? In other words, one must still specify what *additional* capacity ("art") has been selected for.[6]

Additionally, a closer look at some hypotheses reveals that they neglect important features of the arts in premodern societies. *Contra* the sexual selection hypothesis, in many traditional societies arts are typically if not always conservative. Originality and

5
The position thus unwittingly resembles the "anything can be art" stance of cultural constructivists.

6
This objection pertains also to the penchant of archaeologists to consider art as a subset of the ability to make and use symbols. But one can make a symbol that no one would consider art—a scrawled map, a cross or mandala casually drawn with the forefinger on a fogged windowpane. The question similarly remains: what is the difference between an artful and non-artful symbol? When and why does one make the map, cross, or mandala art and what makes it so?

creativity, so important in Western arts, are often discouraged (Aiken and Coe, 2004; Coe 2003). Traditional arts may not necessarily be even beautiful (Van Damme 1996) or skilled, as in Yupik painting where stylized simple representation to accompany a story is valued over aesthetic effect (Himmelheber 1993 [1938], 11, 28; see also Horton 1965, 39–40; Stott, 1975, 38). Often several arts occur and are experienced concurrently—unlike modern societies' arts, which typically reside in museums, concert halls, and books, created, performed and experienced by specialists who individually practice or appreciate these individual manifestations of paintings, chamber music, or literature. In traditional societies, an entire group may make the art and join in its performance. As Chernoff (1979, 21) says, "[t]he most fundamental aesthetic in Africa [is that] without participation, there is no meaning."

Such considerations suggest that adaptive hypotheses or humanistic proposals for art's function that are based on a single art, a single artist (as "genius" or as fitness-maximizer at the expense of others), or a single (or no) function require modification as do hypotheses that presuppose the necessity to art of beauty or skill.

IV. A COMMON DENOMINATOR OF ART

Scholars versed in historical, anthropological, or philosophical studies of the arts are well aware of the complexities inherent in conceptualizing their subject. They appreciate that orthodox Western notions of aesthetics and art—that art is rare, elite, original, individual, and costly; that it is synonymous with or closely related to concepts of beauty, skill, creativity, imagination, representational accuracy, or self-expression; that it is composed of autonomous objects (paintings, sculptures, ceramics) or activities (dances, songs, performances); that it is the province of specialist "artists"—are derived from Enlightenment ideas (Eagleton 1990) and are by no means universally held or practiced. Moreover, most human societies have no concept of "art" in the Western sense of an overarching category that includes such diverse entities as paintings, carvings, songs, dances, and literature.

Most contemporary evolutionists lack this new and broader understanding of art. In this respect, their assumptions about art and art theory are as outdated and beside-the-point as are most art theorists' assumptions about evolutionary theory. Yet those who have a sophisticated knowledge of art today—the humanists—adhere to the axiom that there cannot be a common denominator that characterizes art: for most such scholars today, art is only a socially-constructed concept.

Unfortunately for an evolutionist who wishes to consider art as an evolved component of human nature, there must be some universal proclivity or feature(s) that selection could have acted on, something that encompasses all instances—premodern, modern, and postmodern—and can be shown to have a plausible evolutionary origin and adaptive function or functions. One worthwhile effort to find such a common denominator is that of Dutton (2000), who in the spirit of Weitz (1959) and Munro (1963), used a "family resemblance" notion of art and made a provisional list of eight characteristics which, in whole or large part, will apply to the practice of art across cultures and throughout historical time: giving pleasure in itself, exhibiting specialized skill, being made in a recognizable style according to formal rules, lending itself to a critical discourse of judgment and appreciation, representing or imitating real and imaginary experience of the world, being the product of conscious intention by a maker, being "bracketed" or set off from ordinary life, and serving as an imaginative experience for both producers and audiences.

Dutton's list is a valiant and useful attempt to delineate universal characteristics of the arts across cultures, but six of the features (i.e., specialized skill, styles and rules, critical evaluative language, representation, conscious intent, and imaginative embodiment) characterize—as Dutton admits—examples of nonart as well.[7] In this respect they are like the features assumed to characterize art by the evolutionary hypotheses described in Section III. Only intrinsic pleasure (self-reward) and bracketing seem more or less restricted to art or artlike activities (such as play and make-believe, or ritual behavior—see Dissanayake 1988, 1992).

Past and present Western theories of art have considered art as an *artifact* (a work or object of a certain kind, say a painting, mask, song, or literary work), an *essential attribute* that makes a work or object art (e.g., disinterested appreciation, beauty, skill, costliness, a preference), a *cue* to something else (e.g., the presence of a deity, virtuosity and creativity which denote good genes), or as an activity or *behavior* (e.g., making or displaying).[8] As explained earlier, however, artifact, essence, and cue are problematic defining features for an adaptationist account of art because they do not pertain to many important instances of the arts in small-scale societies and they beg the question of what art is.

An ethological (biobehavioral) perspective may be helpful here. When studying courtship, parenting, and other characteristic activities of an animal's life, ethologists describe what individuals do or accomplish when they court, parent, and so forth. Art too can be regarded as a behavior by describing what people do or accomplish when they make something art—when they "artify."[9] It is easier to conceptualize art as behavior if we think of art as music (chanting, singing, playing an instrument) or performing (dancing, reciting, miming, acting, telling a story), since these arts take place, like "behavior," in time. In a similar way, one can also think of the plastic or visual arts as making, marking, image-making, adorning (in any medium)—that is, as the process or activity rather than the product or outcome of the artifying. But it is not immediately evident what—if anything—these various activities accomplish or have in common.

7
As Weitz (1959) and Munro (1963) noted, if an object or event has many of the eight features and possesses them to an exceptional degree, most Westerners would consider it to be "art."

8
Art has also been called "a label" bestowed upon certain works by an institutionalized "artworld" (Danto, 1964; Dickie, 1974).

9
Coe (2003, 76) defines visual art as a behavior: "the modification of an object or body through color, line, pattern, and form that is done solely to attract attention to that object or body."

10
Carroll (2004, 159) proposes an "elemental, universal [human] motive" that evolutionists have neglected to address sufficiently: the need to create cognitive order.

In earlier publications (Dissanayake 1988, 1992, 1995), I suggested a common denominator for a behavior of art that I called *making special*. I claimed that in all instances of this behavior, in all times and places, ordinary experience (e.g., ordinary objects, movements, sounds, utterances, surroundings) is transformed, is made *extra*ordinary. For example, in *dance*, ordinary bodily movements of everyday life are exaggerated, patterned, embellished, repeated—made special; in *poetry*, the usual syntactic and semantic aspects of everyday spoken language are patterned (by means of rhythm, rhyme, alliteration, assonance), inverted, exaggerated (using special vocabulary and unusual metaphorical analogies) and repeated—made special; in *song*, the prosodic (intonational and expressive) aspects of everyday language (the ups and downs of pitch, pauses or rests, stresses of accents, louds and softs, fasts and slows) are exaggerated (sustained), patterned, repeated, varied, and so forth—made special; in *visual display*, ordinary objects like the natural body, the natural surroundings (e.g., cave walls, logs, anthill mud), and common artifacts (e.g., house walls, canoes) are made special by cultural shaping and elaboration that make them more than ordinary. The notion of making special is congruent with similar formulations by others—e.g., the notion of "bracketing" (Dutton 2000), or "defamiliarization" ("making strange") and "foregrounding" in literary studies (e.g., Shklovsky 1965 [1917]; Mukařovský 1964 [1932]; Miall and Kuiken 1994a, 1994b).

I propose that making special (which I now use interchangeably with "artifying") is the ancestral activity or behavior that gave rise to and continues to characterize or imbue all instances of what today are called the arts. The term "making special" can be substituted for "art" in the six characteristics of an adaptation (Section I) and it avoids the inadequacies and problems noted in the latter part of Section III. It describes an important human propensity that other evolutionists have not seriously considered or examined.[10] Although it does not deny the functions proposed by hypotheses A, B, and C described in Section III, the concept of making special strongly supports hypothesis D—that artification is important in reinforcing sociality (see V–C). Unlike many of the hypotheses, the concept of making special proposes answers to the proximate questions *when* or *why* as well as to the operational question of *what* is art.

V. WHAT, WHEN, AND WHY
IS SOMETHING "MADE SPECIAL"

"Making special," not "beauty" or "display," explains the difference between a collection of decorated yams and a field of wildflowers, or a headdress composed of the colored feathers of thousands of birds and the feathers on the bird itself. Beauty, virtuosity, skill, and costliness, like individual sensory stimuli or preferences, are *ingredients* of the arts that are used to make something special.

Rather than ask why people have *art* (that troublesome word) or why they create fictions, make music, or paint landscapes, the more fundamental evolutionary, adaptive question is to consider why our ancestors intentionally began, and continued—as we continue today—to make things special or extraordinary. Other species display their charms to prospective mates and make choices according to brain-based perceptual and cognitive preferences. Or, with markings that mimic another species, they deceive predators or rivals. But it is only humans who deliberately make bodies, materials, places, vocal sounds, physical movements, words, stories, and even ideas special. It is *making special*—weirdness, strangeness, and unusualness, as well as beauty, costliness, or excessiveness—that requires evolutionary explanation. When and why do people do this? These are *psychological* more than philosophical or art historical questions and they demand an adaptive answer.

My adaptationist hypothesis about the arts has three strands: *origin, motivation,* and *manifestation.*[11]

A. Origin: *Aesthetic predisposition and the operations of making special*

Studies by developmental psychologists reveal universal features in the interactions of human mothers and their infants. Despite cultural variations, mothers (and other adults) everywhere talk to babies in a characteristically soft, high-pitched, undulant voice, which babies prefer to typical adult conversational speech. Along with this special vocal behavior, adults engage infants' attention by the use of rhythmic body movements (touching, patting, stroking, hugging, and kissing), unusual facial expressions (gaze, sustained smiles, open mouth, widened eyes, raised eyebrows), and characteristic head movements (bobs, nods, and wags) in an almost ritualized way. These vocalizations, expressions, and movements are repeated, often with dynamic variations (loud and soft, large and small, fast and slow) in what can be called a "multimedia performance."

Yet it is more than an individual performance. Minute analysis of videotaped engagements of mothers and babies show that the pair interact in remarkably close temporal unity—responding to each other in subtle yet precise ways (see, for example, Beebe, Stern, and Jaffe 1979; Beebe et al. 1988; Nadel et al. 1999; Papoušek and Papoušek 1981; Stern 1971). The mother varies her pace and rhythm in order maximally to fit in with or gently direct the baby's emotional state. The baby in turn responds to the mother's signals with kicks, hand and arm movements, facial expressions, head movements, and vocalizations of its own—often as if participating in a mutually-negotiated rhythmic pulse with complementary dynamics. Over much of the first year of the infant's life, the pair engage and disengage, synchronize and alternate, practicing their physical, physiological, and emotional "attunement" by means of these multimodal expressive signals.

Because of its spontaneous nature and widespread occurrence, mother-infant interaction as described is assumed to be an evolved, adaptive part of human nature. Among its many practical contributions to the baby's development are assisting emotional equilibrium (Hofer 1990), self- and interactive regulation (Gianino and Tronick 1988), socialization (Aitken and Trevarthen 1997; Papoušek and Papoušek 1979; Schore 1994), language learning (Fernald 1992), cognitive development (Papoušek and Papoušek 1981; Trevarthen 1997), and acquisition of the parental culture.

It is important, though largely unrecognized, that the very components of the interaction are fundamentally aesthetic or protoaesthetic (Dissanayake 2000a). The signals used by adults to infants are formalized (simplified or stereotyped), exaggerated, repeated, and elaborated in visual, vocal, and kinesic (gestural) modalities. These features attract and sustain the infant's attention, maintain the engagement, and serve to bond the partners. They also create and satisfy anticipation. In the early months, babies require predictability, but at about five to six months of age, they start to enjoy suspense and surprise, as in games of "Peek-a-boo," and "This Little Piggy," in which their expectation is manipulated.

I suggest that the innate capacities and sensitivities that evolved originally between adults and babies to make and respond to protoaesthetic temporal and dynamic manipulations (i.e., formalization, exaggeration, repetition, elaboration, and delayed expectancy) comprised a "behavioral reservoir" from which early humans could draw when at a later point in evolution they began deliberately to artify (see V–B, C). Notably, it is these same manipulations or operations that are used—intentionally and in varied ways—by artists in any medium when they artify (make something special). Almost any mask from geographical areas as widely separated as sub-Saharan Africa, the Arctic, and Oceania shows the first four of these features. When masks are danced, manipulation of expectation takes place, like song, oratory, and musical accompaniment, in time. (For additional examples from the visual arts, see the final paragraph of V–C.)

B. Motivation: *Uncertainty, emotional investment ("caring about"), and coping*

Like proponents of the neurocognitivist and evolutionary aesthetics hypotheses (see III–A), I locate the antecedents of the arts in already evolved propensities. Unlike them, I suggest proximate motivations for when and why our ancestors might have gone on to develop these propensities outside their original context—here, for artifying (making special by means of aesthetic operations).

Humans, more than other animals, use wits rather than instincts to address the problems of their lives. For our species, what to do and how to live are rarely instinctive, but must be learned. Over the millennia of hominid evolution, the mind increasingly became a "making sense" organ: interrelated powers of memory, foresight, and imagination gradually developed and allowed humans to stabilize and confine the stream of life by making mental "connections" between past, present, and future, or among different experiences or observations.

Humans could remember or even dwell upon good and bad things and imagine them happening again.[12] One cost of this growing awareness of the desired possibilities and inevitable unpredictability of life was uncertainty, even anxiety. Because the most conspicuous occasion for the arts in small-scale societies of today is in ritual ceremonies, this association of art and ceremony may hold a clue to the original motivation in ancestral humans for the co-opting and further development of protoaesthetic operations.

What do ceremonies concern? The anthropological literature on ritual is vast and varied, but it seems safe to say that most ceremonies are about biologically important things—e.g., assuring or restoring subsistence, safety, fecundity, health, prosperity, and victory or successfully dealing with the bodily changes and emotional and social concomitants of sexual maturity, pregnancy, birth, and death. The "liminal" occasions for ritual ceremony are times of transition and uncertainty (Van Gennep 1960 [1909]; Turner 1969). *I suggest that uncertainty—leading to emotional investment or "caring about"—was the original motivating impetus for the human invention of religion and its behavioral expression, making special* (see V–C).

Religion and art are usually treated by anthropologists as aspects of "culture," which according to conventional theory is opposed to "biology." An adaptationist view, however (see II), views the various components that are called "culture" as outgrowths of evolved psychobiological predispositions. In general, cultural knowledge and practices direct our attention to particular biologically significant things—e.g., ways to become a competent adult, to make a living, to rear children, and to maintain social relationships. Among these "ways" are language and traditions of toolmaking or subsistence practice. At some point, our ancestors had to *care about the outcomes* of these biologically significant and valuable events and states that were not always certain of attainment.

Other animals in uncertain or conflicted circumstances frequently engage in "displacement activities" or evolved ritualized behaviors whose components are drawn from ordinary bodily movements used in everyday contexts such as grooming or locomotion (e.g., scratching, preening, moving back and forth). In the new, uncertain context, these ordinary movements become more stereotyped—that is, exaggerated, patterned in space and time, and regularized (repeated). Such "ritualized" movements reduce the tension of the displaying animal at the same time as they signal its mood and intentions to conspecifics (Lorenz 1982, 249–53). Humans show displacement, sometimes called "comfort movements," when they repeatedly tap a foot, wiggle a knee, or wind a strand of hair around a finger. Caged animals and university lecturers pace.

12
The development of language certainly contributed to the cognitive capacity to simulate the future. In this regard, making special can be considered as being in the same suite of cognitive abilities as language.

13
Several studies find that ritual and artful behavior increased in prehistory at
times of resource stress, as in Mimbres
(Brody 1977, 210), Late Dorset (Taçon
1983) and prehistoric Arnhem Land
(Taçon and Brockwell 1995; Taçon,
Wilson, and Chippindale 1996) populations (see also Hayden 1987; Mithen
1996, 157).

I suggest that in uncertain circumstances that did not call for immediate pragmatic action (that is, were not matters of immediate fight, flee, or freeze responses), our early human ancestors at some point found that performing repetitious, simplified or stereotyped, exaggerated sounds and movements (already part of their behavioral repertoire as described in V–A and noted above as displacement or ritualized movements) felt comforting and ultimately eased tension—particularly when performed in a coordinated fashion among members of a group. Perhaps this behavior first occurred during a frightening storm. Such a response was described in two different Papua New Guinean societies by Mead (1976 [1930]) and Malinowski (1922), when villagers huddled together, chanting charms to calm the violent winds. I further suggest that individuals in groups that responded to uncertainty in stressful circumstances with such coordinative practices would gradually have gained survival advantage over those in groups where each person acted individually or randomly. The tension-reduction capability of coordinated voice and movement is evidenced in infancy, when mother-infant engagement assists biobehavioral self-regulation and the development of infant homeostasis (Gianino and Tronick 1988; Hofer 1990), so it is not farfetched to suggest that the same antecedent mechanisms "worked" for similar ends in ancestral artification of movement and vocalization. Once these became culturally established as ritualized responses to recurrent provoking circumstances, they could become further elaborated and institutionalized as ceremonies.

I suggest that a fifth hypothesis—stress reduction—be added to the four adaptive functions described in Section III: *the temporal arts help individuals psychologically to cope with uncertainty.* Malinowski (1948, p. 60) remarked that the "impetus to do something about our perceived needs is overwhelming; we need to express any strong emotion by some form of action." In times of anxiety one may not know what action to take and in fact there may be no obvious practical course to follow. Prescribed behavioral coordination with others through moving and singing or chanting provides "something to do." It additionally relieves tension and anxiety and instills a sense of coping, as is evidenced in countless ceremonial practices that are meant to address some vital but uncertain occasion (Dissanayake 2000a, 2006b). One sees this function of making special, for example, in performances of the lament, an ancient and widespread response to the loss by death or separation of a person or place to which one is attached, where natural weeping and wailing is subjected to aesthetic operations (formalization and so forth) and becomes a musical-poetic cultural artifact.

Relief of uncertainty or anxiety is not the only function of the arts, but making places and actions special continues to provide "something to do" and a means of coping, as was evident in the spontaneous public responses of Americans to the horrifying destruction of the World Trade Center towers in September 2001.[13]

C. Manifestation: *the invention and functions of ceremonial ritual*

In "traditional" or "subsistence" societies—small-scale groups that are more like ancestral societies than recent, specialized, technologically complex societies with developed agriculture and writing—the primary context for artifications such as singing, drumming, dancing, dramatic performance, poetic language, and visual display is in various kinds of ritual ceremony. Although anthropologists usually conceptualize ceremonies as part of a symbolic cognitive system, here I wish to point out that regardless of what meanings they convey, ceremonies are constituted of arts (again, behavior and artifacts made special) and would not exist without them. In ceremonies, the arts attract attention, sustain interest, coordinate group effort, and provide emotional excitement and satisfaction, plausibly implying that the arts arose in human evolution as adjuncts to ceremonial behavior rather than as independently-evolved activities.

In his essay "Religion and society," Radcliffe-Brown (1952) unwittingly used adaptationist thinking when he claimed that religion has a function in society apart from whether it does for the participants what they want it to do or think it does. He found its ("ultimate") function to be to regulate, maintain, and transmit from one generation to another sentiments on which the continuity of the society depends.[14] Radcliffe-Brown's emphasis on emotion ("sentiments") begs for an additional clause that emphasizes that the arts are the crucial mechanisms in ceremonies for regulating, maintaining, and transmitting these sentiments.

I view ceremonial arts as the behavioral counterpart of religious beliefs. In this I also follow Radcliffe-Brown (1952, 155), who proposed that religion in small-scale societies was less a matter of beliefs than of rites, indeed that belief was an *effect* of rites (which he further described as positive and negative actions and abstentions). Beliefs and doctrines are like black and white outline drawings that require the color of emotion to become psychologically incorporated as a living, forceful presence. The arts in "rites" engage and shape emotion, thereby inducing memory of historical and subsistence information in a nonliterate society where everything must be remembered.[15]

Although art-filled ceremonial practices themselves may or may not resolve the immediate vital problems that are their proximate motivation, they address and satisfy other physical and psychological needs. Through aesthetic operations, ceremonial practices create and reinforce emotionally satisfying and reassuring feelings of belonging to a group (Dissanayake 2000). Further, they provide to individuals a sense of meaningfulness or cognitive order and individual competence insofar as they give emotional force to explanations of how the world came to be as it is and what is required to maintain it (see also Carroll 2007). They coordinate and unify group members in a feeling of "oneheartedness." All these

14
A similar statement can also be found in the *Book of Rites* of Confucius: "ceremonies are the bond that holds the multitudes together and if the bond be removed, those multitudes fall into confusion" (Confucius [Li Ji] 1966).

15
In a similar way, medieval European images are understood by some contemporary art historians (e.g., Hamburger, 1998) as visual instruments of religious experience and as the visual complement of the study of texts concerned with medieval spirituality (Sauerländer, 2002).

effects contribute to psychobiological homeostasis and thus to individuals' survival and reproductive success—i.e., fitness.

For these reasons, I question the explanatory power of the sexual selection hypothesis (III–C) with its emphasis on the arts as originating or persisting primarily as indications of personal fitness. Certainly costly display may indicate fitness and hence sexual desirability, or preferred shapes, colors, and movements may provide criteria for mate-choice. However, it should not be forgotten that costliness (specialness) may also signal "Look at how important this is" and "See how much I [we] care about this." Because in ritual performances the artistic effort that is given to assure good outcomes is "indexical" to the importance they are felt to have (Tambiah 1979), it is not surprising that people use skill, expense, and excess of all kinds to demonstrate their emotional investment in the object or event they choose to artify.

For example, shields that are used for protection in hunting or warfare, as by Maasai men of East Africa or numerous groups in Papua New Guinea, could hypothetically be made of just a plain strong plank of wood. Such shields, however, are invariably decorated—not simply with adaptively-relevant colors and forms but with carefully carved or painted motifs. Although the motifs' power resides in their supposed magical potency, they are not simply scrawled onto the wood. On the contrary, they must be made with care—not to display one's virtuosic painting or carving ability for admiring females but so that they will *work*. Similarly, young males who undergo scarification for rites of manhood are not randomly slashed, although any sort of cut would presumably demonstrate their ability to bear pain manfully. Because what the scars will indicate is important—the state of adulthood—they are placed carefully and symmetrically on the face or body of the initiate. The Trobrianders' ceremonial (*kula*) seagoing canoe (*masawa*) is carved perfectly, whereas carving is often indifferent in fishing canoes and nonexistent in personal ones (Campbell 2002; Malinowski 1922, 113). Beauty, skill, and high cost signal (to higher powers, to others, to one's group, and to oneself) the supreme importance of the artifact or occasion.

VI. IMPLICATIONS OF A "HUMANITY-CENTERED" OR ADAPTATIONIST MODEL OF THE ARTS

Only an adaptationist paradigm can address two important and incontrovertible facts about the implied subject of humanistic study—humanity. First, all people who have lived during the past 250 thousand years have been members of one species and, like other species, share a common nature—human nature. Comprehending this fact is essential for contemporary understanding of world art, as of world history, religion, health, education, or any other human subject. Second, the human mind and the behaviors and artifacts it produces are biologically-based—that is, the result of the electrochemistry and anatomical structure of the brain that has evolved like other parts of the body to help individuals survive and reproduce. Because all individuals have similar emotional needs and motivational structures, it is obsolete and limiting to treat human behavior as being *only* culturally or individually constructed.

Human cultures have developed as ways of addressing and satisfying evolved individual emotional needs and motivations. In other words, all cultures have devised ways of dealing with their members' vital concerns and, as I have shown, the arts are integral parts of this armamentarium. As arts are part of culture, artifying or making special is part of biology.

The concept of making special is congruent with a number of valued premises in contemporary humanistic study. It supports such aims as reexamination and reevaluation of orthodox anthropological and aesthetic assumptions (Marcus and Fischer 1999 [1986], 26), and provides good arguments against hierarchical thinking ("Us-Them") and for pluralism. Whether in or out of the academy, the problem of cultural bias is lessened if we understand that all cultures address biologically-important matters and that the arts have evolved as integral parts of dealing with these.

Additionally, the concept provides a general and superordinate term for a universal human behavior that helps us to understand the different arts in different societies to be instances of the same underlying propensity. Because the behavior is operationalized (as formalization, exaggeration, elaboration, repetition, and manipulation of expectation) one can recognize its manifestations both in the field and as described by earlier scholars. That is, the concept skirts such perennial and insoluble problems as defining art—e.g., are gift-presentation (d'Azevedo 1958, 705–6) or the Japanese tea ceremony "art"? It further makes clear that the arts are not "disinterested" but, as making special, are performative and experienced multimodally as an integral part of life.

Making special shifts the subject of study from art as an object or product, essence, cue, opinion, label, preference, or experience to *what people do or accomplish* (the operations of making special) and it reframes aesthetics to the larger matter of *when and why people do it*. Studies of the arts of an individual or society can be recast within this framework and then compared with similar what, when, and why questions of another individual or society. The ways that different groups artify the various values themselves (e.g., subsistence, safety, prosperity, health, social harmony, reciprocity, social role, status) can also be a relevant basis for comparative studies.

Similarly, the study of meaning (symbols and language) can be enriched with adaptationist understanding of why humans evolved to have and use these capacities and when and why (not only how) meanings are so often artified. "Meaning" ultimately and necessarily reduces to biological meaning, which is felt emotionally.

Because humans generally artify biologically and psychologically important things, artifications are a useful index to the values of a group or individual (see also Van Damme 1996, 56–57) and an additional way of identifying those values.

Finally, an understanding that making special is inherent in all societies and individuals compels awareness that the subject of art is of particular and commanding interest and consequence within humanistic studies *and to human life itself*. The current postulate that art has no biological or functional importance has real-world implications outside academic theory. It echoes the traditional Western elitist assumption of "art for art's sake" and contributes to the broader cultural atmosphere that increasingly reduces support of art programs in schools and communities.

REFERENCES

AIKEN, NANCY E. 1998a. *The biological origins of art*. Westport, CT: Praeger.
—. 1998b. Power through art. In *Sociobiology and politics,* ed. Vincent S. E. Falger, Peter Meyer, and Johan M. G. van der Dennen, 215–28. Vol. 6 of *Research in biopolitics,* ed. Steven A. Peterson and Albert Somit. Greenwich, CT: JAI Press.
—, and Kathryn Coe. 2004. Promoting cooperation among humans: The arts as the ties that bind. *Bulletin of Psychology and the Arts* 5 (1): 5–20.

AITKEN, KENNETH W., AND COLWYN TREVARTHEN. 1997. Self/other organization in human psychological development. *Development and Psychopathology* 9: 653–77.

ALLAND, ALEXANDER. 1977. *The artistic animal: An inquiry into the biological roots of art*. Garden City, NY: Anchor.

BEEBE, BEATRICE, DIANE ALSON, JOSEPH JAFFE, STANLEY FELDSTEIN, AND CYNTHIA CROWN. 1988. Vocal congruence in mother-infant play. *Journal of Psycholinguistic Research* 17 (3): 245–259.
—, Daniel Stern, and Joseph Jaffe. 1979. The kinesic rhythm of mother-infant interactions. In *Of speech and time: Temporal speech patterns in interpersonal contexts,* ed. Aron W. Siegman and Stanley Feldstein, 23–34. Hillsdale, NJ: Erlbaum.

BOYD, BRIAN. 2005. Evolutionary theories of art. In *Literature and the human animal: Evolution and the nature of narrative,* ed. Jonathan Gottschall and David Sloan Wilson. 147–76. Evanston, IL: Northwestern University Press.

BRODY, J.J. 1977. *Mimbres painted pottery*. Albuquerque: University of New Mexico Press and Santa Fe, NM: School of American Research.

BROWN, STEVEN. 2000a. The "musilanguage" model of music evolution. In *The origins of music,* ed. Nils L. Wallin, Björn Merker, and Steven Brown, 271–300. Cambridge, MA: MIT Press.
—. 2000b. Evolutionary models of music: From sexual selection to group selection. In *Evolution, culture, and behavior,* ed. Nicholas S. Thompson and François Tonneau, 231–281. Vol. 13 of *Perspectives in ethology*. New York: Plenum.

CAMPBELL, SHIRLEY F. 2002. *The art of Kula*. Oxford and New York: Berg.

CARROLL, JOSEPH. 1995. *Evolution and literary theory*. Columbia: University of Missouri Press.
—. 2004. *Literary Darwinism: Evolution, human nature, and literature*. New York and London: Routledge.
—. 2007. The adaptive function of literature. *Evolutionary and neuro-cognitive approaches to aesthetics, creativity, and the arts,* ed. Colin Martindale, Paul Locher and Vladimir Petrov, 31–45. Foundations and frontiers in aesthetics, ed. Colin Martindale, Arnold Berleant. Amityville, NY: Baywood.

CHERNOFF, JOHN MILLER. 1979. *African rhythm and African sensibility: Aesthetics and social action in African musical idioms*. Chicago and London: The University of Chicago Press.

COE, KATHRYN. 2003. *The ancestress hypothesis: Visual art as adaptation*. New Brunswick, NJ: Rutgers University Press.

CONFUCIUS [LI JI]. 1966. *The sacred books of China: The texts of confucianism*. Trans. James Legge Delhi: Motilal Banarsidass.

COOKE, BRETT, ed. 2001. *Interdisciplinary Literary Studies* 2 (2). Special issue on Darwinian literary study.
—. 2002. *Human nature in Utopia: Zamyatin's We*. Evanston, IL: Northwestern University Press.

COSMIDES, LEDA, AND JOHN TOOBY. 1992. Cognitive adaptations for social exchange. In *The adapted mind: Evolutionary psychology and the generation of culture,* ed. Jerome H. Barkow, Leda Cosmides, and John Tooby, 163–228. New York and Oxford: Oxford University Press.

CROSS, IAN. 1999. Is music the most important thing we ever did?: Music, development and evolution. In *Music, mind, and science,* ed. Suk Won Yi, 10–39. Seoul: Seoul National University Press.
—. 2003. Music and evolution: Consequences and causes. *Contemporary Music Review* 22 (3): 79–89.

DANTO, ARTHUR C. 1964. The artworld. *Journal of Philosophy* 61 (19): 571–84.

DARWIN, CHARLES. 1871. *The descent of man and selection in relation to sex*. London: Murray.

D'AZEVEDO, WARREN L. 1958. A structural approach to esthetics: Toward a definition of art in anthropology. *American Anthropologist* 60 (4): 702–14.

DIAMOND, JARED. 1997. *Guns, germs, and steel: The fates of human societies*. New York: Norton.

DICKIE, GEORGE. 1974. *Art and the aesthetic: An institutional analysis*. Ithaca, NY: Cornell University Press.

DISSANAYAKE, ELLEN. 1988. *What is art for?* Seattle: University of Washington Press.
—. 1992. *Homo aestheticus: Where art comes from and why*. New York: Free Press, etc.
—. 1995. Chimera, spandrel, or adaptation: Conceptualizing art in human evolution. *Human Nature* 6 (2): 99–117.
—. 2000a. *Art and intimacy: How the arts began*. Seattle: University of Washington Press.
—. 2000b. Antecedents of the temporal arts in early mother-infant interaction. In *The origins of music,* ed. Nils L. Wallin, Björn Merker, and Steven Brown, 389–410. Cambridge, MA: MIT Press.
—. 2003. Art in global context: An evolutionary/functionalist perspective for the 21st century. *International Journal of Anthropology* 18 (3): 245–58.

DUTTON, DENIS. 2000. But they don't have our concept of art. In *Theories of art today,* ed. Noël Carroll, 217–38. Madison: University of Wisconsin Press.

EAGLETON, TERRY. 1990. *The ideology of the aesthetic*. Oxford and Cambridge, MA: Blackwell.

EIBL-EIBESFELDT, IRENÄUS. 1988. The biological foundations of aesthetics. In *Beauty and the brain: Biological aspects of aesthetics,* ed. Ingo Rentschler, Barbara Herzberger and David Epstein, 29–68. Basel: Birkhäuser.
—. 1989. *Human Ethology*. Trans. Geoffrey Strachan. Hawthorne, NY: Aldine de Gruyter.

FERNALD, ANNE. 1992. Human maternal vocalizations to infants as biologically relevant signals: An evolutionary perspective. In *The adapted mind: Evolutionary psychology and the generation of culture,* ed. Jerome H. Barkow, Leda Cosmides, and John Tooby, 391–428. New York and Oxford: Oxford University Press.

GEIST, VALERIUS. 1978. *Life strategies, human evolution, environmental design: Toward a biological theory of health*. New York: Springer.

GIANINO, ANDREW, AND EDWARD Z. TRONICK. 1988. The mutual regulation model: The infant's self and interactive regulation and coping and defensive capacities. In *Stress and coping across development*, ed. Tiffany M. Field, Philip M. McCabe, and Neil Schneiderman, 47–68. Hillsdale, NJ: Erlbaum.

GILMAN, ALFRED. 2003. How should schools teach evolution?: Emphasize the scientific facts. *Reports of the National Center for Science Education* 23 (5–6): 8–9.

GOTTSCHALL, JONATHAN, AND DAVID SLOAN WILSON, eds. 2005. *Literature and the human animal: Evolution and the nature of narrative.* Evanston, IL: Northwestern University Press.

GROSS, MICHAEL. 2002. Red head: US-style creationism spreads to Europe. *Current Biology* 12 (8): 265–66.

HAGEN, EDWARD H., AND GREGORY A. BRYANT. 2003. Music and dance as a coalition signaling system. *Human Nature* 14 (1): 21–51.

HAMBURGER, JEFFREY F. 1998. *The visual and the visionary: Art and female spirituality in late medieval Germany.* New York: Zone Books and Cambridge, MA: MIT Press.

HAYDEN, BRIAN. 1987. Alliances and ritual ecstasy: Human responses to resource stress. *Journal for the Scientific Study of Religion* 26 (1): 81–91.

HIMMELHEBER, HANS. 1993. *Eskimo artists: Fieldwork in Alaska, June 1936 until April 1937.* Trans. D. G. Gunderson and author. [Fairbanks]: University of Alaska Press. Originally published as *Eskimokünstler: Teilergebnis einer ethnographischen Expedition in Alaska von Juni 1936-April 1937* (Stuttgart: Strecker & Schröder, 1938).

HOFER, MYRON A. 1990. Early symbolic processes: Hard evidence from a soft place. In *Pleasure beyond the pleasure principle.* Vol. 1 of *The role of affect in motivation, development and adaptation*, ed. Robert A. Glick and Stanley Bone, 55–78. New Haven, CT and London: Yale University Press.

HORTON, ROBIN. 1965. *Kalabari sculpture.* Apapa, Lagos: Nigerian National Press for: Department of Antiquities.

LORENZ, KONRAD. 1982. *The foundations of ethology: The principal ideas and discoveries in animal behavior.* Trans. Robert Warren Kickert and author. New York: Simon and Schuster.

MALINOWSKI, BRONISLAW. 1922. *Argonauts of the Western Pacific.* London: Routledge and Kegan Paul.
—. 1948. *Magic, science and religion and other essays,* selected and with an introd. by Robert Redfield. Boston: Beacon Press.

MALLOCH, STEPHEN, AND COLWYN TREVARTHEN, eds. Forthcoming. *Communicative musicality: Narratives of expressive gesture and being human.* Oxford: Oxford University Press.

MARCUS, GEORGE E., AND MICHAEL M. J. FISCHER. 1999. *Anthropology as cultural critique: An experimental moment in the human sciences.* 1st ed. published 1986. Chicago and London: The University of Chicago Press.

MEAD, MARGARET. 1975. *Growing up in New Guinea: A comparative study of primitive education.* 1st ed. published 1930. New York: Morrow.

MERKER, BJÖRN. 2000. Synchronous chorusing and human origins. In *The origins of music*, ed. Nils Wallin, Björn Merker, and Steven Brown, 315–27. Cambridge, MA: MIT Press.

MIALL, DAVID, AND DON KUIKEN. 1994a. Beyond text theory: Understanding literary response. *Discourse Processes* 17: 337–52.
—. 1994b. Foregrounding, defamiliarization, and affect: Response to literary stories. *Poetics* 22: 389–407.

MILLER, GEOFFREY F. 1999. Sexual selection for cultural displays. In *The evolution of culture: An interdisciplinary view*, ed. Robin Dunbar, Chris Knight, and Camilla Power, 71–91. Edinburgh: Edinburgh University Press
—. 2000a. The mating mind: How sexual choice shaped the evolution of human nature. New York: Doubleday; London: Heinemann.
—. 2000b. Evolution of human music through sexual selection. In The origins of music, ed. Nils Wallin, Björn Merker, and Steven Brown, 329–60. Cambridge, MA: MIT Press.
—. 2001. Aesthetic fitness: How sexual selection shaped artistic virtuosity as a fitness indicator and aesthetic preferences as mate choice critera. *Bulletin of Psychology and the Arts* 2 (1): 20–25.

MITHEN, STEVEN J. 1996. *The prehistory of the mind: The cognitive origins of art, religion and science.* London: Thames and Hudson.

MORLEY, IAIN. 2002. Evolution of the physiological and neurological capacities for music. *Cambridge Archaeological Journal* 12 (2): 195–216.

MORRIS, DESMOND. 1962. *The Biology of art: A study of the picture-making behaviour of the great apes and its relationship to human art.* New York: Knopf.

MUKAŘOVSKÝ, JAN. 1964. Standard language and poetic language. In *A Prague School reader on esthetics, literary structure and style*, ed. and trans. from the Czech by Paul L. Garvin, 17–30. Washington, DC: Georgetown University Press. Originally published as Jazyk spisovný a jazyk básnický. *Spisovná čeština a jazyková kultura* (1932): 132–56.

MUNRO, THOMAS. 1963. *Evolution in the arts and other theories of culture history.* [Cleveland:] Cleveland Museum of Art.

NADEL, JACQUELINE, ISABELLE CARCHON, CLAUDE KERVELLA, DANIEL MARCELLI, AND DENIS RÉSERBET-PLANTEY. 1999. Expectancies for social contingency in 2-month-olds. *Developmental Science* 2 (2): 164–73.

PAPOUŠEK, HANUŠ, AND MECHTHILD PAPOUŠEK. 1979. Early ontogeny of human social interaction: Its biological roots and social dimensions. In *Human ethology: Claims and limits of a new discipline: Contributions to the colloquium*, ed. M. von Cranach et al., 456–78. Cambridge: Cambridge University Press.
—. 1981. Musical elements in the infant's vocalization: Their significance for communication, cognition, and creativity. In *Advances in Infancy Research*, vol. I, ed. Lewis P. Lipsitt and Carolyn K. Rovee-Collier, 163–224. Norwood, NJ: Ablex 1981.

PINKER, STEVEN. 1997. *How the mind works,* New York: Norton.
—. 2002. *The blank slate: The modern denial of human nature.* New York: Viking.

POWER, CAMILLA. 1999. "Beauty magic": The origins of art. In *The evolution of culture: An interdisciplinary view,* ed. Robin Dunbar, Chris Knight, and Camilla Power, 82–112. Edinburgh: Edinburgh University Press.

RADCLIFFE-BROWN, ALFRED REGINALD. 1952. Religion and society. In *Structure and function in primitive society.* Glencoe, IL: Free Press, 153–77. Originally published in *Journal of the Royal Anthropological Institute* 75 (1945) 1–2: 33–43.

RAMACHANDRAN, V. S., AND WILLIAM HIRSTEIN. 1999. The science of art: A neurological theory of aesthetic experience. *Journal of Consciousness Studies* 6 (6): 15–51.

SAUERLÄNDER, WILLIBALD. 2002. Images behind the wall: Review of *The visual and the visionary: Art and female spirituality in late medieval Germany* by Jeffrey F. Hamburger. *The New York Review of Books* 49 (7) April 25: 40–42.

SCALISE SUGIYAMA, MICHELLE. 1996. On the origins of narrative: Storyteller bias as a fitness-enhancing strategy. *Human Nature* 7 (4): 403–25.
—. 2001a. Food, foragers, and folklore: The role of narrative in human subsistence. *Evolution and Human Behavior* 22 (4): 221–40.
—. 2001b. Narrative theory and function: why evolution matters. *Philosophy and Literature* 25 (2): 233–250.
—. 2001c. New science, old myth: an evolutionary critique of the Oedipal paradigm. *Mosaic* 34 (March): 121–36.
—. 2003. Cultural variation is part of human nature: literary universals, context-sensitivity, and "Shakespeare in the Bush". *Human Nature* 14 (4): 383–96.

SCHORE, ALLAN N. 1994. *Affect regulation and the origin of the self: The neurobiology of emotional development.* Hillsdale NJ: Erlbaum.

SHKLOVSKY, VICTOR. 1965. Art as technique [1917]. In *Russian formalist criticism: Four essays,* ed. and trans. by Lee T. Lemon and Marion J. Reis, 3–24. Lincoln: University of Nebraska Press.

SOLSO, ROBERT L. 1994. *Cognition and the visual arts.* Cambridge, MA: MIT Press.

STERN, DANIEL. 1971. A microanalysis of mother-infant interaction. *Journal of the American Academy of Child Psychiatry* 10: 501–17.

STOREY, ROBERT F. 1996. *Literature and the human animal: On the biogenetic foundations of literary representation.* Evanston, IL: Northwestern University Press.

STOTT, MARGARET A. 1975. *Bella Coola ceremony and art.* Ottawa: National Museums of Canada.

TAÇON, PAUL S. C. 1983. Dorset art in relation to prehistoric culture stress. *Études Inuit/Inuit Studies* 7 (1): 41–65.
—, and Sally Brockwell 1995. Arnhem Land prehistory in landscape, stone, and paint. *Antiquity* 69 (259): 676–95.
—, Meredith Wilson, and Christopher Chippindale. 1996. Birth of the rainbow serpent in Arnhem Land rock art and oral history. *Archaeology Oceania* 31 (3): 103–24.

TAMBIAH, STANLEY J. 1979. A performative approach to ritual. In *Proceedings of the British Academy, London LXV.* London: British Academy; Oxford: Oxford University Press, 113–69.

THORNHILL, RANDY. 2003. Darwinian aesthetics informs traditional aesthetics. In *Evolutionary aesthetics,* ed. Eckart Voland and Karl Grammer, 9–38. Berlin: Springer.

TOOBY, JOHN, AND LEDA COSMIDES. 2001. Does beauty build adaptive minds?: Toward an evolutionary theory of aesthetics. In *On the origin of fictions: Interdisciplinary perspectives,* ed. H. Porter Abbott. Special issue, *SubStance: A review of theory and literary criticism* 94/95, vol. 30 (1–2): 6–27.

TREVARTHEN, COLWYN. 1997. Fetal and neonatal psychology: intrinsic motives and learning behavior. In *Advances in perinatal medicine,* Proceedings of the Fifteenth European Congress of Perinatal Medicine, ed. F. Cockburn, 282–91. New York: Parthenon.

TURNER, VICTOR. 1969. *The ritual process: Structure and anti-structure.* London: Routledge and Kegan Paul 1969.

VAN DAMME, WILFRIED. 1996. *Beauty in context: Towards an anthropological approach to aesthetics.* Philosophy of History and Culture 17. Leiden, New York, and Cologne: Brill.

VAN GENNEP, ARNOLD. 1960. *The rites of passage.* Trans. Monika B. Vizedom and Gabrielle L. Caffe. London: Routledge and Kegan Paul. Originally published as *Les rites de passage* (Paris: Nourry, 1909).

VOLAND, ECKART. 2003. Aesthetic preferences in the world of artifacts—adaptations for the evaluation of "honest signals"? In *Evolutionary aesthetics,* ed. Eckart Voland and Karl Grammer, 239–60. Berlin: Springer.
—, and Karl Grammer, eds. 2003. *Evolutionary aesthetics.* Berlin: Springer.

WATTS, IAN. 1999. The origin of symbolic culture. In *The evolution of culture: An interdisciplinary view,* ed. Robin Dunbar, Chris Knight, and Camilla Power, 113–46. Edinburgh: Edinburgh University Press.

WEITZ, MORRIS. 1959. The role of theory in aesthetics. In *Problems in aesthetics,* ed. Morris Weitz, 145–56. New York: Macmillan.

ZAHAVI, AMOTZ, AND AVISHAG ZAHAVI. 1997. *The handicap principle: A missing piece of Darwin's puzzle.* Oxford: Oxford University Press.

ZEKI, SEMIR. 1999. *Inner vision: An exploration of art and the brain.* Oxford and New York: Oxford University Press.

JOHN ONIANS

Neuroarthistory: Making More Sense of Art

In many ways there is nothing new about neuroarthistory as a way of making more sense of art as a worldwide phenomenon. It has long been an implicit aspect of the agenda of art historians, anthropologists, and archaeologists, and it has become a more explicit element in the work of practitioners of visual and material culture studies with their heightened interest in theory. After all, any notion that the making or viewing of art is affected by what goes on in the head of the artist or the viewer is implicitly neuroarthistory. This is true whether we are talking of older ideas of artistic genius or stylistic influence or newer theories of Marxism or feminism, structuralism or poststructuralism, semiotics or critical theory. Since everybody agrees that all mental activity takes place in the brain, whenever we make use of such notions, we all make assumptions about what goes on inside that organ. What distinguishes neuroarthistory is only a more conscious commitment to look behind such assumptions and find out as much as possible about what it is that goes on in our brains, how it goes on and why.

Perhaps the first art historian who took a consciously neural approach to art was Michael Baxandall, although few people realize this. For example, it is in explicitly neural terms that he presents his famous concept of the "period eye" in *Painting and Experience in Fifteenth Century Italy* 1972. He begins the famous chapter in which he introduces the concept by pointing out how "rays from an object are received by the retina's network of nerve fibers. It is at this point human equipment for visual perception ceases to be uniform, from one man to the next. The brain must interpret the raw data about light and color that it receives from the cones and it does this with innate skills and those developed out of experience…. Everyone in fact processes the data from the eye with different equipment" (Baxandall 1972, 29). More recently, in the

1990s, Baxandall has gone further, using a deepening knowledge of the neuroanatomy of the sense of sight to explain our response to paintings such as Piero's *Resurrection* and Braque's *Violin and pitcher*, and becoming the first art historian to use diagrams of neural networks to illustrate his writings. Baxandall is thought of as a social art historian, but he is in fact a neuroarthistorian (Onians 2007, 178-88).

More recently he has been joined by a surprising ally, Norman Bryson. Bryson spent the last two decades of the twentieth century as a poststructuralist vehemently attacking the perceptualist account of art associated with Baxandall and my teacher, Ernst Gombrich. Recently, though, he has reversed his opinion, becoming a convert to a neural approach. In 2003 he not only welcomed neuroscience as a "wholly original paradigm for thinking through cultural history and the philosophy of the human subject" (Bryson 2003, 11), but went on to assert that it also exposes the shortcomings of the assumptions underpinning much of recent cultural theory: "The radicalism of neuroscience consists in its bracketing out the signifier as the force that binds the world together: what makes the apple is not the signifier 'apple' … but rather the simultaneous firing of axons and neurons within cellular and organic life" (Bryson 2003, 14). As he says, poststructuralist thought, "by concentrating on the signifier as the basic unit of description … commits itself to an intensely *cognitive* point of view." And this is not a good thing. The result is a tremendous loss. "Feeling, emotion, intuition, sensation—the creatural life of the body and of embodied experience—tend to fall away, their place taken by an essentially *clerical* outlook that centers on the written text. The signifier rules over a set of terms whose functions are primarily textual in scope: the analysis of ordinary language (Wittgenstein); of the circulation of meaning within the literary text (deconstructive criticism); of the disruptions in the symbolic order that indicate the advent of the unconscious fear and desire in the analysand's speech or in the discourse of the work of art (psychoanalysis). While the family of terms that owe their allegiance to the signifier—*text, discourse, code, meaning*—is brilliantly adept at dealing with questions of signification, it encounters a notable limit when the area that it seeks to understand exceeds the sphere of textual meaning" (ibid.). With these words Bryson not only contemptuously relegates the tools of which he was once most proud, poststructuralism, Wittgensteinian philosophy, deconstruction, and psychoanalysis, to the domain of the purely *clerical,* he heralds neuroscience as a way to make more sense of art because it accommodates the vital categories of human experience bracketed out by the other approaches, "feeling, emotion, intuition and sensation." Bryson, once the apostle of the linguistic and the social, and critic of the biological and the perceptual, now celebrates the neuroscientific. For him it has become clear that neuroscience can indeed help us to make more sense of art, precisely because it requires us to take into account those vital phenomena.

What then would be the essence of the neuroarthistory to which Bryson implicitly looks forward? As he suggests, its core concern would be to understand the making and viewing of art, not metaphorically by reference to language, but physically in terms of the firing of neurons. And at this point it is worth reminding ourselves what persuaded him to change his view so dramatically. The core factor was quite simply the extraordinary growth in neuroscience over the last decade or two. The reason why people such as he had earlier placed so much faith in nonneural approaches such as poststructuralism was quite simply because at that stage there were no other tools available to deal with the problems with which he and others were concerned. What Bryson realized was that the new neuroscience allowed him to answer the questions he was asking, especially questions about meaning, at a much more fundamental level. This was because neuroscientific techniques such as PET, CT, MRI and fMRI had so transformed our ability to monitor brain activity that we can now understand much of our experience, especially visual experience, in neural terms. We used to have to ask people what they were thinking. We can now see not just what they are thinking but we can see all the other vital areas of the brain that are involved, the autonomous nervous system that helps us to breathe, the emotional system that ensures that our actions match the needs of our viscera. The outer cortex of our brains only exists to serve these lower areas and it is in these areas that the most profound meanings are experienced. We cannot understand thinking without understanding feeling.

What then is the new knowledge of the brain that can sustain a new discipline of neuroarthistory? The basic facts are simple, but they reveal an astonishing complexity. We now know that each of us is born with about 100 billion neurons, that each of these neurons can have to up to 100,000 connections with other neurons, and that these connections are constantly being made and falling away during our life (Fig. 1). We also know increasingly which neurons or groups of neurons support which physical or mental activity. For example, we know which groups deal with signals from each of our senses, with the area of the brain that deals with sight being placed at the back of the head and that which deals with hearing at the side. We also know how the distribution of the separate groups of neurons dealing with somatosensory signals from our limbs relates to those that send out signals to perform motor actions. We know that these arrangements of collections of neurons with specialized function are determined by the genetic coding of our DNA and that the same coding establishes the principles by which the connections between individual neurons will form or fall away in response to experience, their so-called plasticity. Fig. 2, for example, shows how neurons in the human visual cortex establish connections in the first two years of life, and it is now known that this process continues until we die. We can, thus, see how repeated use of the tips of our fingers to touch causes their sensibility to increase dramatically, being directly associated with an enlargement of the areas of the brain receiving inputs from those fingers, caused by the proliferation of connections between the neurons involved. More importantly for anyone studying any type of art, that is any type of visually interesting artifact, we know that the more often we look at an object, the more connections will be made between neurons to help us to see it (Tanaka 1993, 685–88). This is of enormous relevance, because it means that whatever the landscape we are brought up in, whether sand or jungle, ice or rock, whatever the plants, or animals or man-made objects we look at, the more we will develop neural networks to help us to do so. The networks so formed will give us a preference for looking at—and indeed for making—configurations that share the properties of that landscape-type, plant-type, animal-type or object-type, a knowledge which acquires particular significance given that we also know that the brain contains separate areas in and around the inferotemporal cortex devoted to such phenomena as faces, bodies, places, organic and inorganic objects, and so on (Kanwisher 2004). We know less about the brain's chemistry, the role of neurotransmitters in communication between neurons and the processes by which hormones, such as the pleasure-giving dopamines, are released at different times in the brain's basal ganglia to affect mood and emotions, such as the pleasure we feel in looking at something or the desire that makes us reach out to touch it, but we know they hold the key to explaining why we do what we do. The area of our ignorance is still vastly greater than that of our knowledge, but even that limited knowledge has so transformed our ability to understand the mind that it is increasingly helpful to think of it in neurophysical terms.

And, fortunately for those studying art, this is particularly true of the mental operations of the maker or viewer of art, because the area at the back of the brain that deals with sight is much bigger than that dealing with any other of the senses and it is the best understood, thanks to the work of neuroscientists who have shown how this area is divided into subareas, such as $V1$ where signals from the eye first arrive and $V4$ and $V5$ where slightly later color and movement are processed (Zeki 1999). Thanks to neuroscientists we also know that, although each of the senses is principally dealt with in a distinct area of the brain, they are in fact all connected, so that, for example, information gathered from the sense of sight is collated with any available from the senses of touch, hearing and smell when it first arrives and these correlations become part of our memory; so that if we experience the same object more than once the sensory associations established earlier are liable to be recalled. For the brain the senses are only separate in terms of the distinct locations where signals from the outer sense organs arrive. If we consider the brain as a whole they are cross-connected.

Figure 1
Neuron, drawing by O. Deiters,
1865.

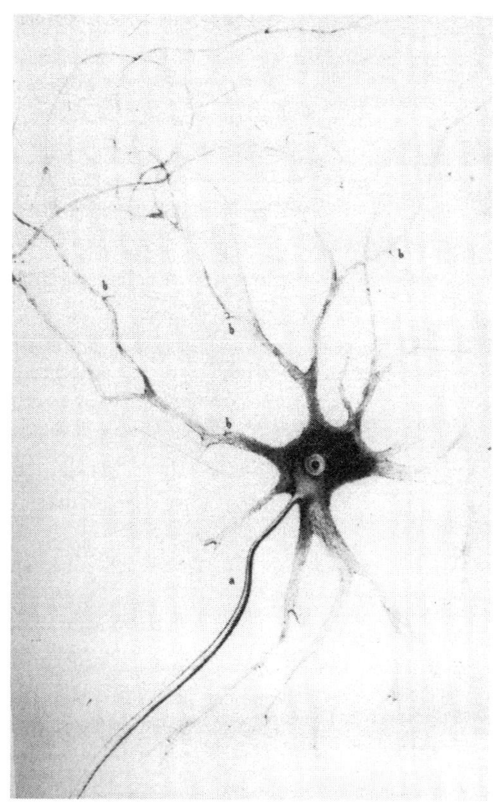

Figure 2
Neuronal connections in the human brain: (from top to bottom)
at birth, three months, fifteen
months and two years.

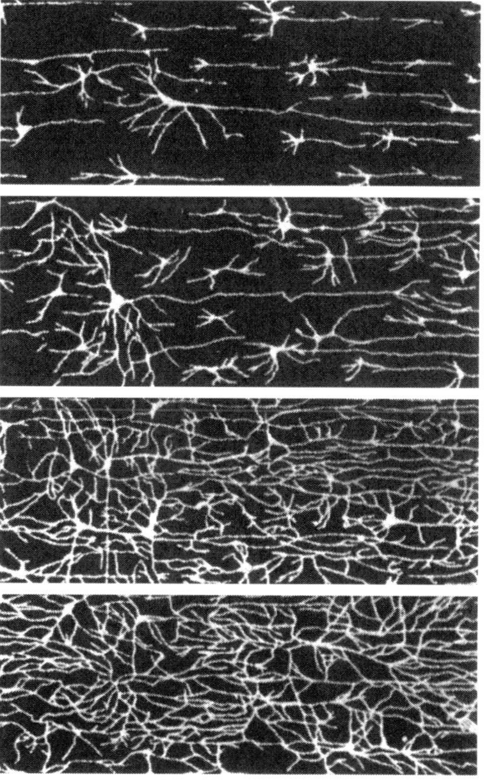

The reason why the brain is constantly collating information from the different senses has to do with the reason why we have a brain in the first place, and that is also something the neuro-arthistorian needs to understand because it explains much about art's importance to us. Plants don't have brains and animals do simply because animals need to move in order to survive, that is in order to find food and a mate and to protect themselves. There is even the famous case of the sea squirt which has a brain until it has a place where it can meet all its needs and then consumes it, effectively giving up the life of an animal and becoming a plant. Otherwise each creature's nervous system, like the rest of its particular sensory and motor resources, is selected for by evolution to enable it to survive in its particular ecological context. This is well illustrated by the nervous system of the frog, which contains neurons that fire when exposed to a dot, because that is likely to be a fly, and a similar specialization is found in other creatures with restricted needs.

Our own nervous system is also specifically adapted to help us to survive, but is much more complex because survival for us requires much more complex skills. One way we acquire those skills is by learning from and imitating our elders and betters, and we have neurons that cause this to happen without us knowing. These are called "mirror neurons" and were first recognized in the temporal area of the brains of macaque monkeys just ten years ago (Rizzolatti, Fadiga, Gallese and Fogassi 1996). What experimenters in Parma, Italy, noticed was that these neurons in the premotor cortex which normally fired before the monkey makes a particular movement of the fingers also fire when the monkey sees another monkey or man do the same thing, or even when it just hears a peanut being cracked, and all this happens without the monkey itself moving (Fig. 3). It is now clear that possession of such mirror neurons in all us apes allows us not only to acquire the motor actions of those around us without moving, but gives us insight into why the motor action is performed. This gives us obvious advantages. Our mirror neurons ensure that we follow and understand the motor preferences of our elders, whether they involve moving our eyes or our hands. They thus ensure that we acquire vital skills quite spontaneously.

Those skills become permanent because of the plasticity of our motor cortex and in the same way the plasticity of our visual cortex ensures that our knowledge of good and bad things and people becomes embedded too. We are neurologically predisposed to have particular emotional and motor responses to particular configurations and shapes, because if we didn't we would not find and ingest food, identify and consolidate friendships, or select and keep our mates. These properties of our brains are vital tools in our battle for survival, they are also vital tools for the neuro-arthistorian. If we understand the principles that underlie their operation, we can apply them to any circumstance in which motor or visual preferences are involved, wherever in the world, whatever the place, and whatever the period.

This is why neuroarthistory can help art historians, anthropologists and archaeologists answer questions such as why a particular artist, or group of artists, makes a particular work at a particular time in a particular essay, and why a particular community or a particular individual patron has an interest in such art, as will be shown in the remainder of this essay. But before moving to this stage it will be helpful first to apply this neuroscientific knowledge to the explanation of an art-like behaviour in another species. This example, by illustrating both how important neural equipment can be for any species and how useful a knowledge of neuroscience can be for the study of that species' activities, provides a powerful demonstration of the universal applicability of neuroarthistory's principles. In Fig. 4a we see a man standing outside an aquarium and looking in on a family of dolphins. He is smoking and happens to puff a cloud of smoke.

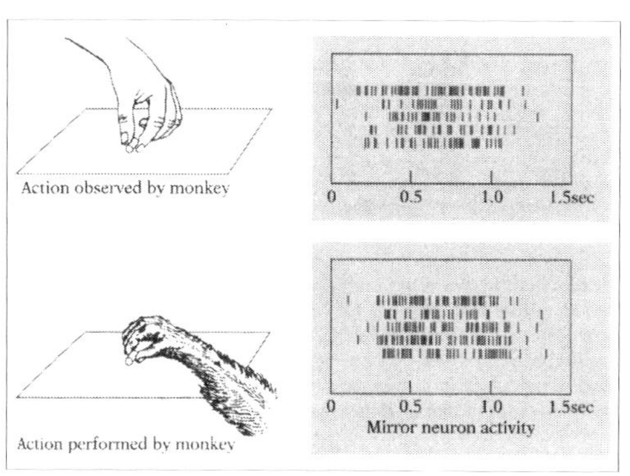

Figure 3
Functioning of mirror neurons.

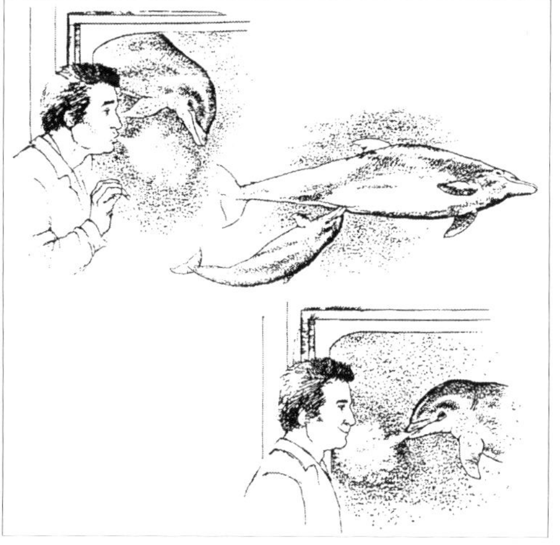

Figure 4 a-b
An infant dolphin blowing milk
to mimic a human's puff of
cigarette smoke,
drawing by P. Barrett.

In Fig. 4b we see what happened next. A young female dolphin inside the aquarium saw what he did. To his surprise she next swam off to her mother took a suck of milk and then coming back to him blew a cloud of milk exactly like his own cloud of smoke. There are many aspects of this event which are remarkable. For example, the young female dolphin evidently not only has the capacity to see a cloud shape as a particular thing, she also remembers having produced a similar effect when milk leaked from her mouth, and has sufficient motor control of her mouth to produce the effect deliberately. But much the most astonishing thing is that she does all this without any instruction or any inducements. We may ask why she does it, and the answer is surprisingly simple. We have mirror neurons to help us learn complicated activities by watching our elders and betters and so does she. It is some equivalent of mirror neurons in the dolphin's brain, their effect reinforced by some rewarding brain chemical such as dopa-mine, that causes her to do something that is extremely difficult, that is reproduce the effect of smoke suspended in air using milk suspended in water. She is effectively doing what humans have to go to art school to learn, how to represent something made using one medium on one type of support by using another medium on another type of support. There can hardly be a more eloquent illustration of at least two neural resources, the neural networks in the visual cortex that enable us to see, identify and reproduce shapes, and the neural networks in our motor system that enable us to reproduce actions. What we have effectively been able to explain is why a particular individual made a particular work of art with a particular subject in a particular medium on a particular support in a particular place at a particular time, and we have been able to do so only thanks to neuroscience. No other existing approach from the positivist to the postmodernist, from the structuralist to the Marxist, could have offered us any help in answering these classic questions. So, having found it useful to applying the method of neuroarthistory to dolphins, we can now at last apply it to humans, taking examples from the beginning, the middle and end of art's history to date.

In what follows we will take account of neurally based tendencies that are both inborn and acquired and we will make use of knowledge of several neural phenomena that have already been introduced and which are likely in the long run to transform all the disciplines dealing with art. One is neural plasticity, and especially the way repeated exposure to any object or configuration makes us better at seeing it and so gives us a preference for look at it. If we know what things a person has been looking at intently and repeatedly, we will have some guidance on the visual preferences which will influence their hand movements if they are makers of art and their visual interest if they are viewers. Another is mirror neurons, which allow us unconsciously to acquire the bodily dispositions and movements of those around us to whom we give attention. If we know who are the most admired individuals in a particular community, we will have a line on whose body language is most likely to be adopted by other members. Other neural phenomena, too, will appear during the discussion.

One challenging but appropriate area of art for the application of a neuroarthistorical approach is the earliest, that from the Chauvet Cave in the Ardeche, to the west of the Rhone in Southern France. There is certainly a need for a new approach to this material, as existing ones can make no sense of it. This is immediately obvious if we consider that the paintings in the cave are at once the earliest, that is about 32,000 years old, in other words twice as old as Lascaux, and also, in many ways, the most photographically naturalistic. Not only do individual representations, such as those of hunting lions or this bear (Fig. 5), exploit such features as three-quarter perspective which is almost unknown before the ancient Greeks, thirty thousand years later, they have a life-likeness in their capturing of those animals' intent and intelligent movement that is unknown in all later art, as comparison with a drawing of a bear by Leonardo indicates. The Lascaux animals, too, look like stuffed toys by comparison. Indeed, the lifelikeness of the Chauvet animals is only paralleled in wild-life filming. The same is true of large compositions. Whole walls are covered with such vivid processions of painted animals that we are confronted with a scene that captures the chaotic movement of different species in a landscape better than anything before a David Attenborough film on the Serengeti. All existing approaches assume that the first art must have been schematic and that it only became more naturalistic as a result of social pressures and conscious effort by artists. Such approaches can only accommodate the art of Chauvet by assuming that there was a lot of earlier schematic art that was lost, although we have no evidence for it. They have no way to explain why such naturalism, once realized, was never achieved again. Current approaches also assume that any such large investment of effort must testify to society's reliance for its well being on a belief system involving shamanism or myth. But, however applicable such theories might be to later art, such as the measured rows of bulls in Lascaux or Altamira, it would be impossible to find a belief system that was served by Chauvet's representation of nature's natural complexity and disorder.

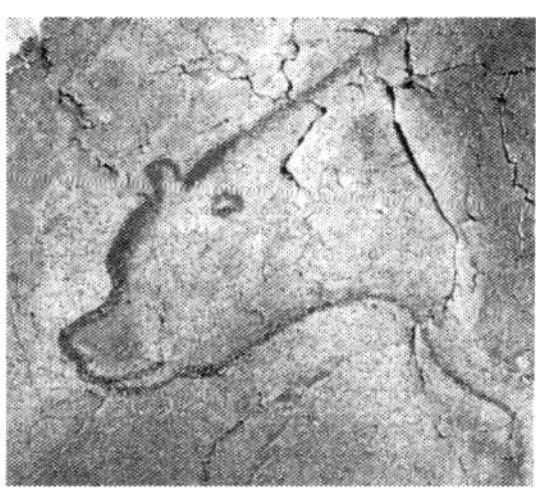

Neuroscience on the other hand can suggest explanations for both why this is the earliest art and why it is the most naturalistic. So, if this is the earliest art, what made humans make it in the first place? It clearly has something to do with their biology, since the art appears soon after the new slender type of *Homo sapiens*

arrives in South Western Europe displacing the earlier Neander-
thal population. But it must also have something to do with the
specific environment, cold and at the limits of human habitability,
since specimens of the new human type did not make such art
earlier on the travels out of Africa after 100,000 years ago.

One clue may lie in something noted seventy years ago, that
in later caves, such as Pech Merle, human marks and especially
hand marks are found next to the marks left by cave bear claws.
For this is also a particular feature of Chauvet. Indeed, the team
who published the cave have shown how in several cases cave bear
claw marks are succeeded on the same spot by representations
made by human engravings (Fig. 6). Elsewhere in the cave there is
another parallel between human and bear activity. Bears sometimes make brown marks on the wall of the cave with their muddy
paws, and nearby humans have left hand prints. Neuroarthistory
can make sense of this, as mirror neurons make such a sequence
not just comprehensible but almost predictable. The same neural
equipment that led humans to spontaneously imitate the actions
of their elders would also have led them to imitate those of an animal which also stood upright and whose size and power they must
have particularly admired and envied. The two techniques used by
the Chauvet artists, engraving and painting, can thus both be seen
to be techniques accidentally employed by the bears. Human neural networks led them to imitate the big bears, just as the young
female dolphin's neural networks led her to imitate a human adult.

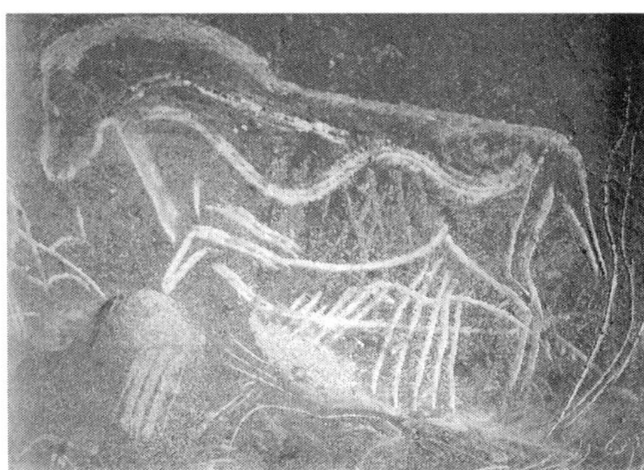

Of course, humans had always been living with animals and
the new slender human type that made this art had lived with
animals all the time during its movement out of Africa and through
Eastern Europe, but never before had the coldness and difficulty
of their environment caused them to look at other creatures, such
as the bear, lion, mammoth and rhinoceros that are so prominent
in these paintings, with such envy of their kits of tools, their claws,
their horns, their fur coats, and above all the neural resources in
their heads, their intelligence. If mirror neurons first led them to
mark the walls, the plasticity of their neural networks determined
what shape they gave those marks. The networks formed as a
result of the repeated visual attention they had given such beasts

would have meant that theirs would have been the first shapes they would have tended to see in the shifting surfaces of the cave's colored walls. The outlines of many of the animals at Chauvet, as elsewhere in Palaeolithic art, appear to have their origin in some chance feature of the cave surface, and this is certainly what happened in the case of our bear, whose presence was first suggested by the chance resemblance of markings on the wall to the silhouette of a bear's forepaw. Just as releases of pleasure-giving dopamine would have been prompted by the first sight of an envied animal in the wild, so similar releases would have followed both the first recognition of the shape in the wall and each enhancement of the image until no further enhancement was possible, that is at the moment when the painted image matched exactly the optical memory in the inferotemporal cortex.

Again, of course, humans would have entered many such limestone caves in South Western France, but for some reason they didn't make any art; so what was it in the neural apparatus of those that entered this particular cave that set them apart? The answer probably lies in the rock arch that spans the Ardeche river just below the site. Such an arch is unparalleled not just in France but in the world and it is likely to have been exploited as a safe bridge by all the animals that were forced to migrate seasonally in the then tundra habitat (Fig. 7). As a result, those who lived nearby would have been more often exposed to the sight of processions of groups of animals than humans anywhere in the world, with all the consequences that had for the further strengthening of their neural networks. Confirmation that the unique talents of the makers of this art were indeed the product of watching animals cross the unique bridge comes from the unparalleled nature of compositions on two of the cave walls, both of which are arranged around niche-like configurations that recall the rock arch (Fig. 8). Indeed, in the most striking case the mammoths seem to be climbing up the arch so as to cross. The neural apparatus of those who made such images had been affected by the sight not just of animals passing over the arch but of the arch itself. If this explanation is right, and the first great work of art in human history is the product of nothing more than the first exposure of the new and improved neural apparatus of *Homo sapiens* to a particular place in a particularly stressful environment, then neuroarthistory can indeed make more sense of art.

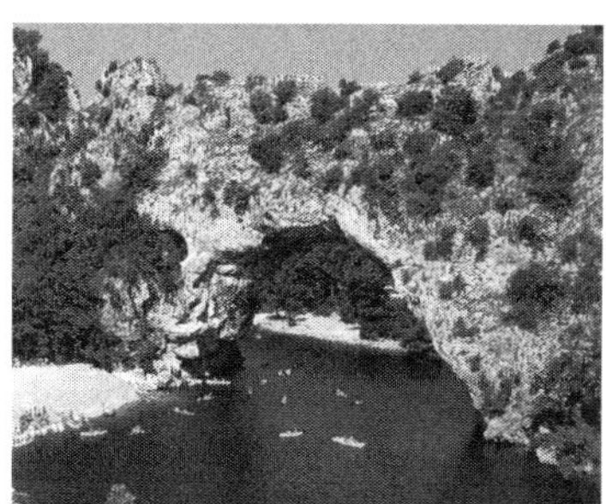

Figure 7
Rock arch, Vallon Pont d'Arc.

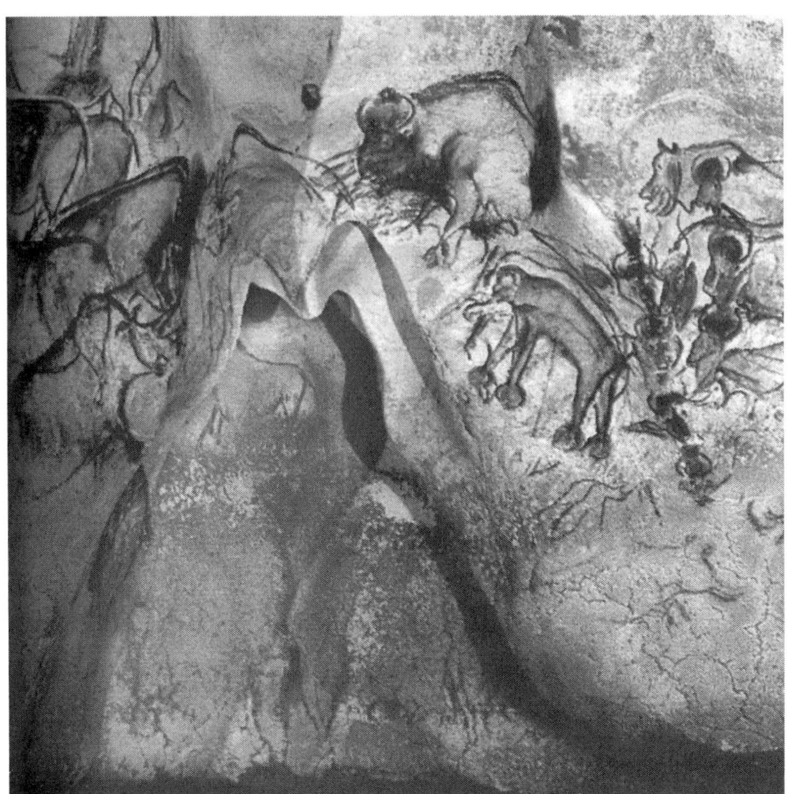

Interestingly, it also makes sense of art's subsequent decline. The life-likeness of the art at Chauvet is due to the fact that the visual cortex of those who made it had been exposed only to live animals. From the moment the first paintings of those animals were made they would have started to affect their viewers in a similar way, and would have given them a preference for more schematic outlines. Each new image would have been infected by a greater influence from art rather than nature, producing an inevitable decline in naturalism. Indeed, we can see this process happening in the series of lion or rhinoceros paintings, each more stiff and exaggerated in its features than the next. The process we see here in which a first stage of attentive looking at nature produces great life-likeness, only to be followed by an increase in schematization, is one that has been repeated a thousand times in the history of art, as the history of figure painting in Italy after Giotto or Michelangelo, or that of landscape painting after the Sung dynasty in China, well illustrate. Giotto and Michelangelo, like the Sung artists, had neural networks more formed by exposure to nature. Those of their followers were more exposed to the schematizations of art. Of course, the observation of the phenomenon is not new, but the neuroscientific explanation which allows us to see the same principle at work both at the dawn of art and 30,000 years later, well illustrates the way neuroarthistory can strengthen existing methods.

It is one thing to apply neuroarthistory's revelations of the power of unconsciously formed neural networks to the explanation of the origin of artistic activity 30,000 years ago. It may seem less appropriate to apply it to the ancient Greeks, whose new self-consciousness and intellectual freedom is supposed to be the source of their art's excellence. And, of course, the importance of these new elements resulting from a particular social formation are not to be denied. Neuroarthistory does not replace existing art history, it only gives it another resource and dimension, as in the case of Greek sculpture, where it can again suggest that neural attributes acquired passively may have been as important for its quality as active, conscious effort. Thus, the reason why Greeks of the fifth century BCE made life-size and life-like representations of themselves in stone and bronze may have more in common with the background to Chauvet than we might like to think. After all, if the formation of the neural networks of the artists of Chauvet was due to a combination of unique stresses and unique opportunities, the same may have been true of ancient Greece.

Humans had, of course, always had the opportunity to look at the human body, but only in Greece was looking intently at the young male body an essential part of experience. The reason why this came to be true is already suggested by the outline of Greece, so much more broken up and indented than the outline of the other peninsulas entering the Mediterranean, Asia Minor, Italy and Spain. Greece has that indented shape because it is made up of many narrow valleys cramped between high rocky mountains and this had powerful implications for those who grew up in those valleys after 1000 BCE. As villages became towns, and towns cities, populations grew and soon ran out of fertile soil. Each community coveted the land of its neighbors, just as its neighbors coveted theirs. In this dangerous situation, where there were no allies to call on because all communities were potential rivals, the only way for a city to protect itself was to train and arm their young men as no communities had ever done before. Everyone watched the young men as they trained, making sure that they were strong and fit and disciplined enough to fight in the phalanx, and such watching was formalized as an activity at such Great Games as those of Olympia. The inevitable neurological consequence was that frequent exposure to the sight of the young male body, associated with intense attention to the particular physical attributes which made the body effective in war, would have meant that their neural networks dealing with the human body would have been richer and more complex than those of the members of any community earlier. In the brain of a sculptor, those networks would have ensured that his chisel would produce a figure of exceptional lifelikeness. The Greek sculptor would have got as much pleasure out of a sculpture of a life-like man as the artists of Chauvet got out of a life-like bear or lion. The only difference was that since the Greeks' neural networks were also shaped by exposure to existing representations of bodies, whether their own geometric imagery or that of Egypt, it took at least two hundred years, from 600 to 400 BCE, for repeated exposure to the real thing to allow artists who were now competing to please their clients to achieve a comparable level of naturalism.

One of the aspects of artistic activity about which existing approaches, whether art-historical, anthropological or archaeological, have little to say is the physical response to the artifact, and in the case of Greek statues this is something on which neuroscience can help directly from two points of view. For one thing, the fact that there are neurons in V5 that respond to and so treat as moving not only moving objects but static ones, such as the representation of an athlete in preparation for movement, would have meant that the effect of the statue would have been more vivid than the viewer, either then or now, is consciously aware of. Even more significant would have been the impact of mirror neurons. Since the way these operate means that, just by looking at someone doing something, the premotor cortex of our brain goes through the same motions and so prepares us to do the same thing, viewing a famous Greek statue such as a Tyrant-slayer, a Discobolus or a Doryphorus would have had a powerful unconscious effect on the viewer. Simply by being exposed to such a figure the viewer would have acquired a predisposition to hold himself and move in a similar way, while, since those who paid for such statues would have unconsciously been affected by them in similar ways, it is not surprising that they invested so much money in them. By their effect on young male members of the community such statues repaid the investment in them not just as memorials of the famous but as contributors to the training of a defence force. By giving insight into the response to art, neuroarthistory makes more sense not just of art-making but of art-expenditure.

Once the Greeks had shown the importance of the fighting man, other Europeans continued to invest in them more prestige than other communities, and this has some surprising consequences for the history of art, adding a further dimension of neuroarthistory's potential. One of these can be illustrated by a sixteenth-century print showing a painter in a typical pose (Fig. 9). The artist stands in front of a panel vertical on an easel, his brush in his right hand and palette in the left. It is easy for a European to take such a pose for granted as somehow normal, but it isn't. No artists anywhere else in the world stood like that. If, however, we recognize in the pose an imitation of the knight with his sword and shield we understand what is going on—a correlation strengthened by the artist's choice for subject of a knight in his ultimate glory. Knowledge of the way mirror neurons affect bodily deportment would suggest that Renaissance artists would have been inclined to imitate knights for exactly the same reason that Paleolithic artists imitated bears, or for that matter why the young female dolphin imitated the adult human smoker, because knights were in crucially important ways more effective and materially successful than were painters.

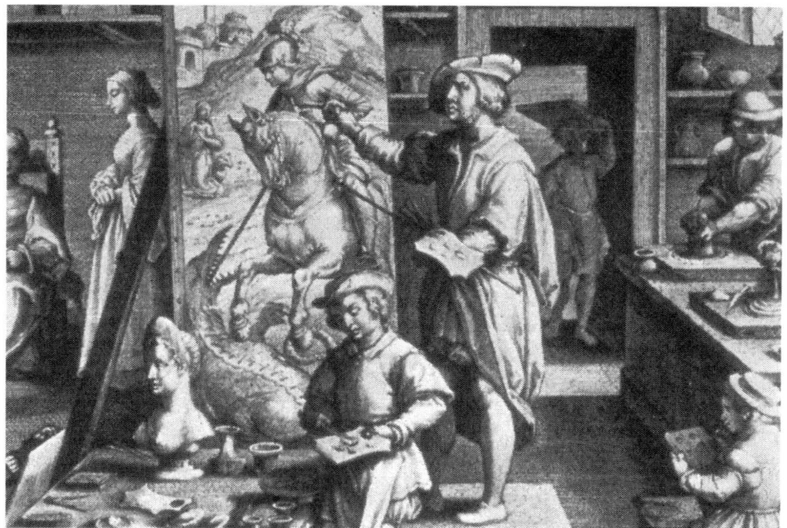

Figure 9
Painter in his studio, sixteenth century.

Neuroarthistory works not by aperçu but by principle. This invites us to explain the artistic poses typical of other communities in a similar way, and challenges us to use the same knowledge of mirror neurons to explain the typical pose of the Chinese ink painter. While in Europe, where military values since the Greeks had been supreme, ink was always applied with a sharp instrument such as a pen, even more like a sword than a brush, in China it was just as consistently applied only with a brush, whether it was being used for painting or for writing. This contrast in implement was matched by a contrast in pose, since the artist sat and dragged ink from a pool-like container onto a horizontal sheet of paper or silk. In asking whose body language the artist might be imitating, I decided some time ago that it was probably that of the farmer irrigating his rice field, since that was the prime source of wealth for rich and poor, and, although neuroarthistory does not rely on texts to come to its conclusions, I was not disappointed when I discovered that the character for painting in Chinese script is built around the sign for field. Evidently it was as natural for the Chinese artist to feel that his activity was analogous to that of a farmer as it was for a European artist to think of it as analogous to a knight. And it is worth reflecting on what this means in terms of the artist's sense of himself. The European artist stabs at his canvas or panel like a fencer, while a Chinese artist gently waters his sheet like a field to make it more fertile for his imagination.

The contrast in the body languages of the European and Chinese artist caused by the action of mirror neurons reminds us that there is a related contrast between the painting styles of Florentine and Venetian artists, which is due to the neural plasticity of the visual cortex. It has been recognized since Vasari that Venetian art is associated with "color" and Florentine with "line" and we can now explain the neuroscientific basis of the polarization. Surrounded by buildings made of stone from the mountains with which their city was ringed, in the company of statues made from marble from not far away, the Florentines looked at, drew their confidence from and so had their neural networks configured by hard angular shapes. In Venice, on the other hand, the principal element in the environment was the calm water of the canals and the lagoon, which reflected the colors of sky and clouds as well as buildings made of red brick and polished colored marble. The neural networks shaped by exposure to the colored reflections of the water, were reinforced by further experience of things for which those same neural networks had given them a preference. Exposure to reflections from water endowed them with a neurally-based taste for the marbles they found in the ruined Roman cities of the Eastern Mediterranean, for the silks and other luxury textiles they imported from the East, and it also encouraged the establishment of mosaic and glass industries. All these artistic preferences, most of which are captured in Gentile Bellini's painting of St Marks square of 1496, were the consequence of a neurologically determined progressive intensification of particular sensual preferences.

We are familiar with the distinctions in the visual preferences produced by these different exposures, as represented by the linear paintings of Botticelli and the coloristic works of Titian, but we should be as aware of the parallel differentiations in the sense of touch as they are represented by the contrast between Titian's *Flora*, her fingers fondling embroidered silk, and Michelangelo's *David*, his muscled fist clenched on a stone. Neuroarthistory reminds us that in the making and experiencing of art we have to consider all the senses, and not just sight.

Neuroarthistory helps us to understand why environments, such as those of Venice and Florence, which are basically constant, are still capable of having a particular impact on the art produced in them at particular times, and the same is true of Britain. There, although clouds and aerial humidity had always been a feature of the environment, they only become a prominent feature of painting around 1800 in the art of Constable and Turner, as we see in Constable's cloud studies and Turner's skies. A neuroarthistorian would expect such heightened interest to be the result of a new exposure to vapors and that is exactly what we find around 1800. Not only had the growth of London and the increased use of coal for heating in the metropolis caused such a change in the city's atmosphere that it became known as "The Smoke," but the new steam engines gave both smoke and steam a new aura of power.

People who lived in England at this time would all have been exposed to vapors more than anybody anywhere in the world, and their constant exposure to such a defining attribute of their new commercial dominance would have given them a neurologically based preference for looking at them, just as was to happen a century or so later in China (see Onians 1999, 690–715).

Of course, again we have to understand differences as well as similarities, and the exposures of Constable and Turner were not identical. Constable was brought up in an East Anglian river valley, where clouds and mist would have been predominant, and it was thus clouds that always attracted him most, even after he arrived in London. Turner, on the other hand, having been brought up just off the Strand near Covent Garden, would have been more accustomed to vapor laden with particles, which is why his attention focused on smoke and the heavier suspensions of rain and snow. Of course smoke, steam, and snow do not just have vaporousness in common, they are also sharply differentiated in smell and temperature and so carry neurally recorded associations with other senses than sight. Neuroarthistory not only helps us to understand the similarity of the subjects and to some extent the styles of two important artists. It also helps us to understand the way the differences in their childhood homes is a source of significant differences in their painting. In both these ways, as in its constant reminder of the interconnection of the senses in the brain, neuroarthistory here as so often helps us to make more sense of art.

When we come to the nineteenth century we are also arriving at the time when medical science was for the first time becoming conscious of the refinement of the nervous system and it was probably some awareness of this development that allowed Ruskin to emerge as one of the first true neuroarthistorians. He is indeed the first person to associate the prevalence of fog in Turner's paintings with his youthful exposure and to see his preference for many more incidental elements, not just patched sails and dark walls, but oranges, and even litter, as due to his childhood visual experiences off Covent Garden, even developing a general theory of the importance of early exposure in a remarkable comparison of Turner and Giorgione called "Two boyhoods" (Ruskin 1888, 292–93). Ruskin was only going by intuition, and that intuition can now be confirmed by neuroscience.

Ruskin believed that the reason why it was particularly in great artists that early experiences in fields such as landscape or female beauty were so important was because at the start of their careers they looked more intently than others, and his observation is consonant with the latest neuroscience. This confirms both that neural plasticity is greatest when we are young and that it is the intensity of our engagement at any age that critically determines the effect of any experience on our neural resources. This is why when studying any artist it may be useful to know what they looked at intently in their youth. Each reader of this essay may

come up with their own potential correlation between early environmental experience and later artistic style and seek to test its
merits against other explanatory models. If they are lucky they
may even have the opportunity of trying them out on the artist
concerned, although most artists are either unconscious of the importance of early experiences or hostile to the notion that such
passive exposure might have a substantial influence on their art. I
certainly felt myself to be lucky when I had the opportunity of
trying out such an explanation on Jasper Johns, when I once sat
next to him at dinner.

Being anxious to apply a neuroarthistorical approach to all
periods and places, I had wanted to find a neurally based explanation of why so many American abstract expressionist artists of his
generation favored a new type of large featureless canvas spread
with relatively monotonous colors and textures (Fig. 10). Wonder-
ing what early visual experience might have led to the formation of
neurally based preferences for such surfaces, I had come to the
conclusion that it was perhaps pictures of the dustbowl, the disastrous desertification of the prairies in the 1930s that seemed emblematic of the impoverishment that followed the depression. Certainly photographs of the dustbowl filled the pages of publications
such as newspapers and *Life* magazine, as they did those of my
own early geography text books (Fig. 11). Anyway, having come up
with this idea, I couldn't resist the temptation to try it out on Jasper, who took me more seriously than he might have done because
it was a small dinner party in the house of a billionaire patron. His
reply was not exactly what I wanted but it came close. What he said
was, "I cant speak for the other guys, but I come from southern
farming stock and in my own case I vividly remember being taken
out of town by my uncle in the spring and being shown fields that
to me all looked empty. What impressed me was that my uncle
looked at the same fields and said 'Jasper, that'n s going to be good.
That'n aint. That'n I don't know.' That was certainly a powerful
experience for me." It is inherent in the nature of neuroarthistorical explanations that we can't prove or disprove the connections
suggested either by my general hunch or this story, but, just as it
was convenient to my explanation of the body language of the Chinese painter to find that the character for painting was based on
that for field, so it pleased me to know that Johns's paintings of the
type that interested me bore titles such as *Flag on Orange Field*.

Figure 10
Jasper Johns, *Flag Painting*,
1955.

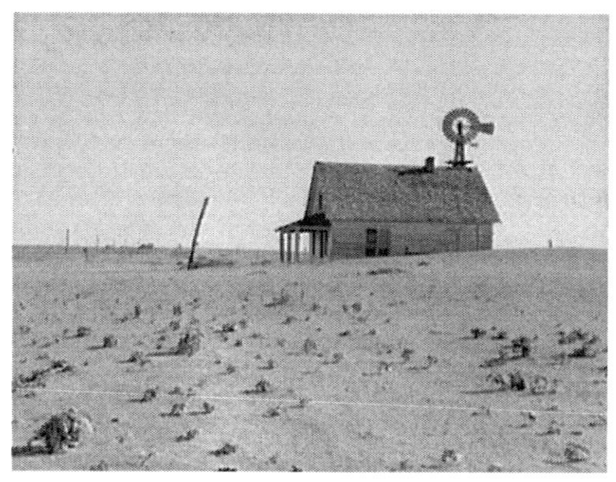

When discussing Ruskin a little earlier, I referred to a potential parallel between developments in the territories of neuroscience, art and art history, and there is an intriguing parallel between the neuroarthistorical trend represented by Baxandall, Bryson, and, indeed, myself, and some core concerns of the so-called YBA's, or Young British Artists. It was at exactly the same time in the 1980s and 90s when those art historians were starting to attend to neurobiology that the YBA's were producing the art that featured so prominently in the 1996 *Sensation* show at the Royal Academy with its many references to the body and feeling. The cover of the exhibition's catalogue announced these themes by its pairing of a cold wet tongue and a dry potentially hot iron, and many of the works in the exhibition were calculated to engage the neural networks of viewers in similarly compelling ways, though only a neuroarthistorian would realize the extent to which this was happening. Thus the power of the Chapman brothers' sculptures must lie at least partly in the way the abnormal bodies would stress our mirror neurons, while Sarah Lucas's *Au Naturel* with its use of organic and inorganic objects to represent the naked male and female body on a mattress would equally stress those areas of the brain where different sets of neurons are designed to deal with different object-types. Fig. 12, for example, shows how one area responds to faces, another to bodies and their parts and yet another to places, while other areas that have been identified are those that respond respectively to animate and inanimate objects. Clearly Lucas's installation presents the brain with a puzzle since the two bodies, for instance, are represented using objects normally responded to by other areas (see Kanwisher 2004).

When I put the word "more" in the title of this essay, I did so above all in order to make clear that neuroarthistory is not a replacement for any existing approaches to art, only an additional resource. All that it does is add something to them by taking note of the neuroscience which has become available since all the other current approaches were developed. What it adds is above all a new set of insights into the unconscious mental formation of both artists and art-users, as comes out particularly clearly in our last examples. Neuroarthistory tells us more about what went on in the mind of the artist, by reminding us that when Jasper Johns was painting *Flag on Orange Field*, the movements of his hand were to some extent influenced by his experience of looking at newly planted fields in South Carolina with his uncle. The unconscious memory of the appearance of the empty fields, and the uncertainty about their yield at the time of the tragedy of the Dustbowl, contributed a special urgency to his search for color and tone and texture. Neuroarthistory also tells us what goes on in the mind of the viewer. It tells us that we have to understand that each viewer sees a work of art differently because they have different neural resources built up by different experiences. It tells us that the more we know about those experiences, the better we can understand the individual viewer's response. In the case of the Lucas's work it also reminds us that there are universal visceral and emotional responses to different categories of objects, which all viewers are likely to share. And that brings out the most important way in which neuroscience makes more sense of art. It reminds us that our entire neural apparatus is designed by evolution with one purpose, to help us to transmit our genetic material, by maximizing the effective use of all the senses. This is why the making and viewing of art are such vital activities.

The examples in this essay are taken from the traditions of European and Chinese art, but they could as easily have been taken from the art of the Arctic Inuit or the Aboriginal inhabitants of Australia, from that of the Aztecs or Incas in the Americas, or of the Bantu or the Tuareg in Africa. And this brings out why a neuro-scientific approach is likely to contribute so much to world art studies. While other disciplines, such as art history, anthropology, or archaeology, or visual and material culture studies, all rely on methods that reflect the differential availability of information relating to different cultures, methods that usually are difficult to apply to materials for which they were not designed, neuroarthistory, or for that matter neuroanthropology or neuroarchaeology, allow all art to be treated equally. If we know something of the factors that might have affected the unconscious mental formation of the makers and viewers of art in a particular place at a particular time, neuroscience helps us to understand how those factors might also have affected the appearance of that art. This is why neuroscience helps us to make more sense of art.

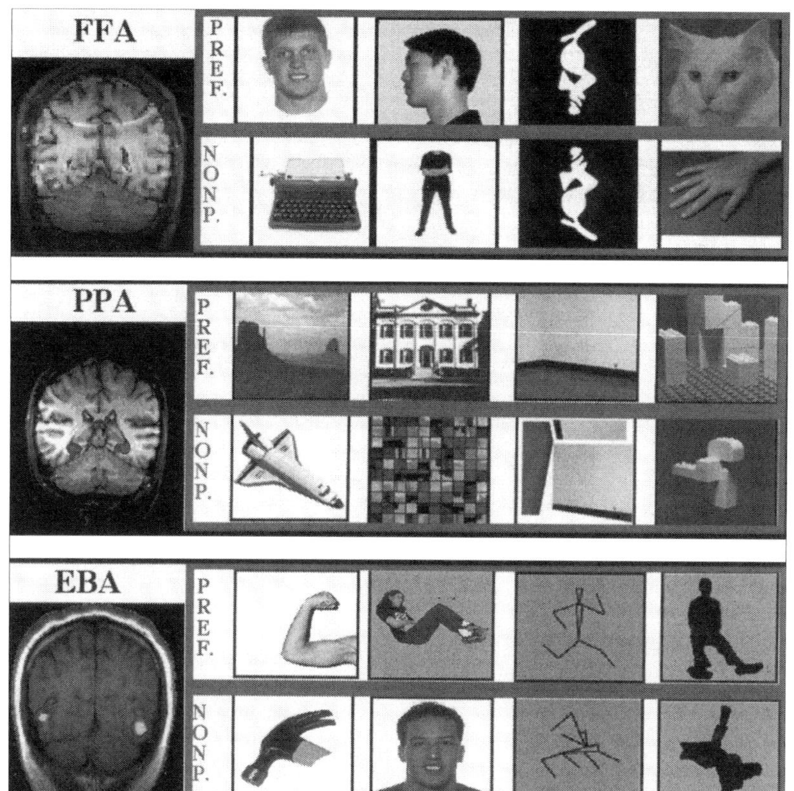

Figure 12

Three category-selective regions of the extrastriate
cortex, those for faces, for places and for body parts.

REFERENCES

BAXANDALL, MICHAEL. 1972. *Painting and experience in fifteenth century Italy: A primer in the social history of pictorial style.* Oxford: Clarendon Press.

BRYSON, NORMAN. 2003. Introduction to *Blow-up: Photography, cinema, and the brain*, Warren Neidich, 11–19. Riverside, CA: California Museum of Photography.

KANWISHER, NANCY. 2004. The ventral visual pathway in humans: Evidence from fMRI. In *The Visual Neurosciences*, vol. 2, ed. Leo M. Chalupa and John S. Werner, 1179–89. Cambridge, MA: MIT Press.

ONIANS, JOHN. 1999. The nature of art in Lin Fengmian's China: a neuropsychological perspective. In *The approach of Lin Fengmian: The centenary of Lin Fengmian*, 690–715. Hangzhou: China Academy of Art Press.
—. 2007. *Neuroarthistory: From Aristotle and Pliny to Baxandall and Zeki.* New Haven, CT and London: Yale University Press.

RIZZOLATTI, GIACOMO, LUCIANO FADIGA, VITTORIO GALLESE, AND LEONARDO FOGASSI. 1996. Premotor cortex and the recognition of motor actions. *Cognitive Brain Research* 3 (2): 131–41.

RUSKIN, JOHN. 1888. *Modern painters*, vol. 5. Orpington: G. Allen.

TANAKA, KREIJI. 1993. Neuronal mechanisms of object recognition. *Science* 262 (5134): 685–88.

ZEKI, SEMIR. 1999. *Inner vision: An exploration of art and the brain.* Oxford and New York: Oxford University Press.

IV

Comparative Approaches: Differences and Commonalities

Intercultural Comparison and Art

Human groups, one might assume, have long compared their appearance, products, customs, and beliefs with those of others—those people living across the river, on the other side of the mountains, or said to inhabit strange and distant lands. In such intergroup comparisons, commonalities might first be taken for granted, while differences are stressed, and the farther away other people live, the more different and less human they are usually made out to be. Increased trade, improved means of transport, and intergroup conflicts often both facilitate and necessitate a deeper understanding of a growing range of other human populations and the ways they shape their lives. Although not necessarily, this frequently entails an increasing acceptance of other people's humanity, for all their differences, making comparisons the more poignant and interesting. If we are all humans, then exactly what do we share and what not? How does one account for commonalities, and why is it that we differ? The visual arts, in their ubiquity and local embeddedness, present a particularly fruitful field for pursuing intercultural comparative questions.

While intergroup or intercultural comparisons must have been made throughout human history, we generally know very little about the forms they took or the effects they had. For more recent history, however, various sources are available. As for the West, we know that in the ancient Greek city states, with their maritime trade, colonies, and extra-Hellenic wars, differences and commonalities among human populations were reflected upon. The thinker Protagoras (c. 481–c. 411), a contemporary of the traveling reporter Herodotus, provides a case in point. His comparative deliberations appear to have led to what one might call, perhaps somewhat anachronistically, a cultural relativistic stance. Protagoras developed an attitude that involves seeing one's own tradition or culture as merely one among many others, all equally particularistic (for a variety of constitutive reasons) in their local outlook, organization of social life, and various forms of cultural expression.

It has been argued that the "modern" Western interest in intercultural comparison emerged during the period known as the Renaissance. This interest is said to have been prompted first and foremost by the rediscovery of the cultures of Western Antiquity. Scholarly engagement with these ancient cultures, which were deemed sufficiently different to invite comparison, would then have provided models for dealing with the increasing number and variety of foreign cultures, arts, and crafts coming to the attention of Europeans after 1500 CE (Rowe 1965).

It may be noted that such major extensions of the horizon of known forms of human living and cultural products have of course occurred elsewhere, too, as when the followers of Mohammed conquered vast and culturally varied territories to the north and the west of Arabia in the seventh and eight century CE, when the Mongol khans expanded their realm in the thirteenth century CE to include most parts of Eurasia, when the Chinese admiral Zheng He set out to explore insular Southeast Asia and the Indian, Arabian, and African coasts in the early fourteenth century CE, when the Inca built their empire in South America from 1438 CE onwards, and so on. Further examination, and indeed comparative analysis, of the ways in which human groups worldwide have accumulated and compared information on other groups, artistic products included, would make for a fascinating and timely study.[1]

In the West, the unprecedented large-scale introduction to other ways of living subsequent to the "voyages of discovery" and everything that followed in their wake (trade, missionary activities, colonization) was to gradually leave its mark on scholarly writings in what we would call today the social sciences and humanities. Although the data coming in from ever-larger parts of the world were often superficial, factually incorrect, and biased by their collectors' Christian outlook, scholars increasingly added an intercultural comparative dimension to their analyses of such topics as religion and social and political organization.

Intercultural comparative perspectives were occasionally applied as well to visual arts and architecture. In addition to the efforts of De Las Casas and others, briefly mentioned in the introduction to this volume, one may note, for example, that in the second half of the sixteenth century a dozen or so costume books were published that attempted to provide "a global mapping of dress" (Ilg 2004, 33), incorporating examples of costume from all the then known parts of the world. As for architecture, in the third quarter of the seventeenth century the Jesuit scholar Athanasius Kircher speculatively compared the monumental buildings of Babylonia, Egypt, China, and Mexico (Greenhalgh 1978, 95ff).

The interest in intercultural comparative analysis generally becomes especially clear in the eighteenth century, known as the age of the Enlightenment. For example, in his *De l'esprit des lois* (On The Spirit of the Laws, 1748), Montesquieu considered and compared the then available data on both ancient and contemporary cultures worldwide in his examination of the ideal form of government, resulting in his famous *trias politicas* suggesting the separation of legislative, executive, and judicial powers. By introducing European audiences to other worldviews and ways of living, the writings of the French *philosophes* and other European scholars contributed to an increasing secularization and cultural relativization. As an example one might mention Diderot's *Supplément au voyage de Bougainville* (Supplement to the Voyage of Bougainville, 1772), where the author imagines a conversation between a Frenchman and a Tahitian on such matters as the different religious and sexual mores of the two traditions concerned.

It is in the eighteenth century also that references to the visual arts from cultures outside the West start turning up somewhat more frequently in European writings (see Kaufmann 1999). The mostly casual intercultural comparisons that resulted were often of an evaluative nature. Although various forms of decorative art, or what was interpreted as such, occasionally received praise, the three-dimensional art forms of foreign cultures were generally compared unfavorably to those of the West, being usually denounced as "grotesque idols." In this respect, Frances Connely (1995) argues for the emergence in the eighteenth and nineteenth centuries of a "primitivist" paradigm that applied to nearly all visual arts from outside the West, but also included most "non-classical" arts from the Western tradition. In her analysis, Connely draws on various sources, including art criticism, the popular press, and the comments of artists, but provides only limited references to the developments in Western philosophy and art history during this period, as briefly mentioned in the introduction to this volume.

Comparative scholarship may take many forms, including either more implicit and informal comparisons or more explicit and systematic ones (thereby typically avoiding an evaluative stance). In the eighteenth century, the idea of a systematic comparative *method* was associated especially with anatomy. By comparing the anatomy of various organisms, scholars wanted to investigate their biological relationships, proposing that commonalities point to descent from a common source. The idea of comparison thus had a strong diachronic flavor. The same applies to the then budding science of comparative linguistics, especially after 1786, when the British scholar William Jones suggested that Latin, Greek, and Sanskrit were systematically related and must, therefore, share a common origin.[2]

The success of the comparative method, especially in anatomy, resulted in diachronically oriented comparisons becoming a staple in various forms of Western scholarship in the nineteenth

2
For observations on intercultural comparative studies and their intellectual histories, especially in anthropology, see Sarana 1975; Holy 1987; Gingrich and Fox 2002; Trigger 2003, 16ff.

Matthew Rampley (2000) has argued that at the end of the nineteenth century there was not yet any clear-cut distinction between anthropologists and art historians in the study of art.

century. This included the emerging discipline of cultural anthropology, where scholars would attach relatively great importance to a particular type of visual art. The first generations of professional anthropologists in the second half of the nineteenth century compared cultures and their products in order to assign them a place on an alleged evolutionary ladder that led from "savage" to "civilized." Human societies outside the West were assumed to represent various stages of cultural development that Western civilization had already gone through. Examining these "living fossils" was thus thought to provide the data needed to reconstruct an evolutionary history that culminated in late-nineteenth-century Western culture. In this mode of thought, traveling in space meant traveling in time, although the "armchair anthropologists" of the period usually left the collection of data to others, particularly colonial officials, missionaries, and traders.

By asking about the origins and development of the various aspects of human culture, such as kinship, marriage, and religion, evolutionist scholars continued a project (as did a small number of historians focusing on "universal history") that has deep intellectual roots in European thought and that had been foregrounded by eighteenth-century thinkers, starting with the Italian scholar Giambattista Vico, whose *Nuova Sienza* (The New Science, 1725) suggested the outlines of a "history of civilization."

Since many first and second generation professional anthropologists were based in so-called ethnographic museums that were being established all over Europe in the second half of the nineteenth century, it is not surprising that a form of visual culture or art played a prominent role in these anthropologists' evolutionist comparative analyses. Numerous studies were devoted to the question of the origin and development of what was typically referred to as "ornament." With relatively little archaeological data available at the time, anthropologists relied on a cross-cultural sample of contemporary motifs or designs found on objects in ethnographic museums, for example, and held to be representative of various cultural stages.

Art historians, who would examine these topics until well into the twentieth century, shared the anthropological interest in comparing designs worldwide in order to establish their origin and evolution.[3] In time they would add to their analyses the notion of cultural diffusion that was gaining ground in anthropology as a reaction, or at least as a complement, to evolutionism. The idea of diffusion also reflected to some extent the diachronic line of reasoning in comparative anatomy and linguistics. (For more on the interest in ornaments and the various theories of development that were proposed, see Anderson, Halbertsma, Pfisterer, this volume.)

At the turn of the nineteenth to twentieth century, then, intercultural comparison may be seen as an integral part, however modest, of the emerging disciplinary study of art. In particular, the systematic field of *Kunstwissenschaft* explicitly sought to add a cross-cultural dimension to its endeavors (see Pfisterer, this volume). The art historical interest in intercultural comparison did not, however, lead to the establishment of a subdiscipline in its own right, as did happen in related fields in the humanities. Indeed, at the turn of the previous century both musicology and literary studies developed intercultural comparative branches or subdisciplines, labeled "comparative musicology" and "comparative literature," respectively. Within the humanities, "comparative philosophy" and "comparative aesthetics" were to follow suit a few decades later.

However, rather than dealing with systematic intercultural comparison, these various new subdisciplines tended to concentrate on studying relevant phenomena in cultures outside the West, cultures that had hitherto been largely ignored by their home disciplines (not necessarily because of ethnocentrism, but also because of a lack of information). To be sure, in musicology, especially, explicit intercultural comparisons were carried out prior to World War II (see Schneider 2006). But even then the relative lack of such efforts led "comparative musicologists" in the 1950s to change the name of their subdiscipline to "ethnomusicology."

Unlike musicology, the various other "comparative" branches in the humanities, moreover, tended to limit their attention to so-called Oriental or Asian cultures. Towards the end of the twentieth century, it was increasingly felt, however, that an intercultural orientation should include in principle all human cultures in time and space. Together with the absence, by and large, of explicit comparisons, this resulted in reconceptualizations in the 1990s such as "world literature," "world philosophy," and "transcultural aesthetics" as academic fields of study, despite the older labels remaining in use to this day.[4] As with world art studies, intercultural comparison may then be conceived as one type of research to be undertaken within these larger fields.

Rather than with these various humanistic endeavors, however, the idea of intercultural comparison is associated especially with the Western discipline of cultural anthropology, which sets out to study human cultures worldwide. Indeed, intercultural comparison is frequently mentioned as a key characteristic in the definitions that anthropologists provide of their discipline. Yet many scholars in this field have for the last century or so expressed serious reservations about the project of comparing cultures, or culture-traits, especially on a global scale. One could suggest various reasons for this anthropological skepticism about comparisons, some of which may be briefly discussed here.

To begin with, intercultural comparison raises some thorny theoretical issues: What do we actually mean by intercultural comparison? What would be the units between which we compare, and what do we in fact compare, i.e., what would be our *tertia comparationis*? Can we ever devise a conceptual apparatus that is neutral enough to be employed in likening phenomena from disparate cultures or contexts? And if intercultural comparison

4

As for the study of history, "universal history," too, came to be generally regarded as not inclusive enough (focusing as it did on literate traditions) and gave way to "world history," particularly from the 1980s onward (an early and classical example is McNeil 1976; the *Journal of World History* was launched in 1990; for a survey of the field, see Manning 2003). In that same decade, it was suggested that a new field of study, "global history," focus specifically on processes of globalization and the emergence of a global awareness in the present and the recent past (see Mazlish and Buultjens 1993). Then there is "big history," which usually starts with what is currently known as the "big bang" (see, e.g., Christian 2004).

would indeed be feasible, then how should we in effect proceed, on the basis of which data, on the number and type of which samples, and on what scale?[5]

Also, from an intellectual-historical perspective, the idea of intercultural comparison would from the beginning of the twentieth century become negatively associated with the ethnocentric and speculative endeavors of nineteenth-century evolutionist anthropology. In the early twentieth century, Western anthropologists decided that it was imperative for them as academic professionals to "go out into the field" in order to study living foreign cultures themselves, rather than leaving this job to amateur ethnographers (as had been the case in the previous century). "Fieldwork," or *in situ* research, was strongly promoted by, among others, the influential anthropologist Franz Boas, whose emphasis on cultures' historical particularity, moreover, was not conducive to the idea of intercultural comparison. Indeed, in Boas's wake, many "field-workers" would argue for the specifity and at times even the incommensurability of cultures, thus rendering the whole idea of intercultural comparison misguided and pointless (however much this conclusion is in itself the outcome of comparison).

Boas himself, however, was not ultimately opposed to the comparative study of cultures, but suggested that this scholarly enterprise could only be effectuated in earnest when enough valid data about the world's many existing cultures became available. Although some twentieth-century anthropologists have carried out intercultural comparisons (for discussions, see, e.g., Sarana 1975; Holy 1987; Gingrich and Fox 2002), the majority of them focused on individual cultures or societies.

In addition to theoretical problems, the early association with evolutionist anthropology, and the paradigmatic shift to local research with its frequent particularistic emphasis, a more recent impediment to the development of intercultural comparative research in anthropology (and other disciplines) must be mentioned. This concerns the influence at the end of the twentieth-century of postmodernism and postcolonialism. The skepticism that was raised in these fields about the scholarly validity of cross-cultural data-gathering, let alone generalizations on any grand scale, would effectively discourage the undertaking of comparativist projects.

Recently, however, a group of anthropologists, postmodernists among them, have advocated a rehabilitation of intercultural comparison in anthropology (Gingrich and Fox 2002; compare also De Munck 2002). While still generally opposed to global comparisons, they argue for the importance of cross-cultural generalizations, suggesting that such propositions, while giving added value to primary data through secondary analysis, legitimize anthropology as the scholarly discipline that studies humankind and its sociocultural institutions. In order to avoid some of the shortcomings of earlier comparisons, it is suggested that, rather than likening culture-traits that have been unduly isolated from their settings for

   World Art Studies IV Comparative Approaches

analytical purposes, scholars proceed by comparing phenomena in their sociocultural contexts. This is precisely what the anthropologist Donald Brown does in his intercultural comparative analysis for the present section when he examines whether particular visual properties of portraits (specifically, their naturalistic or stylized appearance) can be related to features of the sociocultural environment of their creation and use.[6]

Any cross-cultural study of portraits faces the more general comparativist problem of how to define the object of analysis in such a manner that a heuristic starting point is provided for its examination in various contexts in time and space. Art historian Jean Borgatti, who has pioneered the intercultural investigation of portraits (and, indeed, in so doing has pioneered world art studies), solves the problem of adequately defining her *tertium comparationis* by conceiving of a portrait as any visual creation that references a specific human being. In her contribution to this section, Borgatti elaborates on a cross-cultural classification or typology she drew up earlier, distinguishing between representational portraits (which present a physiognomic likeness of an individual), generic portraits (which may be individualized by various means, including context of presentation, the addition of personal belongings, or inscriptions), and emblematic portraits (which refer to an individual by way of characteristic emblems or attributes) (see Borgatti and Brilliant 1990).

Besides portraits, numerous other topics concerning the visual arts could be interculturally compared as well. Topics could range from the more tangible to the more conceptual: from raw materials and techniques, through visual appearance, theme or subject matter, use and function, producers and patrons, to aesthetic evaluation and philosophies of art. In some of these areas, the first steps to intercultural comparative analysis have already been made.

In 1971, the anthropologists Jacques Maquet (see also Maquet 1986) and Robert Plant Armstrong (see also Armstrong 1981) each published a monograph promoting an intercultural comparative perspective in the study of art and aesthetics. Armstrong's studies, foregrounding the concept of "affecting presence," prefigure in a sense both David Freedberg's (1988) analysis of the "power of images" as a worldwide phenomenon (although Freedberg discusses mainly Western examples) and Alfred Gell's (1998) focus on artistic objects' "agency," illustrated with reference to various cross-cultural cases. Gell's work has inspired research exploring, and at least implicitly comparing, art objects as "presences" in a variety of cultures worldwide (see especially Osborne and Tanner 2007, as well as Maniura and Shepherd 2006; compare also Helms 1993, analyzing the power and prestige that in communities all over the globe are ascribed to finely made and exotic objects). In a related sense, Hans Belting (2001) discusses the social and psychological function of anthropomorphic images in various cases across time and place, suggesting that such

---

6

For another example of intercultural contextual comparison, see Van Damme 1996, where an attempt is made to account for cultural differences in visual preference by systematically relating aesthetic predilections to the sociocultural settings in which they occur.

images originated as substitutes for deceased persons.[7]

Variously conceived intercultural comparative perspectives on the visual arts have recently been provided by David Summers (2003), who takes as his point of departure the engagement with space in art and architecture; Nigel Spivey (2005), focusing on such themes as the representation of the human body and nature in art; and Esther Pasztory (2005), whose work was briefly discussed in the introduction to this volume. Also, in his comparative analysis of seven "early civilizations" worldwide, Trigger (2003) devotes a chapter to a discussion of the materials, styles, themes, and uses of what he calls the "elite art and architecture" of the cultures studied (ancient Egypt and Mesopotamia, Shang China, the Aztec, the classical Maya, the Inca, and the Yoruba). Another recent and explicitly comparative study is the ongoing Boabab Project, directed by Suzanne Blier at Harvard University. This project investigates why innovation in the arts occurs more in some cultural contexts than in others.[8]

Aside from the topics to be investigated, intercultural comparison could take many forms, in terms of scope, method, and goal. Comparisons could be regional or global, synchronic or diachronic, or feature a combination of these. Intercultural comparison could proceed inductively, when cross-cultural data are examined in order to arrive at generalizations, but it could also have a more deductive flavor, when hypotheses concerning the visual arts are tested by drawing on available data from a variety of cultures. Intercultural comparative analysis could bring out differences, and indeed have the establishment of cultural specifity as its aim (e.g., Holy 1987, 15), but it could also search for commonalities on various levels of analysis, which is what most studies in this field in fact do (Trigger 2003, 16).

In this section, Ben-Ami Scharfstein adds to the discussion by outlining and comparing various cultures' ways of thinking about artistic quality. He proposes that, underlying the variety of the traditions examined, there is a "common humanity" that manifests itself in the evaluation of the arts worldwide (see also Scharfstein 2008 for the most comprehensive intercultural comparative analysis of art and artists to date).

—WvD

REFERENCES

ABRAMSON, J. A. 2000. *Art in nonliterate societies: Structural approaches and implications for sociocultural and system theories.* Kalamazoo, MI: Western Michigan University; New Issues Press.

AIKEN, NANCY E. 1998. *The biological origins of art.* Westport, CT: Praeger.

ANDERSON, RICHARD L. 2004. *Calliope's sisters: A comparative study of philosophies of art.* 2nd, rev. ed., 1st ed. published 1990. Upper Saddle River, NJ: Prentice Hall.

ARMSTRONG, ROBERT P. 1971. *The affecting presence: An essay in humanistic anthropology.* Urbana: University of Illinois Press.
—. 1981. *The powers of presence: Consciousness, myth, and affecting presence.* Philadelphia: University of Pennsylvania Press.

BEDAUX, JAN BAPTIST, AND BRETT COOKE, eds. 1999. *Sociobiology and the arts.* Amsterdam, Atlanta: Editions Rodopi.

BELTING, HANS. 2001. *Bild-anthropologie: Entwürfe für eine bildwissenschaft.* Munich: Wilhelm Fink.

BIEBUYCK, DANIEL P., AND NELLY VAN DEN ABBEELE 1984. *The power of headdresses: A cross-cultural study of forms and functions.* Brussels: TENDI.

BORGATTI, JEAN M., AND RICHARD BRILLIANT. 1990. *Likeness and beyond: Portraits from Africa and the world.* New York: The Center for African Art.

CHRISTIAN, DAVID. 2004. *Maps of time: An introduction to big history.* Los Angeles: University of California Press.

COE, KATHRYN. 2003. *The ancestress hypothesis: Visual art as adaption.* New Brunswick, NJ: Rutgers University Press.

CONNELY, FRANCES S. 1995. *The sleep of reason: Primitivism in modern European art and aesthetics, 1725–1907.* University Park: Pennsylvania State University Press.

DE MUNCK, VICTOR C. 2002. Contemporary issues and challenges for comparativists. *Anthropological Theory* 2 (1) : 5–19.

DEAL, DAVID M., AND LAURA HOSTETTER. 2006. *The art of ethnography: A Chinese "Miao Album."* Seattle: University of Washington Press.

DISSANAYAKE, ELLEN. 1988. *What is art for?* Seattle: University of Washington Press.
—. 1992. *Homo aestheticus: Where art comes from and why.* New York: Free Press, etc.
—. 2000. *Art and intimacy: How the arts began.* Seattle: University of Washington Press.

DUTTON, DENIS. 2008. *The art instinct: Beauty, pleasure, and human evolution.* London: Bloomsbury.

EIBL-EIBESFELDT, IRENÄUS, AND CHRISTA SÜTTERLIN. 2007. *Weltsprache Kunst: zur Natur- und Kunstgeschichte bildlicher Kommunikation.* Vienna: Brandstätter Verlag.

ELBERFELD, ROLF, AND GÜNTER WOHLFART, eds. 2000. *Komparative Ästhetik: Künste und ästhetische Erfahrungen zwischen Asien und Europa.* Cologne: Edition Chora.

EMIGH, JOHN. 1996. *Masked performance: The play of self and other in ritual and theatre.* Philadelphia: University of Pennsylvania Press.

FORTY, ADRIAN, AND SUSANNE KUECHLER, eds. 1999. *The art of forgetting.* Oxford and New York: Berg.

FREY, DAGOBERT. 1949. *Grundlegung zu einer Vergleichenden Kunstwissenschaft: Raum und Zeit in der Kunst der afrikanisch-eurasiatischen Hochkulturen.* Innsbruck and Vienna: Friedrich Rohrer Verlag.

GELL, ALFRED. 1998. *Art and agency: An anthropological theory.* Oxford: Oxford University Press.

GINGRICH, ANDRE, AND RICHARD G. FOX, eds. 2002. *Anthropology, by comparison.* London: Routledge.

GOMBRICH, ERNST H. 1979. *The sense of order: A study in the psychology of decorative art.* 2nd ed. 1994. London: Phaidon.

GREENHALGH, MICHAEL. 1978. European interest in the non-European: The sixteenth century and Pre-Columbian art and architecture. In *Art in society*, ed. Michael Greenhalgh and Vincent Megaw, 89–103. London: Duckworth.

HELMS, MARY W. 1993. *Craft and the kingly ideals: Art, trade, and power.* Austin: University of Texas Press.

HOLSBEKE, MIREILLE, ed. 1996. *The object as mediator: On the transcendental meaning of art in traditional cultures.* Antwerp: Ethnographic Museum.

HOLY, LADISLAV, ed. 1987. *Comparative anthropology.* London: Blackwell.

HUSSAIN, MAZHAR, AND ROBERT WILKINSON, eds. 2006. *The pursuit of comparative aesthetics: An interface between the East and the West.* Aldershot and Burlington, VT: Ashgate.

ILG, ULRIKE. 2004. The cultural significance of costume books in sixteenth-century Europe. In *Clothing Culture: 1350–1650,* ed. Catherine Richardson, 29–48. Aldershot and Burlington, VT: Ashgate.

KAUFMANN, THOMAS DACOSTA. 1999. Eurocentrism and art history?: Universal history and the historiography of the arts before Winckelmann. In *Memory and oblivion: Proceedings of the XXXIXth International Congress of the History of Art*, ed. Wessel Reinink and Jeroen Stumpel, 35–42. Dordrecht: Kluwer.

MANIURA, ROBERT, AND RUPERT SHEPHERD, eds. 2006. *Presence: The inherence of the prototype within images and other objects.* Aldershot: Ashgate.

MANNING, PETER. 2003. *Navigating world history: Historians create a global past.* New York: Palgrave Macmillan.

MAQUET, JACQUES J. 1971. *Introduction to aesthetic anthropology.* 2nd ed. 1979. Reading, MA: Addison-Wesley.
—. 1986. *The aesthetic experience: An anthropologist looks at the visual arts.* New Haven, CT and London: Yale University Press.

MAZLISH, BRUCE, AND RALPH BUULTJENS, eds. 1993. *Conceptualizing global history.* Boulder, San Francisco, and Oxford: Westview Press.

MCNEILL, WILLIAM H. 1976. *Plagues and peoples.* Garden City, NY: Doubleday.

MILLER, GEOFFREY. 2000. *The mating mind: How sexual selection shaped the evolution of human nature.* London: Heinemann.

MORPHY, HOWARD, ed. 1989. *Animals into art*. London: Unwin Hyman.

NAPIER, A. DAVID. 1986. *Masks, tranformation, and paradox*. Berkeley: University of California Press.
—. 1992. *Foreign bodies: Performance, art, and symbolic anthropology*. Berkeley: University of California Press.

OSBORNE, ROBIN, AND JEREMY TANNER, eds. 2007. *Art's agency and art history*. London: Blackwell.

PASZTORY, ESTHER. 2005. *Thinking with things: Toward a new vision of art*. Austin: University of Texas Press.

RAMPLEY, MATTHEW. 2000. Anthropology at the origins of art history. In *Site-specifity: The ethnographic turn*, ed. Alex Coles, 138–63. London: Black Dog Publishing.

ROWE, JOHN HOWLAND. 1965. The Renaissance foundations of anthropology. *American Anthropologist* 67 (1): 1–20.

RUBIN, ARNOLD, ed. 1988. *Marks of civilization: Artistic transformations of the human body*. Los Angeles: Museum of Cultural History; University of California.

SARANA, GOPALA. 1975. *The methodology of anthropological comparisons: An analysis of comparative methods in social and cultural anthropology*. Tuscon: The University of Arizona Press.

SCHARFSTEIN, BEN-AMI. 1988. *Of birds, beasts, and other artists: An essay on the universality of art*. New York: New York University Press.
—. 2008. *Art without borders: A philosophical exploration of art and humanity*. Chicago and London: The University of Chicago Press.

SCHNEIDER, ALBRECHT. 2006. Comparative and systematic musicology in relation to ethnomusicology: A historical and methodological survey. *Ethnomusicology* 50 (2): 236–58.

SPIVEY, NIGEL. 2005. *How art made the world*. London: BBC Books.

SUMMERS, DAVID. 2003. *Real spaces: World art history and the rise of Western modernism*. London and New York: Phaidon.

TRIGGER, BRUCE G. 2003. *Understanding early civilizations: A comparative study*. Cambridge: Cambridge University Press.

VAN DAMME, WILFRIED. 1996. *Beauty in context: Towards an anthropological approach to aesthetics*. Philosophy of History and Culture 17. Leiden, New York, and Cologne: Brill.

VOLAND, ECKART, AND KARL GRAMMER, eds. 2003. *Evolutionary aesthetics*. Berlin: Springer.

WU, JIA-HUA. 1994. *A comparative study of landscape aesthetics*. Lewiston, NY: Edwin Mellen Press.

ZIJLMANS, KITTY, ed. 2006. *Site-seeing: Places in culture, time and space*. Leiden: CNWS Publications.

JEAN M. BORGATTI

Constructed Identities: Portraiture in World Art

Portraiture, if by this we mean the indexing of a particular personality through material objects, is as old as Jericho, where overmodeled skulls have been excavated dating to 5000 BCE,[1] and widely shared across world cultures—from the Asmat and Kamoro of Irian Jaya where families erect ancestor poles bearing named figures[2] to the Antanosy of Madagascar where grave markers give a visual biography of the deceased (Mack 1986, 90–92), from the Moche of Peru where startlingly realistic pottery vessels (c. 500 CE) chart the aging of an individual (Donnan 2004, 56–68) to China's Ming Dynasty in the sixteenth century where portraits of ancestors, teachers or priests remarkable for their realistic rendering of face and costume competed with less formal portraits that conveyed identity through cues embedded in the setting but not in the human figure itself (Cahill 1982, 114–16).

Whether representational or conceptual, portraits represent particular people and spring from a common impulse to remember and be remembered, whether the reasons are personal or political, ritual or social. It was accepted without question in the court circles of sixteenth century Europe "that one of the chief functions of art was to serve as a 'weapon against oblivion,'" a notion traced to classical sources (Jenkins 1947, 4). When New York gallery owner Holly Solomon saw Warhol's nine-panel portrait of her, she exclaimed: "Oh, my God, this is fabulous! ... Long after I'm dead ... it will be hanging" (Bourdon 1975, 42). "They give us history," said Iyawo Obamina, an African woman, in regard to her aunt's

[1] Breckenridge 1968, 15–16 (Fig. 5). We do not know the particular use of these skulls, except that they were used in burial rituals. Our assumptions are based on analogies with later cultures. The skulls, however, seem to be the oldest extant artifacts of their type and belong, if not to portraiture, than to a kind of proto-portraiture in which an individual was referenced by his own remains.

[2] Smidt 1993, 23–24. Mamapuku and Harple (2003, 97) note an Asmat *bis* pole in which government official Hein van der Schoot is represented.

commemorative mask (quoted in Borgatti 1990a, 80) (Fig. 1). Similarly, a verse ("If only I had had the time, To draw a picture of my dear wife…. Looking at it I would long for her") written by a Japanese frontier guard in 755 CE (Mori 1977, 95) highlights the relationship between portrait and memory in a way curiously similar to the legend of Butades and the silhouette drawn by his daughter of her departing lover. Recounted by Pliny, it is regarded as the founding myth of Western portraiture.[3] Such commentary and numerous examples given throughout this essay make it clear that the impulse for remembrance informs portraits across a spectrum of world cultures.

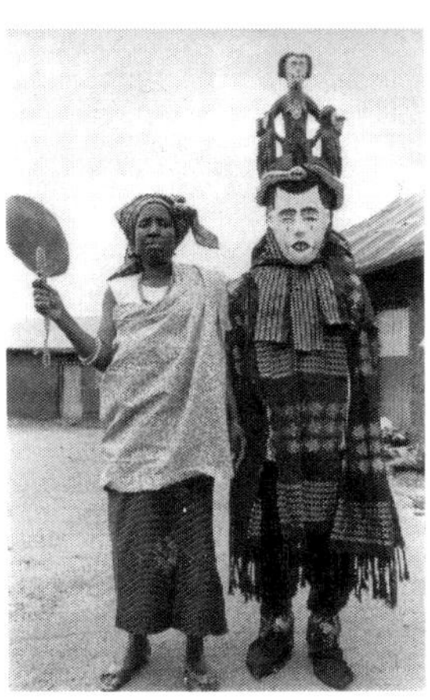

Figure 1
Memorial portrait mask of Idebua with her niece, the 1970s custodian, Mrs. Iyawo Obamina (now deceased). Okpella, Afokpella (Imiamune Quarter), Nigeria. The mask itself is attributed to the carver Asume, alleged to be Lawrence Ajanaku of Ogiriga-Okpella, and made c. 1970.

Okpella memorial masquerades display attributes of wealth and status to honor their subjects. They bear the names of their subjects and accompanying custodial relatives emphasizes personal identity.

THE CONSTRUCTION OF IDENTITY

How identity is constructed and presence evoked differs from culture to culture, though, subject to concepts of individualism, a prevailing aesthetic, and a host of social or ritual beliefs particular to a given time or place. Nonetheless, three general categories of image emerge from a survey of portraiture across many cultures and time periods. The most widespread method of portrayal is by means of a generic human representation made correct by its attributes of wealth and status but not necessarily bearing physical resemblance to the subject. Many cultures also use symbolic or emblematic images to evoke the individual through various associational characteristics as site, clothing, and literary convention, that is, through visual reference to the subject's name in acronym or proverbial form. Finally, portraiture includes works based on likeness, the result of a confrontation between artist and subject —or some facsimile in the case of posthumous portraits. The three categories of image—generic, emblematic, and representational—are not mutually exclusive.

THE LENS OF LIKENESS

Idiosyncratic physiognomic likeness, name, accoutrements and context are all strategies employed for asserting identity and conveying character in portraits. Since physiognomic likeness is the strategy most favored historically in Western art, it is the lens that refracts all views of portraiture as a subject in Western discourse.[4] Such is the persuasive nature of the lifelike that the distance between the generalized imagery associated with portraiture in many cultures and the idiosyncratic representational images of post-Renaissance Europe is linked to an easy acceptance that the general image cannot be specific but that the representational one must be. Our eyes convince us, even though there may be evidence to the contrary.

The faces of Chinese ancestor portraits display a painstaking realism, making it easy for us to accept these images as physical descriptions of real people. Yet, we know that professional Chinese portrait painters made use of prefabricated "likenesses" (Fig. 2) to preserve the illusion that the portraits were likenesses identifying their subjects even though specificity of site (homes or temples), inscriptions on the paintings or their association with spirit tablets bearing the ancestors' names provided their actual identifications (Vinograd 1992, 2).[5] Similarly, the furrowed brow, balding head and sunken cheeks of a verist Roman portrait are conventions to indicate character in a responsible head of household (Nodelman 1975, 27–33) and are not necessarily based on the subject's actual face. They are eminently believable images, though, as are the naturalistic terra cotta and bronze heads of twelfth-century Ife (Yoruba) in Nigeria (see Willett 1967 for illustrations, plates I, II, VII, VIII, IX). We have little difficulty believing that they represent real people, though we have no definitive proof that they did. We have a much harder time thinking of the highly stylized Yoruba (Nigeria) commemorative images for dead twins known as *ere ibeji* as portrayals of individuals (Fig. 3), despite good documentation that they are (Drewal 1984). The substitution of photographs for sculpture in twin shrines today (Fig. 4) merely underlines the equivalence of memorial sculpture and subject (Sprague 1978, 58).

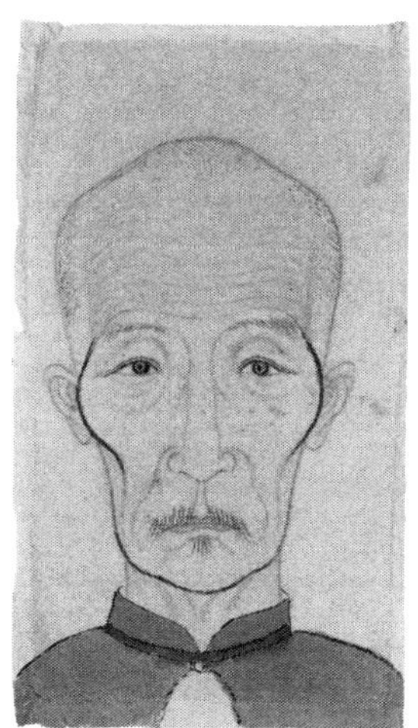

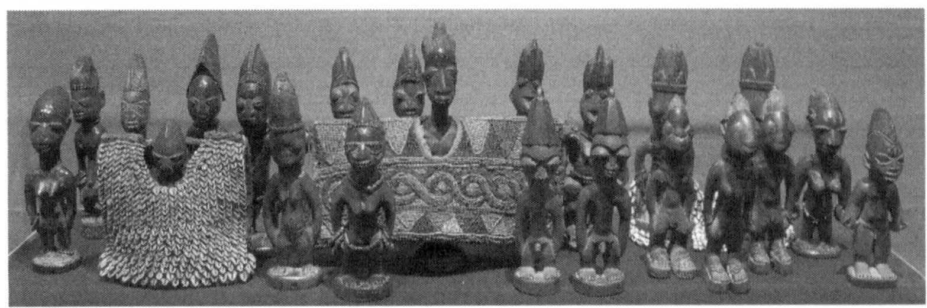

Figure 3
Memorial portraits of twins (*ibeji*).

For generations, Yoruba families have preserved the memory of deceased twins within the lineage by commissioning standardized but gender specific figurines given the dead twins' names.

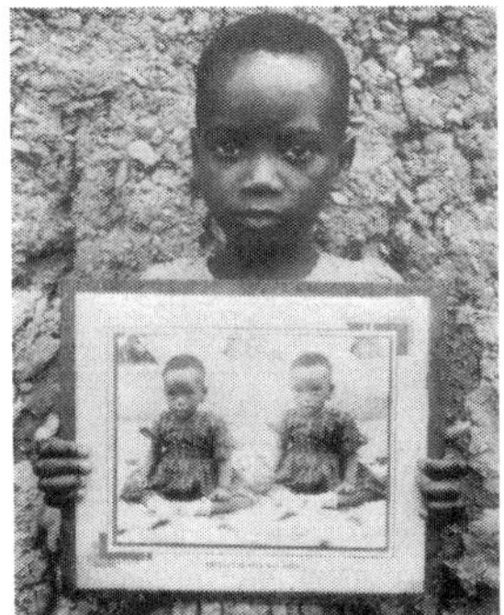

Figure 4
Memorial photograph of twins held by surviving twin whose image has been double printed. Yoruba, Ila-Orangun, Nigeria, 1975.

The indexical quality of twin carvings (*ere ibeji*) is confirmed by the integration of photographic portraits into Yoruba twin rituals in recent years.

To establish common ground across cultures within this genre then depends first upon differentiating between realism as a mode of depiction, that is, as an artistic convention, and description as an aspect of portraiture, and second, on recognizing the evocative quality of the work for its intended audience, however that is achieved. Western culture emphasizes individual identity, Western art features representation, and the portrait canon stresses physiognomic likeness—incorporating the idea that personality may be communicated through idiosyncratic facial features and expression. Thus we accept nameless but representational images as portraits, whether or not we have the documentation to provide us with a specific identity, and we create imaginary portraits of historic individuals, witness the statue of John Harvard in Harvard Square.

SOCIAL ROLE AS A STRATEGY FOR IDENTIFICATION

Most of the rest of the world emphasizes social identity, a more generalizing aesthetic, and distinctive conventions for constructing and conveying personal identity. In the Japanese tradition, for example, it was the sketch drawn from life that lent authenticity to the final idealized image—and the more sketches, the greater the authority of the portrait as an embodiment of the individual

(Phillips 2000, 163–64). Yet, neither a lifelike representation nor a desire to portray the inner spirit of the subject was the purpose of the portrait. Rather, a portrait was meant to celebrate an individual's achievements, and "anyone worthy of having his portrait painted was worthy of being given perfected form and features" (Browne 1985, 31).

In the case of Africa, the aesthetic is a generalizing one with a consequent stress on ideals of expression and comportment.[6] The disfavor with which Africans viewed realistic representation in portraits is made clear in a story that explains the relative hierarchy of artists' guilds in Benin City (Nigeria), with the upstart but idealizing brasscasters given preference over the senior but verist ivory carvers by the mid-fifteenth-century Oba Ewuare.[7] Only in rare instances is physiognomic likeness considered to individuate the traditional African portrait, and even in those instances, the image tends to be idealized or transformed according to the particular aesthetic of time and place (Fig. 5).[8]

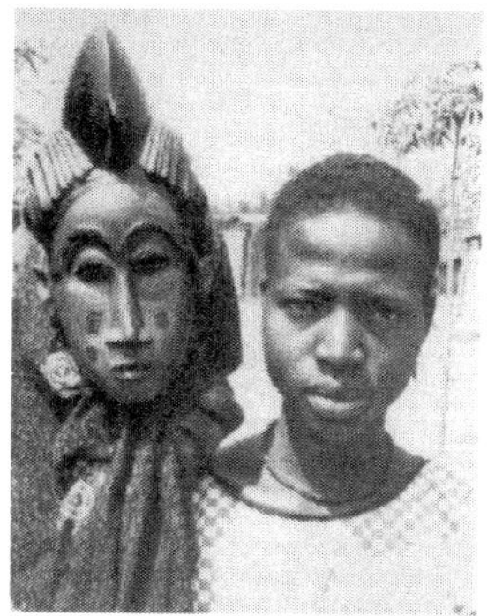

Figure 5
Baule. Abone Amui of Akukro Village, Ivory Coast, holding her portrait mask, carved by Tano Ndri. 1968.

Baule portrait masks are intended as likenesses, though transformed by Baule artistic convention. The subjects of these masks accompany their "doubles" in performance, and the masks bear their names — establishing incontrovertibly their identities for the audience.

NAME AS A STRATEGY FOR IDENTIFICATION

Naming is an important aspect of identifying the subject of a portrait everywhere, but it is crucial to particularizing the image in Africa and other preliterate societies. In the West, labels were a commonplace adding authenticity to the image after the fifteenth century, whether inscribed on the surface of the picture or attached to the frame.[9] Similarly, portrait practice in both Japan and China included 'legible iconographies of identity' through inscriptions added over time (Phillips 2000, 167; Stuart and Rawski 2001, 143–48), and in Mayan culture, glyphs converted generic images into individuals by giving them names and histories (Martin and Grube 2000) (Fig. 6).

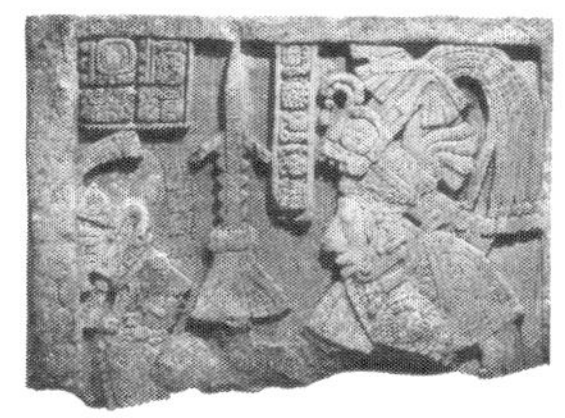

Figure 6
Bird Jaguar IV with his wife Lade Wak Jalam Chan Ajaw. Classic Maya, 755 CE.

Mayan rulers chronicled their achievements in monuments that provided name and narrative for those portrayed.

6
See Borgatti 1990a for a full discussion of African portraiture; see also Borgatti ed. 1990 and Borgatti ed. 1991. The essays in these two guest-edited issues of the journal *African Arts* represent case studies of portraiture in Africa and are based on papers written in response to using a definition of portraiture that included specificity of the subjects and intentionality of the artists/patrons.

7
Ewuare, one of the great Warrior Kings of Benin, ruled during the mid-fifteenth century when the physical and structural organization of the present-day kingdom of Benin was taking shape. When Ewuare grew old, he asked the members of both the casters' and carvers' guilds to make an image of him. The casters depicted him as he appeared in the prime of life, but the carvers showed him as he was at the time of the commission, in his old age. Ewuare was furious with the carvers and demoted them, proclaiming that they would never again be as important as the brasscasters (Ben-Amos 1980, 24).

8
A particularly good example is provided by the experiment in portraiture conducted by Hans Himmelheber in 1971. He commissioned portrait masks from Senufo, Baule, Guro and Dan artists. All the masks show Himmelheber's characteristic high forehead and heavy browline but each is governed by the parameters of its local style. See Borgatti 1990a: Fig. 20 — Himmelheber with four portrait masks. See also Himmelheber 1977.

West 2004, 53–54. West gives the example of a portrait of Native American Pocahontas dating from 1616. She suggests that the use of words to establish the identity of the sitter tends to "authenticate" the image as a likeness in the West, but notes how misleading this can be. Although the use of words identifying Pocahontas confirms the historical placing of the sitter, it proves deceptive regarding the authenticity of the likeness since the portrait in question was a third-hand image, copied from a print that had been in turn copied from a drawing.

10
As Samuel Johnson (1921, 78–89) notes, a birth name (*oruko*) comments on the circumstances surrounding his origins, a totem name (*orile*) fixies his lineage and occupation; and praise names (*oriki*) acquired throughout life elaborate upon personal attributes and accomplishments.

11
Among the Kongo, a baby is merely a "stomach-that-works" until the family welcomes it into the human community by giving it a name two or three months after birth. Subsequently, names acquired over time chart an individual's progress through life, link him to his forebears, and note birth situation (Balandier 1968, 227–28).

12
Elite men would have "milk" names as infants; after approximately three months of life, they would receive a personal name (*ming*); upon coming of age, they took the names by which they were known among their peers (*zi*). A man could also select a literary or studio name (*hao*) or receive such from others. Finally, if of high rank, he would get a posthumous name (*shi, shi hao*), and this was the name inscribed on the gravestone and on the spirit tablet (Stuart and Rawski 2001, 151).

13
Smidt 1993, 20. Smidt's use of the term "likeness" should be understood in the context of the problematic discourse on portraiture, and taken not to indicate a naturalistic representation but a named representation of the subject.

In preliterate societies especially, name and context encouraged memory, evoking a presence rather than simulating it. At the risk of digressing, it is worth pointing out that memory has its own histories in Western and non-Western societies, with recent research suggesting that memory, like portraiture, is a cultural construction. In non-Western cultures it may be seen as active, always in the present, a transaction or negotiation rather than a reproduction (Roberts and Roberts 1996, 29)—much as African and Oceanic portrait figures and masks indicate rather than replicate their subjects.

The power of names to particularize images relates to the significance of names in a given culture. In many African cultures names form an integral part of an individual's personality, often placing a person socially and giving him historical reality. Traditional Nigerian Yoruba names are biographical,[10] as they are among the Kongo of the Democratic Republic of Congo.[11] A comparable situation obtained in Chinese culture, where "identifying" an individual meant knowing his or her name, although women often did not have personal names—referred to only by birth rank or marital status, and only men's names charted their paths through life.[12]

Marilyn Strathern (1997) notes the particular complex interaction between head, name, and individual among the Asmat, where name equals life force and is transferred by the severed head of its owner to another, so that a living person stands in for the deceased, although not as an evocation or memorial, and therefore not as a portrait. The Asmat do create personally referential images to evoke the memory of the dead, however, immortalizing in sculptural form community members who have died. According to Dirk Smidt (1993), Asmat canoe prows, paddles, paint vessels, sago bowls, drums and headrests, and other more pedestrian objects are often named after ancestors. Sometimes they are carved with representations of specific ancestors, or schematic motifs representing individuals. However, the most important of these memorial sculptural forms are ancestor poles, shields, and free standing figures (Fig. 7). All serve as constant reminders that a death needs to be avenged. "Men have been known to carve the likeness of an unavenged relative into the knob on the end of their canoe paddles, so with each stroke, the reminder is staring them in the eye."[13]

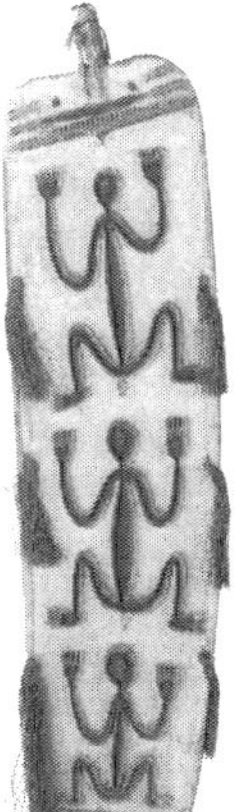

Figure 7
Shield made by Tjokotsj, Atjametsj village, Central Asmat.

The shield portrays several members of the carver's family. The small figure at the top represents Twerawiutsj, an elder sister of the carver, Tjokotsj. The relief figures depict (from top to bottom): Ewomber, Tjoktosj's elder brother; Jiirtinaq, Tjokotsj's younger brother; and Jiwei, Tjokotsj's elder sister.

Names themselves may have a concrete value or be so intrinsically a part of the individual that they may not be shared indiscriminately, if at all. In southwestern New Britain among the Rauto, the word *anine* signifies "name," meaning both personal name and social status. That one's name is an important part of one's identity is confirmed formally by the belief that a person should not touch or go near someone who shares his name. A person who takes the same name as a fellow village or hamlet resident is thought to be taking something away from that person, for by sharing his name, a person loses a bit of himself (Maschio 1994, 46–48). Elsewhere in New Britain, the word for name is the same as the word used for soul and shadow, and the son of a recently deceased man will impersonate with mask and dance his dead father, evoking him through performance and saying that he is dancing in his dead father's name.[14]

The spoken word attributes a name to a person. Text or glyphs lend form to the name, as do masks, figural sculpture, paintings or assembled goods. They give physical reality to the reference[15] and therefore (in the case of portraits) to the identity it represents. Such was the power of the inscribed name that in Egypt, the identity conferred by name on a pharaonic image could be altered by changing the name (Breckenridge 1968, 50 and footnote 42). The physical object, like text or glyph, is a more efficacious name than the spoken word because it is less ephemeral. The Kalabari Ijo of southern Nigeria say that the spirits come and stay in their names, meaning their particular sculpted figure or headdress (Horton 1965, 8–10; Barley 1988, 17). It is the name itself that invests the image with identity, substituting for physical resemblance, in many African contexts, endowing the image with reality and evoking the presence of the portrayed to those who knew the individual.[16] Thus, the living elders of Okpella (Nigeria) recognize and greet their dead kin by name when they return during the Festival of All Souls (*Olimi*), using the greeting form for an individual returning from a long journey (Borgatti 1990a, 81).

When name and context are key factors in personalizing a work, not only do human images work as portraits, but also such widely disparate visual configurations as antelope headdresses and dressed houses in Africa, shields among the Asmat of Irian Jaya or wooden posts wrapped in bark cloth in Fiji. The Kurumba (Burkina Faso) startle their Western audience by depicting their subjects in the guise of an antelope totem. Like other African ancestral images, they bear their subjects' names and help to preserve the memory of the deceased by providing a physical reminder of the dead elders' achievements (Roy 1987, 198–202). In Northern Togo, Batammaliba and Moba families honor their deceased elders during funeral celebrations, evoking them as they were in their prime by portraying them in house form and draping these symbolic bodies with the garments of initiation (Fig. 8).[17] The Moba also portray individual women through an assemblage of possessions during funeral celebrations (Fig. 9).[18]

14
Hesse and Aerts 1996, 26–27. Indicating a similar significant relationship between name and individual identity, the Okpella of southern Nigeria give a woman's name to her memorial mask only after she dies, even though that mask may be carved and danced publicly during her lifetime (Borgatti 1990a, 41).

15
For example, in Okpella (Nigeria), an individual's personal name should not be written down without the permission of the bearer, just as photographs should not be taken of individuals without their consent—both script and image referencing that person's identity in a concrete way (Borgatti 1990a, 41).

16
For a discussion of this in the Yoruba context, see Lawal 1977, 52. See also Borgatti 1990a.

17
Blier 1987, 130. Blier discusses the houses as "architectural self-images" on pp. 118–39. See also Kreamer n.d. [2001]—point made in relation to slide pair 5 (dressed house), where she notes the house also serves as a surrogate body for the deceased which can be dressed for the event as a man or woman, depending on the gender of the deceased.

18
In this ritual, a calabash called *kumang* stands in for the deceased—making a journey from the compound of her husband to the compound of her parents, in order to say farewell. The woman is identified by her cloth, hat, beads and other ornaments as well as her associates and the goal that is her parents' compound. She socializes during her journey, stopping to shop or drink beer at a local market. Her family accompanies her, and she dances for joy upon reaching her destination—the calabash being twisted and turned in a way that directly references Moba dance style (Kreamer, n.d. [2001]).

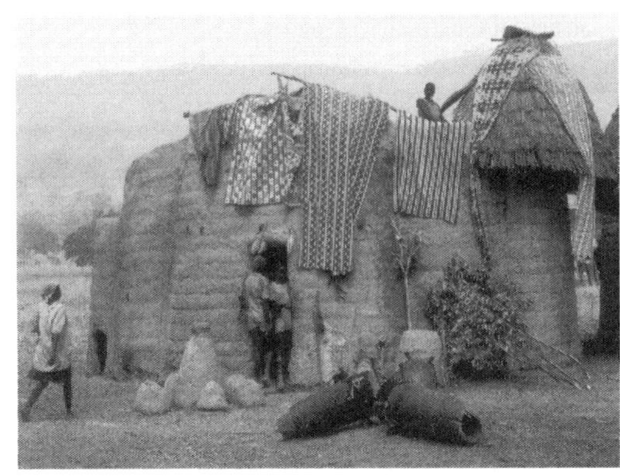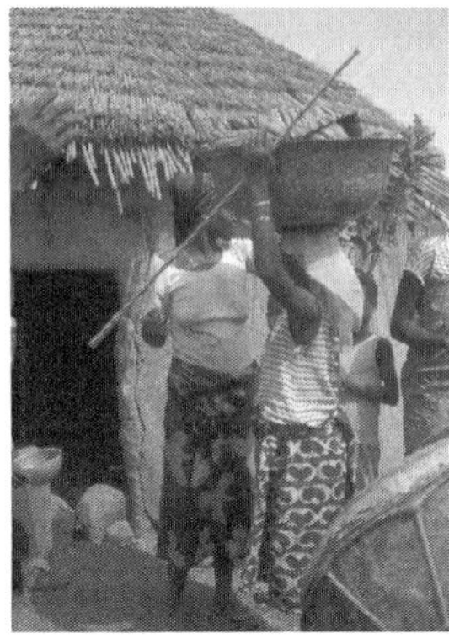

Among the Asmat, a human figure representing a dead relative may be carved at the top of the shield, giving the shield that person's name (Smidt 1993, 23). The patterns carved on the front of the shield often refer to other relatives of the deceased. For example, a shield made by Tjokotsj from Atjametsj village and collected in 1961 by Adrian Gerbrands (1993, Plate 8.8) depicts the carver's elder sister Twerawiutsj while the relief figures from top to bottom represent an elder brother Ewomber, a younger brother Jiirtinaq, and another sister Jiwei, respectively (see Fig. 7).

Fijians memorialize important dead with posts wrapped or bound with coconut-husk fibre and then dressed with barkcloth wrappings, sash and turban. Steven Hooper writes of a 1955 memorial image for Adi Arieta Kuila at Tubou, one in 1962 made for Ratu Sir Lala Sukuna, another in 1969 for Ratu Tevita Uluilakeba, but most recently, one constructed in 1995 for Ratu Sir Peniaia Ganilau, the paramount chief of Cakaudrove and former president of the Republic of Fiji. Hooper notes a striking difference between this and earlier ones, though, in that a head was sculpted at the top of the post. He says that it does not appear to be a likeness but it was a conscious attempt to anthropomorphize the image and make explicit the Fijian's conception of the memorial as a human image by clearly identifying it with the body of the deceased (Hooper 2002; personal communication, January 2005). In other words, it indexed the individual to evoke his memory, making it a portrait.

Naming happens in various ways, as already indicated, but using a mask to reveal rather than conceal identity is a mechanism noted in memorial practice in several cultures. Thus we see the subjects of Kalabari Ijo memorial screens (see Barley 1988, 24 and plates 1, 2 and 3 for examples) and Japanese woodblock prints identified by masks worn or roles played by the individual during his performing life.[19]

THE DISCOURSE

There are many fewer studies of portraiture in the so-called non-Western world (in English) and fewer still of portraiture from what are frequently termed preliterate societies.[20] The subject has been discounted and portraits themselves rendered almost invisible given strong limitations on literal likeness within the portrait genre in non-Western modes of representation. For this very reason, these studies raise important questions about the nature of portraiture, not so much about who is portrayed, but how the portrayal is achieved—providing a view alternative to that of the self-centered historical discourse of the West.

In China and Japan there are longstanding traditions of portraiture and a dialogue on art recognized, if not entirely comprehended, by Western scholars. Chinese portraiture presents a complex and intriguing programmatic history, almost the obverse of Western portraiture, since the 'lifelike' portrayal carries very different connotations. Both Chinese and European ancestral portraits emphasize face and body by having them dominate the picture plane (Figs. 10 and 11). Faces and costumes are constructed with painstaking detail, although with greater dependence on line in the Chinese and Japanese cases than on the volumes that characterize painting in the West. Chinese ancestor portraits startle us with their extraordinarily realistic faces, their lifelike quality enhanced by the artificiality of pose and pattern. The point of these images is not the replication of appearance as much as it is the "construction of an ancestral presence" (Vinograd 1992, 11)—rendering them much more like African portraits conceptually than Western ones.[21] Informal portraits in China tend to use a completely different compositional format in which the figure is much smaller within the field of illustration, and the field itself may be filled with landscape and pictorial narrative. Although there is an effort to convey likeness through facial representation, it is only one means used by the artist, and indeed, it tends to be overwhelmed by other pictorial elements that assist in the construction of identity and the communication of the individual's inner reality, so valorized in the Chinese discourse.[22] Such elements as landscape, posture, interaction with other figures, and various accoutrements that signify biographical data or psychological insight assume much greater importance (Fig. 12).

19
See, for example, *Shunkosai Hokushu, Actors Bando Mitsugoro III as Lady Iwafuji and Nakamura Matsue III as Churo Onoe, 1821*, from *On Stage in Osaka: Actor Prints from the MFA Collection* (Boston, April 5, 2006–January 3, 2007). This exhibit focused on prints from nineteenth-century Osaka that concentrated almost exclusively on the Kabuki theatre tradition unlike the better known works made in Tokyo from the late seventeenth to the early twentieth centuries where subjects were more diverse, including beautiful women, historical scenes, and landscape as well as actors. http://www.mfa.org/exhibitions/, accessed June 6, 2006.

20
Indeed, a quick search of Northwestern University's on-line book catalogue using the terms "portrait" or "portraiture" and limited to the art library resulted in 2001 hits. Of these, only 20 referred to portraiture in non-Western cultures. Moreover, a direct question to Professor Michio Yonekura, who offers a seminar on Japanese Portraiture at Sophia University in Tokyo, elicited the response that he had no suggestions whatsoever for articles in English, though it would not be difficult to give me a list in Japanese (personal communication, June 2005).

21
It should be noted that this is also a feature of the social history of portraits in the West. Portraits legitimated dynasty (cf. Jenkins 1947), and the acquisition of old portraits by *nouveau riche* in England in the nineteenth century to provide an aura of family history is a vestige of this function and an example of the social dimension of the power of ancestral presence.

22
According to James Cahill (1982, 106), pictures of people, whether types or individuals, real or imaginary, made up the larger part of Chinese painting until the tenth century when landscapes and other themes from nature became the focus not only for most artists but also the best artists. Figure painting and portraiture came into vogue again in the late Ming period, from the end of the sixteenth century. Those who painted ancestor portraits for ritual use continued to work throughout, and the effigy portrait remained the dominant portrait form, despite their authors' being relegated to the status of mere artisans because they produced realistic images rather than transforming what they saw.

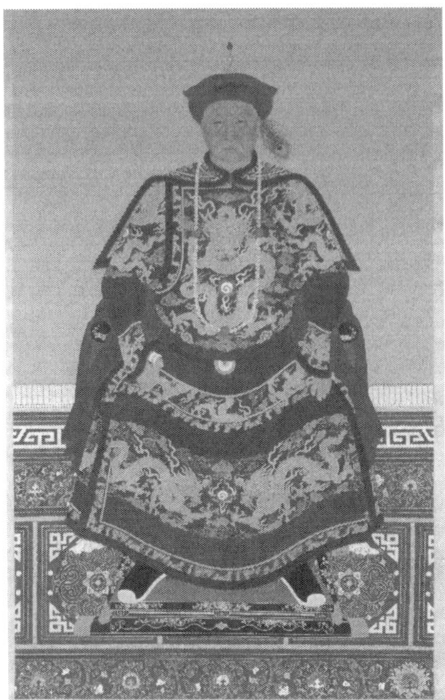 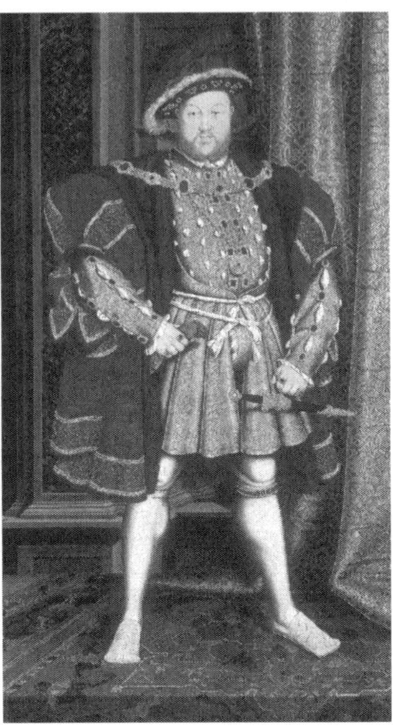

Figure 10
Portrait of Oboi (died 1669), Qing dynasty (1644-1912).

Figure 11
After Hans Holbein the Younger, Henry VIII, post 1537.

European ancestral portraits like their Chinese counterparts place great stress on the accoutrements of wealth and
status and emphasize face and body by having them dominate
the picture plane.

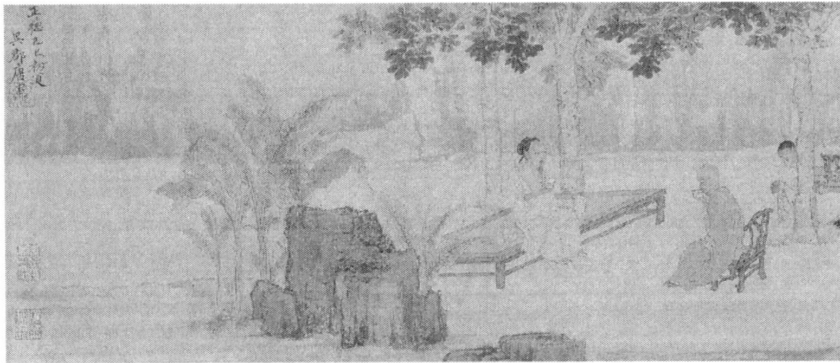

Figure 12
The Bamboo Stove (detail), 1509 (Ming Dynasty, 1369-1644).
Attributed to T'ang Yin (1470-1523). Chinese, from Suzhou,
Jiangso province.

Informal portraits, considered "art works," in China use a
different compositional format from ancestral portraits,
considered "ritual objects," with the figure occupying only
a small space within a field of illustration filled with
landscape and pictorial narrative.

In Japan, a distinction *was* made between image and likeness. Only images of historical and living figures were referred to as likenesses, in recognition of a belief in a verisimilitude established by nonmystical knowledge of the subjects, that is, by actual observation, and transmission of a true appearance acquired through sketching or copying (*utsutsu*) the individual (or appropriate facsimiles) from life.[23] The end product of this observation was transformed into an appropriate representation, not necessarily one true to life (Phillips 2000; Browne 1985)—but this issue of likeness has framed those studies of the genre in English until relatively recently,[24] as it frames or intrudes upon all studies of portraiture, simply because the narrowest spectrum of specifically referential personal images has been subject to the broadest literary treatment under the hegemony of Western scholarship.

In Africa, portrait images fall into three broad but overlapping categories in terms of actual art practice. Almost all are memorial figures. All are specified by name, whether that naming is done by verbal attribution understood by community members, by visual reference to hairstyle, distinctive body markings, clothing or other accoutrements associated with the subject, placement in a family compound in the case of a stationary work or among family members in the case of a masquerade. Almost all have gone unrecognized because of the lens of likeness (see Borgatti 1990a, 1990b, 1991 and Borgatti, Grove Art Online).

A PORTRAIT IS IN THE EYE OF THE BEHOLDER

That non-Western portraiture has suffered from lack of recognition is part of a larger problem of cross-cultural misunderstanding. Cues suggest different interpretations across societal frameworks as anthropologist Laura Bohannan (1966) demonstrates in an amusing but significant example in her article "Hamlet in Africa,"[25] and James Cahill reinforces with anecdotes in relation to Chinese art.[26] Despite gaps in understanding, literacy privileged the arts of China, Japan and India in the European mind. Portraits, if disparaged for their lack of presence, were nonetheless identified, and a respect for art and culture accorded.

In contrast, Europeans have characterized the material objects of preliterate cultures variously over the last five hundred years as exotica, fetish, specimen and only recently, as art. Not until the mid twentieth century did these objects migrate from natural history museums into art museums, having been recognized by early modern artists as innovative (in European eyes) formal solutions to sculptural problems. Rather than bringing understanding, recognition as art merely extended the projection of European fantasies upon these objects (Blier 2001; Vogel 2001). The colonial period attitude that traditional art was the relic of primitive superstition or the product of lack of ability and training is sufficiently

23
Phillips 2000, 154. Phillips notes that the verb *utsusu* means either *to sketch* or *to copy*, but cautions that *to copy*, in modern English usage, implies a degree of exactitude, mechanicalness and even mindlessness in replication that need not be assumed in the Japanese context. Premodern Japanese usage allowed for considerable transformation of the model in the act of *utsusu*.

24
Hishashi Mori (1977, 17) begins his now classic work on Japanese portrait sculpture, originally published in Japanese in 1967 and in English in 1977, with the statement: "There are portraits that reflect an outlook similar to the Western concept of individualism, but there are also statues, regarded as objects of worship, that exhibit only vestigial traces of the qualities that were characteristic of the individual subjects, the depiction of which is essential to true portraiture"—the prevailing concept of the true portrait, i.e., the "depiction of the individual in his own character" emerging in the work of John Pope-Hennessey, *The Portrait in the Renaissance* (1967), and quoted by Ishibashi in the introduction to his translation of Mori's work (Mori 1977, 11).

25
Having argued with an Oxford cohort over the universality of Shakespeare when he declared that Americans might misunderstand the particulars in this very English author's work and so misinterpret the universal, she retold the story of Hamlet to an audience of Tiv (Nigeria) elders. The Tiv interpretation of events as they unfolded drew the story out along quite different lines than Bohannan had anticipated, for the Tiv elders were appalled by Hamlet's consorting with a ghost, since in Tiv belief there is no such thing as a good ghost, and applauded Claudius for his exemplary behavior in marrying his brother's widow, since this would have been the honorable course of action for any Tiv man. What Bohannan concluded from this exercise about Americans understanding Shakespeare is not clear, but certainly she demonstrated that placing events in an alternative and radically different cultural framework most certainly led to a distinctive interpretation.

26
In the context of the West and China, Cahill (1982, 71–74) notes the problem of "intercultural incomprehension" because imagery, style or technique fail to meet expectations, citing Jesuit missionary Matteo Ricci's seventeenth century journal observation: "The Chinese use pictures extensively ... but in the production of these ... they have not at all acquired the skill of Europeans.... They know nothing of the art of painting in oil or of the use

entrenched that many well-educated Africans remain uncomfortable with works of art derived from received tradition. African portraits, whether painted or sculpted, now follow accepted Western models based on mimesis, whether done by university trained artists or self-taught sign painters (Fig. 13).[27]

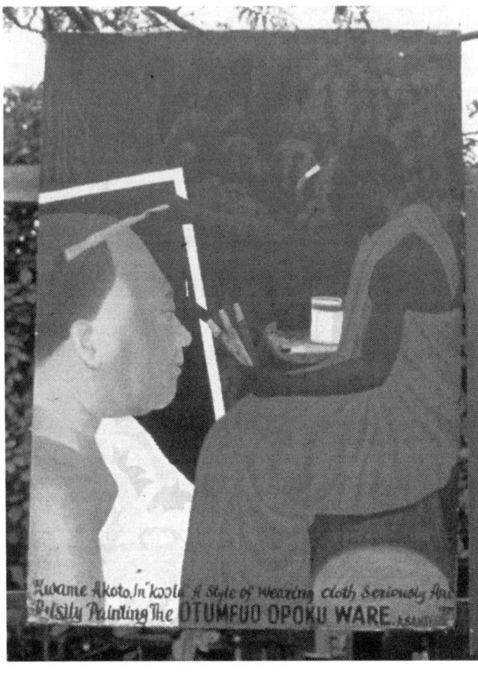

Figure 13
Kwame Akoto. Double portrait entitled *Kwame Akoto in* koola, *a style of wearing cloth, seriously and busily painting the Otumfuo OpokuWare, Asantehene.* Kumasi (Ghana), December 14,1997. Kumasi (Ghana), December 14, 1997.

Kwame Akoto, the master of the Almighty God Art Works, shows himself making a portrait of the Ashanti paramount chief to tout his credentials as a portrait painter.

Because of the equation between likeness and image that stands at the forefront of Western attitudes about portraiture, Euramericans — government officials, businessmen, missionaries or anthropologists — often failed to recognize images from other cultures identified with particular people, dismissing those works described as portraits by their owners. They were unable to see the likeness, transformed as it was by the indigenous aesthetic, and African or Oceanic portraits do not tell us their names, unlike their counterparts from literate societies.[28]

ICON AND INDEX

Portrait photography is a subject too broad to be included in this essay, but photography itself has had the consequence of moving portraits to a more representational program in many non-Western cultures and to a less representational one in the West. Thus, in the latter part of the twentieth century, previously generalized images have become more physiognomically correct — as Nigel Barley (1995, 128–30) indicates in his account of the Tau Tau figures of southern Sulawesi — underlining the relationship between sculpture and subject that had been subordinate to the artistic conventions of an earlier period (Figs. 14 & 15). Today, photographs tag and therefore identify less representational images, as in the Bwa (Burkina Faso) effigy photographed by art historian Christopher Roy in 1985 (illustrated in Borgatti 1990a, 77), or they may be used as substitutes, as in several Yoruba contexts, notably replacing sculpted images for deceased twins (see Fig. 4) or paraded as part of a funeral procession (illustrated in Borgatti 1990a, 59).

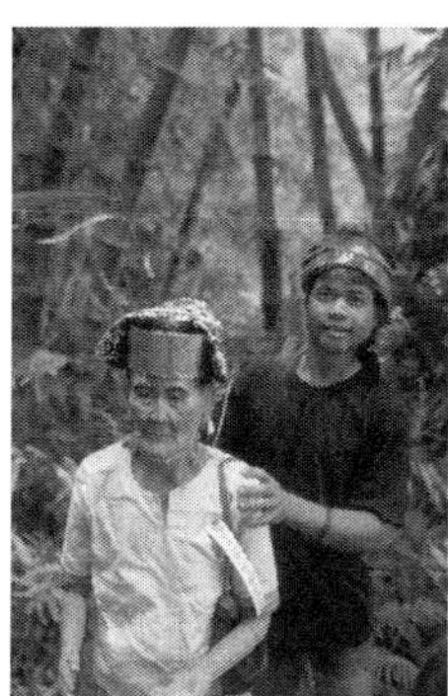

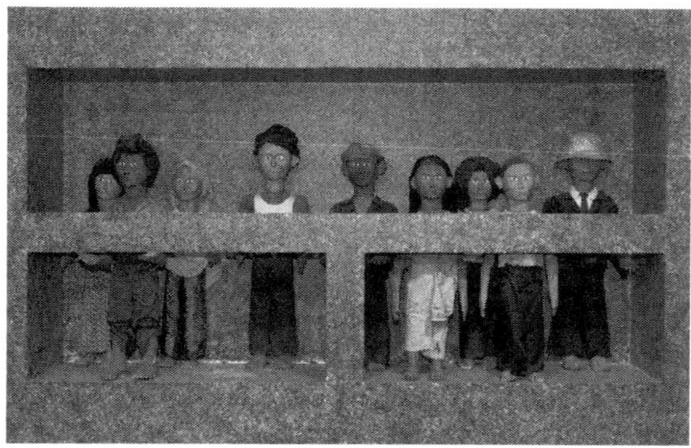

Figure 14
A grandson poses by the *tau tau* of his Grandmother on the occasion of her funeral. Toraja region, South Sulawesi, 1992

Figure 15
Tau tau or memorial figures (Toraja, Indonesia) placed in niches in rock walls near burials. Display of figures recreated by the Tropenmuseum, Amsterdam.

Among the Toraja of southern Sulawesi (Indonesia), previously generalized images have become more physiognomically correct.

If many non-Western societies have moved towards an increased naturalism in their portraits, by the late twentieth century, the combination of likeness and revelation that characterized the flowering of Western portraiture had split into discrete phenomena glossed by the terms icon and index (Brilliant 1990, 171; West 2004, 231). Iconic representations refer to their subjects mimetically to make that person present. Indexical works don't claim presence, they evoke it through referential means (Van Alphen 2004, 250), as has been the case with much world portraiture historically. Such emphasis on external characteristics, not excluding likeness, on social rather than personal identity, and an aesthetic preference for the general and ideal have been properties associated with much Western portraiture as well, even when the portrait resulted from a confrontation between artist and subject.[29]

Indeed, numerous studies of Western portraiture, both general and period specific,[30] discuss the changing nature of the personal image from its early history in ancient portraiture through the present. Thus the plastic realism of Rome gave way to the stylization and symbolism of Byzantine and Early Christian

the circumstances surrounding the portrait's origin (Strong 1969), as did Daimyo portraits in Japan from the same period (Shimizu 1988). In Mayan culture, glyphs convert generic images into individuals by giving them names and history (Martin and Grube 2000).

29
West's discussions of "likeness and type," "the functions of portraiture," and portraits as exemplars of "power and status" provide numerous illustrations from Western art (West 2004, 21–104).

30
General studies include West 2004, organized thematically and providing an excellent annotated bibliography, and Brilliant 1991, providing a more theoretical view. Beyer 2003 makes a chronological journey through Western portraiture, and Woodall 1997 gives a succinct discussion of the issues as an introduction to a series of case studies. More period or theme specific are Breckenridge 1968, on ancient portraiture; Strong 1969 on Elizabethan portraiture; Jenkins 1947, on state portraiture, to name a few.

31
West (2004, 24) notes that it was common practice in the sixteenth century for artists to paint portraits of sitters they had not seen for some time or might not have seen at all. In the 1530s, Isabella d'Este had Titian paint her portrait. Rather than sitting for him, she sent him a portrait by Francesco Francia to copy. This portrait had itself been copied from another 25 years previously. Thus Titian's portrait was a copy of a copy, without direct reference to the real age and appearance of the individual who commissioned it.

32
See Picasso's 1910 portrait of Henry Kahnweiler, for example, illustrated in Pointon 1997, 191. Brancusi's portrait is illustrated in Brilliant 1990, 26.

art, exemplified by the two-dimensional, glittering mosaic portraits of Justinian and his Queen Theodora. These conventionalized images, informed by neo-Platonist aesthetics, intended to represent a truth "not, to be sure, of direct visual facts, since such facts were metaphysically discredited, but of an ideal, extrasensory reality" (Steinberg 1972, 14). Closer examination of portraits as a class in any particular period or location in Europe reveals a standardization of the imagery and a reliance on artistic convention in the rendering of background, costume, posture, and expression, as well as physiognomy, to create an image that fulfills the expectations of the patron. Prototypes take on a signal importance with a particular painting of an individual becoming the model for subsequent paintings, the repetition creating a specious verisimilitude in the painted description of the subject.[31] West (2004, 29–32) notes that while it is possible to trace a gradual shift from portraits that stress identity through external signs to those that focus on character or personality, the attempt to reconcile the inner life with outer appearance was visible in portraits from the Renaissance onwards, becoming common after nineteenth century Romanticism fuelled the idea of a personality cult focused on celebrated individuals.

However, perspective on the unfamiliar, whether art from the past or from other cultures, changes from generation to generation. Developments in Western art have altered and continue to alter expectations about the nature of works of art and of representation itself. Thus portraits of the Elizabethan and Jacobean period could be described as "frights" by a daughter of George III in the late 1700s and subsequently in terms of their "lost loveliness" (Strong 1969, 57). Certainly the history of non-Western art in the West reflects the changing boundaries of art in Western culture rather than changes in the art itself (Goldwater 1967; Rubin 1984).

It's the circumscribing of literal representation that renders the image not recognizable—as in Picasso's cubist portraits or Brancusi's portrait of Mlle. Pogany.[32] In such portraits, the use of a single attribute to identify the subject, the large eyes of Mlle. Pogany, for example, recall the conventions of African portraiture, which play upon a recognizable feature of the individual portrayed to cue the audience—the heavy browline in African portrayals of Hans Himmelheber, for example, or the distinctive hairstyle and facial markings in Akan memorials (Borgatti 1990a, 35, 44–45). Thus, the referential becomes a strategy to evoke individual identity, replacing the mimetic in some portraits. Ernst van Alphen argues forcefully that Christian Boltanski's portraits of Holocaust victims created by their discarded clothing are more powerfully evocative of identity and biography than photographs of the children themselves (Fig. 16). He attributes their success to the exchange of a traditional component of portraiture for a different semiotic principle. Similarity has gone. Contiguity is proposed as the new mode (Van Alphen 1997, 250). It is a mode of portraiture that has long existed in non-Western cultures—as Battamaliba or

Moba (Togo) dressed houses or Kurumba (Burkina Faso) antelope headdresses illustrate (Borgatti 1990a, 28).

Figure 16
Christian Boltanski, The Clothes of François C., 1972.

The photographs of the clothes raise the question of the identity and where-abouts of the owner, through refer-ence, that is, through their indexical rather than their iconic qualities.

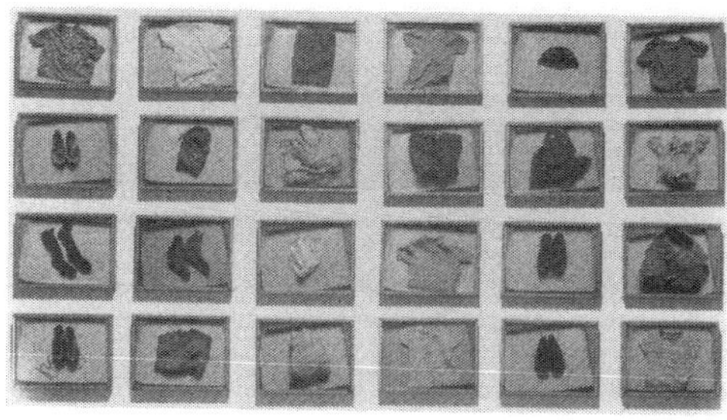

Exposure to non-Western art forms at a critical juncture in Western history gave artists an alternative view of formal construc-tions that catalyzed profound changes in the art of the West and the way we see. So too has the changing conception of the individ-ual contributed to the wealth of portrait images in the modern and postmodern periods that convey personal identity without re-sorting to literal physical description. Such emblematic portraits "do not beguile us by physiognomic verisimilitude into thinking we know the subject" (Aiken 1987, 178), demanding instead an effort on the part of the viewer to recognize the subject or acquire the knowledge that enables him to do so.

CROSS-CULTURAL ANALOGUES

A reliance upon literary reference and indirection creates a con-ceptual and cross-cultural bond across several traditions: Fon ap-pliqué portraits draw upon the imagery of a proverb to suggest name and character (discussed in Borgatti 1990a, 69–70); Chinese commemorative paintings illustrate literally the characters that spell out the patron's *hao* or praise name;[33] and such works as Charles Demuth's *I Saw the Figure 5 in Gold*, a symbolic portrait of William Carlos Williams that refers to his poetry (Aiken 1987), or Marsden Hartley's portrait of Gertrude Stein, *One Portrait of One Woman* (illustrated in Borgatti and Brilliant 1990, 94), make connections to other media or works.

In still other portraits from these periods, artists evoke the subject's personality through an assemblage of memorabilia or the clustering of artifacts rather than through recording physical ap-pearance. Consider Eleanor Antin's attribute portrait of Margaret Mead consisting of a director's chair (with her name on it) and such paraphernalia as a thermos flask, umbrella and binoculars as-sociated with her in her later years, part of a study entitled *Eight New York Women* (Goldin 1975), Armand Arman's *Portrait of Warhol*, comprised of characteristic costuming including a hank of white hair, the tools of his trade, and a visual reference to an idio-syncratic method of accounting (illustrated and discussed in Borgatti and Brilliant 1990, 86–87), Katherine Dreier's abstract portrait of Marcel Duchamp that she describes as representing his character in a more pleasurable way to those who understood than an ordinary portrait (Dreier quoted in West 2004, 200), and Tracey Emin's confessional portrait, *Everyone I Have Ever Slept with 1963–1995,* that is oriented towards self-exploration characteristic of artist self-portraits but through radically different means (West 2004, 212). Emphasis on name and personal artifact recall African modes of portraiture, the Dead Mothers of Okpella, for example, whose generically correct images are identified by name; the effigy portrait in which the person is evoked by the use of his or her actual clothing (Battamaliba, Bwa, Mossi, northern Edo, Yoruba, Antaimoro); or a style of representation which includes the last used goods of the deceased along with his or her image (Ibibio; Kongo) (Borgatti 1990a, 43–57). Nailing down the identity of the effigy is accomplished by siting it appropriately, on the rooftop of the elder's compound in an example drawn from the Northern Edo, and adding personal paraphernalia like hunting equipment and even a photograph of the deceased in the Bwa case (illustrated in Borgatti 1990a, 77).

Certain modes of portraiture from Asia solve the problems of identifying and personalizing images in ways similar to those used in Africa. Sculpted Japanese devotional portraits of Buddhist monks (Fig. 17) carry relics from the body of the deceased and other relevant items inserted into a large cavity in the image; they wear his clothing and take up residence in his house. The home of the deceased becomes a shrine to be visited in order to facilitate a sense of identity between the monk and his followers (Mori 1977, 18–26). Relics and siting of statuary identify figures from Kongo "cluster" portraits while the presence of sculpture at grave sites lends the cemetery even greater significance as a place for pilgrims to visit, communing with the deceased and paying their last respects as well as seeking justice on occasion (Thompson and Cornet 1981, 95–96).

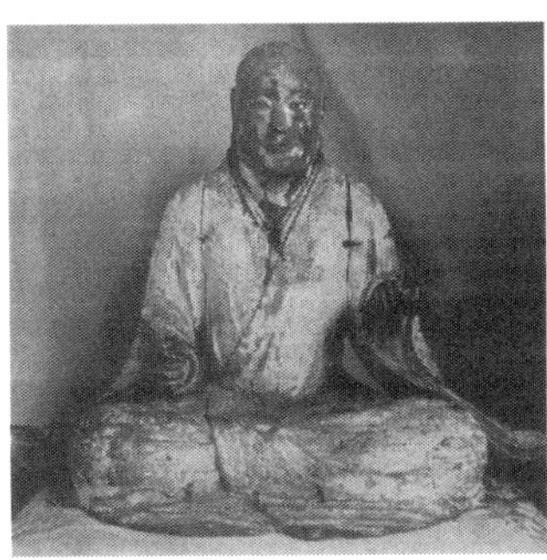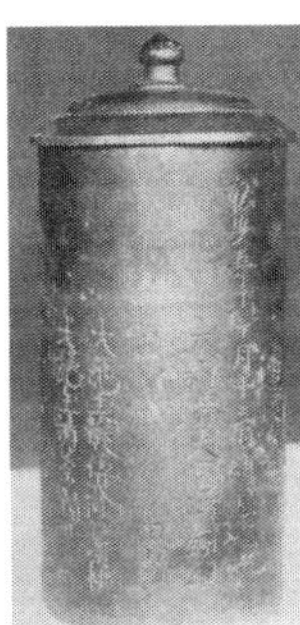

Figure 17
Portrait sculpture of the monk Nichiren with reliquary containing his ashes (retrieved from the interior). Hommon-ji, Tokyo, 1288.

Devotional portraits of Buddhist monks are "named" not only by carrying relics from the body of the deceased in their bodies, but by wearing their clothing and residing in their houses.

One of the most striking analogies between African and Asian modes of portrayal occurs in the conceptual correspondence between Fon sculptural tableaux (Fig. 18) and the early sixteenth century Chinese portrait in a landscape (Fig. 12) of which the *hao*

          World Art Studies IV Comparative Approaches

portraits mentioned above are one variation. Both are commemorative in function and metaphoric in style, using a diminutive and generic, but culturally appropriate image to portray the subject. A Fon ancestor is honored with royal form; a Ming subject is dignified by his depiction as a scholar-gentleman. In both traditions, visual references to the profession or *métier* of the subject may be made; one Fon altar shows a merchant standing by his cloth display (illustrated in Bay 1985, 31 and Borgatti and Brilliant 1990, 113), another the minister of "foreign affairs" (illustrated in Borgatti 1990a, 31 and Blier 2004, 106–7); in a commemorative painting by T'ang Yin, *Auspicious Clouds over Yeh-t'ing*, the subject's family profession and medical skills are suggested by a servant carrying a hoe and basket, attributes of the herb-gatherer or apothecary.[34]

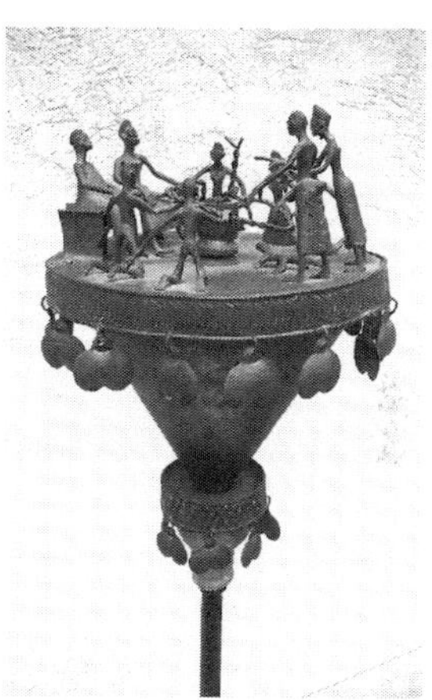

Figure 18
Fon memorial tableau by Aloxa Agbakodji of Abomey.

This work may be the only completely documented Fon altar in the literature, since the true meaning of these forms are known only to the commissioner and the artist, and revealed only once in a narrative when the altar is publicly placed or "planted." The memorial tableau here commissioned by historian Edna Bay takes as its subject Bay, her family and in-laws — showing all the characters as typical Fon figures with the narrative of family and lineage expressed in Fon symbolic terms. The reference to non-African subjects is completely opaque to the uninformed viewer.

Texts explicate the imagery in both traditions. Songs and chants are performed at the formal presentation (planting) of a Fon memorial; a preface written for the Chinese work introduced the subject and provided biographical data on lineage, career, and significant incidents in his life. In each case, the actual imagery is cryptic, following a program conceived by the donor or patron and executed by the artist (or the artist in collaboration with a calligrapher and a poet). The notion that only artist and patron fully understand the message encoded in the forms of a Fon tableau applies equally well to the understanding of imagery in these sixteenth-century Chinese "portraits disguised as landscapes." The major difference centers on the literacy of one culture and its lack in the other. In the Fon context, no effort is made to remember the material that places the tableau into a fully narrative context while in the Chinese example, the textual material is prized as an enrichment of the piece, proving its commemorative function.

THE POWER OF THE IMAGE

Ancestral portraits serve to validate position cross-culturally—not only through the message conveyed by costume and props, but by

their very existence. This is very clear in the Cameroun Grassfields'
context, where the possession of ancestral portraits is an important aspect of reinforcing political authority (Fig. 19). A comparable
motivation may underlie Elizabethan collections of portraiture,
described as not aesthetic but dynastic (Strong 1969, 44). So, too, do
Yoruba (Nigeria) *ako* figures reconstruct the social image of the
deceased, and by extension the heirs, demonstrating chiefly status
in the choice of attire and music as well as the richness of the
cloth (Abiodun 1976) and statuary (as opposed to uncarved sticks)
indicates status within the Oron Ibibio (Nigeria) social hierarchy
(Nicklin n.d.).

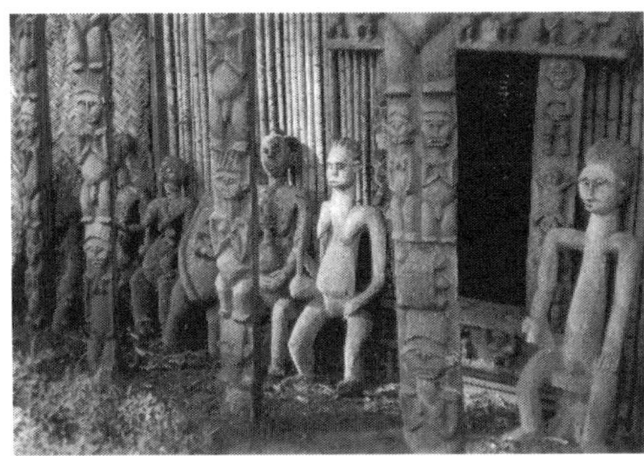

Portraits, too, legitimate dynasty in China. Jan Stuart (2001,
44) points out that the monopoly exercised by a new dynasty
over portraits of its predecessors goes back at least to the Mongol
conquest when captured Song portraits were moved by the Yuan
rulers to their capital not merely for aesthetic reasons but as part
of their claim to being the legitimate heirs of the dynasty. The fall
of the Yuan caused ownership of Song and Yuan portraits to be
transferred to the Ming, while in 1644 all of these portraits became
the property of the Qing imperial household. After 1911, when
the Qing dynasty ended, the portraits became the property of the
new republic and after 1949 were transferred by the Guomindang
government to Taiwan, where 152 imperial portraits are currently
located in the National Palace Museum.

Providing a visual genealogical record especially in cultures
that did not keep records in written form was a particularly important function for portraiture. There is no question that in Africa and
other preliterate areas, portraits were works of history as well as art,
preserving information and facilitating its transfer from person to
person, across the generations. The capacity of art in such societies
to provide not just a mnemonic but to shape ideas becomes explicit in Benin, where "to cast a plaque" (*saey-ama*) not only means
literally "to pour metal into a mold" (Melzian 1937, 83), but also
carries the extended meanings of capturing an image (as in a photograph) and establishing a monument or tradition (R. Agheyisi, personal communication, 1968, quoted in Ben-Amos 1983, 14). Thus
portraits serve as genealogical reference points (captured images)

and as public statements (monuments). Royal portraits, emblematic or representational, recall not only specific monarchs and their achievements, but also principles of governance (Fig. 20). Even in politically decentralized societies, portraits may be read simultaneously as individually referential—or indexical—and as iconic, helping people to remember significant community leaders as well as to provide models of ideal behavior and comportment.

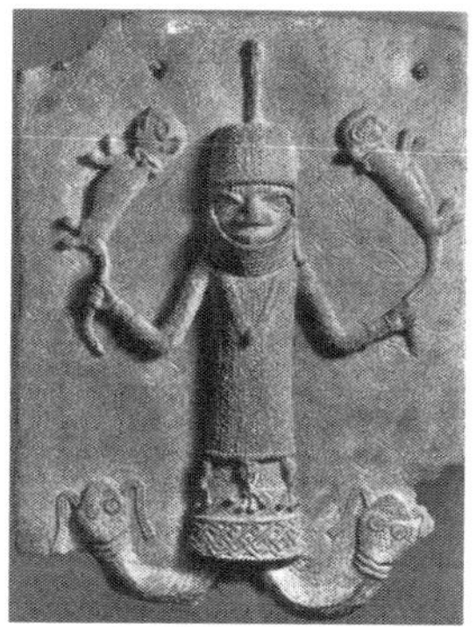

When the last generation who knew the portrayed personally passes on, all portraits lose their power to evoke an actual, though not necessarily an imagined, personality—retaining authority as examples of virtue and achievement. In the words of Quitman Phillips (2000, 170) regarding Japanese portraiture of the late fifteenth century: "Even with an identifying text, time deprives the image of its core of recognizable likeness and it is more readily explained as the product of general circumstances and practices than as a particular act of representation." Vinograd (1992, 14) suggests that at this point the portrait has become an object, but that it does not necessarily cease to be an event, since different audiences will bring distinctive expectations to the image.

Particularly pertinent here is the extended event—and the kinds of recognition, identification, psychic or imaginative captivation that occur as the object becomes increasingly decontextualized over time. Representational images tend to be interpreted like photographs, as generally faithful reconstructions of physical form —and we use our imaginations to construct a story. We may recontextualize the image intellectually, decoding symbolic attributes specific to the period and place, making an effort to locate biographical and historical information. Changing interpretations of images find their way into art historical studies, or, in the case of Chinese "scholar painting," onto the work itself, since tradition permitted successive viewers to make physical and symbolic alterations to them in the form of inscriptions and colophons (Vinograd 1992, 14).

CONCLUSION

Greater globalization and an expanded discourse on portraiture that takes into account the range of strategies employed to establish individual presence means that the recognition of portraits is no longer narrowly confined to those produced by Western artists or based on likeness. Much non-Western portraiture was invisible to the West because it did not conform to a mimetic ideal, identified instead by name and association. Like "abstract or nondescriptive portraits" from the modern and postmodern periods, non-Western portraits challenge our assumptions that easy visual recognition is an essential requirement and attack the importance of physical resemblance as the criterion for assessing quality or insightfulness (Brilliant 1991, 15). Just as much non-Western sculpture was not recognized as art until the forms were appropriated by Western artists, many non-Western portraits have been unrecognized and unappreciated. It is not without irony that a principle long established in many parts of the world underlies the new paradigm forming for Western portraiture—that the power of the image depends upon its being unseen (Byatt 2000, 1).

ACKNOWLEGDMENTS

I was drawn into a study of portraiture in traditional African art by the evocative power of named masquerade images that I observed among the Okpella of southern Nigeria. This essay has evolved from the catalogue essay written for the exhibition *Likeness and Beyond: Portraits from Africa and the World* that I curated for the Center for African Art in New York in 1990. I am grateful to my colleague Wilfried van Damme for inviting me to participate in this volume, and so giving me the opportunity to extend my research and thinking on this topic, and to support by the Sainsbury Research Unit at the University of East Anglia (2005) that enabled me to make a beginning, although this project was merely an adjunct to other work on aesthetics and social change that I was carrying out under their auspices.

REFERENCES

ABIODUN, ROWLAND. 1976. A reconsideration of the function of Ako: Second burial effigy in Owo. *Africa* 46 (1): 4–20.

AIKEN, EDWARD A. 1987. I saw the figure 5 in gold: Charles Demuth's emblematic portrait of William Carlos Williams. *Art Journal* 46 (3): 178–84.

BALANDIER, GEORGES. 1968. *Daily life in the kingdom of the Kongo.* New York: Pantheon Books.

BARLEY, NIGEL. 1988. *Foreheads of the dead: An anthropological view of Kalabari ancestral screens.* Washington, DC: Smithsonian Institution Press.
—. 1995. *Dancing on the grave: Encounters with death.* London: John Murray.

BAY, EDNA. 1985. *Iron altars of the Fon people of Benin.* Atlanta, GA: Emory University.

BEN-AMOS, PAULA. 1980. *Benin art.* London: Thames and Hudson.
—. 1983. Introduction: History and art in Benin. In *The art of power— The power of art: Studies in Benin iconography,* ed. Paula Ben-Amos and Arnold Rubin, 13–16. Los Angeles: UCLA Museum of Cultural History.

BEYER, ANDREAS. 2003. *Portraits: A history.* New York: Harry N. Abrams.

BLIER, SUZANNE P. 1987. *The anatomy of architecture: Ontology and metaphor in Batammaliba architectural expression.* Cambridge: Cambridge University Press.
—. 2001. Africa, art, and history: An introduction. In *A history of art in Africa,* Monica Blackmun Visona et al., 14–23. New York: Harry N. Abrams.
—, ed. 2004. *Art of the senses: African masterpieces from the Teel collection.* Boston: Museum of Fine Arts.

BOHANNAN, LAURA. 1966. Shakespeare in the bush. *Natural History* 75 (7): 28–33.

BORGATTI, JEAN. 1990a. African portraits. In *Likeness and beyond: Portraits in Africa and the world,* Jean Borgatti and Richard Brilliant, 28–83. New York: The Center for African Art.
—. 1990b. Portraiture in Africa. In *Portraiture in Africa, Part I,* ed. Jean Borgatti, 34–39, 101. Special issue, *African Arts* 23 (3).
—, ed. 1990. *Portraiture in Africa, Part I.* Special issue, *African Arts* 23 (3).
—. 1991. African portraiture: A commentary. In *Portraiture in Africa, Part II,* ed. Jean Borgatti, 38–41. Special issue, *African Arts* 23 (4).
—, ed. 1991. *Portraiture in Africa, Part II.* Special issue, *African Arts* 23 (4).
— 1996. Portraiture in African art. In *The dictionary of art* at Grove Art Online, accessed December 18, 2007, http://0-www.groveart com.
—, and Richard Brilliant. 1990. *Likeness and beyond: Portraits in Africa and the world.* New York: The Center for African Art.

BOURDON, DAVID. 1975. Andy Warhol and the society icon. *Art in America* 63 (1), 42–45.

BRECKENRIDGE, JAMES. 1968. *Likeness: A conceptual history of ancient portraiture.* Evanston, IL: Northwestern University Press.

BRILLIANT, RICHARD. 1990. Portraiture: A recurrent genre in world art. In *Likeness and beyond: Portraits in Africa and the world.* Jean Borgatti and Richard Brilliant, 10–27. New York: The Center for African Art.
—. 1991. *Portraiture.* Cambridge, MA: Harvard University Press.

BROWNE, MICHAEL L. 1985. Portraits of foreigners by Kawahara Keiga. *Ars Orientalis* 15: 31–35.

BYATT, ANTONIA S. 2000. *Portraits in fiction.* London: Chatto and Windus.

CAHILL, JAMES. 1982. *The compelling image: Nature and style in seventeenth century Chinese painting.* Cambridge MA, Harvard University Press.

CLAPP, ANN 1991. *The painting of T'ang Yin.* Chicago and London: The University of Chicago Press.

DONNAN, CHRISTOPHER B. 2004. Moche portraits: Masterpieces from ancient Peru. In *Retratos: 2000 years of Latin American portraits,* Marion Oettinger, Jr. et al., 56–65. New Haven, CT and London: Yale University Press.

DREWAL, HENRY. 1984. Art history and the individual: A new perspective for the study of African visual traditions. In *Iowa studies in African art I,* ed. Christopher Roy, 87–114. Iowa City: School of Art and Art History, The University of Iowa.

GERBRANDS, ADRIANUS A. 1993. Atjametsj: Unique collection of statues and shields. In *Asmat art: Woodcarvings of southwest New Guinea,* ed. Dirk Smidt, 115–35. New York: George Braziller in association with the Rijksmuseum voor Volkenkunde, Leiden.

GOLDIN, AMY. 1975. The post-perceptual portrait. *Art in America* 63 (1): 79–82.

GOLDWATER, ROBERT. 1967. *Primitivism in modern art.* New York: Vintage Books.

HESSE, KARL, AND THEO AERTS. 1996. *Baining life and lore.* Port Moresby: University of Papua New Guinea Press.

HIMMELHEBER, HANS. 1972. Das Porträt in der Negerkunst. *Baessler Archiv* 20: 261–311.

HOOPER, STEVEN. 2002. Memorial images of Eastern Fiji: Materials, metaphors and meanings. In *Pacific art: Persistence, change, meaning,* ed. Anita Herle et al., 309–22. Honolulu: University of Hawaii Press.

HORTON, ROBIN. 1965. *Kalabari sculpture.* Apapa, Lagos: Nigerian National Press for Department of Antiquities.

JENKINS, MARIANNA. 1947. *The state portrait: Its origin and evolution.* New York: College Art Association.

JOHNSON, SAMUEL. 1921. *The history of the Yorubas.* Lagos: CSS Bookshops, reprint 1969.

JORDANOVA, LUDMILLA. 2000. *Defining features: Scientific and medical portraits 1660–2000.* London: Reaktion Books in association with the National Portrait Gallery.

KREAMER, CHRISTINE M. [2001]. *Women's work: Everyday utensils and daily work as symbols of Moba women (Northern Togo).* Paper presented at the Triennial Symposium on African Art, St. Thomas, Virgin Islands.

LAWAL, BABATUNDE. 1977. Art and immortality among the Yoruba. *Africa* 47 (1): 52–60.

MACK, JOHN. 1986. *Madagascar: Island of the ancestors.* London: British Museum Publications.

MAMAPUKU, METHODIUS, AND TODD S. HARPLE. 2003. Ancestral heritage and the essence of life. In *Kamoro art: Tradition and innovation in a New Guinea culture*, ed. Dirk Smidt, 22–23. Amsterdam: KIT Publishers.

MARTIN, SIMON, AND NIKOLAI GRUBE. 2000. *Chronicle of the Maya kings and queens: Deciphering the dynasties of the ancient Maya*. London: Thames and Hudson.

MASCHIO, THOMAS. 1994. *To remember the faces of the dead: The plenitude of memory in Southwestern New Britain*. Madison: University of Wisconsin Press.

MELZIAN, HANS. 1937. *A concise dictionary of the Bini language of Southern Nigeria*. London: Kegan Paul and Trench Trubner.

MORI, HISHASHI. 1977. *Japanese portrait sculpture*. Trans. and adapted by W. Chie Ishibashi. Tokyo, New York, and San Francisco: Kodansha International and Shibundo.

NEVADOMSKY, JOSEPH. 1997. Contemporary art and artists in Benin City. *African Arts* 30 (4): 54–63, 94–95.

NICKLIN, KEITH. N.d. *Guide to the National Museum, Oron*. Lagos: Federal Department of Antiquities.

NODELMAN, SHELDON. 1975. How to read a Roman portrait. *Art in America* 63 (1): 27–33.

PHILLIPS, QUITMAN S. 2000. *The practices of painting in Japan, 1475–1500*. Stanford, CA: Stanford University Press.

POINTON, MARCIA. 1997. Kahnweiler's Picasso; Picasso's Kahnweiler. In *Portraiture: Facing the subject*, ed. Joanna Woodall, 189–202. Manchester and New York: Manchester University Press.

POPE-HENNESSEY, JOHN. 1967. *The portrait in the Renaissance*. Princeton, NJ: Princeton University Press.

ROBERTS, MARY, AND ALLEN ROBERTS. 1996. *Memory: Luba art and the making of history*. Munich: Prestel Verlag for the Museum for African Art.

ROY, CHRISTOPHER. 1987. *Art of the Upper Volta rivers*. Meudon: Alain and Françoise Chaffin.

RUBIN, WILLIAM S., ed. 1984. *"Primitivism" in 20th century art: Affinity of the tribal and the modern*. 2 vols. New York: The Museum of Modern Art.

SHIMIZU, YOSHIAKI, ed. 1988. *Japan: The shaping of Daimyo culture 1185–1868*. Washington, DC: The National Gallery of Art.

SMIDT, DIRK. 1993. The Asmat: Life, death and the ancestors. In *Asmat art: Woodcarvings of Southwest New Guinea*, ed. Dirk Smidt, 15–25. New York: George Braziller in association with the Rijksmuseum voor Volkenkunde, Leiden.

SPRAGUE, STEPHEN F. 1978. Yoruba photography: How the Yoruba see themselves. *African Arts* 12 (1): 52–59, 107.

STEINBERG, LEO. 1972. *Other criteria: Confrontations with twentieth-century art*. New York: Oxford University Press.

STRATHERN, MARILYN. 1997. Pre-figured features: A view from the Papua New Guinea highlands. In *Portraiture: Facing the subject*, ed. Joanna Woodall, 259–68. Manchester and New York: Manchester University Press.

STRONG, ROY C. 1969. *The English icon: Elizabethan and Jacobean portraiture*. New Haven, CT: Yale University Press.

STUART, JAN, AND EVELYN S. RAWSKI. 2001. *Worshiping the ancestors: Chinese commemorative portraits*. Palo Alto: Stanford University Press in association with the Smithsonian Institution, Washington DC.

THOMPSON, ROBERT F., AND JOSEPH CORNET. 1981. *The four moments of the sun: Kongo art in two worlds*. Washington DC: The National Art Gallery.

VAN ALPHEN, ERNST 1997. The portrait's dispersal: Concepts of representation and subjectivity in contemporary portraiture. In *Portraiture: Facing the subject*, ed. Joanna Woodall, 239–56. Manchester and New York: Manchester University Press.

VINOGRAD, RICHARD. 1992. *Boundaries of the self: Chinese portraits 1600–1900*. Cambridge: Cambridge University Press.

VOGEL, SUSAN. 2001. *Fang: An epic journey*. New York: Prince Street Productions.

WEST, SHEARER. 2004. *Portraiture*. Oxford: Oxford University Press.

WILLETT, FRANK. 1967. *Ife in the history of West African sculpture*. New York: McGraw-Hill.

WOODALL, JOANNA, ed. 1997. *Portraiture: Facing the subject*. Manchester and New York: Manchester University Press.

DONALD E. BROWN

Portraiture and Social Stratification

Faces or face-like images capture the attention of infants at very early ages. Shortly after a child is born, its eyes will only focus at about the distance of a nursing mother's face. The human face is wondrously expressive, and humans scan faces for the faintest cues. Humans recognize very large numbers of distinct faces, even in seriously degraded images. Recognizing human faces is so important that a portion of the human brain is dedicated to that task. It is not surprising then that realistic representation of the human face (photographs included) is so much a part of our world. However, as common as such representations are in all modern settings, they are rare in the wide range of societies known to ethnography and history. To some extent this must reflect the relatively undeveloped artistic skills that result from a minimal division of labor and/or no leisure class—conditions that characterized the great bulk of human societies over countless generations of human history. The well-known cave paintings and rock art that have survived do depict humans but do not show realistic human portraiture, even though some of this art shows skill levels that might well have sufficed for caricature.

There must be various reasons why there may have been little interest in realistic portrayal of faces in the very considerable majority of human societies known to archaeology, ethnology, and history. However, the aim of this essay is to offer an explanation for why some peoples who surely did possess the relevant skills—such as the ancient Egyptians over many centuries—do not seem to have shown much interest in the realistic representation of distinct individuals. I will argue that part of the explanation for the absence or presence of realistic portraiture in premodern societies lies in the alternative patterns of their social stratification: where it was hereditarily closed, as in caste-organized societies, realistic portraiture was inhibited; where the social strata were open to social climbing and descent, as in most if not all modern societies, realistic portraiture could flourish. This argument, initially formulated in a study of the various implications of caste organization (Brown 1988), builds upon, confirms, and extends positions set forth in Breckenridge's (1968) uncommonly extensive survey of early portraiture. The argument shares the comparative approach and the stress on the intimate connection between art and the basic structures of society advocated by Pasztory (2005).

The reasoning that lies behind my argument will be discussed at the end of this essay. First I will define my terms with respect to societal types and then present the relevant case materials. A caste-organized society is one that is stratified into a hereditary upper caste or set of castes that is or are a numerical minority (but not merely a kingly line) and a lower caste or set of castes that constitutes the larger part of society. In such a society there is no expectation that one can be born to low estate and rise to the top depending on one's achievements or good fortune. The maintenance of such a society has quite stringent cultural and social requirements.

In contrast with the caste-organized societies are those that are also stratified but with mobility of individuals or groups from one stratum to another considered normal, as in most if not all modern societies. These may be called openly stratified. Societies that have notions of caste, but apply them to low-caste minorities only, so that the bulk of the populace consists of a single and dominant great category within which up and down movement is considered normal, for the concerns of this essay are effectively openly stratified.

In either case one is speaking of ideal types or ideological conceptions of societies. In reality, social mobility occurs to some degree in caste organized societies just as there are limitations on social mobility in the openly-stratified societies. However, the ideals may well be crucial in their impact on cultural productions such as the literary and visual arts.

Let us look now at some of the record, starting with cases from the Americas. In each case portraiture will be discussed first, then the pattern of social stratification.

REALISTIC PORTRAITURE DID OCCUR IN PRELITERATE SOCIETIES BEYOND EUROPE AND ASIA

The fullest flowering of realistic[1] portraiture in the ancient world came first, as is well-known, with the Greeks. But realistic portraiture apparently developed independently elsewhere, at least in the Americas—among the Olmec, Moche, and Maya—and possibly in the West African kingdom of Benin (all cases are discussed comparatively in Pasztory 2005).

"Olmec" refers to an archaeologically identified cultural tradition that flourished in Mexico in the two millennia BCE. In that culture colossal human heads were carved from stone as early as 1500 BCE. The heads are sufficiently realistic in appearance that there is a general consensus that they are probably the portraits of actual rulers. The portrait heads appear suddenly and are most realistic in the earlier versions (Pasztory 2005). Interestingly, Pasztory uses the words "caste" and "rigid" (2005, 146–48) in describing the apparent social order of the ancient Mexican culture represented at Teotihuacan, which—in contrast to the Olmec—produced far more abstract representations of the face. However, in my opinion too little is known about the social organization of the Olmec or that at Teotihuacan to make a confident judgment of whether they were or weren't caste organized.

The Moche, who existed from c. 100 to c. 800 CE in northern coastal Peru, are also known only archaeologically, but their remains are extraordinarily rich in pottery that depicts many facets of their lives and culture. Among the pottery finds are numerous vessels in the form of human heads—nearly always male and produced only in certain Moche areas in a fairly delimited period of time. Many of these heads are sufficiently realistic that they may be actual individuals. The depiction of the emotion of fear is evident in some of the portrait heads, and some show facial decorations, signs of age, and marks of disease. In most cases there is no way of telling whether these heads are of distinct individuals who were alive at the times the portrait vessels were made, though some of the vessels clearly depict the same real or imagined individuals, identifiable by their physical form, clothing, and objects held (Borgatti and Brilliant 1990; Breckenridge 1968; Donnan 1978, 2004).

In a carefully studied sample of Moche portrait heads 750 individuals were identified, 75 of them represented by two or more portraits, and many others by fifteen or more. One individual appeared in over forty portraits. This individual, identified by a distinctive scar on his upper lip, appears at differing stages of his life, starting at about age ten and continuing into his midthirties (Donnan 2004).

Since the Moche and their contemporary neighbors left no written documents, there is no historical record to guide us in interpreting the portrait heads or determining whether the Moche were or weren't caste-organized (Donnan 1978, 2004). However, the Moche archaeological record's richness has allowed attempts to reconstruct their social order. A study of Moche burial patterns that specifically looked at evidence for social stratification found a more or less continuous gradation of inequalities and no evidence of class boundaries (Milliare 2002). A broad survey of the fuller range of Moche archaeological remains argues that elites developed and reached their zenith during the period when the portrait heads were produced and that the portraits ceased to be made in a period that shows both decline and an apparent rigidification of hierarchy evidenced by the introduction of walls and barriers in Moche settlements that clearly separated the upper strata from the masses (Bawden 1996). The conclusions of both of these studies are consistent with the absence of caste among the Moche—except possibly during the very period when the production of Moche portraiture came to an end.

The Classic Maya of the Yucatan Peninsula, in the period from c. 250 to 800 CE, present a somewhat different picture. On the one hand, having existed for many centuries, they have left a far richer archaeological record, replete with sculpture and paintings as well as pottery. Moreover, the Maya still had functioning societies when contacted by Europeans. Finally, as recent break-throughs in the reading of their writings have revealed, the Maya produced histories that allow us to identify some of their por-traits with particular named individuals. At least two of these portraits—sculptured heads of Pakal the Great (seventh century CE) and his son—are realistic (Drew 1999; Martin and Grube 2000; Schele and Freidel 1990).

However, in spite of the Maya's advanced ability to accur-ately and movingly depict emotion, along with body build, region-al physiognomy, state of health, and of course sex and age, the overall thrust of much of their art is to depict the highly stylized and elaborate costume and paraphernalia that symbolized high station. While it is notable that Pakal the Great was an individual who rose to the top (by founding a dynasty in a period marked by the rise and fall of rival polities), there is no overall conclusion confidently to be drawn either about the realism of their portrait-ure or their system of stratification. Suffice it to say that they did produce some realistic portraiture of identifiable individuals in a period for which there is evidence of the dynastic rivalry that al-lows substantial social mobility, and that there is no clear evidence of caste among the Maya.

The West African Kingdom of Benin flourished from around the thirteenth century onward. Judging by later practices, each ruler on his accession to the throne had a brass head of his prede-cessor cast. Heads that were produced earlier—in both brass and terracotta—are highly realistic, while those produced later are much less so. Unfortunately, the earlier heads were discovered archaeologically and there is considerable uncertainty whether they depict particular individuals. Judging by its later periods, Benin was not caste-organized. There is no reason to suspect that things were different earlier, and the fifteenth and sixteenth cen-turies, an "age of warrior kings" that was marked by revolution and upheaval, and an age in which the arts flourished (Ben-Amos 1995), seems particularly unlikely to have been caste-organized (Ben-Amos 1995; Bradbury 1957; Borgatti and Brilliant 1990; Breckenridge 1968).

REALISTIC PORTRAITURE OCCURRED ONLY IN DELIMITED PERIODS IN ANCIENT EGYPT

Egyptian art is much more elaborate than any of those so far discussed and was produced for a much lengthier time. The technical skill of Egyptian artisans was maintained at a very high level over many centuries. Portraits with the names of their subjects were produced throughout Egypt's history, and in some infrequent cases Egyptians produced remarkably life-like portraits. But until Egypt was conquered by Alexander in the fourth century BCE there is no clear evidence that any of these portraits was the actual image of the person it was claimed to portray (Breckenridge 1968). Close examination shows that either two or more portraits of the same subject do not resemble each other, or the same physiognomy is imposed on more subjects than are likely to have shared a family likeness. Some very life-like masks that have been found are thought to have been armatures upon which idealized faces would normally have been fashioned. As Frankfort says, "Egyptian monuments ... consistently hide the individuality of the kings" (1961 [1948], 46–48).

Certain qualifications to the above should be noted. One is that the more realistic portraiture tended to come early in Egyptian history and to disappear in later periods. Thus Breckenridge (1968, 44) finds that "the portraits of the Old Kingdom [c. 2700–2200 BCE] are the most individualized and naturalistic of any major period of Egyptian history." Wilson (1951) sees a degree of realism up to the end of the Empire (1165 BCE). Both these authors note a distinct upsurge of realistic portraiture in the Amarna period, ushered in by Akh-en-Aton (r. 1352–1344 BCE).

There is evidence both for social mobility and for the hereditary transmission of status throughout Egyptian dynastic history, which stretches over more than two and a half millennia. However, publicly supported egalitarian ideals were swept away in a period of dynastic breakdown from 1800 to 1550 BCE. "Class cleavage" then became marked and it was rare "to move upward on the social scale" (Wilson 1951, 186). There was a brief break in this situation when Akh-en-Aton came to the throne, followed by a "swarm of parvenus" who eclipsed the old bureaucracy and priesthood (Wilson 1951, 207). In the following reign, however, the old priesthood and hereditary bureaucrats reasserted their authority. The tendency to hereditary rank then remained strong throughout the Empire Period (c. 1465–1165 BCE). And after about 1100 BCE Egypt began to "petrify": "The formation of society into rigid classes, with priests and warriors constituting castes of special privilege ... became more and more important from that time on" (Wilson 1951, 306–7, 308). When Greek travelers came to Egypt they found claims of hereditary succession to a variety of offices that stretched back for hundreds of generations.

To summarize this more complicated case, there is a loose fit on a very long-term basis between degrees of realism and degrees of stratificational openness, and a short-term but tighter fit in the Amarna period.

REALISTIC PORTRAITURE DEVELOPED IN CLASSICAL IONIAN GREECE, BUT NOT IN DORIAN SPARTA

Classical Greek sculptors were initially more concerned to depict ideal human figures but by the fourth century BCE realistic portraiture reached its fullest development (Ashmole 1964; Breckenridge 1968; Starr 1968). In his important survey of portraiture, Breckenridge argues for a nexus between individualism, literary characterization of concrete individuals, science, and a materialistic philosophy in ancient Greece. He finds this nexus epitomized in a portrait of Aristotle: "the first portrait of an individual in the strongly realistic sense of the word" (1968, 120). For Aristotle, mind and soul could only be apprehended through the physical appearance and action of the individual, thus establishing "the fundamental premise of the scientific method" (Breckenridge 1968, 123). "Only when such an attitude toward physical reality is accepted," Breckenridge (1968, 123) suggests, "is portraiture in its most fully developed sense a possibility."

Those conditions were not found in Athens' rival, Sparta. Although the Spartans did commission portrait sculptures at Delphi at the end of their war with Athens (404 BCE), none of the artists appears to have been Spartan. In general, the once flourishing arts of Sparta languished after the sixth century BCE (Breckenridge 1968; Jones 1967; Michell 1952).

In the epic poems of ancient Greece both kingship and nobility were hereditary and traced their descent from the gods. The social gap between them and others was rarely crossed (Finley 1962). The nobility and the masses were thought to be distinguished from each other by character, way of life, and physical appearance (Baldry 1965). But the development of cities, trade, and industry ushered in new classes, and by the sixth century BCE the basis was laid both materially and legally for stratification by wealth (Baldry 1965; Finley 1962; Starr 1968). The principle that merit, not birth, determined nobility was enunciated by various thinkers of the time, so that by the fifth century BCE in Ionic Greece the idea of nobility by birth was "finally crushed" (Baldry 1965, 34).

In Athens—the spiritual and political center of Ionia—there was a large slave population, but anyone could become a slave and slaves could and did rise to great wealth and high status (Finley 1959; Westermann 1955).

In the sixth through fourth centuries BCE, conditions were very different in Athens' Dorian rival, Sparta. The term "caste" is regularly used in describing Sparta's ruling stratum, the Spartiates: "the most exclusive economical and political caste in all Greece" (Michell 1952, 29). Beneath them was a category called *periokoi* ("dwellers around"), and beneath them was a large serf-like category called helots. The *periokoi* inhabited areas conquered by the Spartans and could not easily become Spartan, if at all. The helots were tied to the soil and could be neither sold nor manumitted. There is some evidence that the Spartans considered the *periokoi* and helots to be "aborigines" whom the Spartans as an invading race had conquered; some modern authorities consider *periokoi* and helots to have been Dorians who were reduced to their low status (Chrimes 1942; Jones 1967; Huxley 1962; Michell 1952).

REALISTIC PORTRAITURE FLOURISHED IN REPUBLICAN ROME BUT DECLINED IN LATE IMPERIAL ROME (AND INTO THE EUROPEAN MIDDLE AGES)

Roman portraiture probably had its roots in the wax death-masks of high-ranking Romans. Originally Roman portraits were not realistic, but in the second century BCE, and under the influence of Greek patterns, they became so (Breckenridge 1968). Eventually they became extremely realistic, "as far removed as possible from the generalized and the typical" (Breckenridge 1968, 143).

As in Greece, Breckenridge (1968) sees in Rome too a connection between realistic portraiture—which in Rome became the predominant form of sculpture, produced for common citizens as well as heroes—and the individualism fostered by materialistic philosophies. Breckenridge (1968, 185) says that "a naturalistic art would seem almost an inevitable concomitant" of the individualism and materialism that characterized the Stoicism and Epicureanism of the time. Biography developed along with portraiture, so that "toward the end of Cicero's life, [when] portrait sculpture in Rome reached a new level of vividness and psychological penetration, we know the faces as well as the minds of some of the prominent men of the time" (Rawson 1975, xiii).

However, "from Constantine [r. 306–337] onwards, there is no longer anything which has any worth: there are only lifeless images in the Oriental frontal style" (Lot 1961 [1937], 138). Berenson (1954, 34), too, traces the decline of realistic portraiture to the lifetime of Constantine, and wonders if the artists hadn't suddenly deserted Rome, "leaving mere artisans" to do their work (see also Brown 1971; Ullmann 1966b).

The dominant theme of early republican Roman history is a two-century "struggle of the orders" in which plebian Romans by 287 BCE achieved effective equality with patricians, who had hitherto monopolized high office (Hammond and Scullard 1970). In the middle of the republican period successes in the Punic Wars gave Rome a larger control of the Mediterranean region, and as Rome's power grew so did the scope it provided for amassing wealth and achieving upward social mobility. A whole new "middle class" emerged, ultimately crystalizing around the equestrian order, in opposition to the Roman senatorial class (Hill 1952; Wiseman 1971).

From early times Rome was legally stratified into classes based on wealth, and high office was confined to those who met specified wealth standards. With the decline of the patricians, high status was determined by wealth, education, family, and office holding (Hammond and Scullard 1970; Gelzer 1969 [1912]; Hopkins 1974; Wiseman 1971). Mobility was possible even for the common man (MacMullen 1974).

So too with slaves. Freeing slaves was considered normal, because Romans recognized individual merit. Rates of manumission were high. Some freedmen became very wealthy and in the early imperial period some rose to high office (Hopkins 1974, 1978; Treggiari 1969; Weaver 1974).

Roman citizenship was progressively expanded, and by 212 CE all Roman subjects were citizens (Hammond and Scullard 1970).

According to two careful studies, the early Imperial period was one of unprecedented and explosive social mobility. The rise and fall of competing dictators and emperors enhanced the opportunities for the meritorious (or unscrupulous) to rise (Treggiari 1969; Wiseman 1971; see also Syme 1979).

Social mobility in the republican and early imperial periods received considerable ideological support from the likes of Cato, Sallust, and Cicero, and from Stoicism, with its belief in the essential unity of humanity. Although Romans were at all times highly conscious of rank, and the social pyramid was steep, social mobility was ubiquitous and consciously defended in republican Rome and well into the imperial period (Hammond and Scullard 1970; Hopkins 1974, 1978; MacMullen 1974; Syme 1958; Treggiari 1969).

But in late imperial Rome, for example the reigns of Diocletian (284–305) and Constantine, the emperors began to tie the members of various occupational groups to their tasks hereditarily, so that historians begin to use the word "caste" in describing Rome's social order (e.g., Lot 1961 [1937], 84). At first certain military posts were made hereditary, then some mining occupations, minters, armorers, smiths, muleteers, grooms, cartrights, veterinary surgeons, postmen, weavers, and others were not only hereditarily bound to their professions but their children were forbidden to marry outside their occupational caste. The serfdom of Europe's Middle Ages was set in place when Constantine bound agricultural workers to their estates or villages. Agricultural slaves were similarly bound to the lands they worked, and could only be sold if the land was sold (Jones 1956; Lot 1961 [1937]).

It was not only the lower strata who were made hereditary, but so too the upper and middle class elements of Roman municipalities (Lot 1961 [1937]; Hammond and Scullard 1970). "[T]he arrangement of society into 'orders' or closed classes brought almost to a complete standstill the upward movement from class to class" (Lot 1961 [1937], 124–25). "Class hardened almost to the point of caste … in the late Empire" (MacMullen 1974, 126). And those who argue for at least "gradual mobility" at that time, note that it was "unsupported by any major ideology of advancement"; "the dominant ideology praised aristocratic birth, blood and nature above all else" (Hopkins 1974, 117).

PORTRAITURE REMAINED IN DECLINE UNTIL LATE IN THE MIDDLE AGES

In the European Middle Ages artists showed more interest in the "garments and paraphernalia" of office than in the features of the individuals who held them (Ullman 1966a, 44). This was not due to any lack of ability but to a lack of interest (Ullman 1966a, 1966b).

Given that Europe was highly decentralized during the Middle Ages and that travel was difficult between its regions, there was substantial variation from region to region as well as through time. There is considerable debate about the extent of caste organization, but the authors in two recent works on the topic indicate an early development of a hereditary nobility in Europe's Germanic and Frankish core, as an amalgam of late Roman and barbarian institutions (Cheyette 1968; Reuter 1978). In an attempt to summarize, Reuter (1978, 28) stresses the "importance of blood" in defining the medieval nobility. Initially knighthood could be gained or lost, but it "contained the seed of inheritance" from the beginning and rapidly became a closed, hereditary class (Duby 1968). Medieval nobility shared the "heritable charisma" of royalty; "nobility was acquired by birth, certainly" (Tellenbach 1978, 204). Such social mobility as did occur was often hidden by mythical genealogical claims (see, e.g., Bosl 1978; Genicott 1968; Schlesinger 1968).

There was substantial regional variation, with the peripheral areas, such as England and the Norman regions, showing considerably lesser signs of caste organization (Bloch 1961; Haskins 1966). Where states centralized, hereditary principles were weaker (Murray 1978). And by the turn of the millennium (in response to the northward movement of monetization and intellectual ferment initiated in the Muslim world), and especially between 1100 and 1300, there were signs of increased vertical mobility, a consciousness of it, and, ultimately, defenses of the idea that rank should be based on merit rather than birth (Murray 1978).

IN CONTRAST WITH THE MIDDLE AGES, REALISTIC PORTRAITURE FLOURISHED IN THE RENAISSANCE, ESPECIALLY IN FLORENCE, LESS SO IN VENICE

Reflecting the period's individualism, portraiture (and biography) flourished in the Italian Renaissance (Kristeller 1961, 1965). Realistic portraiture was particularly associated with Florence. The Florentine Giotto's (c. 1266–1337) "school set art on a new course of realistic representation;" Giotto's "figures are not, as in earlier medieval painting, symbolic emblems of biblical persons but men and women with perceptible body and weight, displaying visible emotions" (Holmes 1975, 143). From Giotto onward there was progress in Florence in rendering facial expression (Berenson 1967). The Florentine painters were the most addicted to figure studies, particularly with conveying a tactile sense of the material solidity and motion of the body, and were obsessed with scientific naturalism and the development of technique to render one's subject ever more naturalistically (Berenson 1967). Martines (1979) sees the distinctive features of Florentine art, including its naturalism and emphasis on individuals, as direct reflections of the Florentine republican ideals that will be discussed below.

But Renaissance art was slow to come to Venice (Bouwsma 1968; Berenson 1967). When individual portraiture was commissioned, it subdued individualism by, for example, avoiding the full face: "In the portraits of the Doges ... Venice wanted the effigies of functionaries entirely devoted to the State, and not of great personalities, and the profile lent itself more readily to the omission of purely individual traits" (Berenson 1967, 17). Even when the techniques of individual portraiture were fully developed in Venice, as in the works of Giorgione (1478?–1511), "the least apparent object was the likeness, the real purpose being to please the eye and to turn the mind toward pleasant themes" (Berenson 1967, 18). In subject matter, Venetian painting was markedly concerned with pageantry (Berenson 1967; Martines 1979).

At the turn of the millennium the communes of northwestern Italy began their rise into independent and thriving enterprises that could throw off the control of medieval nobility. As a result, social stratification in Renaissance Italy (Venice excepted) came to show "the sharpest contrasts to medievalism" (Burckhardt 1954 [1860], 265).

In many respects Florence stood at the forefront of the European Renaissance. The essentials of its story include a thriving urban and capitalist economy (with its inherent ups and downs), successes in warfare, and a sustained and effective movement against the power and authority of rural nobles and urban magnates. Conditions became so onerous and dangerous for magnates that many of them renounced their status (Becker 1967, 1968b; Schevill 1936). Individual merit became the ideological and legal criterion for social advancement. All this was accompanied by measurably high rates of actual social mobility.

A 1328 revision of the Florentine constitution specifically stated that "public offices should be accessible to all those who by their way of life have been shown fit to hold them" (Rubinstein 1968, 451). From 1343 to 1382, a "golden age in democracy" in Florence, unprecedented numbers of "new men," many of whom had not even been born in Florence, rose to government offices (Becker and Brucker 1956). "This society was the creation of successive waves of immigrants who flocked to the cities in hope of increasing their patrimony and augmenting their status" (Becker 1968a, 93).

Humanist thinkers of the time emphasized the importance of achieved status: that "true nobility was dependent upon deeds rather than birth" was the "capstone" of "consciously pursued ideals" in Florence (Becker 1967, 3, 39). "Florentine diaries, memorials, and manner books are replete with prudent counsel for the social climber" (Becker 1967, 26).

As in other parts of Italy, a new class of the commercially wealthy arose in Venice in the few centuries after the turn of the millennium. This class successfully contested the powers of the old nobility and the Duke (Doge) of Venice, but late in the thirteenth century closed its own ranks to new admissions, converting itself into a "caste-like … nobility" (Davis 1962, 15; see also Brown 1907, 54). This act is called the *serrata*, the "closing" of the Great Council of Venice, whose members ruled the city-state. Consisting of about 5 per cent of the populace, the Great Council admitted virtually no new members for more than the next two and a half centuries (Bouwsma 1968; Brown 1907). Members needed proof that a "paternal ancestor had at some time sat in the Great Council" (Brown 1907, 64). Nobility and membership in the Council became synonymous, and a variety of steps—such as regulating marriages, excluding illegitimate sons, and recording births and marriages in "Golden Books"—were taken to prevent contamination of the body (Bouwsma 1968; Brown 1907; Davis 1962). The Venetian chroniclers promoted a myth of an "eternal Venice" that "had always been governed by noble families" (Cochrane 1981, 65). Thus, in the late Middle Ages and early Renaissance social mobility did in fact occur in Venice, but as the Renaissance progressed mobility into the ruling stratum was stopped and the existence of the actual mobility was officially denied.

IN CONTRAST WITH CHINA, REALISTIC PORTRAITURE WAS LARGELY ABSENT IN HINDU INDIA BUT WAS MORE CLOSELY APPROACHED IN BUDDHIST INDIA AND FLOURISHED IN MUGHAL INDIA

Realistic portraiture had almost no place in Hindu India (Coomaraswamy 1931). Realism in general was rare in Indian art, and artists were usually anonymous (Rowland 1953). However, early Buddhist paintings (e.g., the seventh century work that is the frontispiece to Basham 1959) did show considerable realism in depicting humans (Wilkinson 1949).

In the period of the Mughal Empire (sixteenth to eighteenth centuries) and under the direct patronage of its rulers, who were Persian-influenced Muslims of Mongol-Turkic origin, a distinctive style of miniature painting developed. Coomaraswamy (1975 [1916], 74) contrasts Mughal painting with a derivative but Hindu style, the (Hindu) Rajput: "Portraiture is the typical mode of

Mughal painting. Its predominance there and comparative subordination in Rajput art, exactly reflect the characteristic bias of the Mughal and the Hindu culture—the one deeply interested in individual character and in passing events, the other in ideal types and symbols. Even human figures … stand essentially as symbols of ideas [in Rajput art].… [Mughal portraiture achieved] perhaps the highest level that miniature portraiture has ever reached, [exhibiting] penetrating insight into the character of the individual represented."

Not only do the Mughal paintings delineate individuals but many are individually signed. Interestingly, the majority of the painters apparently were Hindu, possibly because of the considerable ambivalence among Muslims about the religious correctness of images of living things. When the Mughals ceased direct patronage of the painters, individualistic realism disappeared (Brown 1975 [1924]; Wilkinson 1949).

By contrast with Hindu India, Chinese portrait art has a long and distinguished history, although the Chinese artist often attached no great importance to achieving a precise physical likeness of his subject, seeking rather to represent the inner spirit or essence of the individual portrayed. Only in the case of ancestral portraits was an attempt made at accurate physical representation, and these works were not considered art; many were combinations of stock types of noses, eyes, etc. (Lancman 1966). The antiquity of Chinese attempts at portraiture—or at any rate their sense of individual differences—may readily be seen in the life-size figures found at the site of the tomb of the Ch'in Emperor, the first to unify China. Each figure, and there are thousands of them, appears to have a distinct and realistic visage, showing age, mood, and regional variations in physiognomy. It may be that, like the ancestral portraits, these faces are actually the many combinations possible from relatively small numbers of fixed and variable components and are artistic renderings on the range of possibilities seen in real soldiers of the time. Although some are inscribed with the name of the artisan who produced them, none has the name of a person depicted (Fu 1989; Hearn 1979; Zhang 1996). Whatever the case, Chinese portraiture is a larger and more realistic art form than its counterpart in India, though considerably less realistic than the more life-like examples of Western portraiture.

The ancient and enduring caste system of India may well be its best known feature. In a volume devoted primarily to questioning the prevailing assumption of rigid and hereditary stratification in India (Silverberg 1968), a summary article states that Hindu India's "socioreligious values and ideologies express what is probably as extreme a disapproval of mobility as is possible, and … they have in fact worked to reduce very greatly the amount of mobility in Indian society" (Barber 1968, 29).

Although founded in India and for a time widespread there, Buddhism did not persist in India. The Buddha considered caste irrelevant and he belittled the pretensions of the Brahmins who claimed to cap the Hindu caste system. The Buddhist monastic order was open to all (men) and advance within it was based on merit (Chakravarti 1987).

According to Von Grunebaum (1961, 171), "the fundamental assumption of Islam [is the] leveling [of] all distinctions of birth." Historically there have been various lapses from or exceptions to this ideal, and in the earliest century or so of the Islamic world it did not prevail, for pre-Islamic Arabs emphasized the importance of birth, and Muslim Arabs initially held themselves above those they conquered. But in time these old patterns were swept away, and much of the Islamic world conformed to fundamentally egalitarian ideals (see an extended discussion in Brown 1988). This does not, of course, imply that Muslim societies were not stratified. The Mughal states were stratified yet highly centralized, and the rulers were relatively free to appoint whom they would to high office. This included appointing Hindus as well as Muslims to very high office. The Mughal ruler Akbar (r. 1556–1605), a principal patron of the portrait artists, made "no distinction of caste or creed in the conferment of high titles and offices" (Sharma 1940, 331–32).

The ideal of a basic human equality (at least of men) has been longer and more consistently at home in China than in the West. "What is unique about China is the agreement on all sides that men are naturally equal;" this ideal "is central to any deep understanding of the Chinese world view" (Munro 1969, 22). The ideal was incorporated in the Confucian doctrine that merit should be the sole basis for political advancement (Munro 1969).

To facilitate this ideal, by the first century BCE the Chinese had instituted examinations for the recruitment of bureaucrats. These examinations remained in use throughout much of China's history, persisting into the twentieth century. The folklore of China has been "filled with success stories of self-made men" who, though from poor families, succeeded in passing the examinations by dint of heroic effort. Rates of social mobility in China's Ming and Ching periods (1368–1911) were as high or higher than in the modern West (Ho 1964).

REALISTIC PORTRAITURE EMERGED IN THE KAMAKURA PERIOD OF JAPAN

Portraiture dates back to the eighth century in Japan and for centuries was particularly associated with Buddhism. In the Kamakura period (roughly, thirteenth and fourteenth centuries) portraits became more common, reached a very high degree of realism (in the face), and began to be commissioned for secular figures (Mori 1977). "Unlike the emphasis on elegance and idealization prevalent in the art of the [previous period], the Kamakura aesthetic stressed realism in the arts and sought to invest works of art with a vigorous naturalism more in keeping with the expansive spirit of the period itself" (Mori 1977, 105).

The upsurge in social mobility (and instability) in the Kamakura age is a central theme of Souyri's *The World Turned Upside Down* (2001). "The rise of the warrior classes" and "social mobility" "were prominent phenomena of this period" (Souyri 2001, 4). The Japanese term for this condition indicated "the lower commanding the upper" (Souyri 2001, 4). "Japanese society during this time was relatively dynamic and open, bringing in its wake a period of exceptional cultural creativity" (Souyri 2001, 5).

DISCUSSION

The foregoing cases, and comparisons both between and chronologically within them, support the following observation: in premodern societies caste organization appears to inhibit the realistic portrayal of individuals, while open systems of social stratification appear to readily allow if not actually promote such realism. Before offering an explanation for these differing consequences of the two opposed patterns of social stratification, let me note an important qualification. Whereas caste appears to be a *sufficient* condition to suppress realistic portraiture (in the premodern world), it is not alone in this. Although they were not explored here, other conditions—such as the Muslim ban on images—may also suppress realistic portraiture. It follows that although open stratification may be a *necessary* condition for the emergence of realistic portraiture, it is not in itself a sufficient condition.

By way of explaining the contrasting consequences of the two patterns of stratification, let me describe the larger clusters of ideological and cultural traits that, in literate premodern societies, tend to accompany those patterns. I list first the traits that accompany open stratification and refer in parentheses to the opposed tendencies that accompany closed stratification (i.e., caste). In the societies with open hierarchies the members, or the considerable bulk of them, are all culturally considered to be a single species of humanity (rather than a graded series of race-like castes); individualism is greater (as opposed to caste stereotyping); there is greater scope for humanistic secularism (as opposed to hypertrophied ritual and supernatural concerns); the scope for science is greater (versus lesser); there is more historical (rather than mythical) mindedness; there is more biography (rather than hagiography); and realistic portraiture (rather than iconography) may flourish. These contrasting patterns, as I have argued elsewhere (Brown 1988), emerge out of the stringent requirements of maintaining a hereditarily closed society as opposed to the tendencies or potentials allowed by conditions of social fluidity.[2]

While the traits in each of these clusters are interrelated in various ways, the most important connection with portraiture, I will argue, is with the contrasting conceptions of humanity or human nature. Barring differences of sex and age (and allowing that people might be different in other societies), human nature is fundamentally single or uniform in the case of the open societies, multiple in the caste-organized societies. The typical indigenous explanation or justification for the hereditary inequalities of caste is that the members of the different castes are innately, intrinsically different in character. Rather than the bulk or all of the members of the society sharing a common humanity they form a graded series of human types that are understood, in effect or literally, as different races or species with inherent stereotyped behaviors and capacities — with those on top being nearer to divinity. The character of each individual, thus, is a matter of which caste he (or she) was born into, and is essentially a given — not something uniquely acquired by each individual through the myriad effects of time, place, circumstance, accident, and effort. This inherited character is also usually thought to be externally manifest in physical features. In the European Middle Ages, for example, the caste-like order of nobles were conceived as tall, slender, and elegant while peasants were short, grotesque, even monstrous (Friedman 1981).

As near as can be told from modern studies of these racialist axioms of caste organization they are false or mythical, particularly in the sense that character is *not* determined by line of descent. Individuals of course do differ from one another, but not in the way and for the reasons that caste ideology posits. Accurate representations of individuals — whether written or visual — would expose the ideology as false. Maintenance of the caste ideology relies on representations of the myths, not of reality. Hence, in a caste-organized society one should expect iconography rather than realistic portraiture.

In the openly-stratified society the concern is not how to justify inherited and unchangeable inequalities but rather is to confront the problem of the social placement, fate, and effect of the individual where social inequalities are substantial but birth is not perceived as deciding who will be placed high and who low. Confronting this problem provides a rationale for keeping account of individual actions in concrete circumstances (history and biography), and thereby promotes a focus on the individuals who make history: who they were, what they did, and what they were like. This is the context in which realistic portraiture of particular individuals finds a rationale.

Recall now that I earlier cited Breckenridge's argument for a nexus between individualism, biography, and a materialist/ scientific philosophy, with the latter a necessary condition for the fullest flowering of portraiture. What I hope to have shown is not only that his argument is correct, but that it is part of a larger pattern that engages the basic structures of society (as Pasztory 2005 would argue). In a caste-organized society, realistic portraiture would be subversive, and hence is curtailed. In an openly-stratified society, realistic portraiture is not subversive, and is more likely to develop or even flourish.

REFERENCES

ASHMOLE, BERNARD. 1964. *The classical ideal in Greek sculpture.* Cincinnati, OH: University of Cincinnati.

BALDRY, H.C. 1965. *The unity of mankind in Greek thought.* Cambridge, MA: Cambridge University Press.

BARBER, BERNARD. 1968. Social mobility in hindu India. In *Social mobility in the caste system in India: An interdisciplinary symposium*, ed. James Silverberg, 18–35. The Hague: Mouton.

BASHAM, ARTHUR L. 1959. *The wonder that was India: A survey of the culture of the Indian sub-continent before the coming of the muslims.* New York: Grove Press.

BAWDEN, GARTH. 1996. *The Moche.* Cambridge, MA: Blackwell Publishers.

BECKER, MARVIN B. 1967. *The decline of the commune.* Vol. 1 of *Florence in transition.* Baltimore, MD: Johns Hopkins University Press.
—. 1968a. *Studies in the rise of the territorial state.* Vol. 2 of *Florence in transition.* Baltimore, MD: Johns Hopkins University Press.
—. 1968b. The Florentine territorial state and civic humanism in the early Renaissance. In *Florentine studies: Politics and society in Renaissance Florence*, ed. Nicolai Rubinstein, 109–39. Evanston, IL: Northwestern University Press.
—, and Gene A. Brucker. 1956. The *arti minori* in Florentine Politics, 1342–1378. *Medieval Studies* 18: 93–104.

BEN-AMOS, PAULA. 1995. *The art of Benin.* Washington, DC: Smithsonian Institution Press.

BERENSON, BERNARD. 1954. *The arch of Constantine: Or the decline of form.* New York: Macmillan Co.
—. 1967. *The Italian painters of the Renaissance.* London: Phaidon Press.

BLOCH, MARC. 1961. *Social classes and political organization.* Vol. II of *Feudal society.* Trans. L. A. Manyon, Chicago and London: The University of Chicago Press.

BORGATTI, JEAN, AND RICHARD BRILLIANT. 1990. *Likeness and beyond: Portraits from Africa and the world.* New York: The Center for African Art.

BOSL, KARL. 1978. Noble unfreedom. The rise of the ministeriales in Germany. In *The medieval nobility: Studies on the ruling classes of France and Germany from the sixth to the twelfth century*, ed. Timothy Reuter, 291–311. Amsterdam: North Holland Publishing Co.

BOUWSMA, WILLIAM J. 1968. *Venice and the defense of republican liberty: Renaissance values in the age of the Counter Reformation.* Berkeley: University of California Press.

BRADBURY, R. E. 1957. *The Benin kingdom and the Edo-speaking peoples of South-Western Nigeria.* London: International African Institute.

BRECKENRIDGE, JAMES D. 1968. *Likeness: A conceptual history of ancient portraiture.* Evanston, IL: Northwestern University Press.

BROWN, DONALD E. 1988. *Hierarchy, history, and human nature: The social origins of historical consciousness.* Tucson: The University of Arizona Press.

BROWN, HORATIO F. 1907. *Studies in the history of Venice*, vol. I. New York: E. P. Dutton and Co.

BROWN, PERCY. 1975. *Indian painting under the Mughals, A.D. 1550–A.D. 1750.* 1st ed. published 1924. New York: Hacker Art Books.

BROWN, PETER R. L. 1971. *The world of late Antiquity, AD 150–750.* London: Harcourt Brace Jovanovich.

BURCKHARDT, JACOB. 1954. *The civilization of the Renaissance in Italy.* Trans. S. G. C. Middlemore. New York: Random House. Originally published as *Die Cultur der Renaissance in Italien: ein Versuch* (Basel: Schweighauser, 1860).

CHAKRAVARTI, UMA. 1987. *The social dimension of early Buddhism.* Delhi: Oxford University Press.

CHEYETTE, FREDRIC L., ed. 1968. *Lordship and community in medieval Europe.* New York: Holt, Rinehart, and Winston.

CHRIMES, KATHLEEN M. T. 1942. *Ancient Sparta: A re-examination of the evidence.* Manchester: Manchester University Press.

COCHRANE, ERIC. 1981. *Historians and historiography in the Italian Renaissance.* Chicago and London: The University of Chicago Press.

COOMARASWAMY, ANANDA K. 1975. *Rajput painting: Being an account of the Hindu paintings of Rajasthan and the Punjab Himalayas from the sixteenth to the nineteenth century: Described in relation to contemporary thought.* 1st ed. published 1916. New York: Hacker Art Books.
—. 1931. Foreword to *Portrait sculpture in South India*, T. Aravamuthan, xi. London: India Society.

DAVIS, JAMES C. 1962. *The decline of the Venetian nobility as a ruling class.* Baltimore, MD: Johns Hopkins University Press.

DONNAN, CHRISTOPHER B. 1978. *Moche art of Peru: Pre-Columbian symbolic communication.* Los Angeles: Museum of Cultural History; University of California, Los Angeles.
—. 2004. *Moche portraits from ancient Peru.* Joe R. and Teresa Lozano Long Series in Latin American and Latino Art and Culture. Austin: University of Texas Press.

DREW, DAVID. 1999. *The lost chronicles of the Maya kings.* Berkeley: University of California Press.

DUBY, GEORGES. 1968. The nobility in eleventh- and twelfth-century Mâconnais. In *Lordship and community in medieval Europe*, ed. Fredric L. Cheyette, 137–55. New York: Holt, Rinehart, and Winston.

FINLEY, MOSES I. 1959. Was Greek civilization based on slave labor? *Historia* 8: 145–64.
—. 1962. *The world of Odysseus.* Rev. ed. Harmondsworth: Penguin Books.

FRANKFORT, HENRI. 1961. *Ancient Egyptian religion: An interpretation.* 1st ed. published 1948. New York: Harper and Brothers.

FRIEDMAN, JOHN BLOCK. 1981. *The monstrous races in medieval art and thought.* Cambridge, MA: Harvard University Press.

FU TIANCHOU, ed. 1989. *Wonders from the earth: The first emperors underground army.* Rev. ed. San Francisco: China Books and Periodicals, Inc.

GASCOIGNE, BAMBER. 2002. *The great Moguls: Indias most flamboyant rulers.* Rev. ed., 1st ed. published 1971. New York: Carroll & Graf Publishers.

GELZER, MATTHIAS. 1969. *The Roman nobility*. Trans. Robin
Seager. Oxford: Basil Blackwell. Originally published as *Die
Nobilität der Römischen Republik* (Leipzig, etc.: Teubner, 1912).

GENICOT, LÉOPOLD. 1968. The nobility in medieval Francia:
Continuity, break, or evolution? In *Lordship and community in
medieval Europe*, ed. Fredric L. Chyette, 128–36. New York: Holt,
Rinehart, and Winston.

HAMMOND, NICHOLAS D., AND HOWARD H. SCULLARD,
eds. 1970. *The Oxford classical dictionary*. 2nd ed. Oxford:
Clarendon Press.

HASKINS, CHARLES HOMER. 1966. *The Renaissance of the
twelfth century*. 1st ed. published 1927. Cleveland: World
Publishing Co.

HEARN, MAXWELL K. 1979. An ancient Chinese army rises from
underground sentinel duty. *Smithsonian* 10 (8): 38–51.

HILL, HERBERT. 1952. *The Roman middle class in the republican
period*. Oxford: Basil Blackwell.

HO, PING-TI. 1964. *The ladder of success in imperial China: Aspects
of social mobility, 1368–1911*. New York: John Wiley and Sons.

HOLMES, GEORGE. 1975. *Europe: Hierarchy and revolt, 1320–1450*.
Sussex: Harvester Press.

HOPKINS, KEITH. 1974. Elite mobility in the Roman empire. In
Studies in ancient society, ed. Moses I. Finley, 103–20. London:
Routledge and Kegan Paul.
—. 1978. *Conquerors and slaves*, Cambridge: Cambridge University
Press.

HUXLEY, GEORGE L. 1962. *Early Sparta*. Cambridge, MA:
Harvard University Press.

JONES, A. H. M. 1956. Slavery in the ancient world. *Economic History
Review* 9: 185–99.
—. 1967. *Sparta*. Cambridge, MA: Harvard University Press.

KRISTELLER, PAUL O. 1961. *Renaissance thought: The classic,
scholastic, and humanistic strains*. New York: Harper and Collins.

LANCMAN, ELI. 1966. *Chinese portraiture*. Rutland: Charles E.
Tuttle Co.

LOT, FERDINAND. 1961. *The end of the ancient world and the
beginnings of the Middle Ages*. 1st ed. published 1937. New York:
Harper and Row.

MACMULLEN, RAMSEY. 1974. *Roman social relations, 50 B.C. to
A.D. 284*. New Haven, CT: Yale University Press.

MARTIN, SIMON, AND NICOLAI GRUBE. 2000. *Chronicle of the
Maya kings and queens: Deciphering the dynasties of the ancient
Maya*. London: Thames and Hudson.

MARTINES, LAURO. 1979. *Power and imagination: City-states in
Renaissance Italy*. New York: Alfred A. Knopf.

MICHELL, HUMFREY. 1952. *Sparta*. Cambridge, MA: Cambridge
University Press.

MILLAIRE, JEAN-FRANÇOIS. 2002. *Moche burial patterns:
An investigation into prehispanic social structure*. Oxford:
Archaeopress.

MORI, HISHASHI. 1977. *Japanese portrait sculpture*. Trans. and
adapted by W. Chie Ishibashi. Tokyo, New York and San Francisco:
Kodansha International Ltd. and Shibundo.

MUNRO, DONALD J. 1969. *The concept of man in Early China*.
Stanford, CA: Stanford University Press.

MURRAY, ALEXANDER. 1978. *Reason and society in the Middle
Ages*. Oxford: Clarendon Press.

PASZTORY, ESTHER. 2005. *Thinking with things: Toward a new
vision of art*. Austin: University of Texas Press.

REUTER, TIMOTHY, ed. and trans. 1978. *The medieval nobility:
Studies on the ruling classes of France and Germany from the
sixth to the twelfth century*. Amsterdam, New York; Oxford: North
Holland Publishing Co.

ROWLAND, BENJAMIN. 1953. *The art and architecture of India*.
Baltimore: Penguin Books.

RUBINSTEIN, NICOLAI. 1968. Florentine constitutionalism and
Medici ascendancy in the fifteenth century. In *Florentine studies:
Politics and society in Renaissance Florence*, ed. by Nicolai
Rubinstein, 442–62. Evanston, IL: Northwestern University Press.

SCHELE, LINDA, AND DAVID FREIDEL. 1990. *A forest of kings:
The untold story of the ancient Maya*. New York: William Morrow.

SCHEVILL, FERDINAND. 1936. *History of Florence from the
founding of the city through the Renaissance*. New York: Harcourt
Brace and Co.

SCHLESINGER, WALTER. 1968. Lord and follower in Germanic
institutional history. In *Lordship and community in medieval
Europe*, ed. Fredric L. Chyette, 664–99. New York: Holt, Rinehart,
and Winston.

SHARMA, SRIPAD RAMA. 1940. *Mughal empire in India:
A systematic study including source material*. Rev. ed. Bombay:
Karnatak Publishing House.

SILVERBERG, JAMES, ed. 1968. *Social mobility in the caste system
in India: An interdisciplinary symposium*. The Hague: Mouton.

SOUYRI, PIERRE FRANÇOIS. 2001. *The world turned upside down:
Medieval Japanese society*. Trans. by Käthe Roth. New York:
Columbia University Press.

STARR, CHESTER G. 1968. *The awakening of the Greek historical
spirit*. New York: Alfred A. Knopf.

SYME, RONALD. 1958. *Tacitus*. 2 vols. Oxford: Clarendon Press.
—. 1979. *The Roman revolution*. Oxford: Oxford University Press.

TELLENBACH, GERD. 1978. From the Carolingian imperial nobility to the German estate of imperial princes. In *The medieval
nobility: Studies on the ruling classes of France and Germany from
the sixth to the twelfth century*, ed. by Timothy Reuter, 203–42.
Amsterdam, New York; Oxford: North Holland Publishing Co.

TREGGIARI, SUSAN. 1969. *Roman freedmen during the late Republic*. Oxford: Clarendon Press.

ULLMAN, WALTER. 1966a. *The individual and society in the Middle
Ages*. Baltimore, MD: Johns Hopkins University Press.
—. 1966b. *Principles of government and politics in the Middle Ages*.
New York: Barnes and Noble.

VON GRUNEBAUM, GUSTAVE E. 1961. *Medieval islam: A study in cultural orientation*. 2nd ed. Chicago and London: The University of Chicago Press

WEAVER, PAUL R.C. 1974. Social mobility in the early Roman empire: The evidence of the imperial freedmen and slaves. In *Studies in ancient society*, ed. by Moses I. Finley, 121–40. London: Routledge and Kegan Paul.

WESTERMANN, WILLIAM L. 1955. *The slave systems of Greek and Roman antiquity*. Memoirs of the American Philosophical Society 40. Philadelphia: American Philosophical Society.

WILKINSON, JAMES V.S. 1949. Introduction to *The Pitman gallery of oriental art: Mughal painting*, ed. by Basil Gray. New York: Pitman Publishing Corp.

WILSON, JOHN A. 1951. *The culture of ancient Egypt*. Chicago and London: The University of Chicago Press.

WISEMAN, T. PETER. 1971. *New men in the Roman senate, 139 B.C.–A.D. 14*. Oxford Classical and Philosophical Monographs. London: Oxford University Press.

ZHANG, WENLI. 1996. *The Qin terracotta army: Treasures of Lintong*. London: Scala Books and Cultural Relics Publishing House.

BEN-AMI SCHARFSTEIN

The Common Humanity Evident in European, African, Indian, Chinese, and Japanese Aesthetic Theory

I prefer what appears to me a common-sense universalism to the kinds of relativism most usually taught by symbolic anthropologists and by those who are called "postmodernists." Summarily, I believe that, for all their differences, human beings are much alike. This is because elementary sensations and perceptions, including at least some general aesthetic preferences, are roughly alike among human beings; because basic human emotions are in the beginning of all human lives much alike; and because different cultures invent similar modes of response for the most essential social purposes. In order not to appear simply prejudiced in favor of an

1
The present essay is taken, with deletions and other changes, from a chapter of my book *Art without Borders: A philosophical Exploration of Art and Humanity* (Scharfstein 2008). The text there is more detailed.
2
See Pinker 1997, 268–275. Pinker refers to Biederman 1995. For a different, more phenomenological account of visual construction, see Willats 1997.

outmoded traditionalism, given time and space enough, I would elaborate on the following points—all directly relevant to art and aesthetics—to which I only here and there append a bibliography to lend support to what is no more than a sketch, beginning with a brief reference to the brain.[1]

I contend the following:

1. The very ability of the brain to construct three-dimensional objects from the two-dimensional forms on the retina and to recognize these forms as the objects that in practice they are is a universal human ability, based on the nature of the visual system that human beings (and many other creatures) share.[2]

2. Whatever the cultural variations, humans all perceive, respond to, and make use of symmetry and balance, and of geometrical shapes such as the square, oblong, triangle, circle, oval, and spiral, which exemplify symmetry and balance and invite the effects that come from their reiteration or contrast, their motion or stillness, their complication, and their disturbance.

3. Whatever the cultural variations, humans all also perceive, respond to, and make use of rhythms, whether seen, heard, or felt. In rhythms, too, the effects of symmetry and balance, of motion and stillness, of contrast and sameness, are simplified or complicated, and disturbed and restored.

4. Whatever the cultural variations, humans all perceive, respond to, and make use of the shapes, widths, and other characteristics of lines and planes—their straightness, crookedness, sharpness, jaggedness, curvature, wandering, their relative and absolute size, and so on. Three-dimensional objects also evoke similar uses of and responses to their different kinds of bulk.

5. Whatever the cultural variations, humans universally perceive, respond to, and make use of the textures of things—their roughness, raggedness, prickliness, stickiness, wrinkling, smoothness, softness, hardness, and so on. Whatever the use or interpretation of these textures, they are perceived in much the same way and recall objects with similar textures and the experiences in which these textures played a part.

6. Whatever humans' cultural variations, the neurology of vision gives almost all of them the ability to see and react to different colors and color combinations. These responses include the differences between dark and light colors, especially black and white, between saturated and unsaturated colors, between colors that are graduated (as from light to dark) and ungraduated, between colors that are graded into other colors and into ungraded colors, and between colors that are complementary.

7. The constancy of color—its tendency to be perceived as the same in different light—is universal among humans.

8. In different cultures, the colors that are recognized by being given explicit names vary greatly, but they tend to be chosen from among a small basic group in a way that is explained by a (controversial) "evolutionary" scheme.[3]

9. The colors and color combinations that are favored vary in different cultural areas, but in ways that can be more or less systematically understood in relation to one another.[4]

10. Various emotional qualities are widely equated, though in different ways, with the various colors. What is universal is often not the relation between a particular emotion and a particular color but the felt closeness between color as such and emotion as such.[5]

11. Whatever the cultural variations, the development of art tends everywhere to oscillate between extremes of (relative) simplicity and complexity, seriousness and playfulness, realism and abstraction, literalness and symbolism, and tradition and individualism.

12. In average or "normal" persons anywhere, the sensory or perceptual responses I have called universal are only roughly the same—every individual senses somewhat differently from every other. These responses are conditioned by experience, especially early experience, when the brain is at its most plastic, but such conditioned experience is often the similar result of similar matur-ation. The personal associations that the responses accumulate, however different in detail, are often variants of the universal, primary responses.[6]

13. I have repeated the catchall phrase, "whatever the cultural variations," a number of times. It is here taken to imply that the responses based on the nature of human perception are subject to different uses and interpretations, but that these uses and interpretations are often similar. Their differences and similarities, so to speak, color one another, and the differences, I argue, are not simply random.

14. Whatever the cultural variation, the association of blue with the sky, of brown with the earth, of green with plants, and of red with fire and blood, seems unavoidable (though an anthropologist gives a counterexample from the lower Congo, where blood, she says, is not at all associated with red).[7] White can be an indication of purity and innocence, or of mourning, or of much else, but the diametrical opposition of black and white (as well as the obvious contrast of both with red) seems to be unavoidable and must at

3

For an account of the anthropological investigation of color terms, see Berlin and Kay 1969. Berlin and Kay's research led to a series of responses and researches that, as usual, multiplied questions and made clear, definitive answers hard to reach. See, e.g. Gage 1993, chaps. 2, 7; Gage 1995 is rather skeptical of Berlin and Kay (it is not clear to me what is meant by "the assimilation of white to black," the phrase attributed to the anthropologist R. E. MacLaury on p. 187 of Gage's article). Barnes 1987, 119–26, is highly skeptical of Berlin and Kay J. Lyons, who is relatively favorable, asks for more careful formulation of the hypothesis (1995, 201, 222). See also Lakoff 1987, 24–38. For an evolutionary hypothesis, see Shepard 1992. Hoffman 1998, chap 5, deals with the process of color perception.

4

Two general books on color: Lamb and Bourriau 1995; and Riley 1995. For the history of the use of color in Western painting, see: Gage 1993, thoroughgoing, though limited to European art. Gage 1999 contains wide-ranging essays. Pastoureau 2001 is the social history of the color blue in Europe.

5

On the Lüscher test and the emotional qualities attributed to colors, see the brief account in Gage 1995, 189–91.

6

For a sharp, well-informed criticism of most of the kind of universalizing tendencies I show here, see Needham 1981. For Africa in particular, see the essays in Lloyd and Gay 1981. The essays are under the general headings of "Perception," "Cognitive Development," and "Language."

7

See Jacobson-Wedding 1979. I owe this reference to Needham 1981, 47.

many times and places have stimulated a symbolic polar response for the same perceptual reasons.[8]

15. Whatever their cultural variations, the basic emotions are universally felt and are expressed everywhere in similar ways. Research shows this to be most likely true of fear, anger, sadness, disgust, happiness, and surprise, of their combinations, and of the varied wealth of their representations in art.[9]

16. It is nearly universally true that the human face and figure have been of primary importance in visual art—the Islamic tradition against representing humans in visual art has often been defied by the Muslims themselves. As art in many places has shown, there is a strong natural tendency to be attracted to young, symmetrical, unblemished faces, and to young, strong, graceful, symmetrical bodies.

17. Art everywhere serves as an instrument of memories. The memories it serves are the usual social ones, the celebrations, rituals, and memorials that are needed to establish social identity. It also endlessly serves the memories of individuals. These, for all their differences, tend to be of the same general kinds, that is, memories of one's family and friends, of the stages of one's life, of one's work, travels, adventures, and so on.

18. Whether or not the sensitivities and responses I have described are fully recognized as important to art—which may not be recognized as a separate interest or activity—they remain implicit in everything that we see or learn to see as art. They tend to exert their influence almost regardless of cultural differences and changes in fashion. The test of this statement cannot be made from literary evidence alone or traditional doctrines alone.

If the preceding contentions are more or less persuasive, it should not be surprising if there were a perceptual, emotional, and social overlap among cultures that would be reflected in an at least potential resemblance in their art, which would in turn be reflected in whatever implicit or explicit aesthetic doctrines were held in these cultures. These resemblances in aesthetic doctrines are the subject of the present essay. In the attempt that follows to compare the humanity common to the aesthetic theories of Europeans, of at least some Africans, and of Indians, Chinese, and Japanese, I have done my best not to force the evidence but to allow it to reveal itself by means of a description that is in principle objective, I mean, meant to be based on careful evidence, to be subject to indefinitely prolonged correction, and to have the ascertainable truth as its ideal. The feeling that keeps this ideal alive is compounded of hope, humility, pride, and a stubborn curiosity.

8
I quote from Pastoureau 2001, 7, 9, 10. On white, black and red in European antiquity, see Pastoureau 2001, 14–16 and the entry "colours, sacred" in Hornblower and Spawforth 1996, 366 (quoting E. Wunderlich, 1925). In some contradiction to the impression left by Pastoureau, who says that in Europe up to the twelfth century blue was an uncommon color (p. 13), who points out that the Greeks had no simple, unambivalent word for blue, and notes that Latin authors were indifferent or hostile to the color blue (p. 26), see Gage 1993, 11 (blue and yellow were often used in early Greek painting), 12 (for Aristotle, deep blue was one of the five unmixed intermediate colors), 14 (Lucian speaks of bright blue), 15 (Greek painters use blue and green), 16 (mosaics from Pompeii and Hercula-neum use vivid blues (also Pastoureau 2001, 30 [Latin had eight terms for blues], 30 [in painting, the Greeks used bright, satur-ated blues], and, 27–29).

It is said, however, that there are non-European languages in which "black is assimilated to white." Michel Pastoureau (2001) goes so far as to say, "Color is first and foremost a social phenomenon. There is no transcultural truth to color perception." He stresses the danger, especially to the art histor-ian, of anachronism. "For centuries," he says, "black and white were considered to be completely separate from the other colors; the spectrum with its nat-ural order or colors was unknown before the seventeenth century … and the contrast between warm and cool colors is a matter of convention and functions differently according to the period and society in question (in the Middle Ages, for example, blue was a warm color)." But while it is true that color symbolism has varied greatly, I am sure that Pastoureau goes too far and himself oversimplifies when he says, "human biology, and even nature are ultimately irrelevant to this process of ascribing meaning to color." A dif-ferent emphasis on the evidence, much of it literary, can leave a rather differ-ent impression.
9
But see Lutz 1988, 5, 8. The universalist attitude she objects to is exemplified by the research that I depend on, of Paul Ekman and his associates. See, e.g., Ekman 1982. See also the later sum-mary of his work in the introduction, afterward, and commentaries to his edition of Charles Darwin, *The Expres-sion of the Emotions in Man and Ani-mals* (Darwin 1998 [1872]). A few, among many, relevant books or articles (I omit books studying Chinese, Jap-anese, and Indian emotion or personal-ity): Fridlund and Duchaine 1996, 259–84; Heelas 1996, 171–99; Kleinman and Good 1985; Lakoff 1987; Lazarus 1991; Marks and Ames 1995. Lutz 1988 makes the claim, not uncommon now in

     World Art Studies IV Comparative Approaches

EUROPE: AESTHETICS WITH
NEOPLATONIC INCLINATIONS

I should have preferred to begin with a more adequate account of the European or Western aesthetic tradition. This is because this tradition is likely to be dominant in the reader's mind and to be both a conscious and unconscious standard of judgment. A rich tradition, it is filled with uncountable nuances and endless disagreements. But given the constraints of space, I will say little about this tradition, except that, until relatively recently, the dominant impulse has been the one that comes from Plato and Plotinus and can be called, for short, the Neoplatonic. In the case of Plato himself, I am referring to his belief, as I take it to be, that love for the beauties of the body reflects love for the beauties of the soul, and love for the beauties of the soul reflects the vision of superlative, everlasting beauty.[10] In the case of Plotinus, I am referring to his belief that the artist can grasp sublime archetypes, "the logoi from which nature derives." He therefore says, "Phidias did not make his Zeus from any model perceived by the senses; he understood what Zeus would look like if he wanted to make himself visible."[11]

Medieval aesthetics was always closely related to the Neoplatonic themes (Panofsky 1968, 36ff). During the Renaissance, the emphasis on anatomy and perspective did not change the primacy of Neoplatonic attitudes. It is true that Alberti, like other theorists of the early Renaissance, was not a transcendentalist, and he and others like him contented themselves with an emphasis on harmony, proportion, and the idealizing of merely human beauty (Panofsky 1968, 49–52, 58–59). But Marsilio Ficino, an influential Neoplatonist, defined beauty as a "victory of divine reason over matter" (Gombrich 1972, 172ff; Panofsky 1968, 53–54; Chastel 1959, 102ff). Neoplatonic theories like Ficino's became prominent in art theory from the second half of the sixteenth century. According to these theories, the artist is the person who gives nature a more than natural perfection (Panofsky 1968, 93–95). Michelangelo accepts Plotinus's view that the sculptor reveals the beauty already inherent in the stone (Panofsky 1968, 115–16). The earlier comparison of the artist with God is extended and allows the artist to pride himself (or, more rarely, herself) on some measure of godliness.

I cannot list the many later artists, writers, and musicians who have accepted or resisted the influence of Neoplatonism or its analogues.[12] The secularism induced by science was often tinged with nature mysticism. Beginning in the late nineteenth century, Neoplatonic ideas were varied and both reinforced and contradicted by those imported from India by Schopenhauer and others, while Buddhism, at first in its more simple forms and later in Zen or in the more florid, magical, forms of Buddhism, played its skeptical-believing role.[13] Physics stimulated the imaginations of the mystical-minded no less than the secular-minded. The creators themselves of twentieth-century physics, Einstein, Bohr, Schrödinger, and Dirac, expressed views either compatible with

anthropology, that "emotional meaning is fundamentally structured by particular cultural systems and particular social and material environments." Her fieldwork taught her, she says, that "emotional experience is not pre-cultural but *preeminently* cultural." To assume "that emotion is simply a biophysical event and that each emotion is universal and linked neatly to a facial expression (of which even careful and intentional masking leaves unmistakable cues)" is to refuse to see that emotion is "woven in complex ways into cultural meaning systems and social interaction...." Yes, but the study of the social complexity of emotional expression and its weaving into cultural meaning systems should not cause us to forget the common psychophysical basis. Diseases and the reactions to them are also woven into cultural meaning systems, but this is not good enough reason to neglect them as the objects of study by contemporary medicine. It is not insignificant that people born blind smile for the same reasons that sighted people do.

10

E.g., *Republic* 424, 596ff; *Laws* 656ff; as against the *Symposium*.

11

Plotinus 1953, 149 [Plotinus 5.8.1].

12

In addition to Panofky 1968, see, e.g., Abrams 1971, 27, 29, 31, 169. Mysticism in modern art: Besançon 2000 (chap. 8 is on Kandinsky and Malevich); Barasch 1998, 293–371; Tuchman 1986; Golding 2000 (on Mondrian, Malevich, Kandinsky, Pollock, Newman, Rothko, and Still).

13

Von Glasenapp, 1960; Schwab 1950; Schopenhauer e.g., Schopenhauer 1969 [1819], para. 34. Theosophists: Campbell 1980, 168–71.

14
Mysticism and European abstract painting: Besançon 2000 (from roughly Plato to Kandinsky and Malevich); Golding 2000 (on Mondrian, Malevich, Kandinsky, Pollock, Newman, Rothko, and Still); Harrison and Wood 1992 (a number of relevant texts); Moszynska 1990 (comprehensive, brief, general); Tuchman 1986 (from my standpoint, the fullest and most pertinent account). Individual Europeans: Kupka: Spate 1981, 88–89. Kandinsky: Washton Long 1980; Roethel 1979; Selz 1957, 223–24; but see also Kandinsky 1978, 270. Malevich: Andrea 1990; Fauchereau 1991. Mondrian: Bois 1990; Elgar 1968; Vallier 1967; Milner 1992.

mysticism or explicitly mystical: Einstein identified himself Spinozistically with the universe; Planck adopted a Kant-like thing-in-itself; Bohr favored contradictories in a way reminiscent of Kierkegaard; Schrödinger was an open Vedantist; and Dirac made a Neoplatonic equation of truth with beauty.

Mysticism certainly remained common among artists (Scharfstein 1973; Wilbur 1984). The German Expressionists often voiced mystical opinions, and so, in their distinctive vocabularies, did the Surrealists (see e.g., Vogt 1980, 6–7). Of the pioneering abstract artists, Kupka was mystical in the name of Orphism, Malevich in that of Suprematism, Kandinsky in that at first of the Blue Rider, Mondrian in that of De Stijl or Neoplasticism, Ozenfant and Jeanneret in the name of Purism, and so on.[14] Kandinsky, like some religious Russians, and like Rosicrucians and Theosophists, all of whom influenced him, believed that humankind, about to awaken from the nightmare of materialism, was approaching a utopian era. In a letter he even suggested that brush and canvas could be given up and paintings created by spiritual irradiation alone (Roethel 1979, 18). Mondrian "accepted the Theosophical [essentially Neoplatonic] notion of matter as a denser variant of the spirit." According to him, we gradually "leave material forms behind" and "the representation of matter becomes redundant" (Ringbom 1986, 146; see also Blotkamp 1986). He says that "Plastic art discloses what science has discovered: *that time and subjective vision veil the true reality*" (Mondrian 1945, 14–15).

Many more recent artists have held mystical or semimystical statements. Among the members of the New York School, at least Reinhardt, Pollock, Rothko, Still, and Newman, had mystical inclinations. Newman wanted to dig into metaphysical secrets and by means of symbols "catch the basic truth of life … to wrest truth from the void" (Tuchman 1986, 49; quoted from Hess 1971).

In such an abbreviated account, I have been able to preserve almost nothing of the local color of European aesthetics. This account should be corrected by recalling the secular thought I have neglected, too often supported by brutal governments. My general conclusion is that the thought of European aestheticians and artists has been strongly tinged with mysticism, and when it has attempted to go deep, has become the more mystical.

AFRICA: AN AESTHETICS OF "GOODNESS" AND "CLARITY"

I feel that it is unprofitable to make untested generalizations on so-called "primitives" and therefore restrict myself to indigenous black Africans. Even this restriction does not help much because these peoples are so varied and because there are too few detailed descriptions of their aesthetic thought. However, instead of giving up Africa, I have chosen a brief but interesting description, in which a serious attempt is made to understand the nature of art through the eyes of the particular people involved. I add some general, if conjectural, reflections on the aesthetics of Black Africa.

The African example I have chosen is that described in a recent museum catalogue on the art of the Bamana, who live in Mali (their earlier name, Bambara, has been discarded by anthropologists).[15] Although the Bamana have by now mostly accepted Islam, they retain non-Muslim beliefs and rituals that relate to farming, fishing, hunting, the working of iron, and so on. They believe, as do the nearby Dogon, that everything has a dangerous energy they call *nyama*. In initiation rites, they are taught how to control it in order to further the cultivation of crops, healing of the sick, working of iron, and other essential activities (Colleyn 2001, 122).

Nyama is commanded especially by blacksmiths, who are also healers, circumcisers, and sorcerers. In spite of their professional classification, some blacksmiths specialize in wood sculpture, while the women are potters. Each of the stages of the blacksmiths' work — the finding and extracting of the iron ore, the making of the coke for the fire, the bringing of the ore and coke to the furnace, and the smelting and extraction of the iron — require ritual gestures or sacrifices to ensure that the work goes well. During the collective rite for the trimming of the iron, there are blacksmiths who demonstrate the occult knowledge by which what is "hot" is mastered (Brink 2001, 240; Malé 2001, 156 quoted: see also Frank 2001).

To allow Bamana aesthetics to keep something of its character, I use the admittedly inadequate translations of six of its terms: goodness (*nyumaya*), clarity (*jaya*), way (*cogo*), tastiness or pleasure (*jakaya*), embellishment (*jako*), and identity (*ja*) — more literally, "double," shadow, or mirror reflection. When applied to the arts, the first term, "goodness," designates the qualities that give the arts' forms an identifiable, suitable shape. The "goodness" of the arts' forms is their retention of the cultural identity that has been given them by past generations, this "goodness" having been arrived at or condensed, "dried down," by generations of experiment. Such "goodness" rests on the "clarity" of understanding granted by these generations' accumulated wisdom. Every aesthetic act has a particular "way," the set of instructions for its pattern, appearance, or performance.[16]

So much for "goodness," with its attendant "clarity" and "way." But "goodness" is not enough, because the power or *nyama* of the arts gives them a complementary "tastiness," a term that refers to the qualities that in some way challenge the recognized, traditional forms so as to arouse imagination or stimulate involvement. To arouse, art needs "embellishment," which — unlike "clarity," which "cools" — "heats up" forms. When yielded to without restraint, this power is able to drive the individual back into the primal wildness of the bush. In music and dance, for example, fast tempos help performers to heat performances and stimulate them to improvise.

To link art with tradition and yet recreate it for the commu-

15
The Bamana: Colleyn 2001, 36; Visonà 2000. For a summary (following the Griaule school) of Bamana (still called Bambara) mythology, see Dieterlin 1993a, 1993b, 1993c, 199d. The name Bamana (or Bambara) is more nearly regional than ethnic and has had had shifting connotations, but it marks out the peoples who were relatively resistant to Islam. The name "Bambara," which was applied by Muslims to those "who refuse to pray," was adopted by French administrators, while "Bamana" is what the people call themselves. Confusingly, the first language of Mali is now officially called "Bambara," which is also the official name of the inhabitants of central-south Mali.

16
Brink 2001, 240. In the parentheses I have substituted English for the Bamana words for "dance-step," "musical rhythm," etc.

nity, performers "heat" a form and do their best to lend it the grace of the virtuosity or "suppleness" that renews its energy while retaining the essentials of its form (Brink 2001, 240). Effective performances give those who attend them a sense of their unity as a social group. What mediates between this social group, which is external to the individual, and the individual person's soul is the person's "identity," the "shadow" or reflection of the person's character and intelligence that reveals itself in art. "Art is said to express the person's *ja*, and thus provide access to the creator's identity" (Brink 2001, 239–40).

One safe generalization on black Africa is that its art is intended to ensure fertility, the germination of seeds and the multiplication of animals and human beings (Brink 2001, 62). So African art is intended to help with the process of birth, growth, death, and birth again, which in African eyes constitutes an endless and always precariously balanced process that requires both supplications to and manipulations of the natural powers that be. This ritual art, an art of performance, demands the reciprocity of all the persons involved: performers and audience give one another the encouragement they need in order to invent human responses and to participate in their invention (e.g., Huet 1978; Thompson 1974). The reciprocity is also one between human beings and the capricious forces that inhabit and surround them (Zahan 1979, 1, 154, 156). These forces are caught, invigorated, deployed, and absorbed by the art, that is, the sounding of its music, the symbolism of its masks, the gestures of its dancers, its incantations, and its old, powerful stories. African art is the style in which the powers are mingled and balanced and the visible and invisible are encouraged to enter into a more empathic, life-giving intimacy. Everywhere there are rules for the proper making and use of the ritual objects. The objects' attractive appearance—that of the beauty of beautiful women apart—follows from the care with which they are made and their appropriateness for their roles; but the inevitably spontaneous variations introduced by the impresarios, sculptors, costume makers, and actors, are necessary for the vitality and efficacy of the performance in which they appear. Regardless of the exceptions, most of this art, with all its artfulness, has a magical aim.

Although it is true that African art is highly varied, if we are to accept the view of the expert, Susan Vogel, recent studies of African art lead us back toward the generalizing attitudes of an earlier generation of scholars, so that "the greatest interest of a tightly focused art study … may be precisely in how much light is shed on the place of art in other, distant cultures (Vogel 1997, 288, 292).

INDIA: THE DEPERSONALIZATION OF EMOTIONS

Although each kind of Indian craft-manual invokes its particular patron god, the manuals are mostly compressed, matter-of-fact directions that venture very little, if at all, into philosophical justification.[17] Aesthetically, the craftsmen were nourished by the old Indian feeling that the energy of the universe is a breathing, *prana,* evident in any instance of motion, change, transmutation, or life (Ray 1974, 177). This feeling appears in the inherent energy of early Indian sculpture and the remnants of its early paintings. The figures, flexible, rhythmic, round-limbed, and sensuous, are often set among twining creepers and touch or lean on trees, as if to take in their own life from the trees' life, from the ground. They all express the fertility of nature, the sculptured forms of which include invitingly beautiful women, amorous couples, copulating couples, and phallus-shaped gods. No doubt, the figures are generally fixed in the attitudes of Indian dance because they reflect danced ceremonial. This relation of visual art to dance and therefore to music is the subject of an old text, which connects them in the following way: one cannot discern the characteristics of images without knowing the rules of *chitra,* that is, sculpture and painting; it is hard to understand the rules of painting without knowing the art of dancing; the practice of dancing is hard to understand for anyone who is not acquainted with music; and without music dancing cannot exist at all. Therefore, "He who knows the art of singing is the best of men and knows everything" (Ray 1974, 266–67 [*Vishnu-dharmmottaram* 3.2.1–9]). This conception of the essential oneness of the arts is consonant with the Indian view that everything expresses the ultimate reality, *brahman* or perhaps the ultimate reality conceived as the god Shiva (Warder 1972, 32–33).

Usually, the hierarchy of the arts is headed not by music, but by drama, regarded as a form of poetry. The scripture, so to speak, of Indian dramaturgy and dance, Bharata's Natya Śhastra (second [some say fourth] century CE) says that the god Brahma, in trying to placate some disaffected demons, created the dramatic art in order to delight and edify gods and humans (and presumably demons) by including within itself all knowledge, every craft, learning, art, practical skill, and activity. Indian drama is, in fact, an art of arts that exert a strong mutual influence on one another. Instrumental music is as essential to a drama's beauty, says Bharata, as color is to that of a drawing. The pattern of its drumbeats is essential to its rhythm and tempo, and singing is essential to its text and the dance and mime to its action.

Every drama has a predominant emotion. The emotions are categorized by Bharata into eight basic emotions paired with eight aesthetic emotions, the latter called *rasas,* flavors. The pairs of emotions may be translated, with the basic of each pair first: love/the erotic, laughter/the comic, sorrow/the compassionate, anger/the furious, energy/the heroic, disgust/the odious, and wonder/the

17
Ancient Indian Aesthetics: Background: Banerjea 1974 [1956]; Desai 1975; Gonda 1975, 65–73; Masselos, Mrnzies and Pasl 1997; Rowell 1992; Ray 1974; Sivaramamurti 1978, 1977. Poetics: De 1963, 1977; Vidyakara 1965; Dhvanaloka 1990; Masson and Patwardhan 1969; Pandey 1950; Ramanujan and Gerow 1974; Warder 1972. Iconography and Canons: Bhattacharyya 1963; Bose 1928.

18
I take these translations of the terms
from Rowell 1992, 329.

19
Warder 1972, 33, cites ancient discussions of music and paintings in relation
to *rasas*.

wondrous.[18] (These invite comparison with the European theory of "affections," including anger, excitement, grandeur, heroism, contemplation, and mystical exaltation, which Baroque musicians and musical theorists took to express their aims, see e.g., Bukofzer 1947, 388–90.)

Each *rasa* predominates in a given poem or play—or, in principle, in a given musical composition, dance, painting, or sculpture.[19] The causes that arouse and the effects that follow from the basic emotions conjoin with those of other, transitory emotions and give rise to a state in which a basic emotion gives pleasure, which is to say, it is relished as an aesthetic emotion, a *rasa*. Although depending for its existence on its basic counterpart, the aesthetic emotion is isolated from the circumstances of real life and therefore from the direct influence of biological and psychological impulses. For this reason, it may be said to be depersonalized or delocalized, or, to put it in positive terms, to be universalized. To the extent that this is so, the whole state of mind of the reader of a poem or spectator of a play has been depersonalized, delocalized, or universalized. A play or poem (or piece of music, picture, or statue) is therefore an autonomous creation, to be appreciated in a timeless, impersonal spirit to which truth and falsity, the criteria of ordinary life, are irrelevant (Masson and Patwardhan 1969, 9).

Each of the character types—the amorous and heroic are the most important—has its typical color (blue/black for the amorous, yellow for the heroic), ornaments, and gestures or poses—thirteen gestures for the head, thirty-six for the eyes, nine for the neck, thirty-seven for the hand, and ten for the body, and so on.

As Bharata points out, the muteness and stillness of a painting or sculpture make them artistically inferior to the full, dynamic expressiveness of a drama (Warder 1972, 16, 32–33, 74; Rowell 1992, 96–98, 112). He reports that Brahma promised that a dramatic representation of the world would embolden the weak, energize the strong, enlighten the ignorant, teach the miserable fortitude and the agitated firmness, and show the materially minded how gains are made. An attuned spectator will relish the drama just as a gastronome relishes an artistically prepared and embellished feast (Embree 1988, 266–68 [*Natya Śastra* 1.113–14, 104–8, and 6.31–32]). As for painting and sculpture, their part in drama, according to the Natya Śhastra, is to decorate the theater and create a suitable general atmosphere for the plays.

With the Natya Śhastra as its main basis, esthetics of a more articulated, philosophical kind began to develop in India about the fourth or fifth century CE. It was a poetics of emotive—not didactic or philosophical—poetry, *kavya,* which ranges from brief lyrics to extensive court epics and dramas, the dramas regarded, one might say, as "spectacle-poems." This poetry was mostly in Sanskrit, by then a mother tongue to only few, but, for the educated, a second, literary language. This language has an extraordinarily large vocabulary and commensurate resources for what the aestheticians called "ornaments," forms of word-play, from figures of speech and kinds of alliteration to puns, similes and metaphors, ambiguities, palindromes. and whatever else linguistic ingenuity could invent and categorize (De 1963, 1977; Vidyakara 1965, 72ff; Pandey 1950; Ramanujan and Gerow 1974).

The often proud writers of this poetry, an occasional woman among them, ado not appear to have felt any special identification with the craftsmen who made stone or metal images (Anandavardhana 1974, xxix; Warder 1972, 118). Yet the orbit of their aesthetics extends, as I have been emphasizing, to all the Indian arts. This is not simply because of the claim that drama occupies the highest position in the hierarchy of the arts. It is, rather, because their conception is the fullest aesthetic expression of the point-of-view of those who dominated all art (except, I suppose, folk art). The poets were court poets writing competitively in the same literary language. Their patrons, like those of painters, sculptors, and architects, were aristocrats and rulers, who might themselves practice one or more of the arts. As a result, there developed a whole aesthetically sensitive culture, much of it based on the two great Indian epics, rather as Greek culture was based on the two great Greek epics. Therefore the themes of painting, sculpture, poetry, and drama drew on the same narrative sources and imagery, and the same general aesthetic principles applied to it. Apart from the cut-and-dried manuals, by nature limited in their vision, the best developed keys to the understanding of the visual arts of India are those found in its literature, because everything in every art is part of a story with a poetic resonance. The attitudes, figures, jewelry, moon-shaded brows, languor, hope, suffering, and extraordinary voluptuousness of the heroines of poetry and drama are those that appear in the sculptures of the time, even on temples, as they presumably appeared in now lost paintings (Desai 1975, 177–82, 184, 187, 195). Ancient Indian sculptures are (at least often) embodiments of literary descriptions, or are the equivalents of word-play, visual puns resembling verbal ones. An example I have read of is a sculptural combination of an elephant and a bull, the trunk and tusks of the elephant forming the bull's hump and horns and the snout of the bull forming the temples of the elephant; another example, related to "wonder," is the Ganges appearing in a sculpture as both as a river and a person.[20]

To return to the development of Indian aesthetics, it was a great step forward when the idea of aesthetic emotion, *rasa*, was connected with the power of suggestion, *dhvani,* that reveals what is above and beyond literal meaning.[21] Its most notable theorist was the Kashmiri named Anandavardhana—Ananda for short— who lived in the ninth century CE.[22] He connects aesthetic emotion with suggestion by distinguishing between three levels of the meaning of words and sentences: the primary or literal meaning, the secondary or contextual meaning, and the tertiary or suggestive meaning. Given suggestion, even the oldest, most familiar

[20]
See Sivaramamurti 1977, 131–32, 134, 135, and elsewhere. Both examples, with associated illustrations, are on p. 132.

[21]
Anandavardhana and Abhinavagupta: Gnoli 1956, 55, 87–96; Vidyakara 1956, 13ff; Anandavadhana 1990; Masson and Patwardhan 1969, 50–55; Pandey 1950, 21; Ray 1974, 31ff.

[22]
In Indian-style, Anandavardhana's *Light on [the Doctrine of] Suggestion* consists of verses, meant to be memorized, and a prose commentary on them, which some modern scholars believe is by another, anonymous author. Because there are no marked discrepancies between verses and commentary, I do not distinguish between their different possible authors.

language, he says, acquires fresh color and elicits an aesthetic reaction in those who have been sensitized by nature and by the study and practice of poetry (Vidyyakara 1965, 5–6; Anandavardhana 1990, 45, 679–89 [*Dhvanyaloka* 4.2]).

Ananda remains faithful to the view, which he attributes to "wise men," that suggestion, *dhvani*, is the soul or essence of poetry, the word that "lights up a beauty" impossible to any literal or merely decorative expression (Anandavardhana 1990, 47–48, 243 [*Dhvanyaloka* 1.1, 1.1.5]). "Anything," he says, "is beautiful if a person's mind rises at it, realizing that something special has suddenly flashed before him" (Anandavardhana 1990, 721 [*Dhvabyaloka* 4.16]). He holds that esthetic emotion, *rasa*, is the essence of suggestion, and suggestion the essence of poetry, or, in reverse, that poetry is based on suggestion and suggestion on aesthetic emotion (Anandavardhana 1974, xxxi).

After Anadavardhana, the most distinguished aesthetician was the great tenth-century Kashmiri philosopher Abhinavagupta (Abhinava for short), who "alone turned poetics into a science."[23] I concentrate on what I take is for him the main point, the ability of poetic technique and knowledge to achieve the universal. It is universalization that distinguishes aesthetic from ordinary experience. The ordinary experience of people is saturated with the pain of illness, the tiredness of long journeys, the death of relatives, and the weakness caused by ascetic practices. Drama, by the pleasure it gives, can neutralize these negative emotions, calm the sad, distract the ill, and give the weary happiness. And it teaches its spectators the ways of the world and so makes them happy and gives them the wisdom to grow (Gnoli 1956, 87–90; Masson and Pawardhan 1969, 56–57; Pandey 1950, 144).

Drama and, with it, poetry (and, in principle, music, the dance, painting, poetry, sculpture, and no doubt architecture) have this effect because the experiences they yield are deeply different from those in ordinary life that they resemble. The sights one sees and sounds one hears in drama and poetry lead to a strange longing that comes from memories that are not fully conscious and are too vague to have an identifiable object. These memories are latent impressions of pleasure or pain, the residues of experiences of an earlier life. For example: in a drama, a character's grief—marked by conventional signs of grief, expressed in metrical, poetically grieving words, and surrounded by the reality-neutralizing decor of a theater—arouses the spectator's own latent memories of grief. This grief by empathic revival of old, vague grief-memories is not grief itself but, by the melting together of all one's thoughts, the taste or *rasa* of compassion. Purified of all direct pain, it is superior to the emotion it is related to (Anandavardhana 1990, 114–16; Masson and Patwardhan 1969, 46–47, 57–58). Like any aesthetic emotion or *rasa*, it cannot be directly perceived because an aesthetic experience, that is, a *rasa*-experience (*rasapratiti*), is possible only when the stimuli that arouse it have been generalized or universalized. The clarity, softness, and vigor of the *rasa*-stimulating words are such that the experience they convey is transcendental (Masson and Patwardhan 1969, 65–67, 70). Summing all this up in a metaphor, Abhinava says that aesthetic experience "opens like a flower born of magic," without any relation with anything in time or space, or relation with the practical life that precedes and follows it (Gnoli 1956, xxii).

24
On Abhinavas's philosophy, see
Pandey 1963, 293ff.

Aesthetic detachment is possible because our response in art, basically our identification with the hero of the drama, is sympathetic rather than selfish. Our identification fails to become aesthetic if it is too personal, in a modern term, too narcissistic, or if it is too concentrated within the individual self. By this aesthetics, art requires one to be as much out of oneself as in oneself and as much in as out, and, for this reason, it requires nothing less than inspiration, poetic genius (*pratibha*), "which has its seat in the poet's heart, and which is eternally in creative motion" (Masson and Patwardhan 1969, 12). So great is the true poet's accomplishment, says Abhinava, that he can be compared to the God whose will creates the world. "In the shoreless world of poetry," he says, "the poet is the unique creator. Everything becomes transformed into the way he envisions it" (Anandavardhana 1990, 120–21; Masson and Patwardhan 1969, 12, 18–19). By means of the poet's genius, the pleasure of the spectator or reader grows so great, so far beyond that of ordinary experience, that the ego is temporarily transcended and the person enters into the unique state of emotion, the higher, undifferentiated pleasure of the peace in which all sensual desire dies, the *rasa* of peace, *shantarasa* (*śantarasa*). The sensitive spectator of a drama, like the mystic, forgets the self, forgets material gain, transcends the subject-object difference, is unconscious of space and time, and at the height of aesthetic experience attains the goal of peace. This verges on and draws toward mystical experience. This is because in aesthetic tranquility we come into contact with the memory of the primeval unity of man and universe, that is, with the primeval spontaneous expression of overflowing bliss that is the creative source of the universe (Anandavardhana 1990, 520–26; Masson and Patwardhan 1969, vii–viii, 130–59; Pandey 1950, 196–206).

Although profoundly mystical, Abhinava accepts the world and the pleasures that humans find in it as real and not, as most often among Vedantic philosophers, as unreal.[24] To him, a follower of Shiva (Śiva), the world is the manifestation of the pure self or supreme consciousness, or, as I would put it, objective subjectivity, that contains but transcends all differences. Like Ananda, he sees the Mahabharata not only as a vast scripture filled with moral examples but also as a profoundly moving work of literature. As an expert in Tantric ritual and a lover of literary drama, it is easy for him to compare human life with a drama or compare the poet with Shiva, who out of purposeless, spontaneous ecstasy, dances world creation, destruction, incarnation, and salvation, although the poet

25
Chinese Aesthetics: Acker 1979, xx-
vii–xxviii; Shou Kwan Lui 1971, 144;
Ching Hao 1974, 3, 20–21, 24–25. See
also Sirén 1936 (sometimes misleading)
and especially Bush 1971; Bush and
Hsio-yen Shih 1985; Lin Yutang 1967
(knowledgeable but very free).

is to create the full semblance of salvation (Masson and Patwardhan 1969, x–xiii, 51–52).

Despite the contentiousness of Indian aestheticians, there is no doubt of the commanding stature and lasting effect of Abhinava on Indian aesthetic thought. The extent of his influence in India is like that I have attributed to Plato and Plotinus in the West.

The Indian philosophy of art and the performing tradition to which it was related remained creative until about the eleventh or twelfth century, when then they were interrupted by invasion. Remarkably, the influence of the old aesthetics became prominent again in the Hindu, that is, Rajput, miniatures of the eighteenth century. These miniatures, the pictorial expressions of a revival of Hinduism, are different in style from the miniatures painted for the Muslim (Mughal) rulers of India. In the Rajput miniatures, there is little if any of the Mughal three-dimensionality or of the hard, realistic Mughal portraiture. In their space, things fit togeth-er metaphorically and emotionally rather than realistically. The themes of the miniatures are likely to be based on the old Indian mythology and poetry. Sometimes a whole series of miniatures is composed of faithful illustrations of the old Sanskrit poetry. The best example of which I know is a series of well composed, mostly brightly colored miniatures that illustrate the famous love story of King Nala and the superlative woman Damayanti (Goswamy 1975; Beach 1992, 174–210). The illustrations are not to the ori-ginal, Mahabharata version of the story, but to that of the twelfth-century court-poet and philosopher Śri Harsha, who elaborates it in the longest, most difficult, most "ornate," pun-filled, purposely ambiguous, wandering, mannered, and perhaps best of the "great" or epic *kavyas,* the *Naisasdhacarita.* One set of these illustrations consists only of drawings to which no color has yet been applied. On the drawings, there are written instructions to the artist that insist on faithfulness to details mentioned in Harsha's poem but left out of the sketch (Beach 1992, 31). The learned person or persons who made these corrections were able to understand the difficult text and able, it may be assumed, of grasping its stylistic expedients, an exhaustive exhibition of the effects taught by the *kayva* aestheticians.

CHINA: THE REVERBERATION OF THE LIFE-BREATH

To approach Chinese aesthetic thought in its own terms, begin with the all-important concept of *ch'i* (*qi*).[25] Considered to be the uni-versal energy, it is present everywhere in different concentrations. Its early meanings include "vapor," "breath," "exhalation," and "life-spirit." *Ch'i* is not at all abstract because, among other things, it is the very air we breathe The source of our life, it increases as we swell in anger, diminishes as we shrink in old age, and disperses as we die. As a concept, it plays an important role in the theory of every Chinese art. In literature, it is the rhythmic force that impels, changes speed, connects, and gives a literary composition its unity (Pollard 1978, 64–65). Elusive though it is, it can be captured if one shares the tension-creating twists and turns by which words are related to one another. A literary composition is considered, as by Herder and other Europeans, to resemble a living organism, and as perhaps literally alive.

For calligraphy and painting, the concept of *ch'i* is most used in combination with *yün*, meaning "reverberation" or "resonance." *Ch'i-yün* (*qi-yun*) is therefore often translated "reverberation of the life-breath." In the first of the famous canons of Chinese art, enunciated by Hsieh Ho (Xie Ho) in the late fifth century CE, this phrase is coupled with another, *sheng-tung* (*sheng-dong*).[26] Its translations are of two kinds. Leaving aside relatively unimportant variations, if one takes the whole to be made up of two parallel phrases, its translation is "the reverberation of life-breath, that is, the creation of movement"; but if one takes the second phrase to qualify the first, the translation is "the reverberation of the life-breath creates life-movement."

It seems that in the early development of Chinese art theory, *ch'i-yün* was used to mean the life-force of the objects that were depicted, which is the force that the painter aimed to capture. The force might be supposed quite real. A fourteenth-century critic believes that success in infusing it into a painting ensures, for instance, that "a painted cat hung on a wall may stop the rats" and a painted "venerable sage or war-god can be prayed to and its voice will answer."[27] As the term widened its meaning, it took on cosmic and moral overtones and came to express the creative force of the universe, in which everything takes part (esp. Acker 1979; Lui 1971). The presence of *ch'i* in a work of art was then equivalent to the presence in it of the vital spirit of the universe, the *tao* (Ching 1974, 20–21, note 13, 225, note 21).

Based on this idea of the unifying vital spirit, Chinese aesthetics tended to specify its subprinciples as polar opposites. Tung Ch'i-ch'ang (1555–1636) emphasizes such compositional principles as "opening and closing" or "open-join" (*k'ai-ho*), "void and solidity" (*hsü-shih*)(*xu-shi*), and "frontality and reverse" (*hsiang-pei*) (*xiang-bei*) (Fong 1962, 171). Ideas like these, clarifications or expansions of earlier ones, continued to be elaborated. For example, to bring out the omnipresent activity called *kai-ho,* which is *chi* as the rhythmically differentiated expansion and contraction of everything within everything, the eighteenth-century critic Shen Tsung-ch'ien (Shen Zong-jian) writes the following:

> From the revolution of the world to our own breathing there
> is nothing that is not k'ai-ho. If one can understand this, then
> we can discuss how to bring the painting to a conclusion.
> If you analyze a large k'ai ho, within it there is more k'ai-ho.
> Even down to one tree and one rock, there is nothing that

26
Acker 1979, 4. Acker gives a carefully explanation of the terms of the canon on pp. xxi–xliii.
27
From Yang Wei-chen, *Precious Mirror for Examining Painting,* completed in 1365; as quoted in Bush and Hsio-yen Shih 1985, 246.

28
In a fuller account it would be necessary to comment on the extraordinarily developed technical terminology of the Chinese criticism of art, which makes it possible to give stylistic descriptions of Chinese paintings an exactness hard to attain in Western criticism. Take for example the sheer number of brushstrokes known as *tsun*, which as a noun is often given the unilluminating translation "wrinkles." *Tsun* are used to shade, model, or give texture to paintings, especially of trees, rocks, mountains, and terrain in general. There are about twenty-five varieties of *tsun*, divided into three main groups. The similes that follow do not of course give an adequate idea of the *tsun*'s formal resemblances and differences. The *tsun* of the first group are compared to differently related hemp fibers and to brushwood, lotus-leaf veins, raveled rope, clouds, cattle hair, torn nets, lumps of alum, whirlpool eddies, and devil's-face wrinkles. Those of the second group are compared with the halves of a split bean, raindrops, and thorns. Those of the third group are compared to small or large axe-cuts, axe splits, severed bands, severed bands dragged in mud, nails pulled up from mud, horses' teeth, and stiff iron wires. For details see March 1935.

does not have both expanding and winding up. Where things grow and expand that is k'ai, where things are gathered up, that is ho … In using brush and in laying out the composition, there is not one moment when you can depart from k'ai-ho (Rowley 1947, 48).

As this passage shows, in China, too, the work of art is regarded as an organism the parts of which have an always changing, always self-restoring balance with one another. Always there is the sense of forces that give life by their harmonized opposition within and between the parts and parts of parts that make up the whole. Always there are expansion and contraction, the alternation of dense and rare, of closed and open, of excessiveness restrained and want supplied, and, if one sees sharply enough, of individual and universe containing and contained within one another.[28]

To end this series of references to Chinese aesthetic principles, I should like to cite the seventeenth-century critic Wang Fu-chih (Wang Fu-zhi), who does not believe in the impossible effort to hold everything poetic under conscious control (Wong 1978, 148–50). Poetry, he insists, is more concerned with life than with literature as such because it is a continuation of the processes of the universe as human consciousness interacts with it, so that poetry helps to recreate the human-universal bond that too many persons have broken.

Wang is surely referring to two doctrines of the Neo-Confucians: the one that the human mind and nature are identical, and the other that the virtue of "humanity" should be widened to fit this identity. In a famous essay of 1527, the Neo-Confucian philosopher Wang Yang-ming wrote, in a traditional but newly elaborated vein, that when a person sees a child about to fall into a well, he cannot avoid alarm and sympathy; and much the same happens when he hears and sees birds and beasts about to be slaughtered; and he cannot help feeling pity when he sees plants broken and destroyed. Evidently, the same humanity that joins him with the child joins him with the birds, beasts, and plants. True, even plants are living things and so they are open to fellow-feeling, but the shattering of tiles and a stone also gives him a feeling of regret, which shows that his humanity unites him with tiles and stones as well. "This means that even the heart of the small (unlearned) man must have this humanity which unites him (potentially) to all things" (Ching 1976, 127). And so, transcending itself, the human heart becomes one with anything and everything, and thereby shows itself to be essentially its innate consciousness of the good (*liang-chih*) (*liang-zhi*) that is the very force of goodness that unites the cosmos—in Neo-Confucianism, as in Neoplatonism, oneness and goodness are identical (Ching 1976, 142–44).

JAPAN: TEMPERING BEAUTY WITH REGRET

Having said what I have about traditional Chinese art theory, I feel it necessary to add some words on Japanese aesthetics.[29] As elsewhere, I abbreviate severely. I also limit myself to classical or "medieval" Japanese aesthetics.[30] The Japanese emphasis on sensitivity to nuances of feeling and expression was characteristic, to begin with, of small, sophisticated groups of aristocrats. Proud of their aesthetic refinement, they depreciated the types and genres of art that were given over to professional artists. It was the aristocrats' shared way of life, as sharply defined as that of the Chinese literati, that made it possible for them to express themselves by means of allusions that would be lost on a less sensitized audience.[31]

In the eleventh century, the most sensitive literature was written by women aristocrats. But from the twelfth century and on, Japanese literature was increasingly sustained by recluses who renounced the world, not mainly to devote themselves to Buddhism but to art. Among the recluses there were nobles who had given up their worldly status (though they probably lived from property they retained). The recluses I am speaking of kept up their passionate interest in art and lost no chance to praise the way the moon looked or describe the blooming and withering of flowers (Tokue 1985, 154).

Yet the aesthetic responses of the Japanese were both richer and more disharmonious than such devotion to aestheticism may imply. One obvious reason, which has been called a "fracture of meaning," is the disharmony between art's Japanese substance and its Chinese forms (Pollack 1986). The great literary scholar Motoori Norinaga (1730–1801) argues that the Japanese should accept the ancient Shinto account of the world's creation and not the mistaken cosmological notions of the Chinese. To him, the "ornateness" of Chinese writing, with its artificially ordered antitheses and its forms divorced from their content, is dull and cold and does not speak to the heart, while the Confucian "logic" of the Chinese, which grasps everything in terms of reward for good and punishment for evil, falsifies the unpremeditated simplicity and beauty of life (Pollack 1986, 43–47).

In keeping with his preference for native attitudes, Norinaga emphasizes the old Japanese sensitivity to *aware*. *Aware* was at first the exclamation, the "ah!" of surprise or delight, said to have been evoked in the ancient poets by, for instance, the birds' melancholy calls or by the rain in the spring. The word *aware* came to be used for whatever was emotionally moving, especially if beautiful. In the later poets, the word means that the joy aroused by beauty is accompanied by the regret that beauty is fragile and short-lived. So to Norinaga, the word *aware* or the phrase *mono no aware* ("mono" is literally "thing[s]") expresses the ancient sensitivity to the perishable beauty of things.[32]

Another basic aesthetic concept is that of *yūgen*, a state of mysterious sad depth. This is the emotion evoked by ideal beauty.

[29] Classical ("Medieval") Japanese Aesthetics: Miner 1985; Keene 1995; De Bary 1995 [1958]; Ienaga 1979 (sketches changing social backgrounds of art); Izutsu and Izutsu 1981, p. 28; Miner, Odagiri and Morrell 1985, esp. the dictionary of literary terms on pp. 270–305. Odin 2001, 99–169; Pollack 1986. Singer 1999; Stanley-Baker 2000 (the footnote below is from p. 10). Stanley-Baker's relevant study (which I have not had the chance to consult) is Stanley-Baker 1992; Ueda 1967, chap. 4; Varly 1990; Ruch 1990. Modern Japanese Aesthetics: Marra, 1999, 2001; Odin 2001.

[30] For Japan, the medieval period is reckoned in different ways. The *Cambridge History of Japan* conceives of the Middle Ages as beginning toward the end of the twelfth century and ending during the middle of the sixteenth. But Jin'ichi Konishi, the learned, original historian of Japanese literature on whom I (somewhat ambiguously) draw in this paragraph, has a much more extended conception of the Middle Ages and, conceiving them as divided into Early, High, and Late periods, begins them in the second half of the ninth century and ends them with the first half of the nineteenth.

Along with attitudes towards aesthetics, Chinese and Japanese painting share so much that it is hard to make a general stylistic distinction between them, especially when the subjects of the paintings are common to both. However, a well-informed historian of Chinese and Japanese art writes, unafraid, "Chinese forms tend to be self-contained and relaxed, while Japanese forms are affected by the overall compositions of a picture, and emotional tension charges both motifs and the space around and between them. The inward-directed motifs of Chinese paintings tend to stress solidity and depth (an effect often achieved by the complex interweaving of brushstrokes), whereas the motifs in Japanese paintings, each conceived as part of a larger emotional whole, tend to reach laterally across the picture-plane in a 'layered' technique and to be drawn together by the treatment of the intervening space. The ease and grandeur of Chinese art generate forms which are malleable: each can be slightly changed in space without disturbing the overall visual harmony. Japanese art, by contrast, is often focused on nuances of emotions, and works tend to be so charged with tension that altering the position of any part would drastically change the overall effect" (Stanley-Baker 1992).

As for literature, according to Konishi, Chinese, Japanese, and Korean lit-

erature are alike in making the assumption that author and audience share the same classic world and sense of what constitutes literature. But Japanese literature is more emotional, that is, more sensitive to mood,
more introverted, and only lyrical, not political. In contrast, Chinese literature, along with the Korean, is "volitional, intellectual, and extroverted." That is, Chinese literature has a greater interplay of the introverted—the Taoist or Buddhist—with the extroverted—the Confucian—and is more explicit and socially critical. These generalizations of course need both examples and qualifications.

31
Konishi 1986, 91–99. For Konishi's periodization, see the chart on p. 66. This chart contradicts the more general chart I, Konishi 1984, 66, which ends the Middle Ages in the late fifteenth century. Konishi's comparison of Chinese, Japanese, and Korean literature is taken, with large omissions, from Konishi 1984, 21–34.

32
De Bary 1995, 44–45; Ueda 1967, 196–213, esp. 199–202. On Norinaga and the intellectual movement
called "national studies" see also Najita 1991, 616–21.

33
De Bary 1995, 55–58; Izutsu and Izutsu 1981, 26–44 (esp. 33); Pollack 1986, 40–53, 223–25; Ueda 1967, 59–66. The quotation, from a translation of Zeami's difficult summary of his views, *The Nine Stages of the No in Order*, is found in Tsunoda, De Bary, Keene 1958, 293.

Etymologically made up of *yū*, "deep," "dim," or "hard to see," and *gen*, *yūgen* refers to the "profound truth" of the universe. It is that which, unseen and indescribable, lies below the perceived surface of things. The emotion that can be expressed by words alone is inevitably shallow. But soundless, colorless, inexplicable, ineffable, *yūgen* can arouse sudden painfully pleasurable tears. It is there in the simple, perfect Chinese vase, in the bright cloud that hides the moon, and in the beautiful flow of sad music. To the great No actor, writer, and theorist Zeami (1363–1443), who was deeply influenced by Zen Buddhism, *yūgen* is the profound inward beauty that manifests itself outwardly. All beauty's elegance, Zeami says, is perishable, and so *yūgen*, which is cosmic truth, invokes feelings of mutability and sadness as well. At the highest stage of the art of No, an actor reaches nonduality. Then "admiration transcends the comprehension of the mind, and all attempts at classification and grading are made impossible," for art has caused the miraculous to flower.[33]

To many other Japanese aesthetic concepts that might be invoked, I add only *sabi*, which in No drama is closely allied with *yūgen*. *Sabi* is the sense of loneliness such as is felt by someone who, traveling in a desolate place, senses the pathos and insubstantiality of life. It is desolation's beloved beauty (Varley 1990, 466–67).

The aesthetic terms and attitudes I have just described are those of the self-consciously aesthetic Japanese, but they are not as characteristic of the people at large nor of the popular painters, sculptors, singers, and dancers, who gave the people less introverted aesthetic pleasures. This popular art was enjoyed by the Japanese regardless of their status in life. In the larger world, from which the smaller aesthetic worlds were not isolated, art might express the feeling that good emerges only from suffering, but also that the gods take compassion on sufferers, that there are magical words that move gods and humans, that the underdog deserves sympathy, that impetuous, sincere acts should be admired, and that one can take great satisfaction in suppressing and sublimating oneself. I cannot complete this list of values, which, like *aware, yūgen,* and *sabi,* are both aesthetic and social, but only note how different they are and how much vitality they lend Japanese art as a whole (Ruch 1990, esp. 541–43).

A COMMON HUMANITY

What not excessively obvious or questionable generalizations can be drawn on the aesthetics of the cultures I have drawn on?

First, the conception of art and, with it, of beauty is highly variable and often implicit rather than explicit. Among the Bamana, for instance, it seems in itself, in the absence of other, deeper values, to be trivial. Everywhere, however, there is the conception of what is well made as against badly made, a conception that has a moral overtone like that of authenticity, honesty, or serious intention. Not infrequently a "well-made" object is the equivalent of what Westerners might consider a "beautiful" one.

Second, non-Islamic Africa and the modern West excepted, there is a general tendency to set the literary arts above the others and to model all aesthetics after that of literature and, in China and Japan, of calligraphy. Initially, Chinese calligraphy owed its importance, which was magical, to the reverence of the sources it transcribed and the magic of the impulse that moved the hand of the author-transcriber, so that at first the scholar-painting of China derived its prestige from the prestige of calligraphy. The great Chinese writer, calligrapher, or painter enjoyed the status of a great personage. But when, as in ancient Greece, India, or China, sculpture was regarded as the work of a professional, who works in terms of traditional knowledge and not spontaneous inspiration, the sculptor might be regarded as an estimable, even important person, but his status as an artist was denied or put into question. In Europe, we know, this attitude began to change during the Renaissance.

Third, in, primarily, non-Muslim Africa, the status of the artist has depended on prestige related to his (or sometimes her) age, initiation into sacred matters, and the importance—sometimes equivalent to the secrecy—of a work's ritual purpose. Often, the importance of the function of a "work of art" far outweighs that of the person who has been chosen to make it. But in Africa too, there have been artists who were regarded or insisted on being regarded as "geniuses." An aggrandizing self-importance is a constant human possibility.

Fourth, at least locally, the style and personality of an artist is recognized as his or hers. Such recognition may have been confined to a relatively small area because of differences in language, the absence of open markets, and the absence of communication and written records. China excelled in its insistence on the individual personality of the writer, calligrapher, or painter, and the classical Indian writers were well aware of it. I have found it remarkable that the Bamana notion of an artist's identity, or double, shadow, or reflection is quite like that that I have myself repeatedly used when characterizing or defining art.

Fifth, there is a consistent likeness in the structures of art. For instance, the aesthetic vocabulary of the Bamana could easily be adapted to the expedients of an improvising jazz musician. In spite of the to us unfamiliar terms, the content of the terms is just what might be expected of Westerners or, for that matter, Indians, Chinese, and Japanese: a received, expectable, that is, conventional structure for each form of art that, to become interesting, has to be imaginatively varied, though never so imaginatively or emotionally—not made so hot, as Westerners too might say—that the structure is destroyed. The Indian theory of inspired suggestion depends on the relatively conventional character of the text that is made fresh again by the poet's power of verbal suggestion. It

34
Odin 2001 is a well-researched and well-thought out exposition of this theme, with examples from modern Western and modern Japanese literature. As is usual, Odin finds the Western origin of the idea in Immanuel Kant, who probably owes the idea to the seventeenth-century empiricists beginning with the Third Earl of Shaftesbury (1671–1713)—"the first thinker to bring the phenomenon of disinterestedness to light and analyzing it"—and continuing with David Hume, Joseph Addison, Edmund Burke, and others (quotation from Odin 2001, 27, from Stolnitz 1961, 100). I think that it was the work of Edward Bullough that made the "psychical distance" well known.

seems to me that everything that has been written here on Chinese art and the life-movement that animates it could be rephrased using the Bamana vocabulary. And for the Japanese and Chinese, sensitivity is adjusted to rising and falling, opening and closing, and every other verbal, visual, and musical rhythmic and compositional device.

Sixth, there are interesting variations in the different peoples' sense of the "psychic distance" of art from mundane reality. Legends of art so realistic or life-infused that they turned literally alive seem to be found everywhere. When the art is sacred, the possibility of an indwelling deity may be accepted. However, at least in India and in Africa, the life of a statue or mask may come to an end: however handsome, an African mask that has served its function and need not be kept for a future performance was likely to be treated as of little value, an attitude that is the reverse of the near-religious respect in other cultures for great works of art as such. In China and Japan, the work of art could be great in itself, in virtue of the quality and immediacy of touch that had created it. But in India and, to a lesser extent, in Japan and Europe, a theory of psychic distance or artistic detachment was developed to account for the artistry of art. In India, the univeralization of emotions was an abstraction from any particular individual's emotion, and the doctrine of *rasadhvani* culminated in the *rasa* of peace, *shantadhvani*, which is one of near-mystical detachment. But while in India impersonal emotion was the essence of art, in China and, with it, Japan, there was detachment from any emotion (in the usual sense) when it was decided that the aesthetic quality—the variable dynamism—of calligraphy was quite apart from the verbal meaning or emotive qualities of the text. Yet in Japan, there was a principle, reminiscent of Buddhism, according to which the goal of art, like that of life, is detachment, so that *aware* and *yūgen* can be equated with tranquility and with Buddhist "suchness" or "emptiness."[34] In Europe, the idea of psychic distance was cultivated by Romantics along with that of the sacredness of art as such and of art for art's sake. As has been shown, the notion of psychic distance (from everyday, realistic experience) has often justified abstract painting and the ascription to it of mystical virtues.

Seventh, in every one of the cultures discussed, everything in art, as understood in Western terms, is in the end dependent on a great, singular, mysterious force and the subforces that can in some way or other be summoned up or blocked. This is of course true if the "art" is part of a sacred ritual, or if the art (like the great classical Greek sculpture of Zeus, or like medieval paintings, or like Michelangelo's Sistine frescoes, or like the great images of the Buddha or Shiva) is itself sacred or the sacred representation of something even more sacred, whose life and power depend on the indwelling life and power of Zeus, Christ, the Buddha, Krishna, or Shiva. This force and its power, like the creative power of any maker, are later assimilated to the inspiration that an artist needs to attain exceptional success. It has been natural to assimilate sacred art to prayer and to hope that art alone or in ritual performance will guard the well-being, in every sense, of the people it represents. When the literal relation to God, Shiva, the Buddha, or any sacred force is weakened or lost, it retains a power in a symbolic sense. I suppose that it is the sense of the possible closeness to a cosmic creator that stimulates the idea that poet or artist is godlike in that he or she creates or recreates a whole living reality. Certainly, this is Bharata's view of the dramatist and Leonardo's of the painter, and something like it animates Wagner's idea of the opera as the total work of art, and must have animated some of the creators of cinema.

Note that in both the sixth and seventh points I have related art to mystical experience, or, at the least, to something transcendental, or to what may be called "fusion," or, on a more modest level, "empathy." These experiences, emphases, and terms all seem to be related to the importance that humans everywhere ascribe to symbolism and to the relation between the cosmic, the social, and the individual human's abilities to create.

In the discussion I have just ended of varying cultural views of aesthetics, I have neither tried nor by accident succeeded in reducing the views to a few easily assimilated generalizations. On the contrary, each generalization has been accompanied by variations and possible exceptions, so my generalizing passion has not at all overcome the specificity of the different cultures. But to the extent that my discussion has been convincing, I have shown that all this is best appreciated as belonging to a common universe of discourse, in which the humanity of the art is never quite eclipsed by its locality, because the locality of the art and its modes of appreciation are best understood by their position beside or within other, contrasted localities and modes, all of which make up a recognizably common world.

REFERENCES

ABRAMS, MEYER H. 1971. *Natural supernaturalism: Tradition and revolution in romantic literature.* New York: Norton.

ACKER, WILLIAM R. B. 1979. *Some T'ang and pre-T'ang texts on Chinese painting.* Westport, CO: Hyperion Press.

ANANDAVARDHANA. 1974. *Dhvanyaloka of Anandavardhana,* ed. and with an introd., trans and notes by K. Krishnamoorthy. Dharwar: Karnatak University.
—. 1990. *The* Dhvanyaloka *of Anandavardhana with the* Locana *of Abhinavagupta.* Trans. Daniel H. H. Ingalls, Jeffrey Moussaieff Masson and M. V. Patwardhan; ed. and with an introd. by Daniel H. H. Ingalls. Cambridge, MA: Harvard University Press.

ARMSTRONG, A. M. 1953. *Plotinus.* London: Allen & Unwin.

BANERJEA, JITENDRA NATH. 1974. *The development of Indian iconography.* 3rd ed., from 2nd ed. 1956. New Delhi: M. Manoharlal Publishers.

BARASCH, MOSHE. 1998. *From impressionism to Kandinsky.* Vol. 2 of *Modern Theories of Art.* New York and London: New York University Press.

BARNES, R. H. 1987. Anthropological comparison. In *Comparative anthropology,* ed. Ladislav Holý, 119–26. Oxford and New York: Blackwell.

BEACH, MILO C. 1992. *Mughal and Rajput painting.* Cambridge and New York: Cambridge University Press.

BERLIN, BRENT, AND PAUL KAY. 1969. *Basic color terms: Their universality and evolution.* Berkeley: University of California Press.

BESANÇON, ALAIN. 2000. *The forbiden image: An intellectual history of iconoclasm.* Trans. Jane Marie Todd. Chicago and London: The University of Chicago Press.

BHATTACARYYENA, TARAPADA. 1963. *The Canons of Indian Art: Or, a study on Vastuvidya.* 2nd ed. Calcutta: K. L. Mukhopadhyay.

BIEDERMAN, IRVING. 1995. Visual object recognition. In *Visual cognition.* 2nd ed, ed. Stephen M. Kosslyn and Daniel N. Osherson, 121–65. Vol. 2 of *An invitation to cognitive science,* ed. Daniel N. Osherson. Cambridge, MA: MIT Press.

BLOTKAMP, CAREL. 1986. Annunciation of the new mysticism: Dutch symbolism and early abstraction. In *The spiritual in art: Abstract painting 1890–1985,* ed. Maurice Tuchman, 89–111. Los Angeles: Los Angeles County Museum of Art; New York: Abeville Press.

BOIS, YVE-ALAIN, et al. 1995. *Piet Mondrian, 1872–1944.* Boston: Bulfinch Press.

BOSE, PHANINDRA NATH, ed. 1928. *Silpa-Sastram.* Saidmitha, Lahore: Moti Lal Banarsi Dass.

BRINK, JAMES. 2001. Dialectics of aesthetic form in Bamana art. In *Bamana: The art of existence in Mali,* ed. Jean-Paul Colleyn. New York: Museum for African Art, etc.

BUKOFZER, MANFRED F. 1947. *Music in the baroque era: From Monteverdi to Bach.* New York: Norton.

BUSH, SUSAN. 1971. *The Chinese literati on painting: Su Shih (1037–1101) to Tung Chi-chang (1555–1636).* Cambridge, MA: Harvard University Press.

—, and Hsio-yen Shih. 1985. *Early Chinese texts on painting.* Cambridge, MA: Harvard University Press.

CAMPBELL, BRUCE F. 1980. *Ancient wisdom revived: A history of the theosophical movement.* Berkeley: University of California Press.

CHASTEL, ANDRÉ. 1959. *Art et humanisme à Florence au temps de Laurent le Magnifique: Études sur la Renaissance et l'humanisme platonicien.* Paris: Presses universitaires de France.

CHING, HAO. 1974. *Ching Hao's "Pi-fa-chi.": A note on the art of the brush.* Artibus Asiae Supplementum 31, ed. and trans. by Kyohito Munakata. Ascona: Artibus Asiae.

CHING, JULIA. 1976. *To acquire wisdom: The way of Wang Yang ming.* New York: Columbia University Press.

COLLEYN, JEAN-PAUL, ed. 2001. *Bamana: The art of existence in Mali.* New York: Museum for African Art, etc.

D'ANDREA, JEANNE, ed. 1990. *Kazimir Malevich 1878–1935.* Los Angeles: Armand Hammer Museum of Art and Cultural Center.

DARWIN, CHARLES. 1999. *The expression of the emotions in man and animals,* with an introd., afterw., and commentaries by Paul Ekman. 3rd ed., 1st ed. London: John Murray, 1872. London: HarperCollins.

DE, SUSHIL KUMAR. 1963. Sanskrit poetics as a study of aesthetics. Berkeley: University of California Press.
—. 1977. *History of Sanskrit Poetics.* Reprint, 2nd rev. ed. 1960. Calcutta: K. L. Mukhopadhyay.

DE BARY, W. THEODORE. 1995. The vocabulary of Japanese aesthetics I, II, III. In *Japanese aesthetics and culture: A reader,* ed. Nancy Hume, 43–47. Albany, NY: State University of New York Press. Originally published in Ryusaku Tsunoda, W. Theodore de Bary and Donald Keene, comp. 1958. *Sources of Japanese tradition* (New York: Columbia University Press).

DESAI, DEVANGANA. 1975. *Erotic sculpture of India: A socio-cultural study.* New Delhi: Tata McGraw Hill, New Delhi.

DIETERLEN, GERMAINE. 1993a. The mythology of the Mande and the choice of the dogon as a subject to study. In *American, African, and old European mythologies,* comp. Yves Bonnefoy, trans. under the direction of Wendy Doniger by Gerald Honigsblum et al., 117–18. Chicago and London: University of Chicago Press.
—. 1993b. Graphic signs and the seed of knowledge: The 266 basic signs in West Africa. In *American, African, and old European mythologies,* comp. Yves Bonnefoy, trans. under the direction of Wendy Doniger by Gerald Honigsblum et al., 118–20. Chicago and London: University of Chicago Press.
—. 1993c. Twins a dominant theme in West African mythologies. In *American, African, and old European mythologies,* comp. Yves Bonnefoy, trans. under the direction of Wendy Doniger by Gerald Honigsblum et al., 121–23. Chicago and London: University of Chicago Press.
—. 1993d. The placenta in West African myths and rituals. In *American, African, and old European mythologies,* comp. Yves Bonnefoy, trans under the direction of Wendy Doniger by Gerald Honigsblum et al., 123–25. Chicago and London: The University of Chicago Press.

EKMAN, PAUL, ed. 1982. *Emotion in the human face.* 2nd ed. Cambridge and New York: Cambridge University Press; Paris: Editions de la Maison des Sciences de l'Homme.

ELGAR, FRANK. 1968. *Mondrian*. Trans. Thomas Walton. London: Thames and Hudson.

EMBREE, AINSLIE, ed. 1988. Sources *of Indian tradition*. Vol. 1, *From the beginning to 1800 (Introduction to oriental civilizations)*. 2nd ed. New York: Columbia University Press.

FAUCHEREAU, SERGE. 1991. *Kazimir Malévitch*. Paris: Editions Cercles d'Art.

FONG, WEN C. 1962. The problem of forgeries in Chinese painting: Part one. *Artibus Asiae* 25 (2–3), 95–119, 121–40.
—, et al. 1984. *Images of the mind: Selections from the Edward L. Elliott family and John B. Elliott collections of Chinese calligraphy and painting at the Art Museum*. Princeton, NJ: Princeton University Press.

FRANK, BARBARA E. 2001. More than objects: Bamana artistry in iron, wood, clay, leather and cloth. In *Bamana: The art of existence in Mali*, ed. Jean-Paul Colleyn, 45–51. New York: Museum for African Art, etc.

FRIDLUND, ALAN J., AND BRADLEY DUCHAINE. 1996. "Facial expressions of emotion" and the delusion of the hermetic self. In *The emotions: Social, cultural and biological dimensions*, ed. Rom Harré and W. Gerrod Parrott, 259–284. London and Thousand Oaks: Sage.

GAGE, JOHN. 1993. *Colour and culture: Practice and meaning from antiquity to abstraction*. London: Thames and Hudson.
—. 1995. Colour and culture. In *Colour: Art and science*, ed. Trevor Lamb and Janine Bourriau, 186–93. Cambridge and New York: Cambridge University Press.
—. 1999. *Color and meaning: art, science, and symbolism*. Berkeley and Los Angeles: University of California Press.

GNOLI, RANIERO. 1956. *The aesthetic experience according to Abhinavagupta*. Rome: Is. M.E.O.

GOLDING, JOHN. 2000. *Paths to the absolute: Mondrian, Malevich, Kandinsky, Pollock, Newman, Rothko, and Still*. Princeton, NJ: Princeton University Press.

GOMBRICH, ERNST H. 1972. *Symbolic images*. London: Phaidon.

GONDA, JAN. 1975. *Vedic literature: (Saṃhitas and Brahmaṇas)*. Wiesbaden: Harrossowitz.

GOSWAMY, BRIJINDER. N. 1975. *Pahari paintings of the Nala-Damayanti theme in the collection of Dr. Karan Singh: Essays and notes*. New Delhi: National Museum.

HALL, JOHN W., et al., eds. 1989–1997. *The Cambridge history of Japan*. 6 vols. Cambridge and New York: Cambridge University Press.

HARRISON, CHARLES, AND PAUL WOOD, eds. 1992. *Art in theory 1900–1990: An anthology of changing ideas*. London: Blackwell.

HEELAS, PAUL. 1996. Emotion talk across cultures. In *The emotions: Social, cultural and biological dimensions*, ed. Rom Harré and W. Gerrod Parrott, 171–99. London and Thousand Oaks: Sage.

HESS, THOMAS B. 1971. *Barnett Newman*. New York: Museum of Modern Art.

HOFFMAN, DONALD C. 1998. *Visual intelligence: How we create what we see*. New York: Norton.

HORNBLOWER, SIMON, AND ANTHONY SPAWFORTH, eds. 1996. *The Oxford classical dictionary*. 3rd ed. Oxford and New York: Oxford University Press.

HUET, MICHEL. 1978. *The dance, art, and ritual of Africa*. New York: Pantheon.

IENAGA, SABURO. 1979. *Japanese art: A cultural appreciation*. Trans. Richard L. Gage. New York: Weatherhill.

IZUTSU, TOSHIHIKO, AND TOYO IZUTSU. 1981. *The theory of beauty in the classical aesthetics of Japan*. The Hague and Boston: Martinus Nijhoff Publishers.

JACOBSON-WEDDING, ANITA. 1979. *Red-White-Black as a mode of thought: Study of triadic classification by colours in the ritual symbolism and cognitive thought of the peoples of the Lower Congo*. Uppsala: Uppsala Universitet.

KANDINSKY, NINA. 1978. *Kandinsky et moi*. Paris: Flammarion.

KEENE, DONALD. 1995. Japanese aesthetics. In *Japanese aesthetics and culture: A reader*, ed. Nancy Hume, 27–41. Albany, NY: State University of New York Press.

KLEINMAN, ARTHUR, AND BYRON GOOD, eds. 1985. *Culture and depression: Studies in the anthropology and cross-cultural psychiatry of affect and disorder*. Berkeley: University of California Press.

KONISHI, JIN'ICHI. 1984. *The archaic and ancient ages*. Vol. 1 of *A history of Japanese literature*, ed. Earl Miner, trans. Aileen Gatten and Nicholas Teele. Princeton, NJ: Princeton University Press.
—. 1986. *The early Middle Ages*. Vol. 2 of *A history of Japanese literature*, ed. Earl Miner, trans. Aileen Gatten and Nicholas Teele. Princeton, NJ: Princeton University Press.

LAKOFF, GEORGE. 1987. *Women, fire, and dangerous things: What categories reveal about the mind*. Chicago and London: University of Chicago Press.

LAMB, TREVOR, AND JANINE BOURRIAU. 1995. *Colour: Art and science*. Cambridge and New York: Cambridge University Press.

LAZARUS, RICHARD S. 1991. *Emotion and adaptation*. New York: Oxford University Press.

LIN, YUTANG. 1967. *The Chinese theory of art: Translations from the masters of Chinese art by Lin Yutang*. London: Heinemann.

LLOYD, BARBARA, AND JOHN GAY, eds. 1981. *Universals of human thought: Some African evidence*. Cambridge and New York: Cambridge University Press.

LUI, SHOU KWAN. 1971. The six canons of Hsieh Ho. *Oriental Art* 17 (Summer): 144–47, 252–55.

LUTZ, CATHERINE. 1988. *Unnatural emotions: Everyday sentiments on a Micronesian atoll and their challenge to western theory*. Chicago and London: The University of Chicago Press.

LYONS, KAY J. 1995. Colour in language. In *Colour: Art and science*, ed. Trevor Lamb and Janine Bourriau, 194–224. Cambridge and New York: Cambridge University Press.

MALÉ, S. 2001. The initiation as rite of passage: The *Jo* and the *Gwan*. In *Bamana: The art of existence in Mali*, ed. Jean-Paul Colleyn. New York: Museum for African Art, etc.

MARCH, BENJAMIN. 1935. *Some technical terms of Chinese paintings*. Baltimore: Waverly Press.

MARKS, JOEL, AND ROGER T. AMES, eds. 1995. *Emotions in Asian thought: A dialogue in comparative philosophy*. Albany, NY: State University of New York Press.

MARRA, MICHAEL F. 1999. *Modern Japanese aesthetics: A reader*. Honolulu: University of Hawai'i Press.
—, ed. 2001. *A history of modern Japanese aesthetics*. Honolulu: University of Hawai'i Press.

MASSELOS, JIM, JACKIE MRNZIES, AND PRATAPADITYA PASL. 1997. *Dancing to the flute: Music and dance in Indian art*. *Sydney*: Art Gallery of New South Wales.

MASSON, JEFFREY MOUSSAIEFF, AND M. V. PATWARDHAN. 1969. *Śantarasa and Abhinavagupta's philosophy of aesthetics*. Poona: Bhandakar Oriental Research.

MILNER, JOHN. 1992. *Mondrian*. London: Phaidon.

MINER, EARL, ed. 1985. *Principles of classical Japanese literature*. Princeton, NJ: Princeton University Press.
—, Hiroko Odagiri, and Robert E. Morrell. 1985. *The Princeton companion to classical Japanese literature*. Princeton, N.J.: Princeton University Press.

MONDRIAN, PIET. 1945. *Plastic art and pure plastic art, 1937 and other essays 1941–1943*. New York: Wittenborn and Company.

MOSZYNSKA, ANNA. 1990. *Abstract art*. London: Thames and Hudson.

NAJITA, TETSUO. 1991. History and nature in eighteenth-century Tokugawa thought. In *Early modern Japan*, ed. James L. McLain and John W. Hall, 596–659. Vol. 4 of *The Cambridge history of Japan*, ed. John W. Hall et al. Cambridge and New York: Cambridge University Press.

NEEDHAM, RODNEY. 1981. *Circumstantial deliveries*. Berkeley: University of California Press.

ODIN, STEVE. 2001. *Artistic detachment in Japan and the West: Psychic distance in comparative aesthetics*. Honolulu: University of Hawai'i Press.

PANDEY, KANTI CHANDRA. 1950. *Indian aesthetics*. Vol. 1 of *Comparative aesthetics*. Banaras [Varanasi]: Chowkhamba.
—. 1963. *Abhinavagupta: An historical and philosophical study*. 2nd ed., rev. and enl. Varanasi, Chowkhamba Sanskrit Series Office.

PANOFSKY, ERWIN. 1968. *Idea: A concept in art theory*. Trans. Joseph J. S. Peake. Columbia: University of South Carolina Press.

PASTOUREAU, MICHEL. 2001. *Blue: The history of a color*. Princeton, NJ and Oxford: Princeton University Press.

PINKER, STEVEN. 1997. *How the mind works*. New York: Norton.

PLOTINUS. 1953. *Plotinus*. Trans. A. M. Armstrong. London: Allan & Unwin.

POLLACK, DAVID. 1986. *The fracture of meaning: Japan's synthesis of China from the eighth through the eighteenth centuries*. Princeton, NJ: Princeton University Press.

POLLARD, DAVID. 1978. Ch'i in Chinese literary theory. In *Chinese approaches to literature from Confucius to Liang Ch'i-chao*, ed.

Adele A. Rickett, 43–66. Princeton, NJ: Princeton University Press.

RAMANUJAN, ATTIPAT KRISHNASWAMI, AND EDWIN GEROW. 1974. Indian poetics. In *The literatures of India: An introduction*, ed. Edward C. Dimock, Jr. et al., 115–43. Chicago and London: The University of Chicago Press.

RAY, NIHARRANJAN. 1974. *An approach to Indian art*. Chandigarh: Publication Bureau, Panjab University.

RILEY II, CHARLES A. 1995. *Color codes: Modern theories of color in philosophy, painting and architecture, literature, music, and psychology*. Hanover, NH: University Press of New England.

RINGBOM, SIXTEN. 1986. Transcending the visible: The generation of the abstract pioneers. In *The spiritual in art: Abstract painting 1890–1985*, ed. Maurice Tuchman, 131–54. Los Angeles: Los Angeles County Museum of Art; New York: Abbeville Press.

ROETHEL, HANS KONRAD. 1979. *Kandinsky*, in collab. with Jean K. Benjamin. Oxford: Phaidon.

ROWELL, LEWIS. 1992. *Music and musical thought in early India*. Chicago and London: University of Chicago Press.

ROWLEY, GEORGE. 1947. *Principles of Chinese painting*. Princeton, NJ: Princeton University Press.

RUCH, BARBARA. 1990. The other side of culture in Japan. In *Medieval Japan*, ed. Kozo Yamamura, 500–43. Vol. 3 of *The Cambridge history of Japan*, ed. John W. Hall et al. Cambridge and New York: Cambridge University Press.

SCHARFSTEIN, BEN-AMI. 1973. *Mystical experience*. Oxford: Blackwell.
—. 2008. *Art without borders: A philosophical exploration of art and humanity*. Chicago and London: The University of Chicago Press.

SCHOPENHAUER, ARTHUR. 1969. *The world as will and representation*. Trans. E. F. J. Payne. New York: Dover. Originally published as *Die Welt als Wille und Vorstellung* (1819).

SCHWAB, RAYMOND. 1950. *La renaissance orientale*. Paris: Payot.

SELZ, PETER H. 1957. *German expressionistic painting*. Berkeley: University of California Press.

SHEPARD, ROGER N. 1992. The perceptual organization of colors: An adaptation to regularities of the terrestrial world? In *The adapted mind: Evolutionary psychology and the generation of culture*, ed. Jerome H. Barkow, Leda Cosmides, and John Tooby, 492–535. New York and Oxford: Oxford University Press.

SINGER, ILANA. 1999. *The charged emptiness and its expression in the Japanese aesthetic*. PhD diss., University of Haifa.

SIRÉN, OSVALD. 1936. *The Chinese on the art of painting*. Peiping [Beijing]: H. Vetch.

SIVARAMAMURTI, CALAMBUR. 1977. *The art of India*. New York: Abrams.
—. 1978. *The painter in ancient India*. New Delhi: Abinav Publications.

SPATE, VIRGINIA. 1981. Orphism. In *Concepts of modern art*. 2nd. rev., ed. Nikos Stangos, 88–89. London: Thames and Hudson.

STANLEY-BAKER, JOAN. 1992. *The transmission of Chinese idealist painting to Japan: Notes on the early phase (1661–1799)*. Ann Arbor,

Center for Japanese Studies, University of Michigan.
—. 2000. *Japanese art*. Rev. ed. London and New York: Thames and Hudson.

STOLNITZ, JEROME. 1961. On the significance of Lord Shaftesbury in modern aesthetic theory. *The Philosophical Quarterly* 11 (43): 97–113.

SYLVESTER, DAVID. 1997. *About modern art: Critical essays, 1948–1997*. London: Henry Holt.

THOMPSON, ROBERT FARRIS. 1974. *African art in motion: Icon and act in the collection of Katherine Coryton White*. Berkeley: University of California Press.

TOKUE, MEZAKI. 1985. Aesthete-recluses during the transition from ancient to medieval Japan. In *Principles of classical Japanese literature*, ed. Earl Miner, 151–80. Princeton, NJ: Princeton University Press.

TSUNODA, RYUSAKU, W. THEODORE DE BARY, AND DONALD KEENE, comp. 1958. *Sources of Japanese tradition*. New York: Columbia University Press.

TUCHMAN, MAURICE. 1986. Hidden meanings in abstract art. In *The spiritual in art: Abstract painting 1890–1985*, ed. Maurice Tuchman, 17–61. Los Angeles: Los Angeles County Museum of Art; New York: Abeville Press.
—, ed. 1986. *The spiritual in art: Abstract painting 1890–1985*. Los Angeles: Los Angeles County Museum of Art; New York: Abeville Press.

UEDA, MAKOTO. 1967. *Literary and art theories in Japan*. Cleveland, OH: Press of Western Reserve University.

VALLIER, DORA. 1967. *L'art abstrait*. Paris: le Livre de poche.

VARLEY, H. PAUL. 1990. Cultural life in medieval Japan. In *Medieval Japan*, ed. Kozo Yamamura, 447–99. Vol. 3 of *The Cambridge history of Japan*, ed. John W. Hall et al. Cambridge and New York: Cambridge University Press.

VIDYAKARA. 1965. *An anthology of Sanskrit court poetry: Vidyakara's "Subhaṣiaratnakosa."* Trans. Daniel H. H. Ingalls. Cambridge, MA: Harvard University Press.

VISONÀ, MONICA BLACKMUN. 2000. Mande worlds and the Upper Niger. In *A history of art in Africa*, Monica Blackmun Visonà et al., 106–29. New York: Abrams.

VOGEL, SUSAN M. 1997. *Baule: African art, Western eyes*. New Haven, CT and London: Yale University Press.

VOGT, PAUL. 1980. *The Blue Rider*. Trans. Joachim Neugroschel. Woodbury, NY: Barron's.

VON GLASENAPP, HELMUTH. 1960. *Das Indienbild deutscher Denker*. Stuttgart: Köhler.

WARDER, ANTHONY KENNEDY. 1972. *Indian kavya literature*, vol. 1. Delhi: Motilal Banarsidass.

WASHTON LONG, ROSE-CAROL. 1980. *Kandinsky: The development of an abstract style*. Oxford: Clarendon Press.

WEBER, MICHAEL JOHN, ed. 1987. *Perspectives: Angles on African art*. New York: Center for African Art: Abrams.

WILBUR, KEN. 1984. *Quantum questions: Mystical writings of the world's great physicists*. Boulder, CO: Shambhala.

WILLATS, JOHN. 1997. *Art and representation: New principles in the analysis of pictures*. Princeton, NJ: Princeton University Press.

WONG, SIU-KIT. 1978. Ch'ing and Ching in the critical writings of Wang Fu-chih. In *Chinese approaches to literature from Confucius to Liang Ch'i-chao*, ed. Adele A. Rickett, 121–50. Princeton, NJ: Princeton University Press.

ZAHAN, DOMINIQUE. 1979. *The religion, spirituality, and thought of traditional Africa*. Trans. Kate Ezra Martin and Lawrence M. Martin. Chicago and London: The University of Chicago Press.

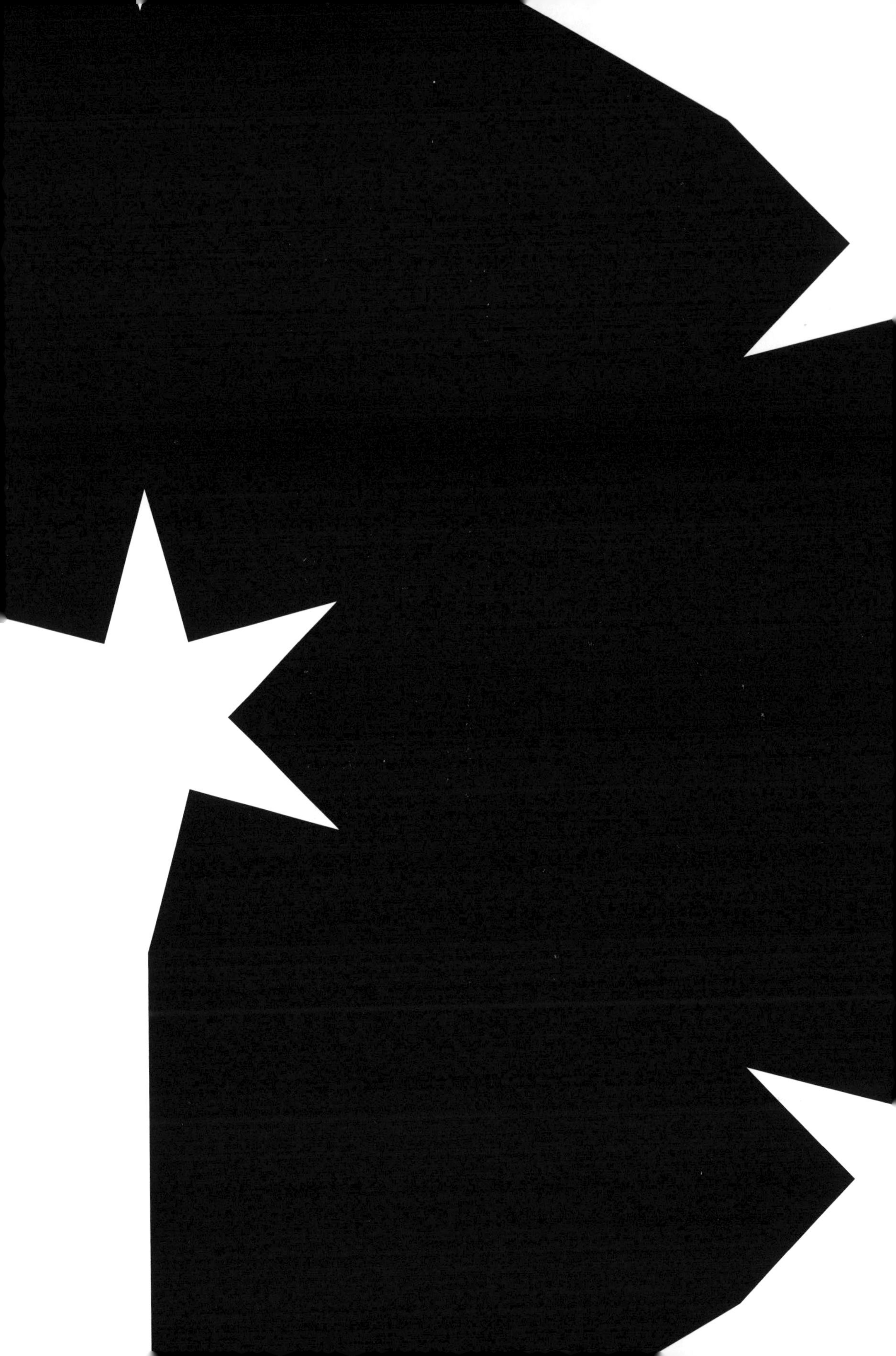

V

Encounters: Intercultural Exchanges

Intercultural-ization in Art: Conceptualizing Processes and Products

In the introduction to the previous section it was noted that, although intercultural comparison might result in emphasizing differences, many studies in this field aim at establishing some form of cross-cultural commonality or regularity, including commonalities that are suggested to underlie observable diversity. Especially in the early days of intercultural comparison, it was commonly assumed that similarities or parallels between individual cultures had come about in a culturally independent manner, meaning that they had resulted from convergent developments or from cross-culturally recurring relationships between particular elements of culture. (Indeed, such similarities in structure and development were ultimately held to demonstrate what nineteenth-century comparativists, their ethnocentrism notwithstanding, referred to as "the psychic unity of mankind," a condition that would allow all cultures to climb the evolutionary ladder.)

However, in 1889, Francis Galton, the inventor of statistics, among other things, charged that, before arriving at the conclusion of culturally independent parallels, one has to convincingly show that these similarities are not the result of other processes, most notably intercultural contact involving diffusion or migration of culture traits. "Galton's problem," as comparativists call it, reminds us that not only have populations throughout history usually been in contact with other populations, but that these contacts regularly imply the exchange and adoption of cultural elements. The visual arts are no exception, and perhaps present even a prominent example of the intricacies involved in the dynamic processes that intercultural encounter and transmission may entail.

It is suggested here to refer to the processes of artistic exchange between disparate contexts as interculturalization in the visual arts. Taking into account recent criticisms of this label's core concept, it needs to be observed that the term "culture" should not be interpreted in any "essentialist" sense, meaning that what are still generally known as cultures tend not to be "monolithic," either diachronically or synchronically. It is indeed easy to see that cultures are not usually static—rather they are dynamic, subject to change as a result of internal and, of special interest here, external factors. Similarly, cultures at any moment in time are not usually uniform or homogeneous—rather they tend to be internally diverse, with their pluriformity potentially being demonstrated, in one example among many others, in the differential responses to outside influences.

In view of a culture's heterogeneity, it should be noted that internal differences may be deemed substantive enough to warrant the use of the label subculture. This could in our case lead to examining processes of "intersubculturalization," for example artistic exchanges between "popular culture" and "elite culture," or between "high" and "low" within what is somehow still perceived as a unity of sorts (historically, linguistically, and so on). One might also point to artistic exchanges within settings referred to as "multicultural," typically implying an intra-regional multiplicity of cultures, frequently with extra-regional or transnational connections. This example also demonstrates that it is difficult today to avoid using the concept of culture in talking about the world's populations and the various worldviews, lifestyles, and material products with which they tend to identify themselves.

In actual analyses of interculturalization in the visual arts, then, culture may be loosely defined as any context or setting in terms of which particular artistic features can, at the time of analysis, be reasonably characterized as either internal or initially external. One way of steering clear of the term culture, incidentally, is by a descriptive approach that typifies the settings or contexts in question by reference to one or more identifying characteristics (spatiotemporal, political, religious, socioeconomic, and so on), for example "the mid-thirteenth-century Mongol court at Karakorum," "avant-garde artistic circles in Paris, c. 1900," or "present-day Islamized urban Mali."

A moment's reflection makes clear that many topics need to be addressed if we want to come to scholarly terms with the phenomenon of interculturalization in the arts. Any attempt at comprehensive analysis also requires theorizing this phenomenon by suggesting ways of conceptualizing its various processes and products. The following interrelated dimensions of analysis are suggested as an attempt to systematize the investigation of the many issues involved: the preconditions of intercultural artistic exchange, including both conditions of availability and conditions of receptivity; the agency of the individuals involved, including both their motivations and their actions; and the resulting products themselves, including both the nature of the observable influences and the impact and role of the objects concerned.[1]

A methodical analysis of interculturalization in the arts, then, must consider the preconditions that allow artistic exchanges to occur. This is in itself already a varied topic with several subtopics. If we look at these preconditions from the receiving end — the context or setting where the incorporation of external elements takes place — we need to analyze the particular circumstances that make the integration of outside features possible. This calls not only for examining the conditions of receptivity of exogenous artistic elements — the climate of acceptance and readiness to incorporate such elements that is in some minimal degree required among at least a few individuals within a society or culture (although artistic absorption may also be forced upon a group by an outside power); in addition to taking account of internal conditions that favor incorporation (some more on that later, when motivations are discussed), the analysis also calls for considering the conditions or factors that make external artistic features available in the first place. In examining the routes via which individuals in a given tradition or setting may have access to outside artistic elements, one may consider at least the following facilitating factors, which tend to be interlinked and are analytically distinguished here for convenience's sake.

The availability of exogenous artistic features may be made possible, for example, by economic factors, most clearly when intercultural trade in various ways provides access to foreign artistic objects and perhaps ideas. The trade along the so-called Silk Road in Eurasia is one prominent instance among various others, but it is also said, for example, that Western artists at the end of the nineteenth century first became acquainted with Japanese book prints as these were used as wrapping paper for Japanese exports to the West.

Then there is the religious factor, as when the introduction to a foreign religion includes the art forms it has developed. The visual art forms spreading in the wake of Hinduism, Buddhism, Christianity, and Islam are well-known examples, but one could mention many other cases, including the imagery that attends the present-day spread of Mamy Wata worship in Africa and beyond — imagery, importantly, that, as in the previous examples, is in itself a continuously evolving and locally varied amalgam of various artistic influences.

1

Anyone interested in the topics addressed in these introductory remarks should look forward to the proceedings of the 32nd conference of the International Committee for the History of Art (CIHA), Melbourne, January 2008, dedicated to the theme of intercultural artistic encounter and exchange (*Crossing Cultures: Conflict, Migration, Convergence*).

In examining the conditions of availability of external artistic features, one might have to consider political or military conquest as well, both in the sense that conquerors introduce their art forms into a given context and in the sense that conquerors become acquainted with the arts of the conquered. The history of Western colonialism, for example, provides various instances of both processes. In either case, the acquaintance may occur in a rather direct yet frequently decontextualized manner in the form of having access to particular artistic objects themselves, or in a more indirect and often distorted way through illustrations of objects in various types of publication.

Finally, to round off this brief survey, one might take into account social factors, specifically human migrations or displacements—phenomena that are frequently described more accurately as socioeconomic or sociopolitical, as the case may be. Again, this often works in two directions, with migrating or displaced humans introducing their art forms to the societies in which they refind themselves, and with diasporic humans in turn becoming acquainted with the arts of the latter. In North America, to give a salient example outside the visual arts, these processes combined to develop jazz on the basis of musical forms of enslaved Africans into which were incorporated Western stylistic influences and instruments. There are of course still other ways in which people may become acquainted with outside artistic features, including individual travel and, more recently, world fairs, museums, exhibitions, documentaries, cultural exchanges, and the internet.

When considering the availability of external artistic elements, one additional level of analysis, especially in synchronic cases, concerns examining whether or not art forms are "actively diffused" by the "source" culture or context. If so, then one may conceptualize the source culture also as the "sender" culture, aiming at a "target" or "destination" culture. (A source culture, of course, may also "passively" exert its influence, as when elements of its artistic tradition are "appropriated" by individuals from another culture or context.) The active diffusion of art forms, while likely to lead to some artistic presence in the intended setting, does not necessarily result in actual impact on local artistic traditions, for this requires particular conditions and decisions at the receiving end, at least in ideal-typical cases of voluntary acceptance of external influences in a "recipient" culture.

All this reminds us that processes of interculturalization in the arts fundamentally imply the agency of individuals or groups of individuals, being concerned not only with receiving and integrating, but potentially with diffusing or exporting artistic features. A basic question then concerns the motivations of the individuals who are involved, directly or indirectly, in these various processes. If we ask, first, why agents in a given context are motivated to incorporate external elements, as artists but also indirectly as patrons or audiences, we may again take into consideration factors having to do with religion (e.g., wanting to apply the stylistic and iconographic prescriptions of a newly introduced faith), politics (e.g., wanting to give support to a foreign or imported ideology through adoption of a particular visual idiom or subject matter in art, for example as part of a strategy in constructing a new collective identity), economics (e.g., wanting to satisfy buyers' desire for novelty or perhaps exoticism), and social considerations (e.g., wanting to boost one's prestige by means of objects that, for example, suggest access to external sources of knowledge or wealth).

Motivations may, however, also be "purely artistic" (e.g., when incorporation results from the desire to draw visual and thematic inspiration, or to solve formal problems of representation and composition, by taking clues from foreign art forms). In a related sense, integration may also result from the desire to communicate artistically to a multicultural audience. In his contribution to this section, Colin Rhodes discusses yet another motivation for incorporating particular exogenous features in art, one having to do with satisfying feelings of romantic or nostalgic primitivism—the longing for a golden age that one situates elsewhere or in the past.

Indeed, at this point it should be observed that, although this preliminary exploration focuses on what are basically synchronic types of interculturalization in the arts, the analysis suggested here in outline may also be applied to diachronic cases, when cultures adopt artistic elements from cultures of the past (belonging to their own tradition or otherwise).

If in discussing the incentives of agency in interculturalization we shift our perspective from incorporating to exporting or diffusing art forms, motivations may once more be found in the spheres of religion and politics (e.g., wanting to deploy particular art styles and themes as visual aids in ideological propaganda and indoctrination abroad), economics (e.g., wanting to create a new market for particular artistic objects), in the social realm (e.g., wanting to extend one's prestige and influence by supporting the export of a given art form or style that one is somehow associated with), or indeed the artistic realm (e.g., wanting others to become convinced of and profit from the possibilities of what are deemed to be more versatile and promising artistic tools and ideas). Again, these motivations may be interrelated, and the list is not exhaustive, potentially including, for example, "socioemotional" intentions, such as making emigrants or colonists feel at home in a foreign environment.

In considering individuals' agency, one also must examine both the concrete behaviors or actions that the various motivations lead to and the effects they have (such as the import or export of artistic influences, as well as their promotion and dissemination). These effects notably include the actual artefacts that result from the various processes discussed, as well as the roles they take on and the impact they have in the context of their occurrence.

To begin with, what is the nature of the influences that can be observed in the resulting products, that is, what do these influences in effect consist of? Many possibilities suggest themselves, since influences may be exerted on the potentially interconnected levels of materials used and techniques employed, style, iconography, symbols, motifs, theme or subject matter, but also use and function. In each case, and in view of each of these categories, it is crucial to ask: Which external features among those available are actually selected for incorporation, and why? For it will be clear that we are not usually dealing with a wholesale artistic take-over of what is on offer from the outside world. Also, elements that end up being selected need not be copied in every detail, and their interpretation and deployment may well be subject to change.

In conjunction with considering the phenomenon of selective incorporation, then, we also need to examine how exogenous features are modified or transformed in the process of local adoption and (re)contextualization. The integration of selected external influences into preexisting frameworks is indeed likely to involve various forms of adaptation or adjustment and hence various degrees of transformation or change (visually, semantically, functionally).

In addition to analyzing the adoption and adaptation of exogenous artistic features into their new settings, one might also try to examine the effects that are wielded by the presence of objects that exhibit these integrated influences. Do these objects indeed have the effects that are anticipated by those who engage in the process of interculturalization? Does the presence of these objects have such unintended side-effects as influencing a society's non-visual art forms, or becoming deployed, positively or negatively, in circumstances that were unforeseen?

The above suggestions for analysis only scratch the surface of a truly complex phenomenon (see also, in this volume, Richard Anderson, who describes recent instances of interculturalization in art; Paula Girshick, who addresses, among other things, the global circulation of objects as a result of present-day intercultural art-collecting, and the role of art objects in "exporting" cultural identities; Thomas DaCosta Kaufmann, who discusses intercultural artistic exchanges in the context of the geography of art, supplying references to recent analyses and attempts at conceptualization; Ben-Ami Scharfstein, who in his Prelude provides examples of interculturalization at work in the output of artists from various times and places; and Kitty Zijlmans, who examines present-day trends toward globalization in the "art system").

Some more and in-depth exploration is provided by John Clark, who in his contribution to this section addresses a kind of "Galton's problem in reverse." Clark suggests that even though the idea of modernity in the art of non-Western cultures is usually associated with imitation or adoption from the West, these "other modernities" in fact often result from developments that are far more autonomous or culturally independent than generally perceived.

The processes of artistic exchange between cultural contexts, as well as the products resulting from this cross-fertilization, have been variously conceptualized, although usually by means of analytical categories used to designate intercultural processes more generally. While passing over here the late-nineteenth-century notion of diffusion that emphasizes the one-way geographical dispersal from a source culture, "acculturation" is perhaps the first concept to have found common application in the West to denote culture contacts and their consequences. Its "classic" definition reads: "Acculturation comprehends those phenomena which result when groups of individuals having different cultures come into continuous first-hand contact, with subsequent changes in the original culture patterns of either or both groups" (Redfield, Linton, and Herskovits 1936, 149).

Following this definition, acculturation coincides with interculturalization as the term is used here—apart from the emphasis on "continuous first-hand contact." However, throughout most of the twentieth century, in the Euro-American sphere at least, "acculturation" has been used in a sense that is virtually synonymous with "Westernization." Colonized peoples and later so-called Third World cultures were supposed to absorb influences from Western cultures and in the process become more like them; likewise, the term was frequently used in the 1970s and 1980s in connection with groups of immigrants who were expected to adapt to the mainstream cultures of their host countries in the West.

Thus, acculturation, in practice, came to describe a one-way process of cultural influence, typically resulting in a "dominated" or "minority" culture moving in the direction of a "prevailing" or "dominant" culture (a phenomenon also known as assimilation, and accompanied by what is sometimes called deculturation). Although usually associated with the recent phenomenon of Westernization, similar and related processes of one-way, assimilative "acculturation" have been described in other contexts in time and space as well—Hinduization in South-East Asia, Lubaization in Central Africa, Chinafication (or Sinafication) in East Asia and beyond, etc.

In contrast, the concept of interculturalization intends to avoid the connotation of one-way traffic that has become attached to acculturation, by describing a potentially two-way process of cultural, in our case specifically artistic, exchange between sociocultural settings. Also used in this context is the concept of "transculturation" (originally coined by Fernando Ortíz in 1940), although it seems slightly less evocative since the prefix "trans," over or across, does not emphasize the possibility of influences traveling both ways as much as the prefix "inter," between, in the sense of going back and forth.

Indigenization is a concept sometimes used specifically to describe processes of integrating or absorbing external features into a given setting. It is a concept that suggests processes, if not of selective incorporation, then at least of contextualization and adaptation to preexisting circumstances—the more or less organic integration of foreign elements into a given sociocultural context (a phenomenon also described as localization). The use of this term seems to be restricted, however, to contexts outside the West, suggesting that indigenization is a concept somehow suited only to designate the absorption of Western (or other non-local) influences into non-Western settings. There seems to be no reason, however, not to describe the adapted incorporation of non-Western influences in local Western contexts in terms of indigenization.

Instead, to denote the "mirror process" of the Western absorption of features from outside the West, the concept of appropriation has been popular in the past two decades or so, especially in relation to the arts. Appropriation, or making one's own, has in this context acquired negative connotations of illegitimate borrowing or stealing, with the use of the term generally implying unequal power relations between the "West and Rest," especially those cultures formerly colonized by European nations. Until recently, the concept was hardly ever used to describe non-Western borrowing or incorporation of Western features, artistic or otherwise (but see Schneider 2003; for an extensive analysis of the concept of appropriation in relation to the arts, see Young 2008).

Equally popular during the last two decades has been the concept of hybridization, together with the accompanying label hybrid for the products resulting from this process. Signifying the merging of influences, these terms, again, have been used almost exclusively with reference to settings outside the West, whenever local and non-local, usually Western, features are blended. Some scholars and critics have employed the term hybridity in a negative sense in art contexts, deploring any sign of Western influence for its impairment of what they consider the authenticity of non-Western artists' works. (The work of Western artists mixing in non-Western elements, as implied above, has not usually been described as hybrid.) Many writers, in contrast, have used the concept of hybridity to celebrate what they see as an invigorating artistic heterogeneity that attests to the dynamism and resilience of formerly colonized cultures, in particular, while at the same time, for some authors, prefiguring a movement of true globalization in the arts.

There are, however, several reasons for being cautious when using the terms hybridization and hybrid as metaphors to characterize the processes and products of interculturalization. In its original meaning as a biological concept, hybridization refers to the blending or mixing of two species, resulting in a hybrid. The latter term especially does seem to have negative connotations: a synonym for hybrid is "bastard," and the paradigmatic example of a hybrid animal is a mule, the infertile progeny of the union between a horse and a donkey (plant hybrids, however, need not be sterile). Also, in biology and genetics, hybridization implies two "pure" species, making a hybrid as a result "impure." Some might

consider this an inappropriate label to attach to art objects showing a mix of influences, especially in postcolonial contexts. Other
critics argue, however, that "pure" is an "essentialist" or a "fascist"
term, making "impure" a compliment. Be this as it may, when
applied to the visual arts, the term hybrid seems to presuppose the
existence of "purebred," prehybrid art forms. The objection has
been raised, however, that there is no such thing as a "pure" art
form—that all art forms are already the composite results of
various influences. Finally, the term hybrid, strictly speaking, implies two, and only two, neatly demarcated sets of influences, each
having an equal share in the mixed end-product, highly unlikely
occurrences in actual cultural and artistic practice.

Various other concepts have been used, and are used still,
to denote the processes of intercultural encounter and subsequent
artistic products. These include the Spanish terms *mestizaje* and
mestizo (deriving from Latin *mixtus*, mixed, they roughly parallel
the concepts of hybridization and hybrid), which are used in the art
history writing of "post-Columbian" South America to denote the
blending of European influences and elements from "pre-
Columbian" traditions (see, e.g., Kaufmann 2004). Also used at
times are the linguistic analogies of pidginization and pidgin as
well as creolization and creole.[2]

One final set of concepts worth mentioning briefly is syncre-
tization and syncretic. Greek in origin, the words are considered to
go back to a combination of *sun* (together) and some term derived
from the verb *kerannumi*, to mix (cf. *krasis*: mixture). In scholarship, these concepts refer especially to the mixing or blending of
elements of various religious traditions, although they may be
used in other contexts as well, deployed as rather neutral (but not
very specific) initial descriptive terms—the same applies to the
word confluence or such current terms as cross-over and fusion.[3]
However, as Arnd Schneider (2003, 217) reminds us, the idea of
syncretism, like hybridity, presupposes the preexistence of nonsyn-
cretic states. This is a problem that seems surmountable, though,
when the term is used to describe actual encounters and exchanges
involving artistic features previously unfamiliar to the various parties involved.

Future scholars of interculturalization in the visual arts will
no doubt critically examine the conceptual legacy briefly described
above, and suggest more nuanced ways forward. In so doing, they
may well draw analytical inspiration from such burgeoning fields
as contact linguistics and the study of intercultural traffic in music.

—WvD

2
When people having no language in
common want to communicate, they
tend to develop a language that combines elements of the various tongues
available (in terms of both vocabulary
and syntax). This process is called
pidginization and the resulting simplified language, pidgin. Pidgin has no
"native speakers" in the sense that it
is a second language for all concerned.
Pidgin may, however, change into a
fully-developed language when it becomes the mother-tongue of a group
of people: a so-called creole language.
3
Compare eclecticism, the bringing
together of selected elements, which is
also used in the study of art, especially
with reference to a combination of
elements of various historical styles
from the Western tradition.

REFERENCES

KAUFMANN, THOMAS DACOSTA. 2004. *Toward a geography of art*. Chicago and London: The University of Chicago Press.

REDFIELD, ROBERT, RALPH LINTON, AND MELVILLE H. HERSKOVITS. 1936. Memorandum on the study of acculturation. *American Anthropologist* 38 (1): 149–52.

SCHNEIDER, ARND. 2003. On "Appropriation": A critical reappraisal of the concept and its application in global art practices. *Social Anthropology* 11 (2): 215–29.

YOUNG, JAMES O. 2008. *Cultural appropriation and the arts*. Oxford: Wiley-Blackwell.

COLIN RHODES

Primitivism: The Primordium Lost and Found and Reinvented

"Our complex culture is demanding for its sustenance a more and more intimate experience of the simplest and remotest manifestations of man's emotional and intellectual life."[1]

"In whatever field it may be, only the first initiative is wholly valid. The succeeding ones are characterized by hesitation and regret, and to try to recover, fragment by fragment, ground that has already been left behind…. The grandeur inseparable from beginnings is so undeniable that even mistakes, provided they are new creations, can still overwhelm us with their beauty."
Claude Lévi-Strauss

In recent years the usefulness of the term, "primitivism" has been challenged in many quarters. This is in part a result of the negative cultural overtones that its root, the "primitive" has acquired, especially in the last three or four decades, and particularly in light of a tendency to privilege its function as a noun rather than an adjective, and where its signification has been reduced to describing "tribal" peoples, thereby implicating its meaning unequivocally with discourses of western imperialism.[2] The adoption of this narrowly specific meaning of the primitive consequently infers that primitivism's range is also rather narrow, both in terms of its referents (the "tribal") and its cultural and historical sweep (more or less consonant with the most intensive period of European colonial-imperialism, for around eight decades from the last third of

1
[Editorial] A word for Caliban 1922, 157.

2
See recently, for example, Flam and Deutch 2003. Flam talks about "a persistent problem" with the term "Primitive art," which by the 1970s had come to be seen as "inherently critical—even insulting—to the peoples who created the art" (xiii). In spite of this, Flam and Deutch "retain" the term because of what they call "its brevity and conciseness" (xiv).

3
This is famously the case in the hugely influential 1984 exhibition at the Museum of Modern Art, New York, curated by William Rubin with Kirk Varnedoe, *"Primitivism" in 20th Century Art: Affinity of the Tribal and Modern*.

4
See, for example: Flam and Deutch 2003; Torgovnik 1990; Barkan and Bush 1995; Sweeney 2004.

5
See, e.g., Campbell 1997, in which the terms are confusingly interchanged.

6
It is worth noting that the "traditional" art and cultural history to which contemporary urban artists turn across the African continent is not necessarily that which relates unambiguously to a direct cultural heritage, but is often an amalgam of borrowings and hybrid traditions. In this way, such primitivism is analogous with, for example, the European modernist infatuation with the Gothic.

7
See, e.g., George Boas: "It will be observed that medieval man did not have the same interest in savages that the Ancients had, probably because medieval man was the savages whom the Ancients had seen fit to eulogize" (*Essays on Primitivism & Related Ideas in the Middle Ages* [1948], as quoted in Friedman 1983, 35).

the nineteenth century).[3] And in so doing, it implicates primitivist discourse emphatically within western racist constructions of otherness.[4] The questioning of primitivism is also in part a result of a common tendency, even among academics, to conflate the words "primitive" and "primitivism," where both are used as descriptive nouns alluding to "primitive" states or to simple technologies.[5] This conflation is unfortunate because it not only turns idea into subject through fusion, but thereby also empties the term primitivism of its agency.

Contrary to this, I want to argue that primitivism is a useful idea that can be effectively applied to art history, and whose articulation can be detected in both stylistic and psychological terms. I will be concentrating on modernist primitivism here as a means of disentangling some of the major theoretical issues involved in understanding the complexity of primitivist discourse as agent of interculturalization. Primitivism relies on an idealized cultural other, and in this sense its intercultural influences are uni-directional. However, it must be made clear from the outset that the notionally primitive subject of one culture is as likely as not to harbor its own primitivist beliefs; and it is not impossible for two cultures to look at each other squarely and for each to regard the other as more primitive. The perception of Japan toward Europe and vice versa in the nineteenth century is a case in point. Similarly, it may be possible to argue that cultural and stylistic primitivism can be discerned in art from many urban centres in contemporary Africa, where artists often fuse a nostalgic yearning for a "purer," more "authentic," agrarian past and stylistic appropriations from "traditional" art,[6] with a gritty urbanism related directly to the modern experience.

Thus, I will argue that primitivism must be understood as an idea whose currency cuts across a much broader timescale and spread of referents, including in the West, cultural tendencies in the postcolonial period, as well as before colonialism's inception. Whilst arguing that primitivism as an idea is generally transhistorical and transcultural, I am also insisting on the recognition of the shifting identity of the notionally primitive subject according to time and cultural specificity, so that nonurban, aboriginal cultures from Africa, the Americas and Oceania are not the *only* focus of primitivist ideas, nor, at times, necessarily part of the primitivizing project at all.[7] In adopting this view of primitivism as a more generally pervasive discourse I am also broadly accepting the specific intellectual construction of primitivism introduced by the great proponent of the History Ideas at the Johns Hopkins University, Arthur Lovejoy in the 1920s and later developed with his colleague George Boas in *Primitivism and Related Ideas in Antiquity* (1935). In spite of the age of their thesis, it continues to have value because it establishes a set of relative predicates whose parameters, though not their definition, are flexible and alter according to historico-cultural specificity. For them the "primitive" is most often used as a rhetorical device or metaphor in opposition to "civilization." As a generally recurring "unit-idea" Primitivism, therefore, is always an event that is concerned with cultural *self-criticism*; or, as Lovejoy and Boas put it, it is "the discontent of the civilized with civilization, or with some conspicuous and characteristic feature of it. It is the belief of men (*sic*) living in a highly evolved and complex cultural condition that a life far simpler and less sophisticated in some or in all respects is a more desirable life" (Lovejoy and Boas 1935, 7). The perception of existing in a state of social, cultural and technological complexity, and discontent with that state, are, therefore, the base conditions for primitivism to arise. Intrinsic to this is a sense of *loss* in the attainment of sophistication. Nostalgia for a simpler and (usually) spiritually healthier cultural past lies at the heart of primitivism; a real or hypothesized primordium, a time or condition of perfect beginnings. But also, crucially, and notwithstanding the fact that similar received knowledge can be at the root of very different ways of viewing the world, if we accept that primitivism is an active discourse, as opposed to a passively acquired institutional attitude, it contains a belief that something can be done to remedy the perceived state of oversophistication.

Although from a contemporary perspective we might perceive omissions and the need for refinement of some of the detail of Lovejoy and Boas's taxonomy of primitivism—for example, in relation to gender—their categories remain valid. They proposed two metacategories of primitivism that they called "chronological" and "cultural," defined respectively as longing for times other than the present and by dissatisfaction with one's own society. These were further refined into a set of subcategories that could serve as anchor points for analysis of individual cases.[8] Crucially, they suggest that subdivisions of cultural primitivism are organized around the "identification of the good with that which is 'natural' or 'according to nature'." The appeal to "nature" is, as they point out, one of the "most potent and most persistent factors in Western thought," yet one that contains a "multiplicity of meanings … in its normative uses" (Lovejoy and Boas 1935, 12). In an appendix they list sixty-six meanings of "nature," which is typical of the systematic character of Lovejoy's general intellectual project.[9] When "nature" refers to the way of life of the humans existing in a "natural" state they further identify two tendencies, which they call "hard" and "soft" primitivism. The first is based on the belief that the peoples in question "wanted less, and therefore knew how to be content with little," bearing hardship "courageously and cheerfully," while the second imagines a person "more free to do as he pleases" and someone "of infinite leisure" (Lovejoy and Boas 1935, 9, 10). In both cases we are dealing with two aspects of the same idea; that of the "noble savage." Needless to say, precisely the same descriptions of "hard" and "soft" primitives have also been utilized variously to illustrate the *undesirability* of the state of nature—

8
For a summary account of these categories, see "Prolegomena," in Lovejoy and Boas 1935, 1–22.

9
"Some Meanings of 'Nature'," in Lovejoy and Boas 1935, 447–56. See pp. 12–13 for their list of meanings of the word "nature" which are "most important in relation to the history of primitivism," including: "[i] That which is true or valid 'by nature' as what is universally known to or accepted by mankind, in contrast with beliefs or standards peculiar to particular nations, periods or individuals.… [ii] The natural state of a living being in its healthy condition, in contrast with conditions of disease and impairment of functions.… [iii] The 'natural' state of any being in its congenital or original condition; hence in the case of mankind, or of a given people, its primaeval state.… [iv] 'Nature' as that which exists apart from man and without human effort or contrivance, in contrast with 'art,' i.e., with all that is artificial or man-made. [v] 'Nature' as that *in* man which is not due to taking thought or to deliberate choice: hence, those modes of human desire, emotion, or behaviour which are instinctive or spontaneous."

although this is an apposite moment to remember that constructing a notional primitive does not in itself denote primitivism.

Primitivism and Related Ideas in Antiquity is concerned specifically with Graeco-Roman literature, but its premises are meant to be broadly applicable to other periods and cultural products.[10] Its potential applications to the cultural mores of later periods has not been lost on other scholars, especially in the field of literary studies, where the Enlightenment has most often been the privileged site for discussion.[11] In art history and aesthetics the book is less well known.[12] The only writer to attempt to deal with a historical sweep that encompasses the Classical period to the twentieth century has been E. H. Gombrich, in *The Preference for the Primitive: Episodes in the History of Western Taste and Art*, published posthumously in 2002.[13] He argues for the pivotal role played by Antique thought in defining the parameters of primitivism in the visual arts as well as literature, especially through his examination of the impact of Classical rhetoric. Gombrich's touchstone is Cicero's *De Oratore*, which describes a primitive turn that is apparently regressive, but actually a conscious strategy; essentially a "stylistic" primitivism, in which simplicity is used as a means of restoring clarity where obfuscation has developed. In spite of his strong interest in the subject, Gombrich himself had no time for those who engage in cultural rejections or social self-loathing; neither does he accept the validity of appeals to more visceral creative wellsprings, remaining committed to western rationalist thought and technological development. Since much of western artistic primitivism in the last century and a half in particular is characterized precisely by such privileging of the intuitive over the rational and levels of cultural despair (most notably, perhaps, in British and German Romanticism, German Expressionism, Zurich Dada, and Surrealism), through omission he thereby created a curiously lopsided picture of the breadth of primitivism in art.

Significantly, aesthetics is the intellectual prime mover for Gombrich, so thinkers are always privileged above artists, who are inevitably presented as either mere users of others' thought or providers (usually unwitting) of the raw material for critical contemplation. And because for Gombrich Primitivism in the arts is properly a *strategy* rather than a mindset, his interrogations of works of art are primarily at a stylistic or technological level, and the notion of primitivizing ideas more fundamentally embodied in a work is largely alien. For example, in his discussion of the British Pre-Raphaelites, Gombrich is quick to point out that, unlike the German Nazarenes, there is little evidence of attempts to return to Primitive Italian styles and methods in their work: "even the most enthusiastic of the medievalizers among artists were rarely carried away by their preferences to depart from the standards of academic accuracy in the rendering of visual appearances." Thus, since Holman Hunt's *The Hireling Shepherd*, for example, "is in no way reminiscent of fifteenth-century art" it does not, according to

Gombrich, "express any preference for the primitive" (Gombrich 2002, 141). Yet, this is to greatly overlook what might be termed its "conceptual" primitivism; that is, iconographically it can be read as an image of the "natural," and moreover of nature as healthy and tumescent. Whilst it stops short of being an evocation of a distant primordium, or Golden Age—the two human protagonists are recognizable as contemporary poor country types by their clothes and the landscape is clearly managed rather than wild—it is nevertheless a celebration of the rural as "natural," healthy and relatively simple, set against the absent, but implied opposite of the industrialized, urban setting as "unnatural," enervating and ove-complex. Similarly, although Gombrich praises Paul Klee for his stylistic orchestrations, the artist's profoundly mystical bent, which springs from primitivist yearnings after the psychological and creative primordium—clear for all to read in his writings as well as see in his art—remains unexamined.

Undoubtedly one of the major reasons that Primitivism came to be widely regarded as a peculiarly modernist discourse in the visual arts is the singularity and deep impact in scholarship and the curatorial world of the first book on primitivism and visual art to follow the publication of Lovejoy and Boas's book, Robert Goldwater's *Primitivism in Modern Painting* (1938).[14] Goldwater was well versed in the history of modernism and acquainted with figures in the contemporary New York and European artworlds, which in the surrealist milieu of the 1920s and 1930s had taken a decidedly "ethnographic" turn. An increasingly self-reflexive attitude toward otherness was therefore evident in much of the art closest to him, enabling more clear-sighted analysis of artistic primitivism's mythologizing tendencies; knowledge about peoples and the world could be more objectively balanced against primitivizing assumptions. His theoretical model owes much to the spirit of Lovejoy and Boas's project, although nowhere does he refer specifically to them and the four metacategories that he introduces—"Romantic," "Emotional" and "Intellectual" Primitivism, and "The Primitivism of the Subconscious"—do not have the same taxonomic rigor as Lovejoy and Boas's. They are also tailored for his specifically art historical project, which means, in Goldwater's case, that even where they are apparently "psychological" in character, the emphasis is on formal issues in the modernist artworks. The intellectual underpinnings of his thesis spring from fin-de-siècle questioning of mimesis and decoration, as exemplified in the writings of critics like Adolf Loos in Austria and Wilhelm Worringer in Germany, and especially artists like Wassily Kandinsky, versions of whose personal credo were, in many ways, institutionalized in the New York artworld of the 1930s. Thus, for Goldwater, as an *idea* primitivism was defined by "the assumption that externals, whether those of a social or cultural group, of individual psychology, or of the physical world, are intricate and complicated and *as such not desirable*. It is the assumption that any

14
Primitivism in Modern Painting was revised and expanded by Goldwater and republished in 1967 as *Primitivism in Modern Art*. A later, posthumous edition (1986), includes two additional essays, "Judgements of Primitive Art, 1905–1965" and "Art History and Anthropology," originally published elsewhere.

15
E. Haeckel, *Anthropogenie oder Entwicklungsgeschichte des Menschen* (1874); quoted in Richards 1987, 191.

reaching under the surface, if only it is carried far enough and proceeds according to the proper method, will reveal something 'simple' and basic which, because of its very fundamentality and simplicity, will be more emotionally compelling than the superficial variations of the surface; and finally that the qualities of simplicity and basicness are things to be valued in and for themselves" (Goldwater 1986, 251). In this view the primitive is therefore that which somehow represents or at least indicates the possibility of a kind of quintessence from which new (western) art styles might be forged. The process of apprehension and artistic creation (and significantly the two are interlinked in Goldwater's conception) might be "intellectual"—approaching the Kantian *Ding an Sich*, as in the case of the Cubists or De Stijl—or irrational—approached either viscerally through raw emotion, as in Expressionism, or psychologically through accessing more primal modes of consciousness, as in Surrealism. Either way, the "abstract" tendency in modern art is privileged above the figurative and especially the mimetic.

Moreover, Goldwater recognizes, but does not expand upon a key evolutionist notion that specifies modernist primitivism when he argues that not only did artists believe that "the further one goes ... the simpler things become; and that because they are simpler they are more profound, more important and more valuable," but also that they sought examples of the primitive that were both historical and contemporary (ibid). This was made possible by the continued general currency of a nineteenth-century Social-Darwinian idea, at the root of which is Ernst Haeckel's "biogenetic law," which states that, "The history of the embryo is an expression of the history of its lineage; or in other words: ontogeny is a recapitulation of phylogeny."[15] By extension, it could be suggested that what the child is to the adult, "primitive" society is to "civilized" society. Implicit in this is the Darwinian idea that evolution *always proceeds from the relatively simple and undifferentiated towards complexity and specialization*. In this way the Rousseauean notion that children are archetypally "natural" beings is seemingly confirmed by science, and they emerge as the "primitive" par excellence around which other notions of the "savage" and "primitive" culture revolve, creating a taxonomy of primitivity that, in the case of material culture, connects disparate artefacts and helps render them amenable to formalist critique. In 1910 Roger Fry characteristically argued that, "The primitive drawing of our own race is singularly like that of children.... The child does, of course, know that the figure thus drawn is not like a man, but it is a kind of hieroglyphic script for a man, and satisfies his desire for expression. Precisely the same phenomenon occurs in primitive art.... The [primitive] artist does not seek to transfer a visual sensation to paper, but to express a mental image which is coloured by his conceptual habits" (Fry 1910, 334). Similarly, G. Baldwin Brown's conflation of history and evolutionism in a 1922 article on the origin of the arts is entirely in keeping with prevalent attitudes: "The *earliest* phenomena of art are partly to be studied among primitive peoples *of the modern world*, who, like the Australian aborigines, the almost extinct Bushmen of Africa, or the Eskimo, are still in the hunter stage." Such expression, he says, demonstrates essentials, because "Painting and sculpture aim not at copying nature, but at producing an aesthetic impression."[16]

By the close of the nineteenth century a strong artistic current had come to prominence that privileged precisely those elements of decoration and conceptual content that the academies largely marginalized. In essence, a tendency gained ground in which a dogma of objectivity, based on the Renaissance mimetic paradigm was replaced by a new individual subjectivity underpinned by emotionalism, or "sensibility." Accordingly, technical virtuosity—which is associated with complexity and specialization—is regarded at best as anterior to that which is proper to art, and untutored expression is privileged. As Fry had earlier put it, "We have to recognise that our admiration of an artist's skill is not aesthetic.… We have to get rid of the idea that our favourable aesthetic judgement of a work of art is a kind of prize conferred on the artist for meritorious effort" (Fry 1917, 226). The "primitive" works to which artists wishing to subvert the academic tradition turned from the 1870s on were, then, precisely those which appeared to privilege directness and intuition over planning and the employment of practiced representational models, ranging from Japanese prints to European Folk and Naïve art, "tribal" sculpture, and psychotic art. The underlying primitivism of characteristic modernist rejections of the idea of artistic training of any kind is perhaps clearest in Kandinsky's 1912 essay, "On the Question of Form" (although ironically Kandinsky himself undertook a long period of training and was a meticulous technician). Along with the visual productions of children and the rural "folk," he considered that self-taught art (not Kandinsky's term) represents an ideal pole of what he called "the great realism," which, he argued, is the result of "an effort to banish external artistic elements from painting and to embody the content of the work in a simple ('inartistic') representation of the simple solid object" (Kandinsky 1912, 161). He placed maximum value on "natural" qualities, rather than bookish learning: "If a man [*sic*] without academic training, free of objective artistic knowledge, paints something, *he never produces an empty sham*" (Kandinsky 1912, 176 [my emphasis]). With the rejection of training we enter the zone of knowledge as a damaging commodity.

In many ways the "primitive" art to which European artists turned from the end of the nineteenth century until the 1920s constituted a kind of *Orbis pictus*; a mélange of cultural and historical forms. Crucially for the received history of modernist primitivism, Robert Goldwater was writing at a moment when the term "Primitive Art" lost its previous primary connection to pre- and early-Renaissance European art and became the generally used category

16
Brown 1922, 91–92. Roger Fry introduces an interesting dimension of class division into the discussion even as he suggests the relative universality of the child's vision. In the English West Midlands, which he describes as an "artistically arid and waterless desert of modern life," he says, "[the art teacher Marion Richardson] has shown that quite average children of lower middle class parents … have in them the same kind of feeling about the life and nature of their surroundings as the primitive artists of, say, fifteenth century Italy" (Fry 1924).

17
In the last three decades or so much informed critical work has been added to the art historical literature on this subject. In the field of museology two groundbreaking studies were: Price 1989 and Coombes 1994.

18
Some of those worth mentioning are: Lippard 1966; Laude 1968; Wiedmann 1979; Lloyd 1991; Rijnders and Martis 1998.

19
Among the most intelligent critical responses to the MoMA show were: McEvilley 1984; Bois 1985; Clifford 1985; Hal Foster, "The "Primitive" Unconscious of Modern Art, or White Skin Black Masks." In Foster 1985, 180–208. For a detailed discussion of the MoMA show and its critics, see Rhodes 1993.

designation for "tribal" and prehistoric artefacts, largely owing to the popularization of the ideas of the anthropologist Franz Boas and his followers. As a result Goldwater considered "tribal" art to be the paradigmatic "primitive" art, although most of the modernist artists under discussion used the term in its older sense; when they referred to "tribal" cultures they tended to use variations on the word "savage." In overlooking this Goldwater effectively closed off a significant aspect of modernist primitivism which was not concerned primarily, if at all with "savage" culture, and remarkably he set a trend in art history that has been a feature of almost all treatments of primitivism in modern art since. Goldwater's position is reinforced by his concern not only with what modernist artists looked for in "tribal" art—both in terms of form and underlying psychology—but also the ways in which a cultural context came about that enabled such an aesthetic interest to become possible in the first place. There are two, essentially prefatory chapters on the growth of ethnographic museums in Europe and the historical development of western evaluations of the material culture of "tribal" peoples, which set the tone in two ways in particular: firstly, they suggest that the "discovery" of the primitive-as-tribal by modernism was fundamentally an aesthetic one—a realization that this was *also* art, like modernism; and secondly, as discovery myths, they ignore the political realities of European colonial imperialism underlying the acquisition of "tribal" material and systemic assumptions about gender and race that lay at the heart of a putatively objective western scientific model.[17]

Subsequent works that deal specifically with primitivism by name are surprisingly relatively few, given its apparent prevalence as an idea among western modernist artists, although those that discuss the impact of "tribal" art on modernism—and in particular Parisian modernism—are many.[18] The single largest and most visible project, the New York Museum of Modern Art's *"Primitivism" in 20th Century Art* (1984) reproduces Goldwater's structure almost exactly in the two-volume book published to accompany the exhibition. Its considerable achievement lay in the scale of the undertaking. Its editor, William Rubin brought together a group of scholars who contributed individual essays according to their specialism across an impressive range of modernist practice thereby broadening, deepening and updating the pool of knowledge uncovered by Goldwater. Yet the key assumptions of *Primitivism in Modern Painting* remained those of *"Primitivism" in 20th Century Art*. Perhaps unsurprisingly in the context of a postmodern New York artworld, the Museum of Modern Art's essentially modernist project was subject to a barrage of mostly hostile criticism, most of which quite legitimately took the project to task for its apparently unquestioning tendency to replicate modernist universalizing and its failure to contextualize "tribal" work.[19] Just as interesting is the fact that only one of the project's critics, Dore Ashton seriously questioned the apparent annexing of primitivism to modernism:

"I question the assumption that ours, the 20th-century Western culture, is the only one to have perceived the primitive as a viable hidden increment in its own culture…. If we take exotic to mean just what it says—all that is other and outside our immediate experience—then the impulse of the modern artists in this exhibition can be seen as continuous with a long and important history" (Ashton 1984). None of its critics, though, question its reductive definition of the primitive as "tribal."

The history of primitivism in the visual arts is analogous with that of primitivism in general precisely because wherever primitivizing cultural discontentedness arises it finds voice across a broad spectrum of activity, from the arts to politics. Primitivism presupposes primitiveness, but it does not necessarily presuppose the wholly primitive character of the creative subject or culture; it is perfectly possible to be technologically primitive and psychologically highly sophisticated. Therefore, at different times and in different places, the "primitive" object of the primitivizing impulse can be partial, residing in some aspect of culture. This has particular resonance in art, where the forms of objects and the cultural information they convey is inextricably linked. As Goldwater rightly pointed out, "supposedly primitive arts are not united by any common qualities of form and composition" (Goldwater 1986, 252). But they are linked by the common qualities of simplicity and purity ascribed to them in the view of the primitivist.

As Dore Ashton points out, exoticism—in the sense of being interested in and learning from that which is outside the parameters of one's cultural paradigm—is a pervasive idea, and moreover not only a "western" preserve. But whilst primitivism necessarily contains some order of exoticism—as a yearning for something one does not have—the converse does not hold, for it is possible for the yearning subject to conceive her/himself as more primitive than or simply different to (without an implied value judgment) the desired other. Thus, in spite of there being very many examples of European artists learning from non-European sources since Antiquity, by no means all of these should be viewed in terms of the primitivizing impulse. Celtic appropriations of features from Classical art, for example, were driven by a desire to develop more sophisticated technologies of representation rather than the opposite. The dynamic interchange of artistic and decorative technologies that took place between the Near East and Italy throughout the Renaissance that has become increasingly well documented in recent years was driven by mercantile activity between two "civilizations." But early-twentieth-century European interest in tenth-century Islamic art was an aspect of modernist primitivism. Similarly, the self-conscious medievalism—in both style and treatment of Christian subject matter—of later work by Sandro Botticelli was the result of a primitivist attempt to expunge his work of pagan humanistic influences and "return" in his practice to a "pure," metaphysical style, which reflected a more general religious primitivism in Florence at the beginning of the sixteenth century. In spite of his own stylistic primitivism, Botticelli is also among those artists commonly referred to as the "Italian Primitives"—because of their status as pioneers, but not perfectors of a new art which took Classical Antiquity as its model—until well into the twentieth century.

In fact, before 1914 in Europe the "savage" was not only not the central notionally primitive grouping, but largely absent in the discourse. Art periodicals that, largely because of improvements in print technologies and particularly photographic reproduction, proliferated at the turn of the century tended to focus on areas other than "savage" art, even when they espoused an interest in primitivizing ideas. In *The Burlington Magazine*, for example, founded in 1903 there was a broad coverage of non-European art and decorative objects from the start. Yet, in spite (or perhaps because) of some of its most influential figures being important players in the European avant-garde, most notably Roger Fry, it is China and Japan rather than Africa that are central to its primitivism. Fry was aware that new ideas and forms often find their way into cultures in decontextualized ways, transforming later through new approaches. As he was to reflect, in reference specifically to Byzantine enamels and Coptic textiles, it was the "collectible" qualities of non-European objects and noncanonical European art, rather than aesthetics which initially allowed artefacts produced outside a perceived Græco-Roman tradition to enter western culture from the end of the sixteenth century. Collectors, he asserted, felt "no need to establish their claims as high art; they were curiosities and they were of precious quality and workmanship" (Fry 1920, 304). By the end of the nineteenth century, though, much of this work was being reclaimed by the European artworld precisely on aesthetic terms; though this was a new aesthetics that was antithetical to what had come to be seen by many as a restrictive post-Renaissance tradition marked by the demand for technical virtuosity and prescriptive hierarchies of genre and subject matter. The process was gradual, though, with artists and collectors usually blazing the trail. For example, although an artist like Paul Gauguin might have laid claim to the aesthetic worth of pre-Colombian pottery in the 1880s, even incorporating formal elements into his own rustic ceramics, its "artistic" incorporation into the dominant cultural psyche was unthinkable at the time and the transformation would not be complete until the 1920s. By the first decade of the twentieth century, however, even mainstream art periodicals could be found trying to convince presumably skeptical readers of its aesthetic worth. Thus a 1910 article on ancient Moche pottery from Peru, written in the wake the British Museum's acquisition of an important private collection begins: "The readers of *The Burlington Magazine* will probably be somewhat surprised at a subject like the present being thought worthy to come within the scope of an artistic publication." But it is quickly made clear these objects were not to be treated as ethnographic specimens, but as art, amenable to conventional aesthetic appraisal: "It may safely be claimed that some of their productions will stand comparison on equal terms, and will not suffer by being subjected to the test of European canons." (Read 1910, 22).

A comprehensive exhibition of early Islamic art in Munich in 1910 was, by the very fact of its staging and its impact, a symptom of changes in aesthetic attitudes. It also awoke a primitivizing interest in Islamic art in many modernist painters and sculptors, not so much because of its exoticism as its analogous status with and influence upon another "primitive" source much in vogue at the time, European Gothic, pre-Colombian and Islamic art had the advantage of being regarded as the products of historical "civilizations"; they were amenable to ratification in European high culture by virtue of its perception of a relatively high cultural context, situated in the past temporally rather than spatially. In particular, at the beginning of the twentieth century, stylistically and culturally they seemed to correspond to European "Primitive" art, such as early Netherlandish and Italian painting, as well as French and English "Primitives" from the sixteenth and seventeenth centuries. This kind of affinity-ism was essential not only to the rehabilitation of a diverse range of hitherto undervalued cultural products, but also in the establishment of a cultural system of values that privileged expression over technical mastery and classical canons of beauty.

Unlike other notionally primitive art forms, tribal objects from West Africa, Oceania and North America could not be recuperated by appealing to their status as historical relic. Aside from the fine bronze work removed from Benin City as a result of the British "punitive expedition" in February 1897, which was generally seen at the time as archaeological—that is, as representative of a past "civilization" since degenerated—objects from these geographical areas were viewed as the products of cultures both pre-sentistic (or ahistorical) *and* in a state of "barbarism" preceding civilization. According to the Social-Darwinist models of evolution that were still current in the first part of the last century, they occupied a place at the wellsprings of cultural development, and their artefacts a kind of embodied creative primordium. In this way they could be viewed as simultaneously both contemporary and "ancient." Without a history that could be mapped against genealogies of artistic development based on a European evolutionist cultural teleology and mechanisms of influence, they were situated inevitably outside art historical discourse. The reappraisal, and admittance of tribal objects into European art history was only made possible by shifts in the language of intentionality and terms of criticism of contemporary European modernist art itself. If Primitive and modernist art are mutually supportive in early twentieth-century artistic discourse, in the absence of a sense of history, tribal art *had* to accord in the first place with the present. Artistic interest in tribal art only really began to gain ground around 1905, in Paris, and then among a relatively closed social group. However, the

20
As quoted in Burgess 1910, 39.

broader acceptance of tribal objects into discourses of *art* as an autonomous subject area was really a postwar event. The immediate postwar period witnessed a surge of interest in tribal art in Europe, largely as a result of the modernist credentials that had begun to accrue to it as public recognition of its role in the development of a post-Impressionist aesthetic deepened. Its wider cultural appropriation, however, was more or less devoid of the cultural primitivism that had produced Picasso's so-called "Negro Period" between 1907 and 1909.

Throughout the second decade of the twentieth century it was common for avant-garde western art to be exhibited alongside "tribal" sculpture, as though they were of the same order of things. The qualities they supposedly shared lay, fundamentally in the intuitive register: expressivity, directness, simplicity. As André Derain told an American journalist in 1910: "These Africans, being primitive, uncomplex, uncultured, can express their thought by a direct appeal to the instinct."[20] But, characteristically, directness and reliance on instinct were also qualities he read into Japanese and Egyptian art. André Salmon perhaps best epitomizes modernist views of "tribal" art and culture in a 1920 article, "Negro Art." He emphasizes "emotional" qualities as against technical and mimetic ones, allying "tribal" art perhaps most closely with the supposed inherent expressiveness of Gothic sculpture: "That which allows the black sculptor to achieve the divine in his interpretations of the human face is his plastic translation of emotion, preferably at its most intense instant" (Salmon 1920, 171). Perhaps unsurprisingly, his analysis maintains close connections between modernist European practice and the "example" of tribal art. That tribal art was seen from the beginning as part of the history of recent European art is underscored by the fact that Salmon authenticated it through modern art, which was in turn authenticated through tribal art. For the timid viewer, he suggested, "It might be better before seeing the collections at the British Museum or the Trocadéro … to study the creations of the modern artists who were the first to place Negro art on a plane not inferior to that of Grecian, mediaeval, or Ancient Egyptian art" (Salmon 1920, 165). He was also clear that it was "Negro sculpture" which provided the lessons to artists suffering from a profound cultural "anguish." People like Picasso, Derain, Matisse and Vlaminck were, he said, "irresistibly drawn towards an art, primitive indeed in a sense, but already highly developed, un-shadowed by any Academy, or by any Renaissance. Such an art, if its logic were studied, was capable of reviving the dried-up sources of the classic" (Salmon 1920, 165–66).

If modern art was, ultimately to provide validation for tribal art, it was itself validated at least partly through comparison with other non-European and Primitive art. An article from 1911 by English critic Arthur Clutton-Brock on "The 'Primitive' tendency in Modern Art" tackles the subject head-on: "A good deal of ridicule has been provoked by the efforts of some modern painters to attain a childish *naïveté*, but these efforts are very like the early Christian efforts in morals…. So nowadays we have grown stale in art; we try to do too much and waste our powers upon what is not essential. Our own past is a burden to us, not because its art was bad, but because … we feel the same need in art as the Christians felt in morals to begin again from the beginning" (Clutton-Brock 1911, 227–28). But it is clear that the "primitive" to which he refers is European: "the word primitive … makes us think at once of the early Italians." And, perhaps, of Byzantium: "Gradually a primitive, living and expressive art ousted the mechanical inexpressive art of the [Roman] empire" (Clutton-Brock 1911, 226–27). Clearly, perceived shifts in contemporary values were regarded at the time as both necessary and part of primitivist disillusionment with European culture. In 1910 Fry defended charges that modern art, as represented by the works in his first Post-Impressionism exhibition was "barbaric" and "regressive" in very similar terms, asking his critics rhetorically why modern artists should "wilfully return to primitive, or … barbaric art," and answering that it was "necessary," if art was to become once again unencumbered by formulas and dogmatism and "regain its power to express emotional ideas."[21] Significantly, though, direct influence is also usually denied; for art to be challenging and valid in this scheme of things, it must not be stylistically derivative. Thus Clutton-Brock argued, "the simplified art of the present is promising because it … is not archaistically primitive; and that is the reason why it shocks and surprises us. We can put up with imitation primitive art, because its originals have prepared us for it…." (Clutton-Brock 1911, 228). In a famous article on "Bushman Painting," Fry once again insinuated a connection to modernism through the Far East: "Japanese drawings … approach more nearly than those of any other civilized people to the immediacy of transcription of Bushman and Paleolithic art…. It is partly due to Japanese influence that our own Impressionists have made an attempt to get back to that ultraprimitive directness of vision—they deliberately sought to deconceptualize art. The artist of today has, therefore a choice before him of whether he will *think* form like the early artists of the European races or merely *see* it like the Bushmen" (Fry 1910, 337–380).

The question remains as to whether primitivism is a feature of progressive art practice in the postcolonial West and whether the means exist to negotiate sensitively the complex relationship between the diverse material cultures of the contemporary world. There is a large body of art produced since 1945 that owes much to children's art, psychotic art, and cultures in the Developing World, but are artists like A. R. Penck, Arnulf Rainer, Annette Messager, or Chris Offili acting upon the same ideas about primitivity as earlier artists? In each case the answer is almost certainly in the negative, insofar as none subscribe to essentialist ideas about human difference or cultural evolutionism—indeed Offili's work is in part a direct critique of such ideas. However, here are four artists whose

21
R. Fry, "The Grafton Gallery – I," *The Nation*, 19 November 1910, as quoted in Green 1999, 123.

cultural discontentedness has found voice and form through some kind of primitivism, whether through a preference for less codified or more chaotic visual cultures, such as graffiti and handmade commercial art, or emotionalism and forms of unreason—both of which are still widely regarded as more primitive aspects of human psychology. The latter is especially apparent in the archaic ritualism of performance artists such as Hermann Nitsch and Carolee Schneemann. Perhaps, though, contemporary western artistic primitivism is nowhere more apparent than in work that reacts against a culture of global capitalism and incomprehensible technological complexity. It is a primitivism that seeks to *go back* to an ethical, spiritually intact time. It is also one that proposes a more Spartan lifestyle, less reliant on consumerism and commodityism. In a contemporary art that is often "issue-based," the models it chooses are cultures reliant on intermediate technologies, or for whom the creative recycling of mass-produced objects is a way of life. No longer perceived as "noble savages" it is still, nevertheless, qualities of simplicity, necessity, frugality, and therefore (because these are perceived as admirable), somehow purity that are read into their practices. Contemporary western art museums nowadays can appear like repositories of detritus reclaimed for art, installations constructed in self-consciously artless ways from ephemeral materials, and collected fragments of an eclectic mass culture that is as if itself already archaeological.

REFERENCES

ASHTON, DORE. 1984. On an epoch of paradox: "Primitivism" at the Museum of Modern Art. *Arts Magazine* 59 (3): 76–79.

BAIRD, JAMES. 1956, *Ishmael*. Baltimore: The Johns Hopkins University.

BARKAN, ELAZAR, AND RONALD BUSH, eds. 1995. *Prehistories of the future: The primitivist project and the culture of modernism*. Stanford, CA: Stanford University.

BIRTWISTLE, GRAHAM. 2000. Wat is er aan de hand met het primitivisme? *Jong Holland* 16 (2): 6–8, 64.

BOAS, GEORGE. 1948. *Essays on primitivism and related ideas in the Middle Ages*. Baltimore, MD: Johns Hopkins Press.

BOIS, YVE-ALAIN. 1985. La pensée sauvage. *Art in America* 73 (4): 178–89.

BROWN, GERARD, BALDWIN, 1922. The origin and early history of the arts in relation to aesthetic theory in general. *The Burlington Magazine* 41 (233): 91–95.

BURGESS, GELETT. 2003. The wild men of Paris [1910]. In *Primitivism and twentieth-century Art: A documentary history*, ed. Jack Flam and Miriam Deutch, 38–40. Berkeley: University of California Press.

CAMPBELL, AIDAN. 1997. *Western primitivism: African ethnicity*. London: Cassell.

CLIFFORD, JAMES. 1985. Histories of the tribal and modern. *Art in America* 73 (4): 164–77, 215.

CLUTTON-BROCK, ARTHUR. 1911. The "primitive" tendency in modern art. *The Burlington Magazine* 19 (100): 226–28.

COOMBES, ANNIE E. 1994. *Reinventing Africa*: Museums, material culture and popular imagination. New Haven, CT and London: Yale University.

DUDLEY, EDWARD, AND MAXIMILLIAN NOVAK, eds. 1972. *The wild man within: An image in Western thought from the Renaissance to Romanticism*. Pittsburgh, PA: University of Pittsburgh Press.

[EDITORIAL] A WORD FOR CALIBAN. 1922. *The Burlington Magazine* 40 (229): 157–58.

FLAM, JACK, AND MIRIAM DEUTCH, eds. 2003. *Primitivism and twentieth-century art: A documentary history*. Berkeley: University of California Press.

FOSTER, HAL. 1985. *Recodings: Art, spectacle, cultural politics*. Washington, DC: Bay.

FRIEDMAN, JONATHAN. 1983. Civilizational cycles and the history of primitivism. *Social Analysis* (14): 31–52.

FRY, ROGER. 1910. Bushman paintings. *The Burlington Magazine* 16 (84): 334–38.
—. 1917. Children's drawings. *The Burlington Magazine* 30 (171): 225–27, 231.
—. 1920. Modern paintings in a collection of ancient art. *The Burlington Magazine* 37 (213): 302–5, 308–9.
—. 1924. Children's drawings. *The Burlington Magazine* 44 (250): 36.

GOLDWATER, ROBERT. 1986. *Primitivism in modern art*. Cambridge, MA: Harvard University.

GOMBRICH, ERNST H. 2002. *The preference for the primitive: Episodes in the history of Western taste and art*. London: Phaidon.

GREEN, CHRISTOPHER, ed. 1999. *Art made modern: Roger Fry's vision of art*. London: Merrell Holberton.

KANDINSKY, WASSILY. 1974. On the question of form [1912] [Über die Formfrage]. In Wassily Kandinsky and Franz Marc, eds., *The Blaue Reiter almanac*. ed. Klaus Klankheit, 147–86. New York: Viking Press, 1974.

LAUDE, JEAN. 1968. *La peintre française (1905–1914) et l'art négre*. Paris: Klincksieck.

LÉVI-STRAUSS, CLAUDE. 1955. *Tristes tropiques*. Trans. John Weightman and Doreen Weightman. Harmondsworth: Penguin, 1992.

LIPPARD, LUCY. 1966. Heroic years from humble treasures. *Art International* 10 (September): 17–25.

LLOYD, JILL. 1991. *German expressionism: Primitivism and modernity*. New Haven, CT, and London: Yale University.

LOVEJOY, ARTHUR O., AND GEORGE BOAS. 1935. *Primitivism and related ideas in Antiquity*, reprint 1997. Baltimore, MD: The Johns Hopkins University.

MCEVILLEY, THOMAS. 1984. Doctor lawyer indian chief. *Artforum* 23 (3): 54–61.

PRICE, SALLY. 1989. *Primitive art in civilized places*. Chicago and London: The University of Chicago Press.

READ, CHARLES H. 1910. Ancient Peruvian pottery. *The Burlington Magazine* 17 (85): 22–23, 25–26.

RHODES, COLIN. 1993. *Primitivism reexamined: Constructions of the "primitive" in modernist visual art*. PhD diss., University of Essex.
—. 1994. *Primitivism and modern art*. World of art. London: Thames and Hudson.

RICHARDS, ROBERT J. 1987. *Darwin and the emergence of evolutionary theories of mind and behaviour*. Science and its conceptual foundations. Chicago and London: The University of Chicago Press.

RIJNDERS, MIEKE, AND ADI MARTIS, eds. 1998. *Expressionisme en primitivisme in de beeldende kunst van de twintigste eeuw*. Heerlen, The Netherlands: Open Universiteit.

RUBIN, WILLIAM S., ed. 1984. *"Primitivism" in 20th century art: Affinity of the tribal and the modern*. 2 vols. New York: Museum of Modern Art.

RUNGE, EDITH A. 1946. *Primitivism and related ideas in "Sturm und Drang" literature*. Baltimore, MD: The Johns Hopkins University.

SALMON, ANDRÉ. 1920. Negro Art. *The Burlington Magazine* 36 (205): 164–67, 170–72.

SWEENEY, CAROLE. 2004. *From fetish to subject: Race, modernism, and primitivism 1919–1935*. Westport, CT: Praeger.

TORGOVNIK, MARIANNA. 1990. *Gone primitive: Savage intellects, modern lives*. Chicago and London: The University of Chicago Press.

WIEDMANN, AUGUST K. 1979. *Romantic roots in modern art*. Surrey: Gresham Books.

JOHN CLARK

Modernities in Art: How Are They "Other"?

The notion of "modern art" is not culturally neutral since the very historical provenance of the term, let alone the advent of modern art in the world, always returns to Euramerica, in a Euramerican-centered version of art history. Yet everywhere in the late twentieth- and early twenty-first century world can be seen modern art which is no longer in Euramerica's conceptual grasp and cannot be conceived as dependent on the insertion of Euramerica into world historical processes. Shall we see these modern arts as merely the extension, imitation or reflection of that found in Euramerica? Are we always to privilege apparent art historical origin over actual art phenomena? Once it is admitted that modernity in art relates to plural phenomena, to modern*ities* within some overall classificatory genus, then we are likely to ask whether these modernities, however much arising out of a situation of originally colonial or quasi-colonial hegemony by Euramerica, are also due to particular kinds of difference which derive from different and very un-Euramerican histories? When we use the term "other," we tend automatically to privilege that which the "other" is "other than," or, as an unseen pole against which otherness is defined. Reciprocal thought is difficult which is constructed between poles and not uni-polar centered, and may even be denied by the very categories of thought formed within natural languages. But coldly and analytically, what is "other than" does not by its otherness privilege that which it is "other from": these are mere positions in an equation of alterity. This logical admission of reciprocality is all the more difficult when it is tied to historical naturalization of origin. It is as difficult to conceive of other things being done with Euramerican modernity, of non-Euramerican modernity not being constituted as a derivation of Euramerica, as it is to conceive of that modernity in itself being of an otherness from Euramerica due to its own historical contingence.

Thus, when we use the phrase "other modernities," perhaps reluctantly because of the in-built tendency to privilege the "Euramerican" as pole, the definition of what is "other," the state of alterity between different modernities, is our target of investigation, not the usually hidden or implicit Euramerican pole which might define this state of alterity. "Other modernities" are not restricted to one discursial space, say that of "Asia" in relation to "Euramerica," but may also be found in different constitutions in "Latin America," "Africa," and the "Middle East." The very differences and similarities within and between these other modernities take on fundamental importance when, as we might posit it, the absence of the historically present Euramerica can be imagined. In this sense the notion of "modernities" not merely being plural but also being "other," carries with it an imaginative leap to a discursial space where all modernities are diacritically positioned relative to each other, and not just to the "Euramerican."

THREE INITIAL ISSUES

At least three issues strike one immediately, from what may be posited as a non-Euramerican-centred position, when one examines the notion of "other modernities" in art (Clark 1998, 11–12).

Firstly, this notion rests on the theoretical position that modernity does not only belong to Euramerica, and on the empirical historical fact that different kinds of modernity have been identified beyond Euramerica. One has to say "in art" because it would be very easy to assume that modernities in other fields such as economics or politics were the same, or were generic for "modernities" as such. This may not be the case. Even if we identify linkages to economic and political changes and modernity, attributing similar or cocausal dynamics would deny the specificity of the field of art in finding that the originating motor for its changes lay outside it, and moreover that the interpretive models applied to explain those exterior changes also would explain those internal to art (Clark 1998, 14).

Secondly, if the first issue of what might be called other-field interpretive dominance over art were not complicated enough, it is inextricably embroiled with the problem of historical precedence and then dependent transfer from Euramerica to the rest of the world of its art-forms. This positions non-Euramerican art within formal art discourses which Euramerican interpretations had "already" privileged as modern. Many cognate issues arise for whatever might be "contemporary" art (Clark, Grove Art Online). The non-Euramerican modern is left simply to trail in the wake of the Euramerican under categories of clever or ignorant local appropriation. Indeed, transfer also lays the non-Euramerican modern open to interpretation through the determinism of stages of development. This concept, under various levels of derivation from Marxist and non-Marxist econometric models, is one where the

"modern" is followed by formal avatars of "modernism" and then
by the "postmodern." A little examination of one or two buildings
in 1870s' Thailand or Japan might make one question why features
of "postmodernism"—such as eclectic freedom to quote other-
cultural architectural styles and own-cultural building techniques
previously encoded in relatively rigid stylistic hierarchies or technical practices—should be found before "modernism" or indeed
before the "modern" itself (Clark 1998, 29).

Thirdly, the precession of the postmodern and the unfamiliar or noncognate historical processes which locate modernity
beyond Euramerica, immediately raises questions of what categories of objects, processes of production, or interpretive discourses
articulate "modernity." This third set of issues concerns the very
specificity of the field of art. The art which became modern in
many Asian societies after the 1850s, and even earlier in, say, late
eighteenth-century Edo or Calcutta, cannot be conceived solely
in terms of a series of appraised and valued fine art objects along
the lines of the kind of works shown in the Euramerican nineteenth-century Salon, itself a relatively recent and highly culturally-
specific phenomenon. The list of objects which are produced by
and fall under categories of visually discursive interpretation is long:
prints, textile designs, upper-class decorative screens, "refined"
literati paintings with their own long and highly erudite critical discourse, "vulgar" folk narrative paintings with complex histories of
belief and borrowed representational styles, photographic portraits, photographic records and journalistic illustrations, *cartes de
visite*, woodblock book illustrations, school text-book lithographs,
town guidebook printed illustrations, various kinds of technical
manual imagery and diagrams, illustrated advertising ephemera,
formal oil portraits, national-mythological paintings, hand-painted
illustrations of deities for sale at religious sites, et cetera. All of
these have to be considered in their relation to an as yet unspeci-
fied concept of "art" outside Euramerica where museum and art
gallery categories, whether or not they include a conception of
"contemporary" art, all collapse under the plethora of these types
of object and practice which produce them (Kinoshita 1993; Canclini 1995). Clearly modernity in art will be located inside discourses
of the visual, several of which are related to literary ones and
some to religious or political ones. In fact much of the relative hys-
teria in the Euramerican academy which has greeted "visual culture" approaches to art seems very misplaced outside it, in Asia in
particular (Krauss et al. 1996; Cherry 2004). No serious student has
ever considered modernity, modernism, and postmodernism in
such contexts to solely refer to a "fine art," or only to an "art" sanctioned or patronized by an aristocracy or property-owning and
entrepreneurial upper middle class (Clark 1998, 152–53).

But the index for much of modernity is found in art practices
of relative specialization or in its institutional development, because if modernity has a cross-culturally generalizable feature it

does seem to lie in the specialization of fields of practice, the training to equip someone to produce objects within them, or indeed to acquire the cultural capital to enjoy or circulate these objects. This is largely because practitioners within the domain of art, the artists, are the subject of a new kind of specialized training, and after certification, of workplace location, which becomes tied to more and more developed and socially complex educational systems.

The artist becomes part of a new class of professionally rather than workshop-trained specialists who have their own reception culture. Thus we also see the advent of such an artist as intrinsically linked to the near-simultaneous development of specialized publics for art, and its interpreters in new collecting and appraising institutions such as museums and art galleries or art critics. The fact that these processes of object-specialization and role-specialization are broadly found in many parts of Asia from the late nineteenth-century points to modernity having generalizable features which support the Euramerican-centered interpretation of a transferred discourse. But they also, and simultaneously, support the fact that culturally-specific and prior conditions for modernity exist broadly and beyond the exclusive grasp of Euramerican transfer theories. It is in the more articulated understanding of the latter set of phenomena, to which we will return, that the conditions for "other modernities" lie.

KINDS OF OTHERNESS

Some thought must be given to what constitutes "otherness" in the context of modernity. One must also, I think, distinguish "logical" from "cultural" kinds of otherness. However, modernity may be analyzed into preconditions or necessary elements, the notion of "other modernities" requires that "modernity" be conceived from the outset as a plural noun.

This is also entailed by the fact that for all modernities the past itself is a nonsingular "other." The modern is constituted from many different reactions to the past, but at the very least it involves the establishing of a notion of what is "not-modern," usually called the "traditional." The "modern-traditional" binary lies at the heart of modernity. The categorization of opposition or mutual relativization between the "modern" and the "traditional" creates a logical plurality. It is a very small extension to see the past as not being singular, despite modernity's attempt to force it into a singular "other" in its own binary constitution, and thus plural pasts will always and necessarily produce plural modernities.

The issue becomes much more complex when the "otherness" is conceived as some kind of cultural difference across different interpretive fields or historical phenomena. The philosophical problem of difference is better conceived as involving both a logical opposition, "same/different," and a deferral of meaning, "not/only and," to elsewhere in a total semiotic structure, away from the binary opposition which logically produces this. But the issue here hangs more on whether one conceives of all cultures as separate, or whether one sees them as subvariations of some wider and more generalizable set of human phenomena. The question of "otherness" in the end is no longer merely one of a formal binary, but according to this "essentialist" viewpoint also of substantial difference which, according to assumptions about the field, becomes a radical or essential incommensurability, even though there are many homologies across cultural difference. This would mean that there was some inalienable or unbridgeable difference between a "Euramerican" modernity and an "Asian" modernity. It might be so, however one conceived it, that similar structural features or historical processes in common allowed each to be classified as cognate with the other, to the extent that comparison of their radical dissimilarity was allowed.

One can also view questions of "otherness" on a short-term and tactically descriptive, or on a long-term and strategically methodological level. On the tactically descriptive level, it makes a lot of pragmatic sense to acknowledge the observable traces of historically conditioned cultural difference which produce a very different face to modernity in different cultural contexts. Modernity then becomes the pattern of those differences articulated into recurrent elements, types, or genealogies of types. On the strategically methodological level one cannot, after recent genomic reinforcement of previous identifications of the essential unity of humankind and its cultures, see cultural difference as anything more than a local, context-based variation within an overall historical set of patterns which have particular structures whose variation is limitable.

TYPES OF "OTHER MODERNITY"

The protocols for switching between the tactical and strategic uses of "otherness" now come into question. These are found via a genealogical tree composed simultaneously from constituting constructions like historical context and substantive or critically defining elements. The context might be the moment and type of contact with Euramerican colonialism, and the substantive elements might be the status of craftsmen vis à vis the role of the premodern intellectual classes which may have contained artists under certain conditions of practice, such as the literati in China.

Such genealogies have two specific branching types, whether or not one deploys Darwinian and Neo-Darwinian models to interpret their variation. The first is of linear branching from a single origin with variation according to the way modernity was accepted and transformed in different contexts. The second genealogy is of multiple and culturally-specific origins for the protomodern preconditions of modernity which when it arises is placable within a single set of comparable but parallel modernities. These often appear to have multiple and simultaneous subbranchings, and to that extent one may call these "other modernities." The genealogy is thus multilinear but with parallel subtrees. As with all genealogical trees the crucial issue is what accounts for, and what happens at, a moment of subbranching. In the Darwinian models this subspeciation was in the establishment — via long stochastic processes of systemic adjustment to environmental conditions over very many reproduction cycles — of replicable characters between generations of a species which were identifiable from an originary species.

In cultural phenomena, replication of isolable characters does not work via information exchanged at reproduction. In any case so many multiple and variable sets of data are exchanged between a putatively cultural "species" and a "subspecies" that the Darwinian interpretive model is inapplicable, despite a tree-like structure working to classify variation. A way of conceiving the changes at branching is to conceive of their dependence on some sorts of colocation conditions — like contact with or subjection to colonialism, the rise of a modern state with specific art-education systems, the birth of critical audiences. These form the preconditions for a change of state which starts off a local variation of modernity which, because of specific and long-seated local preconditions, such as the highly developed codes of visual appraisal in Indian or Chinese painting of various kinds or the complex urban life of Edo Japan, then produces a phase-change to become a modernity. This is so culturally specific it may be constituted as an "other" to modernities in different parts of the same tree.

Three important topographical features of genealogical relations need to be kept in mind for comprehending this "otherness" of modernities. There are, first of all, horizontal relations of similarity and difference between parallel branchings of the genealogical trees. Sometimes these horizontal relations are actually causative of changes in other modernities, such as the Japanese relationship with new Bengali painting before and around the First World War. But other conditions may have intervened, such as colonial structures which allowed but only in 1947 actually resulted in fulfilment of Indian nationalism. Another element was the cultural aggression implicit in the ideology of those Japanese sympathetic to Indian nationalism, like Okakura Kakuzô (Clark 2005). Other horizontal relations of similarity can also be of a lack, such as the lack of an artistic world autonomous of political intervention in China and Vietnam until very recently.

Secondly, vertical relations habitually designate those of origination and derivation from a temporally antecedent state or branching situation in a genealogical tree. This is the topographical feature which has been most often translated to mean derivation from and subsequent dependence on Euramerican modernity as the cause for the initial existence and subsequent structuring of non-Euramerican modernities. In a shorter time-scale, vertical relations constitute a model for dependency between higher, more powerful and lower, less powerful domains in an international to local cycling of art works, artists, and curators. These are usually considered as unilateral higher-to-lower flows which constitute part of the connection between the international and local art worlds.

There is at least a resemblance if not a homology between the vertical relations of typological genealogy and the developmental model of modernity; whereas horizontal relations point towards families or difference or groupings of "other modernities" more characterized by their structural resemblance than their common origin (Bydler 2004; Quemin 2002; Linde 2001).

Indeed, interpretive models which stress horizontal relations, tend to let the initial phase state of modernity remain clouded and the vertical genealogical link to pre- or protomodern conditions, the inheritance of past discourses of art practice or visual interpretation, to be left as constituents of a temporally synchronic mixture of elements whose causal connection is not specified, or is not thought to require further specification. Their causal interrelation is left vague, but is presumed to serve as a foundation for the inception of a modernity which is "other," or, "ours."

Thirdly, different types of modernity defined horizontally by comparison against others and vertically by relation to originary contexts, or indeed to the futures these contexts would appear to proleptically envisage, also include interspaces. The notion of interstitiality, originally used of the spaces in between the molecular structure of some compounds, was extended by several writers in the 1980s and 1990s to indicate spaces in the gaps between cultures where necessary differences also produced fused cultural states whose genealogical descent—vertical relation—was imponderable from any given cultural prescription (Bhabha 1994; Brah and Coombes 2000). The notion of interstitiality was linked on the personal level to cultural hybridity. Such linkage was important for actors in the art world such as artists and curators who were often resident or worked outside their primary culture of affiliation.

But the condition has been returned to the vertical and developmental genealogy by its being associated with postmodernism and postcoloniality. The latter ideological position as much as art world tendency, has also become the territory of formerly colonial artists and theorists who justify their ideas or artistic practice at the previous colonial centres. The latter move has thus had the additional effect of returning interstitiality to interpretation in terms of vertical relations of development, as against the potential of hybridity to remain a hermeneutic space for a kind of freedom interior to the structure of history and the genealogies of the modern itself.

As seriously, postcoloniality has resituated the previous colonial centres in the metropolitan discourses of Euramerica as the sites from which to interpret the modernities of the world beyond Euramerica. This is surely a further denudation or removal of the horizontal space for "other modernities" which could only be seen from outside Euramerica. It would appear in practice to be the case whether one is talking about cultures formerly under direct colonial rule, indirect colonial rule through implanted advisers and structures of economic dominance, or quasi-autonomous colonial rule through settler colonies. One perhaps unforseen consequence of the passing of actually existent communism, and the rise now over more than fifty years of newly independent ex-colonial states, is that the sense of a closely but differently related common positioning against the old imperial metropolises has been lost between the successor cultures to these types of older colonial rule. This has the serious consequence of artists, curators, and critics, not now realizing and strengthening their horizontal linkages, but instead looking for new kinds of vertical link to the old metropolises or their presumed successors and becoming its "stars" (Desai 2003). The situational actuality of "other modernities" in parallel contexts may be being replaced by the sometimes intentionally achieved singularity of one modernity in multiple global contexts.

STRUCTURAL CONTENTS OF "OTHER MODERNITIES"

In the second part of this essay I will look at some of the actual contents of one particular pair of "other modernities" to identify why they should be seen as other-than-Euramerican modernities, as much as mutually differentiated. The analysis is largely based on part of the conclusion for a comparative study of modern art in China and Thailand during the 1980s and 1990s (Clark 2008).

It is clear "other modernities" refers to particular cases of modernity within some general genus of modernities, even thought the fact that modernity is articulated through local, or endogenous discourses, that is internally generated discourses as opposed to externally or exogenously generated ones. The notion of endogeneity means that the driving forces and even types of articulation of modernity are not always the same as those found under Euramerican conditions. These conditions are not clearly recognizable from the position of universal or "exogenous," discourses. Although not widely accepted in Euramerica, these kinds of modernity have their own contingencies and evolutionary trees. That they exist now means that certain kinds of replication and adaptation or adjustment to local environments have taken place by "styles." This term simply denotes types of form and the practices used to produce them which have both an identifiable existence over time and an ability to modify themselves in certain environments. Thus it becomes inevitable that in the self-replicating human environments we call "cultures," a style will survive or functionally subsist only if it has in some replicable way adjusted to that environment.

The following analytical scheme categorizes and discriminates cognate kinds of art discourse in Asia.

A COMPARISON OF ASIAN ART DISCOURSES IN THE 1930s

Degree of State autonomy \ Type of Discourse Structure	A Euramerican art as modern art discourse-initiator	B Syncretism: contiguity of disparate discourses	C Parallel-discourses: neo-traditional & neo-Euramerican art
1 independent			*Japan*
2 neocolonial		*Thailand*	
3 semicolonial	*Philippines*	*China*	
4 fully-colonial	*Indonesia, Malay States*	*India*	*Taiwan, Korea*

The scheme allows the discrimination of similar but very different kinds of modern art, but it does not clarify vertical or horizontal, or interstitial positions, even merely theoretical ones (Clark 1995). One cannot see how A moves into B, or how 4 transforms into 1, and what the consequences of the interstitial gaps might be for any "final" or "resolved" structure of relations between discourses. These gaps need to be recognized under a notion of cultural contradiction between formal expression and how styles perform, that is their function in art discourses.

This kind of typological analysis requires a recognition of formal parallels or similarities between discourses and their correlation with function. These correlations are not necessarily obvious or clear along Euramerican lines. Modern discourses may be *formally* disparate but *functionally* cognate.

In a more general perspective, "peoples make themselves modern by creating indigenous and culturally informed 'functional equivalents' to meet the imperatives of modernization" (Gaonkar 2001, 18). It is these "functional equivalents" which make a culture modern endogenously. Some, like Gaonkar, think that modernity has travelled to places other than Euramerica and these "functional equivalents" are a local translation of what has travelled.

"Modernity has travelled from the West to the rest of the world not only in terms of cultural forms, social practices, and institutional arrangements, but also as a form of discourse that interrogates the present" (Gaonkar 2001, 14).

I see endogenous modernity rather differently, as an internal transmogrification of processes already *in a state of coming into being* but which "Western" modernity may have catalytically set off, and in whose guises they so superficially appear, or, to change the metaphor, whose alluring clothes they so bewitchingly disport.

The problem of modernity is that, however much one specifies how it has resulted from a specifically cultural and not a neutral or a-cultural process (Taylor in Gaonkar 2001, 82) we are dealing with processes which standardize as much as they create difference. That is, modernization may produce difference as much as the resultant modernity may seem to be the same across many different cultures (Gaonkar 2001, 23). Moreover, we cannot avoid

noticing the consequences of interpretive intentionality, for as
Mayo remarks, with the events in China of June 1989 no doubt in
mind, "There is much scope for misusing the concept of alternative
modernities and it may even appear as a justification for acts of
repression, under the guise that each version of modernity has its
own autonomous logic" (Mayo 2008).

Now that understanding other modernities has for perhaps only
a brief moment gained the attention of Euramerican academies,
one cannot help noticing that those who argue for the cultural
specificity of modernity in the "West" have very little output concerned with the "Non-West," and on the other hand, much of the
other-than-Euramerican writing is concerned with single culture
rather than comparative or multiple cultural work.

PRODUCTS AND INTERVENTIONS
ON "THE NATIONAL"

The nation-state is the progenitor but also the product of modernization processes which relativize both the past and the structures
of legitimation and authority which it inherits and transforms for
its own purposes. Non-Euramerican countries like China and Thailand are very different in the historical base from which the modern nation-state was constructed. But they are very similar in that
the nation-state both naturalizes its domination over the inherit-
ances of the past as well as creates hermeneutic hegemony over
how this domination is to be expressed in various social representations. This is why, unlike in Euramerica, the state as an organ of
power has actively or passively set the conditions for the representations of "the national" due to its own actual domination, but also
to the need to produce and perpetuate this. While we may identify
real and immediate differences in the way these conditions are
set, all art activity occurs under the proviso of state intervention as
to the method, content, and display of representations. Art is thus
not an autonomous domain of discourse which may criticize reality
and by extension the nation-state's domination of the past or of
its claim to be able to realize different futures. It is the awareness
of the real possibility of direct state intervention in China which
made so-called "unofficial" artists so careful in their post June 4th
1989 activities. It is a sign of the passive awareness of state intervention in Thailand which restricted art with a critical message
until the end of the 1990s.

But there are important horizontal differences between
non-Euramerican countries like China and Thailand, not merely
in the scale and regionalized structure of the population and
organization of the state, but in the actual historical experience of
modernization. These have direct consequences for art. Individual
artists by and large develop from individual art students. They have
a life history which runs along with the history of events in their

nation-state. For example, in China, despite the interpretive
hegemony claimed by the state, each artist has their own detailed
and intense personal history beyond the direct sway of this hegemony. It incorporates their personal history of Chinese modernization, particularly on the part of art students who became artists
before or after the Cultural Revolution. Such personal history is
particularly accentuated in China because the hegemonic practice
of the art world, with several important expressive variations, was
Soviet socialist realism from the mid-1950s to the mid-1980s. Thus
all Chinese artists, including so-called "unofficial" artists have a
deep and personally experienced sense of history, as well as a long-
practiced knowledge of one particular trajectory of representation
to express this.

Such is not the case in the other country of this comparative
pair, Thailand, where paradoxically the hegemony of the state
has seen extensive, and at times in 1973 and 1992 effective counter-
interventions by sections of the population, including particularly
students. The paradox is that this historical success, if tentative
and always subject to the risk of oligarchic reversal in Thailand,
has not been accompanied by a series of historical representations
in art. This may be due in Thailand to both the lack of history
painting as a subject since the late nineteenth century, but also
probably to the occupation of the space of public and dignified
representation by a discourse of royal images. For various reasons
to do with the official and other institutional manipulation of
"Thai" values, this discourse has rarely been subject to critique, let
alone overthrow.

Above and beyond the state organs which actually secure
hermeneutic hegemony, the basic resemblance between China and
Thailand is that there is presumed to be a set of values which define the state and nation. This might not be the case in many
Euramerican nation states where despite there being a baseline of
presumed "common beliefs," such values might be expected to
emerge during negotiated conflicts between disparate or opposed
sets of values supported by particular groups. In China and Thailand, modernization has made this presumed set of values concrete
through policy. It can be seen through political acceptance of
explicit values in China, or in Thailand through essentialist or perhaps "culturalist" acceptances of a nonspecific, and in important
areas diffuse, set of "Thai" values. This can mean a greater clarity
of political lines relating to arts in China and ambiguous vague, or
underarticulated policies in Thailand.

The role of artists as conscience-bearers for the nation is very
different. The artists have this in China partly because of their restricted access to highly elitist art education, and also partly because
of habits of premodern Chinese literati individualism where the
artist could be positioned as a moral seer willing to make personal
sacrifice or to go into internal exile. Thai artists do not appear to
be accepted as members of the modern intellectual class in this way,

and are unable to call on this premodern legitimation of their critiques.

ENDOGENOUS AND EXOGENOUS

The main constituting feature of almost any kind of modernity or causative processes of modernization is their relational construction to the "West." Endogenous discourses have always been bracketed by the exogenous discourses they refer to. This has made it very difficult to conceive of, say, "Chinese" or "Thai" modernity as "theirs" when to a Euramerican eye "theirs" always appears in the guise of, and therefore as an imitation of, "ours." This is probably doubly problematic because modernity is founded on relativization of the past, and the past is always "other" and plural. So the endogenous position from which "our past" is rendered other to Chinese or Thai discourses is not, without extensive understanding and analysis, available to the exogenous.

The problem of perspective is also related to external perception of endogenous phenomena, such as stylistic cycling. Criteria of cycling time based in the historical experience of exogenous discourses are applied to the endogenous: the time-base for stylistic accession such as, "before" and "after," "origin" and "reception," "new" and "old," may be assigned downwards from the exogenous. Even the concept of relation between exogenous and endogenous discourse tends to note where and when they merge. This may be taken solely from an exogenous position shown by the application of terms such as "up to speed" or "in sync" and "out of sync."

But intervention via the time base applied in appraisal overlaps the selective nature of exogenous interventions. Foreign interest in Chinese nonofficial art has always been much greater than for radical art in Thailand. *Politically* preferred art which was the antithesis to official taste was hardly the concentrated subject of foreign purchase in Thailand, as it may reasonably be said was the case in China, certainly in the early 1990s.

More profound difficulties for the relation between the exogenous and the endogenous come from within the lived experience of artists themselves. If in the Euramerican past the relation between art cultures could be described if not explained by relations between the stylistics of works, with increasing flows of information and mobility of artists the major change in the setting of the terms of inside and outside actually comes in the life of the artist. Or, in the sense that the "artist" is him or herself a complex kind of cultural good, it comes in the way they are handled by exogenous and endogenous discourses. I think the major impact of globalism on Chinese and Thai artists has come in their personal identities and the way they organize degrees of affiliation to the national in their daily lives. This is all the more so when artistic practice may involve the circulation of similar installations or similar participant work-events between distant sites over a period of eighteen months to two years.

If the art work no longer has a monolineal cultural descent
and the artist has not one but several cultural affiliations if not
full-blown identities, how could anyone except the bearer of a
peculiarly Euramerican-centred view of the world conceive of
modernity as belonging to one series, or to one hierarchy? Perhaps
this singularity is possible only at the location of groups which
have been marginalized because of their exogenous origins and
who find themselves or have put themselves into the Euramerican
discourses (Araeen 1989; Asbury and Baddeley 2000). This does
not mean that in any sense their representation or translocation of
the endogenous discourses into the exogenous ones is a remanifest-
ation of those endogenous discourses themselves. But it does
mean the terms of negotiation of the exogenous with the boundaries and sites for endogenous discourses have changed.

STYLISTIC DISCOURSES

Stylistics also frequently challenges the notion of a monolineal
descent tree for modernity. Dimensions which descriptively map
the space of modern art styles in both China and Thailand, would
not derive from the mapping, the distribution or the advent of
Euramerican modernities (Clark 2008, Chapter Three). This mapping does not allow for any facile antithesis between the "modern"
and the "traditional." Moreover, it changes what might have been
the formal quality of works into features of their context of reception, such as in the antitheses of "confronting rawness" and "com-
fortable newness" on the dimension of "public."

Even stylistic modalities such as allegory seen with highly
codified Chinese leader portraits and Thai royal portraits indicate
very different genealogies, historical conjunctions, and historical
motivations. This does not render the *function* of the allegory or
even the *practice* by which the allegory is often deployed very
different. Indeed, it is surprising how alike their functions and application are despite broad differences in the connotations of the
figures portrayed.

The art system in both China and Thailand produces the new
by its demonstration of a special ability to access the exogenous
world, in a way which allows the transformation for the purposes of
discourses we can still only call endogenous. The exogenous loses
its "exogenous" aura and becomes "nested" within endogenous
discourses as a kind of emplaced criterion within an existing set of
values. This "nesting" does not imply external hegemony nor exogenous interventions in the same way as Euramerican monolineal
genealogies of the modern are habituated to construct it.

It remains to ask what group is to perform the function of
further innovation, a potential to relativize not just history but a
previous and already modern position which is peculiarly privileged by modernity itself. If criticism is rarely public and even then

may be indirectly muted, those with educational privilege may suggest alternate views of reality. For artists this is more the case in China than in Thailand. The position seems to institutionalize the avant-garde, rather than make them a special social group who are the temporary bearers of a social and aesthetic consciousness thrown up by the conflicts of their times.

INSTITUTIONS

The bounding feature of modern art in countries like China and Thailand is that it is an institutional practice. Even in China where for political reasons a kind of anti-establishment "unofficial" art developed in the 1990s, the artists involved were overwhelmingly trained in the art establishment or were reacting to its educational curricula, exhibition practices, and stylistic codes. The elaborate series of feedback reinforcements of styles or in reaction of opposing tendencies means that stylistic acceptance and transformation does look like a series of stylistic species' adaptations. Despite the totalism of the Chinese state, its hegemony can never be absolute because of the size and variety of the populations its territory includes. Thus there are indeed the equivalent of environmental niches where quite different kinds of stylistic expression for undominated artistic practice may find their expression.

The Thai case in some respects presents an opposite situation. On the one hand there are the art schools and competitive exhibition institutions which reinforce an educationally sanctioned practice and a public discourse of images which allow various kinds of dignified expression. On the other, there is a kind of laissez-faire indifference which seems to lack formal or socially accepted feedback mechanisms to reinforce stylistic adaptations. Sometimes there appears to be elite tolerance of difference, such as the licensed radicality allocated to some artists, or there is a feigned ignorance of the full meaning of some criticism.

Another reinforcing institution is the market. There has only recently arisen a class of entrepreneurs and higher-paid professionals in China who buy contemporary art or otherwise support it. Actual art sales are still mainly concentrated in overseas buyers, or in market speculation via auctions. Although in the case of auctions, prices have since 2000 crept up for nameable contemporary artist figures, it is unclear if these auction sales are mainly to foreign or overseas Chinese buyers.

Probably the most significant kind of institutional reinforcement of contemporary art has been through educational investment, with contemporary art in various manners from the decorative to the conceptual being accepted in the 1990s as status markers of public display in Thailand, and one thinks also in China from the early 2000s. Educational investment increases the number of artists, and around them a cohort of socially interested persons. It is perhaps the most significant marker of modernity in an art world.

This index puts Thailand with 1–2 graduates per 100,000 population and China with 0.1–0.5 graduates per 100,000 population
in quite different bandings. It is intellectually unattractive to think
there may be such a simple correlation between the modernity
of an art world and the relative size of its population of artists. Yet
when one thinks of the relativization of art values via curricular
encoding, the ideological thrust and system of compliance controls
of modern educational systems, the intergenerational conflict over
art styles, and the very reactions possible against such formaliza-
tions, the conclusion is hardly surprising. Perhaps the educational
cohort-driven features of modernity and their subsequent transformation are much clearer in China and Thailand than in Euramerica. In China the forcefulness and persistence of ideological goals
may lead to a certain ferocious clarity with which contemporary or
"unofficial" art reacts against the institutional hierarchy. In Thailand the passive tolerance or casuistic ignorance—stemming from
Theravadin precepts perhaps—may allow greater decorative
play, one which can descend into merely attractive ornamentalism.

But China and Thailand are alike in that recent developments in new media have facilitated the incorporation of art into
consumer fashion and mass marketing stylistics. This in itself
leaves much similar room for critiques of consumerism through
displacement or traducing of consumer symbols–the exaggeratedly
"Thai" Pizza or Thaified Kentucky Fried Chicken, the Chinese
Macburger or Coke as political symbol. But contemporary art,
whilst it has sometimes referred to urban poverty, has rarely yet in
either country made a topic of the urban poor dragged in from
the countryside to service the grand manufacturing machines of
desire which fuel urban consumption. This is unlikely just to be
due to political sensitivity, but also to the career investment of contemporary artists in the very urban spectacles they might otherwise look behind or try to overturn.

HISTORIES, PERIODS

Two kinds of periodicity seem to govern art practice as a characterizing element of "other modernities" in Asia as I have discussed
above in the opening section. These may be found particularly in
China, but with certain qualifications they are also the case in Thailand. One is the formation and transmission through the art system
of artistic cohorts. The second is the formal exploration and much
later official acceptance of new types of practice, such as installation and performance art. Imbricated within these periodizations is
the acceptance of formerly censored or tabooed subject matters.
Radical or avant-garde qualities in art may thus be governed as
much by the inclusion of content as the stylistically problematic use
of given media or work-events.

These period-generators exist alongside a very marked
political history which is subject to the intervention of political

parties, military oligarchs, and wider societal tendencies to democratic rule. Indeed, it is the close correlation of various changes in stylistic discourse in China with political subsequent economic changes which appears to differentiate it from Thailand. However, closer examination of the Thai material indicates there are correlations of a similar but not so obvious kind, particularly in the 1990s. The main difference is that the Thai oligarchy's compromise with the left in the early 1980s took the political wind out of realism as an oppositional stylistic discourse, and despite the subsequent rise of issue-oriented political activity by NGOs, this does not seem to have produced any major radicality in art.

Both China and Thailand differ in the way the heritage of the past is to be historically worked out, and specific artistic tendencies incorporated in art practice. In China the socialist past may be ironized about by major artists, even those accepted in the art establishment. This is an irony not linked to the overthrow of the state or the upturning of officially hegemonic ideology. In Thailand the heritage of the past is broadly conceived along the lines of a nexus of "Thai" values, in fact established as state ideology in the 1930s, but not given any explicit permanent or recurrent ideological statement. Thus claims to continue or support "Thai" heritage are up for grabs from almost any quarter ranging from monarchists, to the Fine Arts Department's theme-park-ification of archaeological heritage sites (Peleggi 2002, 2005), to *Chang* [elephant] Beer TV commercials. One beer advertisement for Singha beer, even implies that it is "the" Thai beer, representing the quintessence of "Thai" values.

Perhaps the major difference between China and Thailand is that it is always available to Chinese artists, or the specific ideological positions of Chinese educational and cultural policies, not merely to regard "China" as simply the equal of the "West" but also as its cultural superior. This externally projective aspect of "other modernities" which now actually only applies to China, has not often attracted attention partly because Japan was the only power strong enough and integrated into the world system closely enough to advance it in the 1930s and 1940s. In Thailand this sense of a superior "other modernity" does not seem to be the case, except for a certain cultural superiority in sinking back into the presumed self-sufficient and moral virtues of the ideal "Thai" village. This had its education and oral transmission of values organized through the temple and its rulership in the hands of benevolent monarchs. It is a place of mental repose into which a certain "Thai" mentality seems to retreat in fantasy when under exogenous pressure, as after 1997. We may respectively describe these as positions of active-aggressive and passive-introspective endogeneity.

CONCLUDING REMARKS

It would seem that the habitual suppositions of Euramerican modernism in art do not apply in all "other modernities" such as modern and contemporary Asian art, either because of different functionalities in innovation in stylistic discourse, or due to different conceptualizations of practice. In the latter, these are still produced in teleological terms to privilege Euramerican art, whereas in the former far greater room is given, under various constitutions, for "nested endogeny" that indicates a less-than-automatic assumption of priority of the exogenous. Fairly predictably, changing markets and economic competition as well as simply style-fatigue may switch Euramerica towards recognizing contemporary Asian art, but this is unlikely to lead to the recognition of the 150 years or so of "other modernities" in Asian art it has so far ignored.

In Asia new emphases on the national, tribal, or the religious as projects seeking a new identity unleashed on or by the state, may cause the rejection of the assimilation of the exogenous into the endogenous. This could in future indicate a family of modernities fundamentally "other" to the Euramerican ones, where the role of the exogenous in stimulating the endogenous relativization has recurrently taken place.

Some artists are fully aware of the ironies and contrasts between these systems: Huang Yongping's model made out of sand of a precommunist Shanghai Bank (Fig. 1) may stand as a concrete allegory for the whole aporia of the "modernity" of an "Asian art," and of "other modernities" in general.

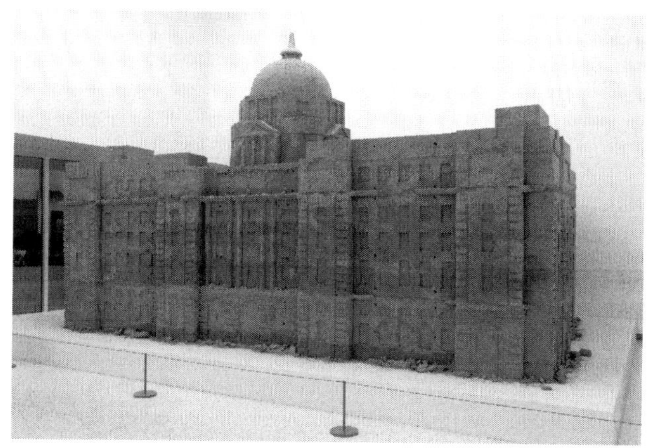

Figure 1
Huang Yongping. Bank of Sand, Sand of Bank. 2000-2005.

Bank of Sand, Sand of Bank consisted in building a "bank," (6 x 4.3 x 3.5 m) out of sand in the main hall of the entrance lobby of the museum. The model for this bank was the former British HSBC (Hongkong and Shanghai Banking Corporation) building, constructed in 1923. This "bank of sand" was composed of four wooden molds, reinforced and fixed together with long screws. Dry sand mixed with cement was poured into the molds. Subsequently, water was sprayed on it, and it was pressed down with a wooden post to make it compact and solid. After it dried, the "bank of sand" would eventually crumble down.

REFERENCES

ARAEEN, RASHEED. 1989. *The other story: Afro-Asian artists in post-war Britain*. London: The South Bank Centre.

ASBURY, MICHAEL, AND ORIANA BADDELEY. 2000. *Other modernities*. London: The London Institute Gallery.

BHABHA, HOMI K. 1994. *The location of culture*. London: Routledge.

BRAH, AVTAR, AND ANNIE E. COOMBES, eds. 2000. *Hybridity and its discontents: Politics, science, culture*. London: Routledge.

BYDLER, CHARLOTTE. 2004. *The global art world inc.: On the globalization of contemporary art*. Figura nova series 32. Uppsala: Acta Universitatis Upsaliensis. PhD diss., Uppsala University.

CANCLINI, NÉSTOR GARCÍA. 1995. *Hybrid cultures: Strategies for entering and leaving modernity*. Trans. Christopher L. Chiappari and Silvia L. López, Minneapolis: University of Minnesota Press.

CHERRY, DEBORAH. 2004. *Art: History: Visual: Culture. Art History* 27 (4): 479–93.

CLARK, JOHN. 1995. Yôga in Japan: Model or exception? Modernity in Japanese art, 1850s–1940s: An international comparison. *Art History* 18 (2): 253–85.
—. 1998. *Modern Asian art*. Sydney: Craftsman House; Honolulu: University of Hawai'i Press.
—. 2005. Okakura Tenshin [Kakuzô] and aesthetic nationalism. *East Asian History* 15 (29): 1–38.
—. 2005. Modern and contemporary Asian art. In *The dictionary of art* at Grove Art Online.
—. 2008. *Modernities compared: Chinese and Thai art in the 1980s and 1990s* Sydney: Power Publications.

DESAI, VISHAKA, APINAN POSHYANANDA, AND OKWUI ENWEZOR. 2003. Looking ahead: Dialogues in Asian contemporary art: Transcription. *Yishu: Journal of Contemporary Chinese Art* 2 (2): 112–121.

GAONKAR, DILIP PARAMESHWAR, ed. 2001. *Alternative modernities*. Durham and London: Duke University Press.
—. 1999. On alternative modernities. *Public Culture* 11 (1): 1–18.

KINOSHITA NAOYUKI. 1993. *Bijutsu to iu misemono, aburae-chaya no jidai*. Tokyo: Chikuma Shobo.

KRAUSS, ROSALIND, ET AL., ed. 1996. Visual studies questionaire. *October* 77 (Summer): 27–28.

LINDE, ROHR-BONGRAD, et al. 2001. *Kunst=Kapital: Der Capital Kunstkompass von 1970 bis heute*. Cologne: Salon Verlag.

MAYO, LEWIS, WITH JOHN CLARK. 2004. Statements about art and modernity in People's Daily since 1990. In *Modernities compared: Chinese and Thai art in the 1980s and 1990s* Sydney: Power Publications.

PELEGGI, MAURIZIO. 2002. The politics of ruins and the business of nostalgia. Bangkok: White Lotus.
—. 2005. Royal antiquarianism, European orientalism and the production of archaeological knowledge in modern Siam. In *Asia in Europe, Europe in Asia*, ed. Srilata Ravi, Mario Rutten, and Ben-Lan Goh. IIAS/ISIAS series on Asia. Leiden: IIAS; Singapore: ISEAS.

QUEMIN, ALAIN. 2002. *L'art contemporain international: entre les institutions et le marché (le rapport disparu)*. Nîmes: Éditions Jacqueline Chambon/Artprice.

TAYLOR, CHARLES. 2001. Two theories of modernity. In *Alternative modernities*, ed. Dilip Parameshwar Gaonkar, 172–96. Durham and London: Duke University Press.

ABOUT THE AUTHORS

RICHARD ANDERSON is Professor of Cultural Anthropology in the School of Liberal Arts of the Kansas City Art Institute. Since joining the Institute in 1974, his research has focused on the anthropology of art and cross-cultural aesthetics. In addition to many journal articles, he is the author of *Art in Small-Scale Societies* (2nd edition, 1989), which focuses on the first topic; and *Calliope's Sistes: A Comparative Study of Philosophies of Art* (2nd edition, 2004), which deals with the second. *American Muse: Anthropological Excursions into Art and Aesthetics* (2000) examines popular art and vernacular aesthetics in the United States. Since 2004, Anderson's chief interests have been the art and culture of Mexico and the effects of globalization on world art.

JEAN M. BORGATTI is a Research Associate (Visual and Performing Arts) at Clark University in Worcester, Massachusetts, where she taught from 1984–2004. She is currently a free-lance lecturer and consultant in African, Black Atlantic World, Oceanic, and Native American Art History. Her main interests are cross-cultural frameworks for understanding art and aesthetics, masquerades in social and historical contexts, and individual artists who might be described as "contemporary" traditionalists. Publications include *From the Hands of Lawrence Ajanaku* (1979), one of the first monographs on a traditional African artist; *Portraiture in Africa, Parts I & II*, special issues of the journal *African Arts* (1990–1991); and *Likeness and Beyond: Portraiture in Africa and the World* (with Richard Brilliant, 1990). She is currently working on analyzing a major longitudinal study of Okpella (Nigeria) aesthetic preference.

DONALD E. BROWN is Professor Emeritus of Anthropology at the University of California, Santa Barbara. His main interests have been the social structure and history of the Sultanate of Brunei; the implications of social structure—especially hereditary rank—for history, historical mindedness, and culture in general; human universals and their implications; and the comparative study of ethnicity. His principal publications include *Hierarchy, History, and Human Nature: The Social Origins of Historical Mindedness* (1988) and *Human Universals* (1991).

CAO YIQIANG is Professor of Art History and Director of the Advanced School of Art and Humanities at the National Academy of Art in Hangzhou, Professor of Historiography at Shanghai University and Nanjing Normal University, and Editor-in-Chief of *New Arts*, People's Republic of China. He has published several books, including *Art and History* (2001) and *New Perspectives on Art History* (2007) (in Chinese), as well as numerous articles. His current research focuses on the visual dialogues between the Euro-American world and China.

JOHN CLARK is Australian Research Council Professorial Fellow at the University of Sydney and founding director of the Australian Centre for Asian Art and Archaeology. Among his books are *Modern Asian Art* (1998), *Modernities of Chinese Art* (2008), and *Modernities Compared: Chinese and Thai Art in the 1980s and 1990s* (2008). From 2004–2006 he worked on the new Biennales in Asia, and in 2008–2012 he will conduct a new comparative study of "The Asian Modern."

ELISABETH DE BIÈVRE has taught at the University of East Anglia, University College London and UCLA, and delivered the Baldwin Lectures at Oberlin College. She is concerned with art in the Netherlands and art as a worldwide phenomenon. Her publications include "The Urban Subconscious: The Art of Delft and Leiden," *Art History* (1995) and "The alchemy of wind and water, Amsterdam 1200–1700," in *Time and Place: The Geohistory of Art*, ed. Thomas DaCosta Kaufmann and Elizabeth Pilliod (2005).

ELLEN DISSANAYAKE is an independent scholar and Affiliate Professor in the School of Music at the University of Washington, Seattle. Her work draws upon experiences from more than fifteen years residence in countries outside the West, including Sri Lanka, Nigeria, and Papua New Guinea, and it synthesizes knowledge from diverse fields—cultural and physical anthropology, developmental and cognitive psychology, Western arts and cultural history, and evolutionary biology. Her viewpoint provides a broader understanding of the arts than is customary in most theoretical approaches: the arts are integral to human nature and they evolved to help individuals adapt to their physical and social environments. She is the author of *What Is Art For?* (1988), *Homo Aestheticus* (1992)—translated into Chinese and Korean— and *Art and Intimacy* (2000).

JAMES ELKINS is E. C. Chadbourne Professor in the Department of Art History, Theory, and Criticism, School of the Art Institute of Chicago. He writes on art and non art images; his recent books include *Visual Studies: A Skeptical Introduction* (2003), *What Happened to Art Criticism?* (2003), and *Master Narratives and Their Discontents* (2005). He is editing two book series for Routledge: The Art Seminar (conversations on different subjects in art theory) and Theories of Modernism and Postmodernism in the Visual Arts (short monographs on the shape of the twentieth century); currently he is organizing a seven-year series called the Stone Summer Theory Institute.

PAULA D. GIRSHICK is Professor of Anthropology and African Studies at Indiana University. She did research for 20 years in the Kingdom of Benin, Nigeria, on issues of art, history and politics, and is currently working in South Africa on two projects: post-apartheid monuments and national identity and the history of the African art market in that country. Her publications include The *Art of Benin* (rev. edition, 1995), *Art, Innovation, and Politics in 18th Century Benin* (1999), and "Ncome Museum/Monument (KwaZulu Natal): From reconciliation to resistance," *Museum Anthropology* (2004).

MARLITE HALBERTSMA is Professor of Cultural History at the Department of Cultural Studies, Erasmus Universiteit Rotterdam. She has published on various subjects, including the cultural history of Rotterdam, city culture in general, and the methodology and history of art history. She is presently leading the research program "Globalisation and Cultural Heritage," financed by the Dutch Science Foundation. Recent publications include *Interbellum Rotterdam, kunst en cultuur 1918–1940* (coedited with Patricia van Ulzen, 2001), "Fremde Welten und vertraute Methoden: die deutsche Weltkunstforschung des frühen 20. Jahrhunderts,"

Kritische Berichte (2003), and "The Call of the Canon: Why Art History Cannot Do Without," in *Making Art History: A Changing Discipline and Its Institutions*, ed. Elizabeth C. Mansfield (2007).

THOMAS DACOSTA KAUFMANN is Frederick Marquand Professor of Art and Archaeology at Princeton University. A member of the Swedish, Flemish, and Polish Academies of Science, as well as Fellow of the American Academy in Rome, he is the recipient of many fellowships and honors for his work on Central Europe, art, science and humanism, and the historiography and geog-raphy of art. He is at present complet-ing a book on Giuseppe Arcimboldo, and involved in a research project on the Dutch in Asia, part of a larger interest in global exchange in art. Among his numerous pub-lications are *The School of Prague: Painting at the Court of Rudolf II*, which won the Mitchell Prize for 1988; *Court, Cloister and City: The Art and Culture of Central Europe 1450–1800* (1995), and *Toward a Geography of Art* (2004).

JOHN ONIANS is Emeritus Professor in the School of World Art Studies at the Univer-sity of East Anglia, Norwich, and has taught and lectured in many countries around the globe. He is a specialist in Classical Art, Italian Renaissance Architecture, and World Art, and is now developing Neuroart-history. He was founding editor of the journal *Art History* (1978), and editor of the first *Atlas of World Art* (2004). His books include *Bearers of Meaning: The Classical Orders in Antiquity, the Middle Ages and the Renaissance* (1989) and *Neuroarthistory: From Aristotle and Pliny to Baxandall and Zeki* (2007).

ULRICH PFISTERER is Professor of Italian Art History at the Ludwig-Maximilians-University in Munich. His research focuses on the relationship between artistic practice and theory in Early Modern Europe, and the history and methodology of the dis-cipline of art history. His publications in-clude *Donatello und die Entdeckung der Stile, 1430–1445* (2002), *Metzler Lexikon Kunstwissenschaft. Ideen, Methoden, Begriffe* (2003), and "Altamira – oder: Die Anfänge von Kunst und Kunstwissenschaft," *Vorträge aus dem Warburg Haus* (2007).

COLIN RHODES is Professor of Art History and Theory and Dean of Sydney College of the Arts, the visual arts Faculty of the University of Sydney. He has published ex-tensively, including the acclaimed book *Primitivism and Modern Art* (1994) and the groundbreaking *Outsider Art: Spontaneous Alternatives* (2000). He has a particular interest in expressionism and its contexts. His recent publications include "Burlington Primitive: Non-European Art in The Burlington Magazine before 1930," *The Burlington Magazine* (2004).

BEN-AMI SCHARFSTEIN is Professor Emeritus of Philosophy at Tel-Aviv Univer-sity, where he established the department of philosophy. This department offers an unusually wide variety of courses, including elementary and advanced courses in Chi-nese and Indian philosophy. The nature of his interests, which can be summed up most easily under the rubric "comparative culture," is evident from the subjects of his books, which include *A Comparative History of World Philosophy: From the Upanishads to Kant* (1998), *Birds, Elephants, Children, and Other Artists: An Essay in Interspecies Aesthetics* (in Hebrew, 2007), and *Art without Borders: A Philosophical Exploration of Art and Humanity* (2008).

WILFRIED VAN DAMME is Lecturer in World Art Studies at Leiden University and teaches African Art at Ghent University. His scholarly work has mainly focused on visual aesthetics. Among his publications are *Beauty in Context: Towards an Anthro-pological Approach to Aesthetics* (1996); "Universality and Cultural Particularity in Visual Aesthetics," in *Being Humans:*

Anthropological Universality and Particularity in Transdisciplinary Perspectives, ed. Neil Roughley (2000); and "World Aesthetics: Biology, Culture, and Reflection," Compression vs. *Expression: Containing and Explaining the World's Art*, ed. John Onians (2006). His current interests include the history of Western scholarly engagements with visual arts from outside the West.

KITTY ZIJLMANS is Professor of Contemporary Art History and Theory, Leiden University. Her main interests are in contemporary art, theory, and methodology. In her work she also focuses on the particular contribution of women to art and culture, as well as on processes of globalization and the increasing role of intercultural dimensions in art and the art world. Her publications include *CO-OPs. Interterritoriale verkenningen in kunst en wetenschap / Exploring New Territories in Art and Science* (coedited with Rob Zwijnenberg and Krien Clevis, 2007); *Site-Seeing: Places in Culture, Time and Space* (ed., 2006); and "Pushing Back Frontiers: Towards a History of Art in a Global Perspective," *International Journal of Anthropology* (2003).

REFERENCES

A

ABIODUN, ROWLAND. 1976. A reconsideration of the function of Ako: Second burial effigy in Owo. *Africa* 46 (1): 4–20.

—. 1987. Verbal and visual metaphors: Mythical allusion in yoruba ritualistic art of Orí. *Word & Image* 3 (3): 252–70.

—. 1990. The future of African art studies: An African perspective. In African art studies: *The state of the discipline*, Rowland Abiodun et al., 63–89. Washington, DC: The National Museum of African Art.

—, Henry J. Drewal, and John Pemberton. 1991. *Yoruba: Art and aesthetics in Nigeria*. Zurich: Museum Rietberg.

ABRAMS, MEYER H. 1971. *Natural supernaturalism: Tradition and revolution in romantic literature*. New York: Norton.

ABRAMSON, J. A. 2000. *Art in nonliterate societies: Structural approaches and implications for sociocultural and system theories*. Kalamazoo, MI: Western Michigan University; New Issues Press.

ACKER, WILLIAM R. B. 1979. *Some T'ang and pre-T'ang texts on Chinese painting*. Westport, CO: Hyperion Press.

ADEPEGBA, CORNELIUS O. 1992. *Ona*: The concept of art among the Yoruba. In *Yoruba culture*, Cornelius O. Adepegba et al., 1–6 Ibadan: The Nigerian Field Society.

ADLER, GUIDO. 1885. Umfang, Methode und Ziel der Musik wissenschaft. *Vierteljahrsschrift für Musikwissenschaft* 1: 5–20. (See Mugglestone 1981 for an English translation)

AIKEN, EDWARD A. 1987. I saw the figure 5 in gold: Charles Demuth's emblematic portrait of William Carlos Williams. *Art Journal* 46 (3): 178–84.

AIKEN, NANCY E. 1998. Power through art. In *Sociobiology and politics,* ed. Vincent S. E. Falger, Peter Meyer, and Johan M. G. van der Dennen, 215–28. Vol. 6 of *Research in biopolitics,* ed. Steven A. Peterson and Albert Somit. Greenwich, CT: JAI Press.

—. 1998. *The biological origins of art*. Westport, CT: Praeger.

—, and Kathryn Coe. 2004. Promoting cooperation among humans: The arts as the ties that bind. *Bulletin of Psychology and the Arts* 5 (1): 5–20.

AITKEN, KENNETH W., AND COLWYN TREVARTHEN. 1997. Self/other organization in human psychological development. *Development and Psychopathology* 9: 653–77.

ALLAND, ALEXANDER. 1977. *The artistic animal: An inquiry into the biological roots of art*. Garden City, NY: Anchor.

ALLEN, NGAPINE. 1998. Maori vision and the imperialist gaze. In *Colonialism and the object: empire, material culture and the museum,* ed. Tim Barringer and Tom Flynn, 144–52. London: Routledge.

ALLESCH, CHRISTIAN G. 1987. *Geschichte der psychologischen Ästhetik: Untersuchungen zur historischen Entwicklung eines psychologischen Verständnisses ästhetischer Phänomene*. Göttingen, etc.: Verlag für Psychologie Hogrefe.

ALPERS, SVETLANA. 1983. *The art of describing: Dutch art in the seventeenth century*. Chicago and London: The University of Chicago Press.

ALSOP, JOSEPH. 1982. *The rare art traditions: The history of art collecting and its linked phenomena wherever they have appeared*. New York: Harper and Row.

AMBROSE, STANLEY H. 1998. Late Pleistocene human population bottlenecks, volcanic winter, and the differentiation of modern humans. *Journal of Human Evolution* 34 (6): 623–51.

—. 2003. Did the super-eruption of Toba cause a human population bottleneck? Reply to Gathorne-Hardy and Harcourt-Smith. *Journal of Human Evolution* 45 (3): 231–37.

ANANDAVARDHANA. 1974. *Dhvanyaloka of Anandavardhana,* ed. and with an introd., trans and notes by K. Krishnamoorthy. Dharwar: Karnatak University.

—. 1990. *The Dhvanyaloka of Anandavardhana with the Locana of Abhinavagupta*. Trans. Daniel H. H. Ingalls, Jeffrey Moussaieff Masson and M. V. Patwardhan; ed. and with an introd. by Daniel H. H. Ingalls. Cambridge, MA: Harvard University Press.

ANDERSON, BENEDICT. 1991. *Imagined communities: Reflections on the origin and spread of nationalism*. London: Verso.

ANDERSON, RICHARD L. 1979. *Art in primitive societies*. Englewood Cliffs, NJ: Prentice Hall.

—. 1989. *Art in small-scale societies*. 2nd, rev. ed. of *Art in primitive societies* (originally published 1979). Englewood Cliffs, NJ: Prentice Hall.

—. 2000. *American muse: Anthropological excursions into art and aesthetics*. Upper Saddle River, NJ: Prentice Hall.

—. 2004. *Calliope's sisters: A comparative study of philosophies of art*. 2nd, rev. ed., 1st ed. published 1990. Upper Saddle River, NJ: Prentice Hall.

ANDRÉE, RICHARD. 1878. *Ethnographische Parallelen und Vergleiche*. Stuttgart: Maier.

—. 1887. Das Zeichnen bei den Naturvölkern. *Mittheilungen der Anthropologischen Gesellschaft in Wien* 12: 98–106.

ANIKOVICH, MICHAEL V., et al. 2007. Early Upper Paleolithic in Eastern Europe and implications for the dispersal of modern humans. *Science* 315 (5819): 223–26.

APPADURAI, ARJUN. 1986. Introduction: Commodities and the

politics of value. In *The social life of things: Commodities in cultural perspective,* ed. Arjun Appadurai, 3–63. Cambridge: Cambridge University Press.

ARAEEN, RASHEED. 1989. *The other story: Afro-Asian artists in post-war Britain.* London: The South Bank Centre.
—, Sean Cubitt, and Ziauddin Sardar, eds. 2002. *The third text reader: On art, culture and theory.* London and New York: Continuum.

ARENS, KATHERINE. 1989. *Structures of knowing: Psychologies of the nineteenth century,* Dordrecht: Kluwer Academic Publishers.

ARMSTRONG, A. M. 1953. *Plotinus.* London: Allen & Unwin.

ARMSTRONG, ROBERT P. 1971. *The affecting presence: An essay in humanistic anthropology.* Urbana: University of Illinois Press.
—. 1981. *The powers of presence: Consciousness, myth, and affecting presence.* Philadelphia: University of Pennsylvania Press.

ARNHEIM, RUDOLF. 2004. *Art and visual perception: A psychology of the creative eye,* rev. and enlarged ed. Los Angeles: University of California Press.

ASBURY, MICHAEL, AND ORIANA BADDELEY. 2000. *Other modernities.* London: The London Institute Gallery.

ASHMOLE, BERNARD. 1964. *The classical ideal in Greek sculpture.* Cincinnati, OH: University of Cincinnati.

ASHTON, DORE. 1984. On an epoch of paradox: "Primitivism" at the Museum of Modern Art. *Arts Magazine* 59 (3): 76–79.

AULINGER, BARBARA. 1996. Social history of art. In *The dictionary of art,* Vol. 29, ed. Jane Turner, 915–17. London: Macmillan.

B

BABCOCK, BARBARA. 1995. Marketing Maria: The tribal artist in the age of mechanical reproduction. In *Looking high and low: Art and cultural identity,* ed. Brenda Jo Bright and Liza Bakewell, 124–50. Tucson: The University of Arizona Press.

BACHELARD, GASTON. 1994. *The poetics of space.* Trans. Maria Jolas, foreword John R. Stilgoe. 1st ed. published 1964. Boston: Beacon Press.

BAHN, PAUL G., AND JEAN VERLUT. 2001. *Journey through the Ice Age.* Los Angeles: University of California Press.

BAILEY, GAUVIN ALEXANDER. 1999. *Art on the Jesuit missions in Asia and Latin America 1542–1773.* Toronto, Buffalo and London: University of Toronto Press.

BAIRD, JAMES. 1956, *Ishmael.* Baltimore: The Johns Hopkins University.

BAKOŠ, JÁN. 1991. Peripherie und kunsthistorische Entwicklung. *Ars* 1:1–12.

BALANDIER, GEORGES. 1968. *Daily life in the kingdom of the Kongo.* New York: Pantheon Books.

BALCH, EDWIN S., AND EUGENIA BALCH. 1920. *Arts of the world: Comparative art studies.* Philadelphia: Lane and Scott.

BALDRY, H.C. 1965. *The unity of mankind in Greek thought.* Cambridge, MA: Cambridge University Press.

BALFOUR, HENRY. 1890. The origin of decorative art as illustrated by the art of modern savages. *Midland Naturalist* 13: 189–201.
—. 1893. *The evolution of decorative art: An essay upon its origin and development as illustrated by the art of modern races of mankind.* London: Rivington, Perceival & Co.

BALME, JANE, AND KATE MORSE. 2006. Shell beads and social behaviour in Pleistocene Australia. *Antiquity* 80 (310): 799–811.

BANERJEA, JITENDRA NATH. 1974. *The development of Indian iconography.* 3rd ed., from 2nd ed. 1956. New Delhi: M. Manoharlal Publishers.

BARASCH, MOSHE. 1998. *From impressionism to Kandinsky.* Vol. 2 of *Modern Theories of Art.* New York and London: New York University Press.

BARBER, BERNARD. 1968. Social mobility in hindu India. In *Social mobility in the caste system in India: An interdisciplinary symposium,* ed. James Silverberg, 18–35. The Hague: Mouton.

BARGELLINI, CLARA. 2005. At the center on the frontier: The Jesuit Tarahumara missions of New Spain. In *Time and place: Essays in the geohistory of art,* ed. Thomas DaCosta Kaufmann and Elizabeth Pilliod, 113–34. Aldershot and Burlington, VT: Ashgate.

BARHAM, LAWRENCE S. 2002. Systematic pigment use in the Middle Pleistocene of South-Central Africa. *Current Anthropology* 43 (1): 181–90.

BARKAN, ELAZAR, AND RONALD BUSH, eds. 1995. *Prehistories of the future: The primitive project and the culture of modernism.* Stanford, CA: Stanford University Press.

BARLEY, NIGEL. 1988. *Foreheads of the dead: An anthropological view of Kalabari ancestral screens.* Washington, DC: Smithsonian Institution Press.
—. 1995. *Dancing on the grave: Encounters with death.* London: John Murray.

BARNES, R. H. 1987. Anthropological comparison. In *Comparative anthropology,* ed. Ladislav Holý, 119–26. Oxford and New York: Blackwell.

BARRINGER, TIM, AND TOM FLYNN, eds. 1998. *Colonialism and the object: Empire, material culture and the museum.* London: Routledge.

BASCOM, WILLIAM R. 1973. A Yoruba master carver: Duga of Meko. In *The traditional artist in African societies,* ed. Warren L. D'Azevedo, 62–78. Bloomington: Indiana University Press.

BASHAM, ARTHUR L. 1959. *The wonder that was India: A survey of the culture of the Indian sub-continent before the coming of the muslims.* New York: Grove Press.

BASSANI, EZIO. 2001. *African art and artifacts in European collections: 1400–1800.* London: British Museum Press.

BASTIAN, ADOLF. 1868. *Das Beständige in den Menschenrassen und die Spielweite ihrer Veränderlichkeit: Prolegomena zu einer Ethnologie der Culturvölker.* Berlin: Reimer.
—. 1874. Review of *Völkerkunde* by Oscar Peschel. *Zeitschrift für Ethnologie* 6: 148ff.
—. 1881. *Die Vorgeschichte der Ethnologie: Deutschlands Denkfreunden gewidmet....* Berlin: Dümmler.

BAWDEN, GARTH. 1996. *The Moche.* Cambridge, MA: Blackwell Publishers.

BAXANDALL, MICHAEL. 1972. *Painting and experience in fifteenth century Italy: A primer in the social history of pictorial style.* Oxford: Clarendon Press.

BAY, EDNA. 1985. *Iron altars of the Fon people of Benin.* Atlanta, GA: Emory University.

BEACH, MILO C. 1992. *Mughal and Rajput painting.* Cambridge and New York: Cambridge University Press.

BECK, HERBERT, AND HORST BREDEKAMP. 1975. Die mittelrheinische Kunst um 1400. In *Kunst um 1400 am Mittelrhein: ein Teil der Wirklichkeit,* ed. Herbert Beck, Wolfgang Beeh, and Horst Bredekamp, 30–109. Frankfurt a. M.: Liebieghaus Museum alter Plastik.

BECKER, HOWARD 1982. *Art worlds.* Berkeley: University of California Press.

BECKER, MARVIN B. 1967. *The decline of the commune.* Vol. 1 of *Florence in transition.* Baltimore, MD: Johns Hopkins University Press.
—. 1968. The Florentine territorial state and civic humanism in the early Renaissance. In *Florentine studies: Politics and society in Renaissance Florence,* ed. Nicolai Rubinstein, 109–39. Evanston, IL: Northwestern University Press.
—. 1968. *Studies in the rise of the territorial state.* Vol. 2 of *Florence in transition.* Baltimore, MD: Johns Hopkins University Press.
—, and Gene A. Brucker. 1956. The *arti minori* in Florentine politics, 1342–1378. *Medieval Studies* 18: 93–104.

BEDAUX, JAN BAPTIST, AND BRETT COOKE, eds. 1999. *Sociobiology and the arts.* Amsterdam, Atlanta: Editions Rodopi.

BEDNARIK, ROBERT G. 2003. A figurine from the African Acheulian. *Current Anthropology* 44 (3): 405–13.

BEEBE, BEATRICE, DIANE ALSON, JOSEPH JAFFE, STANLEY FELDSTEIN, AND CYNTHIA CROWN. 1988. Vocal congruence in mother-infant play. *Journal of Psycholinguistic Research* 17 (3): 245–259.
—, Daniel Stern, and Joseph Jaffe. 1979. The kinesic rhythm of mother-infant interactions. In *Of speech and time: Temporal speech patterns in interpersonal contexts,* ed. Aron W. Siegman and Stanley Feldstein, 23–34. Hillsdale, NJ: Erlbaum.

BEIDELMAN, TOM O. 1992. Authenticity and appropriation [Dialogue section]. *African Arts* 24 (3): 24–26.

BELK, RUSSELL W. 1995. *Collecting in a consumer society.* London: Routledge.

BELKE, INGRID. 1982. Die Begründung der Völkerpsychologie in Deutschland. *Rivista di Filosofia* LXXII (22–23): 192–233.

BELTING, HANS. 2001. *Bild-Anthropologie: Entwürfe für eine Bildwissenschaft.* Bild und Text. Munich: Fink.

BEN-AMOS, PAULA. 1977. Pidgin languages and tourist arts. *Studies in the Anthropology of Visual Communication* 4 (2): 128-39.
—. 1980. *Benin art.* London: Thames and Hudson.
—. 1983. Introduction: History and art in Benin. In *The art of power—The power of art: Studies in Benin iconography,* ed. Paula Ben-Amos and Arnold Rubin, 13–16. Los Angeles: UCLA Museum of Cultural History.
—. 1989. African visual arts from a social perspective. *African Studies Review* 32 (2): 1–53.
—. 1995. *The art of Benin.* Washington, DC: Smithsonian Institution Press.

BENITEZ, EUGENIO, ed. 1997. *The Pacific rim conference in transcultural aesthetics.* Sydney: University of Sydney. (free version available online)
—, ed. 2005. *Before Pangaea: New essays in transcultural aesthetics.* Special issue, *Literature and Aesthetics* 15 (1). (free version available online)

BENJAMIN, WALTER. 1955 [1969]. The work of art in the age of mechanical reproduction. In *Illuminations,* ed. and intro. Hannah Arendt, trans. Harry Zohn, 59–67. New York: Shocken Books.

Originally published as *L'Œuvre d'art à l'époque de sa reproductibilité technique* (1935).

BENTHALL, JONATHAN. 1987. Ethnographic museums and the art trade. *Anthropology Today* 3 (3): 9–13.

BERENSON, BERNARD. 1954. *The arch of Constantine: Or the decline of form.* New York: Macmillan Co.
—. 1967. *The Italian painters of the Renaissance.* London: Phaidon Press.

BERGENTHUM, HARTMUT. 2002. Weltgeschichten im wilhelminischen Deutschland: Innovative Ansätze in der populären Geschichtsschreibung. In *Weltgeschichtsschreibung im 20. Jahrhundert.* Comparativ. Leipziger Beiträge zur Universalgeschichte und vergleichenden Gesellschaftsforschung 12 (3), ed. Matthias Middell, 16–56. Leipzig: Leipziger Universitätsverlag.

BERLIN, BRENT, AND PAUL KAY. 1969. *Basic color terms: Their universality and evolution.* Berkeley: University of California Press.

BERLO, JANET CATHERINE. 1999. Drawing (upon) the past: Negotiating identities in Inuit graphic arts production. In *Unpacking culture: Art and commodity in colonial and postcolonial worlds,* ed. Ruth B. Phillips and Christopher B. Steiner, 178–96. Berkeley: University of California Press.
—, and Ruth B. Phillips. 1998. *Native North American art.* New York: Oxford University Press.

BESANÇON, ALAIN. 2000. *The forbiden image: An intellectual history of iconoclasm.* Trans. Jane Marie Todd. Chicago and London: The University of Chicago Press.

BEYER, ANDREAS. 2003. *Portraits: A history.* New York: Harry N. Abrams.

BEYER, OSKAR. 1923. *Welt-Kunst: von der Umwertung der Kunstgeschichte.* Dresden: Sybillen-Verlag.

BHABHA, HOMI K. 1990. *Nation and narration.* New York: Routledge.
—. 1994. *The location of culture.* London: Routledge.

BHATTACARYYENA, TARAPADA. 1963. *The Canons of Indian Art: Or, a study on Vastuvidya.* 2nd ed. Calcutta: K. L. Mukhopadhyay.

BIAŁOSTOCKI, JAN. 1965. Mannerism and the vernacular in Polish art. In *Walter Friedländer zum 90. Geburtstag: eine Festgabe seiner europäischer Schüler, Freunde und Verehrer,* ed. Georg Kauffmann, 47–57. Berlin: De Gruyter.
—. 1976. The Baltic area as an artistic region in the sixteenth century. In *Hafnia: Copenhagen papers in the theory of art,* 11–23. Copenhagen: University of Copenhagen, Institute of Art History.
—. 1989. Some values of artistic periphery. In *World art: Themes of unity and diversity: Acts of the XXVIth international congress of the history of art,* vol. 1, ed. Irving Lavin, 49–58. University Park, PA: Pennsylvania State University Press.

BIEBUYCK, DANIEL P., AND NELLY VAN DEN ABBEELE 1984. *The power of headdresses: A cross-cultural study of forms and functions.* Brussels: TENDI.

BIEDERMAN, IRVING. 1995. Visual object recognition. In *Visual cognition.* 2nd ed, ed. Stephen M. Kosslyn and Daniel N. Osherson, 121–65. Vol. 2 of *An invitation to cognitive science,* ed. Daniel N. Osherson. Cambridge, MA: MIT Press.

BIRTWISTLE, GRAHAM. 2000. Wat is er aan de hand met het primitivisme? *Jong Holland* 16 (2): 6–8, 64.

BITTEL, KURT, ed. 1966–1983. *Propyläen-Kunstgeschichte: in achtzehn Bänden.* Berlin: Propyläen-Verlag.

BLIER, SUZANNE P. 1987. *The anatomy of architecture: Ontology and metaphor in Batammaliba architectural expression*. Cambridge: Cambridge University Press.

—. 1989–1990. Art systems and semiotics question of art, craft, and colonial taxonomies in Africa. *The American Journal of Semiotics* 6 (1): 7–18.

—. 2001. Africa, art, and history: An introduction. In *A history of art in Africa*, Monica Blackmun Visona et al., 14–23. New York: Harry N. Abrams.

—, ed. 2004. *Art of the senses: African masterpieces from the Teel collection*. Boston: Museum of Fine Arts.

BLOCH, MARC. 1961. *Social classes and political organization*. Vol. II of *Feudal society*. Trans. L. A. Manyon, Chicago and London: The University of Chicago Press.

BLOTKAMP, CAREL. 1986. Annunciation of the new mysticism: Dutch symbolism and early abstraction. In *The spiritual in art: Abstract painting 1890–1985*, ed. Maurice Tuchman, *89–111*. Los Angeles: Los Angeles County Museum of Art; New York: Abeville Press.

BOAS, FRANZ. 1927. *Primitive art*. New York: Dover, 1955 (1st ed. Oslo: Aschehoug).

BOAS, GEORGE. 1948. *Essays on primitivism and related ideas in the Middle Ages*. Baltimore, MD: Johns Hopkins Press.

BOEHM, GOTTFRIED, ed. 2006. *Was ist ein Bild?* Bild und Text 1. 1st ed. 1994. Munich: Wilhelm Fink.

—. 2007. *Wie Bilder Sinn erzeugen*. Berlin: Berlin University Press.

BOHANNAN, LAURA. 1966. Shakespeare in the bush. *Natural History* 75 (7): 28–33.

BOIS, YVE-ALAIN. 1985. La pensée sauvage. *Art in America* 73 (4): 178–89.

—, et al. 1995. *Piet Mondrian, 1872–1944*. Boston: Bulfinch Press.

BORGATTI, JEAN. 1990. African portraits. In *Likeness and beyond: Portraits in Africa and the world*, Jean Borgatti and Richard Brilliant, 28–83. New York: The Center for African Art.

—. 1990. Portraiture in Africa. In *Portraiture in Africa, Part I*, ed. Jean Borgatti, 34–39, 101. Special issue, *African Arts* 23 (3).

—, ed. 1990. *Portraiture in Africa, Part I*. Special issue, *African Arts* 23 (3).

—. 1991. African portraiture: A commentary. In *Portraiture in Africa, Part II*, ed. Jean Borgatti, 38–41. Special issue, *African Arts* 23 (4).

—, ed. 1991. *Portraiture in Africa, Part II*. Special issue, *African Arts* 23 (4).

—. 1996. Portraiture in African art. In *The dictionary of art* at Grove Art Online, accessed December 18, 2007, http://0-www.groveart.com.

—, and Richard Brilliant. 1990. *Likeness and beyond: Portraits from Africa and the world*. New York: The Center for African Art.

BOSE, PHANINDRA NATH, ed. 1928. *Silpa-Sastram*. Saidmitha, Lahore: Moti Lal Banarsi Dass.

BOSL, KARL. 1978. Noble unfreedom. The rise of the ministeriales in Germany. In *The medieval nobility: Studies on the ruling classes of France and Germany from the sixth to the twelfth century*, ed. Timothy Reuter, 291–311. Amsterdam: North Holland Publishing Co.

BOURDIEU, PIERRE. 1984. *Distinction: A social critique of the judgment of taste*, trans. Richard Nice. Cambridge, MA: Cambridge University Press. Originally published as *La distinction: critique sociale du jugement* (Paris: Minuit, 1979).

—. 1990. The intellectual field: A world apart. In *Theory in contemporary art since 1985*, ed. Zoya Kocur and Simon Leung. London: Blackwell.

—, and Alain Darbel. 1990. *The love of art: European art museums and their public*. Trans. Caroline Beattie and Nick Merriman. Cambridge: Cambridge University Press.

BOURDON, DAVID. 1975. Andy Warhol and the society icon. *Art in America* 63 (1), 42–45.

BOUWSMA, WILLIAM J. 1968. *Venice and the defense of republican liberty: Renaissance values in the age of the Counter Reformation*. Berkeley: University of California Press.

BOUZOUGGAR, ABDELJALIL, et al. 2007. 82,000-year-old beads from North Africa and the implications for the origins of modern human behavior. *Proceedings of the National Academy of Sciences of the United States of America* 104: 9964–69.

BOYD, BRIAN. 2005. Evolutionary theories of art. In *Literature and the human animal: Evolution and the nature of narrative*, ed. Jonathan Gottschall and David Sloan Wilson. 147–76. Evanston, IL: Northwestern University Press.

BRADBURY, R. E. 1957. *The Benin kingdom and the Edo-speaking peoples of South-Western Nigeria*. London: International African Institute.

BRAH, AVTAR, AND ANNIE E. COOMBES, eds. 2000. *Hybridity and its discontents: Politics, science, culture*. London: Routledge.

BRECKENRIDGE, JAMES D. 1968. *Likeness: A conceptual history of ancient portraiture*. Evanston, IL: Northwestern University Press.

BREYSIG, KURT. 1896. Über Entwicklungsgeschichte. *Deutsche Zeitschrift für Geschichtswissenschaft* 1: 161–74, 193–211.

BRIGHT, BRENDA JO, AND LIZA BAKEWELL 1995. Introduction: Art hierarchies, cultural boundaries and reflexive analysis. In *Looking high and low: Art and cultural identity*, ed. Brenda Jo Bright and Liza Bakewell, 1–18. Tucson: The University of Arizona Press.

BRILLIANT, RICHARD. 1990. Portraiture: A recurrent genre in world art. In *Likeness and beyond: Portraits in Africa and the world*. Jean Borgatti and Richard Brilliant, 10–27. New York: The Center for African Art.

—. 1991. *Portraiture*. Cambridge MA: Harvard University Press.

BRINK, JAMES. 2001. Dialectics of aesthetic form in Bamana art. In *Bamana: The art of existence in Mali*, ed. Jean-Paul Colleyn. New York: Museum for African Art, etc.

BROCE, GERALD. 1986. Herder and ethnography. *Journal of the History of Behavioral Sciences* 22: 150–170.

BRODY, J.J. 1977. *Mimbres painted pottery*. Albuquerque: University of New Mexico Press and Santa Fe, NM: School of American Research.

BROM, GERARD, AND LAMBREGT ABRAHAM VAN LANGERAAD, eds. 1907. *Diarium van Arend van Buchell*. Amsterdam: Müller.

BROUGH, SONIA. 1985. *The Goths and the concept of Gothic in Germany from 1500 to 1750: Culture, language and architecture*. Frankfurt and New York: Peter Lang.

BROWN, DONALD E. 1988. *Hierarchy, history, and human nature: The social origins of historical consciousness*. Tucson: The University of Arizona Press.

—. 2004. Human universals, human nature & human culture. *Daedalus: Journal of the American Academy of Arts & Sciences* 133 (Fall), 47–54.

BROWN, GERARD, BALDWIN. 1922. The origin and early history of the arts in relation to aesthetic theory in general. *The Burlington Magazine* 41 (233): 91–95.

BROWN, HORATIO F. 1907. *Studies in the history of Venice*, vol. I. New York: E. P. Dutton and Co.

BROWN, PERCY 1975. *Indian painting under the Mughals, A.D. 1550–A.D. 1750.* 1st ed. published 1924. New York: Hacker Art Books.

BROWN, PETER R. L. 1971. *The world of late Antiquity, AD 150–750.* London: Harcourt Brace Jovanovich.

BROWN, STEVEN. 2000. Evolutionary models of music: From sexual selection to group selection. In *Evolution, culture, and behavior,* ed. Nicholas S. Thompson and François Tonneau, 231–281. Vol. 13 of *Perspectives in ethology.* New York: Plenum.
—. 2000. The "musilanguage" model of music evolution. In *The origins of music,* ed. Nils L. Wallin, Björn Merker, and Steven Brown, 271–300. Cambridge, MA: MIT Press.

BROWNE, MICHAEL L. 1985. Portraits of foreigners by Kawahara Keiga. *Ars Orientalis* 15: 31–35.

BRÜCKNER, WOLFGANG. 2004. Museale Kontinuitätskonstruktion von "les arts premiers". In *Gründungsmythen, Genealogien, Memorialzeichen: Beiträge zur intitutionellen Konstruktion von Kontinuität,* ed. Gert Melville and Karl-Siegbert Rehberg, 241–60. Cologne, Weimar and Vienna: Böhlau.

BRYSON, NORMAN. 2003. Introduction to *Blow-up: Photography, cinema, and the brain,* Warren Neidich, 11–19. Riverside, CA: California Museum of Photography.

BUKOFZER, MANFRED F. 1947. *Music in the baroque era: From Monteverdi to Bach.* New York: Norton.

BUNZL, MATTI. 1996. Franz Boas and the Humboldtian tradition: From *Volksgeist* and *Nationalcharakter* to an anthropolocial concept of culture. In *Volksgeist as method and ethic: Essays on Boasian ethnography and the German anthropological tradition.* Vol. 8 of *History of Anthropology,* ed. George W. Stocking, Jr., 17–78. Madison: University of Wisconsin Press.
—. 2003. *Völkerpsychologie* and German-Jewish emancipation. In *Wordly provincialism: German anthropology in the age of empire,* ed. Matti Bunzl and H. Glenn Penny, 47–85. Ann Arbor: University of Michigan Press.
—, and H. Glenn Penny. 2003. Introduction: Rethinking German anthropology, colonialism, and race. In *Wordly provincialism: German anthropology in the age of empire,* ed. Matti Bunzl and H. Glenn Penny, 1–30. Ann Arbor: University of Michigan Press.

BURCKHARDT, JACOB. 1954. *The civilization of the Renaissance in Italy.* Trans. S. G. C. Middlemore. New York: Random House. Originally published as *Die Cultur der Renaissance in Italien: ein Versuch* (Basel: Schweighauser, 1860).

BURGESS, GELETT. 2003. The wild men of Paris [1910]. In *Primitivism and twentieth-century Art: A documentary history,* ed. Jack Flam and Miriam Deutch, 38–40. Berkeley: University of California.

BURKE, PETER. 1992. We, the people: popular culture and popular identity in modern Europe. In: *Modernity and identity,* ed. Scott Lash and Jonathan Friedman, 293–308. Oxford and Cambridge, MA: Blackwell
—. 2003. *Hibridismo cultural.* Trans. Leila Souza Mendes. São Leonardo: Editora Unisinos.

BUSH, SUSAN. 1971. *The Chinese literati on painting: Su Shih (1037–1101) to Tung Chi-chang (1555–1636).* Cambridge, MA: Harvard University Press.
—, and Hsio-yen Shih. 1985. *Early Chinese texts on painting.* Cambridge, MA: Harvard University Press.

BUSSE, KARL H. 1914. Die Ausstellung zur vergleichenden Entwicklungsgeschichte der primitiven Kunst bei den Naturvölkern, den Kindern und in der Urzeit. In *Bericht: Kongress für Ästhetik und Allgemeine Kunstwissenschaft.* Stuttgart: Enke, 79–82.
—. 1914. Vergleichende Entwicklungspsychologie der primitiven Kunst bei den Naturvölkern, den Kindern und in der Urzeit. In *Bericht: Kongress für Ästhetik und Allgemeine Kunstwissenschaft.* Stuttgart: Enke, 232–45.

BUTTERFIELD, HERBERT. 1931. *The whig interpretation of history.* London: G. Bell and Sons.

BYATT, ANTONIA S. 2000. *Portraits in fiction.* London: Chatto and Windus.

BYDLER, CHARLOTTE. 2004. *The global art world inc.: On the globalization of contemporary art.* Figura Nova Series 32. Uppsala: Acta Universitatis Upsaliensis. PhD diss., Uppsala University.

BYSTRYN, MARCIA. 1978. Art galleries as gatekeepers: The case of the abstract expressionists. *Social Research* 45: 390–408.

C

CAHILL, JAMES. 1982. *The compelling image: Nature and style in seventeenth century Chinese painting.* Cambridge, MA, Harvard University Press.

CAMNITZER, LUIS, JANE FARVER, AND RACHEL WEISS, eds. 1999. *Global conceptualism: Points of origin, 1950s–1980s.* New York: Queens Museum of Art.

CAMPBELL, AIDAN. 1997. *Western primitivism: African ethnicity.* London: Cassell.

CAMPBELL, BRUCE F. 1980. *Ancient wisdom revived: A history of the theosophical movement.* Berkeley: University of California Press.

CAMPBELL, SHIRLEY F. 2002. *The art of Kula.* Oxford and New York: Berg.

CANCLINI, NÉSTOR GARCÍA. 1995. *Hybrid cultures: Strategies for entering and leaving modernity.* Trans. Christopher L. Chiappari and Silvia L. López, Minneapolis: University of Minnesota Press.

CANTARES MEXICANOS. 1904. BNMex 1928bis, ff. 1–85.

CARRIER, DAVID. 2008. *A world art history and its objects.* Philadelphia: Pennsylvania State University Press.

CARROLL, JOSEPH. 1995. *Evolution and literary theory.* Columbia: University of Missouri Press.
—. 2004. *Literary Darwinism: Evolution, human nature, and literature.* New York and London: Routledge.
—. 2007. The adaptive function of literature. *Evolutionary and neurocognitive approaches to aesthetics, creativity, and the arts,* ed. Colin Martindale, Paul Locher and Vladimir Petrov, 31–45. Foundations and frontiers in aesthetics, ed. Colin Martindale, Arnold Berleant. Amityville, NY: Baywood.

CASTELNUOVO, ENRICO. 2000. *La cattedrale tascabile: Scritti di storia dell'arte.* Livorno: Sillabe.
—, and Dario Gamboni. 1984. Die Schweiz als Kunstlandschaft: Kunstgeographie als fachspezifisches Problem. *Zeitschrift für Schweizerische Archäologie und Kunstgeschichte* 41: 65–136.
—, and Carlo Ginzburg. 1979. Centro e periferia. In *Materiali e problemi.* Vol. I of *Storia dell' arte italiana: Questioni e metodi,* ed. Giovanni Previtali, 283–352. Turin: Einaudi.

CHAKRAVARTI, UMA. 1987. *The social dimension of early Buddhism.* Delhi: Oxford University Press.

CHASTEL, ANDRÉ. 1959. *Art et humanisme à Florence au temps de Laurent le Magnifique: Études sur la Renaissance et l'humanisme platonicien.* Paris: Presses universitaires de France.

CHERNOFF, JOHN MILLER. 1979. *African rhythm and African sensibility: Aesthetics and social action in African musical idioms.* Chicago and London: The University of Chicago Press.

CHERRY, DEBORAH. 2004. Art: History: Visual: Culture. *Art History* 27 (4): 479–93.

CHEYETTE, FREDRIC L., ed. 1968. *Lordship and community in medieval Europe.* New York: Holt, Rinehart, and Winston.

CHICKERING, ROGER. 1991. Karl Lamprechts Konzeption einer Weltgeschichte. *Archiv für Kulturgeschichte* 73: 437–52.

CHING, HAO. 1974. *Ching Hao's "Pi-fa-chi.": A note on the art of the brush.* Artibus Asiae Supplementum 31, ed. and trans. by Kyohito Munakata. Ascona: Artibus Asiae.

CHING, JULIA. 1976. *To acquire wisdom: The way of Wang Yangming.* New York: Columbia University Press.

CHRIMES, KATHLEEN M. T. 1942. *Ancient Sparta: A re-examination of the evidence.* Manchester: Manchester University Press.

CHRISTIAN, DAVID. 2004. *Maps of time: An introduction to big history.* Los Angeles: University of California Press.

CLAPP, ANN 1991. *The painting of T'ang Yin.* Chicago and London: The University of Chicago Press.

CLARK, JOHN. 1995. Yôga in Japan: Model or exception? Modernity in Japanese art, 1850s–1940s: An international comparison. *Art History* 18 (2): 253–85.
—. 1998. *Modern Asian art.* Sydney: Craftsman House; Honolulu: University of Hawai'i Press.
—. 2004. *Modernities compared: Chinese and Thai art in the 1980s and 1990s* (unpublished book draft).
—. 2005. Okakura Tenshin [Kakuzô] and aesthetic nationalism. *East Asian History* 15 (29): 1–38.
—. 2005. Modern and contemporary Asian art. In *The dictionary of art* at Grove Art Online.

CLIFFORD, JAMES. 1985. Histories of the tribal and modern. *Art in America* 73 (4): 164–77, 215.
—. 1988. *The predicament of culture: Twentieth century ethnography, literature, and art.* Cambridge, MA: Harvard University Press.

CLOTTES, JEAN. 2003. *Return to Chauvet cave: Excavating the birthplace of art.* London: Thames and Hudson.

CLUNAS, CRAIG. 1997. *Art in China.* Oxford History of Art. Oxford: Oxford University Press.

CLUTTON-BROCK, ARTHUR. 1911. The "primitive" tendency in modern art. *The Burlington Magazine* 19 (100): 226–28.

COCHRANE, ERIC. 1981. *Historians and historiography in the Italian Renaissance.* Chicago and London: The University of Chicago Press.

CÓDICE MATRITENSE DE REAL PALACIA. 1906. A facsimile edition of Vol. VI (Part 2) and Vol. VII by Francisco del Paso Y Troncoso. Madrid: Hauser y Menet.

COE, KATHRYN. 2003. *The ancestress hypothesis: Visual art as adaptation.* New Brunswick, NJ: Rutgers University Press.

COLE, DOUGLAS. 1985. *Captured heritage: The scramble for Northwest Coast artifacts.* Norman: University of Oklahoma Press.

COLEMAN, ELIZABETH BURNS. 2001. Aboriginal painting: Identity and authenticity. *Journal of Aesthetics and Art Criticism* 59 (4): 385–402.

COLLEY MARCH, HENRY. 1889. The meaning of ornament, or its archeology and its psychology. *Transactions of the Lancashire and Cheshire Antiquarian Society* 7: 160–92.
—. 1896. Evolution and psychology in art. *Mind: A Quarterly Review of Psychology and Philosophy* 5 (20): 441–63.

COLLEYN, JEAN-PAUL, ed. 2001. *Bamana: The art of existence in Mali.* New York: Museum for African Art, etc.

CONARD, NICHOLAS J. 2003. Palaeolithic ivory sculptures from South-Western Germany and the origins of figurative art. *Nature* 426 (6965): 830–32.
—, et al. 2007. Einmalige Funde durch die Nachgrabung am Vogelherd bei Niederstotzingen-Stetten ob Lontal, Kreis Heidelheim. *Archäologische Ausgrabungen in Baden-Württemberg 2006*, ed. Jörg Biel, 20–24. Stuttgart: Theiss.

CONFUCIUS [LI JI]. 1966. *The sacred books of China: The texts of confucianism.* Trans. James Legge Delhi: Motilal Banarsidass.

CONKLIN, BETH A. 1997. Body paint, feathers, and VCRs: Aesthetics and authenticity in Amazonian activism. *American Ethnologist* 24 (4): 711–37.

CONNELY, FRANCES S. 1995. *The sleep of reason: Primitivism in modern European art and aesthetics, 1725–1907.* University Park: Pennsylvania State University Press.

COOKE, BRETT, ed. 2001. *Interdisciplinary Literary Studies* 2 (2). Special issue on Darwinian literary study.
—. 2002. *Human nature in Utopia: Zamyatin's We.* Evanston, IL: Northwestern University Press.

COOMARASWAMY, ANANDA K. 1931. Foreword to *Portrait sculpture in South India*, T. Aravamuthan, xi. London: India Society.
—. 1975. *Rajput painting: Being an account of the Hindu paintings of Rajasthan and the Punjab Himalayas from the sixteenth to the nineteenth century: Described in relation to contemporary thought.* 1st ed. published 1916. New York: Hacker Art Books.

COOMBES, ANNIE E. 1994. *Reinventing Africa: Museums, material culture and popular imagination.* New Haven, CT and Londen: Yale University Press.

CORBEY, RAYMOND. 2000. *Tribal art traffic: A chronicle of taste, trade and desire in colonial and post-colonial times.* Amsterdam: Royal Tropical Institute.
—, Robert Layton, and Jeremy Tanner. 2004. The archaeology of art. In *A companion to archaeology*, ed. John L. Bintliff, 357–79. London: Blackwell.

COSMIDES, LEDA, AND JOHN TOOBY. 1992. Cognitive adaptations for social exchange. In *The adapted mind: Evolutionary psychology and the generation of culture*, ed. Jerome H. Barkow, Leda Cosmides, and John Tooby, 163–228. New York and Oxford: Oxford University Press.

COTTER, HOLLAND. 2005. Outside In. *New York Times*, March 30, Special Section on Museums.

COWEN, TYLER. 2002. *Creative destruction: How globalization is changing the world's cultures.* Princeton, NJ: Princeton University Press.

CROSS, IAN. 1999. Is music the most important thing we ever did?: Music, development and evolution. In *Music, mind, and science*, ed. Suk Won Yi, 10–39. Seoul: Seoul National University Press.
—. 2003. Music and evolution: Consequences and causes. *Contemporary Music Review* 22 (3): 79–89.

CURRIE, GREGORY. 2004. The representational revolution. *Journal of Aesthetics and Art Criticism* 62 (2): 119–28.

D

D'ALLEVA, ANNE. 2005. *Methods and theories of art history.* London: Lawrence King.

D'ANDREA, JEANNE, ed. 1990. *Kazimir Malevich 1878–1935.* Los Angeles: Armand Hammer Museum of Art and Cultural Center.

DANTO, ARTHUR C. 1964. The artworld. *Journal of Philosophy* 61 (19): 571–84.

DARNTON, ROBERT, ed. 1976. *The widening circle: Essays on the circulation of literature in eighteenth-century Europe.* Philadelphia: University of Pennsylvania Press.
—. 1979. *The business of the Enlightenment: A publishing history of the Encyclopédie 1775–1800.* Cambridge, MA, and London: The Belknap Press of Harvard University Press.

DART, RAYMOND A. 1974. The waterworn pebble of many faces from Makapansgat. *South African Journal of Science* 70 (6): 167–69.

DARWIN, CHARLES. 1871. *The descent of man and selection in relation to sex.* London: Murray.
—. 1999. *The expression of the emotions in man and animals*, with an introd., afterw., and commentaries by Paul Ekman. 3rd ed., 1st ed. London: John Murray, 1872. London: HarperCollins.

DAUM, ANDREAS W. 1998. *Wissenschaftspopularisierung im 19. Jahrhundert: bürgerliche Kultur, naturwissenschaftliche Bildung und die deutsche Öffentlichkeit, 1848–1914.* Munich: Oldenbourg.

D'AZEVEDO, WARREN L. 1958. A structural approach to esthetics: Toward a definition of art in anthropology. *American Anthropologist* 60 (4): 702–14.

DAVIS, JAMES C. 1962. *The decline of the Venetian nobility as a ruling class.* Baltimore, MD: Johns Hopkins University Press.

DE, SUSHIL KUMAR. 1963. *Sanskrit poetics as a study of aesthetics.* Berkeley: University of California Press.
—. 1977. *History of Sanskrit Poetics.* Reprint, 2nd rev. ed. 1960. Calcutta: K. L. Mukhopadhyay.

DE BARY, W. THEODORE. 1995. The vocabulary of Japanese aesthetics I, II, III. In *Japanese aesthetics and culture: A reader*, ed. Nancy Hume, 43–47. Albany, NY: State University of New York Press. Originally published in Ryusaku Tsunoda, W. Theodore de Bary and Donald Keene, comp. 1958. *Sources of Japanese tradition* (New York: Columbia University Press).

DE BIÈVRE, ELISABETH. 1995. The urban subconscious: The arts of Delft and Leiden. *Art History* 18 (2): 222–52.
—. 2005. Alchemy of wind and water: Amsterdam, 1200–1700. In *Time and place: Essays in the geohistory of art*, ed. Thomas Da-Costa Kaufmann and Elizabeth Pilliod, 87–112. Aldershot and Burlington, VT: Ashgate.

DE BLIJ, HARM J., AND ALEXANDER B. MURPHY. 1977. *Human geography: Culture, society, and space.* New York: Wiley.

DE GOBINEAU, J. ARTHUR 1853–1855. *Essai sur l'inégalité des races humaines.* 4 vols. Paris.

DE MUNCK, VICTOR C. 2002. Contemporary issues and challenges for comparativists. *Anthropological Theory* 2 (1): 5–19.

DEAL, DAVID M., AND LAURA HOSTETTER. 2006. *The art of ethnography: A Chinese "Miao Album."* Seattle: University of Washington Press.

D'ERRICO, FRANCESCO, et al. 2003. Archaeological evidence for the emergence of language, symbolism, and music: An alternative multidisciplinary perspective. *Journal of World Prehistory* 17 (1): 1–70.
—, et al. 2005. *Nassarius kraussianus* shell beads from Blombos cave: Evidence for symbolic behavior in the Middle Stone Age. *Journal of Human Evolution* 48 (1): 3–24.

DESAI, DEVANGANA. 1975. *Erotic sculpture of India: A socio-cultural study.* New Delhi: Tata McGraw Hill, New Delhi.

DESAI, VISHAKA, APINAN POSHYANANDA, AND OKWUI ENWEZOR. 2003. Looking ahead: Dialogues in Asian contemporary art: Transcription. *Yishu: Journal of Contemporary Chinese Art* 2 (2): 112–121.

DEUTSCH, ELIOT. 1975. *Studies in comparative aesthetics.* Monographs of the Society for Asian and Comparative Philosophy 2. Honolulu: University Press of Hawaii.

DIAMOND, JARED. 1997. *Guns, germs, and steel: The fates of human societies.* New York: Norton.

DICKIE, GEORGE. 1974. *Art and the aesthetic: An institutional analysis.* Ithaca, NY: Cornell University Press.

DIDI-HUBERMAN, GEORGES. 2002. *L'Image survivante: Histoire de l'art et temps des fantômes selon Aby Warburg.* Paradoxe. Paris: Minuit.

DIETERLEN, GERMAINE. 1993. Graphic signs and the seed of knowledge: The 266 basic signs in West Africa. In *American, African, and old European mythologies*, comp. Yves Bonnefoy, trans. under the direction of Wendy Doniger by Gerald Honigsblum et al., 118–20. Chicago and London: University of Chicago Press.
—. 1993. The mythology of the Mande and the choice of the dogon as a subject to study. In *American, African, and old European mythologies*, comp. Yves Bonnefoy, trans. under the direction of Wendy Doniger by Gerald Honigsblum et al., 117–18. Chicago and London: University of Chicago Press.
—. 1993. The placenta in West African myths and rituals. In *American, African, and old European mythologies*, comp. Yves Bonnefoy, trans under the direction of Wendy Doniger by Gerald Honigsblum et al., 123–25. Chicago and London: University of Chicago Press.
—. 1993. Twins a dominant theme in West African mythologies. In *American, African, and old European mythologies*, comp. Yves Bonnefoy, trans. under the direction of Wendy Doniger by Gerald Honigsblum et al., 121–23. Chicago and London: The University of Chicago Press.

DILLY, HEINRICH. 1979. *Kunstgeschichte als Institution: Studien zur Geschichte einer Disziplin.* Frankfurt a.M.: Suhrkamp.
—. 1988. *Deutsche Kunsthistoriker 1933–1945. Kunstgeschichte und Gegenwart.* Munich and Berlin: Deutscher Kunstverlag.

DIMAGGIO, PAUL. 1991. Cultural entrepreneurship in 19th-century Boston. In *Rethinking popular culture*, ed. Chandra Mukerji and Michael Schudson, 374–97. Berkeley: University of California Press.

DIONISOTTI, CARLO. 1967. *Geografia e storia della letteratura italiana.* Turin: Einaudi.

DIRIWÄCHTER, RAINER. 2004. Völkerpsychologie: The synthesis that never was. *Culture & Psychology* 10 (1): 85–109.

DISSANAYAKE, ELLEN 1988. *What is art for?* Seattle: University of Washington Press.
—. 1992. *Homo aestheticus: Where art comes from and why.* New York: Free Press, etc.
—. 1995. Chimera, spandrel, or adaptation: Conceptualizing art in human evolution. *Human Nature* 6 (2): 99–117.

—. 2000. Antecedents of the temporal arts in early mother-infant interaction. In *The origins of music*, ed. Nils L. Wallin, Björn Merker, and Steven Brown, 389–410. Cambridge, MA: MIT Press.

—. 2000. *Art and intimacy: How the arts began*. Seattle: University of Washington Press.

—. 2003. Art in global context: An evolutionary/functionalist perspective for the 21st century. *International Journal of Anthropology* 18 (3): 245–58.

DOLL, NIKOLA, CHRISTIAN FUHRMEISTER, AND MICHAEL H. SPRENGER, eds. [2005]. *Kunstgeschichte im Nationalsozialismus: Beiträge zur einer Wissenschaft zwischen 1930 und 1950*. Weimar: VDG.

DONNAN, CHRISTOPHER B. 1978. *Moche art of Peru: Pre-Columbian symbolic communication*. Los Angeles: Museum of Cultural History; University of California, Los Angeles.

—. 2004. Moche portraits: Masterpieces from ancient Peru. In *Retratos: 2000 years of Latin American portraits*, Marion Oettinger, Jr. et al., 56–65. New Haven, CT and London: Yale University Press.

—. 2004. *Moche portraits from ancient Peru*. Joe R. and Teresa Lozano Long Series in Latin American and Latino Art and Culture. Austin: University of Texas Press.

DREW, DAVID. 1999. *The lost chronicles of the Maya kings*. Berkeley: University of California Press.

DREWAL, HENRY. 1984. Art history and the individual: A new perspective for the study of African visual traditions. In *Iowa studies in African art I*, ed. Christopher Roy, 87–114. Iowa City: School of Art and Art History, The University of Iowa.

DRÜE, HERMANN. 1983. Die psychologische Ästhetik im Deutschen Kaiserreich. In *Ideengeschichte und Kunstwissenschaft: Philosophie und bildende Kunst im Kaiserreich*. Kunst, Kultur und Politik im Deutschen Kaiserreich 3, ed. Ekkehard Mai, Stephan Waetzoldt and Gerd Wolandt, 71–98. Berlin: Mann.

DUBIN, MARGARET. 2001. *Native America collected: The culture of an art world*. Albuquerque: University of New Mexico Press.

DUBOS, JEAN-BAPTISTE. 1719. *Réflexions critiques sur la poésie et sur la peinture*. Paris: Pissot.

DUBY, GEORGES. 1968. The nobility in eleventh- and twelfth-century Mâconnais. In *Lordship and community in medieval Europe*, ed. Fredric L. Cheyette, 137–55. New York: Holt, Rinehart, and Winston.

DUDLEY, EDWARD, AND MAXIMILLIAN NOVAK, eds. 1972. *The wild man within: An image in Western thought from the Renaissance to Romanticism*. Pittsburgh, PA: University of Pittsburgh Press.

DUTTON, DENIS. 1995. Mythologies of tribal art. *African Arts* 26 (4): 32–43

—. 2000. But they don't have our concept of art. In *Theories of art today*, ed. Noël Carroll, 217–38. Madison: University of Wisconsin Press.

—. 2003. Authenticity in art. In *The Oxford handbook of aesthetics*, ed. Jerrold Levinson, 258–274. New York: Oxford University Press.

—. 2006. A naturalist definition of art. *Journal of Aesthetics and Art Criticism* 64 (3): 367–77.

—. 2008. *The art instinct: Beauty, pleasure, and human evolution*. London: Bloomsbury.

E

EAGLETON, TERRY. 1990. *The ideology of the aesthetic*. Oxford and Cambridge, MA: Blackwell.

EHRENSVÄRD, CARL AUGUST. 1925. *Skriften*. Svenska författare utgivna av Svenska Vitterhetssamfundet, 10, ed. Gunhild Bergh and Andrea Delen. Stockholm. Reprinted in *Carl August Ehrensvärd (1745–1800): An original Swedish aesthetician and an early functionalist*. Holger Frykenstedt. Uppsala, 1965.

EIBL, KARL. 2004. *Bausteine einer biologischen Kultur- und Literaturtheorie*. Paderborn: Mentis Verlag.

EIBL-EIBESFELDT, IRENÄUS. 1988. The biological foundations of aesthetics. In *Beauty and the brain: Biological aspects of aesthetics*, ed. Ingo Rentschler, Barbara Herzberger and David Epstein, 29–68. Basel: Birkhäuser.

—. 1989. *Human Ethology*. Trans. Geoffrey Strachan. Hawthorne, NY: Aldine de Gruyter.

—, and Christa Sütterlin. 2007. *Weltsprache Kunst: zur Natur- und Kunstgeschichte bildlicher Kommunikation*. Vienna: Brandstätter Verlag.

EINSTEIN, CARL. 1920. *Negerplastik*. 1st ed. published 1915. München: K. Wolff.

—. 1928. *Afrikanische Plastik*. Leipzig: Wasmuth.

—. 1981. Afrikanische Plastik. In *Werke 2*, ed. Marion Schmid, 62–144. Berlin: Medusa-Verlag.

EKMAN, PAUL, ed. 1982. *Emotion in the human face*. 2nd ed. Cambridge and New York: Cambridge University Press; Paris: Editions de la Maison des Sciences de l'Homme.

ELBERFELD, ROLF, AND GÜNTER WOHLFART, eds. 2000. *Komparative Ästhetik: Künste und ästhetische Erfahrungen zwischen Asien und Europa*. Cologne: Edition Chora.

ELGAR, FRANK. 1968. *Mondrian*. Trans. Thomas Walton. London: Thames and Hudson.

ELKINS, JAMES. 1998. Different horizons for the concept of the image. *Zeitschrift für Ästhetik und allgemeine Kunstwissenschaft* 43 (1): 29–46.

—. 1998. *On pictures and the words that fail them*. Cambridge: Cambridge University Press.

—. 1999. *Xi fang mei shu shi xue zhong de Zhongguo shan shui hua [Chinese landscape painting as western art history]*. Trans. from the English by Pan Yaochang and Gu Ling. Hangzhou: Zhongguo mei shu xue yuan chu ban she [National Academy of Art].

—. 2000. Review of *Modern art in Eastern Europe: From the Baltic to the Balkans, ca. 1890–1939* by Steven A. Mansbach. *The Art Bulletin* 82 (4): 781–85.

—. 2002. Response [to Anthony Alofsin's letter regarding the review of Mansbach's *Modern art in Eastern Europe*]. *The Art Bulletin* 84 (3): 539.

—. 2002. *Stories of art*. New York: Routledge.

—. 2002. [Why it is not possible to write the art history of non-Western cultures]. Trans. into Chinese by Ding Ning. *Mei yuan/Journal of the Lu Xun Academy of Fine Arts* [Beijing] 3: 56–61.

—. 2002. Why it is not possible to write the art history of non-Western cultures. In *Minulost'v Prítomnosti: Súcasné umenie a umeleckohistorcké myty/The past in the present: contemporary art and art history's myths*, ed. Ján Bakoš, 229–55. Bratislava: Nadácia-Centrum Súcasného Umenia [*sic*: 2003].

—. 2003. Ako je mozné písat' o svetovom umení? [How is it possible to write about the world's art?]. *Ars* [Bratislava] 2: 75–91.

—. 2003. *Visual studies: A skeptical introduction*. London and New York: Routledge.

—. 2004. Review of *Real spaces: World art history and the rise of Western modernism* by David Summers. *The Art Bulletin* 86 (2): 373–80.

—. 2004. Two forms of judgement: forgiving and demanding (the case of marine painting). *Journal of Visual Art Practice* 3 (1): 37–46.

—, ed. 2005. *Art history versus aesthetics*. The Art Seminar 1. New York and London: Routledge.

—. 2006. Afterword. In *Discovering Chinese painting: Dialogues with art historians*. 2nd ed., ed. Jason C. Kuo, 249–56. Dubuque, IO: Kendall/Hunt Publishing.

—. 2006. Writing about modernist painting outside Western Europe and North America. In *Compression vs. expression: Containing and explaining the world's art*, ed. John Onians, 188–214. Williamstown, MA: Clark Art Institute.

—. 2007. Canon and globalization in art history. In *Partisan canons*, ed. Anna Bryzki, 55–77. Durham, NC: Duke University Press.

—. 2008. *Six stories from the end of representation: Images in painting, photography, astronomy, microscopy, particle physics, and quantum mechanics, 1980–2000*. Stanford: Stanford University Press.

—, ed. 2007. *Photography theory*. The Art Seminar 2. New York and London: Routledge.

—, ed. 2007. *Is art history global?* The Art Seminar 3. New York and London: Routledge.

—. Forthcoming. Aesthetics and the two cultures: Why art and science should be allowed to go their separate ways. In *Rediscovering aesthetics*, ed. Julia Jansen, Francis Halsall, and Tony O'Connor. New York: Columbia University Press.

—, and Robert Williams, eds. 2008. *Renaissance theory*. The Art Seminar 4. New York and London: Routledge.

ELSNER, JÁS. 2002. The birth of Late Antiquity: Riegl and Strzygowski in 1901. *Art History* 25 (3): 358–79.

ELSNER, JOHN, AND ROGER CARDINAL, eds. 1994. *The cultures of collecting*. Cambridge, MA: Harvard University Press.

EMBREE, AINSLIE, ed. 1988. *Sources of Indian tradition*. Vol. 1, *From the beginning to 1800 (Introduction to oriental civilizations)*. 2nd ed. New York: Columbia University Press.

EMIGH, JOHN. 1996. *Masked performance: The play of self and other in ritual and theatre*. Philadelphia: University of Pennsylvania Press.

EMONTS, JOHANNES. 1922. *Ins Steppen- und Bergland Innerkameruns: aus dem Leben und Werken deutscher Afrikamissionare*. Aachen: Xaveriusverlag.

ENWEZOR, OKWUI, ed. 2001. *The short century: Independence and liberation movements in Africa 1945–1994*. Munich, London and New York: Prestel.

ERICKSON, BRITTA. 2005. A fleeting introduction to contemporary Chinese art. In *On the edge: Contemporary Chinese artists encounter the West*. Stanford, CA: Iris & B. Gerald Cantor Center for Visual Arts at Stanford University.

ERRINGTON, SHELLEY. 1997. *The death of authentic primitive art and other tales of progress*. Berkeley and London: University of California Press.

F

FABIAN, JOHANNES. 1983. *Time and the other: How anthropology makes its object*. New York: Columbia University Press.

—. 1998. Curios and curiosity: Notes on reading Torday and Frobenius. In *The scramble for Central Africa*, ed. Enid Schildkrout and Curtis Keim, 79–81. Cambridge: Cambridge University Press.

FARAGO, CLAIRE, ed. 1995. *Reframing the Renaissance: Visual culture in Europe and Latin America 1450–1650*. New Haven, CT and London: Yale University Press.

FAUCHEREAU, SERGE. 1991. *Kazimir Malévitch*. Paris: Editions Cercles d'Art.

FEAGIN, SUSAN L., ed. 2007. *Global theories of art and aesthetics*. Special issue, *Journal of Aesthetics and Art Criticism* 61 (1).

FERGUSSON, JAMES. 1865–1867. *History of architecture in all countries: From the earliest times to the present day*. 2 vols. London: John Murray.

FERNALD, ANNE. 1992. Human maternal vocalizations to infants as biologically relevant signals: An evolutionary perspective. In *The adapted mind: Evolutionary psychology and the generation of culture*, ed. Jerome H. Barkow, Leda Cosmides, and John Tooby, 391–428. New York and Oxford: Oxford University Press.

FERNÁNDEZ-ARMESTO, FELIPE. 2001. *Civilizations: Culture, ambition, and the transformation of nature*. New York: Free Press.

FERNIE, ERIC, ed. 1995. *Art history and its methods: A critical anthology*. London: Phaidon.

FIBICHER, BERNHARD. 2005. Kulturelle Partnerschaften, vielleicht auch mehr: zur Rezeption chinesischer Gegenwartskunst im Westen. In *Mahjong: Chinesische Gegenwartskunst aus der Sammlung Sigg*, ed. Bernhard Fibicher and Matthias Frehner, 41–49. Ostfildern: Hatje Cantz.

FINEBERG, JONATHAN, ed. 1998. *Discovering child art: Essays on childhood, primitivism and modernism*. Princeton, NJ: Princeton University Press.

FINLEY, MOSES I. 1959. Was Greek civilization based on slave labor? *Historia* 8: 145–64.

—. 1962. *The world of Odysseus*. Rev. ed. Harmondsworth: Penguin Books.

FLAM, JACK, AND MIRIAM DEUTCH, eds. 2003. *Primitivism and twentieth-century art: A documentary history*. Berkeley: University of California.

FLECKNER, UWE, AND THOMAS W. GAEHTGENS, eds. 1996. *Die Kunst des 20. Jahrhunderts*. Vol. 5 of *Carl Einstein: Werke*, ed. Hermann Haarmann. Berlin: Fannei & Walz.

FLESCH, WILLIAM. 2008. *Comeuppance: Costly signaling, altruistic punishment, and other biological components of fiction*. Cambridge, MA: Harvard University Press.

FONG, WEN C. 1962. The problem of forgeries in Chinese painting: Part one. *Artibus Asiae* 25 (2–3), 95–119, 121–40.

—, et al. 1984. *Images of the mind: Selections from the Edward L. Elliott family and John B. Elliott collections of Chinese calligraphy and painting at the Art Museum*. Princeton, NJ: Princeton University Press.

FONGUE, J. NDEFFO. 2002. The market for works of art: The case of African cultural goods. *South African Journal of Economics* 70 (8): 1320–43.

FORTY, ADRIAN, AND SUSANNE KUECHLER, eds. 1999. *The art of forgetting*. Oxford and New York: Berg.

FOSTER, HAL. 1985. *Recodings: Art, spectacle, cultural politics*. Washington, DC: Bay.

FOUCAULT, MICHEL. 1980. *Power/knowledge: Selected interviews and other writings 1972–1977*, ed. Colin Gordon. New York: Pantheon.

FRANK, BARBARA E. 2001. More than objects: Bamana artistry in iron, wood, clay, leather and cloth. In *Bamana: The art of existence in Mali*, ed. Jean-Paul Colleyn, 45–51. New York: Museum for African Art, etc.

FRANKFORT, HENRI. 1961. *Ancient Egyptian religion: An interpretation*. 1st ed. published 1948. New York: Harper and Brothers.

FRASER, DOUGLAS, AND HERBERT M. COLE, eds. 1972. *African art and leadership*. Madison: University of Wisconsin Press.

FREELAND, CYNTHIA. 2001. *But is it art?* Oxford: Oxford University Press.

FREY, DAGOBERT. 1942. *Das englisches Wesen in der bildenden Kunst*. Stuttgart: Kohlhammer.

—. 1946. *Kunstwissenschaftliche Grundfragen: Prologomena zu einer Kunstphilosophie*. Vienna: Rohrer.

—. 1949. *Grundlegung zu einer Vergleichenden Kunstwissenschaft: Raum und Zeit in der Kunst der afrikanisch-eurasiatischen Hochkulturen*. Innsbruck and Vienna: Friedrich Rohrer Verlag.

—. 1955. Geschichte und Probleme der Kultur- und Kunstgeographie. *Archeologia Geographica* 4: 90–105.

FRIDLUND, ALAN J., AND BRADLEY DUCHAINE. 1996. "Facial expressions of emotion" and the delusion of the hermetic self. In *The emotions: Social, cultural and biological dimensions,* ed. Rom Harré and W. Gerrod Parrott, 259–284. London and Thousand Oaks: Sage.

FRIEDMAN, JOHN BLOCK. 1981. *The monstrous races in medieval art and thought*. Cambridge, MA: Harvard University Press.

FRIEDMAN, JONATHAN. 1983. Civilizational cycles and the history of primitivism. *Social Analysis* (14): 31–52.

FROBENIUS, LEO. 1897. Die bildende Kunst der Afrikaner. *Mittheilungen der Anthropologischen Gesellschaft in Wien* 27: 1–17.

—. 1898. *Der Ursprung der afrikanischen Kulturen*. Berlin: Gebrüder Borntraeger.

—. 1933. *Kulturgeschiche Afrikas: Prolegomena zu einer historischen Gestaltlehre*. Zurich: Phaidon.

FRY, ROGER. 1910. Bushman paintings. *The Burlington Magazine* 16 (84): 334–38.

—. 1917. Children's drawings. *The Burlington Magazine* 30 (171): 225–27, 231.

—. 1920. Modern paintings in a collection of ancient art. *The Burlington Magazine* 37 (213): 302–5, 308–9.

—. 1924. Children's drawings. *The Burlington Magazine* 44 (250): 36.

FU, TIANCHOU, ed. 1989. *Wonders from the earth: The first emperors underground army*. Rev. ed. San Francisco: China Books and Periodicals, Inc.

G

GAGE, JOHN. 1993. *Colour and culture: Practice and meaning from antiquity to abstraction*. London: Thames and Hudson.

—. 1995. Colour and culture. In *Colour: Art and science,* ed. Trevor Lamb and Janine Bourriau, 186–93. Cambridge and New York: Cambridge University Press.

—. 1999. *Color and meaning: art, science, and symbolism*. Berkeley and Los Angeles: University of California Press.

GAMBONI, DARIO. 1987. *Kunstgeographie*. Ars Helvetica: Die visuelle Kunst der Schweiz 1. Disentis: Desertina.

GANS, HERBERT. 1974. *Popular culture and high culture: An analysis and evaluation of taste*. New York: Basic Books.

GAONKAR, DILIP PARAMESHWAR, ed. 2001. *Alternative modernities*. Durham and London: Duke University Press.

—. 1999. On alternative modernities. *Public Culture* 11 (1): 1–18.

GASCOIGNE, BAMBER 2002. *The great Moguls: Indias most flamboyant rulers*. Rev. ed., 1st ed. published 1971. New York: Carroll & Graf Publishers.

GATHERCOLE, PETER. 1987. Anthropology and auction houses: Thatcherite anthropology? *Anthropology Today* 3 (2): 22.

GEISMAR, HAIDY. 2001. What's in a price: An ethnography of tribal art at auction. *Journal of Material Culture* 6 (1): 25–47.

GEIST, VALERIUS. 1978. *Life strategies, human evolution, environmental design: Toward a biological theory of health*. New York: Springer.

GELL, ALFRED. 1998. *Art and agency: An anthropological theory*. Oxford: Oxford University Press.

GELZER, MATTHIAS. 1969. *The Roman nobility*. Trans. Robin Seager. Oxford: Basil Blackwell. Originally published as *Die Nobilität der Römischen Republik* (Leipzig, etc.: Teubner, 1912).

GENICOT, LÉOPOLD. 1968. The nobility in medieval Francia: Continuity, break, or evolution? In *Lordship and community in medieval Europe,* ed. Fredric L. Chyette, 128–36. New York: Holt, Rinehart, and Winston.

GEORGE, KENNETH M. 1999. Objects on the loose: Ethnographic encounters with unruly artefacts. *Ethnos* 64 (2):149–50.

GERBRANDS, ADRIANUS A. 1957. *Art as an element of culture, especially in Negro-Africa*. Trans. Gertrude E. van Baaren-Pape. Leiden: E.J. Brill 1957.

—. 1993. Atjametsj: Unique collection of statues and shields. In *Asmat art: Woodcarvings of southwest New Guinea,* ed. Dirk Smidt, 115–35. New York: George Braziller in association with the Rijksmuseum voor Volkenkunde, Leiden.

GERMANN, PAUL. [1929]. Die afrikanische Kunst. In *Die aussereuropäische Kunst*. Vol. VI of *Handbuch für Kunstgeschichte von Anton Springer,* ed. Curt Glaser, 549–91. Leipzig: Kröner.

GIANINO, ANDREW, AND EDWARD Z. TRONICK, 1988. The mutual regulation model: The infant's self and interactive regulation and coping and defensive capacities. In *Stress and coping across development,* ed. Tiffany M. Field, Philip M. McCabe, and Neil Schneiderman, 47–68. Hillsdale, NJ: Erlbaum.

GILLEN, ECKHART. 2002. German art—national expression or world language?: Two visual essays. In *The two art histories: The museum and the university,* ed. Charles W. Haxthausen, 87–101. Williamstown, MA: The Clark Institute.

GILMAN, ALFRED. 2003. How should schools teach evolution?: Emphasize the scientific facts. *Reports of the National Center for Science Education* 23 (5–6): 8–9.

GINGRICH, ANDRE, AND RICHARD G. FOX, eds. 2002. *Anthropology, by comparison*. London: Routledge.

GLACKEN, CLARENCE J. 1967. *Traces on the Rhodian shore: Nature and culture in Western thought from ancient times to the end of the eighteenth century*. Berkeley and Los Angeles: University of California Press.

GLASER, CURT, ed. [1929]. *Die aussereuropäische Kunst*. Vol. VI of *Handbuch für Kunstgeschichte von Anton Springer*. Leipzig: Kröner.

—. [1929]. Die ostasiatische Kunst. In *Die aussereuropäische Kunst*. Vol. VI of *Handbuch für Kunstgeschichte von Anton Springer,* ed. Curt Glaser, 2–230. Leipzig: Kröner.

GNOLI, RANIERO. 1956. *The aesthetic experience according to Abhinavagupta*. Rome: Is. M.E.O.

GOLDE, PEGGY. 1963. *Aesthetic values and art styles in a Nahua pottery producing village*. PhD diss., Harvard University.

—, and Helena C. Kraemer. 1973. Analysis of an aesthetic values test: Detection of the inter-sub-group differences within a pottery producing community in Mexico. *American Anthropologist* 75 (5): 260–75.

GOLDEN, LAUREN. 2001. Science, Darwin and art history. In *Raising the eyebrow: John Onians and world art studies. An album amicorum in his honour,* ed. Lauren Golden, 79–90. Oxford: Archaeopress.

—, ed. 2001. *Raising the eyebrow: John Onians and World Art Studies. An album amicorum in his honour.* Oxford: Archaeopress.

GOLDIN, AMY. 1975. The post-perceptual portrait. *Art in America* 63 (1): 79–82.

GOLDING, JOHN. 2000. *Paths to the absolute: Mondrian, Malevich, Kandinsky, Pollock, Newman, Rothko, and Still.* Princeton, NJ: Princeton University Press.

GOLDWATER, ROBERT. 1967. *Primitivism in modern art.* New York: Vintage Books.
—. 1986. *Primitivism in modern art.* Cambridge, MA: Harvard University.

GOMBRICH, ERNST H. 1972. *Symbolic images.* London: Phaidon.
—. 1979. *The sense of order: A study in the psychology of decorative art,* 2nd ed. 1994. London: Phaidon.
—. 2002. *The preference for the primitive: Episodes in the history of Western taste and art.* London: Phaidon.

GONDA, JAN. 1975. *Vedic literature: (Saṃhitas and Brahmaṇas).* Wiesbaden: Harrossowitz.

GORDON, BEVERLY, WITH MELANIE HERZOG. 1988. *American Indian art: The collecting experience.* Madison: University of Wisconsin Press.

GORDON, DONALD E. 1984. German Expressionism. In *"Primitivism" in 20th Century Art: Affinity of the Tribal and the Modern,* vol. II, ed. William S. Rubin, 368–403. New York: Museum of Modern Art.

GOSDEN, CHRIS, AND CHANTAL KNOWLES. 2001. *Collecting colonialism: Material culture and colonial change.* Oxford: Berg.

GOSWAMY, BRIJINDER N. 1975. *Pahari paintings of the Nala-Damayanti theme in the collection of Dr. Karan Singh: Essays and notes.* New Delhi: National Museum.

GOTTSCHALL, JONATHAN, AND DAVID SLOAN WILSON, eds. 2005. *Literature and the human animal: Evolution and the nature of narrative.* Evanston, IL: Northwestern University Press.

GRABAR, OLEG. 1982. On the universality of the history of art. *Art Journal* 42 (4): 281–83.

GRABURN, NELSON, ed. 1976. *Ethnic and tourist arts: Cultural expressions from the fourth world.* Berkeley: University of California Press.
—. 1999. Ethnic and tourist arts revisited. In *Unpacking culture: Art and culture in the colonial and postcolonial worlds,* ed. Ruth Phillips and Christopher Steiner, 335–53. Berkeley: University of California Press.

GREEN, CHRISTOPHER, ed. 1999. *Art made modern: Roger Fry's vision of art.* London: Merrell Holberton.

GREENHALGH, MICHAEL. 1978. European interest in the non-European: The sixteenth century and Pre-Columbian art and architecture. In *Art in society,* ed. Michael Greenhalgh and Vincent Megaw, 89–103. London: Duckworth.

GROSS, MICHAEL. 2002. Red head: US-style creationism spreads to Europe. *Current Biology* 12 (8): 265–66.

GROSSE, ERNST. 1897. *Die Anfänge der Kunst.* Freiburg i.Br. and Leipzig: J. C. B. Mohr. *English trans. The beginning of art.* New York: Appleton, 1897.

GUICCIARDINI, LUDOVICO. 1612. *Beschryvinghe van alle de Neder-landen, anderssins ghenoemt Neder-duytslandt.* Trans. by Cornelius Kilianus. Amsterdam: Willem Jansz. Originally published as *Descrittione di tutti I Paesi Bassi, altrimenti detti Germania Inferiore* (Antwerp, 1567).

GUILLAUME, JEAN. 2005. Styles and manners: Reflections on the longue durée in the history of architecture. In *Time and place: Essays in the geohistory of art,* ed. Thomas DaCosta Kaufmann and Elizabeth Pilliod, 37–58. Aldershot and Burlington, VT: Ashgate.

GUTHRIE, R. DALE. 2005. *The nature of Paleolithic art.* Chicago and London: The University of Chicago Press.

H

HAAS, STEFAN. 1994. *Historische Kulturforschung in Deutschland 1880–1930: Geschichtswissenschaft zwischen Synthese und Pluralität.* Münstersche historische Forschungen 5. Cologne, etc.: Böhlau.

HABERLAND, EIKE, ed. 1973. *Leo Frobenius 1873–1973: An Anthology.* Wiesbaden: F. Steiner.

HADDON, ALFRED C. 1895. *Evolution in art: As illustrated by the life-histories of designs.* London: Walter Scott.
—. 1910. *History of anthropology.* London: Watts.

HADJINICOLAOU, NICOS. 1983. Kunstzentren und periphere Kunst. *Kritische Berichte* 11: 36–56.

HAGEN, EDWARD H., AND GREGORY A. BRYANT. 2003. Music and dance as a coalition signaling system. *Human Nature* 14 (1): 21–51.

HALBERTSMA, MARLITE. 1992. *Wilhelm Pinder und die Deutsche Kunstgeschichte.* Worms: Wernersche Verlagsgesellschaft.
—. 2003. Fremde Welten und vertraute Methoden: die deutsche Weltkunstforschung des frühen 20. Jahrhunderts. *Kritische Berichte* 31 (2): 28–36.

HALL, JOHN W., et al., eds. 1989–1997. *The Cambridge history of Japan.* 6 vols. Cambridge and New York: Cambridge University Press.

HALLE, DAVID. 1993. *Inside culture: Art and class in the American home.* Chicago and London: The University of Chicago Press.

HALSALL, FRANCIS. 2007. Niklas Luhmann (1927–1998). In *Art: Key contemporary thinkers,* ed. Diarmuid Costello and Jonathan Vickery, 187–90. Oxford and New York: Berg.
—. 2008. *Systems of art.* Oxford: Peter Lang.

HAMBURGER, JEFFREY F. 1998. *The visual and the visionary: Art and female spirituality in late medieval Germany.* New York: Zone Books and Cambridge, MA: MIT Press.

HAMMOND, NICHOLAS D., AND HOWARD H. SCULLARD, eds. 1970. *The Oxford classical dictionary.* 2nd ed. Oxford: Clarendon Press.

HARDT, MICHAEL, AND ANTONIO NEGRI. 2000. *Empire.* Cambridge, MA: Harvard University Press.

HARNEY, ELIZABETH. 2004. *In Senghor's shadow: Art, politics, and the avant-garde in Senegal, 1960–1995.* Durham, NC: Duke University Press.

HARRISON, CHARLES. 2003. Modernism. In *Critical terms for art history.* 2nd. ed., ed. Robert S. Nelson and Richard Shiff, 188–201. Chicago and London: The University of Chicago Press.
—, and Paul Wood, eds. 1992. *Art in theory 1900–1990: An anthology of changing ideas.* London: Blackwell.

HART, LYNN M. 1995. Three walls: Regional aesthetics and the international art world. In *The traffic in culture: Refiguring art and* anthropology, ed. George E. Marcus and Fred R. Myers, 127–50. Berkeley: University of California Press.

HASELBERGER, HERTA. 1969. *Kunstethnologie: Grundbegriffe, Methoden, Darstellung*. Vienna and Munich: Schroll.

HASKELL, FRANCIS. 1993. *History and its images: Art and the interpretation of the past*. New Haven: Yale University Press.

HASKINS, CHARLES HOMER. 1966. *The Renaissance of the twelfth century*. 1st ed. published 1927. Cleveland: World Publishing Co.

HASSINGER, HUGO. 1910. Über Aufgaben der Städtekunde. *Dr. A. Petermanns Mitteilungen aus Justus Perthes' geographischer Anstalt* 56: 289–94.

HATCHER, EVELYN PAYNE. 1999. *Art as culture: An introduction to the anthropology of art*. 1st ed. 1985. Westport, CO and London: Bergin & Harvey.

HATT, MICHAEL, AND CHARLOTTE KLONK, 2006. *Art history: A criticial introduction to its methods*. Manchester: Manchester University Press.

HAUSER, ANDREAS. 1985. Der "Cuvier der Kunstwissenschaft": Klassifizierungsprobleme in Gottfried Sempers *Vergleichender Baulehre*. In *Grenzbereiche der Architektur. Festschrift Adolf Reinle*, ed. Thomas Bold, 97–114. Basel, etc.: Birkhäuser.

HAUSER, ARNOLD. 1951. *The social history of art*. London: Routledge and Kegan Paul.

HAUSHERR, RAINER. 1970. Kunstgeographie: Aufgaben, Grenzen Möglichkeiten. *Rheinische Vierteljahrsblätter* 34: 158–71.

HAYDEN, BRIAN. 1987. Alliances and ritual ecstasy: Human responses to resource stress. *Journal for the Scientific Study of Religion* 26 (1): 81–91.

HAZAN, OLGA. 1999. *Le mythe du progrès artistique: étude critique d'un concept fondateur du discours sur l'art depuis la Renaissance*. Montréal: Presses de l'Université de Montréal.

HEARN, MAXWELL K. 1979. An ancient Chinese army rises from underground sentinel duty. *Smithsonian* 10 (8): 38–51.

HEELAS, PAUL. 1996. Emotion talk across cultures. In *The emotions: Social, cultural and biological dimensions*, ed. Rom Harré and W. Gerrod Parrott, 171–99. *London and Thousand Oaks: Sage*.

HEIN, ALOIS RAIMUND. 1890. *Die bildende Kunst bei den Dayaks auf Borneo*. Vienna.
—. 1891. *Mäander, Hakenkreuze und urmotivische Wirbelornamente in Amerika: ein Beitrag zur allgemeinen Ornamentgeschichte*. Vienna: Hölder.

HEINE, PETER. 1980. Leo Frobenius als politischer Agent: Ein Beitrag zu seiner Biographie. *Paideuma* 26: 1–5.

HEINRICHS, HANS-JÜRGEN. 1998. *Die fremde Welt, das bin ich: Leo Frobenius: Etnologe, Forschungsreisender, Abenteurer*. Wuppertal: P. Hammer.

HEINZ, RUDOLF. 1970. Zum Begriff der philosophischen Kunstwissenschaft im 19. Jahrhundert. In *Der Wissenschaftsbegriff: Historische und systematische Untersuchungen*, ed. Alwin Diemer, 202–37. Meisenheim am Glan: Hain.

HELD, JUTTA, AND MARTIN PAPENBROCK, eds. 2003. *Kunstgeschichte an den Universitäten im Nationalsozialismus*. Göttingen: Vandenhoeck und Ruprecht Verlag.

HELMS, MARY W. 1993. *Craft and the kingly ideals: Art, trade, and power*. Austin: University of Texas Press.

HENCKMANN, WOLFHART. 1985. Probleme der allgemeinen Kunstwissenschaft. In *Kategorien und Methoden der deutschen Kunstgeschichte 1900–1930. Aus den Arbeitskreisen "Methoden der Geisteswissenschaften" der Fritz-Thyssen-Stiftung*, ed. Lorenz Dittmann, 273–334. Stuttgart: Steiner-Verlag Wiesbaden GmbH.

HENSHILWOOD, CHRISTOPHER S., et al. 2002. Emergence of modern human behaviour: Middle Stone age engravings from South Africa. *Science* 295 (5561): 1278–80.
—, and Curtis W. Marean. 2003. The origin of modern human behaviour: A review and critique of models and test implications. *Current Anthropology* 44 (5): 627–51.

HESS, THOMAS B. 1971. *Barnett Newman*. New York: Museum of Modern Art.

HESSE, KARL, AND THEO AERTS. 1996. *Baining life and lore*. Port Moresby: University of Papua New Guinea Press.

HESSEL, INGO, DIETER HESSEL (Photographer) and GEORGE SWINTON. 1998. *Inuit art: An introduction*. New York: Harry N. Abrams.

HILDEBRAND, GRANT. 1999. *Origins of architectural pleasure*. Berkeley: University of California Press.

HILDEBRAND, HANS. 1885. Beiträge zur Kenntnis der Kunst der niederen Naturvölker. In *Studien und Forschungen, veranlasst durch meine Reisen im hohen Norden: ein populär-wissenschaftliches Supplement zu: Die Umsegelung Asiens und Europas auf der Vega*, ed. Adolf E. von Nordenskiöld, 289–386. Leipzig: F. A. Brockhaus. Originally published as *Studier och forskningar föranledda af mina resor i höga norden: ett populärt vetenskapligt behang till "Vegas färd kring Asien och Europa"* (Stockholm, 1883).

HILL, HERBERT. 1952. *The Roman middle class in the republican period*. Oxford: Basil Blackwell.

HIMMELHEBER, HANS. 1972. Das Porträt in der Negerkunst. *Baessler Archiv* 20: 261–311.
—. 1993. *Eskimo artists: Fieldwork in Alaska, June 1936 until April 1937*. Trans. D. G. Gunderson and author. [Fairbanks]: University of Alaska Press. Originally published as *Eskimokünstler: Teilergebnis einer ethnographischen Expedition in Alaska von Juni 1936–April 1937* (Stuttgart: Strecker & Schröder, 1938).

HIRN, YRJÖ. 1900. *The origins of art: A psychological & sociological inquiry*. London: Macmillan & Co.

HO, PING-TI. 1964. *The ladder of success in imperial China: Aspects of social mobility, 1368–1911*. New York: John Wiley and Sons.

HODGSON, DEREK. 2006. Understanding the origins of Paleoart: The neurovisual resonance theory and brain functioning. *Paleo-Anthropology* 2006: 54–67.
—. 2006. Altered states of consciousness and Palaeoart: An alternative neurovisual explanation. *Cambridge Archaeological Journal* 16 (1): 27–37.

HOFER, MYRON A. 1990. Early symbolic processes: Hard evidence from a soft place. In *Pleasure beyond the pleasure principle*. Vol. 1 of *The role of affect in motivation, development and adaptation*, ed. Robert A. Glick and Stanley Bone, 55–78. New Haven, CT and London: Yale University Press.

HOFFMAN, DONALD C. 1998. *Visual intelligence: How we create what we see*. New York: Norton.

HOLMES, GEORGE. 1975. *Europe: Hierarchy and revolt, 1320–1450*. Sussex: Harvester Press.

HOLSBEKE, MIREILLE, ed. 1996. *The object as mediator: On the transcendental meaning of art in traditional cultures.* Antwerp: Ethnographic Museum.

HOLY, LADISLAV, ed. 1987. *Comparative anthropology.* London: Blackwell.

HONOUR, HUGH, AND JOHN FLEMING. 2005. *A world history of art.* 7th ed. 1st ed. published 1985. London: Laurence King.

HOOPER, STEVEN. 2002. Memorial images of Eastern Fiji: Materials, metaphors and meanings. In *Pacific art: Persistence, change, meaning,* ed. Anita Herle et al., 309–22. Honolulu: University of Hawaii Press.

HOPKINS, KEITH. 1974. Elite mobility in the Roman empire. In *Studies in ancient society,* ed. Moses I. Finley, 103–20. London: Routledge and Kegan Paul.
—. 1978. *Conquerors and slaves,* Cambridge: Cambridge University Press.

HORNBLOWER, SIMON, AND ANTHONY SPAWFORTH, eds. 1996. *The Oxford classical dictionary.* 3rd ed. Oxford and New York: Oxford University Press.

HORTON, ROBIN. 1965. *Kalabari sculpture.* Apapa, Lagos: Nigerian National Press for Department of Antiquities.

HOVERS, ERELLA, et al. 2003. An early case of color symbolism: Ochre use by modern humans in Qafzeh cave. *Current Anthropology* 44 (4): 491–522.

HUET, MICHEL. 1978. *The dance, art, and ritual of Africa.* New York: Pantheon.

HUNT, TERRY L., AND CARL L. LIPO. 2006. Late colonization of Easter Island. *Science* 311 (5761): 1603–6.

HUSSAIN, MAZHAR, AND ROBERT WILKINSON, eds. 2006. *The pursuit of comparative aesthetics: An interface between the East and the West.* Aldershot and Burlington, VT: Ashgate.

HUXLEY, GEORGE L. 1962. *Early Sparta.* Cambridge, MA: Harvard University Press.

HYATT, MARSHALL. 1990. *Franz Boas: social activist: The dynamics of ethnicity.* New York: Greenwood Press.

HYMAN, JOHN. 2006. Art and neuroscience. www.interdisciplines. org/artcognition/papers/15.
—. 2006. *The objective eye: Color, form, and reality in the theory of art.* Chicago and London: The University of Chicago Press.

I

IENAGA, SABURO. 1979. *Japanese art: A cultural appreciation.* Trans. Richard L. Gage. New York: Weatherhill.

ILG, ULRIKE. 2004. The cultural significance of costume books in sixteenth-century Europe. In *Clothing Culture: 1350–1650,* ed. Catherine Richardson, 29–48. Aldershot and Burlington, VT: Ashgate.

INAGA, SHIGEMI. 2007. Is art history globalizable? A critical commentary from a Far Eastern point of view. In *Is Art history global?* The Art Seminar 3, ed. James Elkins, 249–79. New York and London: Routledge.

IZUTSU, TOSHIHIKO, AND TOYO IZUTSU. 1981. *The theory of beauty in the classical aesthetics of Japan.* The Hague and Boston: Martinus Nijhoff Publishers.

J

JACOBSON-WEDDING, ANITA. 1979. *Red-White-Black as a mode of thought: Study of triadic classification by colours in the ritual symbolism and cognitive thought of the peoples of the Lower Congo.* Uppsala: Uppsala Universitet.

JÄGGI, CAROLA. 2002. Ex Oriente Lux: Josef Strzygowski und die "Orient oder Rom": Debatte um 1900. *Okzient und Okzident.* Special issue, *Sanat Tahiri Defterleri [Kunsthistorische Hefte]* (6): 91–111.

JENKINS, MARIANNA. 1947. *The state portrait: Its origin and evolution.* New York: College Art Association.

JOHNSON, SAMUEL. 1921. *The history of the Yorubas.* Lagos: CSS Bookshops, reprint 1969.

JONAITIS, ALDONA, ed. 1995. *A wealth of thought: Franz Boas on native American art.* Seattle: University of Washington Press.

JONES, A. H. M. 1956. Slavery in the ancient world. *Economic History Review* 9: 185–99.

JONES, A. H. M. 1967. *Sparta.* Cambridge, MA: Harvard University Press.

JONES, OWEN. 1856. *Grammar of ornament.* London: Day and Son.

JOPLING, CAROL F., ed. 1971. *Art and aesthetics in primitive societies.* New York: Dutton.

JORDANOVA, LUDMILLA. 2000. *Defining features: Scientific and medical portraits 1660–2000.* London: Reaktion Books in association with the National Portrait Gallery.

JULES-ROSETTE, BENNETTA. 1984. *The messages of tourist art: An African semiotic system in comparative perspective.* New York: Plenum Press.
—. 1986. Aesthetics and market demand: The structure of the tourist art market in three African settings. *African Studies Review* 29 (1): 41–59.

K

KALMAR, IVAN. 1987. The *Völkerpsychologie* of Lazarus and Steinthal and the modern concept of culture. *Journal of the History of Ideas* 48 (4): 671–90.

KANDINSKY, NINA. 1978. *Kandinsky et moi.* Paris: Flammarion.

KANDINSKY, WASSILY. 1974. On the question of form [1912] [Über die Formfrage]. In Wassily Kandinsky and Franz Marc, eds., *The Blaue Reiter almanac.* The documents of 20th-century art 6, ed. and with an introd. by Klaus Klankheit, trans. Henning Falkenstein with Manug Terzian and Gertrude Hinderlie, 147–86. New York: Viking Press, 1974. Originally published as *Der Blaue Reiter* (München: R. Piper & Co. Verlag, 1914).

KANWISHER, NANCY. 2004. The ventral visual pathway in humans: Evidence from fMRI. In *The Visual Neurosciences,* vol. 2, ed. Leo M. Chalupa and John S. Werner, 1179–89. Cambridge, MA: MIT Press.

KAPUR, GEETA. 2000. *When was modernism: Essays on contemporary cultural practice in India.* New Delhi: Tulika Books.

KARLHOLM, DAN. 2004. *Art of illusion: The representation of art history in nineteenth-century Germany.* Bern: Peter Lang.

KASFIR, SIDNEY L. 1992. African art and authenticity: A text with a shadow. *African Arts* 25 (2): 40–53, 96–97.

—. 2003. Thinking about artworlds in a global flow: Some major disparities in dealing with visual culture. *International Journal of Anthropology* 18 (4): 211–18.

KATER, MICHAEL H. 1997. *Das "Ahnenerbe" der SS, 1935–1945: ein Beitrag zur Kulturpolitik des Dritten Reiches*. Munich: Oldenbourg.

KAUFMANN, THOMAS DACOSTA. 1999. Eurocentrism and art history?: Universal history and the historiography of the arts before Winckelmann. In *Memory and oblivion: Proceedings of the XXXIXth International Congress of the History of Art*, ed. Wessel Reinink and Jeroen Stumpel, 35–42. Dordrecht: Kluwer.
—. 2004. *Toward a geography of art*. Chicago and London: The University of Chicago Press.
—. 2005. Adam Miłobędzki: Mapping and the geography of art. In *Rocznik Historii Sztuki* [Yearbook of Art History] XXX, 23–30. Warsaw: Polish Academy of Sciences.
—. 2005. Introduction. In *Time and place: Essays in the geohistory of art*, ed. Thomas DaCosta Kaufmann and Elizabeth Pilliod, 1–19. Aldershot and Burlington, VT: Ashgate.
—, and Elizabeth Pilliod, eds. 2005. *Time and place: Essays in the geohistory of art*. Aldershot and Burlington, VT: Ashgate.

KEENE, DONALD. 1995. Japanese aesthetics. In *Japanese aesthetics and culture: A reader*, ed. Nancy Hume, 27–41. Albany, NY: State University of New York Press.

KEMP, WOLFGANG. 1990. Alois Riegl (1858–1905). In *Altmeister moderner Kunstgeschichte*. Kunstgeschichte zur Einführung. 2nd. ed. 1999, ed. Heinrich Dilly, 36–60. Berlin: Reimer.
—. 2005. Aesthetikkolumne: Die Idee der Weltkunst in East Anglia. *Merkur* 59 (669): 49–55.

KENNEDY, JEAN, et al. 1992. *New currents, ancient rivers: Contemporary African artists in a generation of change*. Washington, DC: Smithsonian Institution Press.

KINOSHITA NAOYUKI. 1993. *Bijutsu to iu misemono, aburae-chaya no jidai*. Tokyo: Chikuma Shobo.

KIRSCHENBLATT-GIMBLETT, BARBARA. 2001. Reflections. In *The empire of things: Regimes of value and material culture*, ed. Fred R. Myers, 257–68. Santa Fe: School of American Research.

KITE, STEPHEN. 2003. "South opposed to East and North": Adrian Stokes and Josef Strzygowski: A study in the aesthetics and historiography of Orientalism. *Art History* 26 (4): 505–32.

KLEINER, FRED S., AND CHRISTIN J. MAMIYA. 2006. *Gardner's art through the ages*. 12th ed., 1st ed. published 1926. Belmont, CA: Wadsworth.

KLEINERT, SYLVIA, AND MARGO NEALE, eds. 2000. *Oxford companion to aboriginal art and culture*. New York: Oxford University Press.

KLEINMAN, ARTHUR, AND BYRON GOOD, eds. 1985. *Culture and depression: Studies in the anthropology and cross-cultural psychiatry of affect and disorder*. Berkeley: University of California Press.

KLIBANSKY, RAYMOND, AND HERBERT J. PATON, eds. 1936. *Philosophy and history: Essays presented to Ernst Cassirer*. Oxford: The Clarendon Press.

KOHN, MAREK, AND STEVEN MITHEN. 1999. Handaxes: Products of sexual selection? *Antiquity* 73 (279): 518–26.

KÖHNKE, CHRISTIAN. 1990. Soziologie als Kulturwissenschaft: Georg Simmel und die Völkerpsychologie. *Archiv für Kulturgeschichte* 72 (1): 223–32.

KÖNIG, CHRISTOPH, AND EBERHARD LÄMMERT, eds. 1999. *Konkurrenten in der Fakultät: Kultur, Wissen und Universität um 1900*. Fischer 14262: Forum Wissenschaft. Frankfurt a.M.: Fischer.

KONISHI, JIN'ICHI. 1984. *The archaic and ancient ages*. Vol. 1 of *A history of Japanese literature*, ed. Earl Miner, trans. Aileen Gatten and Nicholas Teele. Princeton, NJ: Princeton University Press.
—. 1986. *The early Middle Ages*. Vol. 2 of *A history of Japanese literature*, ed. Earl Miner, trans. Aileen Gatten and Nicholas Teele. Princeton, NJ: Princeton University Press.

KÖPPING, KLAUS-PETER. 1983. *Adolf Bastian and the psychic unity of mankind: The foundations of anthropology in nineteenth-century Germany*. St. Lucia, London, and New York: University of Queensland Press.

KOPYTOFF, IGOR. 1986. The cultural biography of things: Commoditization as process. In *The social life of things: Commodities in cultural perspective*, ed. Arjun Appadurai, 3–63. Cambridge: Cambridge University Press.

KRAUSS, ROSALIND, et al., ed. 1996. Visual studies questionnaire. *October* 77 (Summer): 27–28.
—. 1985. *The originality of the avant-garde and other modernist myths*. Cambridge, MA: MIT Press.

KREAMER, CHRISTINE M. [2001]. *Women's work: Everyday utensils and daily work as symbols of Moba women (Northern Togo)*. Paper presented at the Triennial Symposium on African Art, St. Thomas, Virgin Islands.

KREIDE-DAMANI, INGRID. 1992. *KunstEthnologie: zum Verständnis fremder Kunst*. DuMont-Taschenbücher 291. Cologne: DuMont.

KRISTELLER, PAUL O. 1961. *Renaissance thought: The classic, scholastic, and humanistic strains*. New York: Harper and Collins.

KRUFT, HANNO-WALTER. 1985. *Geschichte der Architekturtheorie: von der Antike bis zur Gegenwart*. München: Beck.

KUBLER, GEORGE. 1991. *Esthetic recognition of ancient Amerindian art*. New Haven, CT and London: Yale University Press.

KUGLER, FRANZ THEODOR. 1842. *Handbuch der Kunstgeschichte*. Stuttgart: Ebner & Seubert.

KÜHN, HERBERT. 1923. *Die Kunst der Primitiven*. Munich: Delphin-Verlag.
—. 1976. *Geschichte der Vorgeschichtsforschung*. Berlin and New York: De Gruyter.

KUHN, THOMAS S. 1962. *The structure of scientific revolutions*. Chicago and London: The University of Chicago Press.

KÜHNEL, ERNST. [1929]. Die islamische Kunst. In *Die aussereuropäische Kunst*. Vol. VI of *Handbuch für Kunstgeschichte von Anton Springer*, ed. Curt Glaser, 373–548. Leipzig: Kröner.

KUPER, ADAM. 1988. *The invention of primitive society: Transformations of an illusion*. London and New York: Routledge.

L

LACH, DONALD F. 1970. *Asia in the making of Europe*. Vol. II: *A century of wonder, Book 1: The visual arts*. Chicago and London: The University of Chicago Press.

LAKOFF, GEORGE. 1987. *Women, fire, and dangerous things: What categories reveal about the mind*. Chicago and London: University of Chicago Press.

LAMB, TREVOR, AND JANINE BOURRIAU. 1995. *Colour: Art and science*. Cambridge and New York: Cambridge University Press.

LAMPRECHT, KARL. 1896. Was ist Kulturgeschichte?: Beitrag zu einer empirischen Historik. *Deutsche Zeitschrift für Geschichtswissenschaft* 1: 75–150.
—. 1905. Universalgeschichtliche Probleme vom sozialpsychologischen Standpunkte. In *Moderne Geschichtswissenschaft: Fünf Vorträge*, 103–30. Freiburg im Breisgau: Heyfelder.
—. 1914. Einführung in die Ausstellung von parallelen Entwicklungen in der bildenden Kunst. In *Bericht: Kongress für Ästhetik und Allgemeine Kunstwissenschaft*. Stuttgart: Enke, 75–78.

LANCMAN, ELI. 1966. *Chinese portraiture*. Rutland: Charles E. Tuttle Co.

LANGE, JULIUS. 1899. *Darstellung des Menschen in der älteren griechischen Kunst*, ed. Adolf Furtwängler. Trans. from the Danish by Mathilde Mann. Strassburg: Heitz (1st Danish ed. 1892/1898).

LAUDE, JEAN. 1968. *La peintre française (1905–1914) et l'art négre*. Paris: Klincksieck.

LAVIN, IRVING, ed. 1988. *World art: Themes of unity and diversity (Acts of the 26th International Congress of the History of Art)*. University Park: Pennsylvania State University Press.

LAWAL, BABATUNDE. 1974. Some aspects of Yoruba aesthetics. *British Journal of Aesthetics* 14(3): 239–49.
—. 1977. Art and immortality among the Yoruba. *Africa* 47 (1): 52–60.
—. 2001. *Àwòrán*: Representing the self and its metaphysical other in Yoruba art. *The Art Bulletin* 93 (3): 498–526.

LAYTON, ROBERT. 1991. *The anthropology of art*. 2nd ed., 1st ed. published 1981. New York: Cambridge University Press.

LAZARUS, MORITZ. 1851. Über den Begriff und die Möglichkeit einer Völkerpsychologie. *Deutsches Museum: Zeitschrift für Literatur, Kunst und öffentliches Leben* 1 (July), 112–26.
—. 2003. *Grundzüge der Völkerpsychologie und Kulturwissenschaft*. Philosophische Bibliothek 551, ed. with an introd. by Klaus Christian Köhnke. Hamburg: Meiner.
—, and Heymann Steinthal. 1860. Einleitende Gedanken über Völkerpsychologie, als Einladung zu einer Zeitschrift für Völkerpsychologie und Sprachwissenschaft. *Zeitschrift für Völkerpsychologie und Sprachwissenschaft* 1: 1–73.

LAZARUS, RICHARD S. 1991. *Emotion and adaptation*. New York: Oxford University Press.

LEARY, DAVID. 1977. *The reconstruction of psychology in Germany, 1780–1850*. PhD diss., University of Chicago.

LEDDEROSE, LOTHAR. 1989. Kunstgeschichte und Weltkunstgeschichte. *Saeculum* 40 (2): 136–41.

LEE, MOLLY. 1999. Tourism and taste cultures: Collecting native art in Alaska at the turn of the twentieth century. In *Unpacking culture: Art and commodity in colonial and postcolonial worlds*, ed. Ruth B. Phillips and Christopher B. Steiner, 267–81. Berkeley: University of California Press.

LÉON-PORTILLA, MIGUEL. 1966. Pre-Hispanic thought. In *Major trends in Mexican philosophy*, Mario De La Cueva et al., 2–56. Notre Dame, in: University of Notre Dame Press.
—. 1971. Philosophy in ancient Mexico. In *Archaeology of Northern Mesoamerica*, ed. Gordon F. Ekholm and Ignacio Bernal, 447–51. Vol. 10 of *Handbook of Middle American indians*, ed. Robert Wauchope. Austin: University of Texas Press.
—. 1980. *Toltecáyotl, aspectos de la cultura náhuatl*. Mexico City: Fondo de Cultura Económica.

LEVINSON, JERROLD, AND JENEFER ROBINSON, eds. 2004. *Art, mind, and cognitive science*. Special issue, *Journal of Aesthetics and Art Criticism* 62 (2).

LÉVI-STRAUSS, CLAUDE. 1955. *Tristes tropiques*. Trans. John Weightman and Doreen Weightman. Harmondsworth: Penguin, 1992.

LEVITIN, DANIEL J. 2006. *Your brain on music: The science of a human obsession*. New York: Dutton.

LEWIS-WILLIAMS, DAVID. 2002. *The mind in the cave: Consciousness and the origins of art*. London: Thames and Hudson.

LIDOV, ALEXEI, ed. 2004. *Hierotopy: Studies in the making of sacred spaces: Material from the international symposium*. Moscow: Radunitsa.

LIN, YUTANG. 1967. *The Chinese theory of art: Translations from the masters of Chinese art by Lin Yutang*. London: Heinemann.

LINDAUER, MARTIN S., ed. 1998. *Interdisciplinarity, the psychology of art, and creativity*. Special issue, *Creativity Research Journal* 11 (1).

LINDE, ROHR-BONGRAD, et al. 2001. *Kunst=Kapital: Der Capital Kunstkompass von 1970 bis heute*. Cologne: Salon Verlag.

LIPPARD, LUCY. 1966. Heroic years from humble treasures. *Art International* 10 (September): 17–25.

LIVINGSTONE, DAVID N. 2003. *Putting science in its place: geographies of scientific knowledge*. Chicago and London: The University of Chicago Press.

LLEWELLEN, TED C. 2002. *The anthropology of globalization: Cultural anthropology enters the 21st century*. Westport, CT: Bergin & Garvey.

LLOYD, BARBARA, AND JOHN GAY, eds. 1981. *Universals of human thought: Some African evidence*. Cambridge and New York: Cambridge University Press.

LLOYD, JILL. 1991. *German expressionism: Primitivism and modernity*. New Haven, CT, and London: Yale University.

LOCHER, HUBERT. 1999. Wissenschaftsgeschichte als Problemgeschichte: die "Kunstgeschichtlichen Grundbegriffe" und die Bemühungen um eine "strenge Kunstwissenschaft". In *Disziplinen im Kontext: Perspektiven der Disziplingeschichtsschreibung*. Erlanger Beiträge zur Wissenschaftsforschung, ed. Volker Peckhaus and Christian Thiel, 129–62. Munich: Fink.
—. 2001. *Kunstgeschichte als historische Theorie der Kunst 1750–1950*. Munich: Fink.

LOCHER, PAUL, COLIN MARTINDALE, AND LEONID DORFMAN, eds. 2006. *New directions in aesthetics, creativity, and the arts*. Amityville, NY: Baywood.

LORBLANCHET, MICHEL. 1999. *La naissance de l'art: genèse de l'art préhistorique dans le monde*. Paris: Editions Errance.

LORENZ, KONRAD. 1982. *The foundations of ethology: The principal ideas and discoveries in animal behavior*. Trans. Robert Warren Kickert and author. New York: Simon and Schuster.

LOT, FERDINAND. 1961. *The end of the ancient world and the beginnings of the Middle Ages*. 1st ed. published 1937. New York: Harper and Row.

LOVEJOY, ARTHUR O., AND GEORGE BOAS. 1935. *Primitivism and related ideas in Antiquity*, reprint 1997. Baltimore, MD: The Johns Hopkins University.

LUBBOCK, JOHN. 1870. *The origins of civilisation and the primitive condition of man*. London: Longmans, Green & Co.

LUHMANN, NIKLAS. 1995. *Social systems*. Trans. John Bednarz, Jr., with Dirk Baecker. Stanford, CA: Stanford University Press. Originally published as *Soziale Systeme: Grundriss einer allgemeinen Theorie* (Frankfurt am Main: Suhrkamp, 1984).
—. 1997. *Die Gesellschaft der Gesellschaft*. 2 Vols. Frankfurt am Main: Suhrkamp.
—. 2000. *Art as a social system*. Trans. Eva M. Knodt. Stanford, CA: Stanford University Press. Originally published as *Die Kunst der Gesellschaft* (Frankfurt am Main: Suhrkamp, 1995).

LUI, SHOU KWAN. 1971. The six canons of Hsieh Ho. *Oriental Art* 17 (Summer): 144–47, 252–55.

LUTZ, CATHERINE. 1988. *Unnatural emotions: Everyday sentiments on a Micronesian atoll and their challenge to western theory*. Chicago and London: The University of Chicago Press.

LYONS, KAY J. 1995. Colour in language. In *Colour: Art and science*, ed. Trevor Lamb and Janine Bourriau, 194–224. Cambridge and New York: Cambridge University Press.

M

MACCLANCY, JEREMY. 1988. A natural curiosity: The British market in primitive art. *RES: Anthropology and Aesthetics* 15: 163–76.
—, ed. 1997. *Contesting art: Art, politics, and identity in the modern world*. Oxford: Berg.

MACK, JOHN. 1986. *Madagascar: Island of the ancestors*. London: British Museum Publications.

MACMULLEN, RAMSEY. 1974. *Roman social relations, 50 B.C. to A.D. 284*. New Haven, CT: Yale University Press.

MAHON, DENIS. 1947. *Studies in seicento art and theory*. London: Warburg Institute, University of London.

MALÉ, S. 2001. The initiation as rite of passage: The *Jo* and the *Gwan*. In *Bamana: The art of existence in Mali*, ed. Jean-Paul Colleyn. New York: Museum for African Art, etc.

MALINOWSKI, BRONISLAW. 1922. *Argonauts of the Western Pacific*. London: Routledge and Kegan Paul.
—. 1948. *Magic, science and religion and other essays*, selected and with an introd. by Robert Redfield. Boston: Beacon Press.

MALLGRAVE, HARRY FRANCIS. 1985. Gustav Klemm and Gottfried Semper: The meeting of ethnological and architectural theory. *Res: Journal of Anthropology and Aesthetics* 9 (Spring): 68–79.
—, and Eleftherios Ikonomou, 1994. Introduction. In *Empathy, form, and space: Problems in German aesthetics, 1873–1893*, ed. Harry Francis Mallgrave and Eleftherios Ikonomou, 1–85. Santa Monica, CA: Getty Center for the History of Art and the Humanities.

MALLOCH, STEPHEN, AND COLWYN TREVARTHEN, eds. Fortcoming. *Communicative musicality: Narratives of expressive gesture and being human*. Oxford: Oxford University Press.

MAMAPUKU, METHODIUS, AND TODD S. HARPLE. 2003. Ancestral heritage and the essence of life. In *Kamoro art: Tradition and innovation in a New Guinea culture*, ed. Dirk Smidt, 22–23. Amsterdam: KIT Publishers.

MANDROU, PIERRE. 1978. *From humanism to science 1480–1700*. Trans. Brian Pearce. Harmondsworth: Penguin.

MANIA, DIETRICH, AND URSULA MANIA. 1988. Deliberate engravings on bone artefacts of Homo Erectus. *Rock Art Research* 5: 91–97.

MANIURA, ROBERT, AND RUPERT SHEPHERD, eds. 2006. *Presence: The inherence of the prototype within images and other objects*. Aldershot and Burlington, VT: Ashgate.

MANN, EKKEHARD. 1996. *Untergrund: Autonome Literatur und das Ende der DDR: eine systemtheoretische Analyse*. Frankfurt: Peter Lang.

MANNING, PETER. 2003. *Navigating world history: Historians create a global past*. New York: Palgrave Macmillan.

MAQUET, JACQUES J. 1971. *Introduction to aesthetic anthropology*. 2nd ed. 1979. Reading, MA: Addison-Wesley.
—. 1986. *The aesthetic experience: An anthropologist looks at the visual arts*. New Haven, CT and London: Yale University Press.

MARAINI, TONI. 1989. Morocco. In *Contemporary art from the Islamic world*, ed. Wijdan Ali, 211–18. London: Scorpion Publishers (on behalf of the Royal Society of Fine Arts in Amman).

MARCH, BENJAMIN. 1935. *Some technical terms of Chinese paintings*. Baltimore: Waverly Press.

MARCHAND, SUZANNE L. 1994. The rhetoric of artefacts and the decline of classical humanism: The case of Josef Strzygowski. In *Proof and persuasion in history*. Special issue, *History and Theory* 33 (4): 106–30.
—. 1996. Orientalism as Kulturpolitik: German Archeology and Cultural Imperialism in Asia Minor. In *Volksgeist as method and ethic: Essays on Boasian ethnography and the German anthropological tradition*, ed. George W. Stocking, Jr., 298–336. Madison: University of Wisconsin Press.
—. 1997. Leo Frobenius and the revolt against the West. *Journal of Contemporary History* 32 (2): 153–70.

MARCHIANÒ, GRAZIA, AND RAFAEL MILANI, eds. 2001. *Frontiers of transculturality in contemporary aesthetics*. Milan: Trauben. (free version available online)

MARCUS, GEORGE E. 1995. Middlebrow into highbrow at the J. Paul Getty Trust, L.A. *Looking high and low*, ed. Brenda Jo Bright and Liza Bakewell, 173–98. Tucson: The University of Arizona Press.
—, and Michael M. J. Fischer. 1986. *Anthropology as cultural critique: An experimental moment in the human sciences*. Chicago and London: The University of Chicago Press.
—, and Fred R. Myers. 1995. The traffic in art and culture: An introduction. In *The traffic in culture: Refiguring art and anthropology*, ed. George E. Marcus and Fred R. Myers, 1–51. Berkeley: University of California Press.

MARKS, JOEL, AND ROGER T. AMES, eds. 1995. *Emotions in Asian thought: A dialogue in comparative philosophy*. Albany, NY: State University of New York Press.

MARQUIS, ALICE GOLDFARB. 1991. *The art biz: The covert world of collectors, dealers, auction houses, museums, and critics*. Chicago: Contemporary Books.

MARRA, MICHAEL F. 1999. *Modern Japanese aesthetics: A reader*. Honolulu: University of Hawai'i Press.
—, ed. 2001. *A history of modern Japanese aesthetics*. Honolulu: University of Hawai'i Press.

MARTIN, SIMON, AND NICOLAI GRUBE. 2000. *Chronicle of the Maya kings and queens: Deciphering the dynasties of the ancient Maya*. London: Thames and Hudson.

MARTINDALE, COLIN, PAUL LOCHER, AND VLADIMIR PETROV, eds. 2007. *Evolutionary and neurocognitive approaches to aesthetics, creativity, and the arts*. Amityville, NY: Baywood.

MARTINES, LAURO. 1979. *Power and imagination: City-states in Renaissance Italy*. New York: Alfred A. Knopf.

MASCHIO, THOMAS. 1994. *To remember the faces of the dead: The plenitude of memory in Southwestern New Britain.* Madison: University of Wisconsin Press.

MASSELOS, JIM, JACKIE MRNZIES, AND PRATAPADITYA PASL. 1997. *Dancing to the flute: Music and dance in Indian art.* Sydney: Art Gallery of New South Wales.

MASSIN, BENOIT. 1996. From Virchow to Fischer. Physical anthropology and "modern race theories" in Wilhelmine Germany. In *Volksgeist as method and ethic: Essays on Boasian ethnography and the German anthropological Tradition.* Vol. 8 of *History of Anthropology,* ed. George W. Stocking, Jr., 79–154. Madison: University of Wisconsin Press.

MASSON, JEFFREY MOUSSAIEFF, AND M. V. PATWARDHAN. 1969. *Śantarasa and Abhinavagupta's philosophy of aesthetics.* Poona: Bhandakar Oriental Research.

MAYO, LEWIS, WITH JOHN CLARK. 2008. Statements about art and modernity in People's Daily since 1990. In *Modernities compared: Chinese and Thai art in the 1980s and 1990s.* Sydney: Power Publication.

MAZLISH, BRUCE, AND RALPH BUULTJENS, eds. 1993. *Conceptualizing global history.* Boulder, San Francisco, and Oxford: Westview Press.

MCBREARTHY, SALLY, AND ALLISON S. BROOKS. 2000. The revolution that wasn't: A new interpretation of the origin of modern human behavior. *Journal of Human Evolution* 39 (5): 453–563.

MCCRACKEN, GRANT. 1998. *Culture and consumption: New approaches to the symbolic character of consumer goods and activities.* Bloomington: Indiana University Press.

MCEVILLEY, THOMAS. 1984. Doctor lawyer indian chief. *Artforum* 23 (3): 54–61.

MCNEILL, WILLIAM H. 1976. *Plagues and peoples.* Garden City, NY: Doubleday.

MEAD, MARGARET. 1975. *Growing up in New Guinea: A comparative study of primitive education.* 1st ed. published 1930. New York: Morrow.

MELLARS, PAUL. 2006. Why did modern human populations disperse from Africa ca. 60,000 years ago? A new model. *Proceedings of the National Academy of Sciences of the United States of America* 103: 9831–36.

MELZIAN, HANS. 1937. *A concise dictionary of the Bini language of Southern Nigeria.* London: Kegan Paul and Trench Trubner.

MERKER, BJÖRN. 2000. Synchronous chorusing and human origins. In *The origins of music,* ed. Nils Wallin, Björn Merker, and Steven Brown, 315–27. Cambridge, MA: MIT Press.

MIALL, DAVID, AND DON KUIKEN. 1994. Beyond text theory: Understanding literary response. *Discourse Processes* 17: 337–52.
—. 1994. Foregrounding, defamiliarization, and affect: Response to literary stories. *Poetics* 22: 389–407.

MICHELL, HUMFREY. 1952. *Sparta.* Cambridge, MA: Cambridge University Press.

MILLAIRE, JEAN-FRANÇOIS. 2002. *Moche burial patterns: An investigation into prehispanic social structure.* Oxford: Archaeopress.

MILLER, GEOFFREY F. 1999. Sexual selection for cultural displays. In *The evolution of culture: An interdisciplinary view,* ed. Robin Dunbar, Chris Knight, and Camilla Power, 71–91. Edinburgh: Edinburgh University Press

—. 2000. Evolution of human music through sexual selection. In *The origins of music,* ed. Nils Wallin, Björn Merker, and Steven Brown, 329–60. Cambridge, MA: MIT Press.
—. 2000. *The mating mind: How sexual choice shaped the evolution of human nature.* New York: Doubleday; London: Heinemann.
—. 2001. Aesthetic fitness: How sexual selection shaped artistic virtuosity as a fitness indicator and aesthetic preferences as mate choice critera. *Bulletin of Psychology and the Arts* 2 (1): 20–25.

MILNER, JOHN. 1992. *Mondrian.* London: Phaidon.

MINER, EARL, ed. 1985. *Principles of classical Japanese literature.* Princeton, NJ: Princeton University Press.
—, Hiroko Odagiri, and Robert E. Morrell. 1985. *The Princeton companion to classical Japanese literature.* Princeton, N.J.: Princeton University Press.

MINOR, VERNON HYDE. 1994. *Art history's history.* Englewood Cliffs, NJ: Prentice Hall.

MIRZOEFF, NICOLAS. 1999. *An introduction to visual culture.* London and New York: Routledge.

MITCHELL, W. J. THOMAS. 2005. *What do pictures want? The loves and lives of images.* Chicago and London: The University of Chicago Press.

MITHEN, STEVEN J. 1996. *The prehistory of the mind: The cognitive origins of art, religion and science.* London: Thames and Hudson 1996.
—. 2005. *The singing Neanderthals: The origins of music, language, mind and body.* London: Weidenfeld and Nicolson.

MONDRIAN, PIET. 1945. *Plastic art and pure plastic art, 1937 and other essays 1941–1943.* New York: Wittenborn and Company.

MONTIAS, JOHN, MICHAEL. 1991. Works of art in seventeenth century Amsterdam. In *Art in history, history in art: Studies in seventeenth-century Dutch culture,* ed. David Freedberg and Jan de Vries, 331–77. Santa Monica, CA: The Getty Center.

MORI, HISHASHI. 1977. *Japanese portrait sculpture.* Trans. and adapted by W. Chie Ishibashi. Tokyo, New York, and San Francisco: Kodansha International and Shibundo.

MORLEY, IAIN. 2002. Evolution of the physiological and neurological capacities for music. *Cambridge Archaeological Journal* 12 (2): 195–216.

MORPHY, HOWARD, ed. 1989. *Animals into art.* London: Unwin Hyman.
—. 1994. The anthropology of art. In *Companion encyclopedia of anthropology: Humanity, culture and social life,* ed. Tim Ingold, 648–85. London and New York: Routledge.
—. 1995. Aboriginal art in a global context. In *Worlds apart: Modernity through the prism of the local,* ed. Daniel Miller, 211–39. London: Routledge.
—. 2001. Seeing aboriginal art in the gallery. *Humanities Research* 8 (1), www.anu.edu.au/hrc/publications/hr/issue1_2001/article05.htm.
—. 2008. *Becoming art: Exploring cross-cultural categories.* Sidney: University of South Wales Press.
—, and Morgan Perkins, eds. 2006. *The anthropology of art: A reader.* Oxford: Blackwell.

MORRIS, DESMOND. 1962. *The Biology of art: A study of the picture-making behaviour of the great apes and its relationship to human art.* New York: Knopf.

MORWOOD, MICHAEL J. 2002. *Visions of the past: The archaeology of Australian aboriginal art.* London: Allen and Unwin.

MOSQUERA, GERARDO. 1992–1993. The Marco Polo syndrome: Some problems around art and eurocentrism. In *Theory in *contemporary art since 1985*, ed. Zoya Kocur and Simon Leung, 218–25. London: Blackwell: 2005.

MOSZYNSKA, ANNA. 1990. *Abstract art*. London: Thames and Hudson.

MOULIN, RAYMONDE. 1987. *The French art market*. Trans. A. Goldhammer. New York: Routledge.

MUGGLESTONE, ERICA. 1981. Guido Adler's "The Scope, Method, and Aim of Musicology" (1885): An English translation with an historico-analytical commentary. *Yearbook for Traditional Music*, vol. 13, 1–21. [New York]: International Council for Traditional Music.

MUKAŘOVSKÝ, JAN. 1964. Standard language and poetic language. In *A Prague School reader on esthetics, literary structure and style*, ed. and trans. from the Czech by Paul L. Garvin, 17–30. Washington, DC: Georgetown University Press. Originally published as Jazyk spisovný a jazyk básnický. *Spisovná čeština a jazyková kultura* (1932): 132–56.

MÜLLER, CLAUDIUS. 2003. La reconnaissance des arts premiers en Allemagne: un trajet bien particulier? *Arquivos do Centro Cultural Calouste Gulbenkian* 45: 75–83.

MULLIN, MOLLY H. 1995. The patronage of difference: Making Indian art "art," not ethnology. In *The traffic in culture: Refiguring art and anthropology*, ed. George E. Marcus and Fred R. Myers, 1–51. Berkeley: University of California Press.
—. 2001. *Culture in the marketplace: Gender, art, and value in the American Southwest*. Durham, NC: Duke University Press.

MUNRO, DONALD J. 1969. *The concept of man in Early China*. Stanford, CA: Stanford University Press.

MUNRO, THOMAS. 1963. *Evolution in the arts and other theories of culture history*. [Cleveland:] Cleveland Museum of Art.

MURAWSKA-MUTHESIUS, KATARZYNA, ed. 2000. *Borders in art: Revisiting "Kunstgeographie": University of East Anglia, Norwich, 1998: The proceedings of the Fourth Joint Conference of Polish and English art historians*. Warsaw: Institute of Art.

MURRAY, ALEXANDER. 1978. *Reason and society in the Middle Ages*. Oxford: Clarendon Press.

MYERS, FRED R. 1994. Culture making: Performing Aboriginality at the Asia Society Gallery. *American Ethnologist* 21 (4): 679–99.
—. 1995. Representing culture: The production of discourse(s) for aboriginal acrylic paintings. In *The traffic in culture: Refiguring art and anthropology*, ed. George E. Marcus and Fred R. Myers, 55–95. Berkeley: University of California Press.
—. 1999. Objects on the loose. *Ethnos* 64 (2): 263–73.
—. 2001. The wizards of Oz: Nation, state and the production of Aboriginal fine art. *The empire of things*, ed. Fred Myers, 165–206. Santa Fe: School of American Research.
—. 2002. *Painting culture: The making of an Aboriginal high art*. Durham, NC: Duke University Press.

N

NACHTSHEIM, STEPHAN. 1984. *Kunstphilosophie und empirische Kunstforschung 1870–1920*. Kunst, Kultur und Politik im deutschen Kaiserreich 7. Berlin: Mann.

NADEL, JACQUELINE, et al. 1999. Expectancies for social contingency in 2-month-olds. *Developmental Science* 2 (2): 164–73.

NADLER, JOSEF. 1912. *Literaturgeschichte der deutschen Stämme und Landschaften*. 3 vols. Regensburg: Habbel.

NAJITA, TETSUO. 1991. History and nature in eighteenth-century Tokugawa thought. In *Early modern Japan*, ed. James L. McLain and John W. Hall, 596–659. Vol. 4 of *The Cambridge history of Japan*, ed. John W. Hall et al. Cambridge and New York: Cambridge University Press.

NAPIER, A. DAVID. 1986. *Masks, tranformation, and paradox*. Berkeley: University of California Press.
—. 1992. *Foreign bodies: Performance, art, and symbolic anthropology*. Berkeley: University of California Press.

NEEDHAM, RODNEY. 1981. *Circumstantial deliveries*. Berkeley: University of California Press.

NEICH, ROGER. 1984. Some recent developments in the anthropology of the visual arts. *Pacific Arts Newsletter* 19: 24–42.

NELSON, EDWARD. 1899. *The Eskimo about Bering Strait*. Washington, DC: 18th Annual Report-Bureau of American Ethnology.

NELSON, ROBERT S., AND RICHARD SHIFF, eds. 2003. *Critical terms for art history*. 2nd ed. Chicago and London: The University of Chicago Press.

NETTL, BRUNO. 2002. *Encounters in ethnomusicology: A memoir*. Warren, MI: Harmonie Park Press.

NETTLETON, ANITRA. 1988. The myth of the transitional: Black art and white markets. *South African Journal for Cultural and Art History* 2 (4): 301–10.

NEVADOMSKY, JOSEPH. 1997. Contemporary art and artists in Benin City. *African Arts* 30 (4): 54–63, 94–95.

NICKLIN, KEITH. N.D. *Guide to the National Museum, Oron*. Lagos: Federal Department of Antiquities.
NODELMAN, SHELDON. 1975. How to read a Roman portrait. *Art in America* 63 (1): 27–33.

NORBERG-SCHULZ, CHRISTIAN. 1979. *Genius loci: Towards a phenomenology of architecture*. New York: Rizzoli.

NUOFFER, OSKAR. 1926. *Afrikanische Plastik in der Gestaltung von Mutter und Kind*. Dresden: Carl Reissner.

O

O'CONNELL, JAMES, AND JAMES ALLEN. 2004. Dating the colonization of Sahul: A review of recent research. *Journal of Archaeological Science* 31: 835–53.

ODIN, STEVE. 2001. *Artistic detachment in Japan and the West: Psychic distance in comparative aesthetics*. Honolulu: University of Hawai'i Press.

ONIANS, JOHN. 1996. World art studies and the need for a new natural history of art. *The Art Bulletin* 78 (2): 206–9.
—. 1999. The nature of art in Lin Fengmian's China: a neuropsychological perspective. In *The approach of Lin Fengmian: The centenary of Lin Fengmian*, 690–715. Hangzhou: China Academy of Art Press.
—, ed. 2004. *Atlas of world art*. London: Laurence King Publishing.
—. 2000. The biological and geographical bases of cultural borders: the case of the earliest European prehistoric art. In *Borders in art: Revisiting "Kunstgeographie": University of East Anglia, Norwich, 1998: The proceedings of the Fourth Joint Conference of Polish and English art historians*, ed. Katarzyna Murawska-Muthesius, 27–33. Warsaw: Institute of Art.
—, ed. 2006. *Compression vs. expression: Containing and explaining the world's art*. Williamstown, MA: Clark Art Institute.
—. 2007. *Art between culture and nature*. London: Pindar Press.

—. 2007. *Neuroarthistory: From Aristotle and Pliny to Baxandall and Zeki*. New Haven, CT and London: Yale University Press.

OPPENHEIMER, STEPHEN. 2004. *The real eve: Man's journey out of Africa*. New York: Carroll and Graf.

OSBORNE, ROBIN, AND JEREMY TANNER, eds. 2007. *Art's agency and art history*. London: Blackwell.

OTTEN, CHARLOTTE M., ed. 1971. *Anthropology and art: Readings in cross-cultural aesthetics*. Garden City, NY: Natural History Press.

P

PANDEY, KANTI CHANDRA. 1950. *Indian aesthetics*. Vol. 1 of *Comparative aesthetics*. Banaras [Varanasi]: Chowkhamba.
—. 1963. *Abhinavagupta: An historical and philosophical study*. 2nd ed., rev. and enl. Varanasi, Chowkhamba Sanskrit Series Office.

PANÉ, RAMÓN. 1999. *An account of the antiquities of the Indians*, rev. ed., with an introductory study, notes, and appendices by José Juan Arrom, trans. Susan C. Griswold. Durham and London: Duke University Press.

PANOFSKY, ERWIN. 1963. The ideological antecedents of the Rolls Royce radiator. *Proceedings of the American Philosophical Society* 107: 273–88.
—. 1968. *Idea: A concept in art theory*. Trans. Joseph J. S. Peake. Columbia: University of South Carolina Press.

PAPOUŠEK, HANUŠ, AND MECHTHILD PAPOUŠEK. 1979. Early ontogeny of human social interaction: Its biological roots and social dimensions. In *Human ethology: Claims and limits of a new discipline: Contributions to the colloquium*, ed. M. von Cranach et al., 456–78. Cambridge: Cambridge University Press.
—. 1981. Musical elements in the infant's vocalization: Their significance for communication, cognition, and creativity. In *Advances in Infancy Research*, vol. 1, ed. Lewis P. Lipsitt and Carolyn K. Rovee-Collier, 163–224. Norwood, NJ: Ablex 1981.

PASTOUREAU, MICHEL. 2001. *Blue: The history of a color*. Princeton, NJ and Oxford: Princeton University Press.

PASZTORY, ESTHER. 2005. *Thinking with things: Toward a new vision of art*. Austin: University of Texas Press.

PAUL, BARBARA. 2003. Schöne heile Welt(ordnung): zum Umgang der Kunstgeschichte in der frühen Bundesrepublik Deutschland mit aussereuropäischer Gegenwartskunst. *Kritische Berichte* 31 (2): 5–27.

PEARCE, SUSAN M. 1995. *On collecting: An investigation into collecting in the European Tradition*. London: Routledge.
—. 1998. *Collecting in contemporary practice*. London: Sage.
—, and Christopher B. Steiner 1999. Art, authenticity, and the baggage of cultural encounter. In *Unpacking culture: Art and commodity in colonial and postcolonial worlds*, ed. Ruth B. Phillips and Christopher B. Steiner, 3–19. Berkeley: University of California Press.

PELEGGI, MAURIZIO. 2002. *The politics of ruins and the business of nostalgia*. Bangkok: White Lotus.
—. 2005. Royal antiquarianism, European orientalism and the production of archaeological knowledge in modern Siam. In *Asia in Europe, Europe in Asia*, ed. Srilata Ravi, Mario Rutten, and Ben-Lan Goh. IIAS/ISIAS series on Asia. Leiden: IIAS; Singapore: ISEAS.

PENNY, H. GLENN. 1999. *Cosmopolitan visions and municipal displays: Museums, markets, and the ethnographic project in Germany, 1868–1914*. PhD diss., University of Illinois.
—. 2003. Bastian's museum: On the limits of empiricism and the transformation of German ethnology. In *Wordly provincialism: German anthropology in the age of empire*, ed. Matti Bunzl and H. Glenn Penny, 86–126. Ann Arbor: University of Michigan.

PERETZ, ISABELLE, AND ROBERT J. ZATORE, eds. 2004. *The cognitive neuroscience of music*. New York: Oxford University Press.

PERRY, GILL. 1993. Primitivism and the "Modern." In *Primitivism, Cubism, Abstraction: The Early Twentieth Century*, ed. Charles Harrison, Francis Frascina, and Gill Perry, 3–86. New Haven, CT and London: Yale University Press in association with The Open University.

PETRAGLIA, MICHAEL, et al. 2007. Middle Paleolithic assemblages from the Indian subcontinent before and after the Toba super-eruption. *Science* 317 (5844): 114–16.

PEVSNER, NIKOLAUS. 1956. *The Englishness of English art*. London. Architectural Press.

PHILLIPS, QUITMAN S. 2000. *The practices of painting in Japan, 1475–1500*. Stanford, CA: Stanford University Press.

PHILLIPS, RUTH B. 1998. *Trading identities: The souvenir in Native North America, 1700–1900*. Seattle: University of Washington Press.

PIEPER, PAUL. 1936. *Kunstgeographie: Versuch einer Grundlegung*. Neue deutsche Forschungen 61. Berlin: Junker & Dünnhaut.

PINKER, STEVEN. 1997. *How the mind works*. New York: Norton.
—. 2002. *The blank slate: The modern denial of human nature*. New York: Viking.

PIOTROWSKI, PIOTR. 2000. The geography of Central/East European art. In *Borders in art: Revisiting "Kunstgeographie": University of East Anglia, Norwich, 1998: The proceedings of the Fourth Joint Conference of Polish and English art historians*, ed. Katarzyna Murawska-Muthesius, 43–50. Warsaw: Institute of Art.
—. 2005. Between place and time: A critical geography of "new" Central Europe. In *Time and place: Essays in the geohistory of art*, ed. Thomas DaCosta Kaufmann and Elizabeth Pilliod, 153–71. Aldershot and Burlington, VT: Ashgate.

PITT-RIVERS, AUGUSTUS HENRY LANE-FOX. 1906. *The evolution of culture and other essays*, ed. John Linton Myres, introd. by Henry Balfour. Oxford: Clarendon Press.

PLATTNER, STUART. 1996. *High art down home: An economic ethnography of a local art market*. Chicago and London: The University of Chicago Press.
—. 1998. A most ingenious paradox: The market for contemporary fine art. *American Anthropologist* 100 (2): 482–93.
—. 2004. Anthropology of art. https://ep.eur.nl/retrieve/1335/towse%20/ebook.

PLOTINUS. 1953. *Plotinus*. Trans. A. M. Armstrong. London: Allan & Unwin.

POINTON, MARCIA. 1997. Kahnweiler's Picasso; Picasso's Kahnweiler. In *Portraiture: Facing the subject*, ed. Joanna Woodall, 189–202. Manchester and New York: Manchester University Press.

POLLACK, DAVID. 1986. *The fracture of meaning: Japan's synthesis of China from the eighth through the eighteenth centuries*. Princeton, NJ: Princeton University Press.

POLLARD, DAVID. 1978. Ch'i in Chinese literary theory. In *Chinese approaches to literature from Confucius to Liang Ch'i-chao*, ed. Adele A. Rickett, 43–66. Princeton, NJ: Princeton University Press.

POPE-HENNESSEY, JOHN. 1967. *The portrait in the Renaissance*. Princeton, NJ: Princeton University Press.

POWER, CAMILLA. 1999. "Beauty magic": The origins of art. In *The evolution of culture: An interdisciplinary view*, ed. Robin Dunbar, Chris Knight, and Camilla Power, 82–112. Edinburgh: Edinburgh University Press.

PREZIOSI, DONALD, ed. 1998. *The art of art history: A critical anthology*. Oxford and New York: Oxford University Press.

PRICE, SALLY. 1989. *Primitive art in civilized places*. Chicago and London: The University of Chicago Press.

PRICHARD, JAMES COWLES. 1848. On the relations of ethnology to other branches of knowledge. *Journal of the Ethnological Society of London* 1: 301–29.

PURTLE, JENNIFER. 2005. Placing Chinese painting history: The cultural production of the geohistory of painting practice in China. In *Time and place: Essays in the geohistory of art*, ed. Thomas DaCosta Kaufmann and Elizabeth Pilliod, 135–51. Aldershot and Burlington, VT: Ashgate.

Q

QUEMIN, ALAIN. 2002. *L'art contemporain international: entre les institutions et le marché (le rapport disparu)*. Nîmes: Éditions Jacqueline Chambon/Artprice.

R

RADCLIFFE-BROWN, ALFRED REGINALD. 1952. Religion and society. In *Structure and function in primitive society*. Glencoe, IL: Free Press, 153–77. Originally published in *Journal of the Royal Anthropological Institute* 75 (1945) 1–2: 33–43.

RAMACHANDRAN, V. S., AND WILLIAM HIRSTEIN. 1999. The science of art: A neurological theory of aesthetic experience. *Journal of Consciousness Studies* 6 (6): 15–51.

RAMANUJAN, ATTIPAT KRISHNASWAMI, AND EDWIN GEROW. 1974. Indian poetics. In *The literatures of India: An introduction*, ed. Edward C. Dimock, Jr. et al., 115–43. Chicago and London: The University of Chicago Press.

RAMPLEY, MATTHEW. 2000. Anthropology at the origins of art history. In *Site-specify: The ethnographic turn*, ed. Alex Coles, 138–63. London: Black Dog Publishing.
—. 2005. The ethnographic sublime. *Res: Anthropology and Aesthetics* 47: 251–63.
—, ed. 2005. *Exploring visual culture: Definitions, concepts, context*. Edinburgh: Edinburgh University Press.
—. 2005. Systems aesthetics: Burnham and others. *Vector [e-zine]* b # 12, http://virose.pt/vector/b_12/rampley.html.
—. 2008. Art as a social system: The sociological aesthetics of Niklas Luhmann. *Telos* 142.

RANKE, JOHANNES. 1879. *Anfänge der Kunst: Anthropologische Beiträge zur Geschichte des Ornaments*. Berlin: Habel.

RATZEL, FRIEDRICH. 1904. Geschichte, Völkerkunde und historische Perspektive. *Historische Zeitschrift* 93: 1–46.
—. 1912. *Die Geographische Verbreitung des Menschen*. Vol. 2 of *Anthropogeographie*. 2nd ed. Stuttgart: Engelhorns.

RAY, DOROTHY JEAN. 1977. *Eskimo art: Tradition and innovation in North Alaska*. Seattle: University of Washington Press.

RAY, NIHARRANJAN. 1974. *An approach to Indian art*. Chandigarh: Publication Bureau, Panjab University.

READ, CHARLES H. 1910. Ancient Peruvian pottery. *The Burlington Magazine* 17 (85): 22–23, 25–26.

REDFIELD, ROBERT, RALPH LINTON, AND MELVILLE H. HERSKOVITS. 1936. Memorandum on the study of acculturation. *American Anthropologist* 38 (1): 149–52.

REUTER, TIMOTHY, ED. AND TRANS. 1978. *The medieval nobility: Studies on the ruling classes of France and Germany from the sixth to the twelfth century*. Amsterdam, New York; Oxford: North Holland Publishing Co.

RHODES, COLIN. 1993. *Primitivism reexamined: Constructions of the "primitive" in modernist visual art*. PhD diss., University of Essex.
—. 1994. *Primitivism and modern art*. World of Art. London: Thames and Hudson.

RICHARDS, ROBERT J. 1987. *Darwin and the emergence of evolutionary theories of mind and behaviour*. Science and its conceptual foundations. Chicago and London: University of Chicago Press.

RICHERSON, PETER J., AND ROBERT BOYD. 2005. *Not by genes alone: How culture transformed human evolution*. Chicago and London: The University of Chicago Press.

RIDLEY, MATT. 2003. *Nature via nurture: Genes, experience, and what makes us human*. New York: HarperCollins.

RIEGL, ALOIS. 1892. Review of *Mäander, Hakenkreuze und urmotivische Wirbelornamente in Amerika* by Alois Raimund Hein. *Mittheilungen der Anthropologischen Gesellschaft in Wien* 22: 120ff.
—. 1893. *Stilfragen: Grundlegungen zu einer Geschichte der Ornamentik*. Berlin: Siemens.
—. 1901. *Spätrömische Kunst-Industrie nach den Funden in Österreich-Ungarn in Zusammenhang mit der Gesammteintwicklung der Bildenden Künste bei den Mittelmeervölkern*. Wien: Verlag der Kaiserlich-Königliche Hof- und Staatsdruckerei.

RIJNDERS, MIEKE, AND ADI MARTIS, eds. 1998. *Expressionisme en primitivisme in de beeldende kunst van de twintigste eeuw*. Heerlen, The Netherlands: Open Universiteit.

RILEY II, CHARLES A. 1995. *Color codes: Modern theories of color in philosophy, painting and architecture, literature, music, and psychology*. Hanover, NH: University Press of New England.

RINGBOM, SIXTEN. 1986. Transcending the visible: The generation of the abstract pioneers. In *The spiritual in art: Abstract painting 1890–1985*, ed. Maurice Tuchman, 131–54. Los Angeles: Los Angeles County Museum of Art; New York: Abbeville Press.

RIZZOLATTI, GIACOMO, LUCIANO FADIGA, VITTORIO GALLESE, AND LEONARDO FOGASSI. 1996. Premotor cortex and the recognition of motor actions. *Cognitive Brain Research* 3 (2): 131–41.

ROBERTS, MARY, AND ALLEN ROBERTS. 1996. *Memory: Luba art and the making of history*. Munich: Prestel Verlag for the Museum for African Art.

RODEKAMP, VOLKER, ed. 1994. *Franz Boas (1858–1942): ein amerikanischer Anthropologe aus Minden*. Bielefeld: Verlag für Regionalgeschichte.

ROETHEL, HANS KONRAD. 1979. *Kandinsky*, in collab. with Jean K. Benjamin. Oxford: Phaidon.

ROTHFUCHS-SCHULZ, CORNELIA. 1980. *Aspekte der Kunstethnologie: Beiträge zum Problem der Universalität von Kunst*. Berlin: Reimer.

ROWE, JOHN HOWLAND. 1965. The Renaissance foundations of anthropology. *American Anthropologist* 67 (1): 1–20.

ROWELL, LEWIS. 1992. *Music and musical thought in early India*. Chicago and London: University of Chicago Press.

ROWLAND, BENJAMIN. 1953. *The art and architecture of India.* Baltimore: Penguin Books.

ROWLEY, GEORGE. 1947. *Principles of Chinese painting.* Princeton, NJ: Princeton University Press.

ROY, CHRISTOPHER. 1987. *Art of the Upper Volta rivers.* Meudon: Alain and Françoise Chaffin.

RUBIN, ARNOLD, ed. 1988. *Marks of civilization: Artistic transformations of the human body.* Los Angeles: Museum of Cultural History; University of California.

RUBIN, WILLIAM S., ed. 1984. *"Primitivism" in 20th century art: Affinity of the tribal and the modern.* 2 vols. New York: The Museum of Modern Art.

RUBINSTEIN, NICOLAI. 1968. Florentine constitutionalism and Medici ascendancy in the fifteenth century. In *Florentine studies: Politics and society in Renaissance Florence,* ed. by Nicolai Rubinstein, 442–62. Evanston, IL: Northwestern University Press.

RUCH, BARBARA. 1990. The other side of culture in Japan. In *Medieval Japan,* ed. Kozo Yamamura, 500–43. Vol. 3 of *The Cambridge history of Japan,* ed. John W. Hall et al. Cambridge and New York: Cambridge University Press.

RUNGE, EDITH A. 1946. *Primitivism and related ideas in "Sturm und Drang" literature.* Baltimore, MD: The Johns Hopkins University.

RUSHING, W. JACKSON. 1995. *Native American art and the New York avant-garde: A history of cultural primitivism.* Austin: University of Texas Press.

RUSKIN, JOHN. 1888. *Modern painters,* vol. 5. Orpington: G. Allen.

S

SACHS-HOMBACH, KLAUS, ed. 2005. *Bildwissenschaft: Disziplinen, Themen und Methoden.* Frankfurt am Main: Suhrkamp.

SACKS, OLIVER. 2007. *Musicophilia: Tales of music and the brain.* New York: Knopf.

SAID, EDWARD. 1978. *Orientalism: Western conceptions of the Orient.* New York: Pantheon.

SALMI, MARIO, et al., eds. 1958. *Enciclopedia universale dell' Arte.* Venice and Rome: Istituto per la Collaborazione Culturale (Published in English as: *Encyclopedia of world art.* New York: McGraw Hill, 1959–1968).

SALMON, ANDRÉ. 1920. Negro Art. *The Burlington Magazine* 36 (205): 164–67, 170–72.

SANDERSON, STEPHEN K. 1990. *Social evolutionism: A critical history.* Cambridge, MA: Blackwell.

SARANA, GOPALA. 1975. *The methodology of anthropological comparisons: An analysis of comparative methods in social and cultural anthropology.* Tuscon: The University of Arizona Press.

SATOV, MURRAY. 1997. Catalogues, collectors, curators: The tribal art market and anthropology. In *Contesting art: Art, politics, and identity in the modern world,* ed. Jeremy MacClancy, 215–41. Oxford: Berg.

SAUER, CARL ORTWIN. 1963. *Land and life: A selection form the writings of Carl Orwin Sauer,* ed. John Leighly. Berkeley, Los Angeles: University of California Press.

SAUERLÄNDER, WILLIBALD. 2002. Images behind the wall: Review of *The visual and the visionary: Art and female spirituality in late medieval Germany* by Jeffrey F. Hamburger. *The New York Review of Books* 49 (7) April 25: 40–42.

SCALISE SUGIYAMA, MICHELLE. 1996. On the origins of narrative: Storyteller bias as a fitness-enhancing strategy. *Human Nature* 7 (4): 403–25.
—. 2001. Food, foragers, and folklore: The role of narrative in human subsistence. *Evolution and Human Behavior* 22 (4): 221–40.
—. 2001. Narrative theory and function: why evolution matters. *Philosophy and Literature* 25 (2): 233–250.
—. 2001. New science, old myth: an evolutionary critique of the Oedipal paradigm. *Mosaic* 34 (March): 121–36.
—. 2003. Cultural variation is part of human nature: literary universals, context-sensitivity, and "Shakespeare in the Bush". *Human Nature* 14 (4): 383–96.

SCHAMA, SIMON. 1987. *The embarrassment of riches: An interpretation of Dutch culture in the Golden Age.* New York: Knopf.

SCHARFSTEIN, BEN-AMI. 1973. *Mystical experience.* Oxford: Blackwell.
—. 1988. *Of birds, beasts, and other artists: An essay on the universality of art.* New York: New York University Press.
—. 2008. *Art without borders: A philosophical exploration of art and humanity.* Chicago and London: The University of Chicago Press.

SCHELE, LINDA, AND DAVID FREIDEL. 1990. *A forest of kings: The untold story of the ancient Maya.* New York: William Morrow.

SCHEVILL, FERDINAND. 1936. *History of Florence from the founding of the city through the Renaissance.* New York: Harcourt Brace and Co.

SCHILDKROUT, ENID, AND CURTIS KEIM. 1998. Objects and agendas: Re-collecting the Congo. In *The scramble for art in Central Africa,* ed. Enid Schildkrout and Curtis Keim, 1–36. Cambridge: Cambridge University Press.

SCHLESIER, KARL H. 2001. More on the "Venus" figurines. *Current Anthropology* 42 (3): 410–12.

SCHLESINGER, WALTER. 1968. Lord and follower in Germanic institutional history. In *Lordship and community in medieval Europe,* ed. Fredric L. Chayette, 664–99. New York: Holt, Rinehart, and Winston.

SCHMARSOW, AUGUST. 1907. Kunstwissenschaft und Völkerpsychologie: ein Versuch zur Verständigung. *Zeitschrift für Ästhetik und Kunstwissenschaft* 2: 305–39, 467–500.
—. 1910. Anfangsgründe jeder Ornamentik. *Zeitschrift für Ästhetik und Kunstwissenschaft* 5: 191–215, 321–55.
—. 1919. Kunstwissenschaft und Kulturphilosophie mit gemeinsamen Grundbegriffen. *Zeitschrift für Ästhetik und Kunstwissenschaft* 13: 165–258.

SCHMIDT-LINSENHOFF, VIKTORIA. 2003. Postkolonialismus. *Metzler-Lexikon Kunstwissenschaft: Ideen, Methoden, Begriffe,* ed. Ulrich Pfisterer, 278–82. Stuttgart and Weimar: Metzler.

SCHNEIDER, ALBRECHT. 2006. Comparative and systematic musicology in relation to ethnomusicology: A historical and methodological survey. *Ethnomusicology* 50 (2): 236–58.

SCHNEIDER, ARND. 1996. Uneasy relationships: Contemporary artists and anthropology. *Journal of Material Culture* 1 (2): 183–210.
—. 2003. On "appropriation": A critical reappraisal of the concept and its application to global art practices. *Social Anthropology* 11 (2): 215–29.
—, and Christopher Wright, eds. 2006. *Contemporary art and anthropology.* Oxford: Berg.

SCHOPENHAUER, ARTHUR. 1969. *The world as will and representation*. Trans. E. F. J. Payne. New York: Dover. Originally published as *Die Welt als Wille und Vorstellung* (1819).

SCHORE, ALLAN N. 1994. *Affect regulation and the origin of the self: The neurobiology of emotional development*. Hillsdale, NJ: Erlbaum.

SCHWAB, RAYMOND. 1950. *La renaissance orientale*. Paris: Payot.

SCHWARZER, MITCHELL. 1995. Origins of the art history survey text. *Art Journal* 54 (3): 24–29.

SCHWEINFURTH, GEORG. 1875. *Artes Africanae: Abbildungen und Beschreibungen von Erzeugnissen des Kunstfleisses Central-afrikanischer Völker: Illustrations and Descriptions of Productions of the Industrial Arts of Central African Tribes*. Leipzig: F. A. Brockhaus; London: S. Low, Marston, Low, and Searle.

SCOTT LITTLETON, C. 1985. Lucien Lévy-Bruhl and the concept of cognitive relativism. In Lucien Lévy-Bruhl, *How Natives think* [1910], trans. Lilian A. Clare, introd. by Lucien Lévy-Bruhl. Princeton, NJ: Princeton University Press.

SCULLY, VINCENT. 1991. *Architecture: The natural and the man-made*. New York: St. Martin's Press.

SEESSELBERG, FRIEDRICH. 1897. *Die früh-mittelalterliche Kunst der germanischen Voelker unter besonderer Berücksichtigung der skandinavischen Baukunst in ethnographisch-anthropologischer Begruendung*. Berlin: Wasmuth; the second volume was published under the title *Die skandinavische Baukunst der ersten nordisch-christlichen Jahrhunderte in ausgewählten Beispielen bildlich vorgeführt von Friedrich Seesselberg*. Berlin: Wasmuth.

SEIDELMAN, HAROLD, JAMES TURNER, AND GEORGE SWINTON. 2001. *The Inuit imagination: Arctic myth and sculpture*. Reprint, 1st ed. published 1994. Seattle: University of Washington Press.

SEIGE, CHRISTINE. 1996. Paul Germann (1884–1966): In memoriam. In *Jahrbuch des Museums für Völkerkunde zu Leipzig*, vol. XLII, 47–79. Leipzig: Harrassowitz.

SELZ, PETER H. 1957. *German expressionistic painting*. Berkeley: University of California Press.

SENGHOR, LÉOPOLD S. 1973. The Lessons of Leo Frobenius. In *Leo Frobenius 1873–1973: An anthology*, ed. Elke Haberland, vii-xiii. Wiesbaden: F. Steiner.

SHARMA, SRIPAD RAMA. 1940. *Mughal empire in India: A systematic study including source material*. Rev. ed. Bombay: Karnatak Publishing House.

SHEPARD, ROGER N. 1992. The perceptual organization of colors: An adaptation to regularities of the terrestrial world? In *The adapted mind: Evolutionary psychology and the generation of culture*, ed. Jerome H. Barkow, Leda Cosmides, and John Tooby, 492–535. New York and Oxford: Oxford University Press.

SHIMIZU, YOSHIAKI, ed. 1988. *Japan: The shaping of Daimyo culture 1185–1868*. Washington, DC: The National Gallery of Art.

SHINER, LARRY. 1994. "Primitive fakes," "Tourist art," and the ideology of authenticity. *Journal of Aesthetics and Art Criticism* 52 (2): 225–34.
—. 2001. *The invention of art: A cultural history*. Chicago and London: The University of Chicago Press.

SHKLOVSKY, VICTOR. 1965. Art as technique [1917]. In *Russian formalist criticism: Four essays*, ed. and trans. by Lee T. Lemon and Marion J. Reis, 3–24. Lincoln: University of Nebraska Press.

SIEBER, ROY. 1962. Masks as agents of social control. *African Studies Bulletin* 5 (11): 8–13.

SILVER, LARRY. 2004. Review of *The atlas of world art* by John Onians and *Toward a geography of art* by Thomas DaCosta Kaufmann. *The Art Bulletin* 86 (4): 783–87.

SILVERBERG, JAMES, ed. 1968. *Social mobility in the caste system in India: An interdisciplinary symposium*. The Hague: Mouton.

SILVERMAN, ERIC. 1999. Tourist art as the crafting of identity in the Sepik River (Papua New Guinea). In *Unpacking culture: Art and commodity in colonial and postcolonial worlds*, ed. Ruth B. Phillips and Christopher B. Steiner, 51–86. Berkeley: University of California Press.

SIMON THOMAS, MIENKE. 1996. *De leer van het ornament: Versieren volgens voorschrift 1850–1930*. Amsterdam: De Bataafsche Leeuw.

SINGER, ILANA. 1999. *The charged emptiness and its expression in the Japanese aesthetic*. PhD diss., University of Haifa.

SIRÉN, OSVALD. 1936. *The Chinese on the art of painting*. Peiping [Beijing]: H. Vetch.

SIVARAMAMURTI, CALAMBUR. 1977. *The art of India*. New York: Abrams.
—. 1978. *The painter in ancient India*. New Delhi: Abinav Publications.

SMIDT, DIRK. 1993. The Asmat: Life, death and the ancestors. In *Asmat art: Woodcarvings of Southwest New Guinea*, ed. Dirk Smidt, 15–25. New York: George Braziller in association with the Rijksmuseum voor Volkenkunde, Leiden.

SMITH, PETER F. 2003. *The dynamics of delight: Architecture and aesthetics*. London and New York: Routledge.

SOLSO, ROBERT L. 1994. *Cognition and the visual arts*. Cambridge, MA: MIT Press.
—. 2003. *The psychology of art and the evolution of the conscious brain*. Boston: MIT Press.

SOUYRI, PIERRE FRANÇOIS. 2001. *The world turned upside down: Medieval Japanese society*. Trans. by Käthe Roth. New York: Columbia University Press.

SPATE, VIRGINIA. 1981. Orphism. In *Concepts of modern art*. 2nd. rev., ed. Nikos Stangos, 88–89. London: Thames and Hudson.

SPENGLER, OSWALD. 1923. *Der Untergang des Abendlandes: Umriss einer Morphologie der Weltgeschichte*. 2 vols. Munich: Beck.

SPIVAK, GAYATRI. 1999. *Critique of postcolonial reason: Toward a history of the vanishing present*. Cambridge, MA: Harvard University Press.

SPIVEY, NIGEL. 2005. *How art made the world*. London: BBC Books.

SPOONER, BRIAN. 1986. Weavers and dealers: The authenticity of an oriental carpet. In *The social life of things*, ed. Arjun Appadurai, 195–235. Cambridge: Cambridge University Press.

SPRAGUE, STEPHEN F. 1978. Yoruba photography: How the Yoruba see themselves. *African Arts* 12 (1): 52–59, 107.

SPRINGER, ANTON. 1895–. *Handbuch der Kunstgeschichte*. 6 vols. Leipzig: Seemann.

STAFFORD, BARBARA MARIA. 2007. *Echo objects: The cognitive work of images*. Chicago and London: The University of Chicago Press.

STANLEY-BAKER, JOAN. 1992. *The transmission of Chinese idealist painting to Japan: Notes on the early phase (1661–1799)*. Ann Arbor, Center for Japanese Studies, University of Michigan.
—. 2000. *Japanese art*. Rev. ed. London and New York: Thames and Hudson.

STARR, CHESTER G. 1968. *The awakening of the Greek historical spirit*. New York: Alfred A. Knopf.

STEINBERG, LEO. 1972. *Other criteria: Confrontations with twentieth-century art*. New York: Oxford University Press.

STEINER, CHRISTOPHER B. 1992. Fake masks and faux: The modernity crisis of misrepresentation [Dialogue section]. *African Arts* 25 (3): 18–19.
—. 1994. *African art in transit*. Cambridge: Cambridge University Press.
—. 1995. The art of the trade: On the creation of value and authenticity in the African art market. In *The traffic in culture: Refiguring art and anthropology*, ed. George E. Marcus and Fred R. Myers, 141–65. Berkeley: University of California Press.
—. 1996. Can the canon burst?, *The Art Bulletin* 78 (2): 213–18.
—. 1999. Authenticity, repetition, and the aesthetics of seriality: The work of tourist art in the age of mechanical reproduction. In *Unpacking culture: Art and commodity in colonial and postcolonial worlds*, ed. Ruth B. Phillips and Christopher B. Steiner, 87–103. Berkeley: University of California Press.

STERN, DANIEL. 1971. A microanalysis of mother-infant interaction. *Journal of the American Academy of Child Psychiatry* 10: 501–17.

STERNE, CARUS [ERNST KRAUS]. 1891. *Natur und Kunst: Studien zur Entwicklungsgeschichte der Kunst*. Berlin: Allgemeiner Verein für Deutsche Literatur.

STOCKING, GEORGE W., JR. 1982. *Race, culture, and evolution: Essays in the history of anthropology*. 1st ed. published 1968. Chicago and London: The University of Chicago Press.
—, ed. 1985. *Objects and others: Essays on museums and material culture*. Madison: The University of Wisconsin Press.
—. 1987. *The Victorian anthropology*. New York: Free Press.
—, ed. 1996. *Volksgeist as method and ethic: Essays on Boasian ethnography and the German anthropological tradition*. Madison: University of Wisconsin Press.

STOKSTAD, MARILYN. 2007. *Art history*. 3rd ed., 1st ed. published 1995. Upper Saddle River, NJ: Prentice Hall.

STOLER MILLER, BARBARA. 1983. Stella Kramrisch: A biographical essay. In *Exploring India's sacred art: Selected writings of Stella Kramrisch*, ed. Barbara Stoler Miller, 3–34. Philadelphia: University of Pennsylvania Press.

STOLLER, PAUL. 2003. Circuits of African art/paths of wood: Exploring an anthropological trail. *Anthropological Quarterly* 76 (2): 207–34.

STOLNITZ, JEROME. 1961. On the significance of Lord Shaftesbury in modern aesthetic theory. *The Philosophical Quarterly* 11 (43): 97–113.

STOLPE, HJALMAR. 1927. *Collected essays in ornamental art*. 2 vols. Foreword by Henry Balfour. Stockholm: Aftonbladets Tryckeri.

STOREY, ROBERT F. 1996. *Literature and the human animal: On the biogenetic foundations of literary representation*. Evanston, IL: Northwestern University Press.

STOTT, MARGARET A. 1975. *Bella Coola ceremony and art*. Ottawa: National Museums of Canada.

STRANG, VERONICA. 2006. A happy coincidence? Symbiosis and synthesis in anthropological and indigenous knowlegde (with peer comments). *Current Anthropology* 47 (6): 981–1008.

STRATHERN, MARILYN. 1997. Pre-figured features: A view from the Papua New Guinea highlands. In *Portraiture: Facing the subject*, ed. Joanna Woodall, 259–68. Manchester and New York: Manchester University Press.

STRONG, ROY C. 1969. *The English icon: Elizabethan and Jacobean portraiture*. New Haven, CT: Yale University Press.

STRZYGOWSKI, JOSEF. 1901. *Orient und Rom: Beiträge zur Geschichte der spätantiken und frühchristlichen Kunst*. Leipzig: Hinrichs.
—. 1918. Vergleichende Kunstforschung auf geographischer Grundlage. *Mitteilungen der geographischen Gesellschaft in Wien* 61: 20–48, 153–58.
—. 1923. *Die Krisis der Geisteswissenschaften*. Vienna: A. Schroll & Co.

STUART, JAN, AND EVELYN S. RAWSKI. 2001. *Worshiping the ancestors: Chinese commemorative portraits*. Palo Alto: Stanford University Press in association with the Smithsonian Institution, Washington DC.

STURKEN, MARITA, AND LISA CARTWRIGHT, eds. 2001. *Practices of looking: An introduction to visual culture*. Oxford: Oxford University Press.

SULLIVAN, NANCY. 1995. Inside trading: postmodernism in the social drama of *Sunflowers* in the 1980s art world. In *The traffic in culture: Refiguring art and anthropology*, ed. George E. Marcus and Fred R. Myers, 256–301. Berkeley: University of California Press.

SUMMERS, DAVID. 2003. *Real spaces: World art history and the rise of western modernism*, London and New York: Phaidon.
—. 2005. Arbitrariness and authority: how art makes cultures. In *Time and place: Essays in the geohistory of art*, ed. Thomas DaCosta Kaufmann and Elizabeth Pilliod, 203–16. Aldershot and Burlington, VT: Ashgate.

SVAŠEK, MARUŠKA 1997. Identity and style in Ghanaian artistic discourse. In *Contesting art: Art, politics, and identity in the modern world*, ed. Jeremy MacClancy, 27–61. Oxford: Berg.
—. *Anthropology, art and cultural production*. London and Ann Arbor, MI: Pluto Press.

SWEENEY, CAROLE. 2004. *From fetish to subject: Race, modernism, and primitivism 1919–1935*. Westport, CT: Praeger.

SYLVAIN, RENEE. 1996. Leo Frobenius: From *Kulturkreis* to *Kulturmorphologie*. *Anthropos* 91 (4): 483–94.

SYLVESTER, DAVID. 1997. *About modern art: Critical essays, 1948–1997*. London: Henry Holt.

SYME, RONALD. 1958. *Tacitus*. 2 vols. Oxford: Clarendon Press.
—. 1979. *The Roman revolution*. Oxford: Oxford University Press.

SZOMBATI-FABIAN, ILONA, AND JOHANNES FABIAN. 1976. Art, history, and society: Popular painting in Shaba, Zaire. *Studies in the Anthropology of Visual Communication* 1 (1): 1–21.

T

TAÇON, PAUL S. C. 1983. Dorset art in relation to prehistoric culture stress. *Études Inuit/Inuit Studies* 7 (1): 41–65.
—, and Sally Brockwell 1995. Arnhem Land prehistory in landscape, stone, and paint. *Antiquity* 69 (259): 676–95.
—, Meredith Wilson, and Christopher Chippindale. 1996. Birth of the rainbow serpent in Arnhem Land rock art and oral history. *Archaeology Oceania* 31 (3): 103–24.

TAINE, HIPPOLYTE. 1964. *Philosophie de l'art: Voyage en Italie: Essais de critique et d'histoire*. Ed. Jean-François Revel. Paris: Hermann.

TAMBIAH, STANLEY J. 1979. A performative approach to ritual. In *Proceedings of the British Academy, London LXV*. London: British Academy; Oxford: Oxford University Press, 113–69.

TANAKA, KREIJI. 1993. Neuronal mechanisms of object recognition. *Science* 262 (5134): 685–88.

TANNER, JEREMY, ed. 2003. *The sociology of art: A reader*. London: Routledge.

TAYLOR, CHARLES. 2001. Two theories of modernity. In *Alternative modernities*, ed. Dilip Parameshwar Gaonkar, 172–96. Durham and London: Duke University Press.

TAYLOR, TIMOTHY D. 1997. *Global pop: World music, world markets*. New York: Routledge.

TELLENBACH, GERD. 1978. From the Carolingian imperial nobility to the German estate of imperial princes. In *The medieval nobility: Studies on the ruling classes of France and Germany from the sixth to the twelfth century*, ed. by Timothy Reuter, 203–42. Amsterdam, New York; Oxford: North Holland Publishing Co.

THOMAS, NICHOLAS. 1991. *Entangled objects: Exchange, material culture, and colonialism in the Pacific*. Cambridge, MA: Harvard University Press.
—. 1996. Cold fusion. *American Anthropologist* 98 (1): 9–16.
—. 1997. Collectivity and nationality in the anthropology of art. In *Rethinking visual anthropology*, ed. Marcus Banks and Howard Morphy, 256–75. New Haven, CT: Yale University Press.
—. 1999. *Possessions: Indigenous art, colonial culture*. London and New York: Thames and Hudson.
—. 2001. Appropriation/appreciation: Settler modernism in Australia and New Zealand. In *The empire of things*, ed. Fred R. Myers, 139–64. Santa Fe: School of American Research.

THOMPSON, ROBERT FARRIS. 1966. An aesthetic of the cool: West African dance. *African Forum* 2 (2): 85–102.
—. 1968. Esthetics in traditional Africa. *Art News* 66 (9): 44–45, 63–68.
—. 1971. *Black gods and kings*. Los Angeles: UCLA Museum of Ethnic Arts.
—. 1973. Yoruba artistic criticism. In *The Traditional Artist in African Societies*, ed. Warren L. d'Azevedo, 19–61. Bloomington: Indiana University Press.
—. 1974. *African art in motion: Icon and act in the collection of Katherine Coryton White*. Berkeley: University of California Press.
—. 1983. *Flash of the spirit: African and Afro-American art and philosophy*. New York: Random House.
—, and Joseph Cornet. 1981. *The four moments of the sun: Kongo art in two worlds*. Washington DC: The National Art Gallery.

THORNHILL, RANDY. 2003. Darwinian aesthetics informs traditional aesthetics. In *Evolutionary aesthetics*, ed. Eckart Voland and Karl Grammer, 9–38. Berlin: Springer.

TOKUE, MEZAKI. 1985. Aesthete-recluses during the transition from ancient to medieval Japan. In *Principles of classical Japanese literature*, ed. Earl Miner, 151–80. Princeton, NJ: Princeton University Press.

TOOBY, JOHN, AND LEDA COSMIDES. 2001. Does beauty build adaptive minds?: Toward an evolutionary theory of aesthetics. In *On the origin of fictions: Interdisciplinary perspectives*, ed. H. Porter Abbott. Special issue, *SubStance: A review of theory and literary criticism* 94/95, vol. 30 (1–2): 6–27.

TORGOVNICK, MARIANNA. 1990. *Gone primitive: Savage intellects, modern lives*. Chicago and London: The University of Chicago Press.

TREGGIARI, SUSAN. 1969. *Roman freedmen during the late Republic*. Oxford: Clarendon Press.

TREVARTHEN, COLWYN. 1997. Fetal and neonatal psychology: intrinsic motives and learning behavior. In *Advances in perinatal medicine*, Proceedings of the Fifteenth European Congress of Perinatal Medicine, ed. F. Cockburn, 282–91. New York: Parthenon.

TRIGGER, BRUCE G. 2003. *Understanding early civilizations: A comparative study*. Cambridge: Cambridge University Press.

TRUBNER, HENRY. 1977. Alfred Salmony (10 November 1890–29 April 1958). In *Zur Kunstgeschichte Asiens: 50 Jahre Lehre und Forschung an der Universität Köln*, ed. Roger Goepper, 17–20. Wiesbaden: Steiner.

TSUNODA, RYUSAKU, W. THEODORE DE BARY, AND DONALD KEENE, comp. 1958. *Sources of Japanese tradition*. New York: Columbia University Press.

TUCHMAN, MAURICE, ed. 1986. *The spiritual in art: Abstract painting 1890–1985*. Los Angeles: Los Angeles County Museum of Art; New York: Abeville Press.
—. 1986. Hidden meanings in abstract art. In *The spiritual in art: Abstract painting 1890–1985*, ed. Maurice Tuchman, 17–61. Los Angeles: Los Angeles County Museum of Art; New York: Abeville Press.

TURNER, JANE. ed. 1996. *The dictionary of art*, 34 vols. London: Macmillan.

TURNER, VICTOR. 1969. *The ritual process: Structure and anti-structure*. London: Routledge and Kegan Paul 1969.

U

UBBELOHDE-DOERING, HEINRICH. [1929]. Die indianische Kunst Amerikas. In *Die aussereuropäische Kunst*. Vol. VI of *Handbuch für Kunstgeschichte von Anton Springer*, ed. Curt Glaser, 592–658. Leipzig: Kröner.

UEDA, MAKOTO. 1967. *Literary and art theories in Japan*. Cleveland, OH: Press of Western Reserve University.

ULLMAN, WALTER. 1966. *Principles of government and politics in the Middle Ages*. New York: Barnes and Noble.
—. 1966. *The individual and society in the Middle Ages*. Baltimore, MD: Johns Hopkins University Press.

V

VALLIER, DORA. 1967. *L'art abstrait*. Paris: le Livre de poche.

VAN ALPHEN, ERNST 1997. The portrait's dispersal: Concepts of representation and subjectivity in contemporary portraiture. In *Portraiture: Facing the subject*, ed. Joanna Woodall, 239–56. Manchester and New York: Manchester University Press.

VAN BEVERWYK, JOHAN. 1644, *Epistolicae quaestiones cum doctorem responsis: Accedit ejusdem, nec non Erasmi, Cardani, Melanchthonis, Medicinae encomium*. Rotterdam: A. Leers.

VAN DAMME, WILFRIED. 1996. *Beauty in context: Towards an anthropological approach to aesthetics*. Philosophy of History and Culture 17. Leiden, New York, and Cologne: Brill.
—. 2000. Universality and cultural particularity in visual aesthetics. In *Being humans: Anthropological universality and particularity in transdisciplinary perspectives*, ed. Neil Roughley, 258–83. Berlin and New York: Walter De Gruyter.
—. 2003. Anthropologies of art. *International Journal of Anthropology* 18 (4): 231–44 (adapted version published as Anthropologies of art: Three approaches. In *Exploring world art*, ed. Eric Venbrux, Pamela S. Rosi, and Robert L. Welsch, 69–81. Long Grove, IL: Waveland Press, 2006).

—. 2006. World aesthetics: Biology, culture, and reflection. In *Compression vs. expression: Containing and explaining the world's art*, ed. John Onians, 153–87. Williamstown, MA: Clark Art Institute.

VAN DER WOUDE, AD. 1991. The volume and value of paintings in Holland at the time of the Dutch Republic. In *Art in history, history in art: Studies in seventeenth-century Dutch culture*, ed. David Freedberg and Jan de Vries, 285–329. Santa Monica, CA: The Getty Center.

VAN GENNEP, ARNOLD. 1960. *The rites of passage*. Trans. Monika B. Vizedom and Gabrielle L. Caffe. London: Routledge and Kegan Paul. Originally published as *Les rites de passage* (Paris: Nourry, 1909).

VAN MANDER, KAREL. 1603–1604. *Het schilder-boeck ... Daer nae in dry deelen t'leven der vermaerde doorluchtighe schilders des ouden en nieuwen tyds*. Haarlem.

VANHAEREN, MARIAN, et al. 2006. Middle Paleolithic shell beads in Israel and Algeria. *Science* 312 (5781): 1785–88.

VARLEY, H. PAUL. 1990. Cultural life in medieval Japan. In *Medieval Japan*, ed. Kozo Yamamura, 447–99. Vol. 3 of *The Cambridge history of Japan*, ed. John W. Hall et al. Cambridge and New York: Cambridge University Press.

VATTER, ERNST. 1926. *Religiöse Plastik der Naturvölker*. Frankfurt a.M.: Frankfurter Verlagsanstalt.

VENBRUX, ERIC, AND PAMELA S. ROSI, eds. 2003. *Conceptualizing world art studies*. Special issue, *International Journal of Anthropology* 18 (4).
—, and Pamela S. Rosi. 2004. Confronting world art: An introduction. *Visual Anthropology* 17 (3/4): 217–28.
—, and Robert L. Welsch, eds. 2006. *Exploring world art*. Long Grove, IL: Waveland Press.

VERWORN, MAX. 1907. *Zur Psychologie der primitiven Kunst: Ein Vortrag*. Jena: Fischer.

VIDAL DE LA BLACHE, PAUL. 1926. *Principles of human geography*. Ed. Emanuel de Martonne, trans. Millicent Todd Bingham. New York: Holt.

VIDYAKARA. 1965. *An anthology of Sanskrit court poetry: Vidyakara's "Subhaṣiaratnakosa."* Trans. Daniel H. H. Ingalls. Cambridge, MA: Harvard University Press.

VIERKANDT, ALFRED. 1925. Prinzipienfragen der ethnologischen Kunstforschung. *Zweiter Kongreß für Ästhetik und Kunstwissenschaft: Bericht*. Stuttgart, 338–55.

VINOGRAD, RICHARD. 1992. *Boundaries of the self: Chinese portraits 1600–1900*. Cambridge: Cambridge University Press.

VISONÀ, MONICA BLACKMUN. 2000. Mande worlds and the Upper Niger. In *A history of art in Africa*, Monica Blackmun Visonà et al., 106–29. New York: Abrams.

VOGEL, SUSAN M. 1988. *The art of collecting African art*. New York: Center for African Art.
—. 1988. Introduction. In *ART/artifact*, Arthur Danto et al., 11–17. New York: Center for African Art.
—. *Baule: African art, Western eyes*. New Haven, CT and London: Yale University Press.
—. 2001. *Fang: An epic journey*. New York: Prince Street Productions.

VOGT, PAUL. 1980. *The Blue Rider*. Trans. Joachim Neugroschel. Woodbury, NY: Barron's.

VOLAND, ECKART. 2003. Aesthetic preferences in the world of artifacts—adaptations for the evaluation of "honest signals"? In *Evolutionary aesthetics*, ed. Eckart Voland and Karl Grammer, 239–60. Berlin: Springer.
—, and Karl Grammer, eds. 2003. *Evolutionary aesthetics*. Berlin: Springer.

VOLKENANDT, CLAUS, ed. 2004. *Kunstgeschichte und Weltgegenwartskunst: Konzepte – Methoden – Perspektiven*. Berlin: Reimer.

VON ERDBERG, ELEANOR. 1985. Die Anfänge der ostasiatischen Kunstgeschichte in Deutschland. In *Kategorien und Methoden der deutschen Kunstgeschichte 1900–1930. Aus den Arbeitskreisen "Methoden der Geisteswissenschaften" der Fritz-Thyssen-Stiftung*, ed. Lorenz Dittmann, 185–207. Stuttgart: Steiner-Verlag Wiesbaden GmbH.

VON GLASENAPP, HELMUTH. 1960. *Das Indienbild deutscher Denker*. Stuttgart: Köhler.

VON GRUNEBAUM, GUSTAVE E. 1961. *Medieval islam: A study in cultural orientation*. 2nd ed. Chicago and London: The University of Chicago Press.

VON SYDOW, ECKART. 1921. *Exotische Kunst. Afrika und Ozeanien*. Leipzig: Klinkhardt & Biermann.
—. 1927. *Primitive Kunst und Psychoanalyse: eine Studie über die sexuelle Grundlage der Bildenden Künste der Naturvölker*. Leipzig: Psychoanalytischer Verlag.
—. 1938. *Die Kunst der Naturvölker und der Vorzeit*. 4th ed., 1st ed. published 1923. Berlin: Propyläen-Verlag.

W

WADE, EDWARD L. 1985. The ethnic art market in the American Southwest 1880–1980. In *Objects and others: Essays on museums and material culture*, ed. George W. Stocking, Jr., 167–91. Madison: University of Wisconsin Press.

WADLEY, LYN. 2005. Putting ochre to the test: Replication studies of adhesives that may have been used for shafting tools in the Middle Stone Age. *Journal of Human Evolution* 49 (5): 587–601.

WAITZ, THEODOR. 1863. *Introduction to anthropology*, ed. J. Frederick Collingwood. London: Longman, Green, Longman, and Roberts. Originally published as *Anthropologie der Naturvölker* (Leipzig: Fleischer, 1859–1871).

WALLERSTEIN, IMMANUEL. 1974. *The modern world system: Capitalist agriculture and the origins of the European world economy*. New York: Academic Press.

WARDER, ANTHONY KENNEDY. 1972. *Indian kavya literature*, vol. 1. Delhi: Motilal Banarsidass.
WASHTON LONG, ROSE-CAROL. 1980. *Kandinsky: The development of an abstract style*. Oxford: Clarendon Press.

WATTS, IAN. 1999. The origin of symbolic culture. In *The evolution of culture: An interdisciplinary view*, ed. Robin Dunbar, Chris Knight, and Camilla Power, 113–46. Edinburgh: Edinburgh University Press.

WEAVER, PAUL R.C. 1974. Social mobility in the early Roman empire: The evidence of the imperial freedmen and slaves. In *Studies in ancient society*, ed. by Moses I. Finley, 121–40. London: Routledge and Kegan Paul.

WEBER, MICHAEL JOHN, ed. 1987. *Perspectives: Angles on African art*. New York: Center for African Art: Abrams.

WEIKART, RICHARD. 2004. *From Darwin to Hitler: Evolutionary ethics, eugenics, and racism in Germany*. New York: Palgrave Macmillan.

WEITZ, MORRIS. 1967. The role of theory in aesthetics. In *Aesthetic inquiry: Essays on art criticism & the philosophy of art*, ed. Monroe C. Beardsley and Herbert M. Schueller, 3–11. Belmont, CA: Dickenson. Originally published in *Journal of Aesthetics and Art Criticism* 15 (1956): 27–35. Reprinted in *Problems in aesthetics*, ed. Morris Weitz, 145–56. New York: Macmillan, 1959.

WELSCH, ROBERT L. 2004. Epilogue: The authenticity of constructed art worlds. *Visual Anthropology* 17 (3/4): 401–6.

WENDLAND, ULRIKE. 1999. *Biographisches Handbuch deutschsprachiger Kunsthistoriker im Exil: Leben und Werk der unter dem Nationalsozialismus verfolgten und vertriebenen Wissenschaftler.* Munich: Saur.

WEST, SHEARER. 2004. *Portraiture.* Oxford: Oxford University Press.

WESTERMANN, MARIËT, ed. 2005. *Anthropologies of art.* Williamstown, MA: Clark Art Institute.

WESTERMANN, WILLIAM L. 1955. *The slave systems of Greek and Roman antiquity.* Memoirs of the American Philosophical Society 40. Philadelphia: American Philosophical Society.

WHARTON, ANNABEL J. 1995. *Refiguring the Post Classical city: Dura Europos, Jerash, Jerusalem, and Ravenna.* Cambridge, MA: Cambridge University Press.

WHITE, RANDALL. 2003. *Prehistoric art: The symbolic journey of humankind.* New York: Harry N. Abrams.

WHITFIELD, JOHN. 2002. Art history doubles. *Nature Science Update*, 11 January.

WHITMAN, JAMES. 1984. From philology to anthropology in midnineteenth-century Germany. In *Functionalism historicized: Essays on British social anthropology*, ed. George W. Stocking, Jr., 214–29. Madison: University of Wisconsin Press.

WIEDMANN, AUGUST K. 1979. *Romantic roots in modern art.* Surrey: Gresham Books.

WIESING, LAMBERT. 1997. *Die Sichtbarkeit des Bildes: Geschichte und Perspektiven der formalen Ästhetik.* Reinbek bei Hamburg: Rowohlt.

WIESNER, ULRICH. 1977. Die Geschichte der Abteilung Asien. In *Zur Kunstgeschichte Asiens: 50 Jahre Lehre und Forschung an der Universität Köln*, ed. Roger Goepper, 3–16. Wiesbaden: Steiner.

WILBUR, KEN. 1984. *Quantum questions: Mystical writings of the world's great physicists.* Boulder, CO: Shambhala.

WILKINSON, JAMES V.S. 1949. Introduction to *The Pitman gallery of oriental art: Mughal painting*, ed. by Basil Gray. New York: Pitman Publishing Corp.

WILLATS, JOHN. 1997. *Art and representation: New principles in the analysis of pictures.* Princeton, NJ: Princeton University Press.

WILLETT, FRANK. 1967. *Ife in the history of West African sculpture.* New York: McGraw-Hill.

WILLIAMS, ELIZABETH A. 1985. Art and artifact at the Trocadero: *Ars Americana* and the primitivist revolution. In *Objects and others: Essays on museums and material culture*, ed. George W. Stocking, Jr., 146–66. Madison: University of Wisconsin Press.

WILSON, JOHN A. 1951. *The culture of ancient Egypt.* Chicago and London: The University of Chicago Press.

WINCKELMANN, JOHANN JOACHIM. 1764. *Geschichte der Kunst des Alterthums.* 2 vols. Dresden: In der Waltherischen Hof-Buchhandlung.

WISEMAN, T. PETER. 1971. *New men in the Roman senate, 139 B.C.-A.D. 14.* Oxford Classical and Philosophical Monographs. London: Oxford University Press.

WITHERSPOON, GARY. 1977. *Language and art in the Navajo universe.* Ann Arbor: University of Michigan Press.
—. 1980. Language in culture and culture in language. *International Journal of American Linguistics* 46 (1): 1–13.
—. 1981. Self-expression and self-esteem in Navajo weaving. *Plateau* 52 (4): 29–32.
—, and Glen Peterson. 1995. *Dynamic symmetry and holistic asymmetry in Navajo and Western art and cosmology.* New York: Peter Lang.

WOERMANN, KARL. 1900–1911. *Geschichte der Kunst aller Zeiten und Völker.* 6 vols. Leipzig: Bibliographisches Institut.
—. 1915–1922. *Die Kunst der Naturvölker und übrigen nichtchristlichen Völker einschliesslich der Kunst des Islams.* Vol. II of *Geschichte der Kunst aller Zeiten und Völker.* 6 vols., 2nd. rev. ed., 1st ed. published 1900–1911. Leipzig and Vienna: Bibliographisches Institut.

WOLF, ERIC. 1982. *Europe and the people without history.* Berkeley: University of California Press.

WONG, SIU-KIT. 1978. Ch'ing and Ching in the critical writings of Wang Fu-chih. In *Chinese approaches to literature from Confucius to Liang Ch'i-chao*, ed. Adele A. Rickett, 121–50. Princeton, NJ: Princeton University Press.

WOOD, CHRISTOPHER. 2004. Strzygowski und Riegl in den Vereinigten Staaten. *Wiener Jahrbuch für Kunstgeschichte*, 53, ed. Hans Aurenhammer and Michael V. Schwarz, 217–33. Wien: Böhlau.

WOODALL, JOANNA, ed. 1997. *Portraiture: Facing the subject.* Manchester and New York: Manchester University Press.

[EDITORIAL.] A WORD FOR CALIBAN. 1922. *The Burlington Magazine* 40 (229): 157–58.

WORNUM, RALPH NICHOLSON. 1856. *Analysis of ornament.* London: Chapman & Hall.

WORRINGER, WILHELM. 1911. *Formprobleme der Gotik.* Munich: Piper.
—. 1919. *Abstraktion und Einfühlung.* 8th ed., 1st ed. published 1907. Munich: Piper.
—. 1956. ARS UNA? In *Fragen und Gegenfragen: Schriften zum Kunstproblem: (Zum 75. Geburtstag v. Wilhelm Worringer).* Munich: Piper, 155–63.

WU, JIA-HUA. 1994. *A comparative study of landscape aesthetics.* Lewiston, NY: Edwin Mellen Press.

WUNDT, WILHELM. 1900. *Völkerpsychologie: eine Untersuchung d. Entwicklungsgesetze von Sprache, Mythus und Sitte.* Leipzig: W. Engelmann.

Y

YAI, OLABIYI BABALOLA. 1999. Tradition and the Yoruba artist. *African Arts* 32 (1): 32–35, 93.

YOUNG, JAMES O. 2008. *Cultural appropriation and the arts.* Oxford: Wiley-Blackwell.

YOUNG, ROBERT M. 1995. *Darwin's metaphor: Nature's place in Victorian culture.* Cambridge: Cambridge University Press.

Z

ZAHAN, DOMINIQUE. 1979. *The religion, spirituality, and thought of traditional Africa.* Trans. Kate Ezra Martin and Lawrence M. Martin. Chicago and London: The University of Chicago Press.

ZAHAVI, AMOTZ, AND AVISHAG ZAHAVI. 1997. *The handicap principle: A missing piece of Darwin's puzzle.* Oxford: Oxford University Press.

ZEKI, SEMIR. 1999. *Inner vision: An exploration of art and the brain.* Oxford and New York: Oxford University Press.

ZHANG, WENLI. 1996. *The Qin terracotta army: Treasures of Lintong.* London: Scala Books and Cultural Relics Publishing House.

ZIJLMANS, KITTY, ed. 2006. *Site-seeing: Places in culture, time and space.* Leiden: CNWS Publications.

ZIMMERMAN, ANDREW. 1998. *Anthropology and the place of knowledge in imperial Berlin.* PhD diss., University of California.
—. 1999. Geschichtslose und schriftlose Völker in Spreeathen: Anthropologie als Kritik der Geschichtswissenschaft im Kaiserreich. *Zeitschrift für Geschichtswissenschaft* 47 (3): 197–210.

RIEGL, A. 78, 81, 93, 97, 98
RIVERA, D. 214
RIVERS, W.H.R. 74
ROSI, P. 56
ROTHKO, M. 347, 348
ROWLANDS, M. 56
ROY, C. 315
RUBIN, W. 386, 392
RUNGE, E. A. 388
RUSKIN, J. 281
RUSSELL, B. 121

S

SAID, E. 224
SALLUST 332
SALMON, A. 396
SALMONY, A. 95
SCHAMA, S. 189
SCHARFSTEIN, B.-A. 48, 58, 162, 163, 299, 300
SCHILDKROUT, E. 222, 224, 225
SCHMARSOW, A. 80-83
SCHMIDT-ROTTLUFF, K. 94
SCHNAASE, C. 53
SCHNEEMANN, C. 398
SCHNEIDER, A. 383
SCHOELL-GLASS, C. 85
SCHOPENHAUER, A. 347
SCHRÖDINGER, E. 347, 348
SCHWEINFURTH, G. 79
SEDLMAYR, H. 173
SEESSELBERG, F. 78
SEMPER, G. 72, 77, 78, 81, 93
SENGHOR, L. 99
SHAKESPEARE, W. 263, 313
SHEN TSUNG-CH'IEN (SHEN ZONG-JIAN) 357
SHINER, L. 221
SI MAQIAN 199, 127, 128
SIEBER, R. 205
SILVERMAN, E. 229
SINÉS DE SEPÚLVED, J. 52
SIQUEIROS, D. A. 214
SIRÉN, O. 130
SMIDT, D. 308
SOLOMON, H. 303
SONG LIAN 131
SOTATSU 21
SOUYRI, P. F. 338
SPEARS, B. 145
SPENCER, H. 72
SPENGLER, O. A. 98, 188
SPITTA, P. 25
SPIVAK, G. 109, 113, 116
SPIVEY, N. 300
SPRINGER, A. 53, 83
ŚRI HARSHA 356
STAFFORD, B. 109, 111
STALLABRASS, J. 109
STEIN, G. 317
STEINER, C. B. 222, 223, 227
STEINTHAL, H. 74
STILL, C. 348
STOKSTAD, M. 53
STOLLER, P. 227
STOLPE, K. H. 78, 204
STRANG, V. 49
STRATHERN, M. 56, 308
STRZYGOWSKI, J. 79, 81–83, 93, 95, 188
STUART, J. 320
SUGIYAMA, S. 247, 249
SUKUNA, RATU SIR LALA 310
SULLIVAN, N. 225, 227, 228

SUMMERS, D. 31, 56, 69, 70, 84, 109, 114, 115, 178, 179, 300
SÜTTERLIN, C. 300
SVAŠEK, M. 160, 229
SWOBODA, K. M. 173
SZEEMANN, H. 146
SZOMBATI-FABIAN, I. 223

T

T'ANG YIN 312, 317, 319
TAINE, H. 131, 170, 172, 187
TAN GU 124
TANNER, J. 159
TER KEURS, P. 58
THEODORA, QUEEN 316
THIERS, A. 127
THOMAS, N. 56, 222, 223, 225, 229
THOMPSON, R. F. 212, 213
THUCYDIDES 131
TITIAN 280, 316
TJOKOTSJ 308, 310
TOBEY, M. 20
TOOBY, J. 244
TOULOUSE-LAUTREC, H. 16, 20
TOYNBEE, A. 14
TREVARTHEN, C. 246
TRIGGER, B. G. 300
TSENG CHING (ZENG JING) 18
TURNER, W. 20, 280, 281
TYLOR, E. B. 74, 75, 81

U

ULUILAKEBA, RATU TEVITA 310

V

VAN ALPHEN, E. 316
VAN DAMME, W. 85, 160, 322
VAN DEN ABBEELE, N. 300
VAN DER AST, B. 201
VAN DER HELST, B. 200
VAN GOGH, V. 16, 20
VAN GOYEN, J. 198
VAN MANDER, K. 193
VAN OUWATER, A. 193
VAN RUISDAEL, J. 194
VAN RUISDAEL, S. 191, 194
VAN SWANENBURGH, I. 198
VARELA, F. 141
VARNEDOE, K. 386
VASARI, G. 121, 125, 128, 129, 171, 280
VENBRUX, E. 56
VERMEER, J. 191, 195
VERPOORTE, A. 58
VERWORN, M. 80
VICO, G. 113, 296
VIDAL DE LA BLACHE, P. 177
VIERKANDT, A. 82
VINOGRAD, R. 107, 321
VIOLLET-LE-DUC, E. E. 72
VISCHER, R. 72
VISCHER, T. 72
VITRUVIUS 170, 171
VOGEL, S. 350
VOLAND, E. 247
VON GRUNEBAUM, G. E. 337
VON RUMOHR, K. F. 71
VON SYDOW, E. 100, 101
VOSSIUS, G. 192

W

X

Y

Z

INDEX OF SUBJECTS

LIST OF ILLUSTRATIONS

Thames & Hudson, 2003, p. 131, fig. 126.

P. 279
Fig. 9
Painter in his studio, sixteenth century.

P. 282
Fig. 10
Jasper Johns, *Flag painting*, 1955.

P. 283
Fig. 11
Scene from the dustbowl.

P. 285
Fig. 12
Three category – selective regions of the extrastriate cortex,
those for faces, for places and for body parts.
From: L.M. Chalupa and J.S. Werner, eds., *The Visual Neuro-
sciences*, 2003, Vol. 2, plate 55.

p. 304
Fig. 1
Memorial portrait mask of Idebua with her niece, the 1970s cus-
todian, Mrs. Iyawo Obamina (now deceased). Okpella, Afokpella
(Imiamune Quarter), Nigeria.
The mask itself is attributed to the carver Asume, alleged to be
Lawrence Ajanaku of Ogiriga-Okpella, and made c. 1970.
Photo: Jean M. Borgatti, 1972

p. 305
Fig. 2
Page from a sketchbook of faces, Qing Dynasty, late nineteenth-
early twentieth century.
Ink and color on paper
18.8 x 10.7 cm
Toronto, Royal Ontario Museum, purchased with ROM Founda-
tion funds, 994.31.1.40.

P. 306
Fig. 3
Memorial portraits of twins (*ibeji*).
Providence, RI, The Haffenreffer Museum of Anthropology at
Manning Gallery, Brown University
Photo: Rip Gerry

For generations, Yoruba families have preserved the memory of
deceased twins within the lineage by commissioning standardized
but gender specific figurines given the dead twins' names.

Fig. 4
Memorial photograph of twins held by surviving twin whose im-
age has been double printed. Yoruba, Ila-Orangun, Nigeria, 1975.
Photo: Marilyn Houlberg

P. 307
Fig. 5
Baule. Abone Amui of Akukro Village, Ivory Coast, holding her
portrait mask, carved by Tano Ndri, 1968.
Photo: Hans Himmelheber

Fig. 66
Bird Jaguar IV with his wife Lade Wak Jalam Chan Ajaw. Classic
Maya, 755 CE.
London, British Museum, Lintel 41
After Martin and Grube, p. 129.

P. 308
Fig. 7
Shield made by Tjokotsj, Atjametsj village, Central Asmat.
Wood, lime, red ocher, charcoal, sago leaf, fiber, Abrus seeds
167 cm
Collected in 1961 by Adran A. Gerbrands, RMV 3790-525

Photo: Ben Grishaaver

P. 310
Fig. 8
Symbolic portrait of a man in the form of a house in the village of
Koufitoukou dressed with funeral cloths, March 4, 1977. Batam-
maliba, Togo.
Photo: Suzanne Blier

Fig. 9
Symbolic portrait of a woman. Moba, northern Togo, 1990.
Photo: Christine Mullen Kreamer (outside Nano)

P. 312
Fig. 10
Portrait of Oboi (died 1669), Qing dynasty, mid eighteenth–
twentieth century.
Hanging scroll; ink and color on silk
H. 193.7 cm (image)
Washington, DC, Arthur M. Sackler Gallery, Smithsonian Institu-
tion, Smithsonian Collections Acquisitions Program and partial
gift of Richard G. Pritzlaff, s1991.93.

Fig. 11
After Hans Holbein the Younger, *Henry VIII*, after 1537.
Oil on canvas
233.7 x 134.6 cm
Liverpool, Walker Art Gallery
Photo © National Museums Liverpool, Walker Art Gallery

Fig. 12
The Bamboo Stove (detail), 1509 (Ming Dynasty, 1369–1644).
Attributed to Tang Yin (1470–1523). Chinese, from Suzhou,
Jiangso province.
Handscroll; ink and slight color on paper
H. 23–33/40.5 cm x L. 114.5–108.5/111 cm
Chicago, The Art Institute of Chicago, Kate S. Buckingham
Endowment Fund, 1941.13
Photo © The Art Institute of Chicago

P. 314
Fig. 13
Kwame Akoto. Double portrait entitled "Kwame Akoto in *koola*,
a style of wearing cloth, seriously and busily painting the Otumfuo
Opoku Ware, Asantehene." Kumasi (Ghana), December 14, 1997.
Acrylic on plywood
c. 91.5 x 61 cm
Photo: John Picton

P. 315
Fig. 14
A grandson poses by the *tau tau* of his Grandmother on the occa-
sion of her funeral. Toraja region, South Sulawesi, 1992.
Photo: courtesy of Dr Eric Crystal

Fig. 15
Tau tau or memorial figures (Toraja, Indonesia) placed in niches in
rock walls near burials. Display of figures recreated by the Tropenmuseum, Amsterdam.

P. 317
Fig. 16
Christian Boltanski, *The Clothes of François C.*, 1972.
Black and white photographs, tin frames, glass
Each 22.5 x 30.5 cm
Nîmes, Musée d'Art Contemporain, on loan from the Fonds
National d'Art Contemporain

P. 318
Fig. 17
Portrait sculpture of the monk Nichiren with reliquary containing
his ashes (retrieved from the interior). Hommon-ji, Tokyo, 1288.
Painted wood

H. 85.7 cm
After Mori, 1977.

P. 319
Fig. 18
Fon memorial tableau by Aloxa Agbakodji of Abomey.
Brass, steel, aluminum, copper, paint
Collection Raymond C. Ganga
Photo: courtesy of Edna Bay

P. 320
Fig. 19
Royal portraits, in situ, Bamileke, Cameroun, 1961.
New York, Metropolitan Museum of Art, Robert Goldwater
Library, Paul Gebauer Collection. (PG-291-25).

P. 321
Fig. 20
Relief plaque. Benin City, Nigeria, 1575–1650.
Cast copper alloy
London, British Museum
From: Leiris and Delange.

P. 417
Fig. 1
Huang Yongping, *Bank of Sand/Sand of Bank*, 2000–2005
6 x 4.3 x 3.5 m
Mixed media
Photo © Huang Yongping, 2008

DIFFERENT WAYS OF UNFOLDING
THE GLOBE

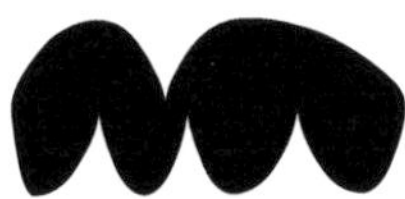

[page 63-66]
GOODE-HOMOLOSINE. John Paul Goode, 1923.

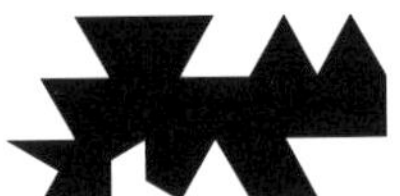

[page 151-154]
DYMAXION. Buckminster Fuller, 1946.

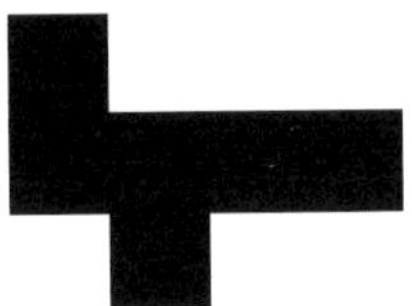

[page 235-238]
CUBE

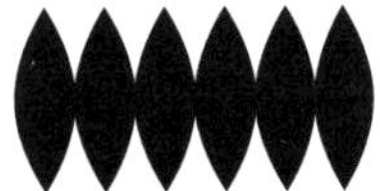

[page 287-290]
POLYCONIC

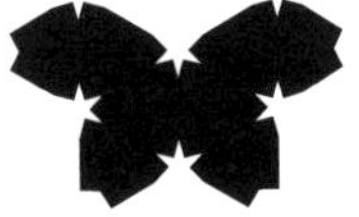

[page 369-372]
WATERMAN "BUTTERFLY". Steve Waterman, 1996.

The shapes above are the "developable surfaces" used for the different map projections.
Idea for insert in this book: Linn Eriksen

COLOPHON

Editors:
Kitty Zijlmans, Wilfried van Damme
Authors:
Richard L. Anderson, Jean M. Borgatti, Donald E. Brown, Cao Yiqiang, John Clark, Elisabeth de Bièvre, Ellen Dissanayake, James Elkins, Paula D. Girshick, Marlite Halbertsma, Thomas DaCosta Kaufmann, John Onians, Ulrich Pfisterer, Colin Rhodes, Ben-Ami Scharfstein, Wilfried van Damme, Kitty Zijlmans
Coordination:
Astrid Vorstermans, Els Brinkman, Amsterdam
English copy-editing of the preface and the text by Cao Yiqiang: Ton Brouwers, Maastricht; of the texts by Marlite Halbertsma, Ulrich Pfisterer, and Kitty Zijlmans: Rosemary Robson, Leiden
Copy-editing:
Els Brinkman, Amsterdam
Graphic design:
Linn Eriksen, Amsterdam, Oslo
Printing:
POD, Scanlaser
Paper:
Biotop 80 gr. (inside); Sulphat Carton 250 gr. (cover)
Publisher:
Valiz, Amsterdam, www.valiz.nl

World Art Studies: Exploring Concepts and Approaches was made possible through the generous support of

Mondriaan Foundation
Prins Bernhard Cultuurfonds

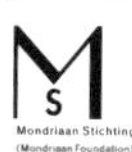
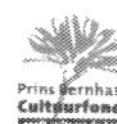

ISBN-13: 978 90 78088 22 6
NUR 646
Printed and bound in the Netherlands

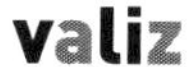

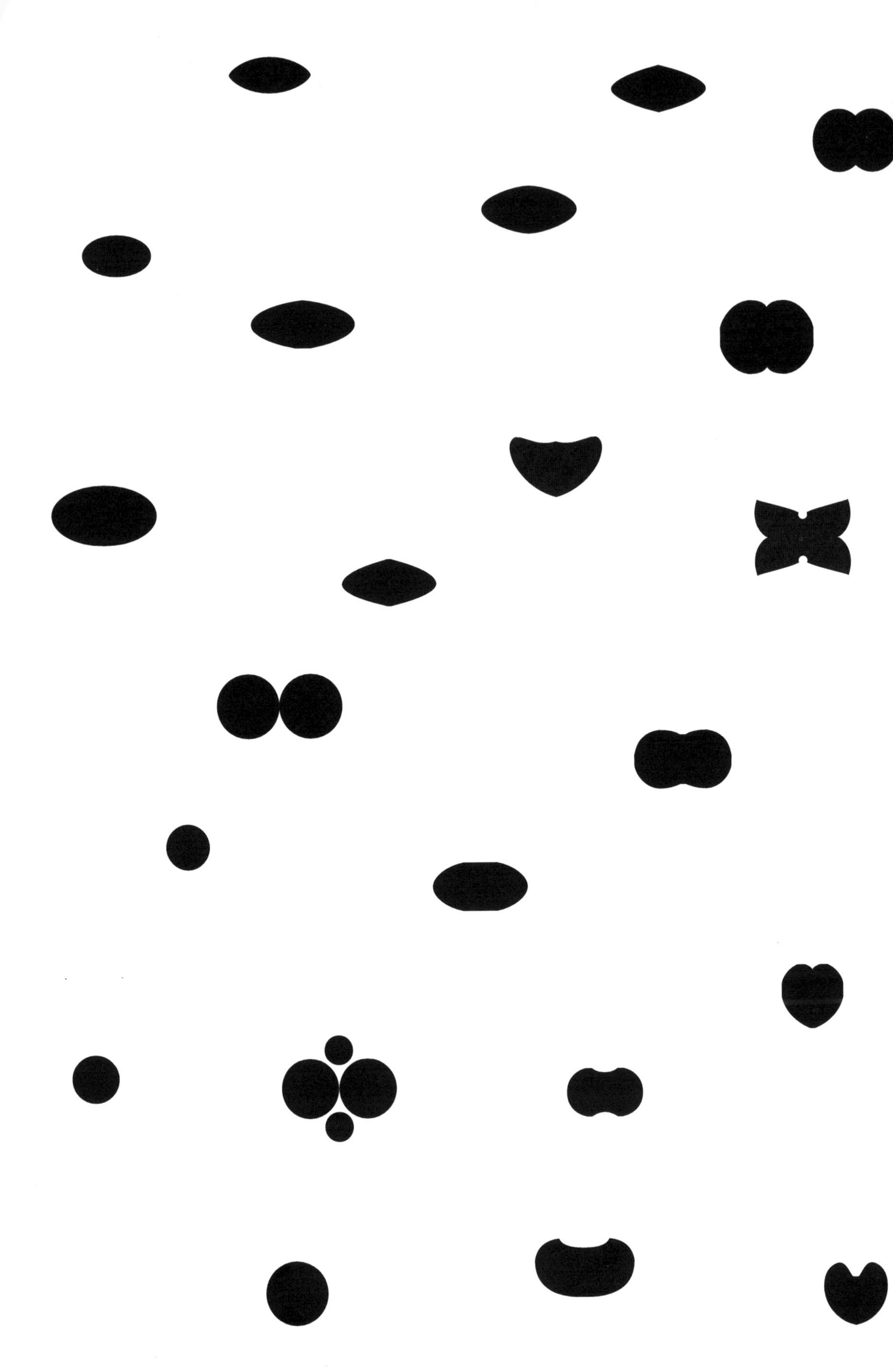